Westminster Pelican Commentaries
Edited by D. E. Nineham

Saint John

Westminster Pelican Commentaries

Saint John

JOHN MARSH

The Westminster Press
PHILADELPHIA

ISBN 0-664-21346-4

Library of Congress Catalog Card No. 77-81619

Published by The Westminster Press
Philadelphia, Pennsylvania   ®

PRINTED IN GREAT BRITAIN

This book is dedicated to the memory of

WILLIAM HEALEY CADMAN

Fellow, Senior Tutor and Yates Lecturer in New Testament Studies at Mansfield College, Oxford. A loyal colleague and gracious friend, he spent his life in the study of the Fourth Gospel, entered deeply into its secrets, lived by its faith, and taught with its aim.

Permission to quote from *The Fourth Gospel* by Hoskyns and Davey, published by Faber & Faber, is gratefully acknowledged.

Contents

Editorial Foreword

Biblical commentaries are of various kinds. Some are intended solely for the specialist; others are devotional commentaries meant simply to help the Christian believer in his prayer and meditation. The commentaries in this series belong to neither class. Though they are based on full scholarly study and deal with technical points wherever necessary, the aim throughout has been to bring out the meaning the Evangelists intended to convey to their original readers. Since that meaning was religious, it is hoped that the commentaries, while being of interest to readers of any religious persuasion or none, and giving a fair indication of the current position in Gospel study, will help Christian readers to a deeper and more informed appreciation of the Gospels.

Technical terms have been avoided wherever possible; where used, they have been fully explained in the Introductions, and readers are advised to read the Introduction to each volume before beginning on the commentary proper. The extended Introduction to the volume on Mark is in some degree intended as an introduction to the series as a whole.

References and Abbreviations

Biblical references are made to chapter and verse, thus: Luke, Chapter 12, verse 24, the first part of the verse (a): Luke 12^{24a}. References which have no name of a biblical book are to the Gospel of St John; thus 12^{24} refers to John 12^{24}.

// means that a synoptic reference has parallels, not always cited.

Some commentaries have been referred to in shortened form. They are:

Dodd: refers to C. H. Dodd, *The Interpretation of the Fourth Gospel*.

Barrett: refers to C. K. Barrett, *The Gospel according to St John*.

Hoskyns: refers to Hoskyns and Davey, *The Fourth Gospel*.

Bernard: refers to the *International Critical Commentary* by J. H. Bernard.

Lightfoot: refers to S. H. Lightfoot, *St John's Gospel: A Commentary*.

The abbreviations of the names of biblical books will be found in the Index of References (pp. 689–701).

ad loc.	*ad locum*, at the place
A.V.	Authorized Version
C.G.T.	*Cambridge Greek Testament*
I.C.C.	*International Critical Commentary*
J.B.L.	*Journal of Biblical Literature*
N.E.B.	New English Bible
N.T.	New Testament
O.T.	Old Testament
R.S.V.	Revised Standard Version
R.V.	Revised Version

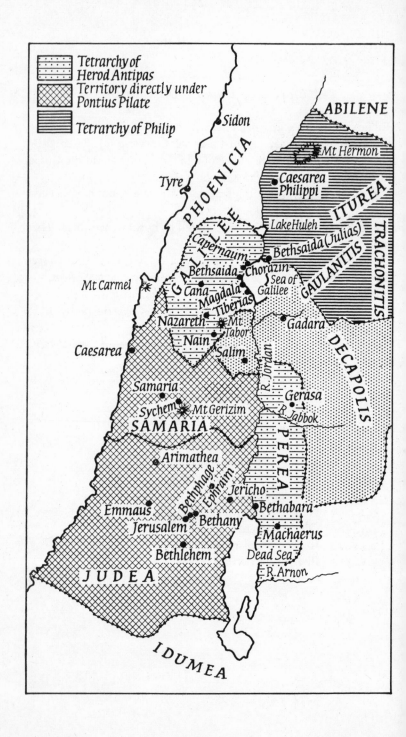

Introduction

Commentary and Gospel

WHAT IS A COMMENTARY?

The publisher and the writer of a commentary on St John's Gospel
share at least two presuppositions: that the gospel itself will be read,
and that at any rate some readers will welcome, though all may need,
a commentary upon it. The first presupposition seems well justified;
the Gospel according to St John is one of sixty-six books of the bible
(one of eighty if the Apocrypha be included) and of all the sixty-six
(or eighty) it may well be the one most distributed, since it is often
issued alone for use by colporteurs, etc. The second presupposition
likewise seems well justified, if the constant succession of biblical
commentaries, and of commentaries on John in particular, is remembered.

But why should any reader need a commentary on what he reads?
What service does a commentary perform? What, in short, is a
commentary? The need for a commentary derives in the first place
from difficulties presented by the text to be read. A work by a quite
modern author (such as the philosopher Heidegger) may profitably
be made the subject of commentary, in view of the difficult style or
the abstruseness of theme. Authors of a previous age may present
similar difficulties, and the passage of time itself may add others.
Shakespeare may take up some Court gossip into a play (as for example
in *A Midsummer Night's Dream*) and unless a commentator makes the
gossip available to the reader, a number of lines will become puzzling
or incomprehensible. A biblical author may name outmoded measures
such as the shekel or omer; he may introduce historical figures
like Cyrus or Claudius; he may use discarded cosmological terms
like 'firmament' or 'the deep'; he may tell stories about people like
Nazirites or places like the 'Holy of Holies'; but unless some
commentator provides an adequate explanation, the reader may find
such references tiresome or even meaningless. Again, a biblical
author may be influenced or even so dominated by a certain religious
or cultural environment that the whole presentation of an important
theme may remain without meaning to the modern reader, unless

13

some commentator provide a key. A commentator may thus be called an expository assistant to the author, seeking to remove any hindrances to the understanding of the text, whether the hindrances be linguistic, stylistic, religious, philosophical or cultural, so that the original author may be able to communicate his message to those who would otherwise be unable rightly or fully to receive it. A commentary is thus no substitute for the original work; rather is it an interpretative introduction to and comment upon it. What really matters is that with the commentator's aid the original work should be enabled to 'speak' effectively.

Such considerations explain the form that a biblical commentary normally takes. Writers of commentaries find it useful to their prospective readers if they discuss the date and authorship, the destination and purpose for which the biblical book was written, and indicate the general world of ideas in which the original author lived, so that the substance of his thought may be grasped through and beyond the particular forms in which it was first expressed. By such means, he hopes that the reader of the commentary will be enabled to read the biblical work concerned with proper understanding.

The phrase 'proper understanding' is used deliberately. It is possible to 'understand' a text by means of a commentary, and yet not be brought to a proper comprehension of what the author originally set out to say. Shakespeare used a good deal of poetry in the writing of his plays; yet for a commentator to confine his observations solely to poetic matters would be severely to mishandle even the poetic parts of a play. The poetry of the play is used in the telling of a dramatic story and the commentator must constantly keep this in mind. Shakespeare's plays inevitably provide a lively documentation of Elizabethan social custom; but to comment on them solely from this perspective would fail in an essential service to the reader of Shakespeare. In the end the commentator has to ask himself, and answer for his reader, what it was that Shakespeare wanted to say in setting out the dramatic material as he did. What did Shakespeare intend to say in those things the actors say, and do, in his drama? The chief task of a good commentator is to help the reader of Shakespeare to arrive at this kind of understanding. A 'proper understanding' of a Shakespeare play is not achieved simply by making the dramatic story plain; it consists in enabling that dramatic story to 'speak' in the commentator's environment as Shakespeare intended it to speak in his. In this sense the 'play's the thing'!

The gospels are manifestly too incomplete to merit classification as biographies. On that point there is general agreement and very little concern. For to tell the message about Jesus it is not necessary to possess or to relate every detail of his biography. But there is contemporary disagreement among scholars, and some concern in Christian circles in the area of discussion about the gospels and history. Are the gospel stories really 'history'? Do they let us know 'how things really happened'? If they do not, why are the narratives related as they are, and can they have any meaning for twentieth-century man? In other words, how are the (historical) stories of Jesus related to the message about him? The question is of the highest importance for the Christian religion, which has not improperly been called an 'historical' religion.

From two very different points of view some contemporary theologians find it difficult to suppose that the stories in the gospels always give accurate information as to 'how things really happened'. The first is held by those who regard some of the events recorded in the gospels as quite impossible, such as those involving miraculous control of nature (the stilling of the storm, the feeding of the five thousand are ready-to-mind examples) or supernatural power leading to otherwise impossible actions (walking on the water, bringing the unquestionably dead Lazarus back to life). Those who take this view may resort to the process of explaining the difficult event in simple and 'acceptable' terms ('acceptable' meaning without straining the credulity of a twentieth-century 'scientific' man, as when, for example, the feeding of the five thousand is explained as the example of one boy's willingness to share his food resulting in a general decision to pool resources and so to discover that there was already more than enough to hand!) or to regarding it as myth and thereafter trying to discover what function the myth was meant to serve in the kindling and development of faith. The second is held by those who have a conception of history as such (in distinction from a conception of what is possible in history) which rules out the possibility of taking many of the gospel stories of Jesus at their face value. Thus Paul van Buren, in his book *The Secular Meaning of the Gospel*, adopts the understanding of history put forward by the Oxford philosopher R. G. Collingwood. 'History, according to Collingwood,' writes van Buren (p. 110), 'is an answering of questions about human actions in the past. The answers are found by means of the interpretation of evidence, and they are sought for the sake of human self-knowledge. Collingwood points out, therefore, that an account of "how God works in history" is not history', for it presupposes part of that answer (i.e. that it was God who was at work, not something or someone to be determined by the interpretation of evidence). 'It is about God's action, not man's and it is investigated for the sake of knowledge of God rather than of man.' Apart from several 'blind spots' in such a view (such as the failure to see that to define history as the place of solely human activity is also to presuppose part of the answer); and that those who believe God to have been and still to be 'at work in history' investigate that story not only for the sake of knowledge of God, but also for the sake of the knowledge of man. Long ago Calvin made it clear* that theology and anthropology are mutually conditioning disciplines: no knowledge of ourselves without knowledge of God; no knowledge of God without knowledge of ourselves. It is quite clear that such a conception of history makes it impossible to accept the evangelists as historians, for each of the four makes it plain that the real reason for writing the stories of Jesus is to proclaim a message about him, the good news (or gospel) that in him, in what he did and what he suffered, God himself was 'at work in history' achieving the fulfilment of his beneficent universal purposes. It is plain that the commentator on John (or any other biblical book) cannot avoid answering the question as to what the gospel is intended to say. What is the story in the stories, the gospel in the gospels? What indeed is 'a gospel'?

WHAT IS A GOSPEL?

There is no need to speculate upon the purposes and intention of John (the name is used at this point simply to indicate the author, and not in any way to settle or prejudge any critical question in advance) in writing his gospel. He has recorded it himself:

Now Jesus did many other signs in the presence of the disciples, which are not written in this book; but these are written that you may believe that Jesus is the Christ, the Son of God, and that believing you may have life in his name (20[30, 31]).

* Calvin, Institutes 1.1.1 and 2.

16

The gospel thus purports to be a record of the 'signs' which Jesus did, admittedly not an exhaustive record, but adequate, in the mind of the evangelist, to convince the readers of the gospel of certain truths about Jesus, and, through such conviction, to bring them to 'life' in his name. It would not be in any way wrong to think that such a statement of intention would equally well apply to Matthew, Mark and Luke. There are certainly very marked differences between the first three gospels on the one hand and the fourth gospel on the other; but however great the differences, the ultimate aim of the four evangelists was the same: to bring men to the knowledge of Jesus as Messiah and Son of God, in order that they might have life.

History and Historiography in the Gospels

But whatever the aim, each evangelist in his gospel tells a story, composed of individual stories, the same story of Jesus, or such parts of it as he believed adequate to achieve his basically religious evangelistic aim. So, whatever opinions may be held about history, it must still be claimed that in some sense or other, the gospels claim to speak of history. But it is not by any means so easily apparent in what precise way they can be reckoned as historical. The twentieth-century reader of the gospels will be very much aware that the gospels, like all historical writings up to the nineteenth century, are not products of a modern 'scientific' approach to history and historiography. The nineteenth century put new tools into the hands of historians and of researchers into the past, and gave them, in a social and political order suddenly more mobile and subject to change, new purposes for pursuing their craft (or, as some would claim, science). History and historiography were subjected to new scrutiny, and in the process had to be purged of marvel and mythology in order to discover *what actually took place*. Yet, were the evangelists themselves to hear some of the modern discussions of their works as valuable historically, it is more than probable that they would protest at the defectiveness and the narrowness of the idea of history by which the gospels are not infrequently judged.

INTRODUCTION

HISTORY AS 'WHAT GOES ON' IN 'WHAT TAKES PLACE'

History may be said to be *what takes place*; in a sense such a description is incontrovertibly true, but in another and truer sense it requires qualification. The qualification necessary can be put in the form that history is what goes on in what takes place, and that the task of the historian is fulfilled when he has used the historiographical devices available to him in such a way as faithfully to indicate what was going on in what took place. An 'annalist' may be content to record simply what takes place, but an historian cannot but make at least some attempt to say what is going on in what takes place. It is this which makes it very difficult to write a history of one's own time; it is nothing like so easy to discern what is going on in what is taking place now, as it is to detect what went on in something that took place a long time ago. This same distinction between what takes place and what goes on also throws light on the work of the evangelists as they use the stories of Jesus (considered as stating roughly *what took place*) to indicate *what was going on* in those stories to constitute the message, the gospel or the good news about him. It also serves to point out the 'story' character, the 'mythical' quality of all historical writing, for to write a history of any kind is to pass beyond the assertion of *what took place* to *what was going on*, from 'how' a thing happened to 'why'. This does not mean that the myth is 'unhistorical', 'unreal', or 'untrue'; but simply that whereas what takes place is conveyed to the mind through the senses, the discernment of what goes on involves mental activity beyond that of the senses. In a real sense, the writing of history is a creative activity, though what it creates is something which has really gone on. The historian cannot recognize or communicate that unless he possess the proper creative insight and power of expression. Many witnesses no doubt saw Jesus crucified on Good Friday. But subsequent events have shown that only those possessed of the creative Spirit of God, the Holy Spirit, were able to discern, proclaim and record, what went on in that crucifixion. Paul put it later on (1 Cor. 12[3]): 'No one can say "Jesus is Lord!" except by the Holy Spirit'.

HISTORIOGRAPHICAL DEVICES

Modern historians have been made very much aware of their dual function, and have fashioned a number of historiographical devices to help themselves to indicate what was going on in the periods about which they write. It is mostly believed that the best historian will try to provide his reader with some criteria by which to judge for himself whether the historian has made a valid estimate of what was going on in the events he relates. The author may print, in the text or in the footnotes or appendices, the sources of his information. He may take considerable pains to indicate where the report of *what took place* stops, and where correspondingly the story of *what went on* begins. He may write a preface or an appendix about the particular perspective from which he writes. His virtue as an historian will be reckoned in proportion to the reasonableness of his conjectures about what went on, and his fairness in indicating their nature and extent.

THE EVANGELISTS' HISTORIOGRAPHICAL DEVICES

Ancient historians in general, and the four evangelists in particular, were of necessity far less self-conscious about the distinctions that modern historians and historiographers have drawn. But they did both recount what took place and affirm what went on. Many statements illustrate the former, e.g. 'There they crucified him' (19^{18}). Others in their various ways illustrate the latter. Some use the form, and possibly also the substance of statements about what took place. Thus Mark (1^6) reports that 'John [the Baptist] was clothed with camel's hair, and had a leather girdle round his waist', which, while reporting what took place, indicates *what was going on*, since the description of the Baptist tallies exactly with the description of Elijah given to King Ahaziah, by which the King knew at once that the man so described was Elijah the prophet (cf. 2 Kings $1^{7, 8}$). Mark in this way identifies John the Baptist with Elijah, who was believed to be about to return to life as the herald of the Messiah. *What took place* was John appearing, in particular his wearing of camel hair cloak and leather girdle; but that pointed to *what was going on* – the Messiah was about to appear, and the Baptist was his herald. A somewhat different use of a known and meaningful piece of past history to indicate through a later event what was going on at the later time is found in for example Matthew's story of Mary and Joseph taking Jesus to Egypt after the visit of the wise men (Matt. 2^{13-15}). The story is stated as something that took place; but its importance for Matthew is not just in its occurrence, but in its ability to point to what was going on. When Israel (or God's son; cf. Hosea 11[1]) first came into historical existence, there was a descent into Egypt, a return through the water, and the receipt of a divine law as the prelude to a new life as the people of God. The repetition of the descent into Egypt is a Matthean historiographical device which informs his sensitive reader that the story of Israel, God's son, God's people, has begun again, finally, in the birth of Jesus at Bethlehem. It may well be noted that Matthew also related how this new Israel, son, or people of God, returns from Egypt, passes through water* (his baptism), receives and prescribes a new 'law' (the sermon on the Mount) as the way to new life of the people of God (the community of Jesus and his disciples) bound together in a new covenant, unbreakable by either sin or death. From even two such examples it is clear that the modern reader would be unwise to dismiss the evangelist's historiography as useless to men in the twentieth century. On the contrary, unless the historiography be properly understood, the gospels themselves will be misunderstood, for then the gospel narrative will not be able to make the affirmations it was intended to make about *what was going on* in *what took place*. More is said upon this in a later section: meanwhile it is necessary to ask questions of an 'introductory' nature about both the author and the book called 'the gospel according to St John'.

St John and his Gospel: The Impossibility of Certainty

In coming to a discussion of the interesting and complicated questions about the fourth evangelist and his gospel one admission is properly and profitably made at the start: there is no problem of 'introduction' about which a certain solution can be found. Who was the 'John' named as the author? Where did he live? For what audience did he write? What sources did he use? When was his work written? About all these questions, and about a good many more, there are divergent judgements, sometimes put forward with great assurance; yet none can claim certainty. Here, as in so many areas of critical study, the choice is not between one solution which has difficulties and others

---

* Matthew 3[13]. It is interesting to recall that Paul refers to the earlier passage through the water as a 'baptism' of Israel (1 Cor. 10[1, 2]).

which have none; it is hardly between one with comparatively few
difficulties and one with very many; it is really a matter of choosing
at what place (and that, of course, believed to be the right place) to
have the difficulties. The best that a commentator can do is to state
the case for and against some of the chief solutions to the various
'introductory' problems, to indicate what might be an acceptable
solution, and to leave the reader largely to make up his own
mind.

WHO WAS THE AUTHOR? THE TRADITIONAL ANSWER

The elusiveness of certainty is admirably illustrated in the discussion
about the author of the gospel. Here, however, one certain element
appears, viz. that the very long tradition of the Church has identified
the author with the apostle John. Irenaeus (A.D. 140–210) said that the
author was 'John, the disciple of the Lord' who gave the gospel to
the elders, and lived at Ephesus until the time of Trajan (A.D. 98–117).
This traditional view has a number of supporting data in the gospel
itself. First, there is a claim that the author is a disciple (21[24]). Second,
the allegedly semitic character of the language supports the view that
the author was a Jew. Third, the knowledge of the geography of
Palestine further supports a Jewish authorship. Fourth, it seems clear
that the fourth gospel actually corrects some statements in the
Synoptics. This would hardly be undertaken by other than an apostle!
Lastly, the tradition of the Church has identified the author with the
beloved disciple, and he in turn has been identified with the Apostle
John.

The tradition of apostolic authorship is thus both ancient and well
supported by internal evidence from the gospel. Yet the tradition
must be questioned. Two considerations have been emphasized. First,
there is an understandable hesitation to suppose that John the son of
Zebedee survived until the reign of Trajan, seeing that he was an
adult at the time of his 'call' by the lakeside in Galilee about A.D. 30;
he would have been a very old man when Trajan's reign began!
Second, there is a tradition that John the apostle was martyred along
with his brother James, whose death is reported in Acts 12[2] – well
before Trajan's time. This tradition may rest on no stronger basis
than the belief that the prophecy of martyrdom for the sons of Zebedee
in Mark 10[39] would not have been recorded unless it had been known

to have taken place. Mark is usually presumed to have written his gospel about A.D. 70*.

Questioning of the long tradition must also be made on the same basis that some support for it was found – the evidence of the gospel itself. To begin with the 'corrections' that John makes to the Synoptic narrative of the life of Jesus. It has been argued that the data are more naturally consistent with non-apostolic authorship. There are such differences between the Synoptic and Johannine narrative, in content as well as in order, that it is impossible to suppose that both derive from the original apostolic witness. If, as our tradition based on evidence from Papias has it†, Mark's narrative embodies in some measure the memories of Peter, is it possible to suppose that another apostle could differ from it so notably as to give an entirely different date to the cleansing of the temple? Further, critics of the tradition point out that the fourth gospel is not only (what some may doubt) the latest biblical stage of a development of Christian thinking, but also that, whatever may be its place in the development of Christian thought, it must be dated at a time when the movement known as Gnosticism had become a powerful influence. That means a date, it is claimed, too late for apostolic authorship.

Another criticism which points in more than one direction, according to the critics of the traditional view, is the knowledge of Palestine and its customs of the time of the gospel story. A notable instance is found, for example, at 18¹³, where the implication is clear that the author believed the High Priest of the time to have held office for one year only. Geographical details are also questioned: for example, the *Sea of Tiberias* was not known by this name until the second century. Finally the claim to apostolic authorship is made only in ch. 21, which is manifestly an addition to the gospel.

If the question be now asked: who can be considered as the author of the fourth gospel if the apostolic authorship be denied? the critic finds another John conveniently to hand in the person of John the

---

* The uncertainties of the whole situation are illustrated by the further reflections that, as Barrett pleads, there may well be other unfulfilled prophecies in Mark; and he cites 9² as an example; and that, against this, it must be remembered that some commentators with a different understanding of eschatology would think that Mark 9² had been fulfilled when he wrote his gospel! Or again, Mark's gospel is held by some to have been written before A.D. 70, and by others much later than that date.

† Cited in Eusebius, Ecclesiastical History III, 39, 15.

Elder. Knowledge of his existence derives from Papias*, quoted by the Church historian Eusebius, and he seems to have lived about the turn of the first century. Papias was bishop of Hierapolis in Phrygia, not far from Ephesus. He does not claim to have any personal acquaintance with John the Elder, or even that he lived in Ephesus. Eusebius, however, does tell of two tombs in Ephesus, each of which was called 'John's'. The most, therefore, that can be said for the claims of John the Elder to be the author of the fourth gospel is that, if he lived in Ephesus, and if he be supposed to have survived from the time of the earthly ministry of Jesus to the reign of Trajan (which supposition about John the son of Zebedee is considered impossible by some), then, though there are even then no positive constraints to cause the critic to identify him as the author of the gospel, it becomes very difficult to disprove such an identification, in the present state of the evidence.

THE TESTIMONY OF THE GOSPEL

If ancient tradition and modern speculation be both put aside, what may be learnt from the statements of the gospel itself? The first thing to note is that, apart from the title of the work (titles being not usually homogeneous with the text) there is no claim in all the twenty-one chapters that it was written by a man named John! The one clue given in the text of the gospel is found in two verses, 21[20, 24], where the disciple following Jesus is identified as *the beloved disciple*, after which it is asserted that *this is the disciple who is bearing witness to these things, and who has written these things*. This cannot mean anything else than that *the beloved disciple* is the author. But of what? Chapter 21 is a very good sample of an appendix added to a work already complete: the conclusion of ch. 20 has all the marks of a gospel ending. Does this leave 21[24] with the meaning that the beloved disciple wrote the additional ch. 21, and no more? Or does the editor (or redactor, as G. H. MacGregor calls him†) intend his readers to understand that this claim to authorship extends to the whole gospel? There is little to guide judgement at this point, though it might be thought more natural to suppose that when ch. 21 was added to the body of the gospel v.24 would not have been included had it not been meant to refer to the writing of the whole gospel.

* Cited in Eusebius, Ecclesiastical History III, 39, 15.
† G. H. MacGregor: *John, in the Moffatt Commentary.*

THE BELOVED DISCIPLE

If the gospel were written by the beloved disciple, who was he? The first candidate whose claims have been advanced is, strangely but understandably, John the son of Zebedee. This is understandable because though the gospel does not mention this son of Zebedee by name, he is the only one of the twelve to bear the name John. It is strange because the identification of Zebedee's son with the figure of the beloved disciple does nothing to ease the difficulties which, as has been shown, the authorship by the disciple John raises (see above p. 21). It must also be noted that it would be highly unlikely that Zebedee's son, a Galilean fisherman, would have been known to the High Priest; and if, as seems reasonable, the anonymous disciple who entered the court of the High Priest (18^{15}) were meant to be the beloved disciple his identification with the son of Zebedee becomes less likely.

Is there yet another John who could fill the role? A suggestion to this effect has been made by Pierson Parker that John Mark would do so admirably.* John Mark has the right name for the part – John. He lived in Jerusalem, was of a priestly family, and therefore possessed a good knowledge of the Temple. He was wealthy, and it is possible, if not indeed probable, that the Last Supper was held in his parental home (cf. Acts 12^{12ff}). Other facts about him consonant with his being the author of the fourth gospel are: he knew the controversy about Judaizing, and had taken part in it; he was influenced by Paul, and associated with Paul and Luke (Acts 12^{25}; $13^{5,\,13}$; 15^{37ff}), whose gospel approximates more to John than either Mark or Matthew. Lastly tradition says that John Mark was an interpreter of Peter, an office which he in fact fulfils in the fourth gospel (e.g. at the Last Supper and at the trial of Jesus) if he be the beloved disciple. But a difficulty about age, similar to that recognized in the identification of John the son of Zebedee, applies to John Mark, though it is less acute if John Mark be further identified with the 'young man' mentioned by Mark as escaping naked from attempted arrest in Gethsemane (Mark 14^{51f}). For the rest the possibility that John Mark was the beloved disciple has much to commend it. It would seem more plausible to recognize him as the person with a background of piety and culture that could, under proper stimuli, become the author of so surpassing a work as the Gospel according to St John.

* *Journal of Biblical Literature* LXXIX, 1960, pp. 97ff.

SPLENDID ANONYMITY

To sum up so far: there are strong and long traditions that John the son of Zebedee was both the beloved disciple and the author of the gospel. There is little to be said against the tradition that he was the beloved disciple until it is coupled with that of his gospel authorship. For then it is not simply a question about an author's age when he wrote his gospel (if, as 21²⁴ can be taken to mean, the beloved disciple was a witness of all the events the gospel records, the problem of the writer's age still applies) but about the probability or improbability of a Galilean fisherman (admittedly a member of a 'family business') called, presumably for good reason, a 'son of thunder', even being able to write or edit and publish, a work so profound and serene as the fourth gospel is*. The suggestion that the author might be John the Elder, though mentioned by Papias, has little to commend it, save that it offers a figure approximately contemporary with John the son of Zebedee who also had the name of John. But we have no evidence positively to support the conjecture, nor can it even be proved that John the Elder lived in Ephesus. As for John Mark, there seem no strong reasons against identifying him with the beloved disciple, and he could conceivably have been possessed of those potentialities which, humanly speaking, would seem to be required in any person able to write the gospel. But again, no positive evidence can be offered for the conjecture, and the conclusion must be drawn, here, as so often in Johannine studies, that no certain hypothesis can be put forward on the basis of the evidence available. The identity of the author must remain, like that of the beloved disciple, wrapped in anonymity. Happily the author's anonymity in no way prevents the splendour of his work from shining out. The identity of the author must remain hidden; the splendour of his genius shines perennially.

The Date of the Gospel

The aura of uncertainty as to the identity of the writer of the gospel also surrounds the date of its appearance. Strong arguments have been advanced, and are still accepted by some, for the view that John was

---

* See Pierson Parker, J.B.L. LXXXI, 1962, pp. 35ff., for an article entitled 'John the son of Zebedee and the Fourth Gospel'.

the last of the gospels to have been written. Extreme representatives of this view have thought that the gospel could not have been written before the middle or latter half of the second century. But equally cogent reasons have been given for thinking that the fourth gospel was much earlier than this, even that it was the first gospel to be produced. In the nature of the case direct evidence is impossible to obtain, and the worth of such evidence as is available is estimated very differently by scholars. What may be called 'direct' evidence, i.e. unmistakable references to the gospel or unquestionable quotations from it, are, of course, accepted by representatives of all views. The difficulties and complexities arise when the attempt is made, and it has to be made, to locate the fourth gospel in its original environment in the first or second centuries A.D.

IGNATIUS AND JUSTIN

Even the presentation of 'direct' evidence is not free from difficulty, as may be seen by consideration of the writings of Ignatius and Justin in their relationship to the fourth gospel. Ignatius was martyred in Rome during the reign of Trajan, and on the way from Antioch to Rome wrote letters to Christians in Ephesus, Magnesia, Tralles, Rome, Philadelphia, and Smyrna, and to Polycarp the bishop of Smyrna. The letters certainly contain something of the same ideas as the fourth gospel. But this does not necessarily imply that about A.D. 115 there was extant a copy of John which Ignatius knew, and which alone could have given him his 'Johannine' ideas. If the letters contained an explicit reference to John's gospel, or some clearly recognizable quotation from it, such an inference might be made. But since the similarity is only in the realm of ideas and not of textual identity, all that can be claimed is that the similarity of ideas is consistent with both Ignatius and John drawing upon the ideas in their contemporary world as well as with the dependence of Ignatius upon John. To be able to affirm the latter as the more likely alternative requires reference or quotation in Ignatius which is simply not there. The same comments apply to the again undoubted similarities between the writings of Justin Martyr (who was martyred about A.D. 165) and the fourth gospel. Justin may have read John and so got his indubitably 'Johannine' ideas; but in the absence of any specific reference to or clear quotation from the fourth gospel, no evidence is available to show more than the sharing of both authors in certain common ideas.

IRENAEUS

The first clear evidence to emerge is provided by a reference to John's gospel by Irenaeus in about A.D. 180 (*Adversus Haereses* 3.1.1). Irenaeus states that after the other gospels had been written, John wrote his while staying at Ephesus. This, combined with another assertion that John remained in Ephesus until the time of Trajan, suggests a date for the gospel before A.D. 117.

THE PAPYRI

In 1935, two ancient papyri were published which may well provide direct evidence about John, taking testimony back before Irenaeus. Rylands' papyrus 457 published by Mr C. H. Roberts contains only John 18[31-33, 37, 38], though it was originally part of a codex (i.e. a book). It has been dated as not later than A.D. 150, though it may well be several decades earlier. It is interesting that it shows no significant variation from the current text of the New Testament. The other papyrus, Egerton papyrus 2, was published in the same year by Dr Bell and Mr Skeat. It is not an edition of John, nor of any other of the canonical gospels, nor, again, of any presently known apocryphal gospel. It contains passages closely similar to John 5[39, 45]; 7[30, 32, 44]; 8[59]; 9[29]; 10[25, 31, 39]. Such similarities can be explained in one of three ways; the papyrus used John; John used the papyrus; both drew on a third source. Professor Dodd has argued the case* for the first possibility with considerable cogency, and while his view cannot be said to be incontrovertible, it seems to the present writer to be sound. If this conclusion be combined with the fact that Egerton 2 was found far away from Ephesus in Egypt it would follow (provided that Ephesus be the place of writing) that John's gospel was in circulation some decade or two before A.D. 150. Admittedly it need not have taken decades to have got a copy of John to Egypt. But if the time needed to do that is combined with time adequate to establish it as an authoritative, citable source, then a decade or two would not be too

* C. H. Dodd, writing in the *Bulletin of the John Rylands Library*, XX, 1936, pp. 56–92.

long. The direct evidence on the whole thus points to a date for the gospel some decade or more before A.D. 150, say between A.D. 100 and 120.

AN EARLY DATE FOR THE FOURTH GOSPEL?

There are considerations of a different and indirect kind which on the whole tend to reinforce an earlier rather than a later date for John. This is really to reverse a trend of scholarly judgement. Even in the critical era, it has been a very widespread assumption that John was the last gospel to have been written. Quite apart from any general considerations of the place John has in the history of thought (his relationship to Gnosticism, for example), it was, and still is, held that he knew and made some use of at least some synoptic material. It was generally conceded that he must have known Mark's gospel, and Luke's, and even, though with much less certainty, that he knew Matthew's. If that were so, then the date of John had to be given as a decade or so at least after the synoptic gospels he was presumed to have known. But in 1938, Gardner Smith of Cambridge, in his work *St John and the Synoptic Gospels*, argued forcefully against this accepted literary judgement and sought to establish an independent origin for the fourth gospel. The possibility of an earlier date for John was thus seen to be more feasible. Dr Dodd's more recent work, *Historical Tradition in the Fourth Gospel* (C.U.P., 1963), has ingeniously and persuasively exploited this new literary territory, and Dr Dodd suggests that an ancient Palestinian tradition independent of the Synoptics and demanding just as serious consideration for an historical reconstruction of the ministry of Jesus lies behind the fourth gospel. Dodd claims that the case he presents, in examining the passion narrative, the account of the ministry, the presentation of John the Baptist and of the sayings in the gospel, is 'cumulative and inter-locking'. If this be so, as the present writer largely agrees, then the critic is presented with some strong evidence in support of an earlier date for John than has often been thought possible. This is illustrated, for example, in the treatment of the Feeding of the Five Thousand, where, in Dodd's view, John has retained the awareness of the highly unstable political situation in which it occurred. He reports that 'they were about to come and take him by force to make him king': by contrast even Mark has been more concerned with a theological

28

interpretation of this incident (obtained in part, it would seem, by employing a double-narrative).* John's gospel may thus well be at this point pre-Marcan in its source material and possibly in its presentation.

There are other critical considerations which may be used in support of an earlier rather than later date for John. Some specialists in Aramaic, the language spoken in Palestine in Jesus' lifetime, claim with C. F. Burney that the fourth gospel was written originally in Aramaic, and only translated into Greek as a completed book. This theory, it is claimed, not only accounts for some of the imperfections of the gospel's Greek style, and for the obscurities of some passages, but also requires a fairly early date for the writing of the original Aramaic gospel: Greek soon became the language of the Church and its writings. But since Dr Colwell has shown (in *The Greek of the Fourth Gospel*, 1931) that the alleged imperfections were characteristic of the koine Greek of the time, and that the obscurities were not so obscure as they had been proclaimed to be, this additional argument has lost a good deal of its force.

JOHN AND THE DEVELOPING THOUGHT OF THE CHURCH

Perhaps the most decisive considerations which persuaded critics to think that the fourth gospel must have a date much later than, for example, the synoptics is the conviction that unless it were placed late it could not be satisfactorily related to the developing thought of the church. It could well be this conviction which moved Clement of Alexandria (about A.D. 150–215) to write: 'Last of all [meaning after the other evangelists] John, perceiving that the external facts had been made plain in the gospel, being urged by his friends, and inspired by the spirit, composed a spiritual gospel' (Eusebius, *Historia Ecclesiastica* 6.14, 5–7). Such a description of the fourth gospel has understandably rooted itself in Christian judgement all down the centuries. For it has seemed obvious to generations of readers and interpreters of the New Testament that such a belief rests upon a natural sequence: the record of what Jesus said, and did, and was, naturally begins with the 'human stories' told about him, and can only then be retold or enlarged or adapted or interpreted so that the readers may understand the 'spiritual' truth that the central person of the record is more than

* See below p. 287.

man. Such a sequence can be seen in the generally accepted chronological order of the gospels. Mark's gospel was the first, simple, factual, brief, but adequate. Matthew and Luke in varying degrees heighten the supernatural and theological elements of Mark and add to them. This they do by including birth narratives with supernatural features (Matthew 1^{18}–2^{23}; Luke 1^{26}–2^{20}); by adding to the number of 'unbelievable' miracles such as raising of the dead (Luke 7^{11-17}) and the provision of a shekel for the temple tax (Matthew 17^{24-27}); and by heightening and interpreting the theological tendencies in the Marcan narrative (Matthew 16^{16}: 'you are the Christ the son of the living God' for Mark's 'You are the Christ'). John as he begins his gospel makes no attempt to hide the fact that his story of the man Jesus is also at the same time the story of the incarnate Word. And as he continues his own narrative he not only heightens and adds to the miraculous, supernatural features* but in a very real way tells his whole story in this transcendent way. His gospel is about the life of the incarnate Word. Seen in this way the four gospels can be seen as constituting a recognizable development from the simple narrative of Jesus and his followers in Mark, through the profounder touches of Matthew and Luke to the fully theological exposition of John. And, it may be added, the process of development went on until it reached the authoritative theological declarations contained in the deliverances of the Councils of the Church in the fourth and fifth centuries.

But history in its reality is rarely as tidy as man's mind would wish! But even if it were, the question could be asked: is the order from the less to the more theological, supernatural, spiritual so manifestly the natural one? Would it not be as likely – and as 'tidy' for human thought – if it were supposed that what would be more likely to be recorded first, if only because rarer, is the supernatural and theological. It is not inherently absurd to claim that it would be precisely the convictions men had about the divinity, the supernatural quality of Jesus, that men first wrote down, largely in the form of the unusual

* For example: he adds the turning of the water into wine; his narrative of a raising of the dead includes the new detail that the resuscitated body had been dead for four days; his account of other miracles parallel to or identical with the synoptics includes an appended discourse which gives them a much profounder significance, as in the case of the feeding of the five thousand, which is interpreted eucharistically, and of the healing of the cripple in Jerusalem, where the reality of the miracle is exposed as giving life where death had reigned.

things he did and said, and that only later on, to give warmth and nearness to the exalted figure they worshipped week by week, were the delightful human stories added. It is surely clear that the only way to decide such questions with integrity is not on any doctrinaire views as to a 'natural' order of development, but on some attempt to understand the history of religious life and thought in the ancient world, and to seek to locate the writing of the gospels, in particular of John, by reference to it. The picture of the world contemporary with the writings of the evangelists is very complex, and it has undergone considerable modification in the light of new discoveries and researches of recent years.

THE BACKGROUND TO THE GOSPEL

In coming to a brief review of the environment in which the fourth gospel might conceivably have been written, it is worth while repeating the warning given by C. H. Dodd. He wrote (*The Fourth Gospel*, p. 6):

'The fact is that the thought of the gospel is so original and creative that a search for its "sources" or even for the "influences" by which it may have been affected, may easily lead us astray. Whatever influences may have been present have been masterfully controlled by a powerful and independent mind. There is no book, either in the New Testament or outside it, which is really *like* the Fourth Gospel. Nevertheless its thought implies a certain background of ideas with which the author could assume his readers to be familiar. How far are we able to reconstruct that background?'

With this salutary reminder a brief review of the background of the fourth gospel may be undertaken.

The Greek Characteristics of John

I. PLATONISM

There is a certain 'Greek' air about the thought and even the precise vocabulary of the fourth gospel, which, as many critics have noted, differentiates it from the synoptics. A popularization of Platonic philosophy had taught men that behind this world of space and time which was always changing and its components 'passing away' there was a real, eternal, changeless world. This led to the contrast between mind and body, spirit and flesh, the world above and the world below, which all have echoes in John. The claim of Jesus to be the *true* or 'real' vine, or to be the one whose judgement is *true* or 'real' (John 15[1]; 8[16]) are likewise echoes of this popular Platonic philosophy: the real vine that bears fruit for God is Jesus himself, and vines in the vineyard are but pale copies of him.

2. STOICISM

Another form of thought, popular in the years when John is likely to have been written, is stoicism. The particular and very important prime point of contact is epitomized in one word, *logos*. For the Stoic, the logos was God, and in some sense also the universe. Yet the Stoics were by no means crude pantheists, for they found seeds of the divine logos in the mind of man, so that there was a possibility of a special relationship between the divine logos and man. The whole duty of man could well be summed up for the Stoic as 'living in accord with the logos'; if that were done, man would become a child of God. What John has to say about the logos in the prologue to the gospel bears certain likenesses to this, though contrariwise, no Stoic would have said that the logos came to his own and was rejected by them (1[11]), or that those who believed in the logos would become children of God by the authority of the logos (1[12]), or most of all, that the logos could be identified with someone in the flesh whose destiny it was to achieve his glory by suffering and death.

These two popular modes of thinking were influential throughout the whole period during which the fourth gospel may be supposed to have been written. Yet neither has made an original contribution to the gospel; rather have both given to the author a useful instrument by which to convey to his readers a belief with both similarities to and yet great contrasts with the ideas of Greek philosophy.

3. THE HERMETICA

Some time at the beginning of the first century B.C. these two streams of Greek thought, the Platonic and the Stoic, were joined in the teachings and writings of the Syrian Posidonius, who eventually settled in Rhodes. But the most notable juncture of the two is to be found in the Hermetic writings, i.e. a collection of works from the second, third, and fourth centuries A.D., in which considerable emphasis is laid upon knowledge. Salvation was really to be found in knowing the truth about God and the world, and about the way to pass through and beyond the world and the heavenly spheres to a final apotheosis. Such language is undoubtedly reflected in the fourth gospel, where much emphasis is placed upon knowing the true God, and Jesus Christ whom he has sent (cf. 17³). There are other ideas common to John and the Hermetica: light and life as the nature of God and as the gifts which his worshippers share, and the regeneration of the believer by a heavenly man or logos who mediates between God and man. But if the fourth gospel is to be dated by reference to these writings nothing more can be said than that both the Corpus Hermeticum and the gospel display patterns of thought that cannot with any certainty be traced back beyond the time possible for the writing of the gospel. A reference to the Hermetica alone would not enable the gospel to be dated much before A.D. 117, when Trajan's reign ended.

4. GNOSTICISM

The quite striking similarities between the fourth gospel and Gnostic ideas has been recognized for a long time. They are evident in the earliest history of the gospel, for John was used both by Gnostic writers to claim apostolic authority for their views, and by the orthodox fathers of the Church to refute Gnostic heresies. It is more than coincidence which lies behind the fact that the first commentary of which reasonably large extracts still survive was the work of a Gnostic, Heracleon, a personal disciple of Valentinus, who used John to indicate what in his view was the basically orthodox character of Gnosticism.

But a careful review of the evidence, such as has been made in the last fifty years by scholars of varying standpoints, leads to one conclusion: no more can be said than that the gospel was written in terms and ideas (knowledge, life, light, truth, the sacraments) that later found expression in the writings of the Gnostics. It is interesting to recall that both polemic against a Gnostic-like heresy and very Gnostic sounding phrases are to be found in Paul's letter to the Colossians, who were evidently being influenced to some degree by 'gnostic' teachers. So Paul says that he writes so 'that no one may delude you with beguiling speech' (Col.2⁴) and warns his readers not to let any make a prey of them 'by philosophy and empty deceit, according to human tradition, according to the elemental spirits of the universe, and not according to Christ' (Col. 2⁸). Such people he adds in another context 'take their stand on visions' and are 'puffed up without reason by their sensuous minds' (2¹⁸). But in the same letter Paul can say that 'in Christ the whole fulness of deity dwells bodily' (2⁹) and that his purpose in writing is that the Colossians may 'have all the riches of assured understanding and the knowledge of God's mystery, of Christ, in whom are hid all the treasures of wisdom and knowledge' (Col. 2², ³). As early as this Gnostic phrases and anti-Gnostic purposes combine in one document.

So the ideas that have gone into Gnosticism have a long ancestry, and found many forms. Without any doubt the world in which the fourth gospel was written, whenever the date may be thought to be, was deeply affected by Gnostic ideas. Yet in spite of many affinities between Gnosticism and the fourth gospel there remains a decisive difference: the Gnostic claims that what saves is knowledge, knowledge of the origins of the world, of man in the world and of the way for man to escape from the world to union with God. But for John (as for Paul) the knowledge that will save is knowledge of the one true God, and of Jesus Christ whom he has sent. Deliverance comes not when a man learns the secrets of the universe and the way through and beyond it; it comes when the Son, given to the world by the Father, gives himself in death for the life of the world. John, no less than Paul, is concerned to preach 'Christ and him crucified', even if John's proclamation be set in a quasi-Gnostic key. The knowledge John would bring to men is not pure intellection; it is a response of mind and heart and will to an acceptance of and trust in what God has done, in the gratitude of obedience and devotion of love.

5. THE MANDAEANS

One particular form of Gnosticism calls for special consideration. Professor Bultmann is the best known exponent of the view that the fourth gospel is a Christian recension of a salvation myth belonging to the Mandaeans. These constituted a Jewish baptist sect, which broke with Judaism in the first century A.D. Some hold that its founder was John the Baptist himself, and regard the incident recorded in Acts 18²⁴–19⁷ as one of a long-continued struggle for supremacy between the Christians and the Mandaeans*. On this view Christianity, founded by Jesus, himself a disciple of the founder of the Mandaeans, John the Baptist, is itself Mandaean in origin! And what is plain to the supporters of the theory is that the ideas of the Mandaeans have contributed considerably to the thought of the fourth evangelist, as he tried to make the Christian message plain to his own contemporaries. The Mandaeans had a cosmological myth, according to which the material world was made by a fusion of light and darkness. The body of man belongs to the kingdom of darkness, but his soul comes from the kingdom of light; though in his earthly life man is a captive to darkness, and stands in need of redemption if he is to attain his true destiny as a child of light. There is also a soteriological myth, according to which the high King of Light sends down to earth his son, his image, suitably disguised in a human form, so that he may reveal to men their heavenly origin, and instruct them in the way to return to their true home. When his work is ended the son returns to heaven, thus opening a way by which those who believe in his teaching can follow him. When such believers die, the son collects their 'sparks' of light, and when they have all returned to heaven, the drama is done. In receiving the teaching of the son, the believer is required to perform the appropriate rituals, a baptism frequently repeated to wash away all impurity and to be invested with the purity of light figured in the white robe worn for the baptismal ceremony.

Not even so cursory a summary as this can hide the quite obvious similarity between Mandaeism and the fourth gospel, or even Christianity itself. But there are still important and decisive differences: The Mandaean view of man considers him 'heavenly' because his real inner self is made of divine light; but in the fourth gospel man belongs to the heavenly world only when he has made a decision in favour of him who is the light. This in Bultmann's understanding of Christian faith is precisely the difference *between* Mandaeism and Christianity, which consists in Christians turning the cosmological mythology of the Mandaeans into the soteriological myth of the Christ. But further points call for modification of such a judgement as

* Dr Dodd makes an apt comment on this (*The Fourth Gospel*, p. 120, 5): 'The amount that has been built upon that meagre and obscure section of Acts by writers of various schools is astonishing.'

to the mythological equivalence of the two forms of thought. The Mandaeans, like the Hermetic writers, hold that man's redemption comes about through the teaching activity of the heavenly mediator, who must teach men the true facts about the world, and of man's way through it. But in the fourth gospel, in spite of a quite clear, and quite normal emphasis upon the indispensable need for the acceptance of the teaching of Jesus*, redemption is not attained through the teaching mission of the heavenly mediator but through his self-offering in death. Finally it must be observed that however close may be the parallels between John and the Mandaean literature, this latter in its present form is of a much later date (the earliest is the seventh century A.D.) than the time at which the fourth gospel was written. This does not mean that the Mandaean scriptures have nothing to say about the world in which the author of the gospel lived; but it does mean that the brilliant attempts by Reitzenstein and Bultmann to read Mandaean ideas back into that period cannot but be conjectural. And as Barrett observes, once Burkitt and others have shown that the Mandaean documents are dependent upon Christian sources rather than Christian on Mandaean, the Mandaean writings become simply 'an interesting and important field for the study of syncretistic religion, and may thus indirectly throw light on John' (Barrett, p. 32, 1).

6. THE MYSTERY RELIGIONS

The reference to the rite of baptism as practised by the Mandaeans leads naturally to a brief reference to another sector of the religious environment of the author of John, viz. the mystery religions. Like the Mandaeans and the Hermetica, each mystery had a salvation myth telling of a saviour-god who by his death and resurrection brought salvation to men as they were initiated into the sacramental life of the religious community, which made them recipients of the divine and immortal life of their saviour-god. It is impossible to deny the similarities between such religions and Christianity, and in particular the similarities to be found markedly in John. But as usual it is the

---

* *He whom God has sent utters the words of God* (3^{34}); *You are already made clean by the word which I have spoken to you* (15^3); *The words that I have spoken to you are spirit and life* (6^{63}), and the closing verses of the Sermon on the Mount, which begin 'Everyone then who hears these words of mine and does them...' (Matt. 7^{24}) and 'Heaven and earth will pass away, but my words will not pass away' (Matt. 24^{35}).

differences that are even more remarkable and significant. Thus, though the heroes of the mysteries were mythical figures, the hero of the Christian 'myth' (if that word be permitted in this context) was an actual historical figure, of quite recent history, whose words and actions could be attested by surviving eye-witnesses. Moreover, however much emphasis John puts upon the sacraments (and opinion varies a good deal on this point) he leaves it perfectly clear that their efficacy is not in themselves, but that their origin, efficacy and substance alike consist of the actual death which Jesus died. This is symbolized for both baptism and eucharist in the blood and water that flowed from the side of Jesus when his dead body was pierced by a Roman soldier (19^{34f}.). What is given to the believer in the Christian sacraments is what has been done for him in history – nothing more and nothing less. So the mystery religions cannot, any more than any other religious movements of the time, be regarded as the source of distinctively Johannine, or even Christian ideas; though they may well contribute to the explanation of John's particular idiom as he wrote about those historical events, in and through which God wrought man's salvation.

Hebrew Characteristics of John

THE DEAD SEA SCROLLS

To conclude this all too brief review of the background of the fourth gospel something needs to be said of the environment disclosed by the writings known as the Dead Sea Scrolls. These are fascinating deposits of the life of an Essene community, which exhibit some remarkably close parallels to the New Testament in general, and to John in particular. Their dating is not yet a matter of universal agreement among scholars, though there is some consensus for the view that they derive from a period between the end of the second century B.C. and the early years of the first century A.D. The author of John then could have read these works, and been influenced by them*. There are indeed some striking similarities, and it is small wonder

* The chief of them are: The Manual of Discipline; the Damascus Covenant; a commentary on Habakkak; the Scroll of Benedictions; the Testimonies Scroll; the War of the Sons of Light against the Sons of Darkness.

that when the scrolls were first discovered enthusiasm outran judgement to claim much more for their influence upon John than now, at a later stage, seems soberly possible. One similarity consists in a dualism between good and evil, between light and darkness. Here the scrolls and John share an ethical dualism as distinct from the metaphysical dualism which is characteristic of later Gnosticism or of the Iranian religions of the time with their two ultimate metaphysical realities of light and darkness, good and evil. But even so, an important difference between John and the scrolls must be noted. For the scrolls the two leaders of the opposed forces of good and evil, light and darkness, were created beings, but John never subscribes in any way to the view that the leader of the forces of good was a created being, but was, on the contrary, goodness itself or light itself come into the world. When the scrolls speak about the actual struggle between light and darkness they envisage a time, fixed by the wisdom of God, when God will intervene in the struggle to destroy all evil, when the wicked will be punished, and wickedness itself be made to disappear for ever. But John's words are much more dramatic than that: '*Now*', he writes, '*now is the judgement of this world, now shall the ruler of this world be cast out*' (12³¹). What is clearly an eschatological event at an as yet unknown future time for the scrolls is for John the realized eschatological event of the lifting up of the Son of man on the cross of Golgotha.

What makes a man one of the 'sons of light'? The answer of the scrolls is quite clear: it is doing the will of God, whose will is revealed in the Torah (the law) which is known in the community of the scrolls. Only a member of the sect could be a 'son of light'. In contrast to this John's teaching is that faith in Jesus Christ is what makes a man a son of light, and faith in him is basically trust in what God has been graciously pleased to do for man in and through Christ's glorification on the cross. It is evident that with the scrolls, as with other religious movements already considered, there is no evidence that any distinctively Christian ideas have been derived from their literature, or from the world of ideas and practices which the literature represents. An earlier excitement about the possible importance of the scrolls for the discovery of Christian origins has not been able to find its expected conclusions. Certainly there is evidence of the use of identical terms (e.g. 'Teacher of Righteousness') and images (e.g. light and darkness), but that does not establish the dependence of either upon the other. What has been established is two-fold: first that there was a widespread movement of religious syncretism in the world of the Scrolls and of the New Testament, and that neither has been unaffected by it: second, that there are quite distinctive Christian assertions made in John (as in the rest of the New Testament) which are concerned with the mystery of the person of Jesus and his mission, and which are wholly without parallel in the Scrolls, or any other literature that is so far known. But in sharing a good deal of common religious language and experience the scrolls shared with John in a world of ideas through which he was able to speak intelligibly to his contemporaries of the central convictions, and central figure, of the Christian faith.

But there is one contribution which the scrolls have made in the understanding of John's gospel which has not been possible before. Until the scrolls were discovered it was not possible to point to an *early* enunciation of ideas which the evangelist used in his statement of the Christian message. It seemed that his thought and language really belonged to that period of the second century when the church was involved in its controversy with Gnosticism. But the Scrolls have given the New Testament scholar a literature in which much of the vocabulary and religious ideas of the fourth gospel are also found. This means that there can no longer be a strong case for saying that an early date for the fourth gospel is impossible merely because its ideas are too developed for the first century A.D. In a most interesting way the scrolls have demonstrated that many of John's ideas hitherto thought to be of necessity an indication of Greek influence, and probably of a late date, are quite explicable in terms of a Palestinian, Jewish movement that was already an established community when Jesus was born. This fact may have important consequences in determining the relationship of John to the Synoptics.

General Conclusions

At the end of a too brief review of the background against which the author of the fourth gospel wrote it has to be noted that the whole period from say A.D. 60 to the middle of the second century was one of immense and intense religious questioning and experiment. The language of popular philosophy, the special and often secret 'gnosis' of Gnostic sects, the myths and sacraments of mystery religions, and the retreat into special 'monastic' communities were all contributing to the general modes in which it was then possible to talk about religious issues. It proves very difficult to trace any direct dependence of John upon any one of the particular traditions examined, though any fair report on the present state of Johannine studies cannot fail to state that advocates for interpreting John in the light of one or the other influence are certainly to be found. Professor Bultmann's commentary is a powerful plea for the Mandaean influence as formative; Dr Dodd believes that 'Rabbinic Judaism, Philo and the *Hermetica* remain our most direct sources for the background of thought' (Dodd, *The Fourth Gospel*, p. 133); Hoskyns and Davey emphasize the Hebraic, biblical and Christian tradition as the dominant influence on John; Barrett (*The Gospel according to St John*, p. 32) believes that Hebraic and Hellenistic influences have been 'fused into a unitary presentation of the universal significance of Jesus'; F. C. Grant (*The Gospels*, p. 160) believes that 'it is from a Gnostic-Christian or Quasi-Gnostic point of view that this book is best understood'.

For the present writer a few points have become relatively clear. First, the Hermetic, Gnostic and particularly the Mandaean literature as we know it was too late in its appearance to have provided John with a source. Second, it is well within the bounds of possibility, so far as dates are concerned, that the literature of the Scrolls, or some quite direct contact with the community, was an influence upon the evangelist. Third, whatever may be said about literary dependence, something quite different has to be said about religious sensitivity. For John shows throughout his writing that he has been very open to the various strands of religious language and experience, both Hebraic and Hellenist, which critics have detected in his work. His tremendous gift has consisted in his ability to put each and all of them completely at the service of Jesus Christ, Son of God and Saviour of the World. The very fact that the fourth gospel can be claimed as Gnostic, Hermetic, Mandaean, Hebraic, etc, is itself an indication not only of a hospitable mind, which might have produced merely syncretism, but of a uniquely creative spirit that could in the crucible of his own profound religious experience fuse all the diverse elements of his contemporary world into one magnificently effective instrument of Christian proclamation.

THE PLACE OF ORIGIN OF THE FOURTH GOSPEL

In reviewing the background of the gospel something must be said about its place of origin. Ephesus has been its traditional 'home'. This view depends almost entirely on the evidence (such as it is) of Irenaeus, and if his testimony be questioned, or the Ephesian residence of the author be doubted, it is difficult to find any confirmatory evidence elsewhere. In fact Irenaeus' evidence has been questioned, and the Ephesian residence of the author has been denied. In this way two other cities of the ancient world have been suggested as homes of the gospel. The first is Alexandria. It was in Egypt that the Rylands and Egerton papyri were found, though as an argument that loses a good deal of its cogency when it is remembered that Egypt provides a uniquely favourable climate for the survival of papyri. But it is also pointed out that Philo lived in Alexandria (and Philonic traces are to be found in the gospel), and some of the Hermetic writings originated there: though the pertinence of these considerations will vary with the judgement made as to the relationship of the gospel to the Hermetica. Alexandria also had a large Jewish population, and if the gospel originated there, its interest in the Jewish-Christian controversy would have a local focus of interest: yet Jewish colonies were known in many other places (cf. the accounts of Paul's journeys in Acts), and interest in the controversy would not necessarily be confined to cities where a large Jewish community existed. Barrett (p. 110) rightly concludes that 'it cannot be said that the case for Alexandria has been made out'.

But if not Alexandria, what of Antioch, which was said long ago by Ephraem Syrus (who died in A.D. 373) to have been the home of the gospel? The suggestion has commended itself to some modern critics of the Irenaean tradition because there are affinities between the theology of John and that of Ignatius of Antioch; because there are similarities between the first epistle of John (presumed here to be by the same author as the gospel) and Matthew (presumed also to have originated in Antioch); and because Theophilus, the seventh bishop of Antioch, seems to have been the first to have mentioned John by name as the author of the first verse of the gospel (in about A.D. 175).

All in all none of the arguments for abandoning the long Irenaean tradition of Ephesus as the home of the gospel possesses real cogency. But if Ephesus were the city in which John was written, an intriguing set of possibilities opens up. In Acts 19$^{1-7}$ the story is told of how Paul came to Ephesus and found some disciples of John the Baptist, who had been baptized into his name, but had not heard of his testimony to Jesus as the Messiah and Lamb of God. On Paul's testimony they became Christians, and were baptized into the name of Jesus. The intriguing possibility concerns the figure of John, the son of Zebedee, whom many students still consider to be the author of the gospel. If he were, and if he wrote it at Ephesus, the fourth gospel might well be seen as his testimony in a later day designed to do what Paul's witness had done at an earlier time – convince the remaining followers of the Baptist that a 'greater than John' had come, and had lived and died for the salvation of the world. Like the Baptist himself, like Paul in Acts, the author of the gospel had as one of his aims to tell men about the appearance, historical and effective, of one who could rightly be called the Lamb of God. The fourth gospel is his telling.

JOHN AND HIS SOURCES

The background against which the fourth evangelist worked is vast and complicated. What can be said when attention is turned from the background to the gospel itself? Are there any indications, as there certainly are in the synoptics, that the author made use of sources? Does the gospel itself give the careful student any clues as to the story of its formation? One thing can be stated with confidence: in complete contrast to Matthew and Luke where verbal reproduction of the text of Mark is widespread, John gives no evidence at all of any such extensive or verbally identical use of Mark – or of Luke or Matthew. In this sense 'source criticism' cannot be applied to the fourth gospel. But two further observations must be made: first, that a number of critics, among whom the most recent and painstakingly careful is C. K. Barrett, believe that there is sufficient literary evidence in the gospel itself to warrant the conclusion that John knew Mark, less certainly Luke, and even, though far less certainly, Matthew; second, that the application of form-critical principles by scholars like Bultmann has resulted in the suggestions of three 'sources' used by John: a sign-source, a discourse or revelation-source, and a Passion narrative independent of the synoptics. A number of scholars have tried to discern from the present state of the Gospel the stages or processes by which it has come to its present form. Thus Hugo Delff

(1899) distinguished the original gospel which contained the report of an eye-witness from the interpolations which were intended to link the original work with the Galilean tradition, the apocalyptic expectations of the time, and with Alexandrian philosophy. Dr Garvie (1922) apportions the gospel thus: most of the 'incidents' of the gospel to the 'eye-witness'; some 'commentary' material to the evangelist, for example, the Prologue, the more heavily 'theological' or 'difficult' utterances of the gospel about Jesus (e.g. 3^{31-6}; 5^{19-29}; $13^{1-3, 18, 19}$); and some particular sections to the 'Redactor' (e.g. ch. 6; ch. 21; 12^{20-36}). To the present writer the various suggestions are interesting, sometimes intriguing, but for the most part lacking in anything approaching real cogency. The renowned critic Strauss put this most clearly when he said of the gospel 'that it was like the seamless robe of which it spoke, which one may cast lots for, but cannot divide'. Yet it must be admitted that all the hypotheses of composite growth have been made in order to identify and preserve as much Johannine material as possible. The present writer will argue that in asking some new questions about the problem of 'historicity' the seamless robe will not need to be rent.

ARE THERE TEXTUAL DISLOCATIONS IN JOHN?

It would be necessary to write a book to deal adequately with all the issues that arise if the question be asked: is the fourth gospel in its present order to be thought of as having had that order when it left its author's hands? The answer frequently given to this question is 'no'; and Dr Moffatt was so convinced of this that when he published his translation of the New Testament he boldly printed the fourth gospel in a revised order, making 8 transpositions in the text.★

Much ingenious skill has been spent on this problem, and it has been directed to enable John to speak as he designed to speak. For all that the present writer believes that Dr Dodd's comment is the most apt at this point (Dodd, p. 290): 'Unfortunately, when once the gospel has been taken to pieces, its re-assemblage is liable to be affected by individual preferences, preconceptions, and even prejudices. Mean-

★ The passages moved, with their new placings, are 3^{22-30} after 3^{12}; 7^{15-24} after 7^{47}; 10^{19-29} after 9^{41}; 11^5 after 11^2; $11^{18, 19}$ after 11^{30}; 12^{44-50} in the middle of 12^{36}; 15 and 16 in the middle of 13^{31}; 18^{19-24} after 18^{14}.

while, the work lies before us in an order which (apart from insignificant details) does not vary in the textual tradition, traceable to an early period. I conceive it to be the duty of an interpreter at least to see what can be done with the document as it has come down to us before attempting to improve upon it.' This is what I shall try to do. I shall assume as a provisional working hypothesis that the present order is not fortuitous, but deliberately devised by somebody – even if he were only a scribe doing his best – and that the person in question (whether the author or another) had some design in mind, and was not necessarily irresponsible or unintelligent. If the attempt to discover any intelligible thread of argument should fail, then we may be compelled to confess that we do not know how the work was originally intended to run. If on the other hand it should appear that the structure of the gospel as we have it has been shaped in most of its details by the ideas which seem to dominate the author's thought, then it would appear not improbable that we have his work before us substantially in the form which he designed. There is every reason for a commentator to write of the book his readers know, and very few, particularly in this instance of a long tradition of textual integrity, for making the book into something different for reasons at best simply conjectural.

JOHN AND THE SYNOPTICS

No reader of the New Testament can for long refrain from asking himself questions about John and the Synoptics. After all the first three gospels tell what is recognizably the same story in approximately the same way. And if the inquiring reader begins to study the New Testament not only more closely, but with the aid of modern manuals of introduction, he will discover that the first impressions of similarity are abundantly confirmed. Mark's narrative turns out to be basic, and all but thirty-one verses of Mark are reproduced in either Matthew or Luke, or both. But when the fourth gospel is read, a very different impression is created. There is none, or very little, of the verbal identity as between Mark and the other two synoptic gospels; and while the fourth gospel is clearly telling the story of the same person known as Jesus the Messiah, the presentation of material, and even the material itself differs widely from that of the synoptics. What is even more puzzling is that at some points, notably the cleansing of the Temple and the Last Supper, John seems clearly to be at variance with the united testimony of the other three gospels. This would in any event be strange, but if the testimony of Irenaeus is to be believed or can be substantiated, that John's gospel was written *after* the other three, then some explanation has to be offered of the discrepancies between John and the Synoptics.

Many scholars would affirm that Irenaeus' statement that John wrote his gospel after the other three is one that can be substantiated. The view was for long accepted, if not on the authority of Irenaeus, at least out of some respect for a very ancient tradition. This assumption was challenged in 1938 by Gardner-Smith (*St John and the Synoptic Gospels*), who argued that John had not read any of the synoptic gospels, but drew upon the same sources of Christian tradition. His views have found some acceptance, and Professor Dodd adopts a similar position in his great work. It is therefore significant that a later scholar, C. K. Barrett, has attempted to restate the case for John's knowledge and indeed use of at least some of the synoptics. He claims that John knew and used Mark; possibly, if not probably, Luke, and with much less certainty, Matthew as well. His argument runs thus: There are at least ten passages which occur in *the same order* (Barrett's italics) in Mark and John. (There is a slight modification necessary since Barrett cites the entry into Jerusalem and the Anointing of Jesus as one Marcan passage, with elements transposed in John!) Further, within those passages there are several instances of quite close verbal resemblances. Barrett is honest enough a scholar to admit that the evidence adduced does not *prove* that John knew and used Mark as a source; but he does claim that it gives plausibility to the view that John had read Mark, and echoed the earlier gospel in writing his own, even if, at times, he be found amending or correcting a tradition found in Mark (e.g. Mark 1^{14f} compared with John 3^{24}; Mark 15^{21} compared with John 19^{17}).

But need it be assumed that John knew and had read Mark to account for the phenomena detailed by Barrett? Could they not equally well be explained by assuming that John had access to the same or even similar tradition about Jesus that lay behind Mark? A good many of the verbal resemblances which Barrett notices are almost inevitable if some particular story is to be told. It would be difficult to tell the story of the feeding of the five thousand without having a verse including a statement that five loaves and two fishes were available. So identity or near identity of language is not necessarily a sign of dependence. It is interesting that Dr Dodd should have followed the lead given by Gardner-Smith rather than attempt to substantiate an Irenaean implication of John's knowledge of the synoptics.

JOHN'S USE OF THE OLD TESTAMENT

There is one further consideration which makes a judgement about John's possible use of the synoptics even more hazardous. It is John's use, and acknowledged use, of the Old Testament. It may well be instructive to examine how John uses an acknowledged source, for it could throw light upon the possibility of his having used an admittedly unacknowledged source, one or more of the synoptic gospels. Such an examination has in fact been undertaken, and the results published, by Charles Goodwin (J.B.L. LXXIII, 1954, pp. 61ff.). The article is entitled: 'How did John treat his sources?' The evidence is clear and unmistakable:

'John's use of his only explicitly acknowledged source shows that he quoted it *rarely*, *loosely* and *confusedly*, often *conflating* two or more passages, *distorting* their *meaning*, and *hiding their context*. We may suspect him of incorporating *alien elements* into them. He appears to have quoted *from memory*, and the attentive reader has seen how elusive are the tricks his memory could play. And whatever was the original intent of the source material used, John has forcibly accommodated everything to his own purposes.'

And the essayist goes on to say: 'Whatever materials he [John] used, his own powerful mind has remoulded everything into a living whole which is all his own.' If then it be asked how, in the light of this example, John could be imagined to deal with a synoptic gospel as a source, and the answer be given in terms that Mr Goodwin says it must be given on the evidence available, it is very difficult to believe that the product would be very different, if at all, from the present gospel of John. It may well be, *pace* Dr Barrett, the very inability to find exact quotations from Mark, Luke or Matthew that is most consistent with John's having known and used them!

THE SYNOPTICS AS SOURCES?

What can be concluded about John's relationship to the synoptics? First a recognition, dependent upon the evangelist himself, that his material is drawn from a much more copious mass of evidence than his own book could hold (20³⁰f; 21²⁵). Whether the material upon which he drew included one or more of the synoptic gospels as we now possess them is something that cannot be determined with certainty. But allowing for the minimal rather than the maximal weight of Mr Goodwin's conclusions, it would seem that John did rely upon the Gospel of Mark, or some work or works very like it. In either case it is possible to suppose that in presenting the material derived from the synoptic or synoptic-like sources, John had some quite clear purpose in his mind as he fused his materials with his own testimony to produce the gospel that bears his name.

JOHN'S PURPOSE

As has been stated John's avowed purpose in writing his gospel was that his readers might 'believe that Jesus is the Christ, the Son of God, and believing, have life in his name' (20³¹). But this purpose is really no different in any fundamental way from that envisaged by Mark, or that detected in Mark by an early editor; for the gospel now begins with the programmatic statement: 'The beginning of the gospel of Jesus Christ, the Son of God' (Mark 1¹). There was a time, not long ago (and possibly not yet over for some), when it was generally supposed that the synoptics in general and Mark in particular told the simple historical story of the life and death of Jesus of Nazareth; and that John, though telling substantially the same story, told it with new and different theological overtones. But it is now generally recognized that Mark is as thoroughgoingly theological as John, even if the implications of this revolutionary conviction are not always perceived. The difference between John and the synoptics is not that John is theological and the synoptics not, but that they are theological in different ways. The consequences of this recognition are extensive and important, and it will be necessary to deal with some of them in the rest of this introduction. But the chief implication is that both synoptics and John, like Paul and other New Testament writers, are concerned to deal neither with mere history (what took place) nor mere mysticism (escape from what takes place) but rather with a reality which partakes both of *what takes place* and of *what goes on*, which is another formulation of the statement that John and the synoptics are all theological. They tell the story of *what took place* (the so-called 'historical') in order to convey to their readers *what went on*. The purpose of the exercise is that the gospel readers should come to have belief in Jesus of Nazareth as Son of God and Saviour, and in that belief find the life that is life indeed.

All this has been excellently stated in Hoskyns and Davey's profound commentary. Before an examination of John and the synoptics is undertaken it is worth quoting the following passages from the end of their long Introduction (pp. 133f.):

'The test that we must in the end apply to the Fourth Gospel, the test by which the Fourth Gospel stands or falls, is whether the Marcan narrative becomes more intelligible after reading the Fourth Gospel, whether the Pauline Epistles become more transparent, or whether the whole material presented to us in the New Testament is breaking up into unrelated fragments. If the latter be the case, we must then go back to speak of Johannine and Pauline theology. Once again we should be compelled to speak of the simplicity of the synoptic gospels, of the complexity of the Pauline ideas, and of the unhistorical mysticism of the Fourth Gospel.'

And a little later:

'A commentary on the Fourth Gospel can therefore be no more than a preliminary work. It leads on to further study of the Pauline Epistles and of the synoptic gospels. For the Fourth Gospel should not be regarded merely as an appendix to other biblical work, as though it lay altogether on the periphery of the Bible. We must be prepared to find that the Fourth Gospel ought to be regarded as a necessary prolegomenon to the understanding, not only of the other books of the New Testament, but of the Old Testament as well. At any rate, we have no right to rule out this possibility *a priori*.'

The present writer believes that this is a true estimate of the significance of the fourth gospel.

THE SYNOPTICS, JOHN, AND HISTORY

In spite of all that has been so wisely written by Hoskyns and Davey, it must be freely admitted that for any reader of John, particularly the modern reader, it is almost fatally easy to suppose that the notable thing about their relationship consists of their differences about certain historical data. If, as many scholars believe, John's is the last gospel, and if, as any reader rapidly observes, there are at least two important and undeniable differences about chronology, then it is easy to understand why the problems of John and the synoptics have been fairly consistently seen as 'historical'. John says that the Temple Cleansing took place near the beginning of the Ministry: The synoptics agree in placing it very near the end. Surely this is the plainest of indications that the difference between them is 'historical'. The conclusion does not follow.

The perception of the difference as historical would be valid if the two sets of documents were historical, but they are not. They are both theological. Or, to put the same point in another way, both synoptics and John are concerned to relate *what took place* so that men may learn thereby *what was going on*. Long ago Bishop Butler said that 'each thing is what it is, and not another thing' and were that maxim observed in dealing with the four gospels the relationship between the synoptics and John would not be so widely misconceived as it is today. There was a time when it was held critically respectable to believe that the synoptic gospels, particularly Mark as the allegedly first of them, provided something approaching a chronological framework for a 'life of Jesus'. That was possible in the days of source criticism. But with the advent of form criticism and the analysis of the synoptic narrative into individual elements of different kinds such a view was no longer tenable. Instead of chronology being, as it were, the thread upon which the pearls of gospel stories were strung in narrative sequence, it became clear that each pearl was a theological counter, and that chronology had much less to do with selection or place than source criticism could ever have imagined. But if even Mark is not constructed chronologically but theologically (i.e. is not concerned simply to report what took place but always to make plain what was going on), then any correction of Mark made by John could not, in the nature of things, be simply chronological. Any 'correction' would primarily be concerned with theology, with meaning, with *what was going on* and only secondarily by implication, as it were, with chronology, with *what took place*. To say all this is not to deny that some plausible chronological deductions can be made from Mark and the other synoptics. Clearly some chronological order is embedded in Mark. The baptism of Jesus and the calling of the disciples are bound to have taken place before the public ministry really began*. There had to be some indication of opposition before Jesus took farewell of the Galilean crowds on the hill of the miraculous feeding. The crucifixion could not come elsewhere than at the end. A minimal outline of this sort, for what it is worth, can be detected. The point that needs to be made is that even among the synoptics themselves, where dislocations of an apparently chronological kind are made, there is always a theological point being made, in and through the chronological change. One or two examples may be quoted by a comparison of the first five incidents in Jesus' career in Mark with their treatment and placing in Luke. Mark's incidents, in his order, are: 1. The baptism (1^{9-11}); 2. The temptation (1^{12-13}); 3. The return to Galilee with the good news of fulfilment (1^{14-15}); 4. The calling of Simon and Andrew, and of James and John (1^{16-20}); and 5. The authoritative preaching and the healing in the synagogue at Capernaum (1^{21-28}). Luke bases his own narrative to some extent upon Mark. He tells in somewhat different terms of the baptism (Luke 3^{21-22}); he then inserts a genealogy which traces the ancestry of Jesus back to 'Adam, the son of God' (Luke 3^{23-38}). This follows the baptism where a voice from heaven had declared that Jesus was the son of God. By the device of the genealogical tree inserted here Luke is on the one hand trying to avoid the false inference that some in fact drew from the baptismal voice – that Jesus did not assume his divine nature and status until the day of his baptism: the son of God did not come into existence on that day! On the other hand Luke is indicating that it was not only a new Israel (or Son) of God that was begun when Jesus was born, but a new humanity. The genealogical tree is thus skilfully placed to make a theological comment on the narrative; it is a means of pointing to what was going on, in the baptism and throughout the ministry. Luke resumes the Marcan order, giving, like Matthew, a somewhat longer story of the temptation, with a shift of theological emphasis to the question 'If you are

* Though even here there may be theological motive behind the place given to the calling of the disciples in Mark. The evangelist may find his present placing of the calling of the disciples (Mark 1^{16-20}) a convenient way of indicating in the very account of what took place that there is no real activity of the Messiah without the prior inauguration of the people of the Messiah. The first miracle is not related until the Messianic community has begun to be formed (Mark 1^{21-28}).

the son of God'. But when Luke reports the return to Galilee, he does not simply report a general proclamation of the arrival of fulfilment time. Instead he follows the report of Jesus' entry into Galilee (Luke 4[14-15]) with the story of the preaching in the synagogue, not at Capernaum, but at Nazareth, according to Luke, his 'patris' or 'native city'. In this story Luke brings out even more vividly than Mark in 1[21-28] the astounding character of the good news of fulfilment. For in Luke it is no longer possible to detect a theme about the arrival of a new age, but instead the reader must grapple with the highly particular claim that the new age is to be identified with the person of Jesus himself. 'The spirit of the Lord is upon *me*,' says Jesus, quoting Isaiah (Isa. 61[1, 2]); and then adds: 'Today this scripture has been fulfilled in your hearing.' Luke has thought it right to indicate at the very start of the gospel that his theological convictions about the new era are focused upon and centre in this particular historical person. Thereafter Luke seems to desert his Marcan model for a time; for though teaching and exorcism in Capernaum follow (as in Mark) and these are followed by the account of the healing of Peter's mother-in-law, and of the healing of the many sick persons at sunset, followed in turn by Jesus' retreat to solitude for the renewal of prayer, and a Johannine-like report of preaching in Judea, it is not until Luke has reached his eleventh incident of the ministry (in contrast to Mark's fourth) that he relates the call of any disciple. He then records the 'call' of Peter. This is a narrative different from Mark's, and much more is involved than in the simple 'call' of Mark. Indeed the response of Peter to the Lord's injunction to 'put out into the deep and let down your nets for a catch' could be taken to presuppose the story of the 'call' recorded in Mark, for Peter replied to Jesus: 'Master, we toiled all night and took nothing.' In this skilful and artistic resetting of Peter's 'call' Luke is trying to make plain to his readers that the bond between the Master and his disciples (for the sons of Zebedee figure at the same time in Luke as in Mark) was from the very beginning rooted in a recognition of something supernatural in the person of the Lord. Such a point is made even more forcefully in John, where the very first approach of any disciple to Jesus follows the witness of the Baptist that Jesus is *the Lamb of God, who takes away the sins of the world* (1[29]). Thus it can be shown that important theological points are, or always may be, involved in dislocations or transpositions of incidents, or in the insertion of new material into the narrative. The wise reader will remain alert to these clues which the synoptists provide as to *what was going on* in *what was taking place*.

Displacement and transposition of order in the synoptics can thus be seen as a means of theological comment. The same point needs to be made in respect of changes of order and content as between the synoptics and John. It is admittedly a difficult point to take, at any rate for a modern Christian. The gospels read so very much like historical narratives of what took place (as indeed to some extent they are) that it requires effort not to treat them exclusively as such, but to understand them as much more concerned to indicate *what was going on* in the narrative provided. It is natural and understandable for any man of any century confronted with the evidence to suppose that John has consciously sought to correct the synoptics in two major points, the position of the Temple Cleansing in the ministry of Jesus, and the date of the Last Supper and the crucifixion. The differences are quite clear. John tells of the cleansing of the Temple at the very start of the ministry (2^{13-22}); the synoptists place it at the beginning of the last week of Jesus' life (Mark 11^{15-19}). For the fourth evangelist the Last Supper took place before the Passover, and Jesus was crucified while the Passover Lambs were being slain in the temple; for the synoptists the last supper was an eating of the Passover by Jesus and the Twelve. It must then freely be granted that a chronological question arises in each instance, and much scholarly care has gone into the understandable attempt to decide which of the two chronologies – Johannine or synoptic – is the more likely in each case. The recognition of the question and the attempt to find a convincing answer are quite proper human enterprises. But it is fatal to suppose that in deciding for one chronology or author, or by producing some reconciliation of the two, the critic has really penetrated to what his text has really affirmed. If the gospels, Johannine or synoptic, are to be treated 'for what they are, and not for another thing', the synoptic narrative must be seen, no less than the Johannine, as a theological document in which what was going on is made clear in the narrative of what took place.

Take, for example, the story of the cleansing of the Temple. Its 'chronological' position in Mark may be right, and John's placing wrong. But even if Mark be right, the chronological position bestows a theological meaning (i.e. something is *going on* in *what takes place*). In the context it is plain that the Temple cleansing was the

occasion of the decision of the authorities to *destroy him* (Mark 11:18)
There is a swift chronological sequence from Temple cleansing to
crucifixion. But the chronological sequence involves a theological
point. The affront to authority consisted in the open condemnation of
the chief priests and scribes as those who, while anxious to preserve
their own knowledge and worship of God, were unwilling to fulfil
God's demands to make his temple a house of prayer for all nations.
What was thus being denied by all the paraphernalia to keep the
Temple worship specifically Jewish was the access of the Gentiles to
Yahweh, a denial symbolized by the presence of money-changing and
animal-selling in the very court where the Gentiles were permitted,
but where they could read at the entry to the holy place 'No Gentile
is to enter on penalty of death'. But when Jesus comes he comes to the
temple to make the religion of the people of God, embodied in
himself and his community, as universal as the prophet's vision which
saw all the nations sharing in the worship of Yahweh. And the
substantive link with the crucifixion is then at once apparent, for it
was by his self-offering in death that Jesus fulfilled his destiny as the
saviour of the world.

In the Johannine placing of the story there is a greater historical
space between the cleansing and the cross. But the theological
proximity to the death and resurrection is no less. As in Mark, those
who preserve the Jewish paraphernalia of worship by selling animals
and changing money are expelled; what is significant is that, in John,
the animals to be used in the sacrifices of Judaism are also driven out
(2:15), leaving Jesus, the one true sacrifice in the temple. The old
temple of animal sacrifices must yield to the new temple and the one
sacrifice. John tells how the authorities ask Jesus what sign he has to
show for his action; he replied by identifying the sign with the
destruction of '*this temple*', and his raising it up in three days (2:19).
That is to say what has really been enacted that day, when the one who
is to become the sufficient sacrifice for the sins of the world expels all
inadequate sacrifice and its signs, is precisely an affirmation of the
reality of Jesus as the perfect sacrifice, which he is only as he gives his
life in death for all mankind. So far, so good! Clearly, by somewhat
different accounts of *what took place* John and Mark have given
common and united witness to *what was going on*. But what of the
chronological difference? Does it have any theological point? The
question is of prime importance. The answer is that John is indicating

by the changed chronological point that the theological depth manifest in the Temple cleansing in Mark was not reached for the first time only a few days before Jesus died: it was there from the beginning of the ministry. The underlying significance of this answer has been admirably stated in Hoskyns and Davey (p. 126):

The true understanding of the history of Jesus – and consequently of all observable history – therefore springs from that God-given perception of which the apostles who *beheld his glory*, and those who share their apprehension (17²⁰), can confidently speak, and it cuts right across the chronological understanding of history. For this reason, in the interests of that history which has been seen to bear witness to God, it has to be detached from its chronological context and narrated non-historically since only so can justice be done to its theological significance. Even the chronological movement of Jesus from His Baptism to the Cross, which in itself, as a chronological movement, is theologically significant, since it bears witness to the return of Jesus whence he came, and to the requisite movement of man to God, has to be rid of any semblance of evolution, lest God should be thought of as an historical end, or His action continued to a distant future.

If the present writer were to attempt to put this point in other words he might say: John is trying to tell his readers that Jesus was 'near the cross' not only at the beginning of the last week of his life, but at the very beginning of his ministry. And it is this 'nearness' which is important. A modern though lesser parallel might help. How near, it might be asked, was the Third World War in 1962 when President Kennedy defied Russia over Cuba? The answer could come in two forms – one chronological, and no precise answer can be given yet, for the third world war has not yet come. But whether a third world war comes or not the world was very near it in 1962. John is saying, in effect, that the cross was 'very near' even from the day when the Baptist first saw Jesus and hailed him with the words *'Behold the lamb of God, who takes away the sin of the world'*. And if such theologizing at the start of the gospel be thought un-synoptic and therefore unhistorical, the reply must be made that Mark's work begins with the theological word: 'The beginning of the gospel of Jesus Christ, the Son of God' and that as early as Chapter 2, in the saying about the wedding guests not fasting while the bridegroom is with them, there is some 'nearness' of the cross at a considerable chronological distance from the crucifixion.

The second 'displacement' can perhaps be more quickly evaluated. John is absolutely unambiguous in his evidence that the Last Supper recorded in 13[1ff] was not a Passover meal, for the simple reason that in 18[28] he reports that the Jews did not enter the praetorium, *so that they might not be defiled, but might eat the passover*; again, in telling the story of the crucifixion he says that *since it was the day of Preparation* (19[31]) for the Passover, the Jews asked Pilate that the legs of the crucified might be broken. In contrast (or conflict?) with this the synoptic tradition is equally unambiguous that the Last Supper was a Passover meal. 'On the first day of Unleavened Bread, when they sacrificed the passover lamb, his disciples said to him, "Where will you have us go and prepare for you to eat the passover?"' (Mark 14[12]). As has already been observed it is possible to ask the chronological question: when did the Last Supper, the crucifixion take place? Very many learned books have grappled with the problem, but certainty has not even so been reached. What the two different chronologies have in common is not just the eating of a meal and the crucifixion of Jesus, which for some unknown reason they place at different chronological points. What is also common is the reference to the Passover and the consequent setting of the death of Jesus in a paschal perspective. Whether the paschal significance of the death of Jesus is brought out by means of the story of the Last Supper, or by the incidents recorded by John at the crucifixion, where Jesus, like a passover lamb, did not have one of his legs broken: what matters is that the paschal theology be made available to the Church so that Christians might be able to understand what God did in giving his son to die for the world. But why should John offer the Church a perspective different from that of the synoptics? The present writer's guess is that it was linked with the eucharistic experience of the Church. The eucharist was, and still is, a rite to be performed 'in memory of' Christ. But what occasion is remembered? Is it the first eucharist after the resurrection, when in a mysterious trinity of wonder, doubt and joy, the earliest disciples were admitted to a new and indestructible communion and community with their Lord? Is it the Last Supper, where before the passion and death Jesus pre-enacted his self-offering for men? Is it the actual event of crucifixion and death itself? It would seem that both John and the synoptics share in the inheritance of the first eucharist. The one whom they remember does not come from it; for he came to it. That being so, it appears that the synoptists have chosen to see the eucharist as the re-enactment of the Last Supper, the pre-enactment; while John sees it as the re-presentation of the act itself. And this is quite in keeping with his whole attitude to history and eschatology. He so writes his story that God, or his coming to men, is not something still to be enacted, but something which happened once for all when Jesus was crucified and so glorified.

The conclusion to be drawn from all this is that it is important for the modern reader to be aware of the differences between modern historiography and that of the evangelists. It is not the case that the first records of Jesus were written down as modern historiography would suppose and require, in a chronologically accurate order, and that later John made some important corrections for sound chronological reasons. Rather the very first order is as theological as the last; and while chronological questions may be quite properly raised, it must always be remembered that chronology was itself a theological tool in the hands of the evangelists. Difficult as it is for the modern reader to realize, there are more important things, even about chronology, than correct chronological order. It is more important to understand why John can say that Jesus' hour has come (12^{23}; 13^1; 17^1) than to determine with irrefutable accuracy the date of the month on which it came!

HISTORIOGRAPHICAL TOOLS: I. TYPOLOGY

John like the synoptists is trying to convey to his readers not only an impression of what took place in the life of Jesus (observable history as Hoskyns and Davey describe it) but also what went on. One tool they shared in common is called typology, which has the dictionary definition: 'the doctrine that things in the Christian dispensation are symbolized or prefigured by things in the Old Testament, as the sacrifice of Christ and the Eucharist by the sacrifice of the Paschal Lamb'. The word doctrine is an exalted description for an historian's tool, and it may well explain why modern historians view the very word with suspicion. Quite unjustifiably! An approach to a better understanding of typology may be facilitated by a modern hypothetical example. If a third world war were to break out between Russia and the Western Powers, and once again large numbers of British troops were to be pushed back to the beaches of north-west France; and if at that time there were to be staged a saving operation akin to that which took place in 1940, it is almost certain that the British press, and possibly the press of the whole Western Alliance, would feature the story with a banner headline: 'Another Dunkirk'. No one would denigrate such journalism (which is the 'contemporary history') as misleading typology; and yet it is precisely this procedure which is followed by the evangelists when they employ an Old Testament saying, person, or even idea to throw light on the story of the New. The phrase 'Another Dunkirk' does no more – and no less – than use a past incident whose 'meaning' or 'significance' or even 'outcome' is well known, and which conveys a whole complex of suggestion, in order to inject into the account of an event not yet so clearly established in its meaning, the significance already established by and attached to the incident from the past. This is precisely what John and the synoptists do as they use the Old Testament typologically. They assume, of course, as any user of typology must, that the meaning of the 'type' they apply is well known – as the Old Testament was to many of the first readers of the gospels. They then invite their readers to see the story they are telling in the light of the meaning the type brings. In another way of putting it they use an accepted witness to what went on in the past to point to what is going on in the story they narrate.

This being so, it is misleading to regard typology as valueless historically. Rather it is an historiographical tool of great value. All history involves meaning: and how can meaning in history be identified better than by recognition of similarities with meanings accepted from the past? It is important to note that typology differs completely from allegory; for typology is a means of being anchored to an historical occasion and to detect the meaning in it, while allegory takes the hearer out of a particular occasion in order to enunciate some universal propositions or rules.

Thus when Augustine deals with the story of the Good Samaritan he sees the injured man as the symbol of humanity; the Good Samaritan as standing for Jesus; the wine and oil as the two dominical sacraments etc. etc. But that is to abstract from the specific situation and seek quite general theological truths. But if Mark's description of John the Baptist in Mk 1⁶ be seen as a typological presentation, then the reader, at each recognition of the type to be applied, is able to enter into that particular situation with a greatly enhanced understanding. He learns, by the quite simple and brief descriptions, that John the

Baptist is 'another Elijah' and that therefore Messiah himself is near (though not identifiable with John); he learns that like Jonathan of old, the new John is gifted with a prevision that in a time of real darkness and defeat can sense an impossible-seeming victory very close at hand.

Typology is thus not a forced literary convention. Quite the contrary! For the evangelist of the first and the journalist of the twentieth century it is a most natural instrument to use. But it has limitations. Its usefulness is confined to those who know the significance of the type. In the imagined third world war situation the headline 'Another Dunkirk' would be either unintelligible or unacceptable to a Russian newspaper reader; and a Tibetan who chanced upon the headline would have no clue from his own nation's history with which to make use of the type. But the Jew of the first century (and many a Gentile convert to the Church) was steeped in the story of the Old Testament and the rich allusiveness of the four evangelists would be most meaningful to him. In any case it is small wonder when the Christian Church came to write about the most important person and the most important event in the whole of human history that it should turn to the Old Testament for types by means of which the account they had to give of what took place should also give something like a worthy account of what went on. Shakespeare wrote of a 'Daniel come to judgement'. The evangelists, using the same device, have tried to say that what went on when Jesus was here could be nothing less than a recital of the mighty acts of God.

HISTORIOGRAPHICAL TOOLS: 2. SYMBOLISM

The author of the fourth gospel had an 'eye' for the symbolic. Again and again he notes some little detail that is full of rich symbolism, and so again a depth of meaning is added to his narrative. One example will illustrate the point. John says that at the wedding in Cana, six jars of water were provided for the customary Jewish rites of purification. Why six? There was no requirement of Jewish law demanding just this number. So why six? Either because six were there, or John chose the number to make a point – or six were there and John saw – and made his point. What point can be made? Six was, for the Jew, near to but short of the 'perfect' number seven; and John is trying to say that Judaism and its rituals is near to but short of the perfection of religion. By its purificatory rites Judaism sought to keep God's people in proper relationship with him, and with its closely guarded marriage regulations tried to secure a proper transmission of that relationship. But Judaism has signally failed. Yet, in the advent of Jesus it could now be said that Judaism could and would be replaced by the only 'purificatory rite' that could make, maintain and transmit a true life for the people of God: the self-offering of Jesus in death, symbolized for ever in the wine of the Christian sacrament. John is richly endowed with this theologically sensitive, almost poetic insight. He is happily unafraid, and unashamed to use it.

John and the Synoptics: Examples and Episodes

One of the most remarkable things about the fourth gospel is that though its author and/or appendicist recognizes that there are very many stories about Jesus that he did not tell, he managed to find room for only seven miracles and very little else by way of incident. This contrasts strongly with the synoptic gospels, where no reference is made to the many stories not published, but where even the shortest gospel greatly surpasses John in the number of stories told. It is worth while quoting Hoskyns and Davey again (pp. 65–6):

'The synoptic gospels consist of a large number of disconnected or semi-disconnected fragments, incidents, episodes, put together by the Evangelists within a broad, roomy framework, capable without serious disturbance to the general plan of the books, of being expanded to hold additional material or contracted in order to render the material more manageable. In the midst of this rich varied gallery the reader can wander about. He is magnificently free. He can pause and admire where he will. He can select an incident, visualize it, meditate upon it, and then preach about it, allegorize it, interpret it, symbolize it, apply it to his own circumstances, use it to pillory his enemies or to encourage himself and his friends. ... And in doing all this he can pride himself that he is acting in obedience to the highest authority, that of the authentic teaching of Jesus of Nazareth, and that he is a true disciple of the "Jesus of History" because he has heard him speak and seen him act. [But] to the reader of the Fourth Gospel no such magnificent freedom is permitted. The selection of incidents has already been made, not at all as we should have made it. The interpretation has been given, and it is in form the interpretation of Jesus Himself, in substance the interpretation of the Holy Spirit of Truth (14^{26}; 16^{12-16}). The Fourth Gospel records not primarily what the crowd of eye-witnesses saw and heard of the Jesus of History, but what the disciples saw of the *glory* of the Word of God (1¹⁴); what they apprehended, as believers, when Jesus *was risen from the dead* (2²²). The Fourth Gospel is less an apostolic witness to history than an Apostolic witness to that which is beyond history, but which is, nevertheless, the meaning of the "Jesus of History", and therefore the meaning of all history.'

All this is finely said. But one important qualification appears necessary to the present writer. It is this: if the comments of Hoskyns and Davey suggest that the synoptists did not set out to do what the fourth Evangelist (in their view) set out to do, and John's work must therefore be taken as in some sense 'correcting' theirs, a seriously false impression is given. For it seems clearer, the more the two traditions, synoptic and Johannine, are studied together, that what John was trying to do was to enable the readers of the synoptic gospels not to go back to them and read them in a Johannine perspective, but to show them that the synoptists' perspective was substantially identical with his own.

In Hoskyns and Davey's terms the synoptics can be termed 'episodic'; so by contrast John can be aptly described as 'exemplary', i.e. he takes a very limited number of incidents and subjects them to a long and penetrating analysis. But the incidents have not ceased to be episodes by being fewer in number or analysed at length. Nor is it in the end possible to maintain a clear distinction between the 'historical' character of the synoptics and the 'theological' character of the fourth gospel. One illustration may suffice: In Mark 3¹⁻⁶ the story is told how Jesus on a certain sabbath day healed a man who had a withered hand. The miracle was performed in a suspicious and hostile environment, and once it was done Pharisees and Herodians planned to destroy Jesus. The fourth gospel does not incorporate this actual story: as will be seen characteristic of it, it selects a typical miracle of this sort and treats it as an example of others. So in John is told the story of the cripple who could not reach the waters of healing, but was brought to locomotive power by the word of Jesus on a sabbath day. John passes in his characteristic way from miracle to discourse expounding it, and in the course of a long analysis it becomes clear that what Jesus had done at the Pool of Bethzatha on that sabbath day was far more than to restore locomotion to impotent limbs: he had given new life to a 'dead' man. Has this not therefore been a grossly exaggerated

Johannine theologizing of a plain Marcan fact? Not at all: for in Mark, before Jesus heals the man in the synagogue he eyes his critical audience and asks them 'Is it lawful on the sabbath to do good or to do harm, to save life or to kill?' (Mark 3⁴). Properly understood the synoptic narrative says, and was intended to say, the same things as John's. The fourth evangelist brings no new meaning to the synoptics but he knows that when a reader of his own gospel turns back to the synoptics he cannot fail to penetrate more closely than before into the very heart of their message, which like his own is concerned to proclaim Jesus as both Messiah and son of God.

The synoptic gospels recount many more 'miracles' than John, and the undiscerning reader might well see the picture of Jesus which emerges as that of a uniquely powerful thaumaturgist. If so, a reading of John might well put him right, and he could return to the synoptics and realize that his previous interpretation was wrong. For the synoptists, no less than John, saw Christ's miracles, and intended their readers to see them, as evidence for the divine nature of the Lord. First it is made clear that the miracles are a sign that with Jesus' activity in miracles the age of fulfilment has at last arrived. What Isaiah foretold, 'In that day the deaf shall hear the words of the book, and out of their gloom and darkness the eyes of the blind shall see. The meek shall obtain fresh joy in the Lord, and the poor among men shall exult in the Holy One of Israel' (Isa. 29¹⁸ᶠ), is taken up into Jesus' own account of his mission: 'Go and tell John what you hear and see: the blind receive their sight and the lame walk, lepers are cleansed and the deaf hear, and the dead are raised up, and the poor have good news preached to them' (Matthew 11⁵). The great messianic age has dawned in fulfilment of its promise in the life and actions of Jesus. Further, it is evident to observant readers of the synoptics that many of the wonders done by Jesus are really activities peculiar to God alone. That Jesus of Nazareth performed such deeds of divinity was itself a testimony to his divine nature. Thus it was Yahweh who 'made the storm be still, and the waves of the sea were hushed' (Psalm 107²⁹); and it was Jesus who said 'Peace! be still!' and the winds ceased and there was a great calm (Mark 4³⁹). Again, Jesus took it upon himself to proclaim the forgiveness of sins, a prerogative that every Jew believed to belong to God alone: and even Christ's adversaries recognized this: 'When Jesus saw their faith he said to the paralytic, "My son, your sins are forgiven". Now some of the scribes were sitting there, questioning in their hearts, "Why does this man speak thus? Who can forgive sins but God alone?" '(Mark 2⁵⁻⁷). And while the Pharisees could number among themselves those who could exorcize demons, Jesus claims that he exorcizes them 'by God's finger', and that therefore the Kingdom of God had come upon men (Luke 11¹⁴⁻²⁰). Similarly for the Jew it was God who gave or permitted health or disease, life or death; that Jesus so manifestly had powers both to restore diseased bodies to health and even to quicken those that were dead is eloquent testimony to the synoptists' intention that he should be regarded not as a mere miracle worker, but rather as the embodiment in one personal human life of a worthy bearer of the name Immanuel, God is with us.

John's purpose is in the end the same. He uses different methods, notably in his treatment of miracles. Indeed John does not talk of 'miracles' but of *signs*. It has already become clear that to use such a word of the miracles of Jesus even as reported in the synoptic gospels would not be an entirely inappropriate thing: no doubt John was aware of this kind of consideration. But for John the works of Jesus are signs in a special way. It is possible to draw a distinction between 'external' and 'internal' signs; an 'external' sign would be something almost arbitrary, as, for example, the colour red as the sign on the hoods of some graduates of Oxford University that their degree is in the faculty of arts: any other colour, historical antecedents apart, would serve equally well. An 'internal' sign is not arbitrary, but in some way an actual part of the thing signified: as, for example, a candidate's examination paper is taken to be a 'sign' of the quality and extent of his knowledge, which cannot all be displayed in any one paper, or set of papers, but which nevertheless enables the examiner to judge fairly about the whole, of which he has only seen a part. The miracles in John are signs in this latter sense. They bring into the particular occasions of Jesus' ministry the reality they represent, which is always the same – his victorious self-offering on the cross. This can be seen in the very first sign, when the water of Jewish purification was changed by Jesus' presence into the wine, which in its sacramental significance stated that in the self-offering on the cross there would be provided the one means of real purification which Judaism had sought, but failed, to provide. The working of the miracles is an 'impossibility' for the modern mind, but what most needs to be said is that however baffling to human reason the story of water into wine may be, the reality of that which is but a sign is even more amazing and 'impossible' – that the Word, creative, divine, eternal, should become flesh, and give himself in suffering and death to make manifest in history the love and the glory of God.

Yet the modern reader may persist 'Did it really happen like that? Were 120 gallons of water really changed into wine?' or, in relation to another sign, 'Was Lazarus really brought back to life after four days dead in the tomb?' To be an understanding interpreter of John means, in the present writer's view, an unwillingness to give an immediate yes or no to these two (or similar) questions. For if either answer is given the questioner may well think his inquiry not only satisfactorily answered, but adequately concluded: whereas to have the question answered without facing the further question of what the author believes history to be, and whether his view of it is justified, is really to treat the record for what it is not, a plain account of 'observable history'. To take the story of Lazarus. Unless careful note is taken of what is said in 11²³⁻²⁶ about resurrection the whole episode is deprived of an indispensable interpretative clue. Jesus met Martha and to her statement that had he been in Bethany her brother would not have died (i.e. Jesus' power was adequate to keep his friends in the historical life-in-the-flesh) Jesus replied that her brother would 'rise again' (11²³). Martha then said she knew he would rise in the resurrection at the last day: to which Jesus replied, giving the interpretative clue for the sign to follow: '*I am the resurrection and the life; he who believes in me, though he die, yet shall he live, and whoever believes in me shall never die.*' Two other scriptures play an interpretative role. Certainly the saying in 5²⁵ (cf. above p. 60) that '*the hour is coming, and now is, when the dead will hear the voice of the Son of God, and those who hear will live*'. And less certainly Luke 16³¹ where Jesus ends the story of the rich man and Lazarus with the words: '*If they do not hear Moses and the prophets, neither will they be convinced if someone should rise from the dead.*' The general import of all this on the sign of Lazarus' *resurrection* is that the real transition from life to death is not be looked for at the point where men pass from 'physical' existence to bodily non-function, but at the point where they turn away from, reject or deny the coming of the word made flesh to bring divine life to men; and the real transition from death to life, if any, is not to be looked for at the point where the dead may be raised in some general resurrection at the last day, for that after all is only an historicization of the essential resurrection, it is to be looked for at the point where men turn to Christ and accept him in faith as God's gift to them of life that is imperishable, unconquerable. The emergence of Lazarus from the tomb is thus much more than a uniquely marvellous resuscitation; it is an enacted confession that Christ holds in his own undying life all those who believe in him, whether physically alive or not. It is only in this context that the 'modern' question can be put without making a Christian response impossible.

The visible, historical Jesus is the place in history where it is demanded that men should believe, and where they can so easily disbelieve, but where, if they disbelieve, the concrete history is found to be altogether meaningless, and where, if they believe, the fragmentary story of His life is woven into one whole, manifesting the glory of God and the glory of men who have been created by Him.*

But if at last the 'awkward' question be faced: did the impossible occur?, the answer has to be that the central part of the Christian gospel to which every part of the gospels refers is itself impossible! The impossible went on in what took place: God was in Christ, reconciling the world to himself. The word became flesh and dwelt among us, and we beheld his glory. He came that we might have life, and have it abundantly. If that central 'impossibility' be believed, then it is less difficult to suppose that even in what took place there would be some uniquely remarkable signs of what was going on. Nor is this so impossible to suppose as it was some decades ago. The universe as men know it today is not a perdurable reality linked throughout its history by uninterruptible sequences of causes and effects, governed everywhere by unchangeable and unbreakable laws. It is rather a universe where pattern and probability are the categories to be used in understanding the world. If so, then instead of having to say of a miracle that it 'breaks the laws of nature' (a notion equally repugnant to the critical inquiring mind and to the Christian understanding of God) it is possible to think that it simply goes outside the familiar pattern that men know, but only for the sake of the ultimate pattern, which is the whole purpose of God. God, that is to say, has a pattern for his world. The existence of evil, itself a mystery to man, creates distortions of that divine pattern. What God has done in Jesus Christ, and this includes the so-called miracles, is to restore the over-all pattern by some further departure from its familiar regularities.

* Hoskyns and Davey, p. 85.

It is, of course, quite possible for a man to accept the witness of John and the synoptics to the person and mission of Jesus, and not to wish to assert that any miracles took place. It is by no means necessary to make belief in Jesus Christ rest upon an acceptance of the miracles as 'observable history'. Indeed the contrary is true: truly Christian belief in the gospel miracles is possible only to those who have a belief in Jesus as Son of God and Saviour, for only those see the miracles as 'signs' of his real nature and mission. There is however no necessary intellectual dishonesty in believing in Jesus and denying the miracles, even if a previous acceptance of the miraculous led to a belief in Christ. The attainment of direct personal relationship with Jesus Christ by any means is properly so satisfying and self-authenticating that the instruments by which the relationship might be begun or explained cease to be of decisive importance. There are more ways than one for a Christian to live with intellectual integrity in the modern world.

THE ORDER OF THE SIGNS IN JOHN

John names only two miracles as *signs*, though this does not mean that only these two are rightly to be so called. Each reader, and each commentator, must therefore make his own judgements as to other signs in John. For reasons which will appear in the course of the commentary the present writer believes there are seven signs in all, six being acts performed by Jesus before the crucifixion, the seventh being the crucifixion itself, which is the mystery of the Word-made-flesh, both sign and thing signified together, and which is both something which Jesus 'suffered' (*there they crucified him* 19^{18}) and something which he did ('*No one takes it – my life – from me, but I lay it down of my own accord*' 10^{18}). All that can be 'seen' at the moment of crucifixion is a man being put to death; but what is really going on is the final victory of God over all the sin and evil of the world. Thus to count seven signs in John involves regarding the walking on the water (6^{16-21}) as part of the sign of the loaves. More is said in the body of the commentary but it may be remarked here that if an independent sign it has even less Johannine commentary than the healing of the nobleman's son.

For the rest it may suffice to say: (1) John's first sign is a comprehensive introduction to the whole body of signs. He uses the sign of

water becoming wine by the act of Jesus to indicate that the whole
religion of Israel as an attempt to keep the people of God pure and
acceptable to him is wholly outmoded and transcended since all its
inadequacy is overcome by the presence and action of the Word-
made-flesh as he gives his life in death for the whole world. For the
future the only adequate means for a man to be acceptable to God
will be the sacrifice which the Son makes in laying down his own life.
(2) John then recounts five signs which echo, and in one instance
repeat, signs already familiar to those acquainted with the synoptic or
synoptic-like tradition. A Gentile's sick boy is healed; a lame man
walks; the hungry are fed; a blind man receives sight; a dead man is
raised. It is impossible to write these sign titles without being reminded of Jesus' answer to the inquiry from John: 'The blind receive
their sight, the lame walk, lepers are cleansed, and the deaf hear, the
dead are raised up, the poor have good news preached them' (Luke
7^{22}). John does not slavishly follow that synoptic catalogue of signs,
but the testimony he advances is clearly of the same order and cogency
as that thought proper by the synoptists. Not least is this true in the
position given to the sign of the raising of the dead, which in John, as
in the synoptics, is given in double form in the raising of a dead person
by Jesus (Jairus' daughter, the widow's son at Nain, Lazarus) and, in the
end, the raising of Jesus himself. John has brought these twin signs
close together as the climax of all the signs. And, it is to be remembered, it was not until Jesus had been glorified that the spirit can be
given and the good news, therefore, be preached to the poor. John's
book of signs, as Dr Dodd felicitously calls it, is designed with great
artistry and profound insight.

THE DISCOURSE IN JOHN

The impressiveness of John's gospel or 'book of the signs'* does not
however lie in the mere fact that he has told six or seven miracle
stories; the synoptists did that, and more! What gives John's gospel its
characteristic impressiveness is undoubtedly his usual practice of

---

* The reader acquainted with Dr Dodd's stimulating and monumental work
The Fourth Gospel will recall his analysis of John into three parts: The Proem
(1^{1-51}), the Book of Signs (2^1-12^{50}) and the Book of the Passion (13^1-20^{31} or
21^{25}). The present writer prefers to see the crucifixion as the last and greatest
sign where sign and thing signified are together. So the whole gospel may be
called a book of signs.

joining the miracle story with a discourse of great profundity, whether that be given (as normally) after the relating of the miracle, or whether before it, as in the case of the cross and glorification. But it must not be too readily assumed that in this John is entirely an innovator. There are miracle stories in the gospels which contain sayings of the Lord, and there have not been lacking critics who believe that the miracle would not have been preserved in the gospel were it not for its conjunction with the saying. With that admitted, it is quite plain that John's use of the discourse is entirely distinctive, and indeed it has been one of the constant difficulties for the critically minded reader, since there is no real parallel to a discourse in any of the synoptic gospels, and since the content of the discourses appears to the judgement of many to leave their 'historicity' very much in doubt. Professor Bultmann is one modern scholar who believes that John drew upon a 'sign source' for his gospel, and, having made his selection, expounded the signs in discourses attached. The hypothesis may in fact be true, but a close scrutiny of the text of John does not enable a confident judgement to be made. The truth is that the signs and the discourses are so closely knit together as to defy any confident separation into material from two sources. It would hardly be over-stating the case to say that miracle story plus discourse constitutes sign-narrative for John. John is not interested in signs merely as 'miracles' or 'wonders' but only as actions embodying as they anticipate the reality of the one great decisive miracle of God's action to redeem his world. In writing of the signs, John has, as always, stamped his own genius upon his work, giving it a unity that is really indivisible.

But not all the discourses in John are linked with miracle. Some sections of the gospel (chs. 3, 4, 7, 8, 10) are discourse or discourse-like material, yet contain no miracle. Yet even this judgement needs some modification, for in 3² Nicodemus says to Jesus *No one can do these signs that you do, unless God is with him,* and the subsequent discourse can properly be taken to bear upon the nature of *signs*. The dialogue with the woman at Samaria is conducted from a starting point where she was expecting what she thought to be a miracle (4¹², ¹⁴). The brothers of Jesus, in ch. 7, want him to go to Judea and 'do his works there'; and when Jesus is in Jerusalem the crowd asked *When the Christ appears, will he do more signs than this man has done?* In ch. 10, the question is asked about Jesus *Can a demon open the eyes of the blind?'* On the other hand there seem to be two miracles with no accompanying discourse; viz. the story of the healing of the official's son, and the report of the walking on the water. The latter miracle is regarded by the present writer as part of the sign of the loaves, in which it plays a subordinate but very important role; for it emphasizes, in a way quite concrete and inescapable, that what Jesus had to give to man is neither food nor political leadership, but himself, which is the heart of the 'eucharistic' discourse of ch. 6. As for the story of the official's son, it closes with a saying linking it with the sign at Cana. Evidently two things were intended: first to indicate that the self-offering of Jesus in his death not only provides for Jews the fulfilment they had hoped for, but also brings to the Gentiles what they long for. Second, that the deed was no mere thaumaturgy, but a veritable manifestation of the giving of life for which the Son had come into the world. This is embodied in the final word of Jesus: *'Your son will live'* (4⁵³). What Jesus brought was not recovery from disease, or renewal of bodily vigour; it was *life*. The story of the healing of the official's son comes between the stories of Nicodemus and the Samaritan woman on the one side, and the lame man being healed on the other. To Nicodemus Jesus speaks of being *born again*; to the woman at the well he promises living water preventing all thirst; the paralytic's new condition he analyses as living instead of dying or dead. It is on all grounds unreasonable to suppose that, for once in his gospel, in so richly allusive a context John should have forgotten all that he sought to do in his gospel, and on this one occasion simply told a story exhausted in thaumaturgy and not therefore pointing through it and beyond it to the divine event of the coming of the Word-made-flesh in glory that could be seen by those whose eyes were opened.

ARE THE DISCOURSES HISTORICAL?

The discourses, peculiar to John, so greatly contrasting with the forms of teaching in the synoptics makes it necessary to ask about them, as about the signs they often elucidate, are they historically reliable? Bultmann supposes a special 'discourse source' from which John drew his material, but in general the homogeneity of theme and language in both signs and discourse has not led a large body of scholars to agree with him. What sort of teacher was Jesus? Did he, as the synoptics suggest, make brilliant use of short parables and telling metaphor, being apt and quick in repartee and controversy; or was he, as the fourth gospel suggests, a much more methodical expositor of ideas, passing his thoughts on by a profound examination of man's world and his own presence and activity in it? The answer first needs to be made in reference to the gospels themselves. The synoptics recount many deeds; John selects six (or seven), including at least three unrecorded by the synoptists. The parallel statements about teaching could well be: the synoptists recount many parables, similitudes, etc. and even extensive blocs of teaching are not homogeneous pieces; John may have a parable, but in the main his teaching is given in different form entirely. The two sets of statement bear interpretatively on each other. It means that, with the teaching as with the actions, the first formulation of modern man's question needs refashioning. The proper question is not 'Did Jesus ever really teach like this?', for to that there may be no possible answer! The better form is: 'Does this matter of presenting the works and words of the Lord really help men to see who he is, and to understand what he did?' If then the question be put 'But did Jesus teach in discourse or parables?' the answer is that both pieces of evidence are before the reader, but that unless both forms of teaching are seen to be means for the disclosure of the truth about Jesus the question of mere historicity is unimportant. It is generally assumed that Jesus would more naturally have used parable rather than discourse. This cannot but be an *a priori* assumption and it would be perfectly possible to argue that one and the same person could do both.

But the form of discourse apart, is it a reasonable assumption that Jesus could have said the kind of things that John reports in the great discourses? Here again, no positive solution is possible: each reader and commentator must decide for himself. But, so it seems to the present writer, the believer who has been persuaded that Jesus is the Christ, the Son of God, will be aware that he cannot state with complete confidence what was and what was not possible to him in the days of his flesh. But believing him to be the Word incarnate, it is possible to suppose that just as his 'omnipotence' was equally consistent with both 'mighty works' and impotence on the cross, so his omniscience could be consistent with utter ignorance of some things (Mark 13²²) and yet with confident knowledge about others. The language of Jesus as reported in the fourth gospel may not have been so inaccessible, in the light of the scrolls, as once was thought.

Thus while the discourse form is peculiar to John among the evangelists and while it must be granted that the compilation of speeches and discourses was a common task of ancient historians, the gospel reader is not precluded from supposing that Jesus used a discourse even if at the same time he admitted that no surviving discourse is likely to be in his exact words. But again, to ask for the *ipsissima verba* of Jesus, even to ask for certainty about the form of his teaching, is really to turn the gospels from being what they are into being what they are not. The discourses stand to the synoptic parables very much as the selected signs stand to the synoptic miracles – they are meant to ensure that when the reader of the discourses goes back to the synoptic records, he will no longer be tempted to treat them as 'observable' (or 'audible'!) history, but will see them, as he cannot but see the discourses, as witnesses to the presence among men of the eternal Word, manifesting his divine glory in the flesh.

A brief consideration of the content of the teaching is needful. Not even a casual reader can fail to be struck by the absence of synoptic themes in John, and Johannine themes in the synoptics. In the synoptics there is considerable teaching about the Kingdom of God, about repentance, and about some future occasion when God's ways with men would be finally vindicated. But in John all this is virtually missing. Only in the conversation with Nicodemus does the *Kingdom of God* find mention ($3^{3, 5}$) and at the trial of Jesus he himself refers to his 'Kingdom' (*Kingship* in R.S.V., 18^{36}). Repentance receives no mention at all, and the eschatological terms found in the synoptics are so rare that when they occur, as they do in ch. 6 ('*raise up at the last day*' $6^{39, 40, 44, 54}$), a scholar like Professor Bultmann has to suggest that they do not really belong to John! What has John done? Has he really distorted the message of the synoptics for something really different? Not at all. The present writer believes that what he has done is to enable the reader of the fourth gospel to move from it back to the synoptics and there to perceive what the synoptic message is. This is done by keeping his readers firmly with the historical Jesus, for it is in him that they can really meet the past, the present and the future. The past means him, that is the real theological justification for typology. If some event in the past, like the exodus from Egypt, throws light (as it does) through the Passover feast on the destiny and death of Christ, it is then seen that as the fulfilment (the achievement once for all in history) of what God sought to do in the Passover is at the cross, the cross itself sheds light back to the exodus. What is going on in the exodus helped many to see what was going on on the cross; but once it is seen what is going on in the event of the cross, then it is seen as what is going on all the time. The cross becomes the meaning, the one event of all history. The future means Jesus Christ too; that is the real essence of eschatology. It is not that the cross was a penultimate act of God, which at some future date will be followed by an ultimate act. Rather is the cross the ultimate act of history. For it is there, and not at some future moment, that men have found the ultimate judgement on the world and the ultimate assurance of the wonder and power of God's love.

So past, present, future, all play their part in the Johannine record, as they do in the synoptic story. But in John they are all linked with the great affirmation 'I am'. 'Before Abraham was, I am' (8⁵⁸); 'I am the light of the world' (8¹²); 'I am the resurrection and the life' (11²⁵). This expounds rather than distorts the whole tenor of the synoptic record. For the synoptics it is typology that focuses the past upon Jesus. As for the future, its reality in him finds statement in two movements – of his own historical person being in the future: the one who is to come and fill the role of the Judge of Jewish apocalyptic is not a new figure but precisely himself as son of man. And during his earthly life the veil of his presence is partly lifted in the strange event known as the transfiguration, which, significantly for this theme, has been called by some critics a 'displaced' resurrection appearance. In fact both John and the synoptics use devices to make it quite plain that the 'historical Jesus' and the risen Lord are not twain but one, the future in the present, the eternal in the temporal, the divine in the human, God become man.

JESUS OF HISTORY AND JOHANNINE CHRIST

Before the implications of this introduction are summarized and assessed, something needs to be said about the Christology of John. What kind of person is the central figure of the fourth gospel? Is he much the same as, or, as is more frequently asserted, very different from, the figure to be found in the synoptics? Is the portrait of Jesus in John a 'credible' historical reality, or has he been so presented by the author as to lose a real claim to historical credibility? And how in the end is the fourth gospel to be used by the theologian? How far does John make a valuable contribution to Christology?

No honest reader of the four gospels can deny that, at any rate on a first reading, the Jesus presented in John seems to differ vastly from the person described in the synoptics. Dr Percy Gardner has made the point briefly and tellingly (*The Ephesian Gospel*, p. 90): 'The greatest contrast exists between the Jesus of the Synoptists who is exquisitely and touchingly human, and the figure which says "*I am the light of the world, the door of the sheepfold, the true vine. Ye are from beneath; I am from above*". The conclusion is unavoidable that such a figure could not have had an historical existence. In his I.C.C. Commentary Dr Bernard said:

'It used to be argued in the middle of the nineteenth century that the christology of John is so markedly different from that of the Synoptists that if we wish to get "Back to Jesus" we shall do well to confine ourselves to the Marcan picture of him as more primitive and less sophisticated than the Johannine narrative.'

Certainly every honest reader of the gospel must admit that, whatever conclusions be drawn from the facts, there are undeniable differences of record and 'atmosphere' alike between the synoptics and John. But if the general position adopted in this commentary be right, it would be possible and indeed right to see John not as adding to, changing or correcting the synoptic(-like) portrait of Jesus, but rather to enable his readers to see, perhaps for the first time, what sort of portrait the synoptists had drawn.

What strikes the reader as he passes from the synoptic narratives to John is, without doubt, something not improperly described as a kind of 'theological' difference. On the very first public appearance of Jesus in the fourth gospel he is hailed as '*The Lamb of God who takes away the sins of the world.*' When one of his first disciples brought Nathanael to Jesus, the evidently supernatural knowledge which he seemed to possess caused Nathanael to say 'Rabbi, you are the son of God.'[*] This theological beginning is sustained throughout John. At his first miracle he can say '*My hour has not yet come*' (2^4). All through the fourth gospel tremendous theological claims are made by Jesus in

[*] The interpretation here given differs from that given in the commentary: but this is the kind of 'natural' interpretation that ordinary readers and learned scholars alike have made.

the first person, and while there are one or two similar sayings in the synoptics* their persistency and profundity in John make the fourth gospel feel a different book. There are the great '*I am*' sayings. '*I am the bread of life*' (6³⁵); '. . . *the light of the world*' (8¹²); '*I am the one who bears witness to myself*' (8¹⁸); '*I am from above*' (8²³); '*I am the door*' (10⁷,⁹); '*I am the good shepherd*' (10¹¹,¹⁴); '*I am the resurrection and the life*' (11²⁵); '*I am the way, the truth and the life*' (14⁶); '*I am the true vine*' (15¹, ⁵). Other transcendent claims are also made by Jesus: '*I and the Father are one*' (10³⁰); '*Before Abraham was, I am*' (8⁵⁸); '*Truly, truly, I say to you, he who hears my word and believes him who sent me, has eternal life; he does not come into judgement, but has passed from death to life*' (5²⁴); '*If any one keeps my word, he will never see death*' (8⁵¹).

Nor is it only about his own exalted nature that Jesus appears to have supernatural sources of knowledge. The 'surface' meaning of his conversation with the Samaritan woman implies that he had miraculous knowledge of her marital history (4¹⁶ff). The repeated saying of '*my time* [or hour] *is not yet*' (2⁴; 7⁶; cf. 7³⁰; 8²⁰) suggests that he had special knowledge of the time of his destined death. And John certainly leaves his readers with the impression that Jesus had foreknowledge of the betrayal by Judas (13¹¹, ²⁷; cf. 6⁷⁰f). He *knew* men (2²⁴f).

The difference is not exhausted in reciting such specific instances as these; there is an 'air' about the fourth gospel that is quite different from that of the synoptics. In the narrative of the passion, for example, the fourth gospel seems to depict a figure who can calmly theologize at the very crisis of his life; the great discourses and the 'High Priestly prayer' seem to belong, not to a recognizably human figure, but to some impassible deity clothed for a while in human flesh. And while that is itself an overstatement about that section of John, and while that passage may not be wholly representative of the rest of the gospel, it suffices to indicate what many readers feel, that in the fourth gospel there is no longer an historical portrait of an historical Jesus, but a theological commentary on aspects of the incarnate Word.

Nothing that can be said can alter the fact of the differences between the synoptics and John. But three things can and must be said to set the facts in perspective. First, the synoptics are far more 'Johannine' than at first appears. If it is substantially only in John that Jesus makes

* e.g. Matt. 11²⁵ff; 12⁴⁷ff.

73

exalted 'theological' claims for himself, it is in the synoptics that he does things which were recognized as being the work of God. The story of the assurance of forgiveness to the man let down through the roof by his friends states that when Jesus said 'My son, your sins are forgiven' the scribes at once questioned in their hearts 'Why does this man speak thus? It is blasphemy! Who can forgive sins but God alone?' (Mark 2[7]). Jesus is reported to have called his disciples together, and appointed twelve 'to be with him, and to be sent out to preach and have authority to cast out demons' (Mark 3[14f]). Mark's gospel is concerned, as all the gospels are, to recount the new beginning, the new creation of the life of the people of God. In the story of the Old Testament people of God there were twelve patriarchs called and appointed by God. In the Old Testament it was God who gave his people the law, and it was the recognition of the divine origin of the law that made men feel unable and unworthy to do any more than expound or interpret it. But in giving the 'new law' of the new people of God in the Sermon on the Mount Jesus does what no believing Jew could do without blasphemy, claim an authority equal with God. 'You have heard that it was said ... But I say to you ...' (Matt. 5[21,27,31,33,38,43]). And if it be thought that the Johannine emphasis upon the great blessings accruing to those who keep Christ's words are uncharacteristic of the synoptics, then it must be noted that the synoptic tradition has the parable of the man who built his house upon a rock (Matt. 7[24f]). The Jesus of the synoptics affirms that he will judge mankind (e.g. Matt. 19[28], with 25[31ff]).

It may be thought that Christ's prevision of the future is much less emphasized and much less present in the synoptics than in John. Less emphasis perhaps; less present, probably not. The voice at the Baptism, '*Thou art my beloved son, with thee I am well pleased*', with its combination of quotations from Psalm 2[7] and Isaiah 42[1] may well be an indication on the part of the evangelist that even at that stage of his life Jesus began to be aware not only of his divine status but also of his destiny as the servant, eventually the suffering servant, of Isaiah's prophecy. And if that be denied, as it may be, then it is significant for the point of early synoptic witness to Jesus' foreknowledge of his death that in answer to the Pharisees' question of Jesus why his disciples did not fast, he answered by saying that the bridegroom would not always be with them. This implied first that he had some sense of an impending removal, and second that he saw himself again in a divine role as God come to claim his bride, Israel. The synoptic gospels are far more Johannine than is commonly supposed.

But likewise the fourth gospel is far more 'synoptic' than is usually perceived. The gospel certainly makes lofty claims for Jesus, but in no other gospel are the human elements so clearly portrayed. John can recount details of occasions not mentioned in the synoptics, as when he reports that Jesus made a whip of cords to clear the temple of cattle and those who sold them, with the money-changers (2^{15}). He reports that Jesus was weary, and that he sat down because he was weary (4^6). He tells how he broke with social custom by addressing a woman (and a Samaritan woman!) to ask her for a drink. He tells how he loved Lazarus, how deeply moved he was, even to tears, when he came near to Lazarus' grave ($11^{33,35,38}$). In the same way John tells of his deeply moved spirit at the moment when he tells the Twelve at the Last Supper that one of them was to betray him – a detail none of the synoptists mentions. The fourth gospel is more 'synoptic' than is usually perceived.

It is often by such means as this that some reconciliation between John and the synoptics is attempted. In so far as they are attempts to show that John and the synoptics are testifying to the same phenomena of what may be called 'observable history', they are interesting, but not theologically very significant. The very fact that all four gospels are about Jesus should be sufficient to establish the view that the same phenomena of observable history lie behind each gospel, even if each gospel makes its own selection of 'observable' data to record. The significant fact about any of the gospels is not its basis in observable history but in its use of a number of devices to indicate that something beyond 'observable history' is being given to the reader. In another word each gospel states some things that took place in order to testify to what was going on. The Jesus who seems so superbly ethical a teacher as he gives the 'Sermon on the Mount' seems to be a very different figure from the Christ who says 'He whom God has sent utters the words of God' (3^{34}); but in fact he is meant to be seen as the *same* person, divine and human together.

It has already been granted that there is a real difference in the way in which the synoptics on the one hand and John on the other try to tell their readers who was among men when Jesus was in the flesh. A suggestion about the reason for the difference may be put forward. It is perhaps best understood in terms of the time at which John wrote and the audience he had in mind. It would seem that the synoptic typology was replaced by a quite different indicator of the divine nature of Jesus. His divinity is not stated for the first time in John; it is only stated in a different way. John is wanting to make two things quite plain: that Jesus really was the *Eternal Word* incarnate in our flesh: and that he really was *in our flesh*. The need for this arose from the religious situation of the time and place of his writing the gospel, when the Gnostic-docetic tendencies were threatening to invade the Church.

Seen in the light of later theological developments the fourth gospel has its own rich contribution to make. Like the two later synoptic gospels, John prefaces the story Mark tells (beginning with John the Baptist) with his own preface. Matthew traced back the beginning of a new Israel to its first beginning with Abraham (Matthew 1^{1-17}). Luke traced the beginning of a new humanity to its first beginning with Adam (Luke 3^{23-38}), but John traces back the beginning of a new creation in Jesus Christ to its first beginning in God before the world came into being (John 1^{1-18}). But it would be wrong to think that John had made a tremendous or isolated innovation in so doing. The idea of the cosmic significance of Christ's coming in the flesh, already on the way to finding statement in the synoptics, was also being developed in the life of the early Church as it tried to clarify to itself what its worship of Jesus Christ as Saviour and Lord meant. The idea is found in Romans, Colossians, Ephesians and Philippians, and the evangelists were only writing their narrative of Jesus in a Church that was increasingly becoming aware of the universal significance of Jesus Christ; or in other words, aware of the universal character of what was going on in the events that took place, when Jesus lived and died and rose from the dead. There is a very moving piece of prose in J. M. Creed's book *The Divinity of Jesus Christ* which seeks to elucidate this profound mystery a little. He writes (p. 139):

Comparison with the Old Testament shows the essential identity of the prophetic and the evangelical religion and at the same time the new and distinctive features of the Gospel. Whereas an Isaiah stands himself as a penitent with the sinful nation over against the holiness of the Lord of Hosts, Jesus Christ is found to stand on the other side of the chasm – or rather, stranger still, he is on both sides at once: 'The friend

of publicans and sinners', yet also 'the Holy one of God'*. That kind
of impression must go back to the very beginning, and it must have
been very nearly, though not quite, at the beginning that the disciples
found here – in this chasm which separated them, yet did not separate
them, from their master – the true explanation of the crucifixion.

The point that needs to be made is that it would be wrong to
separate the historical and theological tasks of either John or the
synoptics. Any attempt to separate the two elements leads, in the end,
to some heretical Christology or theology. True God and true man:
that is certainly John's testimony. It is only if we think that his testimony about the 'observable' must be separated from his witness to
what is beyond observation and yet is 'seen' in the observable that
we find it possible to think him heretical, docetic or Gnostic or
Apollinarian (i.e. with the two natures not properly joined). The
advantage of the distinction between *what takes place* and *what goes on*
is that it does not establish two realms but remains in one. John has
borne witness as to what went on in what took place when Jesus
came, and has provided the Christian theologian with a basis not only
for Christology and in theology, but also for a doctrine of history, in
the place where God is with his world, and with his people in the
world.

Conclusion and Assessments

What then can finally be said about the making of John's gospel, so
long and so rightly venerated as a source for the adoring belief of
Christians? Little can be affirmed with certainty. We cannot know for
certain who wrote it. It may have been written at any time within
seven or eight decades around the turn of the first century A.D. It may
have found publication in any one of three cities. Does it matter? No,
it seems, in the view of the author! 'John' clearly hides behind a
deliberate anonymity (20³¹, *'These are written'* and 21²⁴, *'This is the
disciple who is bearing witness to these things, and who has written these
things'*). But whoever wrote the gospel, at whatever place or what-

* The present writer thinks that an even better point would be to observe
that Jesus goes as a Jew, as a member of the old people of God, Israel-after-the-
flesh, to receive with and for them John's baptism of repentance for the re-
mission of sins! In this way it may be possible to speak of his 'vicarious
repentance'.

ever time it was published, it stands on its own as one of the great books of the world, stamped with the individuality of its author, and beyond that with the wonder and glory of its subject as no other gospel is. But what can be finally said about it, and how is this final word rated in contemporary judgements about John?

If the various strands of evidence are brought together an earlier rather than later date seems required. It is no longer necessary to think that the so-called Hellenistic ideas (such as light and darkness, truth and falsehood) demand a date somewhere in the middle of the second century, where they can be clearly traced in Gnostic literature. It is no longer necessary to demand a date some decade or two after Mark, if it be held that the phenomena of the gospel are explicable, as Dr Dodd believes, though Dr Barrett does not, by supposing John had access to some synoptic-like tradition. For such persons a date perhaps as early as A.D. 70 becomes possible, if no other factor suggests a later date. But if John be thought to have known and used Mark, and at the same time be held to have had access to a tradition parallel to the synoptic, a date say between A.D. 85 and 95 becomes possible. The evidence of the Egerton Papyrus suggests a date either just after the turn of the first century (Barrett) or just before it (Bultmann). The reference to the 'excommunication' (if that be what it is) in 9^{22} would involve a date, it is claimed, after A.D. 90, when the Test Benediction was introduced. But if 5^{43} refers, as few critics nowadays would hold, to the revolt of Bar Cochba, then a date after 132 would be required. The most likely conclusion would be to date John either just before (which the present author prefers) or just after the turn of the first century A.D.

As for the author, certainty is even less obtainable. There are still conservative scholars who plead with skill and cogency for John the son of Zebedee as the author (e.g. Wikenhauser). The general line of argument was admirably used and exemplified in Plummer's commentary (*Cambridge Greek Testament*), where, after establishing the genuineness of the tradition that the author was the son of Zebedee, reinforcement of the tradition is obtained by establishing a series of points: the author was a Jew; he was a Jew of Palestine; he was an eye-witness of most of what he reports; he was an apostle; he was the apostle John. This leads to the statement (p. xxxii): 'We are now on too firm ground to be shaken by isolated difficulties'.

But many scholars have been less certain than Dr Plummer. Some have attributed the work to another John, e.g. John the Elder. Among English scholars there have been von Hugel, R. H. Charles, Canon Streeter and A. H. McNeile. Another 'John' already known in the 'tradition' of the early Church, John Mark, has been identified as the author, and among those supporting this somewhat speculative view the name of Johannes Weiss is found. The present writer's view (see above, p. 24) is that if the gospel is attributed to any John already known, possibly the name with fewest possible objections is that of John Mark, though this is possibly due to the fact that so little is known about him! Dr Moffatt rejected John the Elder as a possible author for the gospel.

Most modern theories of a 'critical' kind detect more than one hand in the production of the gospel. The son of Zebedee, John the Elder, the beloved disciple, the *witness* of 21²⁴ have all been brought into theories of composite production. And perhaps some such suggestion is the most likely to explain the very complex character of the gospel structure and the components of its thought. Such a view need not deny the unity of the gospel as it has come down in the Church: it is meant only to affirm that this rich unity has benefited from the contributions of a number of people, and represents, in the end, a powerful, spiritual, synthetic mind as the final hand at work on the book.

The problem of the relationship of the fourth gospel to the synoptics is also one where opinion is divided. A critic like Bultmann believes John did not know or make use of the synoptics: on the other hand Barrett has more recently argued for the use of Mark, and possibly Luke, and less certainly Matthew. Dr Dodd has pleaded impressively for a recognition that John had access to a source like the synoptics but independent of them. On the whole a view like that of Professor Dodd seems the most likely and to fit the facts best. The attempt to prove that John used Mark, even when made by a scholar of Barrett's skill, always has some air of 'special pleading'. But if Dodd's point be taken two things need to be said. First that John is not just a 'supplement' to the synoptic tradition, adding new material of the same kind; rather must it be seen as an independent contribution given to the world in order to provide a second type of interpretative key to the story of Jesus. Second, that if this be so the fourth gospel provides an independent, and not a dependent witness to the good news centred in Jesus of Nazareth. But if John be independent, what is his aim? Does he wish to correct the synoptics? Historically? Theologically? Scholars have been found to hold these positions: indeed a good deal of debate still turns on the question of 'historical' accuracy. The present writer has argued that the so-called 'corrections' are really historiographical devices aimed at making the central testimony of the synoptics unambiguously clear.

Certain tendencies in the gospel can however be detected. There is, as in the synoptics, a certain polemic against *the Jews*. John's concern is to show that the reality of what the Jews already had and hoped for was to be found in Jesus. He is thus the 'real' temple, the *place* that is to replace both Jerusalem and Samaria as the right place to worship God (4^{21}). He is the 'real' manna sent from heaven, the 'real' passover lamb offered to God (18^{28}); he is the 'real' source of the Law Israel had received (5^{17ff}). The gospel is also engaged, as the synoptics were, in an effort to give a proper account of the mission of John the Baptist ($1^{6-8,\ 20f,\ 29}$; 3^{28-30}). No doubt this reflects a continuation at a later time in the Church's story of the situation recorded in Acts 19^{1-7}, where at *Ephesus* Paul found a group of disciples of John the Baptist. The gospel is said (by Irenaeus, Jerome and other Fathers) to have been written to refute Gnostic errors. The author was so immersed in his task that his own language became to some extent impregnated with Gnostic ideas, which explains both why the Gnostics very quickly made use of it to establish the apostolicity of their faith and why the orthodox were somewhat slow in recognizing John as a gospel alongside the three synoptics.

The sources of John's thought have also been much investigated. Scholars like Hoskyns and Davey have emphasized his great debt to the Hebrew tradition. Dr Dodd has pleaded persuasively and temperately for the basic influence of Hellenism in providing the framework for John's genius to work, though recognizing, of course, other influences as operative. Professor Bultmann has based his interpretation upon the conviction that Mandaean literature is the basic influence on John. What seems to emerge from such a world of such different and sometimes rival claimants is the need to recognize John as endowed with a supreme genius to turn all the varied thought forms of his day into instruments of Christian evangelism and apologetic. He used the various concepts and ideas of his world in a new and Christian way. He may not be said to have become all things to all men, but he can be said to have used all that all men said to make all men learn of the one whom he believed to be the son of God and Lord of all.

Finally what may be said about place is bound up to some extent with what is said about the author and the influences affecting him. Thus Bultmann, with his emphasis on the Mandaean influence on John, is naturally inclined to a view that locates the fourth gospel in Syria (Antioch), where the Mandaeans were strong. Alternatively, J. N. Sanders, holding to the predominant influence of Gnosticism, and impressed by the discovery of Papyrus Egerton 2, has argued for Alexandria as the place of composition, particularly in view of the fact that Alexandrian Gnostics used the fourth gospel.

When all is said and done, then, it is difficult if not impossible to achieve anything more than probability about the various 'critical' introductory problems about John. The present writer believes that it is not impossible to hold, and quite possible to be true, that during the last decade of the first century A.D. a certain John, possibly John Mark, with access to a large amount of material about Jesus, and knowing probably one and possibly more of our synoptic gospels, wrote down a new form of the story of Jesus for his own community, which was both cosmopolitan and affected by the presence of disciples of John the Baptist. He was a deeply sensitive religious spirit, able to fuse together in the crucible of his own ardour for Christ the various sources, materials and ideas he gathered, and transmit them to his world, and ours, in a way which could speak equally well to Jew or Greek, pagan and follower of John the Baptist alike. The eloquence, nobility and persuasiveness of his story have not lessened down the years, for it is still the gospel of John that speaks most tellingly to the simple believer, and also most effectively plumbs the depths of Christian belief and commitment for the highly sophisticated. For all men it still bears the powerful witness that 'Jesus is the Christ, the Son of God', and enables men 'believing, to have life in his name.'

Suggestions for Further Reading

Barrett, C. Kingsley: *The Gospel according to St John* (S.P.C.K., 1955).

Bernard, J. H.: *International Critical Commentary: St John* (Clarke, 1928).

Bultmann, Rudolf: *Das Evangelium des Johannes* (Vandenhoek und Rupprecht, 1957).

Carpenter, J. Estlin: *The Johannine Writings* (Constable, 1927).

Dodd, C. H.: *The Interpretation of the Fourth Gospel* (C.U.P., 1953).

Dodd, C. H.: *Historical Tradition in the Fourth Gospel* (C.U.P., 1963).

Glasson, T. F.: *Moses in the Fourth Gospel* (S.C.M., 1963).

Guilding, Aileen: *The Fourth Gospel and Jewish Worship* (O.U.P., 1960).

Higgins, A. J. B.: *The Historicity of the Fourth Gospel* (Lutterworth, 1960).

Hoskyns and Davey: *The Fourth Gospel* (2nd edition; Faber & Faber, 1947).

Howard, W. F.: *The Fourth Gospel in Recent Criticism* (Epworth, 1956).

Howard, W. F.: *Christianity according to St John* (Duckworth, 1958).

Hunter, A. M.: *The Gospel according to John* (C.U.P., 1965).

Lightfoot, R. H.: *St John's Gospel: A Commentary* (O.U.P., 1956).

Nunn, H. V. P.: *The Authorship of the Fourth Gospel* (Alden & Blackwell, 1953).

Temple, W.: *Readings in the Fourth Gospel* (Macmillan, 1940).

Plan of the Gospel

In dividing the gospel up into sections suitable for commentary and putting titles to them the commentator hopes to make it easier for his reader to enter into the meaning of the text of John. This may or may not prove to be the case. What the commentator cannot help doing is to disclose to his readers a good many of his own views about the gospel.

In the analysis of John which is set out in the Plan of the Gospel it will be evident that the present writer sees the gospel as somewhat symphonic in pattern. There are a number of themes which are separately stated, woven together, and all affirmed together in a final triumphant climax.

The gospel opens with a prologue giving the story about to be told its proper cosmic setting. Then the story of the ministry follows, presented in terms of a number of recognizable and recurrent themes. The New Gospel and the Old World; the Seven Signs; the Deed and the Word; the Rite and the Reality. The last sign for understandable reasons has its 'word' before, not after its deed, and it is thing signified as well as sign, reality as well as rite, a deed done by which God's word was spoken. The commentator can only hope that such a presentation will help his readers to come more easily and quickly to apprehend what John sought to tell the world, so that men might have life in the name of Jesus.

Prologue 1¹⁻¹⁸
The Testimony of John 1¹⁹⁻³⁴
Discipleship – The Beginnings 1³⁵⁻⁵¹
The First Sign: The Bridegroom and the Wine 2¹⁻¹¹
Interlude 1. Capernaum 2¹²
'The Lord will come to his temple': 1. 2¹³⁻²⁵
The New Gospel and the Old World: 1. The Jew 3¹⁻²¹
The Final Testimony of the Baptist 3²²⁻³⁶
Interlude 2. Samaria 4¹⁻⁴
The New Gospel and the Old World: 2. The Samaritan 4⁵⁻⁴²
    5–14 The Woman and the Bride
    15–26 The Bridegroom and the Messiah

John 1¹⁻¹⁸

The Prologue

1 *In the beginning was the Word, and the Word was with God, and the Word was God.* 2*He was in the beginning with God;* 3*all things were made through him, and without him was not anything made that was made.* 4*In him was life,ᵃ and the life was the light of men.* 5*The light shines in the darkness, and the darkness has not overcome it.*

6*There was a man sent from God, whose name was John.* 7*He came for testimony, to bear witness to the light, that all might believe through him.* 8*He was not the light, but came to bear witness to the light.*

9*The true light that enlightens every man was coming into the world.* 10*He was in the world, and the world was made through him, yet the world knew him not.* 11*He came to his own home, and his own people received him not.* 12*But to all who received him, who believed in his name, he gave power to become children of God;* 13*who were born, not of blood nor of the will of the flesh nor of the will of man, but of God.*

14*And the Word became flesh and dwelt among us, full of grace and truth; we have beheld his glory, glory as of the only Son from the Father.* (15*John bore witness to him, and cried, 'This was he of whom I said, "He who comes after me ranks before me, for he was before me." ')* 16*And from his fulness have we all received, grace upon grace.* 17*For the law was given through Moses; grace and truth came through Jesus Christ.* 18*No one has ever seen God; the only Son,ᵇ who is in the bosom of the Father, he has made him known.*

ᵃOr *was not anything made. That which has been made was life in him*
ᵇOther ancient authorities read *God*

'... the preface to the Fourth Gospel, with its movement from the Word to the Son of God, is both an introduction and a conclusion to the whole work. The relation between creation and salvation, prophets and apostles, history and that which lies beyond history, time and eternity, law and grace, death and life, faith and unbelief – these are the themes of the Fourth Gospel, themes that meet and go apart, separate and meet, that is to say, in the human history of the man Jesus, in Jesus Christ, the Son of God, and Word of God.' (Hoskyns and Davey, *The Fourth Gospel*.)

The comprehensive and penetrating insight of the evangelist is immediately apparent in the prologue to the gospel. The author is already acquainted with what the Synoptists have already written of Jesus Christ; he knows the apostolic preaching and some of its development; he is well versed in Jewish learning; he has a profound understanding of the religious thought and practice of contemporary Hellenism. He brings them all to his aid as, like the Synoptists before him, he writes a brief introduction to his gospel. The result is a unified piece of theological writing unmatched in Christian literature.

When Mark set out to write of 'the beginning of the Gospel of Jesus Christ, the Son of God' he found it necessary not only to preface the story of the ministry of Jesus with an account of the work of John the Baptist, but also to present that preparatory mission as itself an embodiment in an actual historical situation of a prophetic oracle (or oracles) from the Old Testament. These two historiographical devices may be summarized for the modern reader by supposing that, were Mark able to address him directly, he would say: 'If you wish to know not only what Jesus did in the course of his ministry, but also to understand it, to know what was "going on" in it, then you must see and understand it as the continuation and the crown of what John the Baptist did; moreover, if you want to know what John the Baptist did and to understand it, then you must go back in Israel's history to two situations in which two great prophets spoke great words about God's provision of his people's needs, words which for the first time begin to find their fulfilment in the historical words and actions of John the Baptist.' The story of Jesus, that is to say, really begins far back in Israel's history.

When Matthew wrote his gospel, so very much modelled on Mark's, he wrote of the 'becoming' (Greek, *genesis*; R.S.V. 'genealogy') of Jesus Christ. He made much use of Mark, but at the beginning of his gospel he traces back the genealogy of Jesus Christ to Abraham, indicating thereby that in the life and work of Jesus, God had now finally, as once in promissory action long ago through the call of Abraham, chosen and called a people into being for himself.

Luke, like the author of the fourth gospel, wrote consciously in relation to a considerable body of tradition (Luke 1¹), and he followed Mark deliberately by telling his readers in his preface that he was, as others before him, intending to 'compile a narrative of the things which have been accomplished (or, "fulfilled") among us'. Luke traced the genealogy of Jesus farther back than Matthew, to the first man Adam; thereby indicating his belief that the story of Jesus really began with the creation of man, and that what God was doing in the life and death of Jesus was to create not only a new Israel, but a new humanity, for himself. As Paul put it, Christ is the second Adam.

Malachi, Isaiah, Abraham, Adam – thus do Mark, Matthew and Luke try to show, at the very beginning of their gospels, by a simple historiographical device, that the story of the gospel does not begin with itself, but for its proper apprehension and understanding demands recognition as the continuation, the crown and the fulfilment of the whole story of the people of God in the Old Testament. John carries this process to its ultimate limit, and, it may be said, even beyond it. The Prologue begins with the same Greek words that were used to open the translation of the Hebrew scriptures into the Septuagint (Greek) version: *In the beginning.* . . . This daring development of the historiographical reference to the beginning of the gospel story is tantamount to a twofold claim: first, that to go back to the real beginning of the Gospel the reader must go back to creation, or even, as Genesis itself cannot be held to do, to what was 'before' creation; and second, that what God was doing in the life, death and resurrection of Jesus Christ was more than simply calling a new people, a new Israel, to himself, more even than making a new humanity, but actually making a new creation. And he made it through the Word, the same Word which framed the first creation, and of which the evangelist now proceeds to give a compendious history, which finds its climax and culmination in v. 14: *The Word became flesh.*

So in the Prologue the evangelist picks up and develops the introductory historiographical devices of the Synoptics. Mark, followed and developed by Matthew and Luke, uses the Old Testament as the scripture whose meanings are already known and accepted, but are now in a new way embodied in an historical situation, in the way of 'fulfilment' in the history of Jesus Christ. With the other three evangelists John sees the Old Testament as that which is fulfilled in the gospel story, though he has his own way of conceiving that relationship.

In forming his own way of exhibiting the relevance of the Old Testament to the facts of the gospel story John is, at least in part, concerned that those who read his gospel shall have no further excuse for reading the Synoptic gospels superficially, or without adequate theological and religious understanding. The long history of the study of the gospels has but served to underline the necessity of his task. It has often been claimed that the Synoptic gospels, particularly Mark, tell the 'simple, historical story' of the life, death and resurrection of Jesus, and that John offers us a 'theological' gospel, one where the facts are all the time given a theological interpretation. We shall see how false this antithesis is, for John again and again makes it clear that in his own selection of material for his gospel he is but making explicit and articulate what had remained obscure and uncertain in the Synoptic narrative.

But John's genius is not concerned simply to restate in profounder and inescapably theological terms the apparently untheological story told by the Synoptists, though that were a sufficiently formidable task in itself; he has also brought into the prologue his own acquaintance with Greek, and particularly with Stoic philosophy, thus making the gospel story meaningful not only to the Christian and the Jewish-Christian reader, but also to the Hellenistic thinker and the Hellenistic religious man. And all this he contrives by his choice of the one term *Word*.

Where does the story of Jesus begin? In his own distinctive way John says 'It begins with the Logos, the Word; for the story of Jesus is the story of the Logos.' In the prologue he first recounts the story of the Word in brief: and then, in the body of the gospel, in a series of selected and significant incidents he tells the story of the incarnate Word. The choice of the term 'Logos' enables him to focus upon his narrative the theological insights of the Old Testament, of Jewish rabbinic tradition, of the apostolic Christian tradition, and of Hellenistic, especially Stoic, thought; he shows how the Christian tradition transcends, even while it uses, the words and ideas of other and apparently irreconcilable traditions.

The Old Testament is summarized in the Johannine teaching about the Word. In Genesis 1, it is stated that when God 'spoke' the creative act took place; and this found many an echo in the rest of the Old Testament, e.g. Psalm 33^6: 'By the word of the Lord the heavens were made.' Jewish tradition had already come to identify the Word of the Lord with the Torah (see Prof. C. H. Dodd, *The Fourth Gospel* 268ff.), and came to absorb into the meaning of 'Word' what its own religious tradition had said about the Memra (= Word) and Wisdom of God. Philo had already begun to use this development to introduce into Judaism some distinctively Greek, particularly Stoic, ideas; and it is significant that John boldly uses the word 'Logos' to express his understanding of the meaning of the Gospel story, so giving the cultured Jew as well as the Gentile intelligentsia an opportunity to understand something of the depth of the Christian interpretation of the life and death of Jesus Christ. So to his interpretation of the Synoptic story John brings from Judaism the ideas of God's effective and indeed creative speech, of his breath, his wisdom and his purpose; from Hellenistic speculation he brings notions about the ideal world and the ideal man. So his prologue is able to indicate to the reader that, far from the gospel story being a series of interesting, even miraculous incidents in the career of a certain Jesus of Nazareth, it is a meeting place, in an historic person, at a specific moment in human history, of time and eternity, of God and man, of all that lies beyond history and what takes place in it.

The prologue gives an outline of the 'history' of the divine Word. It begins with the same words as Genesis 1, and yet does not restrict in any way the 'Word' to God's uttered speech, or even to his creative action. Rather, in the manner of rabbinic Judaism it conceives of the Word, as Judaism thought of the Law or Wisdom, as with God before his creative acts took place. Or, in Hellenistic terms, it sees the Logos as the satisfying rational principle for understanding the universe. The Word may thus be likened to the eternal purpose of God, giving meaning to the whole of existence; and by insisting that such a purpose was, in his sense of the phrase, *in the beginning with God*, John seeks to convey to his readers of every age the conviction that what took place as divine action in the life of Jesus Christ was not some 'afterthought' of God, but the true embodiment in a personal historical life of the whole purpose of God, and of all the meaning of the universe.

The evangelist next states that the Logos that was with God *in the beginning* was also the universal agent of creation. In other words, everything is within the operative area of his universal purpose and control. Nor is the purpose an 'it', but a living person. Indeed the Word thus conceived is really life itself, and we truly share in life as we share in the life of the Logos. The Logos is also the one true source of enlightenment for men, the one real light shining in the darkness of the world, its meaninglessness, and in man's existence in it. The true light of the Logos shines, but the darkness of the world has never quenched it. How can it, since the light is the creative Logos?

These profound reflections now appear to be interrupted by three verses about John the Baptist, who is said to be sent from God to bear witness to the Light, the Logos, so that all men might believe. The interruption is only apparent. The Baptist's central witness is to the Logos incarnate, as he took human flesh and dwelt among men (cf. 1.26–27; 29–34; 36). But in this part of the prologue the evangelist is not writing about the Logos as incarnate (though this view is taken by some commentators) but about the Logos as the true light of the world. He is thus saying, before he records John's testimony to the incarnate Logos, that the Baptist also bore witness to the Logos that had been the true illumination of all men, and especially of God's own people Israel. To recognize the incarnate Logos involved identifying him with the Logos active among God's people in their history and illuminating all men with any true knowledge of God they might have. Thus John's witness is both about the 'old covenant' and the 'new'; to write a 'New Testament' is inevitably to make a new book of the Old. The Baptist stands both in the Old Testament dispensation to witness to the old Israel concerning the Logos who had illumined their way, and in the New Testament era to testify to all men of the incarnate Logos and his work. He affirms the identity of the one Logos in these two operations.

Moreover, none can recognize the Logos, creative, providential or incarnate, without witness, whether that witness be divine and immediate, as with the Old Testament prophets who declared 'Thus saith the Lord' and the Baptist who affirmed 'he who sent me to baptize with water said to me "He on whom you see the Spirit descend and remain, this is he who baptizes with the Holy Spirit"'; or whether that witness be human and mediate, as with all who hear today the preaching of the Word, or in times past listened to the prophet or the preaching of the Baptist and believed.

The evangelist now gives the substance of any true testimony (including that of the Baptist) to Israel as to what God had already done in the work of his enlightening Word. This may be called a brief conspectus of biblical history under the interpretative norm of *the Word*. The basic human situation, such as is depicted in the first twelve chapters of Genesis, is now envisaged as the presence of the true light in the world, with the world failing to recognize him. Into a world of blind men the illuminating Logos next came; came to his own people, his own place, but his own people rejected him. Israel, as a people, was disobedient. But some received him (John here enunciates the Old Testament doctrine of the remnant) and to those was given the right* to become children of God. Such true sonship was not, as the Baptist's Jewish contemporaries held, a matter of human descent, but always and essentially an act and gift of God. In this sentence John has described the situation for mankind, and in particular for God's chosen people, from the call of Abraham to the time of the Baptist's appearance. What follows takes us into the Christian era.

The words next used by the evangelist must have made both Jews and Greeks recoil: *The Word became flesh and dwelt* [tabernacled?] *among us.* In these words John states what he takes to be the story in and behind the Synoptic story, the distinctively Christian view that God became man. The idea of an incarnate Word would have been repulsive to a Stoic, who, though he was prepared to call his god 'logos', could only speak of him as a rational principle explaining the way the world 'worked', and providing for men a proper basis for the direction of their lives through some indwelling of the 'logos' in them. But that the god 'logos' should ever have been incarnate in one personal life would have been a quite impossible and wholly objectionable idea. Yet it offered the evangelist the opportunity of bringing into his Christian thinking whatever was relevant and true in Stoic speculation, and so making more accessible to the Greek mind what it was that Christians believed about God in Jesus Christ.

Similarly with Judaism. A pious Jew was taught to sing that 'by the word of the Lord the heavens were made' (Ps. 33⁶); and so the 'word' was for him creative. The word was also communicative for him, since the great prophets of his religion had prefixed their prophecies with the authoritative affirmation 'Thus says the Lord'. Neither of these concepts in isolation, nor the two combined, come anywhere near the daring thought of a word incarnate; but they at least point in the right direction. There was also further help for the evangelist in later Jewish literature. Wisdom had come to be spoken

* 'Right' rather than 'power' (R.S.V.). To become a 'son of God', whether by creation or redemption, is, in the Bible, always a gift of God, an act of his grace, cf. Paul's use of the phrase 'sons by adoption'. It is important to avoid a translation which suggests that simply by the acquisition of power we can make ourselves into 'sons of God'. Perhaps neither word gives a theologically felicitous translation: the emphasis is on the fact that the right is 'given', 'bestowed', and is not something inherent in man or his deeds.

of in almost personal terms, and was thought of as having almost a personal existence alongside God (cf. especially Wisdom 7$^{22-30}$). The hospitable mind of the Alexandrian Jew Philo had already, in the second century B.C., joined the Greek and Hebraic streams of thought. He borrowed the distinction between the ideal and the real from Plato, and spoke of the world as the *logos* of God. Even more significantly for the fourth Gospel he could identify the logos as the Ideal Man, first or primal man, God's image from whom all mortal men derive.

But if, as seems likely, John's is the last of the four gospels to be written, and if its date is somewhere toward the end of the first century A.D., the author could also draw upon an already developing tradition of Christian usage of the term 'logos'. In the Synoptics it had already come to stand for the whole of the Christian message (e.g. Matt. 13^{19}: 'When anyone hears the word of the kingdom . . .'). Peter and Paul also used the term to signify the Christian message (e.g. 1 Peter 1^{23}: 'You have been born anew . . . through the living and abiding word of God', and 1 Cor. 14^{36}: 'Did the word of God originate with you?'). By joining Peter's notion of the word as living with the Pauline idea of it as God's purpose (cf. Rom. 9^6: 'It is not as if the word of God had failed . . .'), it is possible to come very near to the final step which John now takes in making an explicit identification of the message about Jesus with Jesus Christ himself, and of Jesus Christ with the living and abiding word of God.

But we must not suppose that this analytical method is a bare reversal of John's synthetic labours. We must not imagine him as taking a Jewish idea here, a Rabbinic idea there, a Hellenistic and Stoic idea elsewhere, and then mixing them with some parts of a Christian tradition, and so arriving at his concept of the Logos. That would only be like supposing that Shakespeare wrote his plays simply by mixing medieval chronicle, classical story or historical incident with a few contemporary ingredients and so produced his masterpieces. The truth surely is that John began with a profound insight into the nature and message and work of Jesus, and from that was able to fuse into a new indissoluble unity a conception of Jesus Christ as the Word which spanned the gap between that unutterable time of God *in the beginning* before creation began, and the divine-human life whose story he retells in his gospel, and retells in such a way that for ever after it has remained impossible to read the Synoptic gospels as if they were treating of purely human and temporal magnitudes. Yet, in fastening upon the term *Word* John has provided himself with a means of effective communication with Jew and Greek, Christian and pagan, religious and profane alike.

The Word became flesh and dwelt among us clearly brings the compendious history of the Word to the point which in Luke's and Matthew's gospels is occupied by the nativity stories. The next sentence is a comment on the historic incarnation of the Word: *we have beheld his glory, glory as of the only Son from the Father*. This compresses into a sentence the whole of the synoptic record; what the completed story, from cradle to empty tomb and ascension, really amounts to is precisely that those whose eyes were opened really saw the glory of the Lord. What they saw may seem a paradox to those outside, and that is why testimony is necessary for its present discernment. But the glory was there, and was recognized, as he proposed to show in the narrative of his gospel. The next sentence brings the story of the Word to the era of the Church: *From his fulness have we all received, grace upon grace*. The becoming flesh of the Logos was not a mere theophany, just there for men to see, and to see only when they received the testimony given; it was a gift for all who believe, establishing for them a new relationship to God. In the Old Testament dispensation man could enter into the divine glory only in so far as he could render obedience to the law divinely given; but now, in the community that knows and believes in the Logos incarnate, the undeserved favour (grace) and the unfailing kindness of God have been given to men in their full reality (truth).

The closing sentence of the prologue provides a kind of summary statement of the religion and theology which the Christian church, as the community of the Logos, is bound to affirm: *No one has ever seen God; the only Son, who is in the bosom of the Father, he has made him known*. The evangelist shares with both Jew and Greek the belief that God is not an object of sense; he cannot be seen by mortal eyes. Yet in the incarnation of the Logos, the only Son, the one who, so to speak, sits closest to the Father (in his bosom) has really made God himself known in terms of mortal flesh and life. Yet what they have seen, of which John will remind them in his narrative, is not some being intermediate between God and man, but God himself as man. This is the great wonder and mystery of Christian faith, and with its statement the grand prologue comes to its climax. God has not made himself known in yet another theophany, i.e. in some form of being which is a mere instrument to indicate his activity, but has, in the person of his Son, himself become flesh. God's eternity has been joined to man's temporality in man's history. At last man can truly know God.

So John has begun his gospel in a recognizable restatement of the beginning of the Synoptic gospels, and has done this so that Jewish cognoscenti as well as Hellenistic intelligentsia might, with his Christian readers, learn of the greatness and depth of the mystery which is also reality. His aim here, as declared at the end of the gospel, is 'that you may believe that Jesus is the Christ. and that believing you may have life in his name'.*

The centre of the prologue, as of the whole gospel, is John's conviction that 'the Son of God has come'†. His use of Rabbinic, Stoic or Old Testament terms does not make his work simply an exercise in literary synthesis, or in amateur metaphysics; rather he uses every tool he can to express in as rich and diversified a way as possible his one certain and saving truth – that Jesus Christ, the Son and Logos of God, has indeed come in the flesh as the saviour of the world.

ಚಿಇ

1

In the beginning . . .: This phrase is almost certainly an intentional reference to Gen.1¹, and may well be a deliberate echo of the opening of the Gospel according to St Mark. The evangelist indicates that the story of Jesus Christ really begins with the absolute beginning of all things, with God himself. It is impossible not to comment on the word *was,* for in the Greek language it represents that part of the verb (the imperfect tense) which refers, not to an isolated past event, but to a continuous condition. The evangelist has not yet reached the point of writing about what can in any sense be called 'history', but is concerned with what are the essential and universal conditions of history. Of these the Word's being with God *in the beginning* is paramount.

the Word: We have seen in the exegetical note how many strands of meaning the evangelist picks up with this one term – God's creative power, his purpose, the reason of things, his wisdom and providence. In spite of the somewhat vague sense of the translation *Word,* it is wiser not to replace it by a term with a more definite meaning, for any more

* John 20³¹. † cf. 1 John 5²⁰.

restricted significance would fail to do justice to the rich allusiveness of John's language. Nowhere is it more creatively at work than here.

and the Word was with God: When Mark recounts the story of the rejection of Jesus in his home at Nazareth, he tells us that his fellow-townsmen said 'Is not this the carpenter? . . . and are not his sisters here with us?' (Mark 6³). In a like sense the evangelist intends us to understand that the Word was *with* God, i.e. in his rightful home and place. He also conveys to us that the Word of God is not to be thought of, as a pantheist would think of it, as an undifferentiated part of the divine substance; but rather, as the Christian tradition has always tried to think about the person of the Son in the divine Trinity, a centre of life and being distinguishable from the Father, but abiding with the Father as his natural home, and in a divine unity. The evangelist now crowns his description of the Word with the amazing statement:

the Word was God: This is a statement that exceeded anything that Jewish theologians had ever said about Wisdom or the Law; it exceeded anything that the Stoics said about their Logos. John means us to understand from the beginning of his gospel, as it sets out to retell the synoptic story, that the subject of the story is not simply a Nazarean carpenter, but, in a true sense, the divine being himself.

2
He was in the beginning with God: This is a somewhat typical turn of style in John, a phrase which both resumes what has been said, and yet adds a fresh note. Here John restates the contents of v.1, but in such a way that we cannot suppose that the Word came into being when God began his creative acts. The Word did not come into being when, in terms of Genesis 1, God *said* 'Let there be light'; but he was in the divine being 'before' any creative action occurred. Neither can we think, after reading this verse, that the Word had some existence independent of God before the creation took place, and that the Word, already existent, became associated with God in the act and process of creation. If a temporal framework be used to speak of God and the Word in creation, then it must be affirmed that the Word was with God from and in the beginning.

3
all things were made through him . . . : Judaism and Hellenism each had its own doctrine of a universal agent of creation. John is not stating anything new, save that he is about to say that the agent of creation is also the incarnate saviour.

There is some uncertainty about the end of this verse. It may read

as the R.S.V. translators render it: '*All things were made through him, and
without him was not anything made that was made.*' Or it may be rendered:
'All things were made through him, and without him was not anything
made. What was made was life in him.' The more ancient practice was
to put the full stop after the first 'made'. That sentence ends the account
of the origin of all creation in the Word, which has been stated both
positively and negatively. The evangelist next says explicitly that
created things do not have life in themselves, but only in the Word,
which is thus presented as the agent not only of creation, but of providence as well. The Church Fathers who altered the punctuation were
trying to avoid a possible false doctrine being buttressed by John's
authority: there were those who were trying to speak of the Holy
Spirit as a creation. But today there seems no need to retain the modi-
fied punctuation and so lose the important step forward in John's
account of the Logos.

4

the life was the light of men: Light and life are often connected in the
Old Testament (e.g. Ps. 36⁹; 'For with thee is the fountain of life; in
thy light do we see light'). Light was the first gift of creation, and here
the evangelist is stating that all the light of the world that brings insight
and understanding to men is the work, the presence, of the Logos.

5

The light shines in the darkness, and the darkness has not overcome it: The
first part of this sentence affirms that light, the Logos, always shines,
always illumines the darkness of the world. Though this language no
doubt finds its origin in the biblical creation narrative, it is not simply a
statement about the act of creation; the present tense prohibits any such
interpretation. The light, who is the Logos, shines in the darkness of
the world, a darkness which is by no means only physical, but moral and
spiritual. The light always shines. The darkness *has not overcome* it may
equally be translated 'has not understood'. John probably intentionally
uses the ambiguous word. This statement about the shining of the light
gives the evangelist a point of transition from the eternity of God before
creation (if 'before' be a permissible term) to the history that followed it.
The darkness has not overcome is an historic tense; nothing that occurs in
history can quench the shining of the true, the real light.

6–8: The Witness of John (I).

Before passing to the historical part of the story of the Logos the
evangelist pauses to mention that John had been sent to bear witness to
the light. With the Synoptists, therefore, he shares the view that testimony is necessary to the knowledge of Jesus Christ. But he introduces a
reference to the Baptist's testimony much earlier than any of the

Synoptists. Why? The answer probably is that, granted that the Word incarnate is not simply an object of sense, but the subject of testimony, neither is the Word in Israel an object of simple observation. Or, in other words, the Old Testament, no less than the New, is about the work of the Word that can only be known by testimony given. Such testimony either comes directly from God – *There was a man sent from God* – or indirectly through some divinely-inspired witness, such as John the Baptist. To bear witness to the incarnate Word, and to identify him with the light of God's people Israel, are precisely parallel tasks. To read the Old Testament as the witness to the light that is the Word is itself the fruit of testimony. John, in order to bear witness to the incarnate Word, was necessarily involved in a re-reading of Israel's history, which now stood revealed as the sphere in which the same light operated as that which now shone in the life of the incarnate Word.

6
a man sent from God, whose name was John: John's testimony helped others to believe, but his own belief and therefore his capacity to bear witness to others came by direct inspiration from God. This theme is also recognized in the Synoptics (e.g. Matt. 16¹⁷: 'Blessed are you, Simon Bar-Jona! For flesh and blood has not revealed this to you, but my Father who is in heaven.') and in Paul (e.g. 1 Cor. 12³).

7
He came for testimony: The Greek word for *testimony* can be almost trans-literated into the English word 'martyr'. The evangelist recognizes many persons and acts as witnessing to Jesus Christ. By the time this Gospel was written some of the more tragic meanings of 'martyr' were already being recognized.

9-13
The Light in History and in Salvation-History. This section gives the summary statement of the history of the light or logos. Verse 9 tells us that the light not only shines in the darkness, but also comes into the world; v.10 records the inability of the world to recognize the true light; v.11 speaks of the light as active in the history of God's chosen people Israel; vv. 12 and 13 represent the hope of the faithful remnant of Israel, and so bring the description to the time of the incarnation.

9
The true light . . . was coming into the world: The R.S.V. rightly takes *coming* together with *light*. (The alternative is to take it with 'every man' which, though not unlike similar phrases in Jewish writings, gives too much room to the Stoic idea of the universal light of reason. Moreover, the next verse almost requires a previous statement that the light had come

into the world). The question is, whether this statement is already a reference to the incarnation. This interpretation is possible, and many scholars have commended it. But, while it is possible to take the whole section 9–11 as a description of the world at the time of the incarnation, it seems somewhat artificial to do so, in view of (a) the clearly defined steps of the summary history (the light in creation, in human history, in the chosen people, in the remnant) and (b) the quite different form of speech when the author unmistakably comes to speak of the incarnation in v.14. Here he says *The light was coming into the world*; there he says 'The Word became flesh'. We shall therefore assume that the evangelist is here referring to the fact that the world is the place where the true, the real, or the genuine light has always shone since creation began.

that enlightens every man: If we accept this translation, it must remain something of a mystery why, in the very next verse, John speaks of the world's unbelief! It is better to give the word translated *enlighten* its primary meaning of 'bring to light' or 'shine upon' in the sense that, whether a man believes in the light or not, it shines upon him and shows him up for what he is.

10

He was in the world: World is not an easy term in John. Here it refers to the world of men, and their life in societies and nations. Other meanings of 'world' in John are (a) the whole created order (e.g. 17⁵) and (b) this 'lower' world, in contrast to the world that is above (e.g. 8²³). It is important to recognize what meaning the author is using at each place.

the world knew him not: In John, as in the Bible generally, knowledge is more than intellectual recognition, being much more akin to the sort of knowledge a man may have of his wife, when love and trust and mutual care are at least as important ingredients as the element of intellection. Note that the author does not here refer to the light (which is a neuter noun in Greek) as neuter, but uses a personal pronoun. Grammar is one thing, the reality of the genuine light is another!

11

He came to his own home, and his own people received him not: Came is an historic tense in the Greek. This is not, that is to say, a coming of a general sort, equally true of all men; but an historic coming, in a unique series of historic events. *His own home* reflects a neuter plural in the Greek, and indicates that those to whom he came were rightly to be regarded as his 'property'; the chosen people really belonged to God, by the fact of his choosing them.

his own people: translates a masculine plural. The tenants of God's house (he dwells not in temples made with hands, but with those of

humble heart!), his chosen people, rejected the light that had come to
them.

12, 13

But to all who received him . . . .: This, on the interpretation adopted, refers
to any who were 'righteous' in the midst of an 'unrighteous' Israel;
it included those who came to be known as 'the remnant'. But how
could those who lived B.C. 'receive him'? How could they 'believe
on his name'? The possibility is assumed again in the body of the Gospel
when Jesus says to the Jews that 'Your father Abraham rejoiced that
he was to see my day; he saw it and was glad.' Paul has a similar
thought when he writes of a supernatural rock which followed the
fathers in the wilderness and states that 'the Rock was Christ' (1 Cor.
10⁴). Such language is possible on two conditions: 1. that the same God,
the same Word that was God acts in both Old Testament history and
the New Testament event of the incarnate Word; and 2. that to penetrate behind the observable phenomena of Old Testament events and
see the reality of their divine author was already in basic fact to have
received the Word. Racial descent, legal observance, had never been
the real or adequate bond between God and his people.

he gave power to become children of God: Power is better translated 'the
right' or 'the authority'. The point is that those who believe are children
of God by grace, and not by nature. To believe on the name of Jesus
Christ is to pass from death to life, from alienation from God to a new
adopted sonship; but even that is God's doing, as the figure of 'adoption' indicates, and it is also but the beginning of the attainment of full
glory. As it is put in the first epistle of John, 'Beloved, we are God's
children now; it does not yet appear what we shall be . . .' (1 John 3²).

who were born, not of blood: This phrase underlines, from the divine side,
that the sonship of Christian men is the gift of God. When God begets
us as his sons, it is not through any human descent ('blood' is literally
'bloods' in the Greek, and derives from an ancient belief that blood
was the instrument of procreation) or human sexual desire, but entirely
by means spiritual, in the gift of faith in the name of Christ. Some
give a singular verb to the verse, which then reads 'Who was born,
not of blood . . .' The evidence is not strong and almost certainly
represents an attempt to endue the fourth gospel with some clear
enunciation of the Virgin Birth. Had the evangelist penned the singular
he would almost certainly have been most careful in writing of the Lord's
family in the body of the gospel and left no room for any doubts being
cast upon the Virgin Birth. As it is, he has stated with great care the
essential truth, which is theological, not biological.

14

And the Word became flesh: This is clearly the climax of the prologue, the crown of all the summary history that has been recounted. The Word that created, that shone through creation, that had cast its brightness upon the chosen people of God, in whom the truly 'righteous' had believed, at last came into the sphere of human life as man. He *became flesh. Flesh* means human nature in its totality, not just the physical constituent of a human body. *Became* is a difficult translation, and it is worth noting that the Greek word used here is the same as that used of the appearance of John the Baptist in v.6; perhaps in each case we should translate by some such phrase as 'There appeared (or came) upon the scene the Word as flesh (or, a man sent from God . . .).' The evangelist, who is always most careful in his use of words and phrases, is probably underlining the absolute humanity of the incarnate word in thus using of his coming the same word with which he introduced the Baptist to the reader.

and dwelt among us: A more literal translation would read 'and pitched his tent among us', and would convey the meaning that many have found in the verse, that for a while the eternal word took up temporary residence in the world of men. But the verb never has the implication of a temporary stay in other places in the New Testament. So it is perhaps better to take an even more literal translation, rendering the clause 'and pitched his tabernacle among us'. This has the advantage of taking the mind of the English speaking reader to the Tabernacle described in Exodus (Exod. 25ff.) and to the tent where God came down in the midst of his people (Exod. 33⁷⁻¹¹). The word 'tabernacle' had already become charged with new meaning when the prophets used it to depict the future time when God would finally dwell in the midst of his people. So Zechariah says 'Sing and rejoice, O daughter of Zion; for lo, I come and I will dwell in the midst of you, says the Lord.' John seems to draw these strands together in speaking of the incarnation of the Word. When he came in the flesh it could be said that, like the Tabernacle, there was on earth a human embodiment of an heavenly reality; that, as on the tent of meeting, the glory of God could be seen to rest on him; and that now at last God had indeed taken up residence among his people.

full of grace and truth: These words occur at the end of the Greek sentence, i.e. after the words *glory as of the only Son from the Father*; but they are rightly moved to this position in English, for they really describe the attributes of the Word incarnate. Grace is not a word used in the body of the Gospel, though it was already a treasured Christian word, en-

dowed with deep meaning by Paul, the writer to the Hebrews and
Peter. Its characteristic use is to describe the love of God for men,
stooping to initiate their redemption, in contrast to the legalism of the
Jewish understanding of salvation. It is God's great deed of 'kindness'
that he should give his Son for man's redemption. Truth, by contrast,
is one of the key words of the Fourth Gospel. 'Reality' might be
substituted for it here, and indeed in many places. What has taken place
in the incarnation is no mere 'appearance' of God; Christ did not dwell
among men as some 'phantom', but really took human nature upon
him. Thus the reality of the incarnate Word is not simply that of the
reality of his having a real body of flesh and blood, but of that body
being the 'tent' or 'tabernacle' of the eternal God.

we have beheld his glory: This phrase follows very naturally after a reference to the Word 'pitching his tent' or 'tabernacle' among us, for it
was on the tent of meeting that the bright cloud representing the glory
of God was seen to descend in the days of the wilderness wandering.
The tabernacle especially manifested the glory of God at the time of
sacrifice (Lev. 9$^{6, 23}$). The word glory includes all the manifestations
of the divine majesty and power. God's glory is not only an attribute of
his divine person, but is also his acts, and in the Old Testament it is
spoken of in reference to the miracles in Egypt (Num. 14^{22}), and in the
giving of the Law (Deut. 5^{24}). It is also used to speak of the transcendent
experience of the great men who were privileged to 'see' God in vision;
e.g. Moses (Exod. 33$^{18, 22}$) and Ezekiel (Ezek. 1$^{1, 28}$; 3^{23}; 8^4). To assert that
the glory of God has been seen in the incarnate Word is thus to claim that
in the deeds and in the teaching of Jesus Christ, and perhaps most of
all at the moment of his sacrifice, God has manifested himself to his
people; and that in meeting with him those who had eyes to see knew,
as their fathers of old, that God was dwelling in the midst of his people.
But whereas in the Old Testament the hope of God's coming finally
to live in the midst of his people remained something to be fulfilled in
the future, John means us to understand that in Jesus Christ, the incarnate
Word, that future hope has already taken historical form. This is brought
out in many ways in the Gospel, not least in the thought of his body as
the temple (cf. 2^{21}). The evangelist does not shrink from using the word
'beheld', which implies that what is believed about the incarnate
Word is not derived solely from spiritual insight, but is rooted also in
ordinary sense perception; He will not separate 'spiritual' knowledge
from 'sense' knowledge. The verb *beheld* is in the historic tense; he will
not separate the historic events and the historic person to whom he
witnesses from the knowledge of the eternal God. The use of *we* derives
from the fact that the evangelist is not just speaking for himself, but for

all his fellow believers and eye-witnesses. Christian experience is essentially community experience.

glory as of the only Son from the Father: The meaning of this phrase may be seen if we reflect that the Greek would be more literally translated 'glory as of an only son from a father'. John is making a claim of absolute uniqueness for Jesus Christ. There is none other who can be said to incorporate in his human nature all the transcendent glory of God save this one man, who is thus in the same position as an only son – the one being by whom men can come to know what the father is like. When this conception is lifted from the human to the divine plane, as it is here, then the Church was not in error, once questions had been raised about the nature of Jesus Christ, in translating as in the R.S.V. and most other texts.

15

It is probably an error to put this verse into parenthesis, for it is just as much a part of the whole passage as are vv. 6–8. It is certainly a mistake to translate the verbs 'bore' and 'cried' in the past tense, for, although they have a past form in Greek, their reference is to the present. John the Baptist remains a witness to Jesus Christ. But to what? The usual interpretation is to say that, however mysterious and indeed mystifying it may be, the sense clearly is that John the Baptist testified and continues to testify to the pre-existence of the Son. But if it may be held that in vv. 6–8 the evangelist is making plain that in addition to testimony to him who is the light of the world, John is also involved in witnessing to the presence and activity of that light in the history of Israel, then we may understand these verses as referring to the life and activity of the Word as the crown of Israel's history, out of which history, as its last and greatest exponent, the Baptist spoke. This enables full weight to be given to the temporal meaning of *before* and *after*, without the necessity of supposing that the Baptist taught the pre-existence of the Word, or seeking refuge in the suggestion that *before* and *after* are used here metaphorically, and really say no more than that Jesus is greater than John, and that John knew it.

16

And from his fulness have we all received: This verse resumes the main exposition, and the body of Christian believers bear their joint testimony. They wish to assert that what they obtained from the incarnate Word was not simply a sight of his bodily presence, and the sound of his words in what he taught (and that might be the misinterpretation to which their testimony would be subject), but an actual sharing in what he was, his nature in its fulness.

grace upon grace: Grace is not a once-given and once-received gift or act of kindness. It is a continually renewed giving and receiving, communicated by the personal relationship which the incarnate Word made possible.

17

For the law was given through Moses; grace and truth came through Jesus Christ: Though the light that was the Word had shone in the life of Israel, there is a great difference between that life and the life of the Church. John is about to make this clear in the prologue before he goes on to the body of the Gospel. The law was God's gift to Israel, and as such, to use Paul's words, holy, and just and good; but the gift that God had intended for life, had turned to man's undoing and death. That is the greatest mystery of iniquity, that it could turn a life-giving gift of God into an instrument of death! In contrast to the law, grace and truth have come *through* Jesus Christ. Grace, the kindness of God in receiving to himself those who deserve banishment from his presence, has come, not as an external requirement like the law, but as and in a personal relationship with the only-begotten Son. Hence what has come through Jesus Christ is not only grace, but truth – reality, the reality of that which was intended in the giving of the Law, but which has only found its true embodiment now in the becoming flesh of the Word. So, like the Synoptics before him, John expresses both the continuity and the discontinuity of the new with the old people of God. They are indeed united, but only in the person of him who is Jesus Christ the Lord, the genuine historical embodiment, in life and words and deeds, of that saving act of kindness (grace) which was intended, but, through man's perversity, only foreshadowed, in the law given through Moses.

18

No one has ever seen God: In spite of the stories that in some sense Moses saw God (Exod. 33²³) and that the name Israel means the one who has seen God, it was a fundamental doctrine of Judaism that God was invisible. The targums took special care to avoid any such implication of the biblical text: for example, Isaiah's vision, instead of being reported in the words 'My eyes have seen the King, the Lord of hosts!' is rephrased in the words 'Mine eyes have seen the glory of the shekinah of the King of the ages, the Lord of hosts'. The concept of the invisibility of God was, of course, common to Greek and Jew. John is therefore not trying to say, over against Judaism and Greek religion and philosophy, that God, in Christian eyes, is visible after all. Rather he reaffirms the doctrine in quite uncompromising terms. What he does go on to say is equally forthright, though the text presents difficulties.

the only Son: A more awkward reading would give the translation 'the only God'; and the more awkward reading seems to be the
original, as Hort's exhaustive examination showed.★ Yet it is clear from
the rest of the sentence that what is demanded for the sense is a background to the statement that Jesus Christ had made God known. Two
alleviating comments can be offered. First, the Word has already been
said to be God (v.1b), and the adjective *only* might be translated 'only
begotten': second, the suggestion made by J.H.Bernard resolves the
difficulty, if accepted, that 'only', 'God' and 'he who is in the bosom
of the Father' are three distinct descriptions of him who makes God
known. This involves making 'only' into a noun, and translating
*the only begotten, who is God, who is in the bosom of the Father, he has made
him known.*

who is in the bosom of the Father: This is the position given at a meal to
the specially intimate guest. It was taken, for example, by the beloved
disciple at the Last Supper (cf. 13²³, ²⁵). The Word who has become
incarnate comes, as we might say, from the very heart of God. He
knows all that God knows.

he has made him known: John has chosen a Greek word which is at once
the technical term for the Jew in making known the Rabbinic interpretations of the Law, or for the revelation of divine secrets; and a term
characteristic of Greek religion for the publication of divine truths.
So to Jew and Greek, the evangelist would say, the incarnate Word
brings from the very heart of God a full revelation of what is in his
heart and mind for man and for his world. God remains invisible; the
incarnation is not a chance to see God. But he is no longer unknown or
unknowable; the mystery of his will and purpose has been made known
in the Word who is the Son of God incarnate.

★ F.J.A.Hort, *Two Dissertations*, 1876, pp. 1–72.

John 1^{19–34}

The Testimony of John
Mark 1²⁻⁸
Matthew 3¹⁻¹⁷
Luke 3¹⁻²²

¹⁹*And this is the testimony of John, when the Jews sent priests and Levites from Jerusalem to ask him, 'Who are you?'* ²⁰*He confessed, he did not deny, but confessed, 'I am not the Christ.'* ²¹*And they asked him, 'What then? Are you Eli'jah?' He said, 'I am not.' 'Are you the prophet?' And he answered, 'No.'* ²²*They said to him then, 'Who are you? Let us have an answer for those who sent us. What do you say about yourself?'* ²³*He said, 'I am the voice of one crying in the wilderness, "Make straight the way of the Lord," as the prophet Isaiah said.'*

²⁴*Now they had been sent from the Pharisees.* ²⁵*They asked him, 'Then why are you baptizing, if you are neither the Christ, nor Eli'jah, nor the prophet?'* ²⁶*John answered them, 'I baptize with water; but among you stands one whom you do not know,* ²⁷*even he who comes after me, the thong of whose sandal I am not worthy to untie.'* ²⁸*This took place in Bethany beyond the Jordan where John was baptizing.*

²⁹*The next day he saw Jesus coming towards him, and said, 'Behold, the Lamb of God, who takes away the sin of the world!* ³⁰*This is he of whom I said, "After me comes a man who ranks before me, for he was before me."* ³¹*I myself did not know him; but for this I came baptizing with water, that he might be revealed to Israel.'* ³²*And John bore witness, 'I saw the Spirit descend as a dove from heaven, and it remained on him.* ³³*I myself did not know him; but he who sent me to baptize with water said to me, "He on whom you see the Spirit descend and remain, this is he who baptizes with the Holy Spirit."* ³⁴*And I have seen and have borne witness that this is the Son of God.'*

Each of the four gospels provides information about John the Baptist; yet he remains, for all that, an enigmatic figure; though, as so often with events in the distant past, the enigma persists more in the area of 'historical fact' than in the realm of theological interpretation of the fact. Here, as elsewhere, the Fourth Gospel offers a profound and decisive contribution.

The synoptists agree, and John concurs with them in this (cf. 1¹⁵,³⁰), that the Baptist's ministry preceded that of Jesus.* This gave rise to a situation in which many people, including Herod the Tetrarch, thought that Jesus was but John the Baptist come back to life after his execution. That this was a fairly common view is evident from the fact that all the Synoptists report that before Peter's confession (Mark 8²⁸ ∥) the disciples reported to Jesus that many held him to be John the Baptist. Yet the Synoptists are at one in making it quite clear that Jesus was no mere resuscitated personage from either the near or the distant past, but a being of a quite different order, whom the Church came to worship as the Son of God. The material about John in each Gospel is best understood as each evangelist's attempt to make clear to his readers this important distinction between the Baptist and Jesus Christ.

When Mark introduces John the Baptist he indicates by a description of his clothing (cf. 2 Kings 1⁸) that he was, or claimed to be, Elijah. True, the allusion might escape the unwary, or a Gentile unaware of the Old Testament story, but the allusion is there. Similarly the reference to John's food seems to indicate that like Jonathan in Israel (1 Sam. 14²⁹) the Baptist was possessed of supernatural powers of seeing a great victory of God 'round the corner'. Matthew repeats Mark's Old Testament allusions, and later confirms them in a report of Jesus' teaching (Matt. 11¹⁰⁻¹⁴) and adds an explicit statement, by way of comment on Jesus' conversation with his disciples after the transfiguration, that John the Baptist was Elijah (Matt. 17¹³). Luke is cautious about such a typological use of Elijah. But he does report that before John's birth it was foretold that he would 'go in the power and spirit of Elijah' (Luke 1¹⁷). For the rest Luke omits the Old Testament allusions to Elijah (cf. Luke 7²⁶ᶠ; 9³⁶) in writing of the Baptist, and confines himself to recording his divinely given powers of discernment.

Why should the Baptist be identified with Elijah? Because it was the popular belief of the time that before the great Messiah came to bring final deliverance and victory to Israel, Elijah would return to earth as his herald. In the pattern of events portrayed in Jewish eschatology both Elijah and Messiah had their apportioned roles to play. So to identify the Baptist with Elijah was really to assert that Jesus was Messiah. Yet in the fourth Gospel the Baptist tells the priests

* But at another point John implies that the ministries of John and Jesus overlapped (3²²ᶠ).

and Levites from Jerusalem that he is neither the Messiah nor Elijah. We may well ask why.

John was known as 'the Baptizer'. That this name so easily identified him was due to the fact that he was the first figure in Israel to offer to his followers a baptism performed by another than themselves. The Jews knew a number of 'baptisms' – self-lustrations for purification of one sort or another – but not till now had one appeared offering to baptize other men into discipleship. Yet John's baptism was not simply the gathering of disciples round a teacher; rather was it an attempt to prepare for a rebirth of Israel as the chosen and responsible people of God. John's baptism was one of 'repentance for the forgiveness of sins' (Mark 1⁴; Luke 3³), and the whole setting of the Synoptic narratives emphasizes that repentance was not sought simply in respect of personal shortcomings, but, in the manner of the great prophets of Israel, for sins of national failure to fulfil the responsibilities properly to be discharged by a true people of God.

A number of indications point this way. (1) John's ministry is *in the wilderness*, where the old People of God were prepared for their entry into and life in the land of promise. (2) He baptized his converts 'in the Jordan', and they descended into it, and came from it, in symbolic repetition of the passage of the Israelites of old from the east bank to the west. We know also that other reformers so appeared at this time (cf. Acts 5³ ⁶ᶠᶠ), and Josephus (Antiquities 20⁵,¹ᶠ) tells of Theudas who took his followers to the east of Jordan, and expected the ancient miracle of the river crossing to be repeated; not, of course, for the mere repetition, but to impress upon his followers that, like the Israelites of old, they were now to enter and form anew the life of the people of God. (3) Matthew and Luke report John as warning the Jews, or the Scribes and Pharisees, of 'the wrath to come', and telling them that God was able to raise up his children from the stones in the desert. The wrath of God was exercised upon Israel as a people who had failed to fulfil its reponsibilities as God's chosen means of conveying true faith to the world; and (4) the reference to Abraham's seed is clearly directed away from personal wrongdoing to corporate responsibility. John's baptism was thus a reiteration of the ancient prophetic condemnation of Israel for her unfaithfulness and a new statement that none of the devices offered by her present official religion – purifications of any kind – were adequate to renew the Jews as the true people of God.

To this baptism Jesus came. Mark says that Jesus was baptized by John, and saw a vision as he came out of the water. Matthew reports John's reluctance to baptize Jesus, yet Jesus argues it away. Clearly Matthew wants to underline the complete identification of Jesus with the ancient people of God, even in their disobedience, and his offering as the obedient son, of the one true repentance for Israel's failure to discharge her responsibilities. Matthew's account of the vision reads as if it were visible to all at the time. Luke does not even assert that John baptized Jesus, and reports that the vision (again apparently visible to all) came while Jesus was praying after his baptism.

How does the fourth evangelist deal with this rich tradition about the Baptist? Already in the prologue he has stated that John was 'sent from God'; that his witness to the Word involved a re-reading of the Old Testament story as well as an astounding assertion about Jesus Christ; and that his ministry preceded that of Jesus. Thereafter, although the Baptist is spoken of at some length, the portrait seems very different.

Priests and Levites come from Jerusalem to ask John who he is. The Baptist's replies are all negatives. So much will the evangelist emphasize the synoptists' judgement that John is, theologically speaking, in a different world from Jesus, that he avoids any positive assertion as to his person. '*I am not . . .*' is all that he can say; '*I am . . .*' is to be reserved for Jesus: this is the finality of the contrast that began in Mark between John as Elijah and Jesus as Messiah. '*I am not the Messiah*', says John; and '*I am not Elijah*'. Does this latter denial contradict that Synoptic tradition of John as the returned Elijah? Not necessarily so: for in Mark and Matthew, where the description of John derives from that of Elijah, it is not stated that John made this claim in words. He dressed as Elijah dressed, and many thought he was Elijah *redivivus*, but the only point in Mark or Matthew where this identification is explicit is where Jesus makes it so (Matt. 11^{14}; 17^{12f}). In other words, Mark and Matthew may well be right in asserting that John dressed himself like Elijah, and John correct in stating that he made an open disclaimer that he was Elijah. It is one thing to dress like Elijah, another to put a claim into words before religious officialdom, and still another for Jesus himself to make the identification of John with the prophet. But Luke's position is a half-way stage to John's; for he omits the details of the Elijah dress, and any identification of John with Elijah: indeed he seems to have some concern to present Jesus himself as Elijah returned*. He, like John, tends to assign a lesser status to the Baptist than Mark or Matthew. But John goes further and deeper than Luke. Luke reports that Jesus was baptized, but not that John performed the ceremony: John does not even report the baptism. Like Matthew, Luke describes the vision and the voice at the time of the baptism as publicly visible and audible: John makes it pointedly plain that even the Baptist's ability to understand the significance of the voice and the vision rested upon previous divine preparation (1^{33}) and not upon any 'natural' endowment of the Baptist.

In thus completing the movement of the synoptists, John has achieved two important results: first he has removed the figure of the Baptist from the realm of Jewish apocalyptic, by denying him status as Elijah; and second, as the more important corollary of that, he is able to treat the person of Jesus, from the very beginning of his Gospel, not simply as a human figure with a divinely appointed role to play, not even as a supernatural intruder coming into human history to fulfil his predestined function, but rather as the one divine-human figure, God and man together, the eternal Word made flesh, whose coming into time redeems it, and whose assumption of our human nature opens up new possibilities of being for all men, through the victory-in-tragedy that he is to win.

Jesus in the Fourth Gospel is thus Son of God from the beginning (1^{34}). John the Baptist is but a voice. Indeed it would not be seriously mis-stating the case to say that in the Fourth Gospel the Baptist, for all that it may be true, as Luke tells (Luke 1^{17}), that he would go in the spirit and power of Elijah, is as dependent upon special revelation for his recognition of Jesus (1^{33}) as were the Shepherds in the Gospel of St Luke (cf. 2^{12}). Both John and the Shepherds were told of a recognition-sign; both were privileged to see it; both thereafter bore witness to what they had seen and heard, and told of the person revealed in vision and event, i.e. by revelation.

After the denial by the Baptist that he was Elijah, Messiah, or one of the Prophets (cf. the reports of the disciples as to the popular estimate of Jesus in Mark 8^{28} //), the fourth evangelist reports a further examination of John regarding his baptism (1^{24-28}). The

* See e.g. the discussions in D. E. Nineham, *Studies in the Gospels*, Oxford, 1955, p. 52.

question put to the Baptist was this: 'You admit you have no status as Elijah, Messiah or a prophet reborn. Then whatever significance for God's people can your baptism have? Why are you a baptizer?'

We know from Acts 19$^{1-7}$ and elsewhere that Baptist communities existed for a considerable time after John's death. The Christian Church was under necessity to clarify its position in regard to such communities, and this apologetic necessity probably had a good deal to do with the selection of material relative to the Baptist in all four gospels; and it may well illuminate the development of the treatment of the Baptist between Mark and John. The synoptic answer to such communities was given in such passages as Matthew 11^{11} // , where the Baptist is said to be greater than any born of woman, yet less than the least in the kingdom of heaven. Here, in the Fourth Gospel, in answer to the question about his baptizing, John answers that his is but a water baptism, but that someone is in their midst compared with whom John is utterly negligible. The answer is enigmatic. Yet it clearly points away from the ceremony of baptism, whoever performs it, to the person and nature of one who, at the time of John's speaking, was still to be manifested. Not the rite but the person is important!

The enigma of the Baptist's answer begins to be clarified when the evangelist passes on to report what happened on the next day when John saw Jesus (1$^{29-34}$). As Jesus came towards him John declared:

'Behold the Lamb of God, who takes away the sin of the world! This is he of whom I said "After me comes a man who ranks before me, for he was before me." I myself did not know him; but for this I came baptizing with water, that he might be revealed to Israel.'

'After' and *'before'*. The paradox of these terms expresses the point that not until he who was to come has arrived and been manifested is it possible to know who the Baptist is, or what his function is to be; just as in the Prologue it was made clear that only in the light of the historical coming of the eternal Word was it possible really to understand the history of God's chosen people, Israel. John states explicitly that his baptism was undertaken with one final end only – that the one far superior to John might be manifested to Israel. When John sees Jesus he knows that this purpose has been achieved.

But the evangelist has not yet fully made his point, for it is essential to his presentation of the true significance of John that even John's recognition of Jesus should itself rest upon revelation, and that he should clearly affirm that the true baptism would be a baptism with the Holy Spirit, by him upon whom the Spirit would visibly come and with whom he would visibly stay. Again, this profound insight of the fourth evangelist picks up and develops the growing modification of the Marcan narrative by Matthew and Luke. Mark had reported Jesus as speaking of 'the baptism with which I am baptized' (Mark 10^{39}), and Luke tells of a saying of Jesus, 'I have a baptism to be baptized with; and how I am constrained until it is accomplished' (Luke 12^{50}). It is clear that in the Synoptics the water baptism which Jesus accepted from John was already envisaged as under the necessity of a fulfilment, in the whole event of passion – cross – resurrection. In this part of the fourth gospel it is made plain that the supreme claims made for Jesus are made because the spirit not only came to him at his water baptism, as indeed the Synoptics report, but remained with him. The fourth gospel is written after the first three, and all of them after the resurrection, ascension and the gift of the Spirit. The true baptism is the gift of the Spirit, and the true baptizer is he with whom the Spirit perpetually dwells. The Baptist bears simple and adequate testimony to the descent of the Spirit upon Jesus, and lest any reader of the Synoptics might misconceive the story, his abiding with him. So here is the end of the Baptist's witness to Jesus. He has been at pains to point out that he has far more to proclaim than the occurrence of predestined acts in an eschatological drama, with its figures of Elijah and Messiah: rather is he concerned to assert the insignificance, almost the non-being even of the forerunner and herald of the Word, save as that Word is incarnate in the man Jesus, perpetually indwelt by the Spirit. The person of the forerunner can achieve nothing final: he can at best bear witness – and how significant a witness it is – in his words and his baptizing, to the incarnate Word, the Son of God.

ॐ

19

the Jews sent: The Synoptics report no such embassy, though it is highly probable that some report on all such reformers as the Baptist would be sought by the authorities.

20

He confessed, he did not deny, but confessed . . . .: A typical piece of Johannine style, to give emphasis and weight to what follows, viz. a negative confession of the Christ.

21

'*I am not the Christ . . . Elijah . . . the prophet*': In current Jewish surmise it was hoped that Messiah (Christ) would come. Many had apparently thought that John was he. Elijah was expected, on the basis of Malachi 4^5, as the Messiah's herald. It was further expected that one of the great prophets would return (cf. 1 Macc. 4^{46}; 14^{41}; 4 Ezra 2^{18}). It is clear from Mark 8^{28} that the appearance of Jesus had caused many to identify him with Elijah, or one of the prophets: it is not therefore surprising, nor in any way impossible, that similar eschatological hopes were raised by the activity of John. But the important point here is the evangelist's removal of the whole Baptist–Christ relationship for its interpretation from the realm of such apocalyptic hopes. What is taking place in Christ is not just a scene in a drama, but the coming of the eternal Son into the world of time and history.

23

'*I am the voice of one crying in the wilderness*': For all the impropriety of identifying the Baptist with a figure of apocalyptic Judaism, John now claims before his questioners a significance truly based in the one authority they recognize – the scripture. He is 'a voice crying in the wilderness' – one who speaks from a situation in which the fulfilment of God's promise is still future, as Israel's situation in the days of (second) Isaiah long ago. His cry is '*Make straight the way of the Lord*'. His duty is to prepare for the coming of the Lord – the one God of the Old Testament religion who was shortly to be identified, to the bewilderment of the Jews, with Jesus of Nazareth.

26

'*I baptize with water*': This underlines the relatively insignificant, preparatory, provisional character of John's baptism – and that of Jewish lustrations and purificatory washings. Water cleanses, but temporarily. And in so far as baptism in the water of the Jordan is concerned, neither John nor the Pharisees were of the stature or possessed of the authority to declare any baptism so far practised as the entry into the life of the new people or Israel of God. All that John and the authorities could do belonged to the stage preparatory to the beginning of the new Israel.

'*but among you stands one . . .*': John, supernaturally enlightened for his mission (1^6 cf. Mark 1^7 //; Luke 1$^{15f.}$), knows that the Son – Messiah is among the Jews, though as yet unmanifested. When he is, then John's true non-significant significance will be evident.

27

'*the thong of whose sandal I am not worthy to untie*': This service was a menial one performed by slaves, who had no status and no rights. John is saying that he has no status compared with the coming one, and no rights, even to be a person with no rights in the New Israel of God.

28

This took place in Bethany beyond the Jordan: There is textual support for the name Bethabara, where, according to a local tradition, John baptized. This enables the reader to avoid confusion with the Bethany where Lazarus lived, and whither (according to the evangelist [10⁴⁰; 11⁶ᶠ]) he went from the place where John first baptized. But it is as easy to understand the evangelist's statements in 11¹ᶠᶠ as a careful attempt to differentiate for the reader between two places with the same name.

29

The next day: This is the first of a series of time notes in ch. 1, during which four days are said to elapse – five if we accept an alternative reading in 1⁴¹. It would seem therefore than in some such way as Mark tried to give an account of a 'day of the Lord' as he opened his gospel (Mark 1¹⁶⁻³⁴) John has tried to present the week of the beginning of the new creation by the Word at the commencement of his narrative. The marriage feast at Cana then occurs on the seventh day after John received the official deputation from Jerusalem.

'Behold the Lamb of God': Evidently this is a profound and important saying. Scholars are much divided as to its meaning. The chief lines of interpretation understand the title in terms of

1. Exodus 12, the Paschal lamb. But this lamb was not held to take away sin! Nor is the Greek word used here for 'lamb' the same as that used in Exod. 12.

2. Isaiah 53⁷, the Servant Lamb, though this would be to pick up one, incidental characterization of the servant, and leave unexplained why the fourth gospel fails to report the silence of the Lamb (Jesus before his accusers) at the trial.

3. Leviticus 16²¹ᶠ which was a goat sent into the wilderness on the day of Atonement to take away the sins of the (Jewish) people. But this achieves expiatory significance at the cost of losing the word Lamb.

4. The Lamb offered in the daily sacrifice in the Temple – but this also had no connexion with the taking away of sin.

Therefore some scholars look beyond the Old Testament, and add

5. The Paschal Lamb as reinterpreted in the Christian Eucharist: and in view of the fact that the Gospels come from the Church which celebrated the Eucharist, and further that since John has already left it clear about the person and status of the Baptist that his proper place cannot be seen until the 'coming one' has been manifested, we may

expect that a title drawn from the Eucharist, which is *after* the confession of John, should be the only adequate one to indicate his nature and office.

6. The use of another Greek word for *Lamb* in the book of Revelation where the Lamb, sacrificed for man's redemption, is nevertheless the divinely appointed ruler of God's people, and he is all victorious in his wars against the enemies of God. The book of Revelation comes from the same area as the fourth gospel, and this would suggest the idea of the conquering lamb was well known to its readers. Dr Dodd argues that in the context here *lamb of God* is manifestly a synonym for Messiah.

But we are surely not compelled to confine ourselves to one only of the interpretations offered. We have already discovered in John's writing of the Prologue how skilled he is in gathering into one term significant allusions from diverse backgrounds. The same thing has most probably happened here, and in this one word *Lamb* the evangelist has drawn together from within the eucharistic experience of the Church overtones of meaning from O.T. prophecy and ritual, current temple practices, and the developed apocalyptic hopes of both Jews and Christians.

But a question remains: is any such statement, rich and profound though it be, an historical possibility; or, on another level, is it compatible with the Synoptic story, where according to Matthew (11^{2-15}) and Luke (7^{18-28}) John sent some of his followers while he was in prison to ask whether Jesus were really 'the coming one', and where the recognition of Jesus as Messiah and Lord does not occur until much later in the narrative? The answer to this lies partly in the evangelists' historiography (see Introduction pp. 18ff) and partly in the consideration that, looking back on the story of the Baptist and his first encounter with Jesus from the much later days and the much more considered experience of the Ephesian Church, the evangelist could now see that there was something different, indeed unique, even about that first meeting, something which was in its essence, if not in all its appearances, a real acknowledgement by the Baptist that he had been confronted by the saviour of the world. Such revisions of reminiscence are not unknown to any generation and they are properly defensible as bringing a proper if further dimension into the understanding of an historical situation.

'*who takes away the sin of the world*': John and the Pharisees were concerned about the life of God's chosen people. Their rites and ceremonies were directed to dealing with their sins. But Jesus is not only to effect what Pharisees and Baptist could only prepare for, he was to bring that same reality of forgiveness to the whole world (see on v.32).

30

'*This is he of whom I said . . .*': These same words have been quoted also in the Prologue (1^{15}) and the evangelist does not inform us as to when they were first spoken. Hence we may understand that the anticipation of the manifestation of the one who was to come was characteristic of the Baptist's essential message (cf. Mark 1^7//).

32

And John bore witness, 'I saw the Spirit descend as a dove from heaven': In Mark the Spirit and the dove appear to be an object of Jesus' experience only. Matthew and Luke write as if they were public phenomena whether their significance were grasped or not. Here it is John who reports, and John who interprets, the twin signs, and he can do so only because their meaning has been given to him in revelation. The dove is equated with the spirit. Dr G. F. Knight in his Torch Commentary on Jonah has made the interesting suggestion that since the Hebrew word for 'dove' is 'Jonah', we are to see in the dove an assertion of universal mission at the very beginning of the ministry of Jesus. This would be wholly appropriate here after the evangelist has passed from the narrow efficacy (if any) and hope of John and the Pharisees to the universal gospel and achievement of Jesus Christ.

33

'*I myself did not know him; but he who sent me to baptize with water said to me, "He on whom you see the Spirit descend and remain, this is he who baptizes with the Holy Spirit"* ': John was sent to baptize with water: i.e. a new people of God must be gathered by repentance and baptism in readiness for the real baptism – sharing in the Spirit which was to remain on Jesus.

'*descend and remain*': a reminder that synoptic readers must never suppose that the Spirit came and went at Jesus' baptism; in other words, Jesus is not at the mercy of moods or circumstances, but his divine nature and endowment are permanent.

34

'*And I have seen and borne witness that this is the Son of God*': For the word *Son* certain texts have 'Elect' – an idea present, e.g., in the Lucan story of the transfiguration (Luke 9^{35}). It is the more likely to be the original reading, for it would be hard to see why the reverse change should be made. 'Elect' or 'chosen' fits the context well. Israel of old reckoned herself the chosen people or 'son' of God. John testifies that the only real occurrence of a chosen 'son' or 'person' is in the man Jesus of Nazareth.

John 1³⁵⁻⁵¹

Discipleship –
The Beginnings

Mark 1¹⁶⁻²⁰; 2¹³⁻¹⁴
Luke 5¹⁻¹¹
Matthew 9⁹
Luke 5²⁷⁻²⁸

³⁵ *The next day again John was standing with two of his disciples;* ³⁶*and he looked at Jesus as he walked, and said, 'Behold, the Lamb of God!'* ³⁷*The two disciples heard him say this, and they followed Jesus.* ³⁸*Jesus turned, and saw them following, and said to them, 'What do you seek?' And they said to him, 'Rabbi (which means Teacher), where are you staying?'* ³⁹*He said to them, 'Come and see.' They came and saw where he was staying; and they stayed with him that day, for it was about the tenth hour.* ⁴⁰*One of the two who heard John speak, and followed him, was Andrew, Simon Peter's brother.* ⁴¹*He first found his brother Simon, and said to him, 'We have found the Messiah' (which means Christ).* ⁴²*He brought him to Jesus. Jesus looked at him, and said, 'So you are Simon the son of John? You shall be called Cephas' (which means Peterᵃ).*

⁴³ *The next day Jesus decided to go to Galilee. And he found Philip and said to him, 'Follow me.'* ⁴⁴*Now Philip was from Beth-sa'ida, the city of Andrew and Peter.* ⁴⁵*Philip found Nathan'a-el, and said to him, 'We have found him of whom Moses in the law and also the prophets wrote, Jesus of Nazareth, the son of Joseph.'* ⁴⁶*Nathan'a-el said to him, 'Can anything good come out of Nazareth?' Philip said to him, 'Come and see.'* ⁴⁷*Jesus saw Nathan'a-el coming to him, and said of him, 'Behold, an Israelite indeed, in whom is no guile!'* ⁴⁸*Nathan'a-el said to him, 'How do you know me?' Jesus answered him, 'Before Philip called you, when you were under the fig tree, I saw you.'* ⁴⁹*Nathan'a-el answered him, 'Rabbi, you are the Son of God. You are the King of Israel.'* ⁵⁰*Jesus answered him, 'Because I said to you, I saw you under the fig tree, do you believe? You shall see greater things than these.'* ⁵¹*And he said to him, 'Truly, truly I say to you, you will see heaven opened, and the angels of God ascending and descending upon the Son of man.'*

a From the word for *rock* in Aramaic and Greek, respectively

It seems clear from these texts that there is as much difference between

the synoptic and the Johannine accounts of the calling of the first
disciples as there was between their accounts of the Baptist. And the
differences are largely of the same kind. The story as told by Mark
and Matthew can well be read as if the association between Jesus and
the disciples began in an almost casual and certainly not profound
manner, passed through a stage of growing intimacy and development which had its climax in Peter's confession at Caesarea Philippi,
was tested and found to be tragically inadequate at the time of the
trial and crucifixion, only to be renewed and re-established after the
resurrection and ascension. For John the story of Master and disciples
begins from the profound witness of the Baptist that Jesus is *the Lamb
of God*. But the Synoptic picture is neither as simple nor as superficial
as this bald contrast suggests. Thus Mark's placing of the story is
itself of profound significance. He has related John's witness to Jesus
(Mark I[7,8]), his baptism – when Jesus saw the heavens open and the
Spirit descend upon him – and heard the heavenly voice (Mark I[10–11]),
his temptation when Jesus routed *the* adversary (Mark I[12,13]), and his
proclamation in Galilee that the Kingdom of God was at hand. Then,
before the newly given life of the new people of God begins, Mark
tells how the one in whom that life is now finally to be incorporated
and realized gathers to himself and makes part of his own activity
certain men of Galilee. Before any public messianic work is done, the
Messiah begins to gather to himself the people of the Messiah. So
Mark's account of the calling of the first disciples must be judged not
merely by the simplicity of the story, but by the profundity it obtains
by its place in the story of the new people of God.

Again, while there is not explicit testimony of Messiahship by any
of the disciples, Jesus' call to them is in the words: 'Follow me and I
will make you become fishers of men' (Mark I[17]). That is to say, the
call to the disciples is to leave their own work and to begin to share
in the distinctive work of him who has come to 'gather the scattered
people of God'. The response to such an invitation is not made
without some appreciation of its profundity.

As in the account of John the Baptist Luke writes a report that
seems to lie between the Marcan and Matthean version and that found
in John. Luke omits entirely the brief passage in which Mark (followed
closely by Matthew) tells of the call of Simon and Andrew, and James
and John. And what material he does preserve for his readers is
inserted at a later point in the Marcan framework. After telling of the

temptation Luke writes of a preaching in Galilee (Luke 4¹⁴,¹⁵), the rejection in Nazareth (Luke 4¹⁶⁻³⁰), and of an exorcism of a demon at Capernaum. Then he takes up the narrative of Mark 1 with the story of the healing of Peter's mother-in-law; and it is not until Luke has mentioned Jesus' departure into a lonely place to pray that he gives his readers any information on the calling of disciples. That is to say, Luke would have us perfectly aware that when a disciple is called it is on the assumption of knowledge already attained of the Messianic acts that Jesus has begun to perform. We cannot know Luke's motives for thus altering the emphasis of Mark, but he may well wish to obviate the superficial supposition that Peter and the other disciples answered Jesus' call without any adequate realization of the issues involved.

Luke certainly gives a very different setting to his narrative of Peter's call to discipleship from that offered by Mark. Luke first tells of the miraculous draught of fishes (Luke 5⁴⁻⁷), which is evidently meant to be more than a straightforward nature miracle, but is reported to show how much, even in the natural task of the fisherman, a man is properly dependent for true success upon the superior knowledge and power of the Messiah; and to offer thereby the reflection that the Messiah's power and knowledge will not fail in the more difficult and important task of fishing for men. Luke does not at this stage present Peter as able to voice the positive confession of Jesus as the Messiah which he later made at Caesarea Philippi (Luke 9²⁰), but he tells of Peter's awesome awareness of a strange difference between Jesus and himself: 'Depart from me, for I am a sinful man, O Lord' (Luke 5⁸). It is against such a probing background that Luke introduces Mark's saying about the disciples becoming 'fishers of men', though he gives it a somewhat different form, and applies it to Peter only. Jesus answers Peter's request that he should depart by saying 'Do not be afraid; henceforth you will be catching men' (Luke 5¹⁰). So Luke makes a comment of the utmost artistry and profundity on the theological meaning of Mark's narrative. The disciple shares in the divine task of the Messiah as a fisher of men, but only as he recognizes his own sinfulness, and accepts what Messiah can do to free him from its inhibiting power.

In the fourth gospel John may be said to resolve to have the best, even more than the best, of both these Synoptic worlds. On the one hand, he preserves Mark's theologically important order: before

Messiah performs any Messianic act he begins to surround himself, as in Mark, with the people of the Messiah, or better, and in more Johannine terms, before Jesus is manifested in his glory (2¹¹) he is given some of his brethren by his Father (cf. 6³⁷ff, ⁶⁵; 10²⁹; 17⁶ff). On the other hand, whereas Luke leaves the reader in some sense to draw the inference that when Peter was called he already knew something of the truly Messianic powers of Jesus, John leaves his reader in no doubt at all: Andrew constrains Peter to come to Jesus with the statement: *'We have found the Messiah'* (1⁴¹).

In the light of the evangelist's introduction so far, it is wholly understandable that his narrative of the calling of the disciples begins with a reassertion of the testimony of the Baptist. John was 'a man sent from God' (1⁶) who was given direct divine illumination (1³³) in order that he might bear witness to the true light of the world (1⁷,³¹⁻³⁴). No other disciple or witness bears this relationship to the incarnate Son; every other disciple is dependent upon a human witness for the reception of divine illumination about the true nature of Jesus. The Baptist thus fulfils a unique function in the divine economy, though he does not share in the evangelistic mission of the Church. So John embodies in his narrative the judgement of Luke and Matthew that 'among those born of women there has arisen no one greater than John the Baptist; yet he who is least in the kingdom of heaven is greater than he' (Matt. 11¹¹; cf. Luke 7²⁸).

John now writes that on the day after the Baptist's first confession of Jesus as the Lamb of God, it was repeated by him in the presence of two of his disciples (1³⁶f). Such divine testimony, coming through but not from John (cf. 1³³), turns the two men to follow Jesus. When Jesus, testing the integrity of their intentions (1³⁸), asks them what they are seeking, they inquire where he is staying, and go to spend the rest of the day in his company. Thus two essentials of discipleship for John, following and abiding, have been evoked by the Baptist's witness to Jesus.

Of the two disciples, one was Andrew. It was probably on the next morning (see notes below) that he sought his brother Simon and brought him to Jesus with the words: *'We have found the Messiah'* (1⁴¹). So the evangelist accomplishes two more important theological objectives; he brings together the ideas of the Lamb of God and of the Messiah (see above p. 124), and pursues the theological modification of Mark's story to its logical conclusion. Peter comes to Jesus

upon hearing that he is Messiah: could any serious discipleship begin
save on that foundation? When Jesus and Peter meet, the disciple is
given a new name. It can hardly have escaped the evangelist's notice
that in the Old Testament a decisive encounter with God is sometimes
the occasion of a new name being given. The deceiver Jacob becomes
Israel, the man who has seen God: Abram, exalted father, becomes
Abraham, the father of a multitude. So now Simon ('heard') becomes
Peter (the 'rock man' – so, happily, Moffatt). To meet thus with the
Word incarnate is to receive a new nature, and so to need a new name.

On the following day (now the fifth successive day recorded by
John) Jesus decided to go to Galilee. First he looked for Philip, a
fellow-townsman of Andrew and Peter. Of him alone is it recorded
in the fourth gospel that Jesus used the simple formula of Mark:
'Follow me.' Philip followed, but his response was not elicited by the
simplicities, or apparent simplicities, of the situation that Mark
described in his account of the call of Peter. John has already introduced Jesus as the Lamb of God, and as the Messiah who has already
begun to gather around him the people of the Messiah. This is what
Philip now sees, and that to which he responds, for he at once looks
for Nathanael, whom he greets with the words: 'We have found him
of whom Moses in the law and also the prophets wrote, Jesus of Nazareth,
the son of Joseph.' It is significant that John thus makes Nathanael's
discipleship begin at the point where the two disciples on the road to
Emmaus in Luke are still under instruction; for Luke writes that in
response to their puzzled statements, Jesus 'beginning with Moses and
all the prophets, interpreted to them in all the scriptures the things
concerning himself' (Luke 24²⁵⁻²⁷). Nathanael's first reaction was to
ask a scornful question: 'Can any good thing come out of Nazareth?' for
no discernible reason other than the jealousy of one small town for
another. Philip tells him to come and see for himself. As the gospel
unfolds that there is much concern with what can be 'seen' of Jesus as
the Son of God, the Messiah. But certainly, whatever qualifications
have to be put upon it, John holds that something can be seen; and
Nathanael goes out to see.

The conversation between Jesus and Nathanael cannot be followed
without recalling some Old Testament material, and remembering
that John has already established that the calling of the disciples
involves some recognition of Jesus' Messianic stature. Jesus' first
statement (1⁴⁷) like his last (1⁵¹) brings in the figure of Jacob, the

guileful deceiver, who was enabled to 'see' God, and whose nature was changed. 'Look,' says Jesus as Nathanael approaches, 'here is a genuine Israelite, possessed of no guile' (1⁴⁷), and therewith implies that Nathanael will 'see'.* Nathanael's question is a successful attempt to uncover in what terms the observation of Jesus has been made: '*How do you know me?*' (1⁴⁸). Jesus' reply to that is to tell Nathanael that as he sat under the fig tree before Philip had reached him he had given Jesus the picture of the genuine Israelite in the Messianic age, as that picture had been drawn, for example, by Micah: 'In the latter days . . . they shall sit every man under his vine and under his fig tree, and none shall make them afraid' (Micah 4⁴). Nathanael catches and accepts the Messianic reference and claim, and replies 'Rabbi, you are the Son of God! You are the king of Israel!' (1⁴⁹). The guileless heart of Nathanael had seen, what the guileful hearts of Israel's leaders were not to see, that Jesus, now gathering his Messianic people about him, was more than another figure in the life of God's people; he was the true king of Israel, indeed, in some way Israel itself, which could be called in Old Testament terms itself the 'son' of God (cf. Hosea 11¹f). Jesus was thus recognized as bringing to new birth the life of God's people, Israel, and as Israel's true head and king.

But, as Jesus goes on to instruct so wise an Israelite, this is by no means the last or the greatest thing to be said of himself. He assures Nathanael that a greater vision than he has already had will come to him as the follower of Jesus. He will not only see in him the reality, the new life of Israel, but will come to recognize him as the reality and the new life of the whole of humanity. This will at last fulfil the vision that Jacob saw long ago. The traffic which the patriarch saw taking place between heaven and earth was not, as generations of Israelites had supposed, concerned simply with their destiny as God's chosen people; it was concerned with the destiny of the whole world.

ॐ

35
with two of his disciples: The evangelist makes it plain that some of the earliest converts to Christianity came from the circle of the Baptist's disciples. This was an important fact for the early Church to remember.

37
and they followed Jesus: The verb *follow* has a more than locomotive

---

* It is tempting to see here an enacted instance of Matthew's beatitude 'Blessed are the pure in heart, for they shall see God' (Matt. 5⁸).

sense. With what meanings it is charged becomes clear when it is used again in the final chapter to Peter himself, where, we may suppose, John thinks that at last he is able fully to interpret the situation which Mark describes in the first chapter of his gospel.

38

'*Rabbi*': John normally reserves this form of address for those who misunderstand or misinterpret Jesus, and he may here be trying to retain something of the tension which Luke's story preserves. The transference of loyalty is profoundly based, though not yet fully self-conscious or perfected.

39

... *it was about the tenth hour:* i.e. about 4 p.m., and socially, as well as by day-reckoning, near the 'end of the day'; it is natural to suppose that the two men did not leave Jesus that day.

41

He first found his brother Simon: There is uncertainty about the text, with three possibilities open: *First* may be masculine, giving the meaning that Andrew found Simon before the other disciple found his brother. It may be neuter, indicating that Andrew found Peter before doing anything else after meeting Jesus. Or *first* may be a corruption of another word to be translated 'early', implying that Andrew spent the night in Jesus' company, and set out early the next morning to find Simon. This seems to the present writer, as to Bernard (I.C.C.), the most likely solution.

44

Philip was from Bethsaida, the city of Andrew and Peter: Jesus' decision to go to Galilee confirms the Synoptic report that his public activity began there. Philip's presence near the Jordan, like that of Andrew and Simon, may have been due to an interest in, or discipleship of, John the Baptist. Bethsaida was not really in Galilee, but to the north-east of the Sea of Galilee; yet the names for areas changed so much that Bethsaida may well have been reckoned as in Galilee at the time of the writing of the gospel.

45

Philip found Nathanael: the name *Nathanael* means 'God gives', or 'God has given'. He is sometimes identified with the 'Bartholomew' of the Synoptics, for no greater apparent reason than that Philip's name is coupled with his in the lists of the apostles (cf. Luke 6[14]). Nathanael is mentioned in John only: that, and the rarity of the name in rabbinic writings may justify the suggestion that John cites his name more for theological meaning than historical exactitude, and intends the reader to realize that Nathanael was one of the disciples whom the Father was now giving to the Son (see above, p. 107).

the son of Joseph: another instance of the artistry of John's historiography. For Philip can here say, in this part of his statement about Jesus, no more than the Jews who reject Jesus state concerning him in 6^{42}; yet later it is clear that the true disciple must, like Philip, learn about the divine Father who cannot be seen, and about the divine sonship of him who came from a carpenter's home (cf. 14^9).

49

'Rabbi, you are the Son of God. You are the king of Israel': After a very brief exchange, Nathanael comes to the confession that Philip had not achieved. But it is not yet in the sense of fully developed Christian insight, but rather in the manner of applying to Jesus a great messianic title of Judaism. The title *king of Israel* is likewise taken from contemporary Jewish messianism.

50

'Because I said to you, I saw you under the fig tree, do you believe? You shall see greater things than these': Jesus' reply to Nathanael is still couched in terms of Jewish messianism (see above, p. 121), but he now adds that the real bond between him and his disciples will rest on greater, profounder realities than that.

51

'you will see heaven opened, and the angels of God ascending and descending upon the Son of man': Nathanael used terms from current Jewish messianism. Jesus does the same, but the title Son of man applied to him is the only name that derives from his own application of such a title to himself. Jesus speaks in the plural, i.e. not to Nathanael alone, but to all disciples, and what he has to say is that they shall see in him far more than the person cast for the role of Messiah in the hoped-for final drama of Jewish history, someone who in himself is the instrument of unity between heaven and earth, between time and eternity. The language echoes the story of Jacob's dream in Gen. 28^{12}, but significantly replaces the ladder as the means of communication between heaven and earth with the figure of the *Son of man*. A somewhat later rabbinic exegesis of the Genesis story did portray Jacob, instead of the ladder, as the means of the ascent and descent of the angels (Gen. R. 68^{18}), and the idea may well have been current in the Judaism of John's day. The evangelist expresses the same thought later in the gospel: 'Jesus knew that he had come from God and was going to God' (13^3). Nathanael had spoken of Son of God and king, but had related these terms to Israel; Jesus uses a new term about himself, and does not restrict its significance. How

widely it is to be applied and interpreted the narratives to come will make plain: the circle of divine descent and return is not simply concerned with the restoration of the old Israel in its exclusiveness, but with the creation of a new Israel, indeed of a new humanity inclusive of all: for 'God so loved the world that he gave his only Son, that whoever believes in him should not perish but have eternal life' (3[16]).

John 2¹⁻¹¹

The Bridegroom and the Wine —
The First Sign

2 On the third day there was a marriage at Cana in Galilee, and the mother of Jesus was there; [2] Jesus also was invited to the marriage, with his disciples. [3] When the wine failed, the mother of Jesus said to him, 'They have no wine.' [4] And Jesus said to her, 'O woman, what have you to do with me? My hour has not yet come.' [5] His mother said to the servants, 'Do whatever he tells you.' [6] Now six stone jars were standing there, for the Jewish rites of purification, each holding twenty or thirty gallons. [7] Jesus said to them, 'Fill the jars with water.' And they filled them up to the brim. [8] He said to them, 'Now draw some out, and take it to the steward of the feast.' So they took it. [9] When the steward of the feast tasted the water now become wine, and did not know where it came from (though the servants who had drawn the water knew), the steward of the feast called the bridegroom [10] and said to him, 'Every man serves the good wine first; and when men have drunk freely, then the poor wine; but you have kept the good wine until now.' [11] This, the first of his signs, Jesus did at Cana in Galilee, and manifested his glory; and his disciples believed in him.

This story is linked to the narrative about the calling of the disciples by its opening words: on the third day, and is thus intended by John to be the last of the series of incidents concerned with the beginnings of discipleship. We must note carefully that the evangelist brings the calling of the disciples to its proper climax at the end of this story, in the words his disciples believed in him (see below), and that he has evidently intended that the stories of the calling of disciples should overlap with what Dr Dodd has called 'The Book of Signs'. It may prove impossible to use that title with precision, but it is enough to remind us that for John there can be no hard and fast line drawn, either here where discipleship begins as the Messiah performs his first sign, or later when the time of 'signs' is ended, and the reality signified transpires. For when the story of the crucifixion is told, it is told in the same form as a sign, with an account of a 'wonder' and a discourse attached (even though the discourse about the crucifixion precedes instead of following the event), and it transpires in the end that all that can be seen to occur is but a sign of a reality that cannot be seen, even though ultimate blessedness depends upon believing in its power.

But now, at the beginning of the gospel, John tells of the first sign. In doing so he has characteristically drawn together allusions from many sources, from the Old Testament, from Rabbinic thought and literature, possibly from Hellenistic concepts and beliefs, and certainly from the area of Christian experience, particularly sacramental experience. In light of this it would be foolish to insist upon asking which of several interpretations is the right one; John almost certainly intended his allusions to be manifold, picking up religious experience from several fields in order to point to the reality that lay at the heart of the Christian's faith in God through Christ.

The story of the miracle at Cana of Galilee is not in the synoptic gospels; every commentator knows that. But it is important to recognize that the story of the wedding at Cana serves an interpretative function parallel to certain material in the synoptics; and the evangelist can scarcely be unaware of this. He announces his subject in the first verse: *On the third day there was a marriage at Cana in Galilee* (2^1), and that serves to give an interpretative setting to the whole of what follows. For the central issue of this narrative is not the miracle of changing water into wine, if that wonder be isolated from its setting in John's story, but is rather the amazing thing that happens when he who is the bridegroom, the real, the genuine bridegroom, attends the festival of a Jewish wedding, a marriage ceremony among the people of God, and transforms it. The evangelist puts the important datum first, and we must interpret what follows in the light of it.

In other words, John, like the synoptics before him, tells his readers very early in his narrative that Jesus of Nazareth is *the* bridegroom. Mark (Mark 2$^{19, 20}$) followed both by Matthew (Matt. 9^{15}) and Luke (Luke 5$^{33-35}$), tells us that Jesus, in reply to a Pharisaic inquiry as to the failure of his disciples to fast, answered 'Can the wedding guests fast while the bridegroom is with them?', and added, with an obvious reference to his death, 'The days will come, when the bridegroom is taken away from them, and then they will fast in that day.' The reference in Mark alludes to a common Old Testament metaphor of

Yahweh as the husband of Israel. Israel has been unfaithful, and now the bridegroom has come for his bride, and has indeed begun to find response in the following of the disciples. Other passages in the synoptics and other books of the N.T. carry the idea of the marriage of God and his people further. Matthew twice associates the marriage ceremony with the kingdom of heaven (Matt. 22$^{1-10}$; 25$^{1-13}$). Luke, who tells of the great feast without identifying it with the kingdom of God, states that Jesus, in the course of the same meal at which he told that story, tells the pushful guests seeking the top places at the table 'When you are invited by anyone to a marriage feast, do not sit down in a place of honour ... but ... go and sit in the lowest place ... for everyone who exalts himself will be humbled, and he who humbles himself will be exalted' (Luke 14$^{8-11}$). It is hard to suppose that Luke did not consciously here connect the incident with the life of the kingdom in which the king himself is amongst his people 'as one who serves' (Luke 22^{27}); and the service, seen in Luke at the table of the Last Supper, is the king's death for all.

John's use of the figure of the bridegroom is thus more by indirect implication than by direct statement. He relates how the true, the genuine bridegroom comes to a private festival of marriage in the life of the ancient people of God. It is inevitably transformed, and John makes clear how it is transformed.

The incident takes place *on the third day* after Jesus' conversation with Nathanael. The phrase 'on the third day' is admirably suited to provide both a backward and a forward reference. It clearly points back to the series of stories about the disciples, and beyond them to the first occasion when John bore witness to Jesus as the Lamb of God, which was the first of the seven momentous days at the commencement of John's narrative. It points forward, quite as clearly, to the end of his narrative when 'on the third day', as every Christian account of the resurrection affirmed, Jesus was finally manifested in his death-conquering glory. The first sign that John tells thus not only comes as the climax and crown of the first calling of the disciples, bringing them to real belief (2^{11}), but also as a symbol and sign of that final event which would also take place 'on the third day', when the final glory of the Son would be manifested, and belief could be claimed of all men in his name.

John's story, like that of the synoptists, begins in Galilee. It seems that Philip had been asked to accompany Jesus to Galilee (1^{43}), and

Cana was Nathanael's home (2^2). These, among others, were with Jesus. The mother of Jesus, we read, *was there*. It is not stated that she was invited; she finds it possible to give orders to servants in the house, and they obey her; perhaps she was related to the bridegroom, or at least an intimate friend of his family. The absence of Mary's name is characteristic of John. Some commentators have supposed that we must infer that he is using her presence figuratively, to represent, in a highly symbolic situation, the Judaism that 'bore' Jesus according to the flesh. We need neither reject the symbolism out of hand, nor reject the quite simple possibility that Mary was present at a wedding feast with her son and his disciples. It would be quite like John to focus two meanings into one set of words, and so gain in allusiveness and depth.

Jesus was invited with his disciples, and this is the astounding paradox of the story. The true and genuine, the only bridegroom of Israel, is present as an invited guest. And yet he does not come alone, but with his disciples. Messiah is no true historical figure without a people of the Messiah; the new Israel, like the old, consists not in God in aweful isolation, nor in a people apart from their God, but with both conjoined. That dual reality has appeared, and it comes, with startling effects, to a simple marriage festival.

The narrative proceeds as if it were the most natural thing in the world for the wine to have failed – as it was if the wine were not just a drink for the feasting but also a symbol of the reality of divine communion. For within the life of the old Israel communion with God could not, and did not, proceed continuously or for ever. Israel's life with God had to come to a stop. Jesus' reply to his mother is, as some commentators have failed to see, entirely respectful; he addresses her in the same way from the cross (19^{26}). The strange phrase '*What have you to do with me?*' derives from the Old Testament (cf. Judg. 11^{12}; 2 Sam. 16^{10}), though its meaning can be seen from the New, when the demons claim independence of Jesus, e.g. Mark 1^{24}, and perhaps more particularly Matthew 8^{29} where there is a reference, as here, to the future. Jesus is claiming that the time has come when his actions derive no longer from Mary's parental guidance and authority but are, as the story in Luke 2^{41-51} foreshadowed, from his own relationship with his heavenly Father.

When Jesus asserts that his hour is not yet come, he is again, in typical Johannine fashion, combining more meanings than one. The time has not yet come when he can assist the marriage festivities; it has not yet come for him to make a public manifestation of himself, in spite of his public appearance with his disciples; it has not yet come for him to offer himself as the Lamb of God for the sins of the world. The use of the word 'hour' in John makes it impossible not to read this last reference even into this early saying in the gospel. And the justification for doing so becomes clearer as the story proceeds.

In writing of Mary's direction to the servants John is following the Lucan tradition about the mother of Jesus, for in the third gospel Mary knows from the earliest time something of the divine destiny of her son (Luke 1^{35}; $2^{19, 51}$). And if we accept the statement as indicating a simple historical act of communication, we may also see in it two possible indications of a theological kind. In the first place the word used for *servant* is not the one that is usual; John's word transliterated as 'deacons' is still used of the Christian ministry, and supports the view that this whole incident is coloured by the sacra-mental experience of the Christian Church. Second, the figure of Mary, particularly since she is not named, may be intended to refer not only to the Lord's mother, but to Judaism as such, in whose 'womb' Jesus was conceived. By a reference such as this the evangelist would be trying to indicate that the proper attitude of Judaism to the Church would be to point away from itself, to require no further obedience to itself, but to resign all its authority to Jesus Christ. This suggestion, as we shall see (cf. note on 19^{25ff}), can be pursued in the account of Jesus' word to his mother from the cross.

The flow of the pure narrative is interrupted at this point to tell the readers of the presence of six large stone jars, used to provide water necessary for purificatory rituals by the guests. There is little need to question the strictly historical intention behind the statement, but it may well be the case that here, as elsewhere, the evangelist has also had some symbolic purpose in mind. He had, as we have suggested (see above, p. 58), 'an eye for' the symbolic elements in a situation, and the number six may have suggested to him the less-than-the-perfect number seven, as indicative of the perpetual inadequacy of all the purificatory rites of Judaism, an inadequacy clearly seen by John the Baptist. The water in the jars had already been in use, for they were now in a condition when they could be filled up (fulfilled?), and their use had been intended to make the participating guests worthy, by ritual lustration, to share in the solemnities of the marriage feast.

They stood there, a perpetual reminder to all that no one was worthy without purification to enter into the joy of such a feast. But on this occasion of a wedding among God's people there is present not only the bridegroom who is to marry his Galilean bride, but *the* bridegroom who has come to claim as his true bride all the scattered people of God.

The wedding feast lacked wine, not water; yet it is precisely to the water, concerned with the admission to the feast by purification, that Jesus turns to supply the deficiency of wine. And this is the significant part of the miracle. That which had, as water, never been able, and never would be able, in any quantity, large or small, to prepare men by an adequate purification to enter worthily even into an earthly marriage or union of persons, was to turn, in the presence of the true bridegroom, and by his grace and power, into the very substance of the joy of the divine marriage between God and his people. The inadequate and insufficient preparatory water became the more than adequate and superabundant wine of actual celebration and enjoyment.

The details reported underline the point. Jesus tells the servants to fill the jars with water (2^7) – he will supply all that is necessary, and there will be no need, and indeed no room, for any other to supply any more. He asks for all the jars to be filled, and not just one; and in the absurdly large provision of some 120–180 gallons of wine he indicates that this kindness of God is full and overflowing: 'from his fulness have we all received, grace upon grace' (1^{16}).

Jesus next directs the servants to draw out some of the water/wine and take it to the steward. So does he always use human intermediaries in conveying his gracious gifts. The servants (deacons) of course know how the wine was procured, but the steward does not know. This indicates the position of the Jews and the disciples in the rest of the gospel, and in the story of the Church: it is the Church's privilege to know whence true grace, true unity flows; but this is not seen by typical Jewry.

The final act in the miraculous drama arrived when the steward called the bridegroom and spoke of the unusual habit of keeping the good wine to the last. There is a world of silent comment in the sentence. Of course the bridegroom marrying the Galilean woman knew nothing of the source of the new, good wine. But *the* bridegroom knew. And, as the synoptic writers themselves confessed,

Jesus knew of the historical reality symbolized in the divinely-given wine at the feast. The same complex of ideas – the last being greater than the first, and the ignorance and opposition of the Jews – is exhibited in the parable of the vineyard in Mark 12^{1-11}, and the parallels in Matthew and Luke.

The evangelist adds his final comment: *This, the first of his signs, Jesus did at Cana in Galilee, and manifested his glory; and his disciples believed in him* (2^{11}). The phrase *first of his signs* is happily ambiguous. It may have an axiological as well as a chronological reference; and it almost certainly is intended to have both. This is not only the first sign that Jesus did, before he did any others, but it is also the one which, before the evangelist reproduces a sign like any reported by the synoptists, indicates the profound theological meaning involved in the whole ministry of signs.

That Jesus *manifested his glory* is almost impossible adequately to expound. The evangelist is picking up the great phrase from the Prologue 'we beheld his glory'; he is perhaps beginning to fulfil the promise to Nathanael that he would 'see greater things', for in this miracle John is already setting out the divine drama and victory of the cross and resurrection as the marriage and union between God and his people. That his disciples believed in him is a statement to be taken at its full force. And to believe in him is quite evidently not to believe that he can turn water into wine, but rather that he is the real bridegroom who will replace the inadequate rites of purification established among the Jews with the reality of a communion (marriage) with God achieved through his own sacrificial death for all.

Such an interpretation involves the reader in taking the wine not only as an actual beverage provided for an actual wedding where the wine had run out, but as a symbol of the Christian eucharist. This mode of interpretation does no sort of violence to John. As Professor Dodd has said*: 'He [John] has not chosen to speak directly about the sacraments, but for the Christian reader the allusions are inescapable.' It is inevitable, indeed, that in a setting of the life and worship of the church at Ephesus the original reader of this gospel should at this point of the narrative think about the eucharist. For the evangelist has already underlined the provisional, preparatory character of John's baptism. He will go on immediately to tell of Jesus' 'cleansing' of the temple in Jerusalem, and an enigmatic

* C. H. Dodd, *The Fourth Gospel*, p. 138.

identification of himself with a new temple. He will pass to a discourse to Nicodemus about birth by water and the Spirit. Then he will write of the conversation about truly living water for the woman of Samaria. And so he will come to the feeding of the five thousand, with its discourse ending in a declaration of the necessity to eat the flesh and drink the blood of the Son of man. And here John is saying the water of Judaism is always inadequate, but the wine of Jesus Christ is always more than enough; Jewish water is always an anticipation; Christian wine is for all time the reality. The one is but a promise, the other is fulfilment. And yet the two must not be wholly seen in antithesis, for the person of Jesus, coming out of Judaism by human descent, is the very substance of the reality which fulfils the promise. In him a human wedding with its power to make of twain one flesh is seen as itself dependent upon, and anticipatory of, the one union that makes a unity in diversity – the union to be effected by the sacrifice of the Lamb of God.

২৩

1

On the third day: If we accept the suggestion that the correct reading in 1^{41} was 'early' and not 'first' then this dating brings us to the seventh day after John's first recognition of Jesus. It has been supposed (e.g. by Bernard, I.C.C., p. 72) that if the two disciples who 'stayed with Jesus' (1^{39}) did so on and because it was the Sabbath, then the day of the wedding would be Wednesday, the very day prescribed in a Talmudic direction for the marriage of a virgin.

2

with his disciples: There is no indication as to how many disciples accompanied Jesus. It may have been the Twelve, though the evangelist does not say so. But that a specific group is intended seems implied by the phrase *with his disciples* rather than 'some of his disciples'.

6

six stone jars: Stone jars were held not to suffer contamination of uncleanness.

for the Jewish rites of purification: presumably for washing of hands before and after meals (cf. Mark 7^3) and other cleansing rites.

8

draw some out: It has been suggested that the Greek verb used here implies that Jesus sent the servants, not to the jars filled with water, but to the well from which they had been filled. But there is evidence that the verb was used for drawing water from other sources than wells or springs (see Bernard, I.C.C. pp. 77–8). Even if the suggestion be right, the same theological comment could be made, for the full vessels, untapped as a source of the new wine, would stand revealed as wholly inadequate to mediate the joy of the one real marriage between God and his people.

the steward of the feast: This is a post unknown to any Jewish background that is known to us. He was, it would seem, either the head-waiter (so Hoskyns, p. 189) whose duties included placing the couches, arranging the courses, and tasting the food and wine, or (so Barrett) the toast master, chosen by lot from the guests to preside over the banquet.

9

the water now became wine: Allusions to Hellenistic religion have been detected here, notably by Estlin Carpenter. There were certainly miracles of such change attributed to Dionysus at certain shrines. Similarly commentators, notably Professor Dodd, have seen an allusion in the story to the figure of Melchizedek in Philo, who sees in that strange figure of Genesis 14^{18} who 'brought out bread and wine', a figure of the Word who would, in Philo's language 'bring forth wine instead of water, and shall give your souls to drink . . . that they may be wholly occupied with a divine intoxication, more sober than sobriety itself' (Philo, *Legum Allegoriae* III, 82). It seems that no literary dependence can be proved in either case; what seems clear is that any reader knowing either Greek mythology or Philo's writings would see in this story something surpassing and fulfilling what he already knew.

10

Every man serves the good wine first: Dr Dodd points out (*The Fourth Gospel,* p. 84) that in Rabbinic Judaism wine is a symbol of the Torah. Therefore it is possible that when the steward speaks of the superiority of the later wine over that provided earlier in the feast he may well be held to make a veiled allusion to the superiority of the Gospel over the Torah. Christ would thus give the true wine, as he gives the true bread.

11

Jesus . . . manifested his glory: The glory of Jesus was something he shared with the Father before the incarnation (17$^{5, 24}$) and to which he was to return thereafter. But while he was on earth that glory was from time to time made manifest. In the synoptics it was shown to a limited company at the transfiguration (Mark 9$^{2-8}$//), and in John in Christ's miracles (here and at 11$^{4, 40}$). The meaning of the noun is brought out by the use of the verb 'glorify', which has its special application in this gospel as a fact of the crucifixion (7^{39}; $12^{16, 23}$; 13^{31f}). This is an added reason for supposing that the evangelist believed himself, in the narrative of the first sign, to be setting out something about the triumph of Christ in and through his death.

John 2¹²

Interlude 1: Capernaum

[12]*After this he went down to Caper'na-um, with his mother and his brothers and disciples; and there they stayed for a few days.*

One of the notorious differences between the fourth gospel and the synoptics is that while the earlier tradition gives much place to an account of a Galilean ministry, John sets the great part of his story in and around Jerusalem. There are, of course, theological reasons for this. But John shows that he is neither ignorant of the Galilean ministry, nor unaware of its significance. He has already indicated that Galilee saw the start of the public ministry of Jesus (1^{43}; 2^2), and has revealed, to those who can see his meaning, that from the start that ministry was, to use a Synoptic figure, 'putting new wine into new skins' – i.e. making a quite new start in the life of the people of God. In this single verse between the story of the first sign and that of the cleansing of the temple, John lets his readers know that he is not unaware of the Galilean residence of Jesus, nor unappreciative of the fact that his family ties were there.

John names Capernaum as the place where Jesus, his mother, brothers and disciples *stayed for a few days.* Even though the synoptists speak of Nazareth as the Galilean home of Jesus, they also write confidently of Capernaum as a centre of his activity. Jesus' mother disappears from the narrative at this point, only to reappear at the cross. His brothers are mentioned by John in ch. 7, where, as in the synoptics, they are not among those who believe in him. This is also much in the synoptic tradition, for Jesus himself knew what it meant that his coming involved separations and divisions inside a man's own family (cf. Matt. $10^{35, 36}$).

One manuscript puts a singular verb in the last phrase of this verse and omits the reference to the disciples intending, apparently, to suggest that while Jesus stayed in Capernaum a few days only, his mother and brothers remained there after he had gone to Jerusalem for the Passover; and that, by contrast, the disciples, now becoming part of the new Israel of God, were naturally from henceforth to share the Lord's journeyings with him.

John 2¹³⁻²⁵

¹³ *The Passover of the Jews was at hand, and Jesus went up to Jerusalem.*
¹⁴*In the temple he found those who were selling oxen and sheep and pigeons,
and the money-changers at their business.* ¹⁵*And making a whip of cords, he
drove them all, with the sheep and oxen, out of the temple; and he poured out
the coins of the money-changers and overturned their tables.* ¹⁶*And he told
those who sold pigeons, 'Take these things away; you shall not make my
Father's house a house of trade.'* ¹⁷*His disciples remembered that it was
written, 'Zeal for thy house will consume me.'* ¹⁸*The Jews then said to
him, 'What sign have you to show us for doing this?'* ¹⁹*Jesus answered them,
'Destroy this temple, and in three days I will raise it up.'* ²⁰*The Jews then
said, 'It has taken forty-six years to build this temple, and will you raise it up
in three days?'* ²¹*But he spoke of the temple of his body.* ²²*When therefore he
was raised from the dead, his disciples remembered that he had said this; and
they believed the scripture and the word which Jesus had spoken.*

²³*Now when he was in Jerusalem at the Passover feast, many believed in
his name when they saw his signs which he did;* ²⁴*but Jesus did not trust
himself to them,* ²⁵*because he knew all men and needed no one to bear
witness of man; for he himself knew what was in man.*

When Mark began his gospel he used two Old Testament texts to
head the narrative. One of them was quoted from Malachi: 'Behold,
I send my messenger before thy face' (Mark 1²). In the original the
text continued: 'and the Lord whom you seek will suddenly come to
his temple' (Mal. 3¹). It is not wholly outside the bounds of possibility that John, and the synoptists before him, saw an actual enactment of that prophecy in the story of the cleansing of the temple.

But the reader of the fourth gospel must put two questions to
himself as he comes to this story. First, why has John so changed the
content of the story? He has done this, not by the addition of some
details, such as the mention of a whip, and of the sheep and oxen,
but by the application of quite different Old Testament references,
and by the introduction of a saying of Jesus about the destruction of
the temple. And second, why has John placed this strange incident

at the very beginning of his narrative, instead of keeping it, as the other evangelists do, to the last days of Jesus' life? The two questions, though distinct, are not unrelated.

Mark tells that Jesus came into the temple after he had been welcomed by the crowds as a messianic king (Mark 11^{1-10}). Upon entering the temple Jesus 'began to drive out those who sold and those who bought in the temple, and he overturned the tables of the money-changers and the seats of those who sold pigeons; and he would not allow any one to carry anything through the temple' (Mark $11^{15, 16}$). This action has often been interpreted as a protest in unmistakable deed against the commercialization of the sacred temple. And one part of John's narrative seems to support such an understanding. But in view of Mark's scripture

> And he taught and said to them, 'Is it not written, "My house shall be called a house of prayer for all nations"? But you have made it a den of robbers' (11^{17})

it seems erroneous, particularly if the question is asked as to what sort of justification the action gave to the chief priests and scribes in their consequent decision to destroy Jesus (Mark 11^{18}). The major premiss of Jesus' argument in the temple consists of the quotation from Isaiah (56^7): 'My house shall be a house of prayer for all the nations.' It has often been unnoticed or forgotten that what Jesus did in the temple was to rid it of the obvious removable symbols of a Judaism that kept its temple to itself. There was a 'court of the Gentiles' at the temple! Beyond it no Gentile dared venture, under threat and penalty of death. So little was God's temple a house of prayer for all nations! Again the presence of money-changers in the temple precincts was not objectionable for the sole and superficial reason that it was degrading to introduce commerce into a holy place, but because the need for money to be changed rested upon the Jews' insistence that their religion must not be defiled by having the animals required for sacrifice in the temple paid for in Gentile money. Gentile coins, as well as Gentile persons, were intolerable to the Jews in their temple. If the following quotation from Jeremiah (7^{11}) is interpreted in this light, then the accusation of becoming a den of thieves is seen to be, not a protest at the 'robbery' of commerce, conducted well or ill, but a condemnation, as in the context of Jeremiah, of those who commit injustice and think that, by preserving the outward symbols of religion, and particularly the worship of the temple, they can escape the judgement of God. In a word, the double quotation of scripture means that Jesus is protesting that Israel has failed to fulfil her universal mission to mankind, and has thought that she could 'get away with it' by preserving the mere externals of ceremonial and sacrificial worship in the temple. Such a protest, directed at the roots of the accepted religion of the day, not unnaturally evoked the final hostility of the religious leaders. Jesus sought a radically new direction to religious life; officialdom neither accepted his criticism nor, be it acknowledged, saw its validity.

Against this synoptic background John's account is manifestly an attempt to probe somewhat deeper, not indeed in order to add something new, but rather to expose the fundamental elements in the situation the synoptists had recorded. The first indication of his purpose is found in the statement that Jesus found in the temple *those who were selling oxen and sheep* as well as those selling pigeons (2^{14}). Sheep and oxen were required for the sacrifices of the temple, and by emphasizing their place in the story John is indicating that it was not simply an advance from particularism to universalism that Jesus was demanding, but also a passage from sacrificial to spiritual worship. *'Take these things away'* (2^{16}) expresses this, and so becomes the major premiss for the reference to *trade*, as the quotation from Isaiah had been in Mark's gospel. The buying and selling that was necessary if the sacrificial worship of Judaism was to continue in the situation of Palestine as a Roman-occupied territory would be entirely superseded when the demand for sacrifice was done away.

At this stage of his narrative John records what was the interpretation of the incident made by the disciples at the time. They remembered the scripture 'Zeal for thy house will consume me', a quotation from Psalm 69^9. In this Psalm the writer is deeply afflicted, and traces his troubles to the fact that he has been zealous for the house of God. The whole Psalm is worth reading as a background to its use here, for it suggests that the disciples not only perceived that Jesus was concerned for the honour of the temple, but that he could not act as he did without bringing suffering upon himself. It may even be that, like the Psalmist, they had some confidence that, even if God were to permit their master to suffer, that would not be the end of the story, but that finally he would 'praise the name of God with a song . . . this will please the Lord more than an ox, or a bull with horns and hoofs'

(Psalm 69$^{30,\ 31}$). However that may be, John is emphatic in stating that later on, after the resurrection, the disciples came to see even more profound meaning in the cleansing of the temple (cf. 2^{22}).

After Jesus had driven out the animals and men concerned with the traffic in the temple the Jews asked him for his warrant: '*What sign have you to show us for doing this?*' (2^{18}). Though this is not recorded in Mark at the same time as the cleansing itself, the evangelist records an interrogation of Jesus by the authorities on a following day. 'By what authority are you doing these things, or who gave you this authority to do them?' Mark records an answer to this question by which Jesus silences his opponents: he asks them for their opinion as to the source of John's baptism! But in the fourth gospel the answer as to the 'sign' goes to the heart of the evangelist's understanding of the gospel.

John has replaced Mark's question about authority with one about a 'sign'. That is not only to keep to the language of the earlier parts of Mark's narrative, where Jesus had been asked for a sign (cf. Mark 8$^{11,\ 12}$ // etc.), but to advance into the rich and profound vocabulary of the fourth gospel. In Mark (8^{11}) the Pharisees asked Jesus for a 'sign from heaven', meaning that if he could produce some heavenly portent which it was not in the power of an ordinary mortal to produce then they would be able to accept what he did as the work of someone superhuman. Mark reports that Jesus replied that no sign would be given. In a real and profound sense John echoes that answer from Mark. But when Matthew (12$^{38,\ 39}$) and Luke (11^{29}) take up Mark's narrative they enlarge upon Jesus' answer by making him say: 'No sign shall be given . . . except the sign of the prophet Jonah' (Matt. 12^{38}; Luke 11^{29}). The two evangelists differ in their interpretations of this further saying, but Matthew interprets it as referring to the resurrection (Matt. 12^{40}). John has evidently drawn from a diversity of synoptic material to imbue his story of the cleansing with its essential meaning. And he adds one further synoptic saying to round off his commentary. To the Jews' request for a sign Jesus answered: '*Destroy this temple, and in three days I will raise it up*' (2^{19}). Neither Mark nor Matthew give an occasion when this saying was uttered, but offer it as the substance of the evidence given against Jesus at his trial (Mark 14^{58}; Matt. 26^{61}). Thus they are not required to offer an interpretation of it, though, to Christian ears at least, the very phrase *in three days* would have recalled the miracle of the resurrection. John openly identifies the meaning with a foretelling of the death and resurrection of Jesus.

The resurrection, then, was to be the sign that Jesus would offer to his people, the Jews, as his warrant for cleansing the temple, and for cleansing it in such a way that both synoptic and Johannine interpretations would be fulfilled. For by his death and resurrection the narrow, nationalist and particular religion of the Jews would be replaced by the universal, inclusive gospel of Jesus Christ; and the repeated, animal, sacrificial offerings of Judaism would be replaced by the one and once-for-all offering of himself by Jesus Christ, the Son of God, in death and resurrection. This profound meaning is brought out in a typically Johannine way. When Jesus first utters the saying, the Jews reply, in what is an almost 'natural' misunderstanding: '*It has taken forty-six years to build this temple, and will you raise it up in three days?*' (2^{20}). The evangelist then adds that Jesus *spoke of the temple of his body* (2^{21}).

Whatever else John has achieved by this use of the saying he has at least made it abundantly plain that the sign which Jesus gives is not something apart or different from the thing that is signified, but identical with it. The Pharisees in Mark asked for 'a sign from heaven', and if Jesus had performed some apparently impossible feat not identical with his mission, their credulity might have been captured but no faith in his saviourhood would have been generated. At the cross, Matthew tells (Matt. 27^{42}), the chief priests, scribes and elders mocked Jesus with the taunt: 'He is the king of Israel; let him come down now from the cross, and we will believe in him.' The sign is not at one with the thing signified, any more than, say, the bunting of a national flag is at one with the national heritage that it signifies. But the death of Jesus on the cross and his resurrection after three days is identical with the passing from particular, nationalist religion to a true universalism; it is identical with the passing of the old sacrifices of sheep and oxen and the passage to a religion dependent upon the once-for-all offering of the Son of God in death as the way to life. John is perfectly honest with his readers. The disciples do not at this time have this much insight; at the most they see what zeal for God's house demands, in terms of the Psalmist's agony and triumph. But, as John goes on to say, once the events of the cross and resurrection have taken place, then the disciples can look back to this point and see, for the first time, what significance the event really had.

Similarly, it may be observed, in hearing a piece of music for the first time, the listener cannot know just what the significance of a particular phrase may be; but once he has heard the piece through, its significance is, or can be, clear.

So, as with the record of the miracle at Cana of Galilee, John is deliberately writing his story not as seen from the beginning, but as seen from the end. For only in this way can the story have proper telling. And this leads to two comments: first, that in this way John is to be thought of as still writing under the general reference of Jesus as 'the Lamb of God', and thus to be looking back at all his story from the standpoint, not only of the Jewish Passover, for which Jesus had gone to the temple on this occasion (2^{13}), but also of the Christian Eucharist, where the Lamb of God has replaced the Passover lamb. It is significant in this connexion that the crucifixion in the fourth gospel takes place not after, but at the same time as the killing of the passover lambs in the temple. Jesus went to the temple, and this is recorded so early in the gospel, so that 'these things', sheep and oxen, might be taken away, and himself put in their place. Second, that inasmuch as John is seeing the whole story that the synoptists have magnificently told from its ending rather than from its beginning, it is understandable to us, and certainly useful to him, that he should at this point transpose an incident from the end of the synoptic story and write it at the head of his.

This brings us to the second question that John's narrative puts to the reader: why has he put this incident at the beginning of his gospel instead of at the end? Other commentators have wisely pointed out how, in spite of a plain difference of location, there is a good deal more in the setting of the synoptic gospels that is akin to John than a superficial question of location will disclose. Thus Hoskyns* points out that the cleansing is associated

with the cursing and withering of the barren fig-tree, clearly a parable of Judaism; with the themes of the parable of the Wicked Husbandmen, the destruction of the men who had murdered the son of the owner of the vineyard, the transference of the property to others, and the miracle of the new order raised upon the foundation of the stone that had been rejected; with teaching given to the disciples concerning the imminent destruction of the temple; and with statements concerning the irrelevance of animal sacrifices altogether. All this, moreover, in the Marcan

* pp. 197f.

narrative leads on to the crucifixion of Jesus, not as the death of a man who appeared in Jerusalem as a reformer of Judaism, but as the death of one who claimed to be Messiah, who pointed to the destruction of the temple and to the end of the old covenant, and who by His sacrificial and voluntary death inaugurated the new covenant in His blood.

All this means that John has taken great pains to understand the depth of the synoptic witness to Jesus Christ, and has decided to make that profound understanding more readily available to his own readers. So a story that is capable of introducing some of the chief notes of the Gospel in respect of Christ's ministry in Jerusalem is here used at the very beginning of the narrative in order that the whole may be read in the light, as it were, of the complete synoptic story. In short John is confessing by a simple historiographical device that was available to him that it was impossible to understand even the earliest stories of Jesus save in the light of their end in his cross and resurrection.

John's aim is thus, in our view, religious and theological, not chronological and, in the twentieth-century sense, historical. This does not mean that he is either less or more likely to be right about his placing of this or any other incident. The synoptic accounts are equally unacceptable to our modern standards of dating and chronology, and many theological motives have gone into the determination of their ordering of material. That much is clear from the researches of modern scholars. Thus, while Mark may in fact be accurate in telling of the temple cleansing as an event of the very last phase of Jesus' life, John may equally be right, and Mark wrong. There is no certain historical order which John blameworthily alters to suit his own theological purpose; both synoptic and Johannine gospels are dominated by religious and theological motives. Thus signs, as here, of theological motivation in the placing of a story by John do not necessarily imply that Mark is 'historically' right while John is wrong; the opposite may be the case. And it is possible that neither evangelist is historically accurate in the placing of some incident reported by both. The most that can be said is that in spite of evidence pointing to a temple cleansing at the beginning as well as at the end it is unlikely that the cleansing was undertaken twice by Jesus. The inherent probabilities as well as John's apparent dependence upon Mark make it highly unlikely that we have separate records of two events rather than a double record of one. The evangelist has now prepared his readers for a proper understanding of Jesus' ministry both in Galilee and in Jerusalem. In each case he makes the same point – the old Jewish order is to be replaced by what is quite new in himself. The water of Jewish purification, inadequate even in that of John's baptism, is to be replaced by the wine of the Gospel, i.e. by the self-sacrifice of the Lamb of God. The sacrificial worship of the temple, particularly at the great festival of Passover, is to be replaced by a new spiritual worship offered first by and then through him who will suffer the destruction of the temple of his body only to erect it anew in his resurrection. This is the perspective from which all the narratives of the gospel will be seen. The synoptic story, that is to say, properly understood, is not a tale that begins with self-interpretative events leading on to others of the same nature; rather is it, as the Johannine re-presentation will reveal, a story that shows how from the very beginning the depth and universality of the cross and resurrection were involved. Having made this clear in his own historiography and theology, John is ready to pass on to relate the encounter of him who is the gospel with the three classes of people in the world – the Jews, the Samaritans and, finally, the Gentiles. All this in proper pursuit of synoptist aims, and use of their material.

The evangelist now makes one further introductory remark before he passes to tell the story of the encounter of Jesus with men. He states that while Jesus was in Jerusalem *many believed in his name when they saw his signs which he did* (2^{23}). But, the evangelist adds, Jesus *did not trust himself to them* (2^{24}). John does not suppose, any more than the synoptists, that true belief in Christ is something acquired fully grown at the start. (The synoptists make it plain that the belief even of the Twelve grew. At one level it sufficed to take them from their previous occupation to follow him; at another it caused Peter to confess Jesus as Messiah; and at still another it issued after the resurrection in a new belief at a greater depth than before.) Many believed in his name because of the signs Jesus did. Such belief may or may not issue in full commitment to the Christ; but it could only do so if the believer could, at this stage, hear and accept the proper witness as to who and what Jesus was. Man's belief in Christ, as the Prologue made clear, depends upon witness as to who and what he is. But in the other direction, Jesus needs no witness as to what a particular man is. He knows of himself. Such a knowledge of men was the prerogative and power of God alone, and this is in part the intention

of the evangelist, to emphasize once again, before the great stories of
Christ's confronting the world, that he confronts it as more than man,
as God-in-man, the only Son, the Word incarnate. The believers to
whom Jesus would not entrust himself believed in him because of the
signs which he did. Later in the gospel it can be seen how differently
men react to the signs (cf. e.g. pp. 312ff) but they must not be
thought of as in the end something apart from, or in any other
perspective than, the cross and resurrection. Unless the understanding
of the signs is taken to that depth, seen from that perspective, it will
mislead, instead of disclosing the profound reality of God's saving
love for the world.

ဆ

13

The Passover of the Jews: This is thought by many commentators to be a
form of words used by John because he also knew of a 'Christian'
passover.

Jesus went up to Jerusalem: The verb *went up* is used in all probability on
two levels, as it seems to be in Luke. It reflects the common way of
talking about going to the capital city, in the same way that modern
Englishmen speak of trains going to London as 'up' trains. It also
reflects, in all probability, the early Christian usage of referring to
Christ's 'going up' at his ascension.*

15

making a whip of cords: These details are not in the synoptic record. The
whip was probably one used for driving cattle.

he drove them all, with the sheep and oxen: The *all* in the Greek is masculine,
and the preposition *with* is therefore rightly supplied in English.

he poured out the coins of the money-changers: Temple dues had to be paid
in Tyrian coinage, and the money-changers were thus an essential part
of the temple traffic. By driving out the animals and disposing of the
moneys required, Jesus has, at least for a time, and so as a symbol, made
the sacrifices of the temple impossible.

16

'my Father's house': The phrase constitutes a high, the highest claim.

'Zeal for thy house will consume me': The disciples recall a Psalm regarded
as Messianic, thus picking up the Messianic allusions of 1^{43}ff. The verb

* The considerable authority of Dr Dodd (p. 385, 1) supports this. He asks
'Whether even the banal *to go up to Jerusalem* (2^{13}; 5^1; $7^{10, 14}$), though it is an
expression that every pilgrim to the temple had occasion to use, may not have
had for this writer a suggestion of the "going up" of the Son of Man (3^{13};
6^{62}; 20^{17}).'

consume can also mean 'destroy', and so prepares for the transition to the death and resurrection.

20

'*It has taken forty-six years to build this temple*': The number forty-six presents difficulties. The sentence grammatically means that from the start to the finish of the building of the temple forty-six years elapsed. But Herod's temple was begun in 20/19 B.C., and not finished until about A.D. 63. Forty-six years takes the time interval to A.D. 27/28, which would be a not unsuitable year for the conversation recorded here. Before considering various possibilities it must be pointed out that the evangelist is writing some time after the conversation, and some time even after the completion of the temple, and indeed of its destruction. The possibility of inaccuracy in reference to its dates is thus increased. Three possibilities seem open: (1) In spite of the plain grammar of the sentence it must be taken to refer, not to the completion of the building, but to the length of time building so far has taken. (2) The sentence may be held compatible with some intermediate stage being reached, which could account for the phrase implying completeness. In this connexion it may be useful to note that the word used in vv. 19–21 for *temple* differs from that in vv. 14, 15. The word used here means the sanctuary or holy place; in vv. 14, 15, the word employed refers to the whole complex of buildings. (3) The author, writing at a later date, may have been misinformed by his source or have made a miscalculation himself. On the whole it seems best to adopt the second of these possibilities, since this recognized a not unimportant or unfamiliar theological distinction in the narrative which identifies the person of Jesus with that central body of the temple buildings where the specific sacrifices of Judaism took place. Jesus will, in his own self-giving, replace that and them.

'*will you raise it up in three days?*': Another reminder that John is writing his gospel from the perspective of the completed synoptic story. By the time he wrote, the phrase 'on the third day' had become almost a technical term to refer to the time of the resurrection (see the interesting note by Hoskyns, pp. 199f.).

21

But he spoke of the temple of his body: John knows that the disciples came to see that the real temple of God, the real place where he dwelt was not in the Jewish temple made with hands, but in the body of their Lord. His body, his flesh, was the place where God dwelt. The Father was in him, and he in the Father. Moreover his flesh, thus regarded, was the food upon which his followers lived; and in their becoming one with him, so that the Father could be in them and they in the Father, they came to be reckoned as part of his body. Paul also makes use of the figure of the Body of Christ (e.g. Rom. 12⁴,⁵; 1 Cor. 12²⁷) and of the temple in speaking of believers (1 Cor. 3¹⁶f.; 2 Cor. 6¹⁶; Eph. 2²¹). The resurrection was not just an event that had happened to Jesus; it was an experience through which every believer passed. Paul similarly interprets Christian baptism (Rom. 6³,⁴; Col. 2¹²).

22

... and they believed the scripture: The singular *scripture* normally refers to one particular passage, which the evangelist quotes (e.g. 10³⁵; 13¹⁸; 19²⁴). But here, and at 20⁹, the evangelist fails to quote the particular scripture foretelling the resurrection. It must be assumed either that the scripture in question was so well known as to make its quotation superfluous, or that the evangelist implies that it is the whole Old Testament together to which the Christian looks as the divinely inspired predicter of the resurrection.

23

... at the Passover feast: The Greek, literally translated, reads 'at the Passover, at the feast', almost an hendiadys. Jeremias★ has made a useful and interesting suggestion that the phrase really means 'in the festival crowd', to give the rendering 'Now when he was in Jerusalem at the Passover in the festival crowd . . .'

many believed in his name when they saw his signs which he did: For full belief there must be more than a positive response to the wonders which he worked, a response that might eventuate merely in an assertion of thaumaturgical powers. Full belief requires belief in the scripture and in Christ's word (2²²) – a point which Luke also made (cf. Luke 24⁶, ²⁵ff., ⁴⁴ff.) at the time of the resurrection. The belief that derives from and confines itself to the works that he did in the world of space and time, in our history, is not the belief in the truth that really sets men free. The fact of Christ is not something which is seen simply by observation (cf. Luke 17²⁰); it requires, for its proper discernment, the witness of scripture and of the Spirit, whether mediated through the witness of man or given by divine inspiration. Much of John is concerned to clarify what can be seen, and what, in contrast, cannot be seen. The eternal word has become flesh in the person of Jesus; so everyone who met him had something to see. Yet what was manifested was not 'flesh' alone, but the glory that belongs to the eternal Father; not everyone 'saw' that.

★ J. Jeremias, *The Eucharistic Words of Jesus*, pp. 46–49.

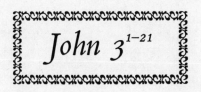

*John 3*¹⁻²¹

The Interview with Nicodemus

3 Now there was a man of the Pharisees, named Nicode'mus, a ruler of the Jews. [2] This man came to Jesus[a] by night and said to him, 'Rabbi, we know that you are a teacher come from God; for no one can do these signs that you do, unless God is with him.' [3] Jesus answered him, 'Truly, truly, I say to you, unless one is born anew,[b] he cannot see the kingdom of God.' [4] Nicode'-mus said to him, 'How can a man be born when he is old? Can he enter a second time into his mother's womb and be born?' [5] Jesus answered, 'Truly, truly, I say to you, unless one is born of water and the Spirit, he cannot enter the kingdom of God. [6] That which is born of the flesh is flesh, and that which is born of the Spirit is spirit.[c] [7] Do not marvel that I said to you, "You must be born anew."[b] [8] The wind[c] blows where it wills, and you hear the sound of it, but you do not know whence it comes or whither it goes; so it is with every one who is born of the Spirit.' [9] Nicode'mus said to him, 'How can this be?' [10] Jesus answered him, 'Are you a teacher of Israel, and yet you do not understand this? [11] Truly, truly, I say to you, we speak of what we know, and bear witness to what we have seen; but you do not receive our testimony. [12] If I have told you earthly things and you do not believe, how can you believe if I tell you heavenly things? [13] No one has ascended into heaven but he who descended from heaven, the Son of man.[d] [14] And as Moses lifted up the serpent in the wilderness, so must the Son of man be lifted up, [15] that whoever believes in him may have eternal life.'[e]

[16] For God so loved the world that he gave his only Son, that whoever believes in him should not perish but have eternal life. [17] For God sent the Son into the world, not to condemn the world, but that the world might be saved through him. [18] He who believes in him is not condemned; he who does not believe is condemned already, because he has not believed in the name of the only Son of God. [19] And this is the judgement, that the light has come into the world, and men loved darkness rather than light, because their deeds were evil. [20] For every one who does evil hates the light, and does not come to the light, lest his deeds should be exposed. [21] But he who does what is true

comes to the light, that it may be clearly seen that his deeds have been wrought in God.

a Greek *him*
b Or *from above*
c The same Greek word means both *wind* and *spirit*
d Other ancient authorities add *who is in heaven*
e Some interpreters hold that the quotation continues through verse 21

John is the only evangelist to write about Nicodemus, though curious minds have tried to identify him with some figure in the synoptic story, notably with the rich young ruler of Mark 10¹⁷ff // . Such an inspired guess may of course be right, for John is not above giving a name to a figure unnamed in the synoptic story (cf. 18¹⁰: 'The slave's name was Malchus'); but certainty cannot be claimed. Moreover it is doubtful whether such nominal links, even if validly established, would lead the reader of the fourth gospel to understand the profound relationship to, and use of, the synoptic material that John achieved in writing his own and final gospel. For even if Nicodemus is not mentioned in the earlier narratives, his position, theological and ecclesiastical, is represented, and not by the rich young ruler alone. It could hardly be otherwise. Christianity was cradled in Judaism (Mary was the mother of the Lord) and the process of achieving separate and independent existence was, as it sometimes is in family life, long and somewhat painful for both parent and child. Almost every book of the New Testament has its own contribution to make to the story of the struggle between Christianity and Judaism, and a very great deal of the synoptic story reflects or embodies it, from the first questioning of Christ's power (Mark 2¹⁻¹² //) to the decision of the Jewish authorities to put him to death. There are similar features in the fourth gospel, though with characteristic differences. But at the beginning of the gospel narrative John, like Matthew before him, sets the old and the new before his readers in a profound dialectical differentiation.

In the Sermon on the Mount two attitudes to Judaism are discernible. On the one hand Judaism brings so much that is positive that Jesus can say 'Think not that I have come to abolish the law and the prophets; I have come not to abolish them but to fulfil them. For truly, I say to you, till heaven and earth pass away, not an iota, not a dot, will pass from the law until it is all accomplished' (Matt. 5¹⁷ᶠ). But on the other hand he has to say quite clearly: 'Unless your righteousness exceeds that of the scribes and Pharisees, you will never enter the kingdom of heaven ... You have heard that it was said to the men of old ... but I say to you' (Matt. 5²⁰, ²¹⁻⁴⁸). That is to say Matthew has taken Judaism at its best, and yet been under the necessity of showing its final inadequacy. So it is with John in the story of Nicodemus; he finds a representative of Judaism at its best; but he cannot but expose his fateful inadequacy.

The discourse with Nicodemus is very skilfully placed. The evangelist has written of the incarnation of the Word. John has borne witness to Jesus as the Lamb of God. Jesus has begun to gather disciples on the basis of his recognized Messiahship. The first sign has demonstrated that the Galilean ministry itself presupposes the final transcendance of all Jewish religion in the self-offering of the Lamb of God, symbolized in the Eucharist. The cleansing of the temple has shown that the whole sacrificial system of Judaism will be replaced by the one true sacrifice in the death and resurrection of the Lord. The report that many believed in Jesus' name because of the signs he wrought, though that was an insufficient basis for Jesus to give himself to them, has already indicated the peculiarly ambiguous situation in which some of the more sensitive Jews would find themselves. It is design, and not accident, that the story of Nicodemus follows immediately. For he is precisely this sort of Jew – ready to believe in Jesus' name, yet really incapable, as a Jew, of full commitment to Jesus as Messiah and Son of God. 'So near, and yet so far' might be a title for the story of Nicodemus, as for that of the rich young ruler, though John lays the roots of difficulty bare with deeper insight.

Nicodemus is presented as a Pharisee (with all the obnoxious synoptic meanings attaching to the word) and a *ruler of the Jews*, which, from the further narrative of 7⁴⁵ᶠᶠ, seems to mean that he was a member of the Sanhedrin. The Jew who comes is thus entirely representative. Not only Christ and Nicodemus, but the Church and Judaism, may be held to meet in this story. Nicodemus comes *by night*; the evangelist here, as at many points in his narrative, has an eye for the symbolic detail. It is likely enough that a member of the Sanhedrin would have been well advised to visit the new Rabbi by night; but equally, in the mind of the evangelist, Nicodemus would have come to Jesus from that world darkness in which the true light of God was now pleased to shine. And Judaism had its own particular darkness, because it deemed itself (see below, pp. 389–390) already to be in possession of the light. But Nicodemus does not come with this as a self-conscious belief; he is a genuine seeker of the truth, hampered only by the religious situation he is already in.

Nicodemus, as the one coming to see Jesus, opens the conversation. If, as the present writer thinks, the setting of the story after the report that many Jews believed in the name of Jesus is significant, then the opening statement by Nicodemus can be viewed as the sort of judgement that intelligent, discerning, religious Judaism could make about Jesus, when exercised at its best. Nicodemus gives Jesus the title of *Rabbi* or 'Teacher' which, though it is common enough in the synoptic gospels, acquires more significance on the lips of a Pharisee and ruler of the Jews. Nicodemus goes on to confess his own belief that Jesus is a teacher come from God, since no one could do the signs that Jesus did unless he were. It is important that the Christian reader be not deceived by this confession. John has already stated that the Baptist was 'a man sent from God', but he cannot be placed in anything like the same category as Jesus, the incarnate Word. Further, the Old Testament, authoritative for Jesus, the Baptist and Nicodemus alike, could speak of many men 'sent from God', deriving their authority from that; but for the evangelist, and for the Christian believer, something transcending all Old Testament mission is present in the person of Jesus Christ. In short, Nicodemus is really in no better situation than the Pharisees who argued about Jesus after his healing of the man born blind (9^{16}). He has all the insight, but also all the limitations which the Old Testament has when isolated from the New.

What Nicodemus said depended upon what he (and/or others) had seen. *No one can do these signs that you do, unless God is with him.* There is no need to ask what the signs were that Nicodemus mentions; for on the one hand each part of the gospel is written from the perspective of the finished story, and, on the other, John can presuppose that his hearers, like himself, are already acquainted with the tradition of the synoptists before they come to read his own profound new interpretation of the story. Jesus answers the thought or the situation of Nicodemus rather than his actual words. The visible signs which he did (i.e. in synoptic and later Christian language, the miracles he wrought) are tokens that in his own person, in his presence as a man of flesh and blood in human history, the final rule or kingdom of God has come to men: 'If it is by the finger of God that I cast out demons, then the kingdom of God has come upon you' (Luke 11^{20} //). Nicodemus has, in one sense, 'seen' the signs; but he has not therefore 'seen' the kingdom of God. He may well (his words suggest he has) so understand what he has seen as to know that they are due to divine activity: thus much the Old Testament can enable him to see. But to see the further thing that Christ's signs convey and are, that cannot be the simple effect of Old Testament insight. Though the Old Testament scriptures bear witness to Jesus (5^{39}) they are not adequate in and by themselves. There is a radical discontinuity between them and the events that constitute the Kingdom, as well as a continuity. Jesus puts these convictions into his comment on Nicodemus' statement: he says: '*Truly, truly, I say to you, unless one is born anew, he cannot see the kingdom of God*' (3^3).

It is clear even at this point that the verb *see* is not used in its literal sense, though its usage includes the act of seeing what there is to be seen. In this saying of Jesus to *see* is to experience, and to experience by possession, or better, by being possessed. To experience the world in terms of Old Testament insights is one thing, and it is very wonderful, and constitutes a real experience of the one true God; but to experience the world in terms of the insights of the New Testament is something very different, not denying the insights of the Old, but bringing them to their proper fulfilment in a newly bestowed insight that both fulfils and radically transcends the old. This radical newness in the Christian experience Jesus likens to being born *anew*. The adverb is deliberately ambiguous, and the course of the conversation depends upon the ambiguity. *Anew*, as Hoskyns remarks (Hoskyns, p. 211), can mean 'from the beginning, completely, utterly' or 'again, a second time'; or it may mean 'from the upper country' (physically speaking) or 'from above', 'from heaven'. The course of the dialogue derives from Nicodemus taking it to mean 'a second time', whereas it is plain that on the lips of Jesus it meant 'from above', birth, that is, of the Spirit. The Christian's 'second birth' is birth of the Spirit.

Once more, it may be suggested, John is showing that the synoptic formulations have a profounder meaning than perhaps some of his contemporaries, and certainly some of ours, would understand. It may well be that John has in mind a saying of the kind which has been printed above (quoting Mark 10¹⁵). Such a saying is surely not properly expounded by any sentimental attempt to extol 'childlike innocence'; what the synoptics are trying to say is that entry into the kingdom is not something into which men grow by physical human development; just as one can only become a man by first being a child, so one can only become a citizen of the kingdom of God by being a child again there – or, in John's sharper phrase, by being born again. Each man therefore is capable of two births: a physical birth which enables him to enter the material world, the world of flesh, and a spiritual birth which brings him into the spiritual realm or kingdom of God. The former birth is 'from below'; a man is begotten of his earthly parents by processes which take place in this world. The latter birth is 'from above', when a man receives that spiritual quickening which enables him to discern in the flesh of Jesus Christ, the historical person of Jesus of Nazareth, the incarnate Word or Son of God. Such vision is never the work of merely terrestrial sight. Paul puts the point in his own way when he writes to the Christians in Corinth: 'No one can say "Jesus is Lord" except by the Holy Spirit' (1 Cor. 12³). To live in the world and recognize that, for all apparent evidence to the contrary, it is still under God's dominion is one thing; and the Jew, with his Old Testament scriptures witnessing to him, can experience the world in this way: but to live in the world and know and experience it as the place where God has come in the flesh to establish his kingdom, that is something quite different, into which Old Testament religion does not 'grow', but into which it must be born. The spirit is the begetter of the child of the kingdom.

Nicodemus might have seemed to start the dialogue with Jesus somewhat auspiciously. He spoke as one who had a profound, if nevertheless limited, spiritual insight. But now, in reply to Christ's reference to 'birth anew', he flounders badly, and thereby exposes the inevitable and almost paradoxical shortcoming of Judaism. From the earliest days the Christian Church has believed, on what it took to be dominical authority, that the scriptures of the Old Testament, *properly under-*

stood, really spoke of, witnessed to Christ.* If so, the Jews should have been able, without more ado, to identify Jesus as the Messiah, once he had appeared. But they did not; and the mission to the Jews remains one of the most difficult of the Church's evangelical tasks. So to be religious, to see and experience the world even in the light of Old Testament insights is still, in some sense, to be 'of this world'. The Old Testament believer believed in another world, he looked for 'an age to come'; the Christian shares both beliefs with him. But what the Christian believes, and the Jew cannot, without some radically new change in his understanding, is that the age to come has already been linked with this present age in the person, the flesh and blood of Jesus of Nazareth. Inevitably, without the radical new change in understanding, Nicodemus, representative in this regard of all his fellow Jews, appears to be, what in fact he is from the Christian perspective, earth-bound, materialist in his whole range of experience. Even the finest religion cannot produce Christian belief, but is exposed as the materialism it is.† Nicodemus replies to Jesus' admittedly hard saying: '*How can a man be born when he is old? Can he enter a second time into his mother's womb and be born?*' (3⁴). This is the measure of the impossibility that Nicodemus perceived in Jesus' claim. Like every good Jew, Nicodemus looked forward to the last days, when God would finally wind up the scroll of history and institute his kingdom or rule. It was impossible for any man living in this world to *see*, to 'experience' that kingdom. So impossible is it that it is more sensible to suppose that Jesus means by *born anew* 'born again' – and that fails to make sense, as Nicodemus knew as he uttered the words.

Jesus' reply to this uncomprehending question leads Nicodemus to ask one of a quite different sort: '*How can this be?*', which should be translated, as Barrett suggests, 'How can these things happen?' The

---

* That the early Church made much use of 'proof texts' in her dialogue with Judaism is well known: it may well be that Matthew's Gospel reflects this practice. Dr Dodd and others have thought that there was a collection of such texts available for the Christian evangelist and apologist. That such a device was thought to have dominical authority can be seen from such passages as Luke 24²⁵, ²⁷, 44–47; 18³¹, ³²; John 5³⁹.

† This is not to label the Jewish religion as 'materialist' in the modern sense; it is to point out that neither Judaism nor any other of man's religions, based or not based on revelation, is able to accept the identification of the eschatological with the historical, the eternal with the temporal, the divine with the human in the way that forms the very starting point of the Christian evangel.

reader might well ask the same question: 'How has Nicodemus been brought to ask his new question?' Jesus begins his answer to Nicodemus' misconception by repeating in fuller, perhaps in stronger terms what he has already stated: *'Truly, truly, I say to you, unless one is born of water and the Spirit, he cannot enter the kingdom of God'* (3⁵). The answer picks up the material already set out in the gospel, and tells Nicodemus that no Jewish purificatory rites, no baptisms by John in the Jordan are adequate to enable men to live in the knowledge and experience of the kingdom of God incorporate in Jesus Christ; something additional is necessary, to which Judaism, in the person of the Baptist, had already witnessed – baptism by the Spirit. And the Christian Church, in whose life of worship and service this story was both preserved and handed on, recognized in this double instrument (water and the Spirit) a description of her own Baptism. She was Judaism baptized by the Spirit. To enter the kingdom is the phrase that most suits the context of the language of new birth; but the phrase is not intended to be applied only to entry, but also to a whole life of experience of the world as the place where God has come in the flesh. Jesus must next underline the distinct 'otherness' of the two worlds. Physical begetting may bring a man to devout religion, but it remains an activity, in the sense described above, within this world; but spiritual begetting enables a man to see the presence of eternity in time, the end in the historical, the divine itself in the human flesh of the Christ.

With this sharp antithesis restated it is natural that Jesus should point out that to describe it language about a new birth is unavoidable. He then proceeds to show how nevertheless the one order is prophetic of the other. Here the English reader must be told that he is at a disadvantage. In the original text the word translated *wind* means, as the marginal note in R.S.V. states, both 'wind' and 'spirit'; and the word translated *sound* can mean both 'sound' and 'voice'. So to get the real force of the saying, it is better set out thus:

'The wind
'The Spirit blows where it will, and you hear the sound of it, his voice,

but you do not know whence it/he comes or whither it/he goes; so it is with every one who is born of the Spirit' (3⁸).

This is the point of the dialogue where the figure of birth and new birth passes over into that of the Spirit, by means of a word that connects with both the terrestrial and the spiritual worlds. The force of the analogy in both senses lies in the fact that the wind (or Spirit) can be likened to a birth because when it blows its reality can be accepted without any knowledge of its origin or destination. Human physical birth is like that: 'Where do you come from, baby dear? Out of the everywhere into here?' We know something about 'where' a baby comes from, though the profounder questions about its origin remain unanswered. Again, human physical birth is like the wind in that when it occurs we do not know what the destiny of the child will be. The same things can be said of birth of the Spirit. There are phenomena in human life which give us some real assurance that the Spirit has been operative. The early Church certainly believed this (cf. Acts. 8^{18}; 19^6; Gal. 5^{22}) and today men still look for evidence of spiritual life. Yet without some further indication we cannot know whence spiritual resilience comes, nor to what destiny it leads. What precedes a man's 'being born of the Spirit' cannot in this life be fully told; whither a spiritual awakening will ultimately take a man, we do not know from his new spiritual activities. Finally it may be reflected that the origin of the coming of the Spirit on to Jesus or whither the Spirit will lead him are not known apart from his own interpretative word. But Nicodemus has heard enough for him to ask the inquirer's question 'How can these things (i.e. spiritual birth) happen?' Or, 'Can it happen to me?'

Jesus' reply indicates that he cannot but expect Nicodemus to be equipped already with sufficient instruments for him to discern the truth of what he has heard; and the Church of which the author is a member and, doubtless, a teacher continued to think that to be instructed in the scriptures of Judaism was to receive some training in the preliminaries to Christianity. An Israelite teacher ought to be aware of the truth of what has already been said. At this point Jesus passes from the use of the first person singular to that of the first person plural: '*Truly, truly, I say to you, we speak of what we know, and bear witness to what we have seen ...*' (3^{11}). On the one hand Jesus identifies himself with his disciples*, and indeed it is only on the basis of his self-identification with them and with humanity in general

---

*This is not uncommon. Cf. Mark 9^{40}: 'He that is not against us is for us' (about someone who had been speaking in Christ's name); Acts 9^4: 'Saul, Saul, why do you persecute me?' The 'we' of the Johannine epistles may likewise be a solidarity of the Lord and his disciples (1 John 1$^{1-4}$; 2 John^2).

that he can speak to Nicodemus at all; and on the other Nicodemus is identified with all his fellow Jews who are in grave difficulty with the gospel. Such a transcendence of the historical, personal relationships is inevitable in the presence of the incarnate Son of God, where he talks to all as he talks to one, and to one as he talks to all.

The witness that the Church gives is thus not a mere theologoumenon received from an inspired teacher, and handed down without deep spiritual appropriation; it is a witness deriving from the Lord himself, from his own Person and his own teaching about his Person, but tested and verified in the life and experience of the Church. This has been the situation from the very start. This word from the solidarity of the Christ–disciple–Church relationship is embedded in the conversation with Nicodemus, and is to be seen as essentially ingredient in it, not a deflection from it. For only on this basis can the Lord continue to Nicodemus: '*If I have told you earthly things and you do not believe, how can you believe if I tell you heavenly things?*' Jesus is still pressing on Nicodemus the fact that either a man stands in the world of his physical, earthly birth, and can attain only to a this-worldly religion; or he has been born of the Spirit, however inexplicably, and then can know the truth of what Jesus says. But there is a further word which may even help Nicodemus in the extremity in which he finds himself; it is the enigmatic word about the ascent and descent of the Son of man.

For the enigmatic word sheds light. If what has been said so far is true, then it would seem impossible for any human being to attain to knowledge of *heavenly* truth.

Even the man who claimed to be 'born anew' of the Spirit might be a deceiver of others, or even more seriously of himself. But Jesus wants to assure Nicodemus that men are no longer left without some objective test about heavenly things. Certainly no man has ever been able to go to 'heaven' and return with first-hand information about heavenly realities; but there is one, the Son of man, a heavenly being now to be found in the flesh among men, who has come from 'heaven' and can therefore speak in confident truthfulness about heavenly realities. The title Son of man recalls Jesus' remark to Nathanael that he would see the heaven opened, and the angels of God ascending and descending upon the Son of man (1⁵¹). It was claimed that this meant that the person of Jesus of Nazareth, born of Mary, yet begotten of the Spirit, was himself the actual vehicle of

communication between heaven and earth, between God and man.
Jesus repeats this assurance for Nicodemus. It is not surprising, seeing
that each incident in the gospel is written from the perspective of the
end, that Jesus should use a past tense about ascension into heaven.
He is both the one who has ascended and who has descended. He is
the incarnate Son or Word, the heavenly Man of contemporary
speculation incarnate, and he speaks of heaven as a man may speak of
his own home. And yet it is not to be by simple verbal testimony
that Jesus will bring the truth home to men, for he continues 'And
as Moses lifted up the serpent in the wilderness, so must the Son of man be
lifted up' (3¹⁴).

It would not be an overstatement to say that in the synoptic gospels
Jesus' path takes him through suffering and death to glory, whereas in
the fourth gospel it leads him to something which is suffering, death
and glory simultaneously. This is detectable in John's language here.
The verb 'lift up' is used actively of Moses raising up the serpent in the
wilderness and passively* of Jesus being raised up on the cross, though
at the same time it serves to refer to his exaltation and glory. It had
already been so used by Luke (Acts 2³³; 5³¹). Passion and action are
spoken of by the same word; defeat and victory, suffering and glory
are particularly together.

Jesus tells Nicodemus that what he has to tell men, as the man who
has come from heaven with authoritative news of the heavenly events
that are to take place on earth, is that they are located at the lifting up
of the Son of man, as long ago the serpent was lifted up by Moses in
the wilderness. The allusion is helpful. For all that Israel now lives in
Palestine, the 'land of promise', she is still, in profounder terms, 'in
the wilderness' (see above, p. 117). The best that Israel-after-the-flesh
had done was to raise up the Baptist to bring a baptism of repentance
for Israel's sins and point to one yet to come, whose forerunner he
was. But John's ministry was an event 'on earth'. But when Jesus
was lifted up, certainly in an event 'on earth', there would also be

---

*There is point in the reflection that the passive voice was used by devout
Jews to speak of God's actions, thus avoiding the necessity of uttering the
divine name. If this be the case here, it accords well with John's theology, in
which the death of Jesus is not 'passion' (it has been well said that there is no
'Passion' in the fourth gospel) but action. Cf. 10¹⁷, ¹⁸: 'I lay down my life,
that I may take it again. No one takes it from me, but I lay it down of my
own accord. I have the power to lay it down, and I have the power to take it
again: this charge I have received from my Father.'

enacted a heavenly reality, in the heavenly dimension, and it is of this that Jesus will tell Nicodemus, though he fears Nicodemus may not believe.

In the story of the serpent, in Numbers 21$^{4-9}$, it is related how those who looked on the serpent were preserved in life. In the developing tradition of Judaism the incident had been subjected to deeper interpretation, and the writer of the Book of Wisdom calls the serpent a 'symbol of salvation' (Wisd. 16^6). Yet even thus reinterpreted the salvation of the serpent benefited only Israel-after-the-flesh, whereas the salvation to be effected by the raising up of the Son of man is to be universal: '*that whoever believes in him may have eternal life*' (3^{15}).

Of course the event of the crucifixion is quite 'earthly': it is as much of the stuff of history as the sack of Rome or the defeat of Hitler. 'Suffered under Pontius Pilate, crucified, dead and buried' is how that earthliness finds proper confession in the creeds. That is to say, any observer there could have seen Jesus die; any person now may read of his death. But just to do that is to see the earthly thing. What the Spirit makes known is that same event as a heavenly thing, i.e. it shows *whence it comes* and *whither it goes*. It is not part of the chain of 'one dam' thing after another'; it has an origin and a destiny. It is itself a place where the Spirit was active. And the same Spirit can enlighten believers. In so doing, the cross ceases to be simply something that just 'happens'; it becomes an event with meaningful antecedents and a satisfying end. It has its origin indeed in the eternal love of God for his creation, and it has for its divinely appointed destiny the salvation of all who believe.

This indeed is the context within which alone we may read and understand the much quoted text of 3^{16}, which has not inappropriately been called a summary of the whole gospel. The serpent was erected in the wilderness for dying Israel, as a life-giving sign. John's baptism of repentance came to Israel 'in the wilderness' as a sign pointing to a reality about to come, the reality of the Son of man lifted up on his cross in that wilderness where all men live a life of estrangement from God. And in that wilderness it is not only a sign of salvation; it is salvation itself. So it has both origin and destiny, if seen under the testimony of the Spirit, of the one who received the Spirit, and with whom the Spirit remained (1$^{33, 34}$).

God so loved the world. This one sentence precludes the Christian from thinking of God's love as some metaphysical attribute of a distant divine being only to be contemplated by the philosophically wise. For God's love is an action in man's history – the Greek uses an aorist tense here, the tense regularly used of historical happenings and actions. God loved, and things happened. But he loved the world. So the witness of the Spirit is making plain the vast origin of the lifting up of Jesus: the divine love which is its origin is not to be confined to one people, race or nation; for God's love embraces the world. The magnitude of the love is matched by the magnitude of the gift: *God so loved the world that he gave his only Son*. God loved all there was, and gave all he had. So the splendid objective of the love of God can be stated only in universal terms: *that whoever believes in him should not perish but have eternal life*. The service of love, then, is not a trivial thing. It is not just a question whether an Israelite will die today on the way to Palestine, or tomorrow within it; it is a question whether in response to the act of love a man will embrace the life that is offered, or finally and utterly perish. The terms *eternal life* and *perish* are, as Barrett observes, 'absolute alternatives'.* The world into which the Son was sent was, and remains, in Paul's phrase, 'in bondage to decay' (Rom. 8^{21}). Man in his inescapable mortality shares the finitude of the whole natural order. But at the cross, seen in the illumination of the Spirit, we learn of the victorious purpose of God's love that has asserted the gift of life in the midst of a dying world. Man has now the possibility of two destinies: life or death. Only God has life in himself. His gift of life to men is thus their own hope of attaining it, and to attain it is to share the fullness of life itself, in never-failing abundance. Its quality is the source of its perpetuity. But outside this life, everything ends in death. The alternatives are indeed absolute.

But this poses a searching question. How can death result from a choice set before men by the God whose love gave his only begotten Son in order that all who believe might live? How can universal saving love be reconciled with the perishing of any single man? Can condemnation have any place in a theology of love? John's answer to this is to reassert that God's act is one of love, and of universal benignity. The condemnation to perish is not the act of God, which is simply the giving of his only Son. Condemnation does not follow from God's action, but from man's. The man who believes is not condemned to

* Barrett, p. 180.

perish. The man who does not believe is not condemned to death by God subsequent to his unbelief; for God has indeed offered him life: he is condemned already *in his unbelief*. The perishing of the unbeliever is not a punishment for unbelief inflicted by a ruthless God; it is the self-determined end of the man who does not believe. In this way John is radically rewriting the Jewish doctrine of judgement, which thought of all such final rewards as being distributed at a 'last day'; and then, inevitably, it was bound to appear that death was the penalty inflicted by God for unbelief. But John tells his readers, as Jesus told Nicodemus, that the real situation is not that the world will go on and at the end the judgement will come, but rather that because God has acted from his universal love and offered to all men the gift of life freely, judgement takes place within history, now. It is not a sentence inflicted by a judge after the commission of a crime, but an inherent part of the choice that some men make when faced by the divine gift. Not that God condemns any man to perish, but that some men so condemn themselves. If we ask how this can be, John helps with an answer. *Light*, Jesus says, *has come into the world*, thus recalling the great words of the Prologue about the Word that is Light ($1^{4,5,9}$) but as the Prologue also leads us to expect ($1^{10, 11}$) some men love darkness rather than the light: the reason? – their works are evil. So John begins to uncover another great metaphor by which he speaks of the significance of the coming of the Word: light and darkness confront each other in the conflicts of the incarnate Son. And that warfare, cosmic in its reach and issue, finds a battlefield in the heart of every man. The evildoer, John acutely observes with the penetration of a modern psychologist, hates the light, for fear of having his evil deeds exposed. But the man who deals with realities, the realities of God's loving and saving act, fashioning his own behaviour in the service of love, he has no fear in coming to the light, but will welcome it, since light can only expose the identity of his deeds with those of the light.

അ

1

named Nicodemus: Nicodemus was a Greek name, used by the Jews, meaning significantly 'conqueror' or 'ruler' of the people. It is an apt name for one in whose discussion with Jesus a number of ideas from the Greek world are to be introduced.

a ruler of the Jews: That Nicodemus was a member of the Sanhedrin appears from 7⁵⁰.

2

came to Jesus by night: probably meant both in its 'earthly' and 'spiritual' meanings – John's eye for a symbolic detail.

'Rabbi': Nicodemus accords Jesus the status he would seek for himself.

'we know . . .': Nicodemus speaks not only for himself, either on the night he went, or at any time since.

'come from God': the words are in a place of emphasis, and may well mean that Nicodemus and his friends were among those who in the synoptic gospels are reported by the disciples to think that Jesus is 'John the Baptist, Elijah, or one of the prophets' – in any event a person of real significance in the life of Israel.

'these signs': cf. 2²³. John has recorded in detail only the sign at Cana so far, but clearly presupposes that his readers knew of others – from the synoptic tradition, or those referred to in 2²³?

'unless God is with him': This is a true perception, but quite inadequate for the central affirmation of the Christian gospel.

4

'How can a man be born when he is old?': The word *old* has suggested to some that Nicodemus was himself an old man at this time. If so, he could not be 'the rich young ruler' as others suppose. It would be more natural to suppose that a member of the Sanhedrin were an old man than a young one.

5

'unless one is born of water and the Spirit': The evangelist picks up his own story of John's identification of Jesus as one who *baptizes* with the Spirit (1³³). The whole notion of spiritual begetting is important for this and other passages in the gospel, see esp. the Prologue 1¹³, as well as for other writers of the N.T. (I Peter 1³, ²³; Titus 3⁵). The language of birth and rebirth was common in Hellenistic religions, which at the time of the writing of the fourth gospel were offering rebirth to men. Yet it seems to the present writer of more significance that John brings this language in to give further definition and contemporary relevance to the language of the synoptists in passages like Mark 10¹⁵ // . The fundamental notions are Hebraic, and the Hellenistic additions serve to make them more widely understood and received.

It is not possible to miss the reference to Christian baptism in the phrase *'water and Spirit'*. John's sacramental theology underlines the term.

8

'so it is with every one who is born of the Spirit': In terms of the exegesis given above this means that it is only as a man learns through the Spirit of the truth and reality of the divine love in Jesus Christ that he can become aware of, or indeed enter into, his origin and destiny in the universal purpose of God. If we are not born of the Spirit we are doomed to be ephemera; but begotten by him we rise to share the eternal life of God.

9

'How can this be?': As Barrett notes (p. 176) this should be translated 'How can these things happen?' and the present writer is inclined to think that this may be intended to betray some personal concern of Nicodemus as he asks the question. 'How can these things happen to me?'

10

'Are you a teacher of Israel?': Again, the translation needs amendment. The literal translation is 'Are you *the* teacher of Israel?' – Jesus acknowledges that Nicodemus was perhaps one of the best and most trusted teachers of the Jewish community.

11

'but you do not receive our testimony': Jesus uses the plural *you* from this point on. It would not be entirely unnatural for this to have been the actual course of the conversation; but again, this, like other incidents, is written from the perspective of the end, not from the moment of occurrence.

12

' earthly things . . . heavenly things': The meaning can only be expounded in the light of the context as it speaks to each commentator. To the present writer it seems that for John an *earthly* thing is an event which may well be, and often is, taken for granted as one of the series of events that go to make up the stream of time, but which when properly seen and understood is recognized to be pregnant with spiritual reality, because it does in fact incorporate in some way divine activity. Physical birth is one such thing; it can be taken as just a fact of nature; but properly and profoundly understood it is a symbol of another sort of begetting, and indeed is not unconnected with such begetting when the story of the life and destiny of a believer is fully told. A *heavenly* thing is an event which, while it may take its place among the things that occur on earth, and are done by men, is nevertheless an event which really has

its origin in the action of God. Thus, the birth of the Son, his being
sent into the world, is a *heavenly* thing; and the lifting up of the Son of
man, the crucifixion, though so plainly a deed wrought by men, is
nevertheless an act of God, originating in his saving love for the world.
This seems to fit the whole context better than by referring to 'earthly'
things as man's condition before rebirth and the 'heavenly' as the
eternal life which follows it; or than interpreting earthly and heavenly
in somewhat Platonic terms as material and spiritual realities.

15

'*that whoever believes in him may have eternal life*': It is better to accept
Barrett's suggestion (p. 179) that *in him* should be associated with
eternal life rather than with *believe*. This avoids difficult grammar, and is
excellent Johannine theology.

Eternal life is a peculiarly Johannine phrase, though it is used by the
synoptists. It is interesting to recall that the rich young ruler asked Jesus
the question '*What must I do to inherit eternal life?*' On the lips of such a
typical Jew (and so therefore to the ears of Nicodemus) the phrase was
really equivalent to 'the life of the age to come', i.e. life in that divine
order that would supervene upon this when history was brought to its
close by God. But for the fourth evangelist the outstanding and characteristic thing is that *eternal life* need not be waited for until this age ceases,
but can be, and indeed is, the gift of God within the present temporal
order. Hence the present tense is used in the next verse, and often afterwards in the gospel, in speaking about begetting eternal life. This is part
of John's 'realized eschatology'. The synoptics sometimes speak of 'life'
absolutely: 'The gate is narrow and the way is hard, that leads to life'
(Matt. 7[14]). It need not be accompanied by the adjective *eternal*. But
what does *eternal* mean? Not 'everlasting' in the sense that it always
goes on, but eternal in the sense that its quality is unassailable by corruption or decay. The emphasis is on the quality, not the duration, of the
life. And the quality is that which the divine life itself has, which God
himself is. John will have much more to say about it as his gospel
continues.

16

God so loved the world: 'The world' is intentionally ambiguous in usage
here, meaning that God has a universal love for his whole creation; but
that properly to reciprocate that love is the gift of God to man.

17

For God sent the Son into the world, not to condemn . . . : The verb translated
sent is associated in Greek with the noun 'apostle'. In John it is a basic
idea that Jesus has been sent (he is *the* great apostle) and that he sends his
disciples as he himself was sent (20[21]).

not to condemn: The thought is often reflected in Paul: 'There is therefore now no condemnation for those who are in Christ Jesus' (Rom. 8^1).

19

And this is the judgement: Or, 'the condemnation'. Here the evangelist makes it plain that it is a reflex of the act of God's love that men may condemn themselves, and not a separate and posterior act of God's judicial condemnation. Even this judgement speaks his love.

21

he who does what is true: Truth = reality; the reality is the act of God. To do the truth is thus to do God's will. Such actions are 'wrought in God'. We are not their sole authors.

> 'And every virtue we possess,
> And every victory won
> And every thought of holiness
> Are his alone.'

John 3²²⁻³⁶

The Final Testimony
of the Baptist

Mark 2¹⁸⁻²⁰
Matthew 11²⁻⁶

²²*After this Jesus and his disciples went into the land of Judea; there he remained with them and baptized.* ²³*John also was baptizing at Ae′non near Salim, because there was much water there; and people came and were baptized.* ²⁴*For John had not yet been put in prison.*

²⁵*Now a discussion arose between John's disciples and a Jew over purifying.* ²⁶*And they came to John, and said to him, 'Rabbi, he who was with you beyond the Jordan, to whom you bore witness, here he is, baptizing, and all are going to him.'* ²⁷*John answered, 'No one can receive anything except what is given him from heaven.* ²⁸*You yourselves bear me witness, that I said, I am not the Christ, but I have been sent before him.* ²⁹*He who has the bride is the bridegroom; the friend of the bridegroom, who stands and hears him, rejoices greatly at the bridegroom's voice; therefore this joy of mine is now full.* ³⁰*He must increase, but I must decrease.'ᵃ*

³¹*He who comes from above is above all; he who is of the earth belongs to the earth, and of the earth he speaks; he who comes from heaven is above all.* ³²*He bears witness to what he has seen and heard, yet no one receives his testimony;* ³³*he who receives his testimony sets his seal to this, that God is true.* ³⁴*For he whom God has sent utters the words of God, for it is not by measure that he gives the Spirit;* ³⁵*the Father loves the Son, and has given all things into his hand.* ³⁶*He who believes in the Son has eternal life; he who does not obey the Son shall not see life, but the wrath of God rests upon him.*

a Some interpreters hold that the quotation continues through verse 36

Understandably and inevitably the present section of the fourth gospel has puzzled commentators. Why does it suddenly jump to an assertion about Jesus and his disciples spending some time baptizing, and doing so, in clear contradiction, it would seem, to all the synoptic evidence (cf. Mark 1¹⁴: 'After John was arrested, Jesus came into Galilee . . .'). Why does the author pass from a passage which

191

may well be reckoned as suitable on the lips of the Baptist, at least as he speaks in the fourth gospel, directly to a passage which it is impossible to suppose that any other than Jesus himself could speak? And why should that final passage of the section be far more related in thought and language to the interview with Nicodemus than with anything the reader has learnt about the Baptist?

Naturally the attempt to answer these questions honestly has produced a number of solutions. Some of them involve a frank recognition that the section is not now in its original place. Thus Bernard (I.C.C.) transposes 3^{31-6} to follow 3^{21}, and leaves the second testimony of the Baptist to follow 3^{36}. This has by no means universally commended itself, and indeed as Prof. Dodd has said:[*]

It is pretty certain that if our MSS. had given verse 31 immediately after verse 21, critics would have pointed out a disjuncture; for there is no immediate connexion between the thought of judgement by the light in verses 17–21 and the supremacy of Christ as the One who descends from heaven and bears witness to what He has seen, which is the theme of 31–2. These verses hark back to 11–14. The whole section, 31–6, is not so much a continuation of the preceding discourse as a recapitulation of its leading ideas, with some additional points. Such a recapitulation is quite in accord with our author's technique, but there is no ground for insisting that such a recapitulation must follow immediately upon the passage which it recapitulates: it may so follow, or it may not.

Dr Dodd goes on to make some interesting suggestions why the author prefaced the recapitulation with the passage 3^{22-6}. It enables him to bring the statement of 3^5 (that unless one is born of water and the Spirit one cannot see the kingdom of God) into association with the two baptisms of Jesus and John, comment on them by means of John's witness that he is but the friend of the bridegroom for Israel (whereas Jesus is the bridegroom himself) and so show baptism by water and the Spirit as indeed the means by which life (rebirth) is possible. Dr Dodd concludes:

'It seems best therefore to regard 3^{22-6} as an explanatory appendix to the dialogue with Nicodemus and the discourse which grows out of it, the whole of ch. 3 being concerned with the idea of initiation into eternal life (or rebirth), in conjunction with a rich complex of ideas which are required for its proper understanding'.[†]

[*] Dodd, p. 309.
[†] Dodd, p. 311.

Dr Dodd is neither so lucid nor so convincing as usual at this point. Dr Barrett simply states that there is no need to make transpositions: 'The whole paragraph is a unity' (p. 183). Some light on the structure of the chapter and on the developing thought of the gospel is again derived by reference to the synoptic tradition. The first thing to notice is that, as many critics have observed, the assertion that Jesus and John conducted some ministry simultaneously seems to contradict the synoptic record. This is particularly so if we note the statement in verse 24, that the simultaneous ministries took place before John was put into prison. Mark reports in 1¹⁴ that Jesus did not go to Galilee to commence his public ministry until John was put in prison. It seems quite pointless to try to find some chronological way round these difficulties, if for no other reason than that it is most probable that the information here given by John was never meant to be a chronological correction of the synoptic story. The author has already made it plain that the Baptist's testimony to Jesus was in part concerned to say that though Jesus came after him, he was before him. That is to say, chronological placing is not the determinative thing. What is determinative for a true judgement of the comparative significance of Jesus and the Baptist is their relation to God and to his great purpose of redemption. Further, it has been shown that John was always concerned to write from the perspective of the 'end', and from that perspective the question was not whether Jesus preceded, or was contemporaneous, even for a time, with the Baptist, but what choice men were to make, even after the crucifixion, between the claims of John and those of Jesus. There is a real and profound sense in which they were offering men their baptisms, different though they were, simultaneously, and that they do so still. There is still a distinction to be made between baptism, even in a Christian church, which is mere ceremonial, and one which is truly a sacrament, i.e. with water *and* the Spirit.

Having stated the simultaneity and therewith the inevitable rivalry between Jesus and John (and no doubt John would have in mind the service that his present passage would render the churches that he knew and loved) the author records a further witness of the Baptist to Jesus. This repays comparison with the synoptic tradition. In Mark 2¹⁸⁻²⁰ // Jesus is himself concerned to draw some distinction between himself and his disciples and John and his disciples. He does this by using the figure of the bridegroom and the bride. The bride is Israel:

the bridegroom is himself.* The friends of the bridegroom, with duties something like a 'best man' at a modern British wedding, are the disciples. But in John, with a much more striking piece of traditional usage of the bridegroom figure, it is the Baptist who uses the metaphor, and sees Jesus as the bridegroom and himself as the friend of the groom. Or again, in Matthew and Luke (Matt. 11²⁻⁶; Luke 7¹⁸⁻²³), we read of John's inquiry from prison whether Jesus was 'the one who is to come', or whether another must be sought. At this Jesus tells John's disciples to report to their master what they have seen and heard when they were with him; the 'signs' would themselves answer John's question. But here in John, at the second witness of the Baptist, it is John himself who states in no uncertainty that Jesus is the Christ, and that while he must grow, John's company must inevitably decrease. So, regarded as material for a Church that had to face surviving members of the Baptist movement, the tradition of the fourth gospel is much more incisive and sure. The fourth gospel is far from simply wanting to correct the synoptics on a point of chronology: it seeks to show that the Gospel is not just subsequent to Judaism, even to its most vital reformed sector, but wholly transcendent of it, as Christ the Son transcended the Baptist and every other born of man.

But can an answer be found to the question why this material about the Baptist should be inserted here, in a chapter devoted to a profound discourse to Nicodemus, and which is, as all readers see, to end in a summary of the discourse? It can. The fourth gospel proceeds on a somewhat thematic plan. If, in terms of the Prologue, it be conceived as the story of the Word incarnate, it is not improper to see that in the earliest chapters the author is dealing with the impact of the Word upon Judaism; and he begins by relating how within Judaism, in the person of the Baptist, there arose some preliminary consciousness of the coming of the Word. He shows how, as a result of the witness of John to Jesus as the Lamb of God, some men, among them disciples of the Baptist, adhered to Jesus himself. He then shows, in two vivid stories, first how Jesus fulfils and therefore replaces all the inadequate purificatory rites of Judaism (by the sign at Cana) and second how Jesus fulfils and therefore replaces all the sacrificial system of Judaism (by the cleansing of the temple). Then, in the third chapter he shows how the Word comes to and deals with Judaism at its best, in the far-

* cf. the story of the wedding at Cana and the notes thereon, pp. 141–150.

seeing but yet inadequate Old Testament faith of Nicodemus. John is about to close the section on the Gospel and the Jews, but before he does so he rightly brings back another example of Judaism at its best, Judaism that did not come from the darkness to seek him, but Judaism that saw itself as his forerunner. The testimony of John must be borne again at this point of the narrative before the author passes on to Samaritans and Gentiles. So, as a last comment on the Word and the religion of the Jews he will write the summarizing passage found in 3³¹⁻⁶. The section will be studied in this light.

Jesus and his disciples, says John, went into Judea and, such is the implication of the Greek, spent some time there and performed baptisms. No such thing has been reported by the synoptics, but there is little inherently impossible in it, unless the reader judges the text by much later ecclesiastical custom and doctrine. John was baptizing not far away. The author is evidently wanting to bring the two into contrast by this juxtaposition, for as Dr Dodd says 'the reader is not to forget that Jesus is he who baptizes with the Holy Spirit' (Dodd, p. 310). But the statement has troubled many commentators, who have remembered that John later says (7³⁹) 'as yet the Spirit had not been given, because Jesus was not yet glorified'. The difficulties of the passage for some ecclesiastical traditions may be granted, and sympathetically understood; but that ought not to prevent the reader from attempting to understand what John is trying to say now. In any case, he has already said that Jesus has manifested his glory (2¹¹); and, for all the clarity of the reference to the cross in the mention of the lifting up of the Son of man, it is not to be supposed that Jesus really thought that Nicodemus could not possibly believe in him until he had been crucified. There is, of course, a profound sense in which that is true. But there is another, not really less profound sense, in which belief is possible to those who meet the Lord before his crucifixion. And they have been 'begotten of the Spirit'.

As John continued his baptism, the disciples began a discussion with some Jew (or Jews) about purifying. It related to the fact that Jesus was also baptizing, and, moreover, was 'drawing the crowds'. John's followers were disturbed. But not so John. He still bore his witness. (Here is a parable of the situation in which the evangelist and some of his contemporaries found themselves, in facing a continuing Baptist sect, and using against it the full testimony of John.) He

reminded his disciples of his former words, and then spoke of Jesus as
the bridegroom, and of himself as the friend of the bridegroom, who
stands and listens for the groom, and rejoices when he hears his voice.
The metaphor of the bridegroom comes home at four distinct levels.
First, by its setting in Jewish social life, it enabled any Jew to understand what John was saying about Jesus. Second, in picking up many
Old Testament sayings, it brought home to the devout Jew the
profound nature of the metaphor, for Yahweh is often called the
husband or the betrothed of Israel (Exod. 34^{15}; Psalm 73^{27}; Hosea 2^{19};
Isa. 54^5). Third, it picks up the synoptists' metaphor used by Jesus in
his statement about his relationship, and that of his disciples, to the
Baptist and his circle, as well as to the Jews. Thus the metaphor has
passed through a social and a theological to a christological stage; and
then finally, and fourthly, the metaphor echoes material already set
out in John, viz. in the story of the wedding at Cana in Galilee (q.v.).
John says plainly that he who has the bride is the bridegroom.
In Jesus Yahweh has come to claim his bride – i.e. his people Israel.
John, for all his concern that the people of God should repent of their
sins, and become a new people of God newly and really given to do
his will, knows very well that he is not the one to whom Israel will be
wedded. That high honour belongs to one for whom he has waited.
But waiting, he has heard the voice of the bridegroom, and that has
brought him the joy of knowing that his own function has been
performed. Of course it is but the fulfilment of God's coming to
claim his bride, Israel, that the bridegroom should gather her to himself. And that is what is really happening as between John and Jesus.
The fundamental question is not simply one of purificatory rites: it is
one about the gathering of the people of God; the marriage of the
Lamb. '*He must increase, but I must decrease*'. That was the lively
witness which the evangelist preserved for the Church as she continued
her ministry of baptism simultaneously with that of the followers of
John.

It is most probable that in verse 31 the evangelist leaves this renewed
testimony of John in order to sum up in a final paragraph both it and
the discourse to Nicodemus. But it is worth observing here a common
feature of the gospel, how impossible it is to be quite certain where the
evangelist really draws boundary lines. To the present writer it is the
evangelist's deliberate purpose to leave them imprecise; here, e.g.
vv. 31 and 32 could as easily belong to the end of the Baptist's witness

as they could to the summary discourse where they are normally placed. If these two verses are compared with what the Baptist said in 1²⁹⁻³⁴, the substance will not be thought to be greatly different, even though the language here has picked up its phrasing from the dialogue with Nicodemus. It has for the most part been held that v. 32 cannot have been spoken by the Baptist, because it affirms that *no one receives his testimony*. But, as every commentator has to recognize, the very next phrase goes on to speak of him who receives his testimony. It could well be argued that the phrase *no one receives his testimony* referred to the Baptist's testimony that Jesus was the lamb, the Son of God (1²⁹, ³⁴), and that the exceptions envisaged are those disciples who moved from the circle of John to that of Jesus. But even so, and it seems a fair point to make, it would be characteristic of the evangelist so to state his point that it applied to Christ himself as well. For that is how John not infrequently takes his text forward.

But whether or not we may suppose that the text of verses 31, 32 has a lower as well as a higher meaning, they are clearly meant to have an ultimate application to Jesus. He who comes as Jesus has come from above, is above all, says the Baptist, says the evangelist, says the Lord (cf. 3¹³). He who is of the earth, who is human, belongs to this world and speaks of it, says the Baptist, says the evangelist, says Jesus. The one who comes from above bears witness to what he has seen and heard, as John did (in 1³²: 'I saw the Spirit descend as a dove from heaven . . . he who sent me said . . .'); as the evangelist does throughout his gospel; as Jesus does, and has already done (3¹¹). This stream of witness is threefold yet really one. And the man who receives it *sets his seal to this, that God is true* (3³³). That is to say, if those who hear the testimony believe it, they are asserting that God has spoken the truth to them. But if they do not receive the testimony they make God a liar (cf. 1 John 5¹⁰). The sealing does not of course either make or add to the truth of what is said. It does, however, commend it as the truth, and is thus in turn itself a witness.

The statement moves now to the crucial summary of what the dialogue between Jesus and Nicodemus, between Jesus and the Baptist, between John and the Baptist sects, between the Church and Judaism amounts to; which is this: The one whom God has sent, Jesus the great apostle, speaks the words of God. Of this we may be sure, because the Father has not given the Spirit to the Son in any stinted measure, but without measure at all. The father indeed loves the Son (the Son is his only-begotten: 3[16]; 1[18]) and has given everything into his hand. That is to say, as the following explanatory verse makes plain, the whole issue of human life and its destiny, the whole question of eternal life or death is involved in man's answer to what the Son says. To believe on the Son of God is, as Jesus has said to Nicodemus, to have eternal life, to be knit anew to God. But to withhold belief, not to obey the Son, is to perish; or, as the point is now stated, to have the wrath of God remain on one. The Greek word 'disbelieve' has the meaning of 'disobey', and gives the evangelist a further opportunity to use a term with some ambiguity in order to express an important idea. Belief for John is not a mere matter of intellectual assent. It involves the setting and direction and persistence of a whole life. So the opposite of 'believing' (which is to yield oneself up to God in Christ) is disobedience. The wrath of God is not mentioned again in the Gospel, though the alternatives life and death are to reappear throughout. The term *wrath* is frequent in Paul, and as Dr Dodd has pointed out in writing of the apostle to the Gentiles, *wrath* in the biblical sense is not 'temper' in the modern meaning of that word. Indeed at this point of the gospel the evangelist is manifestly putting precisely the same point as he made in 3[18]. The wrath of God is the obverse side of his love. Man cannot but deal with God, for God has dealt with man. And in offering man eternal life, God has made rejection both possible and calamitous. Love could not offer life on other terms without forswearing love.

℣℣

22
Jesus and his disciples: Some have speculated on who did accompany Jesus to Judea, seeing, as v. 24 says, it was before John's imprisonment, and therefore before the record in Mark 1[14] had begun. But, as implied above, this is a superfluous question and it need not be supposed that there is any other but the normal gospel meaning to be attached to the term here. He remained with them and baptized: the clear implication of this is that Jesus shared in the baptisms. This is denied in 4[2] in a parenthesis which, as Dr Dodd says (p. 311), 'perhaps has a better claim to be regarded as an "editorial note" by a "redactor" than anything else in the gospel except the colophon xxi, 24–5'.

23
John was also baptizing at Aenon near Salim: It is impossible to give an accurate location to these places, though it is not therefore necessary to

suppose that the evangelist is using metaphorical names; e.g. it has been suggested that the meaning of the names is their only significance, 'fountains (*Aenon*) near to peace (*Salim*)' indicating that the Baptist is preparing for the real peace which Messiah will bring.

25

Now a discussion arose between John's disciples and a Jew: The Greek sentence seems to imply that the discussion arose from the side of John's disciples. *A Jew* is but one reading, the plural 'Jews' being the other. The singular form appears only here in John, and it is thus more likely to be the original. Some have suggested a corruption underlying both readings, and think that some use of 'Jesus' was original, so that the discussion was originally said to be between John's and Jesus' disciples. This fits the context admirably; but as there is no textual basis for it at all, sober scholarship has to stand by *Jew* or Jews.

over purifying: The word is the same as used in the reference to the stone jars at the wedding in Cana (2⁶), and this may be an intentional reference, particularly in a context where the figure of the bridegroom appears.

26

all are going to him: The *all* may be, as Barrett (ad loc.) suggests, an 'historical exaggeration'; but it is more likely to be a means by which the evangelist tells his readers that a new people of God was being gathered, as distinct from even a large number of individual converts. The same comment applies to Mark's account of the Baptist (Mark 1⁵), for he would want his readers to know that the Baptist was concerned with the life of Israel as the people of God, in distinction from individual obedience in private lives.

29

He who has the bride: Not only is this a social, an Old Testament, a synoptic and a Johannine metaphor, but one used elsewhere in the New Testament: cf. 2 Cor. 11²; Eph. 5²⁵⁻³³; Rev. 21²; 22¹⁷; 19⁷⁻⁹.

31

He who comes from above is above all: The synoptics told of a question put by John, 'Art thou he that should come?' (Matt. 11²⁻⁶ //). Here, significantly, the Baptist testifies that he is the one who has come, and come from above. Of course this joins the testimony of Jesus to himself, and of the evangelist to Jesus. But essentially that is what even a synoptic gospel provides!

32

He bears witness to what he has seen and heard: This, as pointed out above, can be well read as coming from the lips of John about himself. But on the lips of Jesus, inasmuch as the speech is passing to him, the evangelist is preparing the reader for a new phase of testimony which Jesus is properly able to bear of himself; and which, in the end, he must bear of himself if the truth be granted, that the earthly man speaks and can but speak of earthly things, and only the man from heaven can speak of heavenly things. See further notes on 5³¹ and especially 8¹⁴.

33
he who receives his testimony sets his seal to this, that God is true: This refers to authentication (cf. Esth. 8⁸), which is a formalized witness. The believer witnesses to God's truth, not to his own ideas.

35
the Father loves the Son: The word for *love* is the same as used in 3¹⁶, and is a word distinctively Christian, indicating a love concerned and actively caring for the beloved. Though it is a new and an 'exalted' word, John can use more familiar ones in the same sort of context as in 5²⁰, where the word '*phileo*' is used.

36
he who does not obey the Son shall not see life: 'Life' is here used in an absolute form parallel with *eternal life* in the earlier part of the verse. Such parallelism of terms is a common feature of Hebrew poetry, and Dr Black has detected a poem behind this section of the gospel.

John 4$^{1-4}$

4 *Now when the Lord knew that the Pharisees had heard that Jesus was
making and baptizing more disciples than John* ²(*although Jesus himself did
not baptize, but only his disciples*), ³*he left Judea and departed again to
Galilee.* ⁴*He had to pass through Samar'ia.*

This note is inserted by the evangelist for two evident reasons. He
wanted to explain why Jesus left Judea and went to Galilee, and he
needed, in view of the next section of the gospel, to bring Jesus to
Samaria.

The reason for the departure from Judea is given in the report that
the Pharisees had heard that Jesus was making and baptizing more
disciples than John. The author has already assumed (3²⁴) that his
readers know at least what the synoptists have reported about the
arrest and imprisonment of the Baptist; so to state that the Pharisees
had heard that Jesus was mounting a movement larger than John's
suffices to suggest the greater hostility with which he would be regarded. Jesus, aware of this, retires to Galilee, for greater quiet,
security and rest. His way lay through Samaria. True, he need not
have gone through Samaria; but, as Josephus tells, the route through
Samaria was the common one for Jews going from Galilee to
Jerusalem for the feasts, and for their return. So the phrase *he had to
pass through Samaria* is charged with more than ordinary meaning, and
we may understand that, as in the synoptics and other places in John,
the word indicates the necessity that the will of God lays upon men,
though it does not necessarily (and does not here) limit the freedom
of choice that men exercise. The divine necessity is complicit in the
deeds of men, notably in the works of Jesus.

The parenthetical statement that Jesus did not baptize is, as Dr
Dodd points out, almost certainly an addition to the original text
(see above, p. 195). It may well be that the scribe who made the
addition was wanting to keep the record from suggesting that Jesus
offered any man simply water-baptism. The Lord's baptism, as John
had testified, and as the discourse with Nicodemus had clarified, was
to be '*with the Holy Spirit*' (1³³).

Samaria is not mentioned at all by Mark, nor does he speak of the Samaritans. Matthew once refers to Samaria: in reporting Jesus' injunction to his disciples not to enter any 'town of the Samaritans' on their evangelistic tour (Matthew 10⁵). But Luke, who has already been recognized in this commentary as being in some ways a half-way stage to the fourth gospel, has much more to say about Samaria and the Samaritans. He reports that Jesus used the present route in reverse as he once went up to Jerusalem (Luke 17¹¹); he tells of one hostile Samaritan village (Luke 9⁵²ff), but also of the Lord's rebuke to the disciples who wanted to punish it; and he tells the parable of the Good Samaritan (Luke 10²⁹⁻³⁷), and also of the Samaritan leper whom Jesus healed, but was the only one of ten who returned to give thanks (Luke 17¹¹⁻¹⁹).

But Samaria had some special category in the theology of missions in the early Church. Luke preserves this in the instructions of the risen Lord to the disciples in Acts 1⁸: 'You shall be my witnesses in Jerusalem and in all Judea and Samaria and to the end of the earth'. It is worth noting that John reports a sequence that can be said to implement this precise programme. Jesus has been to Jerusalem (2¹³–3²¹); he has gone from the city to Judea (3²²–4²); and now he is to be found in Samaria. What he next does in Galilee (Galilee of the Gentiles) is to heal the son of an official, who might well be the Centurion (and so a Gentile) of Matthew 8⁵⁻¹³ // . And even if this is not accepted it remains clear that in the developing story John tells the meeting with the Samaritan woman is a further stage in the definition of the work of the incarnate Son.

John 4$^{5-42}$

4⁵⁻¹⁴   THE WOMAN AND THE BRIDE

⁵So he came to a city of Samar'ia, called Sy'char, near the field that Jacob gave to his son Joseph. ⁶Jacob's well was there, and so Jesus, wearied as he was with his journey, sat down beside the well. It was about the sixth hour.
⁷There came a woman of Samar'ia to draw water. Jesus said to her, 'Give me a drink.' ⁸For his disciples had gone away into the city to buy food. ⁹The Samaritan woman said to him, 'How is it that you, a Jew, ask a drink of me, a woman of Samar'ia?' For Jews have no dealings with Samaritans. ¹⁰Jesus answered her, 'If you knew the gift of God, and who it is that is saying to you, "Give me a drink," you would have asked him, and he would have given you living water.' ¹¹The woman said to him, 'Sir, you have nothing to draw with, and the well is deep; where do you get that living water? ¹²Are you greater than our father Jacob, who gave us the well, and drank from it himself, and his sons, and his cattle?' ¹³Jesus said to her, 'Every one who drinks of this water will thirst again, ¹⁴but whoever drinks of the water that I shall give him will never thirst; the water that I shall give him will become in him a spring of water welling up to eternal life.'

In his thematic treatment of the confrontation of the world by the incarnate Son the fourth evangelist now deals with the Samaritans. This was really a theological necessity. The Jews were the chosen people of God, and when the Word came to them he was 'coming to his own home' (1¹¹). The non-Jews, or the Gentiles, were not the chosen Israel of God, and it might well be thought that John's thematic treatment of the story of the Word made flesh ought to move from the Jews direct to the Gentiles. But the world did not, and does not, divide quite so neatly as that! For there was, and is, a third group, the Samaritans. These claimed, like the Jews, to be true descendants of Jacob, who gave Israel its name. Non-Jews would not think of them as Gentiles, nor Israelites consider them to be Jews. But the Samaritans claimed all the status and all the privileges of the Jews, disputing with them in many matters, theological and ecclesiastical.

Samaria was originally the name of the new capital that the renowned king Omri had built (about 925 B.C.) for the Northern
Kingdom (1 Kings 16²⁴). Later the name was applied to the district
and kingdom itself (cf. Ezek. 16⁴⁶). The city of Samaria was taken by
Assyrian invaders in 721 B.C., the Israelite population being taken into
captivity, and replaced by a number of foreign settlers (2 Kings
17²⁴ff). It appears plain from the historian's account in Kings that
the settlers brought into their new home their old and pagan
religions. Yet to some extent the religion of the Northern tribes was
continued, though when Nehemiah and Ezra led Jews back to
Jerusalem it proved impossible to unite the inhabitants of Samaria
and the restored Jews. Controversy did not lessen with the years, and
by the first century A.D. suspicion and hostility marked the relationships between Samaritans and Jews, as the Gospel records amply
testify. Luke, who tells of the Good Samaritan and of the grateful
Samaritan leper, also reports hostility (see above); and it is significant
that the only other use of the word Samaritan in John is found at the
place where he reports, as the Synoptists do, that the Jews charged
Jesus with being possessed by a demon; John's form of the accusation
is: 'Are we not right in saying that you are a Samaritan and have a
demon?' (8⁴⁸)!

John's unfolding story is thus taken a stage forward when Jesus
talks with a Samaritan. Even the most prosaic eye must see something
symbolic in the confrontation of a Samaritan with the Word made
flesh; and John's highly sensitive eye has seen much more symbolism
in the details of the occasion. Not that, in the view of the present
writer, it is necessary to suppose that the whole incident is allegory
and not real event: there are too many pointers the other way for that.
For example, the language of this chapter does not conform to some
of the general pattern of Johannine dialogue: there is no 'verily,
verily' in the whole length of it; and while that is still compatible
with an allegorical fabrication, it is more likely to be due to respect
for an historical tradition. Yet the story is full of symbolic detail.

Jesus came to Jacob's well near to Sychar. The well for a community
was often at a little distance from the cluster of dwellings. There is
suggestive symbolism that it was Jacob's well – Jacob, whose name
was changed to Israel, and who had dreamed of a ladder between
heaven and earth, which was to be replaced by the person of the Son
of man (1⁵¹). John evidently wants to remind his readers that in the

end through the Person of Jesus, God is in communication with his world. The human being who now comes to be the hearer and bearer of the divine communication is a Samaritan woman. With any Samaritan John could have raised quite easily the questions that are bound to arise as the Hope of Israel meets a representative of this 'third race', which is neither truly Jewish nor wholly Gentile; but the fact that the representative happens to be a woman facilitates the dialogue at one important (and to some commentators inscrutable) point, for Jesus can ask her, who represents Samaria (and Samaria, like any city's name, was a feminine noun!), to fetch her husband – or, in figurative language which the reader of the Gospel has only just heard (cf. the Baptist's testimony that he is the bridegroom's friend), to fetch, to declare her gods. So John has taken for his thematic treatment of the Gospel and the Samaritans one individual who is a representative of her people at their best. She is fully representative, for Jesus can raise through her all the profound issues that affect her people's existence; and she is Samaritanism at its best, because she can in some real sense 'hear the voice' of the 'true bridegroom', and moreover publish her hearing abroad.

In other ways too John is able through this incident to forward the great themes of his gospel. Water has provided the symbol for John to speak of purification, and of initiation into the Christian life and community; now it is to be used to speak of continual renewal in that life. The temple in Jerusalem has been presented already as the place which will eventually be replaced by another 'temple'; now it will be made clear that the new temple is already present and available in the presence of Jesus among men. John has already written things that challenge the Jewish apocalyptic time-scheme, and spoken of a 'final' judgement being involved in the very coming of the Son as the gift of God's love; now it will be made clear that the final *harvest* is already being reaped in the adherence of men to him who is no less than *the saviour of the world*.

Jesus came to Sychar *near the field that Jacob gave to his son Joseph. Jacob's well was there.* Jesus is thus symbolically situated at the very place where Israel may be expected to enter upon her rightful inheritance. Jacob's well was of the usual sort, gathering its water by infiltration. It could thus be thought of as filled with 'running' or *living* water if it were compared with water stored in a hewn cistern that collected nothing by infiltration, just as it could be thought of as quite different from 'running' or *living* water if compared with the fresh, lively water that came rushing down the hillsides in the rainy season. Herein, by a magic stroke of symbolism John portrays the essential ambiguity of Israel's inherited religion. Jesus, weary from his journey, sat by the well. The question that is bound to arise is: Could the weary traveller find refreshment in the water from Jacob's well? Or, to put that into non-symbolic language, can the religion of Israel offer real renewal to Jesus in his weariness? Significantly the evangelist states that it is the sixth hour, the hour at which Jesus was handed over to be crucified (19^{14}); what had the religion of Israel to offer him then?

At this highly symbolic moment, in the highly symbolic setting a woman of Samaria came to the well to draw water. The Son is incarnate in the flesh and it is wholly right, and to be expected, that the greatest spiritual questions should thus be raised by quite simple physical, this-worldly acts. Jesus asks for a simple favour: '*Give me a drink*' (the one request he makes, according to the fourth gospel, from the cross, is for drink: 'I thirst' [19^{28}]). The woman is at once aware of a certain strangeness in the request, and she raises the issue that is relevant on the two levels of the story: '*How is it that you, a Jew, ask a drink of me, a woman of Samaria?*' She has taken him for just an ordinary Jew, which he is not; but for him as an ordinary Jew, the question raises quite profound and ultimate issues, for *Jews have no dealings with Samaritans.* This statement seems an exaggeration in a context that immediately goes on to state that the disciples had gone into the Samaritan town to buy food! Yet the strangeness of the request remains: for, as Dr Daube* has pointed out, the comment reflects a piece of regulation that regarded all Samaritan women as 'menstruants from their cradle'; hence to drink from a common vessel with any one of them was, for a Jew, to incur uncleanness. And the real meaning of the Greek word, Dr Daube points out, is not *to have dealings with* but to 'use together with'. So the simple request for a drink of water itself raises all the questions of uncleanness and purification with which the gospel has been dealing ever since it mentioned for the first time the baptism of John. In particular these questions are raised now in the context of rival claimants to the true inheritance of Jacob or Israel. What can Israel, true or false, do for *the* Israelite in his sixth-hour weariness?

* D. Daube, *Journal of Biblical Literature*, LXIX (1950), pp. 137–47.

The problem raised by rival claims to the status of being the true Israel of God cannot be solved without a realization that it is not what God's people can do for him that is determinative, but rather what he can do for them. Jesus' answer to the woman's not undiscerning question takes the dialogue forward both at the level of a well-side conversation and at the depth of a profound probing into the relationship between sinful man and God. '*If you knew the gift of God, and who it is that is saying to you, "Give me a drink," you would have asked him, and he would have given you living water.*' The phrase *gift of God* is a clear indication of the highly symbolic character of the narrative. It is not an easy one to understand. The best suggestion seems to be that Jesus is referring to the Law, the Torah, which both Samaritans and Jews claimed to honour, and which, as Luke affirms (Luke 24²⁷, ⁴⁴), Jesus himself believed to witness to his passion, death and resurrection. If the woman really understood the scriptures, she would have been able to recognize Jesus for who he was and would have known that, weary though he seemed, he could still give her strength of which, like every human being, she stood in indispensable need. Had she asked Jesus for what he could give, he would have given *living water*. The term *living water*, for all its usefulness in the next part of the conversation, unfortunately keeps the woman's mind on the purely physical aspects of the situation, and she fails to catch the deeper meaning which the Lord's reply contained. Yet the description *living water* raises (see above, p. 207) the wholly ambiguous status of Samaritan religion: compared with pagan cults it looked like Judaism, but seen against Judaism it was plainly partial – just as the infiltrated water in Jacob's well appeared worse or better as it was compared with water from a standing tank or from a running stream. The woman answered in physical terms, and in such a way as to make some defence of her own religion; indeed, her very taking of Christ's saying in a literal sense may have been prompted by her desire (shared doubtless by all Samaritans, and by religious men of any faith) not to have her own religion debased or falsified or destroyed. She first speaks of the water: '*Sir*,' she says, having sensed that Jesus is not quite the ordinary Jew she had first supposed*, 'You have no

---

* The woman passes from a valuation of Jesus as an ordinary Jew to (*a*) a more honourable recognition of him as deserving special respect, to (*b*) a perception of him as a prophet, and finally (*c*) to the point where she wistfully asks 'Can this be the Messiah?' A similar progression in the depth of 'seeing' who Jesus is reveals itself in the story of the man born blind. See the notes on ch. 9.

bucket to draw water and you cannot get water from the well here without a bucket, for the well is deep. Where can *living water*, running water from a stream, be got?' Then she passes to a more radical question, from the merely physical difficulties Jesus had raised to the religious issues she descries ahead. 'Are you greater than Jacob, the great patriarch of our people, who found and dug this well, bequeathed it to his descendants, who have found it good enough for them until the present time? Surely what has been good enough for them needs no replacement now?' Like the guests at the wedding in Cana, like the Jews in the temple at Jerusalem, like Nicodemus in the room at night time, this woman, representative of her people, cannot see that her whole religious life must be started, as it were, all over again. The reply of Jesus takes the conversation to a central and focal point, and makes it plain that what he has to offer is quite without parallel, past, present or future. 'Everyone who drinks of this well water so wisely provided and preserved, will thirst again. But the water I speak of when I speak of *living water* will so quench thirst that a man will never thirst again. What I have to give a man will infiltrate inside of him and become inside him a spring of water, and the end of his taking my gift will be eternal life.' Jesus would draw a contrast between the *water* of the Torah (the Torah was often likened to water, see below, p. 213), which provided a law 'external' to men, and his own *water* of the Spirit, which was internal to men, an interior guide.

The woman seems to persist in a merely physical interpretation of Jesus' words: '*Sir, give me this water, so that I may not thirst, nor come here to draw water.*' Yet later on Jesus is able to pick up even this still crass misunderstanding when he discusses with the woman how both *this mountain* and *Jerusalem* will be transcended by the place in which true (real) worship can take place.

ोॐ

6

wearied as he was: The Greek says 'thus', which the translation probably rightly interprets; but it could equally well mean 'just as he was, without selecting any special place to sit'. John, who most of all four evangelists emphasizes the divinity of Jesus, is least afraid to record his physical frailties, cf. 11[33, 35, 38]; 19[28].

7

a woman of Samaria: The woman was not, evidently, a native of Sychar;

this underlines her position in the story as the representative Samaritan, as Nicodemus had been the representative Jew.

9

For Jews have no dealings with Samaritans: See the exegesis above (p. 210). The R.S.V. prints this sentence as a comment of the evangelist, which it may well be. But the new light thrown on the passage by Dr Daube's observations renews the possibility that the evangelist is recording something that the woman herself said.

10

'If you knew the gift of God': This can be taken to mean the *living water* soon to be mentioned, i.e. the Spirit. But though living water is mentioned in the Old Testament as a metaphor of God's life-giving succour for men (Jer. 2¹³; Zech. 14⁸), the image is much more frequent in Rabbinic writings as an image of the Torah. This makes excellent sense; for Jesus would then be saying to the woman, and to the Samaritan religion through her, that if only she understood the Torah, and could see, because of the understanding it was meant to provide, the reality of his nature, then Samaritans would be among those who came to him for the living water he alone could impart.

11

'Sir': A term of respect, the first indication that the woman is already on the way from a purely 'physical' knowledge of Jesus to one dependent on divine illumination – she is about to be 'born not of blood, nor of the will of the flesh nor of the will of man, but of God' (1¹³).

'the well is deep': The word used for *well* here is different from that in v.6. There it might be translated 'spring' and be intended to refer to the fact that the water seeped into the well from some source. Here the word used is more a 'cistern', for even water that seeps in from elsewhere is not fresh or 'living' as is water that comes from a mountain stream. Samaria's religion is like that; see notes above.

12

'and his cattle': The word translated *cattle* could also mean 'slaves'. The point is that what Jacob left was enough for freeborn, slave and beast; could Jesus improve on that? The answer, already clear from what has already appeared in the gospel, is that he brings salvation adequate for the world.

13

'Every one who drinks of this water will thirst again': The contrast between drink that can only quench the thirst for a short time, and then needs to

be repeated and the drink which, drunk once only, quenches all further thirst, reminds the reader of the contrast in Hebrews between the sacrifices of the old order which had to be repeated daily, and that one sacrifice of the new order which, once offered, is universally and everlastingly efficacious. The point made is in fact the same.

4¹⁵⁻²⁶   THE BRIDEGROOM AND THE MESSIAH

¹⁵*The woman said to him, 'Sir, give me this water, that I may not thirst, nor come here to draw.'*

¹⁶*Jesus said to her, 'Go, call your husband, and come here.' *¹⁷*The woman answered him, 'I have no husband.' Jesus said to her, 'You are right in saying, "I have no husband"; *¹⁸*for you have had five husbands and he whom you now have is not your husband; this you said truly.' *¹⁹*The woman said to him, 'Sir, I perceive that you are a prophet. *²⁰*Our fathers worshipped on this mountain; and you say that in Jerusalem is the place where men ought to worship.'*

²¹*Jesus said to her, 'Woman, believe me, the hour is coming when neither on this mountain nor in Jerusalem will you worship the Father. *²²*You worship what you do not know; we worship what we know, for salvation is from the Jews. *²³*But the hour is coming, and now is, when the true worshippers will worship the Father in spirit and truth, for such the Father seeks to worship him. *²⁴*God is spirit, and those who worship him must worship in spirit and truth.' *²⁵*The woman said to him, 'I know that Messiah is coming (he who is called Christ); when he comes, he will show us all things.' *²⁶*Jesus said to her, 'I who speak to you am he.'*

But before this reply can be woven into the fabric of the dialogue in a positive way, there must be a turn in the conversation, by which the situation of the woman as an individual is exposed as symbolic of that of her people, the Samaritans. Jesus appears abruptly to change the subject, and says '*Go, call your husband, and come here*'. But Jesus, with the supernatural knowledge with which John is sure he is endowed, is not simply exposing the woman's individual matrimonial maladjustment; he is exhibiting, in terms of the metaphor of marriage that has already been strongly embedded in the gospel (2¹⁻¹¹; 3^{29, 30}), the religious situation of the Samaritan people. So the imperative has a second meaning: 'Go, call your God, and come here, i.e. to me, for (as is almost immediately apparent) in me the only real possibility of true worship is to be found'. The woman replies '*I have no husband*', and every commentator has accepted the sad simplicity and truth of the confession. But is it not just as likely, indeed more than likely, that the woman is already trying to escape from the exposure of the ultimate poverty of her Samaritan religion under the inexorable cross-examination by the Jew she had already sensed to be more than an ordinary member of the race? To the present writer such an assumption makes much more sense of the whole course of the dialogue, and in particular gives adequate force to the woman's next answer, that Jesus must be a prophet. For to the woman's confession of her improper matrimonial condition Jesus answered: '*You are right in saying, "I have no husband"; for you have had five husbands and he whom you now have is not your husband; this you said truly.*' The statement of the details of the woman's history, particularly with the added comment '*This you said truly*', seems to point to the fact that both the speakers in the original dialogue, as well as the evangelist who recorded it, were well aware that the stage had already been reached when the double meaning was recognized on both sides. The woman now realizes that she can no longer continue the pretence that the conversation is purely personal, and she proceeds to do what it is necessary to do in order to have the depth of the 'Samaritan–Jewish' question exposed at its Christian depth. She says to Jesus '*Sir, I perceive that you are a prophet*'.

By her use of the word *prophet* the woman showed that she had already understood what Jesus had said in prophetic terms. And while there are instances in the Old Testament of a prophet being engaged in the exposure of matrimonial wrong (e.g. Nathan and David's responsibility for Uriah's death in order to marry Bathsheba [2 Sam. 11, 12]) by far the greater concern of the canonical prophets is to apply the figure of marriage and adultery to the relationship of God's people to God. The use of the word *prophet* at this stage of the conversation indicates that the Samaritan woman has already perceived the prophetic character of the examination Jesus is making. Jesus then recites the damning evidence: the woman has had five husbands already, and is presently living with one who is not her husband. These may well be accepted as facts of the private life of the woman at the well, but the important point which Jesus is making, and which the woman perceives he is making, concerns the validity or otherwise of Samaritan religion. The passage from 2 Kings 17 relates how the king of Assyria, at the time of the sacking of Samaria, repopulated it with alien inhabitants from five other regions, who did not worship the true God of Israel, but the gods of foreign cults. (The passage in 2 Kings lists seven gods as objects of worship, though Josephus is some evidence that the Jewish tradition reckoned the number of foreign gods as five*.) The final point which Jesus makes against Samaritan religion at this stage is that it is not really a worship of the one true God: *'He whom you now have is not your husband'* (4^{18}): in short, Samaritan religion has the externals, or some of the externals of a true religion, but lacks the reality.

At last Jesus has brought the woman to the real issue of the question she so innocently asked him at the beginning of their conversation (4^9). She realizes this, and so asks the fundamental question. Some commentators have suggested that the woman's transition to somewhat theological questions indicates her desire to escape from an otherwise embarrassing pursuit of her matrimonial delinquencies; the present writer would rather see that motive as only one acting upon the woman, who was faced with an awkward exposure whichever course the inquiry now took. She chose to pursue the 'community' rather than the 'personal' theme, though she could not thereby escape the disturbing challenge of vv. 23 ff. However that may be, the woman now states the problem *'Our [Samaritan] fathers worshipped on this mountain; and you say that in Jerusalem is the place where men ought to worship.' This mountain* is Mount Gerizim, which the Samaritans claimed was the one sanctuary enjoined by Deuteronomy as the proper place for Israel's worship of God. But as the conversation is not taking place on Mount Gerizim, the comment gives yet another indication that the dialogue must not be taken too literally, but must be given some allegorical interpretation. In any event, the reference to Mount Gerizim had at last exposed the whole issue between Judaism and the Samaritan religion.

The first three chapters of the gospel have made it clear that the purificatory rites of Judaism, its sacrificial worship, its temple, its offered salvation are all inadequate, and would be transcended by what Jesus wrought. Now he is to make clear that what he will do will transcend the Samaritan religion too. *'Woman'* or, in our more

* Josephus, Antiquities, 9, 288.

modern phrase, 'Madam, *believe me* [the equivalent in this dialogue to the normal "truly, truly" of the discourses], *the hour is coming when neither on this mountain nor in Jerusalem will you worship the Father.*' Once more Jesus speaks to the individual, 'believe thou me': and to many through the individual; '*you will worship the Father*': once more John both records an historical happening, and speaks out of and into a situation in the contemporary church at Ephesus, and to all Christian communities. Then Jesus goes on to say that, even so, there is a real answer, at a certain level, to the questions at issue between Samaritan and Jew: he continued: '*You worship what you do not know; we worship what we know, for salvation is from the Jews*' (4^{22}). It is important to remember that it is Jesus who makes the critical estimate of Samaritan religion, for his accusation of ignorance of the object of worship is in the end only to be made from the perspective of what he is in his own person. (As some commentators have rightly observed, the critique of Samaritanism also applies to Hellenistic religions; indeed, as Acts 17^{23} testifies, some Athenians actually confessed their ignorance.) Judaism was not open to the same radical criticism as Samaritanism, for it had been willing to receive what 'the prophets and the psalms' as well as 'the law of Moses' had to reveal about God – and about himself (cf. Luke 24^{44}). Though he alone brings the absolute truth to light, lesser distinctions are not to be thought trivial or unimportant in their own sphere and on their own level. *Salvation therefore is from the Jews.*

From the Jews: not in them, or by them. There is indeed a new era to come, indeed it has already come, when real worshippers will worship the Father in Spirit and reality. Once more Jesus puts himself as the fulfilment of what has gone before. '*The hour is coming,* AND NOW IS.' It has so far been possible (though doubtless erroneous) to think that the ultimate stage of divinely revealed religion lies still in the future. The miracle at Cana could be interpreted as foreshadowing the transcendence of Jewish purificatory rites; the cleansing of the Temple could with some justification be held to suggest that the final transcendence of Judaism would not take place before the resurrection. It would be a little more difficult, though still possible, to take Jesus' words to Nicodemus as meaning that eternal life was a gift to be received and enjoyed only after this mortal life was over. But now the evangelist makes it uncompromisingly and unmistakably clear that the transcendence of all that has gone before, and of all that survives of what has gone before, is taking place in the very person and presence of the Son of man as himself a man among men. The three words *and now is* can have no other implication than that in virtue of the presence of Jesus himself the 'future fulfilment' of Jewish and Samaritan (and Hellenistic) religion is taking place in an historic human life. Jesus Christ is the 'place' where men of any time or place can at last be free of 'place' in their worship of God; he is the substance, the material by which all men are freed from all materialism in their worship, free to worship God at last *in Spirit.* Jesus is, as the Baptist testified (1[33f]), the one upon whom the Spirit descended – and remained.

But 'in the Spirit' does not imply the vague 'inward spirituality' that some nineteenth-century writers envisaged, as if Christianity were free from everything that ties men to times and places and ceremonies. 'In the Spirit' has precise reference to the Spirit that descended upon and remained with Jesus. The evangelist is not writing of a subjective spirituality but of the Spirit in Christ acting in power to finish the divine work, in Christ and through his Church. Christian worship, worship in reality, is worship in this Spirit, and is precisely tied down to those acts of God in Christ which constitute man's redemption. That is why the Christian religion is at once the most free and the most bound of all. Free in the freedom of the Spirit; bound to scripture, to sacrament, to preaching, to worship 'in his name'. True Christian spirituality is not achieved by abstracting from everything particular, concrete and historical for the sake of what is purely universal, abstract and a-temporal; rather is it the grateful acceptance of a way into the truly eternal through the concrete historical birth, life, death, resurrection and exaltation of Jesus Christ, son of Mary and Son of God.

The Samaritan woman recognized that in his latest answer Jesus had spoken of the ultimate end that her Samaritan as well as his Jewish religion sought and longed for. Yet his full meaning was still beyond her; and she responded: '*I know that Messiah is coming (he who is called Christ); when he comes, he will show us all things*' (4[25]). Little is known about Samaritan Messianism, save that a Messiah, or Taheb, was expected as one who returned and restored. The woman's words suggest that she looked forward to full and authoritative teaching (*show* in the sense of make plain by telling); her messianic beliefs as a Samaritan would lead her to suppose that the Taheb would finally establish Gerizim as the one place of worship for all the nations of the earth. To her supposititious answer Jesus replied '*I who speak to you am he*'.

The English translation fails to do one important service at this point. The Greek can be literally rendered thus: 'I am he; the one who is speaking to thee'. 'I am'. This phrase is of the highest importance in the fourth gospel, and indeed throughout the Bible. It is the name of Yahweh himself (Exod. 3^{14}); it is used in John as a means of making profound statements about the nature and mission of Jesus (cf. 6^{35} etc.; 8^{12,23}; 10^{7,11}; 11^{25}; 14^{6}; 15^{1}; 18^{5}). It is a name which it is blasphemous for mere men to use of themselves; Babylon is condemned by Isaiah for appropriating to herself this title which belongs of right only to Yahweh the one true God, the God of Israel (Isa. 47^{8,10}). Yet John repeatedly puts the words on to the lips of Jesus, and his intention is utterly clear: on his lips the words are not blasphemous, for he is the Son of God, the Word incarnate.

☙❧

15

'*Sir, give me this water*': This is usually thought to betray the same crass misunderstanding as the woman revealed at v.11f. This is very doubtful, if for no other reason than that, had the woman taken Jesus' saying literally, it would be hard to imagine what meaning she could have given to the words '*the water that I shall give him will become in him a spring of water welling up to eternal life*'. It is clear that she does not yet fully understand Jesus; but it seems equally clear that she realizes that the conversation is moving to places where her own personal and her national religious life will be challenged.

16

'*Go call your husband, and come here*': Most commentators have not remarked that Jesus repeats the woman's words about coming here. Thus already he has identified Mount Gerizim with himself. She asked for the water Jesus had to give, in order to avoid *coming here* to draw. But Jesus tells her what it is that alone can obtain for her the living water she more than half knows she wants. She must *bring her husband*, i.e. her Samaritan religion, here, and from Christ she will be able to draw.

17

'*I have no husband*': The woman tries to evade her responsibilities by seeking refuge in a purely personal situation. Jesus turns even this to his own account, and points out how the Samaritan religion has no reality at its heart; it is not wedded to the one true God.

19

'*I perceive that you are a prophet*': This confession has a number of possible causes. The woman may have recognized that Jesus' supernatural knowledge of her matrimonial state betokened him as a prophet: she may have recognized that it was the duty of a prophet to denounce any 'harlotry', any 'adultery' on the part of God's people (though, since the Samaritans did not recognize the validity of the prophets, this is not so likely): or she may have thought that Jesus was *the* prophet foretold in Deut. 18¹⁵. This gives excellent sense, and leads on to the messianic dimension of the dialogue.

20

'*Our fathers worshipped on this mountain*': This mountain cannot but be Gerizim, where, in point of fact, the dialogue was not taking place. This underlines the highly symbolic character of what John doubtless believed to be an historical conversation.

21

'*neither on this mountain nor in Jerusalem will you worship the Father*': Jesus already foresees that some Samaritans will come to worship the Father, and they will do it, as the Jews themselves, not on a particular hill, but in and through a particular person – himself.

22

'*You worship what you do not know*': The Samaritans accepted the Pentateuch; but to accept that without, so to speak, the divine commentary written upon it in the recorded history of Israel and the literature of her wise men and religious poets, was really to remain untutored and therefore ignorant. By contrast the Jews, for all their error and wilfulness, had at least received the testimonies of God.

23

'*in spirit and truth*': C.H.Dodd well puts it 'In Spirit which is the truth'. Truth, as so often in John, could well be replaced with the word 'reality'. As stated in the exegesis the Spirit is not a vague ·'spirituality', but the power that filled and possessed Christ and wrought the works of God in him.

24

'*God is spirit*': This is right. The A.V. is wrong: 'God is a Spirit.' God is not just one of the beings that inhabit the spirit world, he is not just one member of a clan of spirits.

25

'*he will show us all things*': The implication of the Greek word is rather that he will reveal all things by his teaching of the truth, though the word has associations with the cult as well. It is thus admirably suited to the context.

[27]*Just then his disciples came. They marvelled that he was talking with a woman, but none said, 'What do you wish?' or, 'Why are you talking with her?'* [28]*So the woman left her water jar, and went away into the city, and said to the people,* [29]*'Come, see a man who told me all that I ever did. Can this be the Christ?'* [30]*They went out of the city and were coming to him.*

[31]*Meanwhile the disciples besought him, saying, 'Rabbi, eat.'* [32]*But he said to them, 'I have food to eat of which you do not know.'* [33]*So the disciples said to one another, 'Has any one brought him food?'* [34]*Jesus said to them, 'My food is to do the will of him who sent me, and to accomplish his work.* [35]*Do you not say, "There are yet four months, then comes the harvest"? I tell you, lift up your eyes, and see how the fields are already white for harvest.* [36]*He who reaps receives wages, and gathers fruit for eternal life, so that sower and reaper may rejoice together.* [37]*For here the saying holds true, "One sows and another reaps."* [38]*I sent you to reap that for which you did not labour; others have laboured, and you have entered into their labour.'*

At this point, when the woman is about to receive the suggestion that Jesus is the Messiah, the disciples return from the town. They were astonished that he was talking with a woman, for it was considered highly undesirable for a Rabbi to talk with a woman. Yet none of them, such was their trust in him already, said to the woman 'What do you want?' or to Jesus 'Why are you talking with her?' The woman left her water jar at the well, and went into the city. The action is not an indication of absent-mindedness; but rather again, one symbolic element in a highly symbolic situation, for the woman was now able to take her fellow-townsfolk some of the water that could not be drawn from Jacob's well, or any other source of physical water, but could only come from the springing up of the Spirit within a human being as he or she came to know Jesus as the Christ. She summoned her townsfolk to go out and see Jesus for themselves: 'Come, see a man who told me all I ever did. Can this be the Christ?' The woman has gone through the whole gamut of experience possible to men who are confronted by Jesus Christ. At first she took him for an ordinary Jew (4^9); then she recognized that he was a person worthy of special respect, such as a Rabbi would have elicited (cf. her 'Sir' in $4^{11,15,19}$); she perceived that he was a prophet (4^{19}), and now she senses that he may well be the Messiah he claims to be, and senses it sufficiently to take her fellow-Samaritans to the Jew at Jacob's well. So at last the question is answered: 'What can true or false Israel give to the weary Jesus at the hour of his being given over to death?' and the answer is 'Nothing'. On the contrary, it is he who has something to give to them, the water of life, able to spring up in them to eternal life, his own gift of the Spirit. And in that answer, so dramatically set forth, individual need and national aspirations, even of the highest religious kind, alone find their satisfaction.

While the woman was gone to the town and bringing her townsfolk to Jesus, the disciples were engaged in another episode of their training. They had come back to Jesus with the food they had set out to buy; naturally they asked him to eat (4^{31}). The Lord's reply was that he had food to eat of which the disciples did not know; and they, misunderstanding him as the woman had done, asked one another whether anyone had supplied him with food during their absence. Then Jesus plainly stated that his real food, that which really sustained him in his proper integrity, was to do the will of God who had sent him, and to bring his work to its completion. Again, as in using the phrase *and now is* in v. 23, the evangelist is writing from the perspective of the end. Plainly Jesus means that while the disciples have been away he has done God's will and 'accomplished' his work; and he uses for the verb *accomplish* the same Greek word that the evangelist employs to signify, at the crucifixion, that the mission which the Father had given him was successfully accomplished or finished (19^{30}). And indeed the work of the Son was finished in the woman of Samaria, for she had come to acknowledge the man Jesus as the Messiah, and had, moreover, made her own discovery the basis of evangelistic action – she had gone out to bring her neighbours to the Messiah.

Such 'accomplishment' or 'finishing' of Jesus' work itself constitutes a problem, which John again handles from the perspective of the end, and of the end as seen from the situation of the Church in Ephesus. The problem may be posed in the question, 'When will the harvest of the Gospel be reaped?' There are many commentators who find it difficult, if not impossible, to suppose that the harvest can be reaped at all until at least the cross, resurrection and exaltation of Jesus have taken place. Many find it difficult to suppose that anyone in the early church could have supposed the harvest could be reached before the 'Parousia' or 'Second Coming' of Christ. There are others, and among them not a few twentieth-century scholars, who think that the figure of the harvest is one which ought to be used only of a harvest to be reaped at the end of the world. A good deal of 'harvest festival' imagery presupposes this; e.g.

> 'For the Lord our God shall come,
> And shall take his harvest home;
> From his field shall in that day,
> All offences purge away;
> Give his angels charge at last
> In the fire the tares to cast
> But the fruitful ears to store
> In his garners evermore.'
>
> (Harvest hymn)

Many difficult and vast questions arise whenever Christians ask about the end of the world and the relationship, if any, that Christian evangelism has to it. Fortunately the commentator on these verses in John is not called upon to solve these problems, and certainly not to deny their existence. But he has to attempt to expound a train of thought that proceeds very differently from normal philosophical speculation about the end of the world. For these verses embody a view of Christian mission in which beginning and end, seedtime and harvest are brought dramatically together. The commentator is faced with a double difficulty: that of detecting the meaning of the 'proverb' that is quoted at 4³⁵; and that of making sense of a view of history which to some extent makes nonsense of 'chronological time'.

In expounding what he meant by saying that he had food to eat of a secret kind, viz. the doing and the finishing of his Father's will, Jesus began by reminding his disciples of a saying '*There are yet four months, then comes the harvest*'. Whether or not this saying can be used to fix the date of the interview of Jesus with the Samaritan woman (and the present writer thinks it cannot) it would seem impossible to take it simply as a statement in one particular temporal situation; it is evidently a more general saying, applicable in more than one chronological situation. But if so, the saying is not meant to indicate the precise temporal measurement between the time of Jesus' interview with the woman and the reaping of the harvest, but a general space of time between some point and the gathering of the harvest. That point is not too difficult to fix, for the whole period covered between the sowing of the corn seed and the reaping of the crop in Palestine was approximately four months. So what Jesus is doing as he begins to comment on his statement that his food is to finish his Father's work is to refer to a general view that an interval of four months separates sowing from harvesting. He then proceeds '*I tell you*' – reminiscent of the 'I tell you' in the Sermon on the Mount (Matt. $5^{22,28,34,39,44}$) and just as indicative that Jesus is about to say something new and authoritative: what he says is that if the disciples look around them they will see that the harvest is already in a state fit for reaping. (Indeed, it soon appears that had they looked up, as presumably they did, they would have seen the Samaritans coming with the woman to see Jesus, in expectation that he was their Messiah, as he was already the Messiah to the disciples.) The reapers, Jesus continues, already receive their wages – i.e. in gathering a harvest to eternal life; and thus sower and reaper can rejoice together. In comparison with synoptic teaching on the sowing and reaping of the Word, John has made it plain that e.g. Mark does not neccessarily imply in the parable of the Sower (Mark 4^{3-8} //) that a long time must elapse between the work of evangelism and the gathering of its fruits; and that a passage like Matthew 9^{35-37} // means precisely that the harvest of the gospel is fully ready for the reaping. '*Sower and reaper may rejoice together*' says Jesus. In the realm of the Kingdom of God seedtime and harvest are not necessarily separated by a long interval, but, as in some Jewish expectations of the messianic age of which this saying speaks, the time of harvest overlaps with that of sowing, so that there is always fulness of supply and fulness of renewal. This is the situation he implies, with those who are his disciples, his apostles, his ambassadors, his reapers.

Yet, as numerous critics have asked, what is to be said of the very next saying of Jesus: '*For here the saying holds true, "One sows and another reaps." I sent you to reap that for which you did not labour; others have laboured, and you have entered into their labour*' ($4^{37,38}$)? This is not a great difficulty. What Jesus is saying to the disciples is that they must not think that they themselves are widely separated from the patriarchs and prophets of old who sowed the seed of God's word in the

life of God's people. Rather must they think of themselves as already
within the messianic age with him whom they have accepted as
Messiah, and therefore actually in that age when sowing overtakes
reaping. Thus the real, as opposed to the merely chronological
situation is that the prophets and patriarchs of old, who witnessed to
the Word of God to Israel, and thus acted as sowers, are not merely
figures of the past, unable to enter into the joy of the harvest which
Christ and his apostles will now reap, but are indeed fellow sharers of
the joy of the harvest. The disciples have been sent (again a statement
made from the perspective of the end) to reap a harvest which they
did not sow; they are to share its joys with those who did.

༄

27
They marvelled: The word is significant. In the synoptic gospels 'marvel'
is used rarely of Jesus, who 'marvelled' at the faith of the Gentile
centurion. But it is characteristically the word used to describe the
reaction of men to Christ's miraculous deeds (e.g. Matt. 8²⁷; Mark 5²⁰;
Luke 11¹⁴); and it is not at all impossible or unlikely that John is
deliberately using the word here to remind his readers, who may be
assumed to be familiar with the synoptic record, that what he has
recorded of Jesus and the woman of Samaria has in fact been the working of a miracle. More light will be thrown on that as the signs of
healing are examined in due course. The miracle is always that men
come to believe that Jesus is the Christ, the Son of God.

29
'Can this be the Christ?': The Greek form of the question indicates that
the woman puts it tentatively to herself, though with the hope of
receiving an affirmative answer. She evidently receives that, and can
only receive that, in fellowship with her fellow Samaritans.

34
'My food is to do the will of him who sent me, and to accomplish [finish] *his
work':* This saying reminds the reader of the synoptic story of the reply
Jesus made to the tempter: 'Man shall not live by bread alone, but by
every word that proceeds from the mouth of God'. Luke wrote of the
baptism of Jesus being accomplished or finished or fulfilled (Luke 12⁵⁰)
as of the fulfilment or accomplishment of what the prophets had said
about the Son of man (Luke 18³¹). This saying may be taken as the
Johannine equivalent of such declarations, with the typical Johannine
additional comment that the fulfilment has already been achieved in the

present work of the incarnate Son. The end is in the beginning, and exhibited in the process throughout.

35

'lift up your eyes, and see': The harvest is already visible in the figures of those Samaritans who had received the testimony of the woman and had come out to meet Jesus.

4 $^{39-42}$ REAPING THE HARVEST

^{39}*Many Samaritans from that city believed in him because of the woman's testimony, 'He told me all that I ever did.'* ^{40}*So when the Samaritans came to him, they asked him to stay with them; and he stayed there two days.* ^{41}*And many more believed because of his word.* ^{42}*They said to the woman 'It is no longer because of your words that we believe, for we have heard for ourselves, and we know that this is indeed the Saviour of the world.'*

Finally the evangelist reports that many Samaritans from the town believed in Jesus (4^{39}). This was due to the testimony of the woman. But indispensable as personal testimony is and remains, it is not sufficient of itself; this is symbolized in the fact that the faith of the Samaritans takes on a new quality when they have been face to face with Jesus, and enjoyed his companionship for two days. *'It is no longer because of your words'* they told the woman *'that we believe, for we have heard for ourselves, and we know that this is indeed the Saviour of the world'* (4^{42}). This remains true for all really effective religion. It must be, as the Puritan fathers used to say, 'experimental'. That the Samaritans believed Jesus to be the Saviour of the world has surprised some. But it if be remembered that both Samaritan and Jewish hopes for the future centred upon their religious tradition as the one means of communion between heaven and earth, it is not surprising that, in accepting Jesus the Jew as Messiah, the Samaritans should have had more cause than ever before to declare their conviction that Messiah should prove to be the saviour of the whole world.

ଊଌ

39

'He told me all that I ever did': The *all* is not to be interpreted simply in terms of a woman's excited exaggeration. The woman had already stated that her belief was in a Messiah who would 'tell us everything', and that meant not every detail of the future, but everything that really mattered. So here, Jesus had not left untouched any fundamental of her life as it sought, through her Samaritan religion, to find true communion with God.

40

the Samaritans ... asked him to stay with them; and he stayed there two days: Testimony, adequate to bring men to Christ, must give way to personal experience and communion with the Lord. The period of two days is worth noting, being less than the three days which is symbolic in the gospel of the resurrection. John thus underlines the fact that though this harvest has been reaped, and in its reaping is symbolic of the way in which the spiritual realm transcends the time sequences of the physical world, yet there is a time sequence to be got through, one which will entail the death and resurrection of the Son. Yet it must never be assumed that the Jesus whom men met in Galilee, Samaria and Judea was different from the risen Lord whom men can meet in any time or place. It is precisely the identification of what, in modern terms, scholars have come to call the Jesus of history with the Christ of faith that John, the synoptics and Paul, together with all other New Testament writers, are concerned to affirm.

42

'this is indeed the Saviour of the world': This is most appropriately spoken in Samaria, between the testimony of Jesus concerning his universal mission to the Jew Nicodemus, and the healing of the (Gentile?) official's servant in Galilee. It picks up the universalism in the story of Nicodemus, and prepares the way for the account of Messiah's power being freely used for one who could not claim to be 'of the house of Israel'.

John 4⁴³⁻⁴⁵

⁴³After the two days he departed to Galilee. ⁴⁴For Jesus himself testified that a prophet has no honour in his own country. ⁴⁵So when he came to Galilee, the Galileans welcomed him, having seen all that he had done in Jerusalem at the feast, for they too had gone to the feast.

The incident at Jacob's well had interrupted the journey from Jerusalem to Galilee that Jesus had undertaken because of the hostility of the Pharisees (4¹,³). As he brings Jesus to Galilee the evangelist reports him as saying about Jerusalem a word which in the synoptics he is quoted as using about Nazareth: 'A prophet has no honour in his own country' (4⁴⁴; cf. Mark 6⁴; Matt. 13⁵⁷; Luke 4²⁴). What must be said of this apparent contradiction? Some commentators have tried to harmonize it, and suggested that Jesus is about to retire from Jerusalem to Galilee where he will not be under pressure from the eager acceptance of the crowds. Yet in fact the trend of John's gospel cannot support such an interpretation. Jerusalem, for all that many believed on him (2²³), had rejected him (2¹³⁻²¹; 4¹⁻³) at least in the persons of the authorities; he had been received by the Samaritans, and was about to be honoured in Galilee (4⁴⁵) on the very same basis that the Jews in Jerusalem had rejected him. No harmonizing compromise seems possible. John probably knew of the synoptic tradition that Nazareth was the native city of Jesus, and he would expect that his readers would possess the same knowledge. Indeed he has already by implication accepted that view, cf. 1⁴⁵,⁴⁶; 2¹,¹² (cf. also 7¹⁻⁹, 4¹⁻⁴², ⁵²; 18⁵,⁷,⁸;19¹⁹). Why then write now as if Jerusalem were his native city or Judea his fatherland? The answer is that for every true prophet Jerusalem was home, the place where, in the end, all his interests were centred. As Dr Dodd has put it (Dodd, p. 352) 'Jerusalem is the *patris* [home town] of Jesus in the Fourth Gospel'. It is the real locus of all prophetic concern, for there all the issues of Jewish religion are inevitably settled. And yet, having theologized John's point rightly thus far, it seems right to go further, and to say with Hoskyns that the real *patris* of Jesus in the Fourth Gospel is heaven. For he comes 'from above' and thither he is to return (cf. 13³); and it is this fact, basic in reality, that makes him homeless in the place where his earthly religious home, as a good Jew and as a prophet, cannot but be. So while John manifestly does not seek to refute the synoptic statement that Nazareth is Jesus' geographical *patris*, he is at pains to make clear that his true *patris* is in heaven, and that that makes merely geographical or merely Jewish religious considerations of secondary importance. Here is some of the inexorable working out of the sombre words of the prologue, 'He came to his own home, and his own people received him not'. Rejected by authority in Jerusalem; believed on in Samaria; welcomed in Galilee – that was the rueful experience of him who had come to rebuild the temple of Jerusalem in his own death and resurrection.

The Galileans had seen what Jesus had done during the recent Passover feast. And while the Jerusalem authorities rejected Jesus, they now welcomed him. Here too, John is authenticating the synoptic tradition, which spoke of much popular support during the Galilean ministry. 'Jesus returned in the power of the Spirit into Galilee, and a report concerning him went out through all the surrounding country. And he taught in their synagogues, being glorified by all' (Luke 4¹⁴,¹⁵). Yet John will carry his theological estimate of Galilean support further than the synoptics, and is himself about to pass to the telling of a story that raises the question of the status of a faith that depends in some degree upon 'signs and wonders'.

John 4⁴⁶⁻⁵⁴

The New Gospel and the Old World: 3
The Gentile
The Second Sign—
The Official's Boy   Luke 7²⁻¹⁰

⁴⁶*So he came again to Cana in Galilee, where he had made the water wine. And at Caper'na-um there was an official whose son was ill.* ⁴⁷*When he heard that Jesus had come from Judea to Galilee, he went and begged him to come down and heal his son, for he was at the point of death.* ⁴⁸*Jesus therefore said to him, 'Unless you see signs and wonders you will not believe.'* ⁴⁹*The official said to him, 'Sir, come down before my child dies.'* ⁵⁰*Jesus said to him, 'Go; your son will live.' The man believed the word that Jesus spoke to him and went his way.* ⁵¹*As he was going down, his servants met him and told him that his son was living.* ⁵²*So he asked them the hour when he began to mend, and they said to him, 'Yesterday at the seventh hour the fever left him.'* ⁵³*The father knew that was the hour when Jesus had said to him, 'Your son will live'; and he himself believed, and all his household.* ⁵⁴*This was now the second sign that Jesus did when he had come from Judea to Galilee.*

It is unavoidable that this section of the fourth gospel be given a double title, for it belongs both to the author's thematic treatment of the confrontation of the world by the person of the Word incarnate, and to his re-telling of certain typical 'synoptic' or 'synoptic-like' signs or miracles in such a way that they can no longer be taken simply as exciting accounts of extraordinary thaumaturgy, but must be seen as, in reality, part of that which they signify – the gift of eternal life to dying men. John has brought to Jesus a representative both of Judaism and of Samaritanism, each the best of their kind, and now he brings to Jesus a Gentile, again the best of his kind. There is an interesting progression in the gospel to this point. As the representative Jew comes he is hardly aware of his need, or of the great gift which Jesus can give: the Samaritan woman begins by being quite unaware of the status of Jesus, and of her own need, but as her talk with Jesus progresses she becomes increasingly aware of both. Now, as the best representative of the Gentiles comes forward, John shows us a man who, however dimly, already perceives both the depth of his need and the ability of Jesus to satisfy it. The farther Jesus moves from Jerusalem, the farther he goes from the typical Jew, the more he seems to receive the sort of response that he seeks. This fact, disclosed not so much in words as in the actual progression of the gospel story, is John's equivalent to the synoptic estimate of the centurion at Capernaum: Jesus said 'I tell you, not even in Israel have I found such faith' (Luke 7⁹; cf. Matt. 8¹⁰).

In picking up the story of Jesus' return to Galilee John reminds his readers that the Lord went to Cana, where his first sign was done. The evangelist evidently considers the point important, for he refers to it twice (4⁴⁶,⁵⁴).

The present story is umistakably like that in the synoptics of the healing of the centurion's servant. There are some notable differences, however, and the commentator must decide whether John's narrative is to be taken as parallel to that of Matthew and Luke at this point. The assumption seems justified. In the synoptics, as in John, the miracle is wrought after profound teaching about Christ's mission and person (Matt. 8⁵⁻¹³ after 7²⁴⁻²⁷; Luke 7²⁻¹⁰ after 6⁴⁷⁻⁴⁹). In each account there is an appeal by a superior person on behalf of one inferior to him for whom he has to accept some responsibility; there is in each case an effective word of healing spoken by Jesus at some distance from the invalid; and there is also in each instance the faith of the person who seeks Christ's aid. But there are differences: John nowhere states that the *official*, as he calls him, was a centurion, let alone a Gentile; John tells of the healing of the official's son, while Matthew speaks of the Centurion's servant and Luke of his slave; in John Jesus seems at first to question the faith of the official, whereas in Matthew and Luke he praises it immediately; John writes of a fever, while Matthew reports that the servant is paralysed in terrible distress. The evidence on the whole seems more than consistent with the traditional view that John's official is the same as the synoptic Centurion. The form of a traditional story is always affected by the time and place in which it is retold* and that John tells the story for his Church at Ephesus may well account for much of the difference

* The author has known stories told about an absent-minded professor in Edinburgh in 1928 retold with changes of names and places about an equally absent-minded professor in Aberdeen in the 1950s!

between his narrative and that of the synoptics. The following exegesis will therefore assume that John is retelling the story of the healing of the Centurion's 'boy', whether son or servant.

John begins by reminding his reader that the next sign will be performed at the same place as the first sign when water was turned into wine. That remarkable sign signified what was involved for Israel when, as in the coming of Jesus, the true bridegroom of God's people had come to claim his bride. It was revealed that none of the purifications prescribed for or used by the Jews could adequately prepare the bride for her marriage. But when the purificatory rites of Judaism were replaced by the one self-offering in blood of Jesus, then all, and more than all was done to prepare the bride for her husband. This was all finely stated in terms of Jewish symbols and Jewish religion. But what would happen when, as now, a Gentile approached to ask for a share in the rich dowry of God's bride? The story that follows provides the answer. Even a Gentile may share in the true substance of the joy of the real marriage of God and his people, in the life that Jesus brings and gives.

In Capernaum there lived a Centurion whose son was ill, and ill (v. 47) to the point of death. The anxious father went to Cana and asked Jesus to go down to Capernaum and heal his child. This first request, like the first request made at the wedding feast, receives a somewhat abrupt treatment. Jesus probes the character of the belief that has brought the centurion to him. '*Unless you see signs and wonders you will not believe*' (4^{48}). The use of the phrase *signs and wonders* indicates that Jesus is seeking to estimate the faith of the centurion in terms of a common Old Testament term. *Signs and wonders* were the marvels that God wrought in the course of Israel's history, and Jesus is saying that belief based on them is inadequate. This is not to say that true faith cannot find any place for the miraculous, but that faith that cannot believe without a miracle is sadly deficient. In other words, the word *sign* is not at this point being used, as it is in v. 54, in the distinctively Johannine sense. Of belief on account of signs in this sense the evangelist has already recorded (2$^{23-25}$) that Jesus recognized such belief, but did not trust himself to those who had faith only of this sort. The question here is whether the centurion will prove to have faith such that Jesus can 'trust himself' to him. The centurion in answer presses his request: '*Sir, come down before my child dies.*' Even this is not the fulness of belief, for, as becomes most clear in the story of Lazarus, there is much for Jesus to say and to do even when a sick person has passed from life to death. But the reply has demonstrated that the centurion does not first demand a 'sign and a wonder' but trusts Jesus and his power. So Jesus 'trusts' himself to the Gentile and says: '*Go; your son will live*' (4⁵⁰). So it is that the two great themes of the story are clothed in significant incident – belief and life; indeed more than the themes of the story, for these are two of the dominant themes of the whole gospel. To the ear of the Christian well versed in his Old Testament, this saying brings reminiscences of Elijah's word to the woman at Zarephath when he resuscitated her son: 'See, your son lives' (1 Kings 17²³). A greater than Elijah is here! The centurion *believed the word that Jesus spoke to him, and went his way* (4⁵⁰). In this sentence is compressed a great deal of theological evaluation of belief. To believe the word that Jesus spoke is, of course, much more than to accept a statement as true; this particular statement could not be believed as true unless the hearer were ready to 'take Jesus at his word'. That is to say, the departure of the centurion in reliance upon the truth of Christ's word was already an incipient true faith.

His faith was not unjustified. On his way home he was met by his servants and told that his son had recovered, at the very time that Jesus had said to him (the word about life comes strongly into the narrative again) '*Your son will live*' (4⁵³). Then faith that had been incipient becomes more explicit. '*He himself believed, and all his household*' (4⁵³). Such an absolute use of the word *believe* indicates full conversion, as the Church would have put it in the days of her Gentile mission. Indeed, this section of the story at least bears the marks of that particular perspective, for the phrase *and all his household* is one that comes from the missionary story of the Church, and is preserved in the book of Acts, as well as at this point in John (cf. Acts 11¹⁴; 16¹⁵,³¹; 18⁸). This story is a 'sign' that 'the full number of the Gentiles [shall] come in' (Rom. 11²⁵).

The evangelist now repeats his allusion to the sign at Cana (4⁵⁴). Evidently the reader must not forget the first sign as he passes from consideration of the second. In writing of the first sign (see above, p. 146) it was said that, for the Jews at the wedding feast where *the* bridegroom had come, 'that which had, as water, never been able, and never would be able, in any quantity large or small, to prepare men by an adequate purification to enter worthily even into an earthly marriage or union of persons, was to turn, in the presence of the true bridegroom, and by his grace and power, into the very substance of the divine marriage between God and his people. The inadequate and insufficient preparatory water became the more than adequate and superabundant wine of actual celebration and enjoyment.' John has now made it clear that a Gentile is able in true belief to enter into a sharing of the very substance of the divine marriage between God and his people, into sharing the life, the eternal life, that Jesus came to bring to dying men.

So in this one story John has brought his rich thematic treatment to a temporary climax. He has spoken in the Prologue of the exalted nature of the one man Jesus of whom he is to write; he has recorded the witness of John to the divine character of Jesus Messiah; he has written of the beginnings of the community of the Messiah in the persons of the disciples and the quality of their witness. In relating the first sign he has given a revealing clue as to the whole nature of Christ's work in replacing and transcending the religion of the Jews. He has told of the way in which he who is himself the gospel meets with and acts towards the Jewish temple and the Jewish leader; towards the Samaritan temple and the Samaritan woman; and now, finally, towards a Gentile. He has made it abundantly plain that the whole issue of life or death (by that meaning not simply mortal life in this world or passage from it, but eternal life or death) hangs upon the attitude to Christ of those who meet him: if they believe in his name, they receive the gift of life, but if they do not believe, then they place themselves under the condemnation which is death. The last incident of this thematic treatment reflected a synoptic miracle story. As John proceeds with his gospel he selects four further incidents either reproducing (ch. 6) or reminiscent of (ch. 5, 9, 11) synoptic material, and tries to make plain what precisely is involved in acknowledging the supernatural power of Jesus the worker of miracles or signs. These will further expose all that is involved in belief on his name, and in the gift of life eternal, and will prepare the way for the last and greatest sign, when he gives himself to death for all men, to be raised in power and glory as the saviour of the world.

ໜໜ

46
at Capernaum: the town where, in the synoptic record, the whole incident takes place. John links the miraculous power of Jesus very

deliberately with the miracle at Cana, and thus removes it from any chance of being taken for mere thaumaturgy.

47

he ... begged him to come down to Capernaum: In John the centurion goes as far as Cana to fetch Jesus. Matthew tells of his meeting Jesus as he came into Capernaum, while Luke reports that he sent elders from the Jews to make his request for him. John wants a direct confrontation of Jesus and the Gentile.

he was at the point of death: John here begins his exposition of a miracle as in essence the giving of life to dead or dying men, to be crowned first with the raising of Lazarus, and finally by the sign of his own death and resurrection.

48

'Unless you see signs and wonders you will not believe': See notes above. This is the point where it seems that Jesus deprecates the faith of the centurion. Yet if it be remembered that this saying picks up the evangelist's note in 2$^{23-4}$, it is probably right to understand it as putting the centurion in the same place as the Jews who saw his signs in Jerusalem. Jesus did not 'trust' himself to them (the word for 'trust' was the same as that for 'believe', indicating some reciprocal advance between Jesus and the true believer in the act of faith which bound them together). But evidently Jesus is willing to 'trust' himself to the centurion, at least to the extent of making his divine power available to him, once it has been established that he does not seek it simply as a thaumaturgical device, but as the gift of one who demands absolute trust or 'belief'.

49

'come down before my child dies': The centurion, like Martha (11^{21}) and Mary (11^{32}), has as yet no idea of the authority of Jesus that reaches beyond the grave, and so testifies that the life he gives is not temporal but eternal life.

50

'Go; your son will live': The word *live* could well remind the reader of the gospel familiar with the Greek Old Testament, particularly in view of the reference to Moses and the serpent in 3$^{14, 15}$, that in Num. 21^8 the same word is used for 'recovery from disease'. At the same time no sensitive reader of the gospel will suppose that the word at this point is exhausted by that meaning; there is already a reference to eternal life, and a pointing forward to the resurrection. The fact that the phrase is repeated (4^{53}) adds significance to it as a key theological word in the narrative.

51

told him that his son was living: The word used for *son* here is precisely the same as that used for 'servant' in Matt. 8⁶, ⁸, ¹³. The word has this double meaning in Greek, and this may be the cause of the difference between John and the synoptics at this point. The version of the story circulating in Ephesus may well have had the equivalent term 'son' substituted for 'servant' for some reasons irrecoverable by twentieth-century inquirers.

52

'Yesterday at the seventh hour the fever left him': The seventh hour was 1 p.m. If it be asked why had the centurion taken from 1 p.m. through to the next day to travel from Cana to Capernaum, some 20 miles away, the answer could be that a centurion's entourage would take some time to leave Cana, and that the going between the two towns was not easy. Moreover such precision of reference is probably not intended by John. It was common belief that the seventh hour was the critical time for any fever.

53

he himself believed, and all his household: The absolute use of *believed* is deliberate and significant. The Gentile had achieved what neither Jew nor Samaritan had gained. And far from the Gentile mission being a new thing with Paul, its full effect is felt here when the centurion believes with all his house.

John 5¹⁻⁴⁷

Deed and Word: 1
'Then shall the lame man leap like an hart'
The Pool of Bethzatha —
The Third Sign Isaiah 35[5-6a]
Mark 2[1-12, 27, 28]
Mark 3[4]
Luke 13[15, 16]
Matthew 12[5, 6]

The decision to treat ch. 5 in the order of its appearance in the Greek N.T. is justified in part by the considerations put forward in the Introduction (see above, p. 43), and in part by the exegesis of the text that becomes possible. Ch. 5 is thus something of a test of the decision not to change the order of the Greek text, as it is also a test of two further positions adopted in the Introduction (see pp. 47, 67), viz. that John is deliberately offering comment on synoptic situations if not on actual synoptic stories, and that, where a miracle in the gospel is followed by a discourse, the two are really fundamentally one.

The chapter divides itself into five clear and distinct parts: (1) The story of the miracle at the Pool of Bethzatha (1–9); (2) The controversy about work on the sabbath, and the claims of Jesus in that regard (10–18); (3) A profound exposition of the inter-relationships of the Father and the Son (19–29); (4) A first theological examination of the nature of witness (30–36); and (5) A statement on the failure of the Jews (37–47). In each section the author is taking up a theme already begun in the gospel, and carrying its analysis through to a deeper point.

The task of exegesis again faces the commentator with a decision about John's propensity to symbolism. It seems that there are undeniably fashions in this matter, and that at the present time the fashion of interpretation is set against symbolism. Thus Barrett, reflecting the contemporary mood, writes about the five porticoes, that they permit 'the probable identification of the building with remains found between the two portions of the double pool of St Anna. ...

245

This identification *excludes* [italics mine] the view, otherwise improbable, that by the "five porches" John intended to signify the five books of Moses, which were ineffective for salvation'.* Now, however probable the identification of the Pool of Bethzatha with the double pool of St Anna may be – and there is much to be said for it – it cannot, in the view of the present writer, exclude the symbolism of John's narrative; for, if the position adopted by the writer be correct, one of John's most notable characteristics is that he has a very quick eye for the actual elements in any given situation that can be perceived to have a symbolic reference to its meaning. The reader of the gospel is thus not faced with a choice of either rejecting John's symbolism or regarding his historical situations, or the details of them, as allegorical inventions; a reported detail could well be, and in the view of the writer often is, both a true historical reminiscence and a symbolic pointer to an event's significance.

In telling the story of the lame man healed by the Pool of Bethzatha John is not using an actual synoptic incident; nor yet is there one as close to it as was the healing of the centurion's servant to the miracle on the official's son in ch. 4. But it is not without significance that Mark 2^{1-12} has been thought in the long past to be another version of the same story, for it seems clear that John has here treated a synoptic 'situation' rather than a synoptic 'incident'. And he has taken the chance to weave into this incident what the synoptics have in fact spread over a number of happenings in their narratives, particularly in the attempt to indicate the profound christological issues that are bound up, in all four gospels, with both the miracles of healing and with their performance on the Jewish sabbath.

The treatment of this incident is entitled in this study 'The Third Sign'. Admittedly John does not himself use this description. Yet the present author is by no means alone in numbering this among the signs of the fourth gospel (Dodd, Barrett, Lightfoot among recent English writers) and the classification seems well justified in terms of Johannine theology, for vv. 19–30 and 41–47 make it plain that Jesus in this act is doing the work of God and manifesting his glory (cf. 2^{11}).

In passing to the exegesis of the text of the chapter it is as well to be reminded that in making a departure from a synoptic incident John is seeking to offer deliberate comment on several parts of the synoptic record. At first sight it looks as if what he has produced is so different

* Barrett, p. 211.

from anything to be found in the synoptics that it is really past comparison; yet a closer examination shows that even the profoundest points that John makes are by no means absent from the synoptic narratives. John is evidently trying to achieve his twofold aim – to prevent any future reader of the synoptic record from taking it superficially; and to make sure that the readers of his own gospel are led unambiguously into the depth of the mystery of the Word made flesh, wherein lies their salvation.

5 *After this there was a feast of the Jews, and Jesus went up to Jerusalem.* ²*Now there is in Jerusalem by the sheep gate a pool, in Hebrew called Beth-za'tha*^a, *which has five porticoes.* ³*In these lay a multitude of invalids, blind, lame, paralysed.*^b ⁵*One man was there, who had been ill for thirty-eight years.* ⁶*When Jesus saw him and knew that he had been lying there a long time, he said to him, 'Do you want to be healed?'* ⁷*The sick man answered him, 'Sir, I have no man to put me into the pool when the water is troubled, and while I am going another steps down before me.'* ⁸*Jesus said to him, 'Rise, take up your pallet, and walk.'* ⁹*And at once the man was healed, and he took up his pallet and walked.*
Now that day was the sabbath.

a Other ancient authorities read *Bethesda*, others *Bethsaida*
b Other ancient authorities insert, wholly or in part, *waiting for the moving of the water;* ⁴*for an angel of the Lord went down at certain seasons into the pool, and troubled the water: whoever stepped in first after the troubling of the water was healed of whatever disease he had*

John begins his story by telling the reader that Jesus went up to Jerusalem during *a feast of the Jews*. The absence of the definite article is noteworthy. Some manuscripts of the N.T. have provided it, so that it is possible to have a text, which some scholars deem correct, which speaks of *the* feast of the Jews, which would presumably refer to the Feast of Tabernacles, which occurs in the autumn. But a more sober estimate of the evidence confirms that *a* feast is the original reading of John, and the question then to be settled is which feast is supposed by the author to be taking place. Some have said that it was the Passover; and if so, the fourth evangelist tells of four Passovers in his gospel (2¹³; 5¹; 6⁴; 12¹) – not impossible by any means, but the feeling remains that if this were known by John to have taken place at Passover time, he would have stated the fact explicitly. Other scholars have suggested Tabernacles, Purim, Trumpets, and the New Year. The present writer is inclined to the view that since John wrote *a* feast, without mentioning its name, he regarded it as not significant for the reader to be told which feast was being kept, whereas it is clearly important, in John's view, for his readers to know that the feeding of the five thousand took place at Passover time (see below, p. 283). If an opinion has to be expressed the present writer would elect the Feast of Trumpets or New Year*, in the early autumn, presumably between the visit to Jerusalem for the Passover of 2¹³ and the Passover near to which Jesus fed five thousand followers in Galilee.

The evangelist, having omitted to tell his readers which feast was being celebrated, next takes some trouble to lay the scene of the miracle in some detail; which surely means that the details have some significance. In Jerusalem, he says, near the Sheep Gate, there is a pool called Bethzatha, with five porticoes. The scene is laid in Jerusalem and no doubt the reader is invited to recall what took place on Jesus' first visit (2¹³–3²¹), and to compare it with what happens now. Just as the second miracle in Galilee developed the theme that had been begun on the occasion of the first sign, so now in Jerusalem there is to be a development of the situation as between Jesus and his own people (cf. 1¹¹); he has returned to his earthly religious *patris*, and it will be seen how he is indeed without honour there. His miracle was performed near the Sheep Gate and it is perhaps permissible to see that even thus early John is preparing the reader for the self-description of Jesus as the Good Shepherd who gives his life for the sheep, though much is to happen before the disciples can receive such a description of their Master. The Pool is called 'Bethzatha' – at least in the best

---

* Professor Guilding thinks that the feast is that of the New Year, though she accepts the inversion of chs. 5 and 6. The fact that she brings her general thesis to bear fruitfully upon the gospel at this point as well as at others means, if she be right, that it is of importance for the reader to know that the feast in question was the New Year, in order that the Jewish lectionaries for the feast be seen as the background for the miracle and discourse.

texts; though alternative readings are found, e.g. Bethesda (House of Mercy), Bethsaida (avoided because of the well-known town by the lake of Galilee), and Belzetha, which is very near the form of the name by which a north-eastern suburb of the city was known at the time. Bethzatha may mean House of the Olive. The healing took place by the pool Bethzatha, which has recently been identified with the twin pool of St Anna, though previously other identifications have been made, the Pool of Siloam, or the Virgin's Well, which is south of the Temple, in the valley of Kidron. Fortunately the understanding of John's story does not in any way depend upon a correct identification of the Pool in question.

The Pool brings to the reader the substance of water once again. It has been introduced as the material of cleansing, and Jesus showed, by turning it into wine, that his own sacrifice would replace Jewish purifications as the one purification able to prepare men to meet their God. It has been shown as the means of baptism, and Jesus has been hailed as the one who baptizes with water and the spirit. It has been shown as the means of quenching man's ever-recurrent thirst, and Jesus had made it plain that he provides a 'water' that quenches the deepest thirst once and for all, in establishing such a relation between himself and the believer that the only way of preserving the metaphor of water is to say that the believer himself becomes a source of water, with thirst-quenching springs welling up in him ceaselessly. Now water is introduced as the means of healing, and it will be shown forthwith that the word and deed of Jesus have, even in his lifetime, quite superseded water as a healing medium.

The Pool is said to have five porches. It is hard to resist either the mere matter-of-factness of this statement (why should this piece of information be false?) or its symbolic suggestiveness (the five 'porches' of the Pool where sick Jews are gathered symbolize for the sharp eye of the evangelist the five books of the law, in which Jews should have found the way to fulness of life, but have signally failed to do so). At the pool, under cover of the porches, there lay a multitude of invalids, blind, lame, and paralysed. In view of the imminent healing by Jesus the reader may well recall that in Luke's story of the Great Supper Jesus tells his host that when he gives a banquet he should invite 'the poor, the maimed, the lame, the blind' (Luke 14¹³); something is about to be done for such of the world's unfortunates gathered at the Pool. One of the invalids is a cripple, who had been at the Pool hoping for healing for thirty-eight years. Again a simple statement by the evangelist is apt to divide theologians! Some protest that there need be no assumption that John supposed Jesus knew by some supernatural means that the man had been there a long time; could it not have been a matter of common knowledge and gossip that he had been there for thirty-eight years? The comment springs naturally to many a twentieth-century mind, but would have seemed strange to most, if not all, of John's contemporaries. The evident intention is that Jesus is possessed of knowledge about the man, as he had been about the woman at the well, from some source of omniscience, or else that he alone could see the cripple as a symbol of the condition of his people, the Jews. The thirty-eight years are also a matter of argument. Is it an actual number? If so, or even more, perhaps, if not, is the number symbolic? The present writer thinks that here again John has preserved in his gospel a little fact from the tradition he knew which cannot possibly be checked now, but which he preserved just because it was to him not only a fact but a symbol. The man who had waited for his hope to be fulfilled for thirty-eight years was in the precise situation of his people long ago when they wandered and waited for thirty-eight years (Deut. 2^{14}) for the promise of God to be fulfilled to them. Again the man to be healed is representative of his people, and there is nothing strange in the evangelist letting his readers know this indirectly, as was indeed the custom of his day. Yet the symbolism has a purpose, viz., to contrast the barrenness and sterility of the Mosaic law in Jewish tradition with the quickening, life-giving word of Jesus.

Jesus knew that the man had been there a long time, and asked him: '*Do you want to be healed?*' Again the reader can immediately detect the *double-entendre* of the question. It is put to the man as a sick person; after thirty-eight years of waiting to be healed, he had evidently got very used to seeing opportunity after opportunity pass him by, and perhaps his only way of avoiding bitterness was to cease so urgently to want to be healed. His attendance was almost a matter of form, perhaps. The question was addressed through him to the Jew as a man before God – did he want to be healed? Was he really satisfied with what the law of Moses was able to do for him? Was there not something else to which Mosaic religion only pointed, but rightly pointed; did not the Jew want this? Did he really want to be healed? The answer of the man is a quite typical piece of human self-excusing, betraying something of a bad conscience about the past, since he avoided answering the question Jesus had put. But here the superiority of Christ's provision of healing is shown; he says to the man, in words that almost precisely repeat the words of Jesus to the paralysed man in Mark 2^{11}: '*Rise, take up your pallet, and walk*' (5^8). The man was immediately healed, and did as he was directed.

The observant reader will notice that this story has some interesting affinities with, and some significant differences from, the story of the healing of the paralytic in Mark (Mark 2$^{1-12}$). Both men are crippled helplessly: Jesus uses almost identical words to heal them; but – to limit this note to the one important difference – John, for all his apparently greater theological concern than Mark, fails entirely to mention the forgiveness of sin. How is this to be understood? A brief look forward in the chapter, and a reminder that John is dealing with a general synoptic situation rather than a particular synoptic incident, will suffice. For later in the chapter John deals with the question of sin: and it must be recalled that when forgiveness is granted by Jesus the scribes immediately ask 'Why does this man speak thus? It is blasphemy! Who can forgive sins but God alone?' (Mark 2^7), thus raising the same theological issues that are raised in John about the healing at Bethzatha (5^{29}). Moreover, once John has told the story of the miracle he observes that it took place on a sabbath. It is at this point that John is able to bring together the issue that lay behind both miracle and sabbath breaking, for, even in the synoptic record, neither can be understood save as the work of the Messiah, the Son of God. The claim in regard to miracles is explicit, e.g. in Luke 11^{20}: 'If it is by the finger of God that I cast out demons, then the kingdom of God has come upon you'. Sabbath breaking is variously justified in the synoptics. Luke provides what Barrett (Barrett, p. 209) calls the 'humanitarian' argument (Luke 13$^{10-17}$; 14$^{1-6}$); Matthew gives a reason that, after reference to what Israel's priests do in the temple, goes on to affirm that 'something greater than the temple is here' (Matt. 12^6); Mark offers another theological apology by saying that 'The sabbath was made for man, and not man for the sabbath; so the Son of man is lord even of the sabbath' (Mark 2^{27,28}). But these three apparently different arguments all point in the one direction of which John's present exposition is the terminus. Luke's argument concerns in the first place a woman who had been ill for eighteen years, whom Jesus healed in a synagogue on the sabbath. The ruler of the synagogue took sharp exception to this, and stated that there were six days on which work should be done, and that those wanting to be healed should seek healing on some other day. Jesus' reply is twofold: first, an argument *a fortiori* which pleaded that if any Jew was ready to lead his animals to water on the sabbath, then, to fill out the argument, ought not someone who had the relationship of master to ox in regard to the stricken woman to be free and willing to heal her on the sabbath? Second, Jesus used an argument relating to the special status of the Jews: Ought not a daughter of Abraham, a member of God's people according to the flesh, to be loosed from the bond by which Satan had bound her for eighteen years? Again, the claim implicit in the reference to Satan and loosing a woman from his power shows that Luke is offering much more than an humanitarian argument for breaking the sabbath. The point is equally clear about the way in which Matthew and Mark handle the story of David which Jesus used in answer to the charge of sabbath breaking by his disciples as they plucked and ate corn on the sabbath. Matthew refers to what the priests can do in the temple on the sabbath, which elsewhere and by other persons would be 'work' on the sabbath; if then, in the person of Jesus and his fellowship with his disciples there is a 'place' greater than the temple, it follows that the whole question of sabbath keeping and breaking is on another plane, because of the nature of Jesus. Similarly Mark, who pleads that Jesus and the Twelve form some sort of messianic band, and are therefore to be exempted, as David was when he was Israel's anointed king as yet unenthroned, from the laws as they apply to men of ordinary status. Jesus has a quite unique status, that of the Son of man; that is why he can in fact be reckoned 'lord of the sabbath', i.e. not just one who may be granted permission by men to infringe otherwise binding regulations, but one who of his own right and authority is able to make his own provisions about the sabbath. These arguments plainly lead into John's, which consists in a bold and utterly unmistakable claim that Jesus is wholly at one with the Father, the fount of all authority and law.

ಌ

1

After this: This indication of time gives the reader no clue to the interval that it covers; John evidently thought that such information was not really instructive, and intended rather that the reader should know that before he reads ch. 5 he must understand what has gone before and that it was in connexion with a festival at Jerusalem that Jesus undertook his journey.

2

by the sheep gate: The Greek text is uncertain at this point. The chief problem is to decide whether the word *pool* is in the nominative or (like *sheep*) in the dative. If the former, the translation given in the R.S.V. follows, the translator supplying the noun *gate* to agree with *sheep* on the basis of the information given in Nehemiah 3^1; if the latter, the translation would be: 'there is in Jerusalem a sheep pool, in Hebrew called Bethzatha'.

6

'Do you want to be healed?': Jesus takes the initiative, as so often in John, just as Yahweh had taken the initiative in calling Israel to be his chosen people. Both acts appear to be arbitrary, but, as men shall know at the end, the judge of all the earth does what is right and just. The question calls for some response on the part of the man; what the word *heal* meant to him as Jesus spoke it is hard now to recover, though in the context of the fourth gospel it is more than likely to mean all that the synoptics meant by the phrase 'be made whole', i.e. be dealt with at a higher level than the conquest of a bodily disease.

7

'Sir, I have no man to put me into the pool': Contrast the position of the paralytic in Mark 2, who had four men to assist him! Note too that the Jewish pool (symbolic of the Jewish religion) could heal only one invalid at each stirring of the pool, whereas the power of Jesus extended to all whom he willed.

5 $^{10-18}$ THE DAY OF THE DEED AND ITS MEANING

^{10}*So the Jews said to the man who was cured, 'It is the sabbath, it is not lawful for you to carry your pallet.' ^{11}But he answered them, 'The man who healed me said to me, "Take up your pallet, and walk."' ^{12}They asked him, 'Who is the man who said to you, "Take up your pallet, and walk"?' ^{13}Now the man who had been healed did not know who it was, for Jesus had withdrawn, as there was a crowd in the place. ^{14}Afterwards, Jesus found him in the temple, and said to him, 'See, you are well! Sin no more, that nothing worse befall you.' ^{15}The man went away and told the Jews that it was Jesus* *who had healed him.* ¹⁶*And this was why the Jews persecuted Jesus, because he did this on the sabbath.* ¹⁷*But Jesus answered them, 'My Father is working still, and I am working.'* ¹⁸*This was why the Jews sought all the more to kill him, because he not only broke the sabbath but also called God his Father, making himself equal with God.*

The story now switches from the Pool to a place where the Jews tell the healed invalid that it is not lawful for him to carry his pallet on the sabbath. It is unlikely that the man was not already aware of this fact, and probable that his reply reflects his own sense that the one who had cured him with the instruction to carry his pallet had an authority proper to the order; he replies: '*The man who healed me said to me, "Take up your pallet, and walk"*' (5¹¹). But he could give no further information about Jesus save that he was just a male visitor to the Pool; for Jesus, probably to avoid a disturbance on the sabbath, had taken advantage of the crowd and slipped out of sight. But later Jesus sought out the man he had healed and said to him '*See, you are well! Sin no more, that nothing worse befall you*' (5¹⁴). Some scholars have produced the subtle argument that since Jesus at this point says '*sin* NO MORE' he must have dealt with the man's sin at the time of the healing, just as he had dealt with the sins of the paralytic in Mark 2⁵. This seems unimaginative and unnecessary; it cannot be claimed that either evangelist offers his readers an infallibly correct order of all the details of each incident he reports; what each is concerned to do, and each has his own means of doing it, is to lay bare the real issues that lie behind or rather in the stories he tells. Mark has well intermingled the act of healing with the offer of forgiveness; John has separated them, at least to the extent that he tells a story of a healing before he either mentions the sabbath, or speaks about sin. It is almost as if he were saying to his readers, and to some readers of the synoptics, 'You may read the synoptic miracle stories as if they were merely stories of a great healer, which of course they are; and I will, by telling this healing story quite separately, let you see how great healings were done; though, if you have an eye for the symbolic, you will not even then be able to escape the deeper things that are going on. But after what mistaken people might think was the whole story of the healing I will show how in fact it was a great deal more.' So in the discussion of sabbath breaking and all that follows John is really expounding what really was involved in the healing of a lame man.

Sin no more then means that Jesus is not concerned with a mere physical rehabilitation. '*See, you are well*' followed by the injunction '*sin no more*' does not imply that the disease had been the result of sin. This prevalent view the synoptists had reported Jesus to deny (Luke 13¹⁻⁵) and later in this gospel John deals explicitly with the belief (9²,³). When Jesus declares the man *well* he speaks of a wholeness which a paralysed or maimed person does not possess (cf. Matt. 15³¹; 12¹³; Mark 5³⁴). When he adds the warning '*Sin no more, that nothing worse befall you*' he is telling the newly healed man that his new wholeness is not something he may take for granted. Most commentators think that the *nothing worse* must be the Judgement; with temerity the present writer suggests that Jesus is saying something of the same order as is found in the synoptic record of Matthew and Luke, when Jesus speaks of the unclean spirit that had been exorcized returning to the newly swept and ordered home of the man's personality. 'Then he goes and brings seven other spirits more evil than himself, and they enter and dwell there; and the last state of that man becomes worse than the first' (Luke 11²⁶ //). The physical wholeness which Jesus gives is not simply physical, and unless a man made whole renews himself in the life of the Son he will expose his nature to invasion of a demonic kind, and will end up worse than he began.

The man went and told the Jews that it was Jesus who had healed him (5¹⁵). This is not necessarily a matter for condemnation, and in the absence of any adverse comment from the evangelist it is perhaps wrong to think so. The authorities had, after all, only had the man's own story, without any confirmatory evidence; now that this could be supplied, it is natural for the man to offer it. Yet the incident has its dark side; it shows how having dealings with Jesus tends to bring a man into difficulties with the present order. Here we see at work a principle that can be traced in the gospel story from the cry of the babes who were slaughtered at Christ's birth (Matt. 2¹⁶⁻¹⁸) to the saying that the disciples found so hard to accept for themselves, that a man must take up his own cross daily (Luke 9²³ //) if he is to be a worthy disciple of Jesus. The Jews, hearing that Jesus had both occasioned the man's sabbath breaking, and also been a sabbath breaker himself, *persecuted* him (5¹⁶). This is an exact parallel to the synoptic account in Mark 3⁶ where, after a healing in the synagogue on the sabbath, the Pharisees went out and held counsel with the Herodians how to destroy Jesus. Both synoptic and Johannine records, that is to say, portray this opposition as from the start one that had issues of life and death. The cross is foreshadowed here in both traditions.

But in the Johannine tradition there is an immediate precipitation of the issue by Jesus himself, so that the whole nature of the debate can be made unmistakably plain from the start. Jesus answered (the word means to make a public and formal defence*) with some words that bring the charge of blasphemy as did the announcement of forgiveness in Mark 2^5. His words were *'My Father is working still, and I am working'* (5^{17}). The writer comments, *This was why the Jews sought all the more to kill him, because he not only broke the sabbath but also called God his Father, making himself equal with God* (5^{18}). The point to remember is that this saying is stated on the sabbath itself: *My Father is working still*. This was not in itself an offence to the devout and orthodox Jew, who had had to come to terms with the statement in Genesis 2^2 that 'on the seventh day God had finished his work which he had done, and he rested on the seventh day from all his work which he had done'. Philo comments on this thought 'By rest I do not mean inaction, since that which is by nature energetic, that which is the cause of all things, can never desist from doing that which is most excellent.'† Even more, God does not even cease to create: 'God never ceases creating, but as it is the property of fire to burn and of snow to be cold, so it is the property of God to create'.‡ But Philo, and other Jewish thinkers after him, thought it right to modify this position, so that the typical later view was that 'though God ceased from his work on the world [i.e. creation in the narrower sense] he did not cease from his work on the unrighteous and the righteous [i.e. from his moral government of the universe]'§. So there was nothing particularly obnoxious to the Jews or the authorities so far. The obnoxious saying is what follows: 'and I am working'. The whole statement provides support for the view that Jesus had in fact dealt with more than the invalid's bodily ailment. It is not hard to suppose that by the time of Jesus it was already accepted that, whatever 'work' God might be said to do on the sabbath, it would not be the work of actual creation. If then it were already supposed that God could and

---

* The same word is used in the negative sense in the account of the trial of Jesus, e.g. Mark 14^{61}.

† Philo, *De Cherubim*, 87.

‡ Philo, *Legum Allegoriae*, I. 5–6.

§ This quotation is from Rabbi Phinehas (*c.* 360) writing on Gen. 2^2.

did maintain the moral government of his world, dealing with the righteous and the unrighteous, it would be to this activity of God that Jesus laid claim in his emphatic *'and I'* – both words would sound grossly offensive to the pious Jew.

The Jews were not slow to see the implications of Jesus' argument. As quickly as the rulers in the synoptic tradition (Mark 2 ^{6,7}) they detected what was for them his blasphemy. Indeed, in a world where emperors had begun to claim divine honours and natures, it had become a special task of the Jews to expose such blasphemies for what they were worth; and their vigilance was the more to be exercised in that the poison now appeared to have taken root in Judaism itself! How greatly any such claim offended the Jew may be seen from the treatment accorded to Babylon in Second Isaiah, for Babylon took upon herself to speak as only God can speak: 'I am, and there is none beside me' (Isa. 47 ^{8,10}); or to the condemnation of Lucifer who said, 'I will make myself like the Most High' (Isa. 14 $^{12-21}$). Yet for all their misunderstanding there was one thing which, in John as in the synoptics, the Jews are represented as perceiving – that Jesus claimed for himself a special relationship to the Father. Against this the mere question of sabbath breaking took a very second place. *He not only broke the sabbath, but also called God his Father, making himself equal with God* (5 ^{18}). The R.s.v. would have rendered the Greek and the situation a little better if the words 'his own' or 'his very own Father' had been substituted for the simple *his Father*. To the Jews Jesus seemed to be putting himself into a special place in the regard of the Father; and this was rebellious and blasphemous. As a piece of rebellion it would give rise to the phrase *Making himself equal with God*, for in rabbinic teaching a rebellious son was described as 'making himself equal with' his father; that is to say, he assumes charge of his own life as an independent person, and no longer recognizes his father's authority.

✿

10

'It is the sabbath, it is not lawful for you to carry your pallet': The Old Testament references are Exodus 20 ^{10}; Nehemiah 13 ^{19}; Jeremiah 17 ^{21}. But the Mishnah details 39 different offences covered by the general prohibition, of which one is to take anything out of one house into another (Shabbath 7 ^{2}).

16

The Greek uses the imperfect for the verbs in this verse, and for 'sought' in v. 18. The implication is that this was not by any means the only occasion on which Jesus healed on the sabbath, or the Jews sought to deal with him finally.

17

'*My Father is working*': In justifying the thought that, in spite of what is stated in Gen. 2² on God's resting on the sabbath day, his activity continued, some rabbinic arguments pleaded that God could not be held to take anything from one house to another, for the whole universe is his house!

18

he not only broke the sabbath: This does not mean that sabbath breaking was a trivial offence, as Barrett almost says (he uses the adverb 'comparatively'), for the punishment for breaking it was 'cutting off [death] and stoning'; it is only as contrasted with the much more serious offence of blasphemy that it can in any way appear trivial.

making himself equal with God: As Dodd observes, this charge would be understood, though in an entirely different way, by the heathen Greek, who was familiar enough with the idea of a 'divine man'; but for the Jews such a claim was a denial of their basically essential monotheism, real blasphemy.

5^{19–29}   THE DEED, GIVING LIFE

¹⁹*Jesus said to them 'Truly, truly, I say to you, the Son can do nothing of his own accord, but only what he sees the Father doing: for whatever he does, that the Son does likewise.*²⁰*For the Father loves the Son, and shows him all that he himself is doing: and greater works than these will he show him, that you may marvel.*²¹ *For as the Father raises the dead and gives them life, so also the Son gives life to whom he will.*²² *The Father judges no one, but has given all judgement to the Son,* ²³*that all may honour the Son, even as they honour the Father. He who does not honour the Son does not honour the Father who sent him.* ²⁴*Truly, truly, I say to you, he who hears my word and believes him who sent me has eternal life: he does not come into judgement, but has passed from death to life.*

²⁵*'Truly, truly, I say to you, the hour is coming, and now is, when the dead will hear the voice of the Son of God, and those who hear will live.* ²⁶*For as the Father has life in himself, so he has granted the Son also to have*

life in himself, ²⁷*and has given him authority to execute judgement, because he is the Son of man.* ²⁸*Do not marvel at this; for the hour is coming when all who are in the tombs will hear his voice* ²⁹*and come forth, those who have done good, to the resurrection of life, and those who have done evil, to the resurrection of judgement.*

The reply that Jesus gives admirably follows this interpretation of the accusation, for his defence consists in saying first summarily, and then at some length, that as the special Son of the Father he does nothing of his own accord, but only what the Father does. Indeed it might be put that Jesus' defence is that he is the very opposite of a rebellious son, for instead of 'setting himself up as an autonomous personality' he actually has a unity with the Father in which there can be no talk either of Father-actions or of Son-actions, but only actions which, whether here in history or beyond it, both Father and Son share. This reply is introduced with the solemn formula which so often marks the transition to monologue, and sometimes perhaps what the author held to be an authentic saying of the Lord. Certainly in the Johannine gospel the 19th verse is of very great importance, not only as a reply, adequate enough in itself, to the Jews' accusation, but also for a positive summary of John's Christology. The Son does nothing of his own accord. He does only what the Father does, since he sees what the Father does, and does likewise. Here John is expressing in theological symbolic language the idea already inserted into the gospel at 1⁵¹; for here Jesus is making an open claim to be in himself the means by which heavenly things are brought to earth and made real in man's life and history.

To this filial submissiveness the Father offers his love, showing the Son all that he does. So Jesus claims to be the full revelation of God to men, for there is nothing that God does that he does not know, and nothing that he knows that he does not communicate to men. Yet the Jews must not suppose that what they have seen is already an earthly enactment of the greatest thing that God can do, for *greater works than these will he show him, that you may marvel* (5²⁰). What are the *greater works* which John mentions here? The normal answer of the commentator is that the Jews have just witnessed the healing of a disease; but they will see much greater things than this in the future. The present writer differs from this judgement for two reasons: first, it can be adopted only on the assumption that ch. 5 is not the close-knit unity that he supposes it to be and that it appears to be in a sound and profound exegesis; and second, because it cannot give due weight to the somewhat enigmatic phrase *that you may marvel*. To deal with the phrase first. The word *marvel* in the synoptic tradition is closely bound up with the proper reaction of men to the wonderful works of Jesus, and implies some awesome recognition of his supernatural power and nature; typical instances can be found at Mark 5²⁰, Matt. 8²⁷ and Luke 9⁴³, which constitute almost a little series of developing instances, the final one making it quite plain that it connoted some perception of the activity of God. When Jesus healed the demoniac boy whom the disciples had been unable to cure, Luke states that 'all were astonished at the majesty of God' and proceeds without a break 'But while they were all marvelling at everything he did'. We may take it then that the word 'marvel' has, among its theological meanings, this rather special use in recording man's perception that in some things at least which Jesus did there was a more-than-human element. Hence the marvelling. At this point of ch. 5, it is already evident, and it will become more so, that the 'healing of a disease' was by no means the only thing that Jesus did to the paralytic at Bethzatha pool. But none of what he had done had so impressed the Jews that they 'marvelled' at it, discerning some of God's awesome activity among men. Very well, says Jesus, you have not marvelled at what I have done this day in Jerusalem, but there will come a day when the Father will show me a greater work than I have done on this sabbath, and the work that I shall then do will be done to make you marvel – and so, we may add, be saved. That this interpretation is correct is the more certain if v. 28 is considered alongside v. 20. For there, after Jesus has expounded what he had done at the pool of Bethzatha as the giving of life for death, he continues '*Do not marvel at this*' viz. that I can give life to the spiritually dead who are alive in their human physical existence now, marvel rather that the hour is coming when my power will be made manifest in my calling the departed out of the tombs from physical death to the new life that I have to give.

This leads to the consideration of the first reason why it is proposed here to dissent from the usual interpretation of this verse. For if the chapter be a unity, then what Jesus has to say about giving life to the spiritually dead in vv. 21–7 is really a probing of the miracle at the pool to its fundamental character. It is significant perhaps that other commentators write of the 'transition' from the miracle to the discourse; whereas the present writer believes that narrative of miracle and exposition of discourse are really a profound unity, and one means by which John would have his own readers avoid the relatively superficial interpretation of the synoptic healing stories as physical cures and little, if anything, more. Yet as perhaps John himself had in mind, the synoptics themselves give clear clues; and in one sabbath controversy particularly, where the Jews watched Jesus to see whether he would heal on the sabbath day (Mark 3¹⁻⁶). This is a story pitched at about the same critical point in the narrative as the healing at the pool of Bethzatha, for after it the evangelist tells of an alliance between Pharisees and Herodians to accomplish Jesus' destruction. Jesus called the leaders of the synagogue to him, and asked: 'Is it lawful on the sabbath to do good or to do harm, *to save life or to kill?*' (the author's italics, naturally). To restore a withered hand on the sabbath was certainly a 'good turn' (which is what 'to do good' probably means); but Jesus was not a superior 'boy scout', desirous of doing a good turn: he was not content to deal with men simply on the physical level. The synoptics speak of his making men 'whole'; John more explicitly and theologically writes of giving men life. So it is right, or at least possible, to give another interpretation to the *greater works* to which Jesus here refers; it seems that he is looking forward to the time when he will not only give his new gift of life to a living man, but to one who has been in the tomb. And beyond that, and inevitably together with it, he is thinking of the day when his own body will lie in the tomb, and then be raised by the greatest work of the Father in which the Son will share.

In v. 21, Jesus then proceeds to relate what things he has seen the Father do, and has then himself done on this sabbath day. '*As the Father raises the dead and gives them life, so also the Son gives life to whom he will.*' The Jews were familiar with the view that the powers of life and death belonged solely to God (cf. 1 Sam. 2⁶; 2 Kings 5⁷). Elijah, of course, was a strange exception to this rule (cf. 1 Kings 17¹⁷⁻²⁴), though the rule remained accepted as inflexible by the Jews. It was not till very late that even Messiah was thought of as coming with power to raise the dead. But Jesus is stating that this exclusive divine prerogative is one that he shares – he gives life to whom he will. There is a double edge to the phrase *to whom he will*. There had inevitably been an apparent arbitrariness in the healing of the crippled man at the pool in Jerusalem; many invalids were there; why should this man be chosen? If it be replied that he had long been a sick man, it can be assumed that others had also waited a long time; moreover if, as John has already emphasized, the power and grace of Jesus is overflowing and universal, why should only one man be healed? The answer cannot avoid the awkward questions about 'particularity' that are associated with any historic action of God, for, short of exercising his power on all men together, which would really be a denial both of human nature and of history, God cannot act in history save on and in and through individuals. Even the choice of Israel is of this strange kind:

> How odd
> Of God
> To choose
> The Jews!

And the answer, as Paul saw, can only be given at the end, when the whole drama of man's history is concluded in the final victory of God in Christ*. Jesus, to return to the argument following upon the sign at Bethzatha, has healed, i.e. brought to life, *whom he will*, but though that may seem arbitrary to human eyes, it is not a thing done apart from the Father (cf. v. 19).

But, as the discourse with Nicodemus will have taught the reader, the gift of life is an act which paradoxically produces two sets of consequences, so Jesus now states something about God's judgement. *The Father judges no one* is the categorical statement that must not be explained away, but given full force. God can give life, for he is the creator. He can destroy, for the gift of life remains in his hands: yet he does not destroy, or judge in the sense of condemn, without the Son. That is to say, in terms of the biblical account of man, God made man for fellowship with himself, which is man's true life. Man in his sin and rebellion has turned away from God, and seeks to live life on his own terms. But God has not decided on that account to take life from man; rather he has decided to offer man life anew. 'For God so

---

* This theme is the subject of Romans 9–11, where Paul defends the justice of God in reference to the final end he achieves. 'God has consigned all men to disobedience, that he may have mercy upon all' is the general proposition. His means of working that out are past man's knowing fully in this life; but man knows enough of his love and power and justice through Christ confidently to trust God.

loved the world that he gave his only Son that whoever believes in him should not perish, but have eternal life' (3¹⁶). Yet, as was evident in considering ch. 3, this life-saving, life-giving act of God unavoidably has two sides, dependent upon the response of men. Those who believe and accept the gift of life are saved, and share eternal life with God; but those who do not believe reject the gift of life and are thus to be thought of as dead, as 'condemned to death', as 'judged'. The acts of raising the dead and giving life on the one hand, and of judging or condemning to death on the other, are obverse and reverse of the one act of God in which he sent his Son to be the saviour of the world. So it is strictly true to say that the Father judges no one. Every man receives the gift of the Son, and man's response to that gift will determine his destiny, whether of life or of judgement. The Father's activity of judging, that is to say, is wholly to be found in the Son's activity in offering life to men, whereby some are raised and some are 'already judged' because they do not believe on the only Son of God. In this life, then, the whole of a man's relationship to the Father turns upon his relationship to the Son; hence to honour the Son is to honour the Father, and there is no honouring the Father save by honouring the Son. All this, expounded in 5²²⁻²³, is summarized in another 'truly, truly' saying: *'he who hears my word and believes him who sent me has eternal life; he does not come into judgement, but has passed from death to life'* (5²⁴). Thus it is clear that what Jesus did to the crippled man was to bring him from the living death of unbelief to the eternal life of those who believe and trust. The passage from death to life is not necessarily identical with the passage from physical death to resurrection at the last day; it may, and ought to, take place now, in the human historical life which Jesus shared, and in which he offers men the great gift of life. So once more Jesus sums up what he has done in an emphatic saying ('truly, truly') *'the hour is coming, and now is, when the dead will hear the voice of the Son of God, and those who hear will live'*. This 'and now' again exposes what it is that took place at the pool of Bethzatha at its spiritual depth, whether the Jews could discern it or not. And the point is once more rounded off by Jesus' assertion that his ability to do what he claims to do depends entirely upon the fact that he shares one life with the Father; only the Father and himself 'have life in themselves', all other beings must receive it as a gift.

But can a story of a healing such as is reported in 3⁵⁻⁶ really bear this weight of interpretation? It has already been claimed that the synoptic narratives, properly read and understood, make no less signal a claim. It is part of John's religious artistry to join this profound discourse on the ineffable unity of the Father and the Son to a miracle or sign of which the outcome, apart from a physical healing, is not reported. It is as if he would have his reader face the most drastic of contrasts between a mortal physical body disabled and disowned and a person newly endowed with eternal life, for no other act of healing can begin to approach the transforming power displayed here. Yet the power displayed here is recognizably the same as that exercised in the synoptics. The wise student of the gospel is driven to Hoskyns' conclusion: 'The purpose of the Evangelist is to lay bare the theological foundations of the observable history of Jesus, not to impose a "Johannine" interpretation upon it.'* 'Grace and truth came through Jesus Christ'; here is the incredible grace of God, his gift of life to men who, though living, would otherwise die, and it is here 'in truth', i.e. in reality, in the words and in the works of Jesus of Nazareth.

The theological comment on the miracle and on the charge of sabbath breaking and blasphemy is thus completed. But before Jesus leaves it, he picks up the theme touched on in 5²⁰: the greater works that the Father will show the Son, so that the Jews may marvel. '*Do not marvel at this* [at what you have seen and heard today]' he says, '*for the hour is coming* [there is noticeably no 'and now is' in this saying] *when all who are in the tombs will hear his voice and come forth, those who have done good, to the resurrection of life, and those who have done evil, to the resurrection of judgement*' (5²⁹). So far in the discourse Jesus has been speaking of the power he shares with the Father to raise from death and to bestow life (i.e. to be the resurrection and the life) and which he has shown he can exercise in man's historical existence. Now he speaks of the power he will manifest in the future when he will deal not only with the spiritual death in which living men manage to exist, but, much more marvellously, with physical death itself, for all its apparent finality and power. And just as the power of giving life to living men has as its obverse side an inevitable *judgement* or 'condemnation', so has the power of life over physical death: for when men are raised from their tombs they will be raised either to life or to judgement. Three things need to be said. First, that

* Hoskyns and Davey, *The Fourth Gospel*, p. 255.

the authority of Jesus to execute judgement, whether in this age or at some final judgement, is, in terms of v. 27, because he is *Son of man*. The phrase *Son of man* is without articles in the Greek, and it is worth considering why. It is hardly to be supposed that, in a passage so treating of the authority to judge, the evangelist would play down the person of the Son of man to the point where he became just a 'man', which is what the words without articles might mean. The answer to the question why he has dropped the articles here alone in his gospel is probably the twofold one that on the one hand the phrase could not but remind the Jewish reader of the figure from his own mythology called the Son of man, a supernatural figure given authority to judge; and yet, in its form at this point, would also remind the Christian reader that the Son of God really came in the flesh, was really made man, and that in God's love he does not *judge* us from afar, but only as he comes to offer us life and love in his incarnate Son. Second, the saying keeps within the boundaries of Jewish apocalyptic in referring to a double resurrection to life or to judgement based upon the doing of good or of evil.* Yet already John has made serious modifications to the traditional Jewish statement summarized here. The believer does not come into judgement (3¹⁸; 5²⁴); and we must therefore interpret *those who have done good, to the resurrection of life* in terms of what has been stated in 3²¹: 'He who does what is true comes to the light, that it may be clearly seen that his deeds have been wrought in God'. The resurrection to life continues, or makes possible, the continuance of a life that has already in its earthly manifestations realized some unity with that of the Godhead (see further on 14²³; 15^{1–11}; 17^{21–26}). Third, the saying is confessedly prophetic: *the hour is coming* ... The hour that is to come is, in the first place, the hour when Jesus summons Lazarus from the tomb (11⁴³), and in the second, the hour when he leaves his own tomb to ascend to his Father (20¹⁷). The synoptic gospels also have their witness to Jesus' power over physical death during his earthly ministry (the raising of Jairus' daughter, of the widow's son at Nain, and the reply to the disciples of the Baptist: ' ... the dead are raised up'), and they report that on at least three occasions he foretold his death and resurrection (Mark 8³¹; 9³¹; 10³⁴ //).

ಶಾ

* cf. e.g. Daniel 12⁷.

20

the Father loves the Son: The word used for 'love' here is the Greek
word '*phileo*', not the much more distinctively Christian word '*agapao*'.
This latter word is characteristic in John of the love of the Father for
the Son, of the Son's love for the Father, and of both their loves for
men, as of men's for Father and Son, and, in that love of God, of their
love for one another. It may well be that this is just a stylistic variation,
though it might be suggested that the use of the word *phileo* at this
point reflects the fact that so far Jesus has been speaking, as it were,
about the relationships within the 'family' of the Godhead, and uses
phileo to represent that love. Later in the gospel, however, the word
agapao almost entirely replaces *phileo*, at any rate for referring to the
love of God or Christ for men, or of their love for Father or Son.

21

'*as the Father raises the dead, and gives them life*': This is an act of God
which belongs to the eschatological end in Jewish thinking. What Jesus
says modifies this, and transfers into the situation which his coming has
created the issues of life and death which the Jews expect to be dealt
with at the last day, but not before.

22–23

'*The Father judges no one, but has given all judgement to the Son, that all
may honour the Son*': See exegesis for interpretation. Jesus can rightly
claim from men the same honour that they accord to God, and this
itself precipitates the judgement.

25

The aorist participle in *those who hear* indicates that some have already
done so.

26

This verse picks up and restates vv. 19–21.

27

This verse picks up and restates v. 22. The appearance of the title
Son of man without an article may well echo the usage of Daniel,
particularly in view of the Daniel-like quality of the latter part of v. 29.

28

all who are in the tombs: This clearly implies that the authority and power
of Jesus to bestow the gift of life extends beyond the terrestrial existence
in which he has just displayed it in the healing at the pool. It is a matter
for consideration whether the saying implies a 'final' judgement
at the 'end of the world' or whether, at any rate for believers, and possibly for all given the opportunity to believe, the 'final' judgement is
made when a man responds, positively or negatively, to the gospel.

³⁰*'I can do nothing on my own authority; as I hear, I judge; and my judgement is just, because I seek not my own will but the will of him who sent me.* ³¹*If I bear witness to myself, my testimony is not true;* ³²*there is another who bears witness to me, and I know that the testimony which he bears to me is true.* ³³*You sent to John, and he has borne witness to the truth.* ³⁴*Not that the testimony which I receive is from man; but I say this that you may be saved.* ³⁵*He was a burning and shining lamp, and you were willing to rejoice for a while in his light.* ³⁶*But the testimony which I have is greater than that of John; for the works which the Father has granted me to accomplish, these very works which I am doing, bear me witness that the Father has sent me.*

Jesus added but one word after this tremendous prophecy. It concerned himself as judge. Once more he asserts his entire unity with the Father in the eschatological judgement, as he had already asserted his unity with the Father in the judgement his coming precipitates in the lives of those who do not believe. So instead of speaking in the third person of the Son of man, he speaks in the first person, and says: *'I can do nothing on my own authority; as I hear I judge; and my judgement is just, because I seek not my own will, but the will of him who sent me.'* Here at the end of the exposition of the relationship of the Son to the Father Jesus emphasizes again his absolute lack of any independence of God; the two act in complete and transcendental concert.

The turn to the first person singular is skilfully made, for it is much more likely to cause the hearer, and the reader, to ask what support there is for the view that Jesus is who he claims to be. John has suppressed the element of dialogue in this part of the discourse, though it is quite conceivable and indeed probable that some questions were asked by the Jews at teaching such as he had just given.* Verses 31-9

---

* This does not imply that the present writer thinks that the discourse was given on one occasion to Jews who had the opportunity to put their questions; but simply that, if such thoughts as these were part of the tradition that John received as the substance and form of Jesus' teaching, they may well have been set in a context of dialogue which, for reasons of his own, John found less useful for presentation than the monologue of discourse.

contain Jesus' first examination of the concept of witness (another occurs in ch. 8). He begins by stating an accepted Jewish dictum, one which would also be valid in modern communities, as well as the Hellenistic world in which John's gospel first circulated: *'If I bear witness to myself, my testimony is not true'* (5³¹). It repeats the principle enunciated in Deuteronomy 19¹⁵, and accepted (on dominical authority?) by the Christian Church (Matt. 18¹⁶). But Jesus' word goes a little further than any such legal principle of evidence. For the legal principle states that testimony on one's own behalf is inadmissible, as is that of any one witness on his own. Jesus has stated that if he bears witness to himself his witness is just not true. That is to say he agrees with the many critics of his claims since he made them, that any man who claims for himself that he is God cannot be speaking the truth. But Jesus rests his claim nevertheless, and on the admissible basis that others have testified on his behalf. Who were they? The very next verse begins the answer, but poses a problem. *'There is another who bears witness to me, and I know that the testimony which he bears to me is true'* (5³²). Most modern commentators are emphatic in stating that the 'other witness' is the Father, and reject the suggestion that it is the Baptist, though this is as old as Chrysostom. Bernard (I.C.C.) says that to apply it to the Baptist 'makes havoc of the argument which follows'; Dr Dodd asserts that 'the finally valid testimony is that of God himself. It is this testimony (it seems) which is referred to in 32, the following verses, with their reference to the Baptist, being parenthetic'. Barrett writes: 'The witness is not the Baptist (who is dealt with in vv. 33–6) but the Father . . . John returns to the theme of God's witness to Jesus at v. 37.' In spite of this modern harmony, the present writer finds himself bound to disagree. It is to be noted that any attempt to refer v. 32 to the Father forces a break into the otherwise smooth development of the thought of the discourse. This could be justified if necessary by saying that John first states the one true witness he has, and then goes back to reflect on one alleged witness and other forms of the real witness; but there is no need for this, and the much more natural way, as well as the more rewarding exegesis, is to be found by supposing that v. 32 does refer to the Baptist. One of the difficulties that those who reject an application to the Baptist fail to deal with is that, as at other places in the gospel, Jesus uses a form of words which are taken at one level by those who misunderstand, and at another by himself and (the evangelist believes) by the discerning reader. So the present exegesis will assume that in v. 32 Jesus speaks of the Baptist, and affirms that John bore witness to him, and that he (Jesus) knows in his own self that the witness that John bore is true. The evangelist is thus picking up the Baptist's testimony that Jesus was the Lamb of God ($1^{29, 36}$), the one on whom the Spirit descended and remained (1^{33}), the very Son of God (1^{34}). But that witness was not necessarily heard by, or directed to, the Jews as represented now by those who have questioned Jesus about his conduct on the sabbath. He therefore reminds them that they, as a people, inquired of John: '*You sent to John, and he has borne witness to the truth*' (5^{33}). The Jews sent priests and levites to John with certain questions, which John answered as best he could, though the climax of his witness was to tell the Jews that 'among you stands one whom you do not know, even he who comes after me, the thong of whose sandals I am not worthy to untie' ($1^{26, 27}$). This, though not a direct testimony to him as one who possessed the unity with the Father that Jesus had just expounded, is none the less a *witness to the truth*. The next verse is a necessary qualification in view of what Jesus has said and is about to say; it runs: '*Not that the testimony which I receive is from man; but I say this that you may be saved*' (5^{34}). In referring to 'testimony from man' Jesus is drawing a distinction between testimony that men can give, and that which God alone can offer. There is a sense in which John offers both kinds of testimony. On one level and in one sense he speaks as a man. He is indeed a man among men, and the Jewish people who heard what he had to say about Jesus listened to him as to a man. And if it were simply a matter of one man having the exalted things to say about another that Jesus has already said about himself, the situation of absurdity would be repeated again (as at v. 31). But Jesus did not receive John's testimony as just a human opinion, neither did the writer of the fourth gospel. The Baptist was a 'man sent from God . . . to bear witness to the light' ($1^{6,7}$), who had a revelation from heaven about Jesus: 'I saw the Spirit descend as a dove from heaven, and it remained on him' (1^{32}) and 'he who sent me to baptize with water said to me, "He on whom you see the Spirit descend and remain, this is he who baptizes with the Holy Spirit"' (1^{33}). So it is possible for the Jews both to receive John's testimony as a man and not to be convinced by it, and for Jesus and the Christian reader to receive it as of divine inspiration and so to be convinced by it and receive it without error. Jesus then offers a commentary on John: '*He was a burning and shining lamp*': that is to say, he was not a source of light, but a lamp lit from the light (cf. 1⁸: 'He was not the light, but came to bear witness to the light'), and the Jews were glad enough for a while to have him in their midst. Something of this temporary pride of the Jews in the Baptist finds an echo in the synoptic story, when Jesus asks them what they went out expecting to see when they visited the Baptist (Matt. 11⁷ᶠᶠ; Luke 7²⁴ᶠᶠ).

Jesus now at length is able to say fully what the witness to which he turns really is: '*The testimony which I have is greater than that of John; for the works which the Father has granted me to accomplish, these very works which I am doing, bear me witness that the Father has sent me.*' This is to repeat the claim that the works that Jesus has already done make it plain that his claims are justified. And what he has already done (these very works which I am doing) is to raise the spiritually dead to life; and only God has the power to raise from spiritual death and to give the gift of life. The same appeal to the *works* that he did was made in the synoptic record, notably enough at the point where the Baptist sent his disciples to ask whether Jesus were he who was to come, or whether they must wait for another (Matt. 11²⁻⁶; Luke 7¹⁸⁻²³). The evidence of Christ's works is clearly rated highly, but it is not by any means final; there were those in Jerusalem who saw his works at Passover time, and believed in his name, though Jesus would not trust himself to them (2²³,²⁴). Yet to refuse to accept the testimony of the works is culpable.

༒

30
'*my judgement is just*': 'God is a righteous judge' (Psalm 7¹¹) – in spite of many appearances to the contrary! The Psalmist, like Job, finds many facts of life in conflict with what he understands righteous judgement to be. The Christian trust in God has never been able to accept a simple 'justice' of reward and punishment such as governs men's courts of law. Paul has shown how completely the idea of 'justification by faith' (acquittal from a plea of guilty at the divine tribunal) is both nonsensical in a human court and yet actual and *just* (in a new transcendent sense) in the divine court (see especially Romans 8³¹ᶠᶠ, where the prosecuting counsel is to be God, who 'acquits', and the judge to pass sentence is to be Christ, who died, rose and continually intercedes for man!).

31
'*If I bear witness to myself, my testimony is not true*': This seems to contra-

dict 8¹⁴: 'Even if I do bear witness to myself, my testimony is true'.
See exegesis and note.

32

'*I know that the testimony which he bears to me is true*': Some variant
readings have 'You know'. They cannot claim to represent the original
text, but their appearance lends weight to the view that the 'other'
witness is John the Baptist, for Jesus would not at this point of the
discussion tell the Jews that they knew that the witness of the Father
concerning him was true.

34

It would be quite possible, and on the interpretation offered, possibly
better, to translate 'testimony which I receive is from *a* man'.

35

'*you were willing to rejoice for a while in his light*': Rejoice represents a
very strong word in the Greek. The synoptic narratives suggest that
John was very popular for a time, eliciting response from 'all the
country of Judea, and all the people of Jerusalem' (Mark 1⁵). But now
he was forgotten by the Jews.

The Fathers of the early Church applied Psalm 132¹⁷ to the Baptist:
'I have prepared a lamp for my anointed.'

36

'*the testimony which I have is greater than that of John*': One reading
yields the translation: 'I who am greater than John have the witness',
though the point seems really to be that Jesus has a greater witness than
John in that he does works appropriate only to the Father whereas John
did not – and that such works constituted a witness from the Father
himself. Jesus speaks of his works as the Father's 'gift' – another small
but significant indication of the extraordinarily close unity between
Father and Son, for the Son originates no *works* on his own, but only
those given him by the Father.

5³⁷⁻⁴⁷   THE FATHER AS WITNESS

³⁷*And the Father who sent me has himself borne witness to me. His voice
you have never heard, his form you have never seen;* ³⁸*and you do not have
his word abiding in you, for you do not believe him whom he has sent.* ³⁹*You*

search the scriptures, because you think that in them you have eternal life;
and it is they that bear witness to me; 40*yet you refuse to come to me that you*
may have life. 41*I do not receive glory from men.* 42*But I know that you have*
not the love of God within you. 43*I have come in my Father's name, and you*
do not receive me; if another comes in his own name, him you will receive.
44*How can you believe, who receive glory from one another and do not seek*
the glory that comes from the only God? 45*Do not think that I shall accuse*
you to the Father; it is Moses who accuses you, on whom you set your hope.
46*If you believed Moses, you would believe me, for he wrote of me.* 47*But*
if you do not believe his writings, how will you believe my words?'

Witness from John. Witness from works. Next follows witness from
God himself in scripture. Jesus begins by telling the Jews that the
Father who has sent him has borne witness to him. He reminds the
Jews that they had never heard God's voice or seen his form. But God
has a 'word' which he speaks to men. And men who have God's
'word' abiding in them can hear and understand the 'word' that
God speaks. The Jews, for all their spiritual heritage (and that, as
Paul rehearses in Romans 9⁴,⁵ was considerable), cannot be said to have
God's word abiding in them, or they would have recognized the
Word that was God speaking to them in Jesus Christ. Jesus then proceeds to more particular argument: *'You search the scriptures* [i.e. the
whole of the Old Testament] *because you think that in them you have*
eternal life' (5³⁹). A Rabbinical saying on this point runs: 'He who
has acquired the words of the law [Torah] has acquired eternal life'*,
meaning by eternal life an inheritance in the age to come. Jesus
affirms, by contrast, that far from having the secret and gift of eternal
life in themselves, the scriptures do no more than point forward
prophetically to him. There, supremely, in the written word God
gives his word of testimony to the Word incarnate.

From v. 40 to the end of the chapter there is a tragic exposition of
the failure of the Jews. It begins *'Yet'*, or better, 'And yet', for all
the witnesses you have had – John the Baptist, the works I have done,
and the scriptures that speak of me – you will not come to me, where
come is more than physical approach, as 'following' in the synoptics
was more than walking behind Jesus. To come is to believe, and more
than 'mere' belief; it is believing, and trusting, and obeying, to the

---

* *Pirqe Aboth,* 2⁸.

uttermost. The Jews refuse this loyalty and love to Jesus, which would be their salvation. Yet what Jesus is seeking from them is not the sort of applause which leaders often look for and receive from their followers. He does not receive *glory* (here in its secular meaning of repute or honour) from men; he has the only *glory* that matters, the glory which he later says he has shared with his Father since before the foundation of the world (17²⁴). Jesus is not complaining out of any hurt pride, but from deep compassion for his people, who do not have a true love for God in them, for that would constitute for them, as for him, complete freedom from reliance upon the praises of men (cf. Matt. 6¹,²,⁵,⁷,¹⁶ where even the practices of religion have become in fact a display for the applause of men). Jesus has come in the *name*, i.e. in the power and spirit, of God, and the Jews should therefore have received him, as the beloved son of the God they professed to love. But so much are they separated from that love of God that finds its proper satisfaction in his praise and his glory alone, that they reject Jesus, though remaining perfectly ready to accept others who come in their own name, but seeking praise from men, and offering praise in return. Jesus poses the unanswerable question: 'How can men who seek praise from one another really believe in the one who comes with the glory that transcends, as it silences, all mortal search for praise and glory?'

Once more imagination may suppose that some questioner has intervened. He would have seen the force of the argument that Jesus put forward, and thought to himself, and eventually voiced his thoughts: 'What if all that he says is true? What sort of devastating report on us will he be able to make to the Father in the day of judgement?' This is the kind of transition that Jesus now makes. He disclaims any intention of accusing the Jews to the Father. In the great and final judgement he will be the Judge, not the prosecuting counsel! The prosecuting counsel will be Moses, for Moses wrote to bear witness to Jesus, and in rejecting Jesus the Jews are really rejecting Moses and dishonouring the one they think they honour. So the argument has come full circle. The Jews began by using Moses to accuse Jesus; now Jesus pointedly tells them that, far from that being the case, the events of that sabbath in Jerusalem are such that Moses will use as a charge against the Jews, a charge of unbelief, of unbelief in Christ, and consequently of unbelief in the very scriptures they thought to have used on Moses' own authority against him. If they cannot believe what Moses has had to say in prophetic foresight, how can they believe what Jesus says in divine and overflowing fulfilment?

ומם

37
'the Father who sent me has himself borne witness to me': The perfect tense of the Greek, indicating something that has happened in the past with consequences continuing to the present, could reasonably be held to cover the witness that the Father has already borne in the works Jesus had already done; or the prophetic witness which had been so distinctive an element in Israel's history; or the scriptures in which the prophetic testimony to Christ had received permanent form; or possibly all three. It is probable that at this point the evangelist is passing from the indirect witness that God bears to the Son in his works, to the witness that he bears in the hearts of those who accept that indirect testimony. The point is well put in 1 John 5⁹, ¹⁰: 'If we receive the testimony of men, the testimony of God is greater; for this is the testimony of God that he has borne witness to his Son. He who believes in the Son of God has the testimony in himself.' This is the direct witness of the Father to men, what Calvin in a later age called the internal testimony of the Holy Spirit. Paul put the same point in his own way by saying that 'no one can say "Jesus is Lord" except by the Holy Spirit' (1 Cor. 12³). If this be the right kind of interpretation, then the following phrases become quite clear. The Father has borne witness in the hearts of those who have believed on the Son, but this does not include the Jews, because the Jews will not believe. Of course the Jews rightly hold that God is both invisible and inaudible; he neither speaks with a human voice nor appears in a human form so that he could be summoned to court as a witness. 'And yet', for such is the force of the *and* at the commencement of v. 38, in spite of the true witness which the Father is willing to bear, the Jews do not have the internal testifier: his word does not abide in them. To the reader of the gospel this phrase cannot but bring back the teaching of the Prologue about the Word that had tabernacled among men.

39
'You search the scriptures': The verb *search* can be, as to its form, either indicative or imperative. The indicative gives by far the better sense.

'and it is they that bear witness to me': once more for *and* read 'and yet'.

43
This verse repeats, in the circumstances after the sabbath healing, the

truth stated in the prologue at 1^{11}: 'He came to his own home, and his own people received him not.'

'*if another comes in his own name*': Various attempts have been made to identify the 'other' who might be thought to evoke loyalty from the Jews. Bar Cochba (*c.* A.D. 132) has been suggested, but his date is too late if the dating of the gospel accepted in the Introduction be right. It seems quite unnecessary to suppose that any particular personage was in mind, or needed to be in mind. The statement has full significance without.

44

The verse foreshadows the fierce contrast between the glory, the good reputation that men often seek and desire from one another, and the only truly satisfying 'glory' or 'reputation' which, though it count for nothing on earth (Phil. 2^7), is the only real because the only permanent reputation – the *glory* of the Father which Jesus shared eternally (17^{24}).

46

'*If you believed Moses*': The Jews, of course, thought that they knew what Moses said, and that they believed it. They did not really know what Moses said, for he really spoke of Christ, and so they could not be truly said even to believe Moses.

John 6^{1–71}

Deed and Word: 2
'He will feed his flock like a shepherd'
The Feeding of the Five Thousand —
The Fourth Sign

Mark 6$^{30-56}$
Mark 8$^{14-21}$
Exodus 16$^{12-21}$, $^{31, 35}$
Mark 6$^{1-6}$
Mark 14$^{17-25}$
Mark 8$^{27-33}$

In ch. 5 John began his profound retelling of certain typical synoptic 'miracle situations'. He continues this task in ch. 6, though with two important differences: first, he makes use, for the only time in his work, of a miracle story told by all three synoptists; and second, he contrives, at the same time, to use the occasion to bring the Galilean ministry to a close, and to indicate, with more detail and insight, some of the reasons why the Galileans who, according to the synoptic narrative, had much supported him failed to continue to the end.

The fact that this miracle story alone of all such gospel narratives appears in all four gospels is sufficient to assure the reader that he is to engage in a very important task as he tries to understand John's particular treatment of it; it will become clear as the exegesis proceeds what differences there are between John's account and that given in the other three gospels, and what their significance is. But there are one or two matters that are best discussed before the exegesis proper begins. In the first place it must be noted that John follows the versions of Mark and Matthew rather than of Luke; at least in this respect, that he follows the story of the miraculous feeding with that of a miraculous walking on the water. In view of a certain tendency of the evangelist to follow the theological leads of Luke, this needs some examination. Has John kept the story of the walking on the water just out of respect for an older tradition? It would seem not, in view of the fact that he can follow Luke in passing directly from the story of the feeding to that of Peter's confession. If John has kept the difficult story of the water-walking in his narrative of the feeding, before the discourse on it is given, it would seem to indicate that he regarded it as an essential part of the material as he set it down. Yet for the most part commentators have not been successful in discerning such a unity, or even thinking its possibility worth exploring. But if the position suggested in the Introduction (pp. 67ff) be correct, then this whole chapter, with the story of the feeding, of the attempt to make Jesus king, of the walking on the water and with the great discourse is a unity. Such a unity can be not improperly discerned.

John tells his readers how at Passover time (a detail provided only by him, and therefore theologically suggestive) Jesus went up into the hills, followed by a multitude of people. These were fed miraculously upon five barley loaves and two dried pickled fish. Before the miracle took place Philip and Andrew had disclosed their own supposition that Jesus needed some material upon which to work his wonders if the vast crowd were to be fed; and after it the crowd had been so impressed by the ample provision of food that they had tried to make Jesus their (messianic) king. Jesus withdrew alone to the hills, and his disciples set out before sunset for the far shore of the lake by boat. After nightfall they were surprised by a storm, and while it was raging were frightened to see Jesus walking towards them on the sea. He reassured them with the pregnant saying '*I am; do not be afraid*'. It is here that the significance of the walking on the water for John can be seen. Jesus is showing his disciples that he needs no resources outside himself in order to bring to his people the succour and the salvation that they need. The disciples were saved just by his coming. Thus the evangelist prepares for the discourse which is to follow, in which Jesus states that he is himself the real bread by which men really live. And he prepares similarly for other passages later in the gospel in which the bare '*I am*' is followed by a series of predicates: 'the bread of life' (6³⁵); 'the light of the world' (8¹²); 'the door of the sheep' (10⁷); 'the good shepherd' (10¹¹); 'the resurrection and the life' (11²⁵); 'the way, the truth and the life' (14⁶); 'the true vine' (15¹). Jesus is this in and of himself; this fulness is himself; he draws on nothing outside of himself; it is of 'this fulness we have all received' (1¹⁶).

But the walking on the water serves one further purpose in John's narrative. The crowd discover on the following morning that Jesus is no longer on their side of the lake, and that he had had no boat to cross the sea. So they make use of visiting craft, and go in search of him, seeking further light on a second miracle. Thus John gathers them with Jesus and the disciples in the synagogue at Capernaum for the great discourse on the bread of life. The discourse proceeds with majestic rhythm from its simple start to its profound climax. Jesus first establishes in dialogue with the crowd what the real bread from heaven is, and how it is provided (6^{26-33}). When the crowd clamour for such bread he identifies himself as the bread of life and adds for the Galilean audience the truth he had put to the Judean Nicodemus (3^{13}) that he had come down from heaven (6^{35-40}). This in turn occasions some resentment among the Jews, who argue about his family descent; Jesus responds by telling them that such discussion will not produce belief, for which only the instruction of God is adequate (6^{41-7}). He then restates the great theme of himself as the bread of life, and draws out the consequences both for men who receive it, and for himself who gives it. For himself it means yielding up his life in death (6^{48-51}). The Jews not unnaturally engage in sharp dispute as to how Jesus can give his flesh to eat, and Jesus proceeds to enlarge upon this, and finally to draw the last comparison between the inadequate bread given to Israel of old, and the wholly adequate bread of eternal life which he provides in his flesh and blood for the new people of God, his disciples (6^{52-9}).

John next draws many synoptic passages together as he tells of a great sifting of Galilean disciples which resulted from this incident as thus interpreted. Finally the same miracle and teaching is put to the Twelve as the touchstone of their loyalty; and even though Peter protests their desire to remain with their master, Jesus reminds them that they cannot even take his choice of them for granted. For one of those chosen will betray him (6^{60-71}).

It has often been claimed that the discourse in ch. 6 is really a 'eucharistic discourse'. There is certainly a good deal which a Christian worshipper will find speaking to him in terms of his own eucharistic experience; but it is very doubtful if the discourse is about the eucharist as such. Certainly John is writing here, as elsewhere, from what has been called an 'end-perspective' which in this chapter includes the eucharist as well as the crucifixion, the resurrection and the bestowal of the Spirit. But the end-perspective is used to look at an actual historical situation, an occasion when Jesus fed five thousand people miraculously. It is this historical situation that is being examined and exposed, partly through a deft use of synoptic material, and partly through the addition of material from another tradition associated with the same historical situation. The result is to present the occasion in, as it were, a three-dimensional perspective: one perspective is from the past, and the events of the day recorded are set out in terms of the feeding on manna by the Israelites under Moses in the wilderness; another perspective is from the (then) present, and the occasion is set out as over against the contemporary celebration of the Jewish Passover; and the last perspective is the Christian 'end-perspective' which includes the cross, the resurrection, the ascension, the gift of the Spirit, and the celebration of the eucharist in the Church at Ephesus. Thus John is able to give 'body' and 'depth' to the synoptic narrative, and expose for his readers those deeper truths about the historic occasion that they might well have missed had they not been privileged to read his richly annotated description of the feeding and the walking on the water. John, as has been said, 'stays with his historical situation' (Introduction, p. 57); but he stays with it as focused under the triple perspective of past, present and future. And that is possible, and in the end necessary, because Jesus Christ is the Word who was in the beginning with God (1^1), who has been incarnate in the flesh (1^{14}), and is now returned to that glory which he shared with the Father before the foundation of the world (17^{24}). No single perspective, no one dimension, is adequate to portray the deeds and words of him who was the Word incarnate in human flesh in historic time. In setting the deed and the words of Jesus in this triple perspective John has provided a most discerning and valuable commentary on the synoptic record.

THE SIGN OF THE BREAD

6 *After this Jesus went to the other side of the Sea of Galilee, which is the Sea of Tibe'ri-as. ²And a multitude followed him, because they saw the signs which he did on those who were diseased. ³Jesus went up into the hills, and there sat down with his disciples. ⁴Now the Passover, the feast of the Jews, was at hand. ⁵Lifting up his eyes, then, and seeing that a multitude was coming to him, Jesus said to Philip, 'How are we to buy bread, so that*

these people may eat?' ⁶This he said to test him, for he himself knew what he would do. ⁷Philip answered him, 'Two hundred denarii ᵃ would not buy enough bread for each of them to get a little.' ⁸One of his disciples, Andrew, Simon Peter's brother, said to him, ⁹'There is a lad here who has five barley loaves and two fish; but what are they among so many?' ¹⁰Jesus said, 'Make the people sit down.' Now there was much grass in the place; so the men sat down, in number about five thousand. ¹¹Jesus then took the loaves, and when he had given thanks, he distributed them to those who were seated; so also the fish, as much as they wanted. ¹²And when they had eaten their fill, he told his disciples, 'Gather up the fragments left over, that nothing may be lost.' ¹³So they gathered them up and filled twelve baskets with fragments from the five barley loaves, left by those who had eaten.

a The denarius was worth about $9\frac{1}{2}$d

After this, says John, i.e. at some time when all that had been recorded in ch. 5 can be presupposed, Jesus went from the western side of the Sea of Galilee to the eastern. A large crowd, impressed by his healing of those who were diseased, followed him. This Galilean multitude was thus in the same state as were the Jews of 2²³, who had seen certain signs, and had a certain belief, but to whom Jesus did not 'trust himself'. The Galileans had likewise seen signs (6²), and had some sort of belief in Jesus (6¹⁴, ¹⁵), but Jesus did not trust himself to them, knowing what was in them (6⁶⁴). To the Marcan opening of the story John adds two pieces of information – that Jesus went up into the hills or mountains, and that the Passover was drawing near (6³, ⁴). The reference to the hill is John's way of incorporating the statement from Mark that before the feeding took place Jesus taught the people 'many things' (Mark 6³⁴), and of adding to it the rich allusiveness of Matthew's setting of the Sermon on the Mount where Jesus is depicted as a new Moses delivering a new law to the new people of God. This simple but profound historiographical device is given added depth in John who alone of all the evangelists informs the reader that the feeding and the teaching took place as the feast of the Passover was drawing near, so that both action and discourse are to be seen in that particular perspective.

When the disciples rejoined Jesus at Jacob's Well and asked him to eat of the food they had purchased in the Samaritan town, Jesus bade them 'lift up their eyes' and see the 'harvest' of the seed he had been sowing, a harvest made up of Samaritans who had come out from the town to see and hear Jesus for themselves. Now, seated with his disciples on the hillside he *lifts up his eyes* and sees a multitude coming to him. Again he puts a question to his disciples as represented by Philip: '*How are we to buy bread, so that these people may eat?*' (6⁵). After all that had happened at Jacob's Well, it would not have been surprising, and certainly not impossible, for Philip to reply to the effect that to give them real food would be to bring them to obedience to God's will (4³⁴); but Philip has not yet perceived the new situation in this light, and his reply is still on the quite restricted human level: 'It would not be possible to feed them all, not even if we had 200 denarii to spend' (a denarius was a day's wage for an unskilled labourer) (6⁷). Andrew, with somewhat greater insight into the resourcefulness of his master, said, '*There is a lad here who has five barley loaves and two fish,*' but he could not refrain from adding '*but what are they among so many?*' (6⁹). Evidently Andrew thought that even this meagre amount of food was not entirely insignificant in the hands of Jesus, but was not at all sure that his insight was right. But Jesus, keeping the initiative that John has already claimed for him above all the synoptic writers (none of them tell that he first raised the question about feeding the crowd – least of all that he raised it before they had reached him!), asks the disciples to make the crowds recline on the grass as they would recline for a feast, and as, in the synoptic story, Jesus and the Twelve reclined at the Last Supper. So the crowd take their places, and the great marriage supper of the Lamb (Rev. 19⁶⁻⁹) is foreshadowed and pre-enacted on a Galilean hill.

What took place then is reported in such a way as to suggest to the reader that what took place summed up Jewish experience in the past, reflected their own Passover experience, and already partook in some sense of the form and substance of the Last Supper and the Eucharist. The words that appear in 6¹¹ so plainly reflect both the Jewish custom of giving thanks for meat and the Christian practice and ritual of the Eucharist, that the reader cannot suppose that the only, or even the most important, thing that happened was for five thousand physical hungers to have been satisfied. Yet the fact of adequate, and more than adequate, physical satisfaction is clearly stated. When all had eaten their fill (6¹²) Jesus told his disciples '*Gather up the fragments left over, that nothing may be lost*' (6¹²). The reason given for gathering up anticipates the use of the same words in connexion with the work of the Son as he receives from the Father those who are given to him: 'That I should lose nothing of all that he has given me . . .' (6^{39}; cf. 17^{12}). That the disciples should thus be set the task of gathering in the scattered fragments of the Father's provisions is a parabolic anticipation of their sharing in the fulfilment of Christ's sacrifice in 'gathering into one the children of God who are scattered abroad' (11^{52}). Twelve baskets full of fragments were collected, a guarantee of the miraculous nature of the feeding, and of the satisfaction that Jesus had given to the crowd. A notable sign indeed!

ജ്ഞ

1
Tiberias was not built until about A.D. 26, so that mention of it here reflects the situation of the author rather than of the historical participants in the story. The last work done among Galilean disciples is thus placed in Gentile territory.

2
To follow because of signs done is precisely what the Jews in Jerusalem did (2^{23}). Many a potential disciple is in this questing attitude.

4
Though the nearness of the Passover is mentioned for theological rather than historical reasons, there is no need to reject the statement as unhistorical. In particular there is no need, and no grammatical justification for supposing that it refers to a Passover just celebrated: nor is it likely to be the passover at which Jesus was crucified. Rather is this a clear indication, in the fourth gospel, that during his ministry Jesus saw at least three Passovers in Jerusalem before he died.

5
It is important for John to underline that Jesus here, as always, took the initiative.

7
Philip's answer betrays no trace of an idea that Jesus literally had the resources in his own person to satisfy the deepest needs of men, or to provide, in an acted parable, for their physical needs.

9
Only John mentions the barley, which was used to make bread for the poor, and as grain to feed animals. The word translated *fish* was used to describe a dried and pickled fish, eaten as a 'tit-bit' with bread.

12

In the synoptics, the gathering up of the fragments is a rich appendix to the miracle, reflecting, presumably, Jewish custom and possibly 'prophetic' of eucharistic practice. John brings out its significance, which is seen in the parallel to the way he must deal with what God gives in the realm of discipleship – none must be lost (see 6^{39}).

13

Mark alone of the evangelists mentions fragments of fish being picked up. The concentration on the bread is another effect of an 'end-perspective' upon the writing of the gospel story.

6$^{14-15}$ THE RESPONSE OF THE GALILEANS

^{14}When the people saw the sign which he had done, they said, 'This is indeed the prophet who is to come into the world!'
    ^{15}Perceiving then that they were about to come and take him by force to make him king, Jesus withdrew again to the hills by himself.

The notable miracle met with a remarkable response. It seems to have been a quite popular estimate of Jesus that he was a prophet. All three synoptics state that the disciples reported this common view about him when Jesus asked them what men were saying about himself (Mark 8^{28} ∥). Galileans who saw him raise the son of the widow at Nain were convinced that he was 'a great prophet' (Luke 7^{16}); and the chief priests and the Pharisees knew that he was so regarded (Matt. 21^{46}). In the fourth gospel it has already been stated that John the Baptist was, on his own confession, not *the prophet*; the woman at the well perceived that Jesus was *a prophet*; now something more is said: Jesus is '*the prophet* who is to come into the world' (6^{14}). The only comparable incident in the synoptic story is found in Matthew's narrative of the triumphal entry: 'when he entered Jerusalem, all the city was stirred, saying, "Who is this?" And the crowds said, "This is the prophet Jesus from Nazareth of Galilee"' (Matt. 21^{11}) which, if it be punctuated in one way, could be taken as a claim by the crowd that Jesus was the *prophet*. But the Galilean crowd is quite explicit in the fourth gospel: 'This is *indeed* the prophet' where *indeed* means 'really',

286

'genuinely', 'in truth'. The basis for the title of 'the prophet' is probably in Deuteronomy 18^{15ff}, where Moses tells of God's promise to
raise up for his people another prophet like himself. In view of the
part that the figure of Moses plays in the discourse, and the allusiveness of John's placing of the feeding upon a hill, the reader may well
accept this basis, even though only Christians and Samaritans gave
the passage a strictly messianic content. But the crowd's words were
accompanied by action, and Jesus perceived, doubtless in the evangelist's belief by the exercise of his supernatural powers, that the
intention was to make him king. But that was completely to misunderstand his mission and purpose, and Jesus withdrew once more to the
hills. In the later chapters of the gospel John is much concerned with
some exposition of the true kingship of Christ; here the style and
manner of kingship sought for him by the crowd is wholly 'of this
world', and must therefore be rejected.

This incident is peculiar to the fourth gospel. Why has John thought
fit to preserve it, and in particular, why has he woven it into the
narrative of the miraculous feeding? Historically it might be said that
John is presumably dependent upon some tradition known to him in
Ephesus. Theologically a tradition that placed an attempt to make
Jesus king after the feeding of the five thousand would be one which
pointed directly to the great issues raised by the sight of the new
Moses feeding the new Israel with 'bread from heaven'; the whole
issue of whether the kingdom of such a benefactor should be of this
world or not is peculiarly raised by the miracle. Formally it can be
pointed out that just as the Jerusalem ministry had a climax before the
sacrifice of the Son in a triumphal entry where he was hailed as king,
so the Galilean ministry before its close is thus endowed with an
acclamation as eager and as mistaken as that of the Jerusalem crowd.
It has to be said in addition that theologically speaking all the questions of the power, the authority and the purposes of the miracle
worker are raised by any account of such a miraculous multiplication
of the loaves. If Jesus does this miracle, what sort of power does he
exercise?; for what ends will he use it?; and what is his destiny among
men as he uses it? Above all, what sort and dignity of person is he
who can thus command plenty in deficiency? The story is rightly an
indispensable part of the Johannine narrative.

‽

15

The synoptists state that at the end of the Galilean ministry the disciples can report to Jesus that the Galileans believe him to be John the Baptist, Elijah, Jeremiah or one of the prophets – i.e. some figure heralding the expected Messiah. Here the belief is evidently that Jesus is messiah, and must be brought to take his throne. If this be not, as it probably is not, a Johannine parallel to the second temptation in Luke, it at least shows that such a temptation was not an impossibility.

6^{16-21} THE DISCIPLES ON THE LAKE

[16]*When evening came, his disciples went down to the sea,* [17]*got into a boat, and started across the sea to Caper'na-um. It was now dark, and Jesus had not yet come to them.* [18]*The sea rose because a strong wind was blowing.* [19]*When they had rowed about three or four miles,*[a] *they saw Jesus walking on the sea and drawing near to the boat. They were frightened,* [20] *but he said to them, 'It is I; do not be afraid.'* [21]*Then they were glad to take him into the boat, and immediately the boat was at the land to which they were going.*

a Greek *twenty-five or thirty stadia*

The question has not improperly been raised whether this section of the narrative includes a miracle or not. Traditionally it has been generally assumed that when the disciples saw Jesus walking *on the sea and drawing near to the boat*, he was engaged in a miraculous action. But recently some scholars have questioned whether this traditional assumption is right, and not simply on general grounds of suspicion of the miraculous element as such, but on particular grounds of the actual telling of the story. Paradoxically it seems that the main points of the story can be regarded as made whether the walking on the water be regarded as miraculous or not. Bernard in his commentary (I.C.C., pp. 185 ff.) points out that the same Greek words that are used in 6^{19} to state the fact (if such it be) that Jesus walked on the water are used in precisely the same form in 21^{1}, where no one would think of translating them 'on the sea' but only as 'by the sea'. He therefore argues that they should be so translated here, and the commentator must suppose that after rowing some three or four miles in stormy conditions the disciples were not, as they supposed in the overcast darkness, in the very middle of the lake, but, unknown to themselves, almost at the shore. Consequently they could see Jesus walking 'by the sea', even though they thought at first that he was walking 'on the sea'. Further, when they attempted to do what they wanted to do and take him into the boat they found that they were at once at land. So the comforting words of Jesus '*It is I; do not be afraid*' (6^{20}) are set in a quite non-miraculous context, though they lose none of their theological or religious force thereby. Alongside these observations it is stated that had John used the same Greek words but followed the preposition with an accusative instead of a genitive case (as in fact Matthew does in Matt. 14^{25}, the parallel passage in that gospel) it 'would indicate beyond question that Jesus literally "walked on the sea"' (Bernard, p. 186). But not even that point can be made unambiguously, for in this very section of John the narrative begins with the statement that the disciples *went down to the sea* (6^{16}) and that affirmation uses the Greek preposition with the accusative case, though no one would ever suggest that it indicates 'beyond question' that the disciples 'literally "walked on the sea"'. The truth is, of course, that the reader must decide from the context whether a particular combination of preposition and noun must be taken to imply a literal walking on the sea or not.

The present writer is inclined to the view that both the synoptic stories of walking on the water and this in the fourth gospel are intended to be accounts of miracles. The synoptics seem to use them to illustrate their conviction that Jesus possessed the power, ascribed in the Old Testament to Yahweh, of having his way 'through the sea' and 'his path through the great waters' although his 'footprints were not seen' (Psalm 77^{19}); in a word their miracles are basically theological statements about the person of Jesus Christ. And this, with much more manifest self-consciousness, is the purpose of John's narrative. At evening time, before dark, the disciples set out in a boat (thus disclosing that there was not a great number present) and began the journey back to Capernaum. It grew dark, and Jesus was still not with them when a strong wind blew up, and the sea became rough. They had rowed about three or four miles when they saw Jesus *walking on* [or by] *the water* and drawing near to them. They were frightened – the only time in the fourth gospel where this is recorded of the disciples' attitude to Jesus, in contrast to the synoptic story where on several occasions the disciples and others are said to be afraid at the presence, the deeds or the words of Jesus (e.g. Mark 4⁴¹; 9³²; 10³²; Matt. 17⁶; Luke 8³⁵; 9³⁴). In the synoptic telling of this story Mark and Matthew put Jesus' words into a much more 'human' and physical setting: Jesus says to the men in the boat: 'Take heart, it is I; have no fear' (Mark 6⁵⁰; Matt. 14²⁷). The central affirmation of this threefold assurance is composed of the words 'It is I'. These are the words John emphasizes in their spiritual significance by placing them at the beginning of what Jesus said, omitting entirely the more human comfort of the words 'Take heart'. The reasons for this have already been suggested. The disciples did not realize at the time of the feeding that Jesus needed no resources outside himself in order to satisfy men's real needs; all his resources were in himself, were himself, and himself is enough. This is taught by the deed of walking on the water and by the word accompanying it. He comes to them; all then is well, and they are safe at land. This speedy coming to land has been recognized as another 'miracle within a miracle', reflecting in the life and authority of Jesus the power ascribed to Yahweh in e.g. Psalm 107²³⁻³², where distracted mariners are 'brought to their desired haven' by 'the wonderful works' of Yahweh. But this incident is also capable of being woven into a non-miraculous account of the whole episode; for the disciples, on the non-miraculous reading of the narrative, were not in the middle of the lake as they supposed, but very near to the land which they had been unable to see through the stormy conditions. The present writer is confident that the evangelist would not be so concerned with the outcome of a twentieth-century debate about the possibility and extent of miracle as with the question, much more important to him, as to the sole sufficiency of Christ as the satisfaction of the real hunger that men experience as men.

The words that Jesus spoke to the disciples in the boat need further comment. In the story of the Samaritan woman Jesus had used the same verbal form to indicate to the woman that he was indeed the Messiah expected by her own people (see above, p. 219). But at this point John is beginning a series of statements beginning with the great words '*I am*', which are now used without any predicate. 'I am', says Jesus, 'don't be frightened'; and the saying fits both the immediate peril of oarsmen in a storm, and the ultimate peril of death to a human soul. The one and only possible deliverance is in nothing other than the person and the work of Jesus, the Word or Son of God incarnate, who is one with the Father, and who has life in himself. Here in this story it is asserted that 'I am' is with his new people. In later chapters different characteristics of his presence and activity will be stated and described. (See above p. 73, and below, pp. 299, 351, 396ff, 428, 504, 518ff.)

ﬡﬡﬡ

17
The association of darkness and the absence of Jesus is more than coincidental; it represents the condition of all men who try to live without the illumination brought by the Light of the World.

20
'I am': In view of the points made in the exegesis regarding the distinctive treatment that John gives these words when compared with the Synoptists, it is difficult to be content with Barrett's judgement that any 'special associations of the words' clinging to them here 'are overtones at most'!

21
The R.S.V. seems to have accepted a suggestion by Torrey that the verb 'wished', which is the Greek text here, was a mistranslation of an underlying Aramaic word meaning 'rejoiced greatly'. By no verbal device is it possible to avoid telling this story so that both a miraculous and a non-miraculous interpretation is possible.

6²²⁻²⁵   THE CURIOSITY OF THE CROWD

²²*On the next day the people who remained on the other side of the sea saw that there had been only one boat there, and that Jesus had not entered the boat with his disciples, but that his disciples had gone away alone.* ²³*However, boats from Tibe'ri-as came near the place where they ate the bread after the Lord had given thanks.* ²⁴*So when the people saw that Jesus was not there, nor his disciples, they themselves got into the boats and went to Caper'na-um, seeking Jesus.*

²⁵*When they found him on the other side of the sea they said to him, 'Rabbi, when did you come here?'*

This short paragraph is not lacking in confusion. The best way to make sense of it is to translate the verb *saw* as a pluperfect 'had seen'; this leaves the reader with the impression that on the day of the feeding the crowd had noticed that only one boat was at the landing stage, and that they had noticed that Jesus had not gone in the boat with the disciples. This produces considerable curiosity in the crowd which was now aware that Jesus had departed too, though apparently without any transport. What had he done, and where had he gone? They were able to make use of boats from Tiberias, and went to Capernaum to look for Jesus, possibly anticipating that Jesus had wrought another 'physical' miracle. Yet sober criticism can well conclude that v. 23 is a gloss. Barrett writes:

'The narrative use of "the Lord", and the precise reference to the eucharist contained in the repetition of the verb from v. 11, together with the singular "bread" (a reference to the eucharistic loaf?) and the mention of the lately founded Tiberias, are the proofs offered that this verse is a gloss; the last two are not in themselves sufficient.' (Barrett, p. 237.)

In any event the important part of the text is reached when the crowd that had fed upon the miraculous food reached Jesus and found him in the synagogue at Capernaum. They had perhaps been driven to seek him by the prospect of finding that another 'physical' miracle had been accomplished, and indeed the question they put to him seems to seek confirmation of such a view (6^{25}). The evangelist makes it very plain what Jesus did to their curiosity, however it was aroused.

ॐ

23
Bernard may well be right in describing this verse as a later gloss; if so, it is entirely in keeping with Johannine historiography for it sees the feeding from the end-perspective of the eucharist. And why not?

25
on the other side of the sea: The last discourse to the Galileans is about to be given, on Galilean soil. It is parallel to the teaching in the synagogue at Nazareth in the synoptics: his physical, ancestral *patris* rejects him.

²⁶*Jesus answered them, 'Truly, truly, I say to you, you seek me, not because you saw signs, but because you ate your fill of the loaves.* ²⁷*Do not labour for the food which perishes, but for the food which endures to eternal life, which the Son of man will give to you; for on him has God the Father set his seal.'* ²⁸*Then they said to him, 'What must we do, to be doing the work of God?'* ²⁹*Jesus answered them, 'This is the work of God, that you believe in him whom he has sent.'* ³⁰*So they said to him, 'Then what sign do you do, that we may see, and believe you? What work do you perform?* ³¹*Our fathers ate the manna in the wilderness; as it is written, "He gave them bread from heaven to eat."'* ³²*Jesus then said to them, 'Truly, truly, I say to you, it was not Moses who gave you the bread from heaven; my Father gives you the true bread from heaven.* ³³*For the bread of God is that which comes down from heaven, and gives life to the world.'* ³⁴*They said to him, 'Lord, give us this bread always.'*

The discourse which now follows exhibits a natural development in four stages. The first establishes the nature of the food by which God satisfies the real hunger of men (26–34). The second identifies that satisfaction with Jesus Christ himself (35–40). The third deals with the question how are men to recognize Jesus as the divine bread, and states the consequences of such a belief for them, and the tragic cost for Jesus in giving himself as the heavenly bread (41–51); while the fourth expounds how in his self-offering to God on the cross and to men in the eucharist Jesus Christ is and remains the true bread of life (52–59).

Verbal appearances suggest that Jesus was discourteous enough not to answer the question that the crowd put to him when they found him. For instead of telling them when he arrived and how long he had been in Capernaum he reminded them very directly of their estimate of the miracle of the loaves: 'Truly, truly, I say to you, you seek me, not because you saw signs, but because you ate your fill of the loaves' (6²⁶). The solemn opening itself suggests that this is an important statement, and that the evangelist wants his readers, as Jesus meant his hearers, to ponder it fully. In fact reflection on it soon reveals that Jesus has not been 'impolite', but has taken the Galileans just where they were, even though they did not know it. Their eagerness to inquire about the 'second miracle' was not an expression of their awareness that the feeding with the loaves was a profound parable of God's nourishing of the soul, but, as their 'physical' question showed, a direct result of their hope that the supernatural powers Jesus had displayed might be put to their service in providing food and a Jewish empire. Nothing could be done for them or profitably said to them until this grave misconception had at least been exposed. Thus without any direct reference to the problem, John has brought the misconceiving Galileans back from their absence from Jesus, by means of the 'second miracle', so that they may hear from him of their own error, and of his eternal truth. They did not look on the feeding as a sign, but simply as a satisfaction of physical hunger. Here Jesus uses the word *sign* in the sense in which it has already been used of the Jews in Jerusalem who 'saw the signs which he did' and 'believed in his name' (2^{23}). It was not the highest form of faith, for Jesus did not trust himself to the Jews of Jerusalem; but it was an indispensable basis for going any further or any deeper, that the physical actions he did should be perceived as more-than-merely-physical. So Jesus begins where the physical appetites of men are cared for, in their daily toil. The bread which they had eaten yesterday was for them nothing more than the substance for which they toiled day by day. Men of that nation and age, and of every nation and time, know what it is to 'work for their living', to 'toil for bread'. To these Galilean 'breadwinners' Jesus went on to say '*Do not labour for the food which perishes, but for the food which endures to eternal life*' (6^{27}). Certainly the needs of the body must be cared for; but if all the labour of men, whether manual or skilled, has its end only in sustaining the life of the body, human life is mortal indeed. It perishes with the body. But it is possible to *labour* for a *bread* that nourishes something more than the body, something that can endure to eternal life. It is transparently clear that the meaning cannot yet be taken to be that the food to be sought after will endure to eternal life, but that its effect on the eater will be to bring him eternal life. Later in the discourse Jesus identifies himself with the food that bestows eternal life, and then the thought of the *food* enduring to eternal life becomes possible; but that stage has not been reached yet. The food which will have this beneficent and desirable effect will, Jesus states, be given to the Galileans by the Son of man, on whom the Father has set his seal (6^{27}). Whenever John uses the title Son of man he is making a reference, sometimes more, sometimes less direct, to the self-offering on the cross, and the glory that it brings. So here. Already Jesus is preparing his Galilean hearers for the profound truth that it will be by his death and resurrection that they will be able to attain eternal life. The subtlety of John's style is revealed in the tense of the verb '*on him* HAS *God the Father* SET *his seal*'. For the past tense may well be taken, and rightly taken, to refer to some point in the past when God can be thought to have *set his seal* to the self-testimony of the Son (in the sense of 3^{33}, where the word is used of human acceptance of Jesus' testimony as 'setting the seal' to the witness borne to Jesus) and this could well be identified in the fourth gospel with the descent of the Spirit in the form of a dove which was witnessed by John the Baptist (1^{32-34}). But the past tense may equally well stand for what in the Hebrew language is known as the 'prophetic perfect' – a past tense doing duty for a future, to indicate in some human symbol the certainty associated with the prophecy, a certainty normally associated with its having already happened. On this view the seal which the Father has set could be the crucifixion and resurrection, or, in more Johannine terms, the exaltation of the Son of man. It is not impossible, indeed it is probable, that the author made deliberate use of this pregnant ambiguity.

So far Jesus seems to have carried the Galileans with him. For they respond positively and ask: '*What must we do, to be doing the work of God?*' What is the spiritual equivalent of 'earning your bread'? The answer of Jesus is uncompromisingly exclusive; there is but one *work* that earns the food of which he now speaks, that men believe in him whom God has sent (6^{29}). The Galileans manifestly, by their answer, realize that Jesus is making claims for himself in this reply, and they therefore ask him '*What sign do you do, that we may see, and believe you? What work do you perform?*' In this they show themselves to be but children of their time; for this was precisely the attitude that was adopted even at Jesus' crucifixion. The chief priests and scribes said, even if in derision, 'Let the Christ, the King of Israel, come down from the cross, that we may see and believe' (Mark 15^{32}). The required demonstration of supernatural power would doubtless have evoked 'belief' of a sort; but it would not have been the kind that Jesus wanted, or that either the synoptics or John sought to quicken. But the Galileans took their request somewhat further, inspired no doubt by the same 'eye for the symbolic' as animated the evangelist himself. A long time ago in Israelite history, indeed at one of the points where it might be said to have begun, Moses the great leader had taught his followers, and had fed them miraculously in the wilderness. If the new leader were really 'the prophet who was to come into the world', as they had thought yesterday, would he not accomplish some miracles comparable with those recorded of Moses? In particular, was this not highly probable, for there were expectations current that the new Messiah would equal or surpass the wonders of Moses? What would Jesus do?

The reply given corrects the presuppositions of these remarks at the central point. Jesus points out that it was not Moses, but God, who gave the manna in the wilderness, and he adds, within the same sentence, a further important correction, that God's miraculous provision for his people is not rightly to be spoken of in the past tense in which men speak of what has passed into history; it is rightly spoken of in the present tense. And both these corrections are necessary because in the person of Jesus there is present among men not another great, or even greater prophet, but the veritable son of God, the Word incarnate. Moses may be a 'type' of the prophet who is to come; he may even, within a Christian typology, be a 'type' of Christ himself; but if the comparison with Moses results from or issues in a correlation on the human level of Moses and Jesus, then it is more misleading than helpful. Jesus had indeed 'given the bread' on the preceding day; but that did not correlate him with Moses, for it was not Moses who gave the bread to the Fathers in the wilderness. The Father whom Jesus called *mine* in a special way was the giver of that bread, and if Jesus is to be correlated with any figure in the story, it must be with him. Jesus thus stands to the new Israel in the sa relationship as Yahweh had stood to the old. This is the real meaning of what Jesus said, though it was not so understood by the Galileans; but that is normal in a Johannine discourse. Summarizing, Jesus says that '*the bread of God is that which comes down from heaven, and gives life to the world*' (6³³). Commentators discuss whether the relative in the sentence should be translated 'he who' or *that which*, and if a choice has to be made, the difficulty is great. The right answer is that Jesus is certainly intending to convey that the personal reference is right, but the Galileans typically misconstrue him to mean bread for bodily hunger. Like the woman at the well who heard of heavenly water, they ask for constant supplies of 'bread from heaven': '*Sir*, ['Sir' rather than 'Lord'] *give us this bread always*' (6^{34}).

∝∝

26

Instead of reporting on a second miracle (walking on the water) Jesus returns to the one already misunderstood – an emphasizing of its basic importance.

27

'*Do not labour for the food which perishes*': The thought is not far removed from Isa. $55^{2, 3}$.

'*which the Son of man will give*': the reference of *Son of man* is always to his death and resurrection. Hence the future tense of the verb, though Jesus is able even at this stage to satisfy men's ultimate hunger.

29

There is but one work required by God, and it is done, not in one action, but in a life of faith and trust. The Son has been sent to do God's will, and part of the evidence has already been given in the 'sealing' by the spirit at the baptism (cf. 1^{32f}), and part remains to be given by the sealing of the resurrection and exaltation in the end.

The work of God is work that pleases God, a life that conforms to his will and good pleasure.

30

There is a relation between faith and sight, but the Galileans have not conceived it correctly. Cf. 6^{40} and the story of ch. 9, where Jesus bestows sight that can *see* that he is the Son of man (or of God).

31

'*Our fathers*': all the Israelites in the wilderness. The quotation in this verse is probably derived from Neh. 9^{15}, 'Thou didst give them bread from heaven for their hunger' (cf. also Psalm 78^{24}).

32

Moses was not really the giver, and the manna was not really bread! God is the constant giver, and Christ the real food of man (cf. 1 Cor. 10^4). 'And [the fathers] all ate the same supernatural food and all drank the same supernatural drink. For they drank from the supernatural Rock which followed them; and the Rock was Christ'. Paul, like John, believed that Christ was the real substance of the Israelites' experience in the desert.

'*my Father gives you the true bread from heaven*': *True* is 'real' or 'genuine'.

The manna, like the miraculous food of yesterday, was only a parable of the real food God gives.

33

Cf. the statement in 3^{16}. The father gives; the Son comes; the Spirit, as will be seen (cf. 6^{63}), gives life!

6 ³⁵⁻⁴⁰   FOOD AND FELICITY
                          BY FAITH IN CHRIST

³⁵*Jesus said to them, 'I am the bread of life; he who comes to me shall not hunger, and he who believes in me shall never thirst. ³⁶But I said to you that you have seen me and yet do not believe. ³⁷All that the Father gives me will come to me; and him who comes to me I will not cast out. ³⁸For I have come down from heaven, not to do my own will, but the will of him who sent me; ³⁹and this is the will of him who sent me, that I should lose nothing of all that he has given me, but raise it up at the last day. ⁴⁰For this is the will of my Father, that every one who sees the Son and believes in him should have eternal life; and I will raise him up at the last day.'*

The sign done at the Pool by the Sheepgate in Jerusalem led inevitably to a discussion about the relationship of Father to Son, and to some consideration of witness as related to belief. At this point in the discussion of the miracle of the feeding of the five thousand something has to be said again about the nature of belief. For, whether they acknowledge it or not, the Galileans had seen a sign, and an adequate sign; but they had not believed. What can be said about such a situation? In dealing with it John writes for his vastly widened audience, which now includes all who have to face the problem of faith and sight. A simple literary device is one of the instruments used, for now Jesus talks not simply to Galileans, but to *Jews* (6^{41}). The reader must understand that what now follows was valid not only for the Galileans originally involved, but for the whole company of Israel, Galileans and Judeans alike; and by that expansion of the audience to realize that here, as supremely at 20^{29}, he is involved himself. Indeed the modern reader should already have felt himself embraced within those to whom Jesus has spoken; for it is the modern tendency to find the real issue of the narrative in the assertions made about the multiplication of the loaves for the satisfaction of physical hunger; and that issue cannot be avoided. But the evangelist has made it quite plain that whether a synoptic or his own account of the miracle be taken, the real issue and the ultimate stumbling-block to human credulity is not on the level of physical marvel, but on the much higher level of the divine-human nature of him who claimed to be the bread of life.

Jesus now makes explicit what has been the profound meaning of all that he has said so far; and in so doing he clears up, in the words of one commentator, the ambiguity of 6³³; Jesus had begun with the daily toil of his hearers: 'Don't work for meat which perishes, but for food which can issue in eternal life, food which cannot be earned as one earns daily bread, but which is the gift of the Son of man.' To the question what is the work to be done for the special food, Jesus answered 'There is only one work, to believe on the one whom God has sent'. The crowd, perceiving, at least to some extent, the claim Jesus was making for himself, asked what sign he would give them, and reminded him of the sign of bread from heaven that Moses had given. To this Jesus replied that Moses had not given bread from heaven, but that the real 'bread of God' is he who comes down from heaven and gives life to the world. To the persistence of his hearers in their misunderstanding Jesus now claims to be the bread of life. This is a new statement, though implicit in what he has already said. The claim recalls the passage in ch. 5 where Jesus said that the Father has life in himself, and has given the Son to have life in himself also (5²⁶). The bread of life is the bread who has life in himself, and so can bring about a condition of 'eternal life' in those who feed upon him. It must follow that to eat of this bread is to be rid of hunger, the real hunger that is peculiar to man. '*He who comes to me shall not hunger, and he who believes in me shall never thirst*' (6³⁵). In the course of this dialogue, Jesus has been setting the terms hunger, bread, life, and belief in their right relationships: 'real' bread for man is spiritual; so real '*bread from heaven*' is not matter dropping from the sky, but the incarnation of the Son of God. Life is not that which physical bread sustains, but that which is sustained between Jesus and his disciples in the relationship of belief; and this is a life that knows no death. And belief in the Son is possible to men, because the Son is incarnate and can be seen. Yet, as Jesus reminded his hearers, they have seen him and do not believe (6³⁶).

This is a great mystery; and like all other mysteries connected with the coming-in-the-flesh of the eternal Word, it cannot be solved simply in terms of what happens here in the world of time and history, but only by reference to the eternal will and purpose of God as he exercises his sovereignty over the world. In the service of that will and purpose the Word-made-flesh has a duty to perform, and he will fulfil it. The Father will give to the Son those who believe, and the Son's duty is to receive and preserve them to the end: '*All that the Father gives me will come to me; and him who comes I will not cast out*' (6³⁷). The Son's historic mission is not of his own willing or designing, but entirely an obedience to the will of the Father. So, faced by the mysterious unbelief of his hearers Jesus asserts that both they and he are unable to act without reckoning, sooner or later, with the sovereign will of the Father. The Father's will in respect of belief is that all who see the Son and believe should have eternal life. This the Son will ensure, not only in the sphere of history, but in the life of the world to come. In Mark's story of Jesus' visit to his *patris* or native place the final comment is that Jesus 'marvelled because of their unbelief' (Mark 6⁶). The word 'marvel' is characteristically used (see p. 225) for the wonder with which men see the divine, supernatural power of Jesus at work. Here in John, at a point equivalent in design to the Marcan story of the rejection in the (Galilean) *patris*, the same word is again used of Jesus' attitude to unbelief. And John makes clear that there is, in a strange sense, something of divine action even behind unbelief. All who believe do so because the Father has taught them, and Jesus receives them, gives them life, and preserves them. What mystery of the divine will then surround those who do not believe? John has not here provided an answer in terms of what a later theology has called 'double predestination': he has stated enough for human wonder, that God should call any out of their unbelief to belief and life. Nor has John dealt with divine rejection in the way that Paul came to deal with it in Romans 9⁹⁻¹¹ as a mystery that will be comprehended only in the final triumph of the Father's universal will to save (see especially Rom. 11³²). He has not yet traced unbelief to its human or divine source, but has made it quite plain that nothing less than a theological answer can be given to the question of its nature and origin.

35

In this self-identification with bread of life Jesus makes plain that he is the gift he brings. The language, as Dr Dodd reminds readers of the gospel, recalls that used of the servant in Isaiah: 'They shall feed along the ways, on all bare heights shall be their pasture; . . . for he who has pity on them will lead them, and by springs of living water will guide them' (Isa. 49⁹˒¹⁰).

35

bread of life: This is a genitive of apposition, 'bread that is life', and, because it is life, can bestow life on others.

36

The R.S.V. translates the *me* in the verse, but it should in all probability be omitted. If it is, then the remark here made by Jesus refers more directly to what he had already said at 6²⁶. They should have believed, having seen the sign of the loaves; but they mistook the sign for a mere hunger-reducing miracle!

37

To *come to* Jesus is a frequent expression in John, and occurs five times in this chapter, where the parallel expression 'believe in' gives its meaning. See above, p. 272.

In this verse Jesus begins a consideration of the nature of unbelief; but it is plain from the way he approaches it that unbelief cannot be understood on its own, but only after the nature of belief as the work of God has been properly stated and understood.

39

The Son has a mission to perform for the Father, to receive all whom the Father gives him, and to lose none. This is not a statement about the universality or otherwise of the salvation purposed by the Father; it is a consideration relevant to the problem 'Why do some persons not believe in the Son?' Jesus prepares to say something about unbelief by stating the theological character of belief as the Father's giving of a man to Christ.

40

'*every one who sees the Son*': In one sense the *Son* cannot be seen; for all that can be seen is the human Jesus, the son of Galilean parents: yet in another sense the Son may be seen – and even the Father: cf. 9³⁷˒³⁸; 12⁴⁵.

THE TRUE BREAD:
                ITS PROFIT AND ITS PRICE

⁴¹ *The Jews then murmured at him, because he said, 'I am the bread which came down from heaven.'* ⁴² *They said, 'Is not this Jesus, the son of Joseph, whose father and mother we know? How does he now say, "I have come down from heaven"?'* ⁴³ *Jesus answered them, 'Do not murmur among yourselves.* ⁴⁴ *No one can come to me unless the Father who sent me draws him; and I will raise him up at the last day.* ⁴⁵ *It is written in the prophets, "And they shall all be taught by God." Every one who has heard and learned from the Father comes to me.* ⁴⁶ *Not that any one has seen the Father except him who is from God; he has seen the Father.* ⁴⁷ *Truly, truly, I say to you, he who believes has eternal life.* ⁴⁸ *I am the bread of life.* ⁴⁹ *Your fathers ate the manna in the wilderness, and they died.* ⁵⁰ *This is the bread which comes down from heaven, that a man may eat of it and not die.* ⁵¹ *I am the living bread which came down from heaven; if any one eats of this bread, he will live for ever; and the bread which I shall give for the life of the world is my flesh.'*

It is not surprising that the audience, now explicitly enlarged to *the Jews*, declines to pursue so personal an issue as the nature of unbelief. Instead they turn, doubtless with some relief, to a problem that is just as real, but not of personal concern for them (or so they suppose). They began to *murmur* at Jesus because he said (and he had said it not in so many words, but very certainly by implication) *'I am the bread which came down from heaven'* (6⁴¹). But how could this be true of Jesus ben Joseph, whose father and mother were both personally known in Galilee? How can the son of human parents say *'I have come down from heaven'*? This is, indeed, the whole mystery of the incarnation, whatever may have to be said of the doctrine of the virgin birth. Jesus breaks into their discussion: *'Do not murmur among yourselves'*, i.e. 'Do not argue among yourselves about this question, for the question of my heavenly descent will never be settled by discussions, however intelligent or honest, about human genealogical trees!' He then proceeds to reassert the point he had been making before this discussion broke out. Belief in the Son, which is synonymous with coming to him, is the work of the Father drawing men to the Son.

And lest they should find that doctrine unacceptable Jesus reminds them that it comes from their own scriptures, for '*it is written, "They shall all be taught by God*"' (6⁴⁵). But this important scriptural principle must not be pressed to the point of making direct vision of God the essence of religion in this world. There is indeed only one who can claim to speak of God from 'direct vision', the one who has come from him, Jesus the Son, the Word incarnate. So Jesus re-emphasizes the teaching given to Nicodemus at 3¹³, and which was stated also in the prologue to the Gospel at 1¹⁸. With this qualification made, Jesus restates what he has said, drawing out the consequences of his being the bread of life for those who believe (in contrast with those who ate the old 'bread from heaven' under Moses) and for himself. As in the discourse with Nicodemus the statement about having come from heaven is followed by a reference to his destiny on the cross.

This final restatement of the bread of life in the perspective of the Jewish religion begins with the solemn '*Truly, truly, I say to you*'. Jesus then impressively repeats that the man who believes is in possession of (such is the force of the present tense) eternal life. This process is in complete contrast to what happened under Moses, for then the fathers to whom the Galileans had referred ate 'bread from heaven' and yet died (such an adversative sense is given to *and* in 6⁴⁹). But the man who eats of *the* bread which has come down from heaven, bread which is *living*, which has life in itself (himself), will live for ever. So again, in ch. 6 as in ch. 5, it is made plain that what Jesus has done in the miracle is not simply to feed men so that their hunger of a day is stilled; but he has shown himself to be the resurrection and the life; he has given life to those who have fed on his words, who have seen him and believed; and he will raise them up at the last day, to a life that is eternal community with him and the Father. But such rich benefits are not given without cost to the giver, and here Jesus is both giver and gift. '*The bread which I shall give for the life of the world*' he adds '*is my flesh*'. This is not really an addition made in the very last sentence, but rather a making plain that none of what has been said can be understood at all if it be seen solely from the perspective of the Galilean hill; it will only cease to be inevitably and crudely misunderstood if it be seen from the perspective of the end, and the end not only of the cross and resurrection but, as will be seen, of the Christian eucharist also. So the dialogue widens again to include explicitly those it has included implicitly all along – the Christians of Ephesus and the Jews with whom they must live and to whom they must bear witness.

ﬡﬡﬡ

42

Jesus' claim to be the bread of life was evidently held to constitute a further claim about his origin. The Jewish objection is that since Jesus' parentage is known (and normal?) it cannot be the instrument of any divine revelation: for natural process is natural process. See the Introduction for a note on the doctrine of the Virgin birth in John.

'*Is not this Jesus?*': better translated: 'Is not this fellow Jesus?' with a note of offended propriety in the question. Cf. Mark 6² // .

44

Jesus does not deal directly with the objection that had been raised, but returns to expound the nature of belief as the work and gift of God. 6³⁷ had said all that the Father gives will believe; here it is stated that none can come unless sent by the Father.

45

This is an unique – and a vague – scriptural reference for John. Passages that may underlie the statement are, e.g., Isa. 54¹³; Jer. 31³⁴. The prophets, and Jesus, looked forward to what the Puritans, at their best, would have called 'experimental religion', not a religiosity at second hand.

47–51

In this brief but potent paragraph Jesus puts the various terms in their right perspectives and relationships for the last time: bread, life, descent from heaven, manna, belief, eternal life, death, all are said to find their real meaning in reference to him, who is the real living bread that has come down (aorist tense of historic action indicating the incarnation) from heaven. And this bread will be made available for the life of the world in the flesh of the Son of man.

When Jesus says '*the bread which I shall give for the life of the world is my flesh*' he is bringing to its final unveiling the truth that he has been expounding throughout the discourse. From 6²⁷, it has been shown, Jesus has spoken of himself as the bestower of the real food for a man. He had told the Galileans that he must not be likened to Moses, but that his proper counterpart in the Manna story was Yahweh. Here at the end of this part of the discourse (for what follows is about another subject, the eucharist) he forsakes the third person and the present tense, and speaks plainly about himself in the first person as the one who will give the bread of life to men; but that bread will be his flesh. Inasmuch as the eucharist, like the gift of the Spirit, is impossible until he has been glorified, the language must be in the future tense. But that must not be allowed to detract from the spiritual character of the real miracle of yesterday, when he multiplied the loaves for the hungry multitude. The word *flesh* is not associated with the words of the institution of the Lord's supper in the synoptic gospels or in Paul. Its occurrence here is due in part to John's awareness that the eucharist is not yet, and that he writes of a situation midway, as it were, between the feeding and the eucharist; and in part also to the opening of the gospel where the author had written in a magnificent phrase that the Word became flesh. It was moreover a term eminently suitable for sacrificial usage. (See Jeremias, *The Eucharistic Words of Jesus*, pp. 103–7.)

6⁵²⁻⁵⁹   THE REAL FOOD FOR A MAN

⁵²*The Jews then disputed among themselves, saying, 'How can this man give us his flesh to eat?'* ⁵³*So Jesus said to them, 'Truly, truly, I say to you, unless you eat the flesh of the Son of man and drink his blood, you have no life in you;* ⁵⁴*he who eats my flesh and drinks my blood has eternal life, and I will raise him up at the last day.* ⁵⁵*For my flesh is food indeed, and my blood is drink indeed.* ⁵⁶*He who eats my flesh and drinks my blood abides in me, and I in him.* ⁵⁷*As the living Father sent me, and I live because of the Father, so he who eats me will live because of me.* ⁵⁸*This is the bread which came down from heaven, not such as the fathers ate and died; he who eats this bread will live for ever.'* ⁵⁹*This he said in the synagogue, as he taught at Caper'na-um.*

If *the Jews then disputed among themselves, saying, 'How can this man give us his flesh to eat?'* it must be confessed that the question is humanly speaking very understandable. It has been very solemnly debated at times in the history of the Christian Church by theologians, and it is not stating the case too strongly to say that this same question is still a cause of division among Christian people. In the setting provided for it in the fourth gospel it represents another human escape from the personal demands of Christ. 'Coming to' Jesus might well be put off till doomsday if it had to wait for a human rational answer to the question of 'How can he give us his flesh to eat?'! Yet the Jews *disputed* among themselves. Precise knowledge of the terms of the dispute are now irrecoverable, but it is antecedently probable that some thought the statement pure error or nonsense, while others thought that it could be given real meaning if 'spiritualized'. Whatever the argument was, and the Greek word suggests that it was sharp, Jesus dealt with it by making himself more explicit – and more difficult! Again he said that eating of his flesh was necessary in order to have any 'life' at all, but on this restatement he adds to eating the flesh of the Son of man the equal necessity of drinking his blood. Here at last the statement at the beginning of the discourse exhorting the hearers to labour for food which should endure to eternal life is at last brought fully into the 'end-perspective' of the eucharist. The statement as such would have been highly objectionable, if taken literally, to Jews, who were forbidden to take blood. But two points may be noted: first, that John tells of no Jewish reply to this statement of Jesus; it may well be that John thus distinguishes that part of his discourse which he reckoned to represent words offered to the Jews from that which he reckoned as putting the same words more explicitly for Christian readers of the gospel. Second, that in Jewish thinking the twin terms 'flesh and blood' constitute a pair used in reference to the sacrificial giving and taking of life.* So in speaking of eating his flesh and drinking his blood Jesus is saying that unless men come to live by his death, and find their own real life in accepting the destiny that his own life has marked out as characteristic for the disciple, they cannot find the way to the life he has come to bestow. Entry upon 'life' in this world, and an inheritance of *life* in the world to come are both bound up with man's relationship to the self-offering of Jesus in his sacrifice. So it is the conclusion of the discourse that the 'true' food is Christ's flesh, and the 'true' drink his blood: these are what satisfy those hungers and thirsts from which men suffer in distinction from all other earthly creatures. Man's genuine nourishment lies in them; without them the really 'human' person dies, even though he continue to live in the flesh, but with them he lives the life that is really life both here in the course of history, and in that which lies beyond history in the world to come.

This difficult figurative language is then somewhat 'demytholo-

* For a most useful and erudite discussion of this point see the valuable work of Jeremias, *The Eucharistic Words of Jesus*, pp. 103–7.

gized'. Jesus says that the man who eats and drinks in the manner stated 'abides in Christ' and Christ in him. The language is still, of course, figurative, though in some ways less difficult, and perhaps more congenial to twentieth-century man, though the mystery of indwelling of which Jesus speaks transcends what is known elsewhere as 'possession'. To be indwelt by Christ is not to have one's personality divided, but rather for the first time to find true integration. For this indwelling enables the believer to share in the divine unity itself, as will be seen later in the gospel. Jesus adds one explanatory comment. The Father has life in himself: he has sent Jesus to the world with his mission. So Jesus lives here 'because of the Father' i.e. his very life in history is because the Father sent him, and all he does here is for the sake of obeying the Father and serving his will. The mutual indwelling which the eucharistic eating and drinking brings repeats that Father–Son relationship between the Son and the believer: the one who eats Christ will realize that he is in the world only because he has been sent by the Son, and all his life will be given to obey the Son and to serve his will. But in this restatement one other piece of de-mythologizing has taken place: instead of eating flesh and drinking blood, Jesus now speaks of *eating me* (6^{57}). So the whole mystery of the eucharist is opened up at this point for the Christian reader, who knows that his Lord comes to him by sacred tryst in 'the breaking of the bread'.

That the eucharist was very early known as 'the breaking of the bread' seems quite clear (cf. Acts 2^{42,46}; 20^7; 27^{35}). It appears equally, or even more, certain that it derived that name from the habit of actually breaking up a loaf during the rite, which in turn preserved the tradition reported in all three synoptics that at the Last Supper Jesus 'took a loaf, gave thanks, and broke it'. All three synoptists likewise state that at the feeding of the multitude (whether the five or the four thousand) Jesus also 'broke' the bread. John cannot report the breaking of the bread at the Last Supper, for he does not recount the institution of the eucharist at that point. But neither does he mention any breaking of bread in his account of the miracle (cf. 6^{11}). The omission of breaking at the time of the miracle is explicable on one or both of two grounds. John may omit it because he does not report a eucharist, and does not need to make the miracle in Galilee correspond in any way to the Last Supper in Jerusalem. Its omission may also be due to the fact that in the account of the crucifixion John presents Jesus as the true passover lamb, rather than the bread, and one symbolic attestation of this is recorded when the soldiers come to the three crucified figures and, finding Jesus already dead, have no occasion to break his legs (see below, p. 623). This is seen by John as a 'fulfilment' of the scriptural requirement that the passover lamb should have no bones broken.

The discourse ends with a final reassertion of its main structure and theme. The bread which Jesus is has come down from heaven, not as the manna came long ago leaving the fathers to die, but has come to feed men with that genuine divine nourishment that bestows upon them eternal life. The evangelist adds a note that Jesus said this as he taught in the synagogue at Capernaum. This has been discussed at various levels, and reasons have been advanced in the Introduction (see pp. 43ff) for not taking it simply at its literal worth, and concluding from it that the whole chapter is displaced. Professor Guilding has provided what is probably the basis of a right answer, though she would invert the order of chs. 5 and 6 (erroneously, as the present writer supposes). She has pointed out that if the statement as to the discourse being given 'in church' be taken seriously, and that Passover readings be assumed, then Jesus would have been commenting on a number of Old Testament lections that remarkably refer to the themes of the discourse: the gift of manna, the eating that brought death into the world, in contrast to the eating that brings life, the conquest of death illustrated by the walking on the water seen in terms of the destruction of Pharaoh at the Red Sea. The present writer would observe that probably not all the themes handled in the discourse were likely to be treated within one synagogue service, so that the discourse in ch. 6 represents a collection of sermonic material drawn together by its 'passover' theme, much in the same way that Matthew drew together certain 'sermonic' material for the formation of his 'Sermon on the Mount'. If John the author had a tradition of the Lord's teaching at Passover time, which recorded things said in Galilean synagogues, it could well produce just the kind of discourse which he provides in this chapter. But if this be the likeliest hypothesis as to the genesis of the chapter, it must be emphasized that the questions concerning the origin of its form are nothing like so important as those concerning the meaning of its contents.

ಐಐ

54

This verse is the Johannine equivalent to the Synoptic saying to James and John about drinking the cup that Jesus will drink. It is the disciple's privilege and destiny to share the sufferings as well as the glory of Christ.

57

'he who eats me': The metaphor of eating has been slowly brought to a point where it can be transcended. Eating manna, bread, flesh, blood, me – these all point to the reality which is to have unity in communion with the Father through the Son. This is eternal life, so to feed.

6 60-65   THE DIFFICULTIES OF BELIEF:
DESERTION

⁶⁰*Many of his disciples, when they heard it, said, 'This is a hard saying; who can listen to it?'* ⁶¹*But Jesus, knowing in himself that his disciples murmured at it, said to them, 'Do you take offence at this?* ⁶²*Then what if you were to see the Son of man ascending where he was before?* ⁶³*It is the spirit that gives life, the flesh is of no avail; the words that I have spoken to you are spirit and life.* ⁶⁴*But there are some of you that do not believe.'* *For Jesus knew from the first who those were that did not believe, and who it was that should betray him.* ⁶⁵*And he said, 'This is why I told you that no one can come to me unless it is granted him by the Father.'*

Many disciples (who they were or what their numbers John does not specify) heard what Jesus had said, and found it hard to accept. *Hard* (6⁶⁰) not in the sense of difficult to understand; indeed Jesus had made himself almost unbearably intelligible: but hard in the sense of accepting what had been asserted. The *it* in the verse refers to the whole discourse but should probably be read 'him', though the ultimate sense is perhaps the same. The result is clear: Jesus knows (evidently by his supernatural power) that the 'new Israel' is 'murmuring' as did the old, and what they are murmuring about is what he has said to them as an exposition of what he had done. So he asked them 'Are you taking offence at this? What if you were to see something else – the Son of man ascending where he was before?'

The evangelist has evidently left the sentence deliberately incomplete, and its meaning is open to question, and it has been interpreted in two opposite directions. Some have held that it implies that if the hearers were to see the ascending of the Son of man they would find an even greater 'offence' in it; others have supposed that it means that if they were to see the ascending then the offensiveness of what they had seen already would be reduced, because in some way the ascension would ease their present difficulties. In fact, of course, either thing might happen, and it would seem that John has deliberately left the meaning open with an incomplete sentence so that the ambivalence of all that takes place concerning the Son of man might be left unqualified. For those who believe, the ascension would ease the present talk about Jesus being the living bread who gives his flesh for men to eat; to those who do not believe the ascension would be but a further cause of grave difficulty on the plane of physical happenings. But another point must be raised. What does the *ascending* of the Son of man to where he was before itself mean? There is no doubt that it includes what has come to be known in Christendom as 'the Ascension', the return of Jesus to 'heaven' after the resurrection, whether soon after, as in Luke, John, and Mark, or later when Jesus had been for forty days with his disciples, as in Acts. But the verb 'to go up' used here, while it covers what might be called the actual ascension, is also the verb that is used, almost in a technical sense in the gospels, of Jesus 'going up' to Jerusalem, there, as he knew, to be slain in sacrifice (e.g. Luke 19²⁸; Mark 10³²; John 7⁸,¹⁰). And the two ideas may well be mingled here as elsewhere. Dr Dodd has said:

The question may be raised, whether even the banal 'to go up to Jerusalem' (2¹³; 5¹; 7¹⁰, ¹⁴), though it is an expression that every pilgrim to the temple had occasion to use, may not have had for this writer a suggestion of the 'going up' [ascending] of the Son of man?*

If this be so, then the preservation of ambivalence is much more likely. The author has skilfully chosen his words so that both meanings may be carried, one for believers to whom the ascending would be a confirmation and 'easing' of belief, and one for unbelievers, to whom the ascending would be a very great if not a final obstacle to belief.

* Dodd, p. 385, n.1.

However the sentence was intended to be interpreted, the one that follows must follow; for, as 7³⁹ says, *as yet the Spirit had not been given, because Jesus was not yet glorified*. But after the ascending of the Son of man, then the Spirit could be given, and in being possessed by the Spirit, believing men would have the life of which Jesus had spoken. The Spirit that was to be given bestows life; human flesh cannot of itself beget anything called life. In the sentence '*The spirit gives life, the flesh is of no avail*' Jesus is not involved in any contradiction with what he had said about eating the flesh of the Son of man, for his flesh, in contrast to that of ordinary mortals, is 'living flesh', flesh that, in the terms of the Baptist's vision reported in 1^{32ff}, had received the Spirit, and had had it remain. Hence the very words that Jesus had spoken were *spirit* and *life* because he was not just a man of flesh, but a man of spirit as well. Jesus added that some of his Galilean disciples did not believe. That this statement at least was intended by the evangelist to derive from Jesus' supernatural knowledge is clear from the comment he adds: *Jesus knew from the first who those were that did not believe, and who it was that should betray him* (6⁶⁴). The author has so often left the reader to draw his own conclusions about the supernatural origin of the knowledge that Jesus displays that it must be presumed that this is a rather special instance of its exercise. Hence the present writer is disposed to accept the interpretation of those commentators who regard 'from the beginning' as referring back to 1¹ rather than to 1^{39ff}. And indeed on other occasions supernatural knowledge has led Jesus to see elements in a present human situation (e.g. the broken life of the woman of Samaria, 4¹⁶) but here it gives him awareness of God's dealing with men, for those who believe are given to him by the Father. And that this is the proper interpretation seems to be confirmed by the evangelist adding that Jesus then said '*This is why I told you that no one can come to me unless it is granted him by the Father*'.

༚

60

It is the disciples who found, as many still find, the contents of this discourse *hard*! The final phrase should read 'listen to him?' rather than *to it?*

62

'*where he was before*': A plain reference not only to the continuing existence of Jesus after his death, but also to his pre-existence (cf. 3^{13}; 13^3; 17^5).

65

The verb *said* is in the Greek imperfect: 'he kept on saying all the time'. This underlines the importance of $6^{37, 44}$ as basic Johannine doctrines. Belief in Jesus is impossible without the work of the Father. Unbelief is not some strange human behaviour; belief is a miracle of God. 'No one can say "Jesus is Lord" except by the Holy Spirit' is Paul's recognition of the same truth (1 Cor. 12^3).

6^{66-71} DIFFICULTIES IN BELIEF: ADHERENCE

^{66}*After this many of his disciples drew back and no longer went about with him.* ^{67}*Jesus said to the twelve, 'Will you also go away?'* ^{68}*Simon Peter answered him, 'Lord, to whom shall we go? You have the words of eternal life;* ^{69}*and we have believed, and have come to know, that you are the Holy One of God.'* ^{70}*Jesus answered them, 'Did I not choose you, the twelve, and one of you is a devil?'* ^{71}*He spoke of Judas the son of Simon Iscariot, for he, one of the twelve, was to betray him.*

The Galilean ministry comes to an unobtrusive end. The crowd of the feeding time is, as it was in the synoptic gospels, though there without adequate explanation, reduced. John has given his readers enough cause for understanding the profound theological implications of the terse but tragic statement *After this many of his disciples drew back and no longer went about with him* (6^{66}). To 'go about with' has far more than associations of physical propinquity; it means also being devoted as a disciple to a master. In view of the desertion of many, Jesus said to the Twelve: '*Will you also go away?*' John mentions the Twelve only here and at 20^{24}, so much does he assume his readers' familiarity with the synoptic story. The form of the question in Greek carries one of two implications, either of which is possible. It may imply that the questioner expects the answer 'No'; or it may imply that the questioner is quite unsure of what answer he will get. Most commentators seem to prefer the second meaning; but after so elaborate a statement that Jesus knew from the first those who did not believe (6⁶⁴) this seems to be an erroneous judgement. Jesus asks the question, both expecting and knowing the sort of answer he would receive. And he received it, evidently from all the Twelve, though voiced by Peter. The answer is affirmative without being arrogant, sure without being cocksure. Peter said *'Lord, to whom shall we go? You have the words of eternal life; and we have believed, and have come to know, that you are the Holy One of God'* (6^{68, 69}). *To whom shall we go?* must mean *In what other person can we believe?* if, as the evangelist has himself made abundantly clear, 'coming to Jesus' is synonymous with believing in him. This reflection makes the next part of the answer to Jesus more intelligible. *You have the words of eternal life.* This means more than that Jesus has spoken, as indeed he has, about eternal life; rather it means that the very words he speaks are 'quickening', life-giving realities. Grammatically the construction may be called a genitive of apposition, to be translated 'words that are eternal life'; but theologically they bind together in one the Person of Jesus as the living incarnate Word, the Spirit that came and remained with him, and the words that he has spoken: all these three are inextricably bound together in one, in the man Christ Jesus, Word incarnate, eternal Son in an historic man. Peter then relates that the Twelve have believed, and have gone on to know, that Jesus is the Holy One of God. The relation of belief to knowledge is one of perennial interest, and here John regards 'knowledge' as that relationship of conscious communion which ensues upon belief. 'To believe' is, as was seen above (p. 297), in some sense an ambiguous word. It may mean the act of first putting trust in a person or a statement, belief as a single historical act: it may also mean a settled temper and disposition of the whole person and life as it is centred in and given to a person or cause. Here Peter is using believe in the former sense, and keeping the word *know* to serve for what happens to the consciousness of relationship that develops as the believer walks in the life of belief in Jesus Christ. He comes to know something about his Lord, that he is the Holy One of God.

In his *'You are'* Peter echoes in a Christian confession of faith the great *'I am'* of his master. It is here that Peter's confession in John differs verbally from that in Mark and the other synoptics. There is little room for doubting that the title quoted had messianic significance. It was used, according to Mark (Mark 1²⁴ // ; Luke 4³⁴), by the demon which Jesus was about to exorcize, evidently with a messianic significance too. The confession of Messiahship in Mark 8²⁹ // is much more direct than here in John, but this suits the evangelist's purpose at this particular point of his gospel. For Jesus goes on to reply: *'Did I not choose you, the twelve, and one of you is a devil?'* This difficult saying must be seen as it looks both backwards and forwards. As referring to the past it seeks to remind the Twelve that they must, for all their special relationship to Jesus, not 'take it for granted' that the mere fact of being called ensured their cleaving to him in a way superior to the many Galileans who had just deserted him. They walk by faith, and that means a daily renewal of loyalty and belief, even if it also means a daily new bestowal of the Spirit's gifts. They may indeed assume that they are his, but they must not presume upon it! Looking forward, the saying, John indicates, anticipates the 'betrayal'. Again comparison with the synoptics is interesting. After Peter's confession in the earlier narratives it is he who is called 'Satan' because he could not accept the hard teaching about the tragic destiny of his master. In John Jesus does not specify who the devil is; and this accords with the interpretation taken. So far as the Twelve knew, the *devil* might be any one among them; it is noteworthy that when, in the synoptic narrative of the Last Supper, Jesus says that one of the Twelve will 'betray' him, they all begin to ask 'Is it I?'. In John at this point it seems that, whatever may have been the knowledge of Jesus (and the evangelist tells us that he knew about Judas Iscariot [6⁶⁴]), so far as the Twelve were concerned, the issue was not foreclosed. Yet the author closes the chapter and the discourse by one more look at the moment of Peter's confession from the perspective of the end. Discipleship was in itself no security, for many Galileans had ceased to follow Jesus. Neither was being called by Jesus, or being appointed one of the Twelve in itself a security, for one of the Twelve was to betray him. This salutary reminder that no man may take his spiritual condition for granted was made plain to the Twelve after the defection of the Galilean disciples in Capernaum. Yet seen from the perspective of the end Jesus had been speaking not only of the insecurity of them all, but of the severer sifting and the more calamitous defection of Judas Iscariot; *for he, one of the Twelve, was to betray Jesus* (6⁷¹). John does not seek to elaborate on this statement at this point of his narrative; nevertheless it is worth recording that the verbal form in which he here speaks of the betrayal by Judas is the same as that used in some of the synoptic references to the future passion and betrayal of the Lord (Mark 9³¹; 10³³; Matt. 17²²; 20¹⁹; Luke 9⁴⁴). In some mysterious way even Judas' betrayal was within the majestic purpose of God.

The word *betray* is a nasty word in English, particularly when associated with Judas and his deed. Yet the Greek word used means simply 'to deliver up', and were it not for centuries of tradition it is unlikely that a modern scholar would use the word 'betray' in this context (the same word is used in Acts 3¹³ of the whole people of Israel and is translated 'delivered up'). More must be said of this as John's story unfolds. Yet this brief excursion into that strange realm where men not only fail to believe in the Son, but, having believed in him, do him disservice, shows that men's loyalties, even to Christ, are subject to misdirection by demonic powers. The disturbing thought remains that such disservice cannot be so far from any disciple that he can afford to neglect Jesus' present warning to the Twelve. In a word, the constancy of a disciple, like his coming to the Lord, is not his own work, but God's, a precious gift he receives.

ಚಞ

66

After this: offers both a chronological and a logical basis for interpretation. It was after the discourse, and because of it, that many left Jesus.

68

'*Lord*': Here, in contrast to its use in 6³⁴, rightly so rendered. In v. 34 it should read 'Sir'.

69

'*we have believed, and have come to know*': Evidently the reference is to some real 'belief' at 1³⁹ff, that has now grown in depth and in their continuing association has bred the certitude of faith, a knowledge that has an integrity of its own.

70

'*Jesus answered them*': Peter had spoken, but Jesus replied to them all; thus discerning the thoughts of all their hearts, and indicating their common lot in the perils that confront the disciple who is called.

71

The verb used to state that Judas *was to* betray Jesus is capable of two meanings. It can indicate a likely future event, as in 4⁴⁷, where the official's son 'was at the point of death'. Or it may convey a certain inevitability, as at 12^{33}, where the evangelist, having recorded a saying about being lifted up, adds that Jesus spoke it 'to show by what death he was to die'. (There is another possible meaning as at 6^{6}, indicating an intention, but it is not applicable here.) The problem is to decide which of these two meanings applies here, and it seems clear to the present writer that the meaning of inevitability must be taken. In the setting of the chapter from verse 64 onwards, with its emphasis upon the foreknowledge of Jesus, it would be strange indeed if at this very last verse the author were to pass to simple futurity, about a subject which the synoptists and John seem otherwise to recognize as having a certain divine inevitability. More must be said on this as John's record unfolds; for the moment it is clearly affirmed that Judas is the one destined to deliver Jesus up to the authorities.

John 7[1]

Interlude 4: Galilee   Matthew 4[12,23]
17[22]

7 After this Jesus went about in Galilee; he would not go about in Judea, because the Jews[a] sought to kill him.

a Or Judeans

In telling his readers that Jesus *went about* in Galilee John uses a word that is the regular description for a peripatetic Rabbi, and the tense he uses indicates, in the Greek, that this peripatetic activity of Jesus went on for a considerable time. For how long it is impossible to say. Much of the Galilean ministry as recorded in the synoptics would seem to fall outside this reference of John, for the simple reason that John has already described how the Galileans, like the Judeans before them, had largely rejected Jesus after the feeding of the five thousand. Possibly a good deal of the contents of Matthew 14[34]–18[35] could be reckoned as fitting into this Johannine period, and the prediction of the passion quoted above would seem to be a not inappropriate prelude to some of the things that Jesus said in the Temple at the Feast of Tabernacles.

John 7$^{2-52}$

Rite and Reality: 1 Leviticus 23$^{33-6}$
Numbers 29$^{12-39}$
Mark 9^{30}

'He came to his own home, and his own people received him not' (1^{11}). These words from the Prologue are a not inaccurate summary of the whole story of the ministry of Jesus Christ, but they are also, and significantly, just as accurate a summary of the narrative of the fourth gospel up to this point. For John has recounted how Jesus visited both his spiritual and his physical *patris*, both Jerusalem and Galilee, and was rejected in both places (chs. 5 and 6). The peripatetic ministry in Galilee recorded in 7^{1} marks the end of this first cycle of John's gospel story, and it affords an ominous parable of what the whole story will turn out to be. A final rejection awaits Jesus on his final coming to his own 'spiritual' home; and he sets out from Galilee for the last time in ch. 7, decisively and secretly, as Mark reports in his gospel (Mark 9^{30}).

John relates that when he reached Jerusalem Jesus went into the Temple and taught. The controversy that ensued will remind the reader of a previous occasion in Jerusalem when acute controversy arose after the healing of the lame man at the Pool of Bethzatha (ch. 5), and the reminder is necessary for a proper understanding of ch. 7. But it is even more important that the reader should be reminded that John has told of an even earlier visit to Jerusalem and to the Temple (ch. 2), when Jesus drove out the cattle sellers and the money changers from the Temple precincts, and then spoke of the destruction and renewal of the Temple in such a way that after the resurrection the disciples realized that he had, even at that early date, spoken of his death and rising again. It is indispensable to a right understanding of chs. 7–10 that the link between the Temple and the death and resurrection of Jesus be not forgotten.

But what reason could be offered for such a journey to Jerusalem at a time when, as Jesus knew himself, *the Jews sought to kill him* (7^{1}; cf. 5^{18})? John gives his answer to this question in the story of the discussion that Jesus had with his brothers. Human advice, however well-intentioned, is quite inadequate ground for a decision to go to Jerusalem; the only possible reason for the journey is that Jesus should know that *his hour* had come. And when he goes up at that time, the men of Jerusalem and the whole Jewish 'establishment' begin to ask the right questions about him. The ground is being laid for the final question and answer that consists not only of the words spoken at the trial of Jesus, but of the acts perpetrated at his scourging and crucifixion and in the response that the Father made to them.

7$^{2-10}$ JESUS, HIS BRETHREN
                  AND THE JOURNEY

²*Now the Jews' feast of Tabernacles was at hand.* ³*So his brothers said to him, 'Leave here and go to Judea, that your disciples may see the works you are doing.* ⁴*For no man works in secret if he seeks to be known openly. If you do these things, show yourself to the world.'* ⁵*For even his brothers did not believe in him.* ⁶*Jesus said to them, 'My time has not yet come, but your time is always here.* ⁷*The world cannot hate you, but it hates me because I testify of it that its works are evil.* ⁸*Go to the feast yourselves; I am not^a going up to the feast, for my time has not yet fully come.'* ⁹*So saying, he remained in Galilee.*

    ¹⁰*But after his brothers had gone up to the feast, then he also went up, not publicly but in private.*

a Other ancient authorities add *yet*

The Feast of Tabernacles was the most popular of all the great Jewish festivals. It took place in the autumn, after all the harvests had been gathered in, and it looked forward in hope and joy to the new year that had immediately begun. Pilgrims flocked to Jerusalem, and they, together with the inhabitants of the city, lived in the open air for the eight days of the festival, with no more shelter than some very light structures made as 'tabernacles', 'tents' or 'booths'. This custom, which had the effect of inducing an air of equality and anonymity in the crowd, and quite carefree enjoyment, doubtless had its origin in a more primitive agricultural order of society. But it had been re-interpreted, as had other great festivals of the Jews, to commemorate some moment in the great drama of Israel's deliverance from Egypt under Moses. The tabernacles were thus taken to be

tokens of the time when Israel lived in tents during their forty-year
sojourn in the wilderness. The feast began and ended with a day that
was ordained to be a rest day, like a sabbath, and special sacrifices were
prescribed for each day (cf. Num. 29$^{12-38}$). In later times other
ceremonies were added, which throw some light upon the words of
Jesus in the Temple. On each of the first seven days of the feast a
golden vessel was filled with water from the pool of Siloam, and the
water used for libations in the Temple, the words of Isaiah 12^3:
'With joy you will draw water from the wells of salvation' being
used at the rite. Further on the first day of the feast golden candlesticks were set out in the Court of the Women, wicks were made and
the candlesticks lit, 'and there was not a courtyard in Jerusalem that
did not reflect the light of the House of Water-drawing' (Sukk. 5$^{2-4}$).
Jesus, that is to say, in this Johannine allusive historiography, comes
to his people as they re-enact their state as a pilgrim people of God, not
yet having reached the land of promise. But his coming shows that
they are really still a pilgrim people, not yet having attained their
promised inheritance. And as he comes, he brings the real fulfilment
of Israel's promises and hopes. He is not water flowing from a physical
rock to quench a bodily thirst, but a source of *living* water to those
who believe in him so that they too are able to become sources of
living water in him. And he is not only the light of every courtyard
in Jerusalem, but the light of the whole world. And during the feast,
when more animals were slain than at any other, he reminds the
people in the temple that his own death is the inevitable and divine
outcome of the controversy that the Lord has with his people.

It was just before the Feast of Tabernacles that the brothers of Jesus
urged him to go up to Jerusalem. The words that they are reported to
have used need setting in the whole context that John has so skilfully
built up. Jesus has been rejected in Jerusalem already, and at the
present time he is in Galilee just because the Jews are intent upon
killing him. Similarly many Galilean disciples have left him, and yet,
apparently, from the way the brothers talk, Jesus is still going about
in Galilee working signs. But even to brothers who do not, in John's
sense, 'believe', this is an unprofitable way for any person with a
claim to a following to act. To continue so indefinitely in this way
would be to renounce all claim to men's loyalty. So the brethren,
though they do not believe in Jesus as the Messiah, urge him to leave
Galilee and return to Judea. The Feast of Tabernacles would offer

Jesus enthusiastic crowds as a kind of public escort from Galilee to Jerusalem, and if Jesus, going up with a festival procession, were to do some striking 'signs' in Jerusalem, perhaps his position would prove to be not irrecoverable! This offers a quite natural and easy explanation of the text, in contrast with others that require the supposition of some special group of Jerusalem disciples.

The reply of Jesus reminds the reader of his answer to his mother at the wedding in Cana. When she reported to him that there was no wine, his reply was 'O woman, what have you to do with me? My hour has not yet come' (2⁴). Once more Jesus asserts to those who think that his actions are part of the action and counter-action that conditions all human behaviour, that his actions and movements are controlled not by stimuli from without, but from a divine constraint within. Jesus is saying in effect that the sort of reasons which his brothers have advanced for a journey to Jerusalem are quite inapplicable to him; his destiny does not depend upon any human calculation of the prospects of achieving popular esteem. For the brothers, as for any other men, the calculation of probabilities is a not improper exercise, at any time. But for Jesus the situation is not that he has temporarily lost popularity and may regain it, but that already the world has shown its hostility, and that hostility can no longer be avoided. The question is not, is the present time one in which the hostility can be avoided, but at what time and in what way can this hostility be so met and overcome that both it and the divine love that will overcome it may be exposed for what they are. *So saying*, John records, *he remained in Galilee* (7⁹).

But very shortly afterwards, Jesus went up to the Feast *not publicly but in private* (7¹⁰). That is to say he did not go to Jerusalem in one of the many caravans of pilgrims that set out each year for the Feast of Tabernacles. He waited until they had all gone, and then went up on his own. Whether any of the Twelve or any other Galilean disciples went with him it is impossible to say; it certainly cannot be decided by the wording of the text. All that the author conveys is that Jesus did not travel with a pilgrim caravan, or arrive for the opening of the feast. But the journey he takes reflects some elements in the synoptics. All three synoptists tell of a decisive turning from Galilee to Judea and Jerusalem, and Mark 9³⁰ speaks of such a journey being undertaken in secret. For John the secrecy is not merely social, but theological in its reference.

For John is describing a situation that can be viewed in terms of Malachi 3¹, for the Lord, in a divine incognito, is again to appear 'suddenly in his temple'. On the earlier 'sudden' coming (2¹³⁻²²) the Lord had cleansed his temple, using words that spoke, as they realized afterwards, of his death. But now additional symbolism was to hand. The people were engaged in a ritual re-enacting of the days before any temple was built, while they were yet in the wilderness, and not in the land of promise. The Lord's coming, in the phrase of the prologue, to 'tabernacle among them' would reveal that really they were still in the wilderness, short of the promised land of eternal life, which could only be entered by belief in Christ's name. Further, on the last visit to Jerusalem (5¹⁻¹⁸), Jesus had healed a cripple on the sabbath day. The ensuing controversy had plumbed that action to its depth, and Jesus' claim that in essence such action was the exercise of divine powers of giving life to the dead had led to the substitution of a charge of blasphemy for the lesser offence of breaking the law of the sabbath. The present visit is also the basis of controversy, leading to further definition of the nature and destiny of Jesus.

ॐ

2

the Jews' feast of Tabernacles was at hand: This feast began on the 15th Tishri (the seventh month, approximately September). The regulations governing it are in Lev. 23³³⁻⁶, ³⁹⁻⁴³; Deut. 16¹³⁻¹⁵. In the Prologue the evangelist wrote that the Word 'tabernacled' among us.

3

his brothers: Mark names them: James, Joseph, Judas and Simon (Mark 6³), and reports that they had sisters. Nothing in the fourth gospel implies that they were older than Jesus, or offspring of a previous wife of Joseph, though this view, first suggested by Epiphanius (*c.* A.D. 375), has been widely adopted because of its supposed congruity with asserting the virginity of Mary. Another opinion holds that the *brothers* were really cousins; but though this view was held by Jerome, it is hard to conjecture why the evangelist should call a cousin a brother. John, like the other evangelists, pictures the brothers as unable to give credence to Jesus' claims.

'that your disciples may see the works you are doing': This has been taken to imply that Jesus' disciples were in Jerusalem, and had not had opportunity to see his works. But that is inconsistent with 2²³; 5²ff which record 'signs' being done in Jerusalem. Nor can this statement

mean that the Galilean disciples had seen no signs, in view of 2^{1ff}; 4^{46ff}. The most probable interpretation is to suppose that Jesus' brothers are inviting him to do some specially notable signs during the feast, so as to retrieve his position after having lost many who had followed him (6^{66}).

4
The advice of the brothers counsels the precise opposite of what the evangelist reports. Jesus does not embark upon a manifestation of power to attain an easy and compelling victory; rather he suffers 'incognito' and gains a victory recognizable as such only by those who have faith, those who 'not having seen' yet believe.

5
The brothers' unbelief was quite consistent with their conviction that Jesus could perform signs, and attract a following.

6
'*My time has not yet come*': see 2^4. The time for his self-giving in death and glorification has not yet arrived, nor can its coming be calculated in advance in the terms used by the brothers. They can rightly reckon chances for the success they desire; but for his victory he must await the moment of divine destiny.

7
'*The world cannot hate you, but it hates me because I testify of it that its works are evil*': This is more than to acknowledge that Jesus is a moral critic of the world; it is a claim (like that made in 3^{18} etc.) that by his actual presence the world is being judged, judged by its reaction to him.

8
'*I am not going up*': The word for *go up* (*anabaino*) refers both to the physical climb of Jerusalem's hill, and to the Lord's 'ascent' to the Father, i.e. to his glorification.

7^{11-13} THE DIVINE INCOGNITO

^{11} *The Jews were looking for him at the feast, and saying, 'Where is he?'* ^{12} *And there was much muttering about him among the people. While some said, 'He is a good man,' others said, 'No, he is leading the people astray.'* ^{13} *Yet for fear of the Jews no one spoke openly of him.*

Though Judeans and Galileans had refused to believe in Jesus they still looked for him at the feast. They talked much about him in a quiet way; though they had not come to full 'belief' they were still interested to see what 'signs' he might do at the feast. Two opinions dominate the crowd, and in reporting them John reflects synoptic material. One section said of Jesus '*He is a good man*' (7^{12}). This recalls the story of the man who, in Mark's version, ran to Jesus with the question 'Good Teacher, what must I do to inherit eternal life?' (Mark 10^{17}). Jesus answered 'Why do you call me good? No one is good but God alone'. If this reply be taken in its ethical implications, it raises acute difficulty, as Matthew evidently saw (cf. Matthew 19$^{16ff.}$). Did Jesus mean to make public confession that he was not ethically 'good'? Matthew rightly shrank from any such implication, and made the adjective 'good' refer to the questioner's deeds, and made Jesus reply 'Why do you ask me about what is good?', so avoiding offence. But this was achieved only at the cost of the theological meaning of Mark's narrative. For Jesus had not been concerned, in Mark (or Luke), to say that he is not morally 'good', but rather to take the use of the adjective 'good' as a real, if not fully conscious, recognition of his divine nature. It is as if he had said to his questioner: 'Although in the end it is only God who can merit the ascription of goodness, I want to use your application of it to me to point out to you and to all men the exalted nature that I have and claim to bear.' So at this point of the Johannine story one further use of the evangelist's characteristic irony may be detected. One part of the crowd at the feast calls Jesus *good*; yet in so doing they confess, albeit unwittingly, his utter divinity.

Another part of the crowd held that Jesus led the people astray. The actual phrase does not easily bring to mind any particular synoptic statement, though the Greek of Matthew 27^{63} relates that the chief priests and pharisees called Jesus that 'leader-astray' of the people. But without using the same word the synoptists cannot but make it plain that in Jewish official opinion Jesus had led the people astray. They relate how the authorities were unable to move against Jesus when they wished because he had got the ear of the people (cf. Matt. 26^5; Mark 14^2; Luke 20^{19}). The point is perhaps clinched in Luke's report that the accusation laid before Pilate and accepted by him was that 'We found this man perverting our nation' (Luke 23$^{2, 14}$). So John portrays Jesus, in the rich irony characteristic of his writing, as either the one man who can rightly share the divine epithet *good*, or merely one who perverts the life of the people of God. Yet, for all the contrariety of these opinions, the dispute was not yet brought out into the open, for the festival pilgrims 'feared the Jews', which in the context can only mean the authorities.

တလ

11

The Jews were looking for him at the feast: The imperfect tense implies that the search went on for some time. Probably a somewhat hostile search.

13

no one spoke openly of him: Until the authorities had taken their action, and so disclosed their hand, any public commitment was deemed risky!

7$^{14-24}$ 'SUDDENLY IN HIS TEMPLE'

^{14}*About the middle of the feast Jesus went up into the temple and taught.* ^{15}*The Jews marvelled at it, saying, 'How is it that this man has learning,*^{a} *when he has never studied?' *^{16}*So Jesus answered them, 'My teaching is not mine, but his who sent me; *^{17}*if any man's will is to do his will, he shall know whether the teaching is from God or whether I am speaking on my own authority. *^{18}*He who speaks on his own authority seeks his own glory; but he who seeks the glory of him who sent him is true, and in him there is no falsehood. *^{19}*Did not Moses give you the law? Yet none of you keeps the law. Why do you seek to kill me?' *^{20}*The people answered, 'You have a demon! Who is seeking to kill you?' *^{21}*Jesus answered them, 'I did one deed, and you all marvel at it. *^{22}*Moses gave you circumcision (not that it is from Moses, but from the fathers), and you circumcise a man upon the sabbath. *^{23}*If on the sabbath a man receives circumcision, so that the law of Moses may not be broken, are you angry with me because on the sabbath I made a man's whole body well? *^{24}*Do not judge by appearances, but judge with right judgement.'*

a Or this man knows his letters

If John intends his readers to understand his statement with chronological precision it would be on the fourth day of the feast that Jesus entered the temple and taught. But the statement may be imprecise, and merely indicate that the teaching took place neither at the very beginning of the feast, nor as late as the last day (cf. 7¹⁰, ³⁷). The statement of v. 14 may be ambiguous in another way, for the verb 'to go up', which is quite properly used of Jesus, or of any other pilgrim making the ascent to the temple, is also used by John for the departure of Jesus from this world to go to the Father. Some such overtone would be in quite sound Johannine and even synoptist tradition. It would certainly fit the serious nature of the controversy that follows.

When Jesus began to teach in the temple, the Jews began to marvel (such is the force of the imperfect tense in the Greek), and their amazement was due to the fact that a man who had not been trained in the recognized schools should be able to teach and lead discussion as Jesus did. Again, this is a well known theme in the synoptic tradition. Mark's very first account of Jesus teaching in the synagogue is introduced by the comment 'They were astonished at his teaching, for he taught them as one who had authority, and not as the scribes' (Mark 1²²). Later Mark says that when Jesus went to Nazareth and taught in the synagogue many who heard him 'were astonished, saying, "Where did this man get all this? What is the wisdom given to him?"' (Mark 6²). Similar comments can be found in Matthew (Matt. 7²⁸,²⁹; 13⁵⁴) and Luke (4²², ³²), and about Peter and John in Acts 4¹³. The difficulty that the teaching of Jesus and his apostles occasioned for the conventional Jew was that it seemed to be just self opinion. The typical product of the rabbinic schools would always be able to cite authorities for what he said, and the stamp of his master would be detectable in his teaching. But neither of these features was present in the teaching of Jesus. The charge implicit in this observation is not therefore one of complete illiteracy (and there is evidence that Jesus could write) but of incompetence to teach because of lack of proper training in the study of the Law. John now shows how this very factor is a testimony to the divinity of Jesus, for the answer given to the puzzled question of the Jews is '*My teaching is not mine*'. Jesus claims that, like every good teacher of the Law, he has been taught; he is not just voicing his own opinions. But his teacher has been *he who sent* him, so not a rabbi of the schools, but his Father, God. Jesus next reiterates the point made by Peter at his confession (6⁶⁹) when he said that the disciples had believed and then come to know that Jesus was the holy one of God. The man who will really know that Jesus really comes from the Father is the man who really seeks to do the Father's will. No merely intellectual act will be able to decide this question, but only a whole life given to communion with and obedience to God. If Jesus were to speak purely on his own authority, then an intellectual judgement would be adequate; but if he really speaks what the Father himself imparts, then a whole life of obedience is the indispensable basis of judgement. For John the alternatives presented are absolute and exclusive: either he is one who speaks on his own authority or he truly speaks a divine word. There is no other possible alternative.

Jesus next takes up a thought first adumbrated in 5^{41-44}, and claims that any person speaking on his own authority must be concerned with his own reputation (for such is the meaning of the word glory in the context of 7^{18}), whereas in contrast he, who is seeking the glory or reputation (here the two meanings of *glory* blend together) of his Father, is above and beyond the transient, phenomenal matters of human reputation, and deals with what is utterly real, the being of God himself. In such a person there can be no falsehood or unreality, for he speaks that which is absolutely real, the divine word itself.

At this stage of the argument Jesus resumes the debate that had been the cause of bitter hostility-to-the-death on his previous visit. He raises the question of obedience to the Mosaic law. It begins with the statement that in the person who seeks God's glory (i.e. himself) there is no unrighteousness. Yet on his previous visit Jesus had been accused of the 'unrighteousness' of sabbath breaking and of blasphemy. But now, arriving in Jerusalem and the temple under a divine constraint that it was the right time for coming, he himself deliberately raises the question of his alleged unrighteousness again. He makes what seems at first sight an awkward transition to describing Moses as the giver of the law; yet the transition is neither awkward nor unnecessary. Jesus has just said that if any man really sought to do God's will he would be able to discern the divinity that Jesus claimed. But the Jews, who had received the law through Moses and considered themselves as zealous for the law, did not recognize the divinity of Jesus. So the whole situation must be set out in its proper terms. Moses gave the law, Jesus says; yet none of the Jews keep it (here Jesus carries the war into his opponents' territory); then why should the Jews seek to kill Jesus for breaking the law? The crowd in the temple reply that Jesus must have a demon (a charge that was familiar enough to all readers of the synoptics, cf. Mark 3^{21f} // ; Matt. 9^{34}). But, as in the synoptics, John shows that this is but the obverse side of the recognition of Jesus as the Son of God. The crowd continues by disclaiming any intention of wanting to kill Jesus, even though such an escape from the solidarity of the community was impossible for them. Jesus replies that he did one deed, and that the crowd marvelled at it. This is clearly a reference to the healing of the lame man at the pool of Bethzatha. An examination of this situation will be better than a direct answer to the charge of demon-possession. Let us see the course that Jesus' answer takes:

He has been accused of breaking the sabbath. His reply will consist of a denial of that, and a counter-accusation that the Jews themselves permit the breaking of the law about the sabbath, and this is not said to be improper either by Jewish authorities or by Jesus. The instance chosen in John, in contrast to that of the synoptics, who speak of taking an ox or an ass (so Luke 14^5) or a sheep (so Matt. 12^{11}) out of a well on the sabbath, is that of circumcision, which the law permitted to be done on the sabbath. Though this looks like permitting a contravention of the law on the sabbath, the custom was really seen in Jewish eyes as the fulfilling of the law, since it completes the thing for which the law is given – the perfection of man. Jesus then argues that if the law permits circumcision on the sabbath, it cannot but permit him to heal a man on the sabbath when that healing makes a man's body whole and well. The final words of Jesus are '*Do not judge by appearances, but judge with right judgement*' (7^{24}). The crowd must not judge by the superficial appearance of a sabbath healing, which certainly looks like a contravention of the sabbath law; they must see the action 'rightly' and perceive it as one actualization of his mission to bring a final wholeness to men.

ॐ

14
About the middle of the feast: Literally, 'when it was already the middle of the feast'. We are not to suppose that what is now reported took place before the feast was half-way through.

15
'*How is it that this man has learning, when he has never studied?*': The authorities are surprised not at what he says, but that he says it in such

a way as to reveal a scripture knowledge that normally goes with an education 'in the schools': 'How can he talk like a University Graduate, when he has never been there?' So have they missed the substance in surprise at the form.

16

'*My teaching is not mine, but his who sent me*': Jesus drew attention to the substance of his teaching by tracing its form to its divine sources.

17

'*if any man's will is to do his will*': To do God's will is to 'do the truth' (cf. 3^{21}); but it is supremely to believe in Jesus Christ whom God has sent (6^{29}). If a man has a will to believe in Jesus Christ, he knows that it is not a matter of his own decision, but God's gift of faith.

18

'*he who seeks the glory of him who sent him is true*': Jesus does not seek his own glory, but is prepared through his own humiliation to seek the glory of the Father; and the Father will glorify the Son. There is thus no possibility of self-deception about Christ's glory; coming from God's act, it is absolutely real, absolutely true.

19

'*Did not Moses give you the law?*': The reference to Moses is timely here, in spite of those who point out that this fits well on to 5^{47}; for the Jews thought God's will was enshrined in the Law, but could either not perceive, or perceiving, not accept the testimony of the law to Jesus Christ. Their failure to understand the law in this way brought them to the position of those who sought to kill him.

20

'*You have a demon*': This charge is neither pressed, nor answered, with the same force as in the synoptics (cf. Mark 3^{22f} ⫽). John has his own way of showing that to reject Jesus as the one coming with divine authority and power is to be under a judgement of eternal dimensions (compare Mark 3^{28-30} with 3^{16-18}).

21

'*I did one deed*': Evidently the healing at Bethzatha is meant (5^{1ff}).

24

'*judge with right judgement*': The healing of a man on the sabbath looked like setting one part of his body into a healed and healthy condition. But had the crowd been able to see the real character of the healing as a sign they would have recognized that a man had been made whole, made new, been re-created, been brought from death to life, in that apparently merely physical miracle.

²⁵*Some of the people of Jerusalem therefore said, 'Is not this the man whom they seek to kill?* ²⁶*And here he is, speaking openly, and they say nothing to him! Can it be that the authorities really know that this is the Christ?* ²⁷*Yet we know where this man comes from; and when the Christ appears, no one will know where he comes from.'* ²⁸*So Jesus proclaimed, as he taught in the temple, 'You know me, and you know where I come from? But I have not come of my own accord; he who sent me is true, and him you do not know.* ²⁹*I know him, for I come from him, and he sent me.'* ³⁰*So they sought to arrest him; but no one laid hands on him, because his hour had not yet come.* ³¹*Yet many of the people believed in him; they said, 'When the Christ appears, will he do more signs than this man has done?'*

John now records the reactions of some of the citizens of Jerusalem to the dialogue that has been going on. '*Is not this the man whom they seek to kill? And here he is, speaking openly, and they say nothing to him! Can it be that the authorities really know that this is the Christ?*' It is evident from the course of this reasoning that the crowd had already sensed that the struggle going on before them was not simply another example of a law breaker against the authorities; some other explanation was needed, and the suggestion that the authorities must have learnt that Jesus was Messiah demonstrates that the thought was very nearly becoming conviction in themselves. But there was a manifest obstacle to recognition of Jesus as Messiah: his origins were known. The 'knownness' of Jesus was a common synoptic theme (Mark 6³ //) and John makes use of it here for his own purposes. Jesus is known as a man of Nazareth (1⁴⁵; 18⁵, ⁷; 19¹⁹). But the Messiah's origin would not be known. This popular Jewish belief is attested by Justin (Trypho 8), by rabbinic teaching and by apocalyptic writers. Thus Enoch (1 Enoch 48⁶): 'And for this reason hath he [the Son of man] been chosen and hidden before him, before the creation of the world and for evermore', and Ezra (4 Ezra 13⁵¹): 'Then said I, O Lord that bearest rule, shew me this: wherefore have I seen the Man coming up from the midst of the sea. And he said unto me, Like as one can neither seek out nor know what is in the deep of the sea, even so can no man upon earth see my Son, or those that be with him, but in the time of his day.' The fact that Jesus was known to have come from Nazareth would, on these grounds, constitute a refutation to his claim of Messiahship. Yet John is asking his reader to penetrate further. In one sense Jesus' origin is known: he is a man from Nazareth; but, as the evangelist has already made clear, in another sense his origin is not known, and not recognized: he is 'from above', a man from heaven (cf. 3¹³ff, ³¹; 6⁶²). It is precisely in the togetherness of the knownness and the unknownness of the Messiah that the characteristic Christian and Johannine doctrine is to be found. The mystery of the incarnation for the human mind is that the origins of the Son of God can be known. If his origin were really unknowable, there might be reason for asking men to believe that he had come from God; but if men are to believe on him as God's Son while they know his earthly origin, then the characteristic Christian act of faith is called for. John leaves this unequivocally clear.

Jesus takes up with the crowd the question of his known origin. Their remarks brought him to utter a solemn proclamation in the temple. He began by admitting the truth of the crowd's statement that his origin could be and was known. (It seems more in accord with Johannine style not to punctuate the first sentence of direct speech in v. 28 as a question.) But there were things about his real origin in the Father that they did not know. For he was not another instance of a pretender to the Messiahship who came on his own authority for his own purposes; he came as one who had been sent, sent by the Father. The Father is of course invisible, but he can be known, and the fact that the Jews cannot recognize Jesus as the one whom the Father sent is evidence that, although they worship the true God (cf. 4²²), they do not really know the Father. But Jesus does know him, for he has been sent from the Father and comes from (i.e. has his origin in) him (7²⁹). On thus being charged with not knowing God the Jews sought to arrest him, though none of the crowd actually laid hands on him. This part of the story is reminiscent of Luke 4³⁰, where no doubt Luke, like John, realizes something supernatural in Jesus' escape. But it was quite 'natural' that the supernatural escape should have taken place, for *his hour had not yet come* (7³⁰). The reference here is to the final hour of crucifixion and glorification, not (as in v. 6) to the time for visiting the feast. The crowd's last comment reveals its complete misunderstanding of the nature of Jesus' work and person. Some of the crowd, John reports, *believed in him* (7³¹), and said: *'When the Christ* [Messiah] *appears, will he do more signs than this man has done?'* So the populace of Jerusalem remain 'sign-believers' (2²³); and of the worse sort, imagining that the sheer number of signs done is itself a sign, when, contrariwise, one sign properly understood is enough. Indeed in the end only one sign is given, for all the signs now done are themselves 'signs of the sign', signs of the death and resurrection of the Son of man.

২২

25

the people of Jerusalem: The author wants to distinguish the citizens of Jerusalem from the Galilean visitors.

26

'Can it be that the authorities really know that this is the Christ?': Or, 'Can it possibly be that the authorities have themselves recognized that this man is the Messiah?' The fact that Jesus had not yet been arrested suggests this to the citizens of Jerusalem.

27

'when the Christ appears, no one will know where he comes from': Commentators rightly refer to Justin's remark that the Messiahship of the Messiah will not be known until he is anointed by Elijah. The fourth evangelist neither identifies John the Baptist with Elijah (1²¹) nor does he report any baptism of Jesus, even if what he reports presupposes some account such as the synoptists provide of Jesus' baptism (1³²⁻⁴). It seems that the fourth evangelist wants to avoid any possibility of an inference that if the Messiahship be not recognized until the Messiah be anointed, then Messiahship can only be thought to date from the anointing.

28

'You know me, and you know where I come from? But I have not come of my own accord': This makes a better, more Johannine argument if it be in form of a statement. Then Jesus admits that his physical origin can be known, and that the Jews know it; and that nevertheless there is a more important fact about his origin – he has come from the Father.

30

So they sought to arrest him; but no one laid hands on him: cf. Luke 4³⁰ where another evangelist tells of an escape by Jesus which had all the qualities of a miraculous providence.

31

'will he do more signs than this man?': Sign here is in the sense of 'wonder',

337

'miracle' or 'portent'. The Jews have not grasped what the signs signify!

³²*The Pharisees heard the crowd thus muttering about him, and the chief priests and Pharisees sent officers to arrest him.* ³³*Jesus then said, 'I shall be with you a little longer, and then I go to him who sent me;* ³⁴*you will seek me and you will not find me; where I am you cannot come.'* ³⁵*The Jews said to one another, 'Where does this man intend to go that we shall not find him? Does he intend to go to the Dispersion among the Greeks and teach the Greeks?* ³⁶*What does he mean by saying, "You will seek me and you will not find me," and, "Where I am you cannot come"?'*

The Pharisees heard the discussions (muttering in v. 32 does not mean complaint) that were taking place among the crowd, and they combined with the chief priests, who were alone in being able to summon help from police, to send officers to arrest Jesus. The police who came to effect the arrest heard Jesus teach, and failed to act as directed. John, developing in his own way of irony the situation in which the Jews both know and do not know Jesus, now reports teaching not about the origin of Jesus, but about his destiny. '*I shall be with you a little longer,*' he said (7^{33f}), '*and then I go to him who sent me; you will seek me and you will not find me; where I am you cannot come.*' Had the crowd understood that where Jesus came from was not in reality* Nazareth, but from his Father, from above, they would have been able rightly to understand this statement about his destination. But they began to think in the same geographical terms as had led them to picture Nazareth as Jesus' place of origin. So when Jesus says that they would look for him and not find him and be unable to follow him they do not understand that as language about the return to the Father, and they cannot interpret it as speech about a return to Galilee, for thither they would have been able to follow Jesus. So they replied '*Does he intend to go to the Dispersion among the Greeks and teach the Greeks?*' If he doesn't mean this, what does he mean? John has

* cf. the reference to *him who sent me is true* in 7^{18}.

imparted some typical double meaning into the phrase *the Dispersion*. Primarily this was applied to signify the whole body of Jews scattered in many places of the world outside their home in Palestine (cf. Isa. 49^6; 52$^{7-12}$), but it could also be used, as here, to indicate the actual area of the Dispersion (cf. Judith 5^{19}). But in Christian usage the word could denote the members of the one Church or body of Christ scattered throughout the world, as e.g. in 1 Peter 1^1. So John is able to provide another of his double perspectives to a saying of Jesus, which illuminates both the historical situation in which it was spoken, and that in which it was preserved and published as part of a gospel. In John's irony the Jews are postulating for Jesus, and even for the Church, a Gentile mission! It was in this clash of misunderstanding that the police found sufficient reason not to put Jesus under arrest. The Establishment had found an enigma, and had no clue to solve it. Their uncertainty is betrayed in their repetition (v. 36).

ಙಙ

32

the chief priests and Pharisees sent officers: The chief priests were mostly Sadducees, by no means natural or easy allies of the Pharisees.

33

'*I shall be with you a little longer*': The Pharisees and chief priests may resolve to arrest Jesus, but he knows that until his hour comes, and it will come only at the Father's appointment, their decisions can achieve nothing. Yet he knows that his end draws near.

34

'*you will seek me*': They seek him now, but only to arrest him: they will seek him, when he has been glorified, that he might save them.

'*where I am you cannot come*': The Greek word translated *am* may be given a different accenting and then translated 'am going'. This would give quite good and 'Johannine' sense. But the point of *I am* is twofold: first, it links with the 'I am' sayings of the gospel; and second, it underlines the fact that for John Jesus is not glorious only after his glorification, but throughout his life, though that is visible only to the eye of faith.

35

'*Does he intend to go to the Dispersion . . .*': The *Dispersion* here refers to the area of the dispersed Jews. '*Will he teach the Greeks?*' is a contemptuous question indicating the attitude of Jews to Gentiles. Jesus is supposed to be sufficiently careless of Jewish law and custom to go and teach the Gentile Greeks.

36
'*What does he mean?*': The final effect of Jesus' words is to leave people asking questions about him. These had to be answered before the final drama could be enacted.

7^{37–39}   THE GREAT OUTPOURING

³⁷*On the last day of the feast, the great day, Jesus stood up and proclaimed,* '*If any one thirst, let him come to me and drink.* ³⁸*He who believes in me, as^a the scripture has said, "Out of his heart shall flow rivers of living water."*' ³⁹*Now this he said about the Spirit, which those who believed in him were to receive; for as yet the Spirit had not been given, because Jesus was not yet glorified.*

a Or *let him come to me, and let him who believes in me drink. As*

The incident reported in these and the following four verses took place on what John calls *the last day of the feast.* An interesting if somewhat unimportant question is whether this was thought of as the seventh day of the feast proper, or the eighth day which had become a customary addition by the time of Jesus. There is little to assist in a decision, for the whole episode as recorded is explicable on either assumption. The relevant points concern the rite, associated with the Feast of Tabernacles, of bringing water from the Pool of Siloam in a golden flagon and using it for libations in the temple. This was done on the first seven days of the feast, but not on the eighth day. The question which this information does not answer is whether Jesus spoke the words reported on a day when the water was brought from Siloam, or on the eighth day, when its non-performance might well focus attention on it even more strongly. True, evidence for the rite is late, but not therefore to be wholly rejected. Moreover, though the eighth day was not normally called the 'great day' of the feast it was, like the first, a rest day like a sabbath. It seems that whether Jesus' words were spoken on the seventh or the eighth day, they are not inappropriate either as referring to a rite actually going on, or to one that had gone on for seven days, but had now ceased. But even if the uncertainties about the background of the sayings can be not unprofitably left undetermined, they yield in turn to others about the form of words which Jesus spoke.

The setting is festal and solemn; almost momentous. During the feast when the Jews reminded themselves that they depended upon God for the supply of that element which was so essential to the sustenance of life, Jesus stood in the temple and proclaimed in loud tones '*If any one thirst, let him come to me and drink*' (7³⁷). Jesus is in fact beginning to tell the festival crowd in the temple of Jerusalem what he had already told the Samaritan woman at the well by Sychar, that he is the real quenching of thirst that is more than physical, and of which physical thirst, dreadful and critical as it can be, is but a metaphor or symbol. The puzzle about the rest of the words of Jesus can be briefly put thus: Is his saying in the well-known form of Jewish poetry, with a balanced symmetry of expression, or is it somewhat more awkward in form, repeating the teaching of 4¹⁴ about a spring of water welling up in the believer? The text of the R.S.V. translation has assumed the latter solution, which is probably the right one. But the alternative is worth consideration. A translation in terms of it might read 'If any one thirst, let him come to me, and let him who believes on me drink.' This is certainly a neater piece of syntax, and it has a further advantage of allowing the following words to be taken, if that seem necessary, with what follows rather than with what has preceded. Then the words '*Out of his heart shall flow rivers of living water*' need not apply to the believer, and that would be a relief to the Old Testament student, who would find it impossible to cite a quotation making such a statement. But it must be pointed out that the difficulty of finding a suitable scripture quotation even if the words be applied to Christ is still apparently insoluble.

Some writers have suggested that once the connexion with the believer is given up the quotation can best be taken as speaking about Jerusalem. *Heart* in the R.S.V. is 'belly' in the A.V. and the R.V. But 'belly' in the O.T. can be a synonym for 'navel', and Jerusalem is sometimes called the 'navel' of the world. The writers who spoke of the centrality of Jerusalem in the final order which God would inaugurate sometimes pictured Jerusalem as the centre from which flowed life-giving streams of water bringing fertility to the whole outside world. It is suggested that this symbolism gives the real clue to John's meaning here, when Jesus, as the new temple in which Israel shall worship, is also shown to be the true source of the real life of the whole world.

If, over against the not inconsiderable merits of such views, it is decided to adhere to the translation favoured by the R.S.V., the interpreter has the advantage of following the solution generally adopted from the earliest times; moreover, the invitation to drink is much more naturally linked with thirst than with belief. If that leaves the syntax awkward, it is not entirely unusual in the N.T., not even in John; and as for the difficulty of locating a scripture quotation referring to the believer as a source of flowing water, there is some such suggestion in Isaiah 58^{11}: 'The Lord will guide you continually, and satisfy your desire with good things, and make your bones strong; and you shall be like a watered garden, like a spring of water, whose waters fail not.' This is admittedly not the source of a precise quotation in 7^{38}, but it is close enough to provide a relevant reference point. And the final consideration in regard to this line of interpretation is that it provided an offering of the teaching already given to the Samaritan woman in 4^{14}: 'The water that I shall give him will become in him a spring of water welling up to eternal life'.

The evangelist now adds that this saying was really about the Spirit, which was not yet given since Jesus *was not yet glorified* (7^{39}). The statement in the Greek is even more surprising, since if it be literally (though on this occasion it would be inaccurately) translated it would be stating that 'the Spirit was not yet'. Commentators have been quick, and right, to point out that John has no intention of denying that the Spirit existed earlier than the incarnation, but more than this needs to be said. It must be remembered that John is writing from an end-perspective, and from a Church-perspective, and that this yields theological judgements which, if they be translated into historical terms, may cause some unusual statements. What is perfectly plain by the time of the Church, or by the time of the gift of the Spirit to the disciples (which is recounted in John at 20^{22}), is that the Spirit is a gift which includes all the benefits of the incarnation of the Son, and requires that his work on earth be complete and full. That the Spirit cannot come until Jesus be glorified is a theological, not a chronological fact. John is as aware of the activity of the divine nature in the lives of the disciples during the incarnation as are the synoptists. When Peter confessed Jesus as the Christ, Matthew reports that Jesus said to him 'Blessed are you, Simon Bar-Jona! For flesh and blood has not revealed this to you, but my Father who is in heaven.' And if the point be made, as the present writer thinks unnecessary, that Matthew speaks of the 'Father' and not of the 'Holy Spirit' at this point, it is possible to recall that Mark quotes a saying of Jesus himself in which he said that David was inspired by 'the Holy Spirit' (Mark 12³⁶), while Luke preserves a saying of Jesus in which Jesus asks 'How much more will the heavenly Father give the Holy Spirit to those who ask him?' (Luke 11¹³). John's insistence upon the glorification (the crucifixion and exaltation) of Jesus before the Spirit can be given matches, at least in some essential respects, the synoptists' insistence that it is only by sharing the cross of Christ that any man may truly be his disciple. 'No cross, no crown' is a proposition as true of the Lord's disciple as of the disciple's Lord. Only in the sharing of the destiny of the Lord does the disciple acquire the power to become himself, in and with his Lord, a source of life-giving power. The Christian's overflowing spirit of humility, victory and joy cannot be obtained directly, but only in sharing, with Christ, in the agonies of redemption.

ళ

37

On the last day of the feast, the great day: Probably not the seventh, but the eighth day, which was reckoned with those of the feast proper (Num. 29³⁵; Lev. 23³⁶, ³⁹; Neh. 8¹⁸). It was kept as a sabbath, with special sacrifices. Significance would be added to Jesus' words about water if on that day, unlike others in the feast, no water had been brought into the temple from the pool of Siloam. Jesus would then take the place of the water required by the old Jewish rituals, as the source of the real life-sustaining power, which he could give to those who believe on him (cf. 2¹ff).

'If any one thirst': The libation of the water at the feast would not satisfy the thirst of any observer; but Jesus could give what the ritual could not.

38

In addition to what has been said in the commentary it may be useful to refer to what was noted in the Introduction (p. 46) about John's use of his one cited source – the Old Testament. It is not wholly surprising to find that he assumes that he has quoted scripture when, to the precise student, he has not!

39

which those who believed in him were to receive: This is written not only from the perspective of this particular narrative of the gospel but also from the later perspective of the Church, in which every believer has received the Spirit (at baptism).

7⁴⁰⁻⁴⁴   THE CROWD AND THE CHRIST: 2

⁴⁰*When they heard these words, some of the people said, 'This is really the prophet.' *⁴¹*Others said, 'This is the Christ.' But some said, 'Is the Christ to come from Galilee? *⁴²*Has not the scripture said that the Christ is descended from David, and comes from Bethlehem, the village where David was?' *⁴³*So there was a division among the people over him. *⁴⁴*Some of them wanted to arrest him, but no one laid hands on him.*

Hearing this tremendous utterance, the crowd is divided. And little wonder, for the claims inherent in what Jesus had said bordered very close upon the blasphemy for which his life had already been sought in Jerusalem. Two sections of the people took a positive attitude to Jesus. One said that Jesus was *the prophet*, the figure of Jewish expectation who was to appear in the history of Israel to crown and fulfil the work of Moses (Deut. 18¹⁵; cf. 1^{21,25}; 6¹⁴), though by them he was not envisaged as Messiah himself; such people were in the same position as the Galilean crowds on whom the disciples reported to Jesus (in the synoptic tradition) at Caesarea Philippi, holding him to be a figure at most heralding the Messiah, but not Messiah himself. But John tells also of the section of Jerusalemites who because of what he had said believed Jesus to be Messiah himself. But there is a third section of the crowd in the temple who argue very differently: Jesus cannot be the Messiah because he comes from Nazareth, and not, as prophecy foretold, from Bethlehem. Again, this is typical end-writing from John, and a further example of his irony. The scripture hinted at is evidently Micah 5², which is actually quoted in Matthew 2⁶ by the chief priests and scribes in answer to Herod's inquiry as to the birthplace of the king of the Jews. But there is no evidence to support the view that this prophecy was taken to be Messianic before the Christian Church adopted it. So the use of the prophecy here is an example of

John's end-perspective. It illustrates his irony too, because, as one acquainted with the synoptic tradition, John would have been aware of the tradition that Jesus was born at Bethlehem. The Jerusalemites are quite wrong in thinking that, because his home is in Nazareth, he was born there. Once again, and even on a physical level, their ignorance of his origin is exposed. But it is exposed on a deeper level too; for the thing that the Jews are really ignorant of is not just that Jesus was born at, and therefore came from Bethlehem, but that ultimately it has to be said that he came 'from above', from God. John adds that there was a renewed attempt to arrest Jesus by the crowd, but it failed. Once more, his hour had not come.

☙❧

40

'This is really the prophet': This is the figure of Jewish hope, conceived in terms of Deut. 18^{15}. Here it would not be patient of the Messianic interpretation that Peter gave it in Acts 3^{22}.

41

Others said, 'This is the Christ': This is the confession made by Peter at Mark 8^{29}. Even there it is not a final confession of full faith and insight, for Jesus has to go on to rebuke Peter (Mark 8$^{31-33}$); and here too it could lead, as it did in the case of at least some Jews, to a repudiation of all Jesus' claims.

'Is the Christ to come from Galilee?': This and the following sentence are another fine example of John's irony. The Jews were divided as to whether he came from Galilee or from Bethlehem: the difference was quite unimportant beside the all-important fact that he had come from the Father. Not even birth at Bethlehem could be a substitute for that, even if a birth at Bethlehem could be seen, in some sense, as a sign of his coming from the Father.

44
cf. v. 30.

7$^{45-52}$ THE ESTABLISHMENT AND THE ENIGMA: 2

^{45} *The officers then went back to the chief priests and Pharisees, who said to them, 'Why did you not bring him?' * ^{46} *The officers answered, 'No man* *ever spoke like this man!'* ⁴⁷*The Pharisees answered them, 'Are you led astray, you also? ⁴⁸Have any of the authorities or of the Pharisees believed in him? ⁴⁹But this crowd, who do not know the law, are accursed.'* ⁵⁰*Nicode'mus, who had gone to him before, and who was one of them, said to them,* ⁵¹*'Does our law judge a man without first giving him a hearing and learning what he does?'* ⁵²*They replied, 'Are you from Galilee too? Search and you will see that no prophet is to rise from Galilee.'*ᵃ

a Other ancient authorities add 7⁵³⁻8¹¹ either here or at the end of this gospel or after Luke 21³⁸ with variations of the text

John now resumes that part of the story of the Feast of Tabernacles which had begun in 7³² with the authorities sending out police to arrest Jesus. The police had at least heard what Jesus said in v. 33, and possibly also in v. 37f. But whatever they heard had been enough to deter them from making an arrest. They now return to their employers empty-handed, and are asked for an explanation. They reply *'No man ever spoke like this man'* (7⁴⁶). The sentence throws stress on the word 'man', and the implication is that in the view of the police Jesus was more than an ordinary man. This riled the authorities who demanded, *'Are you led astray, you also? Have any of the authorities or of the Pharisees believed in him?'* Again we may detect John's irony, for, as the reader has learnt, Nicodemus had visited Jesus by night, and, as the ensuing incident shows, had not been entirely unimpressed. It may be that the visit of Nicodemus had been kept from the authorities; or it may be that they deliberately chose to ignore it, since Nicodemus · had not publicly professed faith in Jesus. The last sentence of the authorities' reply to the police expresses a radical and far-reaching division in the Jewish community of Jesus' day. Those who were trained in the law, and gave their lives to its observance, the Scribes, Pharisees, Sadducees and others, had a vigorous contempt for the 'poor of the land' who had neither the training nor the time to attend to the keeping of the law in the manner required by authority; this was really a question of being inside or outside the realm of true religion, and therefore of its benefits. So it is the more significant that Nicodemus should at this point 'speak up' for Jesus. What he said was tentative and non-committal, but it was a real attempt to mitigate the clearly fierce opposition now felt by the authorities. *'Does our law'*, Nicodemus asked, *'judge a man without first giving him a hearing and learning what he does?'* So just as Jesus earlier in the chapter had turned an accusation of law-breaking back on to the crowds in the temple (7¹⁹), so now Nicodemus turns a charge against Jesus back on to the authorities. They were surely breaking the law in their proposed course of action? The reply of the authorities is not easy to interpret. The question *'Are you from Galilee too?'* (7⁵²) suggests that unless Nicodemus had come from Galilee there could be no conceivable reason even for his modicum of support for Jesus. The question reveals the depth of the hostility Jesus had already occasioned, and a silent plea of guilty to the implied charge of not keeping the law. The statement about no scripture reference to a prophet rising from Galilee has to be understood without forgetting that Nicodemus, the authorities, and probably the police and some of the crowd, would have known at once that Jonah the son of Amittai who prophesied an extension of Israelite territory in the reign of Jeroboam II had come from Gath-hepher, which, according to Joshua 19¹³, was in what the Jews of Jesus' time knew as Galilee. So the statement cannot be read to mean 'Read the scriptures and you will see that no prophet ever comes out of Galilee', but rather 'Read the scriptures and you will see that there is no prophecy that a prophet will in the future come out of Galilee.' But again, the authorities provide John with a chance to use his irony; Jesus had not come from Galilee; not even, in any ultimate sense, from Judea; he had come from the Father. The real tragedy was not that Jesus must die to fulfil his destiny, but that the Jews could not, as a people, recognize his divine origin.

෧෧

46
'No man ever spoke like this man': The emphatic word is *man.* The sentence could read: 'There never was a man who spoke like this', with the implication that Jesus was really more than human in his nature.

49
'this crowd, who do not know the law': This was their grave defect. Not to know the law was not to be without 'letters', but substantially without 'religion'. The consequences were drastic – and final!

50
'who was one of them': i.e. one of the 'chief priests and Pharisees', one of the Sanhedrin.

51

'*giving him a hearing*': i.e. 'hearing his defence', for which the Greek phrase used is a technical term.

52

'*Are you from Galilee too?*': The question shows the preoccupation of the Jews. Or, to put it another way, it shows how deeply John saw the nature of the conflict between Jesus and the authorities, even at this stage.

'*No prophet is to rise from Galilee*': This is a false statement if it be taken to mean that no prophet has ever come from the northern kingdom. Jonah did, being born at Gath-hepher. The saying was thus probably current and potent at the time of Jesus and/or the evangelist, based upon the strict (Jerusalem) Jews' attitude to 'Galilee of the Gentiles', where, it was felt, the sound if exclusive traditions of Judaism had been hopelessly compromised. 'No prophet will come from Galilee' may well represent a bitter reflection of the strictly conservative Jewish mind of the time.

John 8$^{12-59}$

Rite and Reality: 2
Light

Isaiah 43⁹⁻¹³
Isaiah 60¹ᶠᶠ, ¹⁹ᶠ
Matthew 4¹²⁻¹⁶
Matthew 3⁹
Mark 4²¹, ²²
Luke 2³⁰⁻³²
Luke 3⁸

On a first reading chapter 8 is enigmatic. It begins with one of the gospel's great self-affirmations of Jesus, and though, as shall be shown, the utterance admirably fits the occasion of the Feast of Tabernacles, its theme is immediately dropped, and it seems as if the author resumes a number of themes from earlier chapters, notably those of *witness* and *judgement*, and introduces some quite new matters, e.g. the question of the Jews' descent from Abraham. Apparently it is not until 9⁴ (or even 5?) that the theme of 8¹² is resumed, but by that time all reference to the Feast seems to have disappeared. Yet the enigma is only apparent, for a closer consideration of the text reveals an important progression of thought from 8¹² through the rest of the chapter to 9⁴. It will suffice at this point to indicate the nature of the transition at 8¹², and to leave the rest of the demonstration to the task of exegesis.

In the opening verse of ch. 8 (for it is assumed that 8¹⁻¹¹ is not a true part of the original text, as most modern translators have recognized) Jesus declares '*I am the light of the world*'. At the Feast of Tabernacles four golden candlesticks were lit at night in the Court of Women, and tradition had it that there was not a courtyard in Jerusalem that did not reflect the light. Jesus' declaration thus well fitted the festival. Yet no sooner was it made than it was forgotten, or so it seems; for v. 13 turns from the subject of light to that of witness, which resumes a topic last dealt with in ch. 5. Yet all through ch. 8 there is a connexion, subtle and allusive though it be. For light, in a sense, bears witness to itself, though every other object in the world requires light in order to bear witness to itself. Light always illuminates, is never illuminated; it always bears witness, never has witness borne to it. In this indirect way the validity of a

351

sufficient self-witness is indicated. In the realm of human witness, testimony is always rightly required to be verified by a second witness. This is so even in the case of self-witness; for although introspection is a form of knowledge that no other person can share, a man may even on its basis give false testimony about himself. He may lie; and yet may be ignorant about himself, even if he knows himself in part. But though these reflections apply to all men, they cannot apply to God. In the first place there is but one God, and his self-witness cannot be verified by the evidence of another deity. Second, God is truth, and his witness is therefore true; he does not lie about himself. Third, he knows himself fully and faithfully, and so in speaking the truth about himself cannot mislead his hearers by falsity. The eighth chapter is thus really expounding the character of Jesus as light throughout its course, and provides the evangelist with yet another form in which to establish the high theological claims for the person of Jesus of Nazareth as the Son of God.

Jesus repeats, in the human sphere, the unique position of the Father. Like the Father, he stands alone in his dignity as the Son of God, and so no other man can rightly give testimony to him (cf. 5[33, 34]). Like the Father, he is the truth (1[14, 17]; 14[6]), and so cannot bear false witness, but his witness is 'faithful and true'. Like the Father, he knows himself, his origin and destiny, none of which is hidden from him; so he can speak the truth about himself as men in their ignorance of their own origin and destiny cannot. In all this he is like the light that shines on all other objects and yet receives no light itself; for he reveals in his coming the real situation, the real nature, origin and destiny of all other men, though they cannot reveal anything of his destiny to him. So in this chapter Jesus is naturally found talking about his origin and destiny. He is the true *son of Abraham*; he both comes from and will return to his Father; he comes *from above*; and, as light inevitably casts shadows, so in his coming to proclaim man's victorious destiny in himself, he cannot but *judge*. And yet, for all that he bears witness of himself, seen at its greatest depth his witness is verified by another – by the Father. It is only with such preparation both theological and christological that John is ready to tell how he who is the light of the world made a man born blind to see, or how one who has walked from birth in darkness is brought to travel in the light of day.

8 ^{12}*Again Jesus spoke to them, saying, 'I am the light of the world; he who follows me will not walk in darkness, but will have the light of life.'*

The evangelist resumes his account of the teaching of Jesus at the Feast of Tabernacles (7 ^{39}). There is no indication of any change of time or place; indeed 8 ^{20} reports that the teaching given up to that point was spoken in the temple near the treasury. If John intends his chronological note in 7 ^{37} still to apply, this teaching would be given, as was the great saying of that occasion, on the last day of the Feast. All that was said in the notes then applies equally to this verse. If this were the seventh day, it is possible that in the evening the four golden candlesticks were lit, throwing their glow far beyond the temple precincts. It is reasonably certain that the ceremony took place on the first day of the feast (cf. Sukkah 5 $^{2-4}$), but there is less confidence that it was repeated each night. Even if it were, and this were not the seventh but the eighth day, Jesus' saying would have the force of noting a light conspicuous by its absence. But whatever the chronological setting the force and point of the saying is clear. The world for man is a dark and mysterious place; human life, its origin, its course, and its destiny is shrouded in mystery; Jesus in his coming has brought divine light to play upon the darkness and has shown man the reality of his situation in a final and authoritative act of illumination. With characteristic insight, in using the metaphor of light so firmly associated with the Jewish religion in the Feast of Tabernacles, the evangelist is able to gather up many other theological uses of *light*, from the earlier synoptic tradition (cf. the passages quoted above), from the Old Testament generally (e.g. Gen. 1 ^{3}; 15 ^{17}; Psalm 27 ^{1}; 119 ^{105}; Isaiah 2 ^{5}; 42 ^{6}; 51 ^{4}; 60 ^{19f}), from pagan religions, such as Mithraism, where the sun had a specially divine function ascribed to it, and from Hellenism and its literature. The attention of many readers from many divergent backgrounds would be held and stimulated by this widely prevalent metaphor. *To walk* is a term used in the Old Testament for conduct generally (e.g. 2 Kings 20 ^{3}). *In darkness* gathers its meaning as the argument of the chapter develops. The metaphor rightly suggests that the man who walks in darkness is without guidance; and that, essentially, is the situation of the man who lives without Christ. He alone bestows life; he alone knows whence he comes and whither he goes; so he alone can guide men on their way to the destiny prepared for them by the Father who 'so loved the world'.

სოცს

12

'*he who follows me*': as at 1³⁷ and 21²², to follow is to offer a life in faith and trust.

'*the light of life*': i.e. the light that is life, viz. Jesus himself.

¹³ *The Pharisees then said to him, 'You are bearing witness to yourself; your testimony is not true.'* ¹⁴*Jesus answered, 'Even if I do bear witness to myself, my testimony is true, for I know whence I have come and whither I am going, but you do not know whence I come or whither I am going.* ¹⁵*You judge according to the flesh, I judge no one.* ¹⁶*Yet even if I do judge, my judgement is true, for it is not I alone that judge, but I and he*ᵃ *who sent me.* ¹⁷*In your law it is written that the testimony of two men is true;* ¹⁸*I bear witness to myself, and the Father who sent me bears witness to me.'* ¹⁹*They said to him therefore, 'Where is your Father?' Jesus answered, 'You know neither me nor my Father: if you knew me, you would know my Father also.'* ²⁰*These words he spoke in the treasury, as he taught in the temple; but no one arrested him, because his hour had not yet come.*

a Other ancient authorities read *the Father*

The profound meaning of the great self-affirmation is not directly expounded. Instead, there is a tangential approach through the fact that the great assertion about Jesus as the light of the world has been made by Jesus himself. The Pharisees object that because it is unsupported self-testimony, it is invalid, inadmissible, and untrue. It is interesting to speculate (and no one can do more than speculate) about the connexion of this charge with the statement of Jesus recorded in 5³¹: 'If I bear witness to myself, my testimony is not true.' If this can be in any sense thought of as a Pharisaic quotation of Jesus' words against himself, then they are guilty either of deliberate misapplication (for Jesus immediately went on to say that there was another who bore witness to him, whose witness was true: viz. the Father) or of the shallow misunderstanding so often associated with Jesus' opponents in the fourth gospel. The latter seems to be more in keeping with the narrative and the situation, and in particular because Jesus goes on to expose it for what it is. Yet when he replies to the Pharisees' misapplication of his own words, he seems to contradict his former saying almost outright: *Even if I do bear witness to myself, my testimony is true* (8¹⁴); but does not, as 5³¹ might have led the reader to expect, go on to claim that by virtue of unity with the Father the one witness is really twofold, but states that he knows whence he comes and whither he goes, a knowledge about himself which the Pharisees do not share. But the point is quite valid. To know the facts about the earthly life of Jesus is quite possible, without knowing at all that his story really begins 'with the Father' from whom he came, and ends 'with the Father' to whom he will return. Seen without this knowledge of its setting, the life of Jesus is just another piece of terrestrial history – 'history-knowledge' as Luther rightly called it. But to see those same facts in the great perspective of the eternal being of God is to see them as something quite different, to have 'faith-knowledge', to use Luther's term again, to enter into the knowledge that Jesus had himself, knowledge that he shared with the Father, and that he shares with the believer through the gift of the Holy Spirit. No other man can know, in terms of 'history-knowledge', the ultimate origin and destiny of Jesus Christ. His life remains dark and mysterious to natural man, who has no light to throw upon the story of Jesus to illuminate it and make it meaningful. But Jesus throws light upon it himself; he is the light of the world.

Jesus proceeds: In speaking as they have done, the Pharisees have *judged* him. But they have judged him *according to the flesh*, by the things that can be seen. By contrast Jesus 'judges' no one, a statement which echoes the argument of 3¹⁶⁻²¹, where judgement and light are brought together for the first time in the gospel. Jesus has not come to 'judge' (condemn) the world, but to save it. Yet his very coming to save brings those who reject the light into 'judgement' or 'condemnation' (3¹⁹). Such a condemnation however is not the work of

Jesus alone, Jesus as a mere historical personage, but only of Jesus and the Father together in their indissoluble unity. '*I am*' says Jesus, echoing the great phrase of self-revelation, '*I am the one who bears witness to myself*' and in using the phrase '*I am*', the name of the God of Israel, he can go on readily enough to his further assertion that '*the Father who sent me bears witness to me*' – precisely in his own self-witness!

But the Pharisees still remain, and think, *in the flesh*. '*Where is your father?*' they ask him (8¹⁹). In reply Jesus makes the only possible answer: They do not know whence he comes or whither he goes; therefore they cannot see more in him than just another human historical person. So they cannot really know him, and not knowing him cannot really know his Father with whom he lives, even in the flesh, in an indissoluble unity. The discussion has now been pushed as far as it can go. The quite ultimate gulf that separates Pharisees from Jesus has been disclosed. Nothing more can be said on either side. John simply adds that this teaching took place in the temple *in the treasury*. The treasury was in the court of the women, where the golden candlesticks were lit during the feast. It was also very close to the Headquarters of Judaism, the hall where the Sanhedrin met, and where the final plot against Jesus would be hatched. It was in the same area of the temple that the great vessels were placed to collect the offerings of the people (Mark 12⁴¹⁻⁴⁴). These geographical and religious facts provide motifs for ch. 8 – Jesus, rather than the candlesticks of Judaism, as *the* light, and light of the *world* and not simply of the Jews; the dialogue that follows sharpens the opposition between Jesus and the authorities, who at the end of the chapter are found again in the act of seeking his life.

৩৫

13
The Pharisees exercise a 'fleshly' judgement, based on 'history-knowledge'.

15
'*You judge . . .*': Judge is here almost tantamount to 'reject' (its meaning as 'condemn' may be compared). The rejection by the Pharisees is based upon the evidence of the senses alone, but Christ's judgement is based upon the divine omniscience.

17
This verse is a free reference to Deut. 19¹⁵, which states the law of

witness. '*Your law*' is the way in which, in the dialogues of the Talmud, the Gentiles refer to the law! Jesus is not such an 'outsider'; for as one who is sent by the Father who gives the law (see v.54) he is above it, though not against it.

18

'*I bear witness to myself . . .*': better, 'I am the one who bears witness to myself . . .'

19

The question '*Where is your Father?*' serves to introduce the question of the origin and destiny of Jesus. The answer indicates the foolishness of such a question to anyone who knows the Father!

²¹*Again he said to them, 'I go away, and you will seek me and die in your sin; where I am going, you cannot come.'* ²²*Then said the Jews, 'Will he kill himself, since he says, "Where I am going, you cannot come"?'* ²³*He said to them, 'You are from below, I am from above; you are of this world, I am not of this world.* ²⁴*I told you that you would die in your sins, for you will die in your sins unless you believe that I am he.'* ²⁵*They said to him, 'Who are you?' Jesus said to them, 'Even what I have told you from the beginning.ᵃ* ²⁶*I have much to say about you and much to judge; but he who sent me is true, and I declare to the world what I have heard from him.'* ²⁷*They did not understand that he spoke to them of the Father.* ²⁸*So Jesus said, 'When you have lifted up the Son of man, then you will know that I am he, and that I do nothing on my own authority but speak thus as the Father taught me.* ²⁹*And he who sent me is with me; he has not left me alone, for I always do what is pleasing to him.'* ³⁰*As he spoke thus, many believed in him.*

a Or *Why do I talk to you at all?*

It was, as may not inappropriately be supposed, the last day of the feast, and the pilgrims were thinking, naturally enough, of returning home. Jesus speaks to the preoccupation of their minds by making a statement about himself: '*I go away, and you will seek me and die in your sin; where I am going, you cannot come*' (8²¹). The Christian reader catches easily enough the overtones of the statement, for 'to go away' has become for him a phrase expressive of Jesus' departure from this world and his return to the Father. It was natural enough that Jesus should add that when he had so departed, the Jews would seek him unsuccessfully, and that they would *die in their sin*, the sin, that is, of having rejected the Son of God, and with him their one hope of salvation. '*Where I am going, you cannot come*' then follows as a natural statement, indicating the inability of the unbelieving Jews to enter into the eternal life offered to believers. On a previous occasion when Jesus spoke of the Jews' inability to find him where he will go, the Jews thought that he was making a veiled reference to a mission to the Greeks, a fact which John reports with his characteristic love of irony to indicate the fact that the Church did in fact take the gospel to the Greeks. At the feast of Tabernacles the Jews suppose that Jesus is making a veiled threat of suicide: '*Will he kill himself, since he says, "Where I am going, you cannot come"?*' This is another instance of Johannine irony, for though the charge of suicide could not be laid against Jesus, it can be and has to be said that it was not simply that his life was taken when he was crucified, but that he laid it down of his own free will.

Jesus now passes from speaking of where he was going to saying something, habitual in his teaching (for such is the force of the Greek imperfect which John uses), about his origin. With his accustomed dexterity the evangelist uses words that have meaning and relevance for both Jew and Greek, and yet demand a new interpretation and definition within the ambit of Christian ideas and experience. '*You are from below, I am from above; you are of this world, I am not of this world*' he says (8²³). The Hellenists used this distinction to differentiate between the living and the dead. The Hebrews used it to refer to those who were 'up above' and 'down beneath' this world. Jesus uses the contrast to specify his origin from the Father, and the Jews' origin from their physical father Abraham, and their spiritual father, the devil. The choice that Christ's coming offers the Jews is that of either believing in him as the one who has come from God to bestow the gift of life, or remaining in those sins that focus themselves in the one sin already mentioned (8²¹) – that of rejecting the Son who has come from the Father. Dying in sin(s) can be avoided only, says Jesus, by believing that '*I am he*' (8²⁴ R.S.V.). The saying *I am he* is manifestly enigmatic even as it stands; it is not made any more enigmatic, though the clue to the enigma is more clearly given if the translation be more literal, namely 'unless you believe that I am'. It is difficult, as commentators have noted, to derive any sort of a predicate for 'I am' from the context: the words are evidently meant to bring into the focus of the reader's attention the claim that Jesus made for himself, and that the Christian Church still makes for him, that he stands in relation to the New Israel precisely in the position of 'I am', Jehovah, to the old Israel. Characteristically the Jews miss the profundity of Jesus' statement, and ask him, in effect, to provide a predicate for the verb 'I am . . .': '*Who are you?*', they ask him (8²⁵). Jesus replies that no predicate can be added, because he has always been what he now says he is: 'I am.' The verb 'to be', that is to say, is not used as a simple copula to link a subject and a predicate, but absolutely as a name, precisely as it was used in the name of Israel's God 'I am'. From this standpoint, from this divine perspective, Jesus is able to claim that he can say much and judge much, concerning the Jews. He has been sent by the Father with whom he is one, and whose nature he shares; therefore in declaring what he hears from the Father he speaks the truth. The reliability of the Son's witness is that it is identical with that of the Father, because of the Son's unity with the Father.

Once more, the Jews cannot understand what it is that Jesus is saying, so he continues: '*When you have lifted up the Son of man, then you will know that I am [he],*' (brackets for exegetical purposes from the author) '*and that I do nothing on my own authority but speak thus as the Father taught me*' (8²⁸). No doubt the active form of the verb 'lift up' means that Jesus is referring to the crucifixion, for while it can be said that the Jews crucified Jesus, or shared in doing so, it cannot be said in the same way that they raised him up to heaven. And yet there seems little doubt that the evangelist meant this saying to catch some overtones of meaning from the exaltation (the lifting up) of Christ. It is not mere crucifixion that makes it possible to say 'I, when I am lifted up from the earth, will draw all men to myself' (12³²), but the fact that the one who is crucified and who, through his crucifixion, will draw men to himself, is the Son of man, conqueror of death through death. If then Jesus here refers to his crucifixion, he does so only as Christians have seen the crucifixion as ingredient in and inseparable from the whole complex of events from the 'passion' to the 'ascension and heavenly session'. Yet this only increases the difficulty in understanding the rest of the saying: '*Then you will know that I am* [*he*]' (8²⁸). This is not true as prediction, for many Jews who saw or were complicit in the crucifixion were not converted by it. But John writes from his own perspectives, in particular that of his church at Ephesus, where both the opposition and the conversion of Jews was known (cf. Acts 18¹⁹–19²⁰), and from that of the end of human history when, as Paul could write to the Ephesians, Christ would 'sum up' all things in himself (Eph. 1¹⁰). The power of the crucifixion to bring even the Jews to belief in the Son of man lay in the fact that there, more than anywhere else, it would be made plain that the life he lived with the Father, and that the Father lived with him, was uninterruptible and indestructible. In sequel to such teaching at the feast of Tabernacles, '*many believed in him*' (8³⁰).

אבג

21

'*you will ... die in your sin*': In this verse *sin* is the singular, to indicate, presumably, the great sin of rejecting Jesus, and so cutting oneself off from him who is and has and gives life.

24

'*unless you believe that I am he*': Only trust in Jesus Christ can save men from sin and its consequential death. '*I am*' appears in this verse without any predicate, and it would seem most natural, in the absence from the context of any indication of a predicate (as there is e.g. at 6²⁰), to take the words as a citation of the sacred name of Jehovah, in its Greek form. This would be a claim by Jesus to be of divine stature, and to be so without restriction of time: '*I am*.'. This is the point to which the whole argument now works forward, culminating in v. 58.

25

'*Even what I have told you from the beginning*': The reply Jesus made could be punctuated as a question: 'Why am I talking with you at all?', but this fits the context so ill as to make it quite unacceptable. As a statement three translations are possible: (1) I am from the beginning what I am telling you. (2) I am what I have told you from the beginning. (3) Essentially I am what I am telling you. The R.S.V. and the R.V. support 2, though the words *from the beginning* are not easy to define in that case: they have much greater relevance if taken with *I am*, and that is what the present writer has done. As between '*I am from the beginning ...*' and '*Essentially I am ...*' there is little to choose; they both express the absoluteness that seems the central meaning to be conveyed.

26

'*I declare to the world . . .*': This is the only time in the fourth gospel that this phrase occurs. The mission of the Son from the Father is universal in its scope and intention.

28

'*I do nothing on my own authority . . .*': It seems too much to say, as Dodd does (Dodd p. 254), that the Son speaks the words of God and does his works 'in strict subordination to' the Father. The nature of the relationship as John has already expounded it, and as it will be further expounded, would seem to imply a complete unity in which it would be wrong to use a word to indicate a relationship like 'subordination'. Certainly the Son 'obeys' the Father, but in saying that it must be remembered that a metaphor is being applied, and that the eternal Son does not owe the same sort of obedience as an earthly son to an earthly father. Unity, not subordination is the important theme here as elsewhere in John.

8 31–36   TRUTH AND FREEDOM

31 *Jesus then said to the Jews who had believed in him, 'If you continue in my word, you are truly my disciples,* 32 *and you will know the truth, and the truth will make you free.'* 33 *They answered him, 'We are descendants of Abraham, and have never been in bondage to any one. How is it that you say, "You will be made free"?'*
34 *Jesus answered them, 'Truly, truly, I say to you, every one who commits sin is a slave to sin.* 35 *The slave does not continue in the house for ever; the son continues for ever.* 36 *So if the Son makes you free, you will be free indeed.'*

At this point it is important to put *into English* a subtle difference in the Johannine use of the verb 'believe'. In 8 30 John uses the verb with a preposition: *many believed* IN *him*. But in 8 31 he uses the verb without a preposition: *the Jews who had believed him*. The former use indicates a giving of credence plus intelligent understanding and reliance upon him who is believed. The latter form conveys no more than that credence is given to what has been stated.

So at the end of his discourse in the temple Jesus found many believed in him, giving him credence, and placing personal reliance upon him. The evangelist then relates that Jesus said to those who simply gave credence to his words: '*If you continue in my word, you are truly my disciples*'. Belief is thus not one act of intellection or giving credence; it is much more like placing personal reliance upon another deemed trustworthy. Jesus expresses this in terms of the *word* he has said by saying that true or real discipleship consists in 'continuing with', 'staying with' what had been said. That is to say, it must become a settled point of reliance in the life of the believer, a continuing part of his whole personal attitude. Only as the one who gave credence to, or was stimulated to put reliance upon, Jesus lived by the credence and in the reliance would the truth of what had been said be really known, and the person attain real freedom. Once more John shows his remarkable facility for bringing together into a profoundly Christian statement elements of both Jewish and Hellenistic religious thought. For the Jew the law was truth, and the study of the law made men free. In the Hellenistic world the Stoics taught that man could obtain freedom by regulating his life in accordance with the Logos. For the Jew truth brought freedom from worldly care, while for the Stoic it delivered man from ignorance, error, and final loss of being. For the Christian, at this point of John's gospel as elsewhere freedom was deliverance from sin. But before that point is made clear, the Jews had a comment to make.

'*We are descendants of Abraham*' they claimed '*and have never been in bondage to any one*' (8³³). The comment disclosed a real ability to deal with the argument by metaphor, though it also reveals that the answer is 'on the defensive'. The Jews knew enough about their own history to realize that their claim to freedom from bondage was untrue in the literal sense, for they had been in bondage in Egypt, in captivity in Babylon, and were in Jesus' own day an occupied territory in the Roman empire. The claim never to have been bondsmen must therefore consist in a plea that they had never lost their spiritual autonomy:

> Four walls do not a prison make,
> Nor iron bars a cage.

Yet in making this answer they betray a profound ignorance of their own spiritual situation. There is a similar misconception reported in the synoptics. Jesus ate with tax collectors and sinners, and the authorities questioned his action. Jesus commented: 'Those who are well have no need of a physician, but those who are sick; I came not to call [invite] the righteous, but sinners.' If this be an example of Jesus' irony, it means that the Pharisees are really sick, and need his attendance as the one physician who can cure them, though they believe themselves to be utterly healthy.

Jesus therefore takes the discussion here to its proper depth. The bondage he had spoken of was indeed not physical imprisonment; nor yet was it simply loss of spiritual autonomy or resilience; it was slavery to sin. *'Truly, truly'* (the solemn opening indicates the centrality of what is now said) *'I say to you, every one who commits sin is a slave to sin. The slave does not continue in the house for ever; the son continues for ever'* (8 34, 35). Once more John blends Hebrew and Greek thought, for it was more Greek than Hebraic to think of sin as bondage; the Hebrews more characteristically regarded sin as breaking the law. For Jesus, sin is a manifestation of a state of slavery. And it is at this point that he begins to attack the Jews' confidence in their Abrahamic descent. If to sin is to become a slave and if the Jews are sinners (as they are in their rejection of Christ) and therefore slaves, it follows that they can no longer be free sons of Abraham. The point had particular force, since the Jews were proud to reckon their descent from Abraham through Isaac the free-born, and not through Ishmael the slave-born. But now Jesus shows that they, though free-born, had become slaves, and could not therefore remain as members of a free household. But he, who has remained a true son, remains in the household or family permanently. The slaves, i.e. the Jewish sinners, must be reckoned as outside. But there is still one ray of hope. At the time when a son inherited his Father's property he had special powers to free his father's slaves. Jesus was to enter upon his inheritance as God's Son, through his crucifixion and exaltation. He could really set the Jews free; he could give them real liberty – freedom from sin (8 36).

೧೦

32
'and you will know the truth': So before the devil is denounced as the father of lies, Jesus is presented as the one whose words enable men to know the truth. For John freedom is salvation, deliverance from sin.

33
The pride of Abrahamic descent is reflected much in Jewish literature:

e.g. Psalm 105⁶; Isa. 41⁸; Gen. 22¹⁷; Luke 1⁵⁵. The Church challenged this (Rom. 9⁷) as did John the Baptist (Matt. 3⁹).

35

The freedom, the sonship and the sinlessness of Jesus underlie the thought of this verse. For the story of Hagar and Ishmael see Genesis 17;21.

36

Paul may have this same thought in mind in Gal. 5¹: 'Stand fast in the liberty wherewith Christ has set us free.' *Indeed* is better translated 'really': 'if the Son makes you free, then you will be really free.'

8 37-47   FATHERS AND SONS

³⁷'*I know that you are descendants of Abraham; yet you seek to kill me, because my word finds no place in you.* ³⁸*I speak of what I have seen with my Father, and you do what you have heard from your father.*'

³⁹*They answered him, 'Abraham is our father.' Jesus said to them, 'If you were Abraham's children, you would do what Abraham did,* ⁴⁰*but now you seek to kill me, a man who has told you the truth which I heard from God; this is not what Abraham did.* ⁴¹*You do what your father did.' They said to him, 'We were not born of fornication; we have one Father, even God.'* ⁴²*Jesus said to them, 'If God were your Father, you would love me, for I proceeded and came forth from God; I came not of my own accord, but he sent me.* ⁴³*Why do you not understand what I say? It is because you cannot bear to hear my word.* ⁴⁴*You are of your father the devil, and your will is to do your father's desires. He was a murderer from the beginning, and has nothing to do with the truth, because there is no truth in him. When he lies, he speaks according to his own nature, for he is a liar and the father of lies.* ⁴⁵*But, because I tell the truth, you do not believe me.* ⁴⁶*Which of you convicts me of sin? If I tell the truth, why do you not believe me?* ⁴⁷*He who is of God hears the words of God; the reason why you do not hear them is that you are not of God.'*

Jesus now passes from the description of the Jews as slaves of sin in their rejection of him to a direct challenge to their claim to be true sons of Abraham. He begins by admitting their claim to physical descent from the patriarch. '*I know that you are descendants of Abraham.*' But their sonship is only superficial and not real, for Jesus reminds them that they have already been caught up in the decision to kill him, and the reason is that they have not let his word have any effect on them (8³⁷). There is therefore another contrast between Jesus and the Jews: Jesus speaks of what he has seen with his Father (the language used is that of the immediate and intimate sense of sight) and the Jews do what they have heard from their father (the language is that of the mediate sense of hearing). The Jews, quick to sense this challenge to their true and spiritual as well as physical ancestry, reassert their claim: '*Abraham is our father*' (8³⁹). Jesus reminds them of the implication of their claim: if it be more than simply physical, then it must involve behaviour like that of Abraham. The story behind this observation is evidently that of Genesis 18¹⁻⁸, when Abraham gave generous hospitality to three messengers of God, even though they were 'incognito' – as Jesus had been 'incognito' at the feast, and as he was in a deeper sense 'incognito' in his becoming flesh. Unlike Abraham the Jews not only rejected God's messenger, but actually sought his death. So with a final charge of a different spiritual paternity Jesus said to them: '*You do what your father did*' (8⁴¹).

This is tantamount to a charge of spiritual illegitimacy, and the Jews quickly reject it, and their form of words could well be an attempt to throw the charge back at Jesus. '*We were not born of fornication*' may carry the implication that Jesus was – a thought that was not impossible to a people that could go on to accuse Jesus of being a Samaritan, and so belonging to a people regarded as of illegitimate stock (2 Kings 17²⁴). But though they take the opportunity of a last retort on the physical level, they go on to repeat their claim to honourable descent even in the spiritual sphere: '*We have one Father, even God.*' So they prepare for the exposure of the last and most tragic contrast between Jesus and themselves; for he replies: '*If God were your Father, you would love me, for I proceeded and came forth from God; I came not of my own accord, but he sent me*' (8⁴²). Of course the Jews no more understand this than they have understood his other sayings, and Jesus now probes for the reason. It is given in the assertion that they cannot bear to hear what he says – their conscience painfully accuses them. Then at last comes the final exposure of the real and rival paternities that face each other in and through this dialogue in the temple: '*You are of your father the devil, and your will* [your settled habit

365

of will] *is to do your father's desires. He was a murderer from the beginning, and has nothing to do with the truth, because there is no truth in him'* (8⁴⁴). Here the devil is exposed as anti-Christ, and the reference to him as a murderer *from the beginning* is probably a reference to the story of the 'fall' in Genesis 3, where by the seduction of Adam and Eve he brought death into the world. His falsity is illustrated in the same story for he began his temptation of Eve with a lie: Did God say 'You shall not eat of *any* tree of the garden?' instead of repeating accurately the divine command 'You may freely eat of every tree of the garden; but of the tree of the knowledge of good and evil you shall not eat, for in the day that you eat of it you shall die.' His being the father of lies (8⁴⁴) is shown in the same story, for once he has lied to Eve she replies with a lie: 'We may eat of the fruit of the trees of the garden'; but God said, 'You shall not eat of the fruit of the tree which is in the midst of the garden, *neither shall you touch it,* lest you die' (Gen. 3³). To lie is the devil's nature, as to be the truth is the Father's nature. The children show by their action whose offspring they are! At this point Jesus offers his opponents an argument that would destroy the validity of all that he had said. Could they but show him to be a sinner, then they could reply to his own argument in his own way. If he had sinned, he would be a slave; if a slave, then he would not be a true son of Abraham; and if not a true son of Abraham, then without any claim to be a true son of the Father. But they do not produce any such argument. And again Jesus asks why. Why do they not believe him since they cannot produce any evidence of his falsity? The answer is tragically simple: they are not of God. If they were, they would listen to him: their unwillingness and inability to listen to him shows that they are not of God.

ಬಬ

37
'my words find no place in you': 'fail to operate', 'fail to be effective'.

39
The reassertion of Abrahamic parentage offers the evangelist an opportunity to show that this is not a real theological point; finally the 'parentage' of Jesus and the Jews must be traced beyond Abraham – to God for Jesus and to the devil for the Jews.

'you would do what Abraham did': Some translators and commentators

take this to be an imperative: '*If you are Abraham's children, do what Abraham did.*' But the subjunctive seems better to fit the context.

41

The emphatic position given in the Greek to *we* suggests that the Jews are in fact charging Jesus with being born of fornication.

42

'*I proceeded and came forth from God*': The sense can be better given by some such rendering as: 'I proceeded from God, and here I am' – the latter phrase being held to indicate the arrival of a divine prophet.

43

'*what I say*' . . . '*hear my word*': Behind these translations lie two Greek nouns, one for 'words as spoken,' 'audible speech' (*lalia*) and the other for 'word as message', the divine Word which Jesus both is and conveys (*logos*).

45

'*because I tell the truth, you do not believe me*': It is precisely because Jesus tells the truth that the Jews do not believe him; for if he were to tell them the lies they want to hear, they would believe. The theological basis of their unbelief is in their evil paternity.

8⁴⁸⁻⁵⁹　　　　DEMENTED OR DIVINE?

⁴⁸ *The Jews answered him, 'Are we not right in saying that you are a Samaritan and have a demon?'* ⁴⁹ *Jesus answered, 'I have not a demon; but I honour my Father, and you dishonour me.* ⁵⁰ *Yet I do not seek my own glory; there is One who seeks it and he will be the judge.* ⁵¹ *Truly, truly, I say to you, if any one keeps my word, he will never see death.'* ⁵² *The Jews said to him, 'Now we know that you have a demon. Abraham died, as did the prophets: and you say, "If any one keeps my word, he will never taste death." * ⁵³ *Are you greater than our father Abraham, who died? And the prophets died! Who do you claim to be?'* ⁵⁴ *Jesus answered, 'If I glorify myself, my glory is nothing; it is my Father who glorifies me, of whom you say that he is your God.* ⁵⁵ *But you have not known him; I know him. If I said, I do not know him, I should be a liar like you; but I do know him and I keep his word.* ⁵⁶ *Your Father Abraham rejoiced that he was to see my day; he saw it and was glad.'* ⁵⁷ *The Jews then said to him, 'You are not yet fifty*

years old, and have you seen Abraham?'ᵃ ⁵⁸Jesus said to them, 'Truly, truly, I say to you, before Abraham was, I am.' ⁵⁹So they took up stones to throw at him; but Jesus hid himself, and went out of the temple.

a Other ancient authorities read *has Abraham seen you?*

It would seem that there was no way of escape from the very difficult situation into which Jesus had so inexorably led his opponents. They evidently could not accuse him of sin; they were not prepared to admit his exalted claims for himself or his debasement of themselves (as it seemed to them). But they do light upon a last possible line of defence, which enables them to pick up some of the former points of disagreement. They say to Jesus: *'Are we not right in saying that you are a Samaritan and have a demon?'* (8⁴⁸). The charge was readily at hand, for the Samaritans disputed the Jews' claims to exclusive privilege as Abraham's descendants. So Jesus' attack upon the Jews could easily be ascribed as the mad work of a Samaritan. The accusation also revived the allusion to illegitimacy, for the Samaritans were held to be the product of irregular unions between Israelite women and gentile immigrants (2 Kings 17²⁴ᶠᶠ). As for the charge of having a demon, this gave a certain theological depth to their desire to refute Jesus' accusations; for if he were possessed, then what he said could be properly set aside. Jesus does not take up the Samaritan charge; it would have kept the debate at the physical level; but he does reply to the charge of demon possession. *'I have not a demon; but I honour my Father, and you dishonour* [fail to give due honour to] *me'* (8⁴⁹). The charge of possession is known to the synoptic writers as well, and in all four gospels it is one that is not, in the strict sense of the word, argued out. Indeed it is difficult to see how it can be. But when Mark tells how the scribes from Jerusalem charged Jesus with casting out demons by the prince of demons, Jesus makes a twofold retort: first, he points out the inherent absurdity of an accusation that makes Satan fight against himself. Second, and more profoundly, he says that men's blasphemies are not irredeemable, save that against the Holy Spirit – and by that he means that to call the spirit by which he casts out demons by the name of the prince of demons, to call good evil and light darkness, is in fact to exclude oneself from the possibility of cure. So it is here in John. What Jesus does, in his acts as in his teaching, is to honour his Father. The reaction of the Jews is to fail to give him the honour which they ought to give him as the messenger, the Son of God (cf. the argument of Abraham's action in v. 40). Then, lest this be taken as another piece of pleading by a man for himself, he adds: *'Yet I do not seek my own glory'* – he is not seeking the adulation of men for himself in what he does and says, but only asking from men that they should duly honour his Father. But, he adds, the Father seeks the glory of the Son, and in the end he will give the verdict (*'be the judge'*). The vindication of Jesus lies with what the Father will do. And that this brings Jesus to the very centre of his mission and destiny – his cross – is shown by the fact that he adds: *'Truly, truly, I say to you, if any one keeps my word, he will never see death.'* To keep Christ's word is, of course, more than to keep a commandment, in the usual sense of that phrase. It is to have the whole teaching of Christ dwell within, and to let it be the spirit and power of all action and life. Never to see death is not, at this point, never to undergo bodily death, though that is how the Jews typically misunderstand it; it is rather not to undergo what can be referred to as the death of the soul. This seems to the Jews to give them the opportunity they have been waiting for, and they embrace it with evident eagerness.

'Now we know that you have a demon'. They exult (8⁵²); no one could make such statements unless he were possessed. Though the Jews offer the only alternative to a recognition of the truth of Christ's claims, their assertion is false. But they hasten on with an argument that seeks to rescue their standing as Abraham's true children. *'Abraham died,'* they argue: *'the prophets died. Now you say that if any one keeps your word he shall not taste death'*. Again the Jews have mis-interpreted a saying of Jesus, and turned his reference to the death of the soul to a plain word about the dissolution of the body. They continue, in exulting vein. *'Are you greater than Abraham? Greater than the prophets? Who do you claim to be?'* If Jesus appears to side-step the question, it is only because it cannot be answered on the level at which it is asked; for fundamentally what is at stake now is a strictly theological question, a question about the nature and action of God. *'If I glorify myself'* Jesus replies *'my glory is nothing'*. That is to say that if what he has said seems to be self-glorification, it is in some sense unavoidable that it should. But if it be really self-glorification it will remain simply words. Jesus does not and cannot glorify himself; that act belongs to the Father, who will glorify him when his hour has

come, as the Christian reader knows in advance. Then Jesus makes a statement which, in the plainest terms, identifies his Father with the God of the Jews: '*It is my Father who glorifies me, of whom you say that he is your God*' (8⁵⁴). Yet, for all the grandeur of Israel's history and religion as a traffic of knowledge between God and his people, the Jews have not really known him. But Jesus has known him, and cannot in any circumstances deny his knowledge. He knows the Father and keeps his word: and in so far as that is a reference to the obedience of the Son, it must be recognized that the 'obedience' which Jesus offers flows from an identity of nature and will such as earthly sons, even the best of them, cannot know, but which is nevertheless a pattern of obedience for men in all positions of subordination to authority. Jesus finally takes up the discussion about Abraham again. '*Your father Abraham* [a remark which indicates that it is of their father in terms of physical descent of whom Jesus speaks now, in contrast to 8³⁹] *rejoiced ... to see my day; he saw it and was glad*' (8⁵⁶). This is a final demolition of any attempt to place trust in a physical descent from Abraham. It was one thing to claim such physical descent, and the Jews could claim it validly. But that was not the important or very significant relationship to have with Abraham. Indeed, as the synoptists had pointed out in their stories of John the Baptist, others had challenged the Jewish confidence in their Abrahamic origin '*Do not presume to say to yourselves, "We have Abraham as our father"; for I tell you, God is able from these stones to raise up children to Abraham*' (Matt.3⁹). There was in Judaism the possibility of a far more significant relationship to the great patriarch, and its possibility had been expounded in the Jewish exposition of the scriptures. In commenting on Genesis 24¹ 'Now Abraham was old, well advanced in years' some commentators had interpreted the words translated 'well advanced in years' (more literally rendered 'He went into the days') as meaning that Abraham was shown into the age to come, including the days of the Messiah. It is this scripture and its interpretation that Jesus is using against the Jews at this point, but its use constitutes an overt claim to be the Messiah whom Abraham had seen when he was allowed to 'go into the years'. Abraham's joy is probably derived from Gen. 17¹⁷, when he rejoiced at the disclosure of a future blessing for himself and all the peoples of the world. The Jews perceive with what persistence Jesus refutes them, and their only retort now is to take the words at an absurdly literal level, absurd because the exposition of scripture among the Jews could hardly have been held as literally as now the Jews pressed it back upon Jesus. They said *'You are not yet fifty years old, and have you seen Abraham?'* The reference to fifty years is probably not an indication that Jesus was almost fifty at this time, but rather to what was equivalent to a 'retiring age' for modern men, for fifty was the age at which the Levites retired from active duty. The comment would be *'Are you, still not retired, old enough to have seen Abraham'*, and the comforting conclusion could then be drawn, that no notice need be taken of such a madman's ravings. But Jesus, in a final sentence, convinces them that he may not be so lightly or easily disposed of. The answer he gives is not one which, like their comment, deals with a difficulty of terrestrial time; it is one which firmly and confidently joins terrestrial time and heavenly eternity: *'Before Abraham was* [better – came into existence], *I am'* (8⁵⁸). In a word, Jesus is saying through this response, 'You cannot give yourself grounds for rejecting me by attributing to my saying a quite insoluble problem about time. In fact your problem still remains, for my statement was not about two figures separated by time, but about two figures separated, and also joined, by time *and* eternity.' So he now laid claim not only to be the Jewish Messiah in history, but a being whose real existence was in eternity, though he was now in the flesh in time.

John rounds the story off with a report that the Jews laid hold of stones, ready enough in the temple where building works were still in progress, and meant to throw them at him. But once more, with more than a hint of a miraculous departure, the evangelist records that Jesus hid himself and left the temple. So the story of the visit to the feast of the Tabernacles ended as it had begun, with Jesus in 'secrecy' (the Greek word for 'hide' is the verb of the adjective 'secret' in 7⁴). But this 'secrecy' or 'hiddenness' is more than physical. Jesus had come suddenly to his temple, and had manifested himself. But for all the openness of his self-manifestation, and in particular of his description of himself as the light of the world, what he was and is remained hidden from the Jews. He will come out of this hiddenness only at his glorification, at his cross and resurrection.

There remains one point to discuss about chapter 8. In verse 30 John says that 'many believed in him', and continues in v. 31 to tell what Jesus said to those who gave him credence. But it was at that point that the whole argument about Abrahamic descent began. Has John really got his characters mixed up? And has he therefore slid rather unfortunately from one class of listener to another? Or on the other hand, has he really been aware of what he has done, and has he tried to show what may well be the situation of those who begin by believing, but do not persevere? It has already been apparent that some mystery remains for the reader of the gospel after reading as early as 2²³ of many who believed in Christ's name in Jerusalem because of the signs he did, and after reading of others who believed in him when he was in Galilee (cf. 2¹¹; 4⁵³; 6¹⁴, ³⁴) and in Samaria (4³⁹). The author gives some account of the reason for a falling away of Galilean followers (6⁶⁰⁻⁶⁶), and it would seem not unnatural that he should give a similar, and even a theologically fuller, account of the falling off of some followers from Jerusalem. This would seem to give the better rationale of the narrative of ch. 8, though on such a question each reader needs, and has the right, to make up his own mind.

❦

50
'*he will be the judge*': The Father will in the end vindicate the Son, and this will be the 'judgement' for all those who will not acknowledge the vindication for what it is.

53
The form of the question '*Are you greater ...?*' is such that a Greek would expect the answer 'No'. There is a profound sense in which Jesus must answer 'Yes', though, as his reply indicates, not in any sort of vanity or self-glorification.

'*Who do you claim to be?*' literally, 'What do you make of yourself?'

54
Jesus' reply is that he makes nothing of himself by himself; it is the Father who 'makes' the Son what he is in his glorifying.

57
From the time of Irenaeus this verse has been the reason why some scholars have held Jesus to have been between forty and fifty years old during the years of his ministry. But this is not a necessary inference. If there be any allusion to the years of levitical service, this would imply that the Jews were saying to Jesus, 'If you are still, as you claim "in God's service", you cannot be fifty years old. How can you have known Abraham?'

59
out of the temple: the Lord leaves his temple, where he has 'appeared'.

John 9¹⁻⁴¹

Deed and Word: 3
'The eyes of the blind shall be opened'
Rite and Reality: 3
True Light and True Sight
The Fifth Sign

Isaiah 35^{5-6a}
Mark 8$^{22-26}$
Mark 10$^{46-52}$

In ch. 9 John has skilfully woven three important themes together. First, he carries forward his exposition of the 'signs' of Jesus' messiahship, as these were foreseen in the Old Testament and had begun to be expounded by the synoptic writers: second, he completes his narrative of Jesus as the Lord who came to his temple at the time of the Feast of the Tabernacles and showed himself to be the really living water, the true light of the world, and the true descendant of Abraham and true Son of God: third, he resumes the debate about healing on the sabbath which had been dealt with by the synoptists, as well as partly developed by John in earlier chapters (see notes on chs. 5 and 7). In the story of the man born blind, John relates how he who is the light of the world can bring light to those who are fast enclosed in natural darkness, how the life of the old people of Israel (children of Abraham) finds its fulness in him and those about him, and how the worship of the old temple is replaced by the worship of him who is the *Son of man* (9^{35}) as the *locus* where true worship is offered to the Father (9^{38}; cf. 4$^{20, 23}$). Yet it is not only the messianic fulfilment of Old Testament prophecy, not only the need, as the author saw it, to write safeguarding and explanatory comments on the synoptic material, but also the possibility and apologetic usefulness of presenting Jesus in his works as the crown and fulfilment of Hellenism as well as of Judaism. There is a Greek inscription which reads: 'To Valerius Aper, a blind soldier, the god revealed that he should go and take the blood of a white cock, together with honey, and rub them into an eyesalve and anoint his eyes three days. And

375

he received his sight, and came and gave thanks publicly to the god'
(Dittenberger, Syll. Inscr. Gr. 1173, 15–18). So the author is trying, as
ever, to make the fulness of Christian truth and witness available to
Jews, to Christians already acquainted with the synoptic tradition
and to Greeks who were still within the traditions of Hellenism.

9$^{1-5}$ PROBLEM STATED, ANSWER ANTICIPATED

9 *As he passed by, he saw a man blind from his birth.* ^{2}*And his disciples
asked him, 'Rabbi, who sinned, this man or his parents, that he was born
blind?'* ^{3}*Jesus answered, 'It was not that this man sinned, or his parents, but
that the works of God might be made manifest in him.* ^{4}*We must work the
works of him who sent me, while it is day; night comes, when no one can
work.* ^{5}*As long as I am in the world, I am the light of the world.'*

As Jesus *passed by* he saw a man blind from his birth. The author gives
us no clues save in the setting of the story immediately following the
incidents during the Feast of Tabernacles. It would not be improper,
if it be remembered that locality is subordinate to theology in the
mind of the evangelist, to suppose that Jesus saw the blind man at the
gate of the temple, where, as we know from other biblical stories
(e.g. Acts 3$^{1-10}$ of the healing of a man born lame), sick persons used
to beg. The disciples not unnaturally asked a question about an
affliction that had met a man at his birth. The popular 'theology' of
the time admitted of two explanations of such puzzling mysteries:
either the man must have committed some pre-natal sin, or his
parents had sinned, and the child was being visited with the sins of
the fathers (cf. Exod. 20^5). In a word, they were asking what sort of
happenings in the past could make bearable so apparently intolerable
a burden for man's understanding and loyalty to God. The reply
of Jesus is full and explicit. '*It was not that this man sinned, or his
parents, but that the works of God might be made manifest in him*' (9^3). Or,
in other words, no event in the past can make such undeserved
suffering tolerable to the human spirit; only one thing can make that
tolerable – what God makes of it when he does his work upon it. It
may be reflected that this question is one which is still asked by

contemporary man, and that it remains true that no 'explanation' of innocent suffering in terms of past events can bring relief to human concern about it: Jesus does not even attempt such an explanation. What he does say is that when God has done his work, then some purpose will be discernible in it; and, as we have been led to expect, he proceeds to do 'God's work' upon the sufferer and his suffering, prefacing the deed with a proclamation of nature and purpose.

If the works of God are to be made manifest in the experience of the blind man, then Jesus must do them. *'We must work the works of him who sent me* [i.e. God, the Father], *while it is day; night comes, when no one can work'* (9^4). The coming night is the death which he will die in darkness (the synoptic tradition of actual physical darkness is not recorded in John, see notes ad loc.), and the saying here represents Jesus' sense of impending doom. The more clearly he manifests the Father's glory, the more radical and dangerous is the opposition displayed. Yet, he adds, *'as long as I am in the world, I am the light of the world'* (9^5). He who is the true light cannot but exercise his proper function.

ॐ

3

'. . . but that the works of God might be made manifest in him': This clause which formally suggests that the man was born blind precisely in order that the work of God might be made manifest in him does not really imply such a causal sequence. Both Hebrew and Aramaic languages were characteristically paratactical (putting clauses side by side without thereby implying causal connexions), and the causal forms of classical Greek had given way in popular or Koine Greek to a much looser tie than previously. So what this clause means is that in contrast to the inutility of putting the man's undeserved blindness against parental sin or pre-natal transgression, it will be profitable to set it alongside God's work on it, when it has been done.

4

'. . . while it is day': the day is the earthly life of Jesus, and the night is that dark one in which he is delivered up to men (cf. 13^{30}: 'and it was night').

5

'As long as I am in the world . . .': i.e. while I am in the land of the living. Probably a deliberately ambiguous phrase, for even after the ascending of the Son of man he came back to his own (see 20^{19-29}; 21^{1-23}).

377

⁶As he said this, he spat on the ground and made clay of the spittle and anointed the man's eyes with the clay, ⁷saying to him, 'Go, wash in the pool of Silo'am' (which means Sent). So he went and washed and came back seeing.

The similarity of this healing to that recorded in a Greek inscription has already been mentioned. Clearly John's narrative of a miracle is less full of 'magic' than that of the Greek author, and yet the effect of Jesus' healing is more immediate. These are both effective apologetic points. But more instructive still is the way in which the synoptic record of the direct use of spittle in healing is made by John to assimilate something of the narrative of creation in Genesis 2. Mark twice reports Jesus using spittle: once in the healing of a deaf mute, when Jesus 'spat and touched his tongue' (Mark 7³³), and once when he spat on the eyes of a blind man (Mark 8²³). If a reason be sought why John should add the mixing of clay and spittle to the Marcan form of healing by spittle the answer must surely lie in the fact that, as the evangelist indicated at the healing of the lame man in ch. 5, much more is involved in healing one infirmity than the restoration of one function to a person; rather does Jesus' healing constitute the re-creation of the whole person. This is symbolically represented in the Johannine narrative by the introduction of the clay that is mixed with spittle, reminding the alert reader of the fact that in Genesis God had first made Adam out of the dust of the ground, when it had been softened by rain and mist (Gen. 2⁵⁻⁷). Or as Paul put it in a more theologically worded phrase: 'If anyone is in Christ, he is a new creation' (2 Cor. 5¹⁷). The instructions which accompanied the use of clay made from dust and spittle were that the man should go to the pool of Siloam and wash. No doubt here the evangelist picks up the other thread of Christ's Tabernacle proclamation – that he has living water to offer to men. Here the blind man is sent to water which, in the perspective of the Church, came to be seen as disappearing in him who is the living water himself and in that baptism into his name which remains in the Church as the symbol of man's incorporation into him. The name Siloam is understandably emphasized by the evangelist, for it means *sent*. By this time it has become almost a titular phrase about Jesus himself that he has been sent; it is not unnatural that one who is to become a new disciple should therefore be 'sent' to his baptism, and through his baptism to a new identification with Jesus Christ. So John anticipates in the course of the ministry the charge that Jesus gives to the apostles after the resurrection: 'As the Father has sent me, even so send I you' (20^{21}). The result of these injunctions is swiftly and simply told, and needs little comment: He went and washed and came back seeing (9^7). The light of the world had not only shone upon the blind man, but had shone into and through him so that he could now see the world into which God's light daily shone, and nowhere more than where Jesus himself walked and talked and worked.

᙭

6

As he said this, he spat on the ground: Note that the initiative for the whole miracle comes from Jesus himself. All through this is to be the work of God, sheer grace, sheer kindness.

7

It was from the pool of Siloam that water was drawn for the libations at the feast of Tabernacles. The blind man demonstrates that Jesus fulfils the feast as both the one who commands the life-giving water, and he who shines as the light of the world.

9$^{8-12}$ A CHANGED MAN

^{8}*The neighbours and those who had seen him before as a beggar, said, 'Is not this the man who used to sit and beg?' ^{9}Some said, 'It is he'; others said, 'No, but he is like him.' He said, 'I am the man.' ^{10}They said to him, 'Then how were your eyes opened?' ^{11}He answered, 'The man called Jesus made clay and anointed my eyes and said to me, "Go to Silo'am and wash"; so I went and washed and received my sight.' ^{12}They said to him, 'Where is he?' He said, 'I do not know.'*

When the once blind man resumed his place in Jerusalem, both his neighbours and those who had seen him begging were puzzled. Something had evidently happened, and it was beyond normal understanding. The question troubling them was whether this was the same man; and Johannine irony has never been more quietly or effectively used than in reporting this discussion about the 'new creation' of a man remade by Christ. In answering the question some said '*It is he*', echoing in human speech in the third person that 'I am' which is the divine name, and so suggesting that some contagion of divinity remains with the healed man. Others said 'No, but he is like him'; and both answers can be read as stating some real truth that the speakers do not know. There is a sense in which the man can now join his Lord and say 'I am'; there is a sense in which, by this encounter, he has been made 'like Jesus'. But the man, who is evidently aware of the discussion, though as yet the depth of the meaning is hidden from him, replies '*I am*'. In the synoptic gospels the Twelve had been appointed 'to be with' Jesus (Mark 3¹⁴ //); in the fourth gospel it has already been made clear that to enter into proper relationships with Jesus means that the disciple 'abides in him' and Christ in the disciple. Now by means of a so far almost unconscious bond established between Jesus and the man born blind, the disciple is found using a term that is, strictly speaking, reserved to his Lord. The friends and neighbours of the man then asked: '*How were your eyes opened?*' The reply comes back from the man who has only just begun to use the sight that the light of the world has given to him, '*The man called Jesus made clay and anointed my eyes and said to me, "Go to Siloam and wash"; so I went and washed and received my sight*' (9¹¹). And at this stage of his newly given sight he is unable to say even where Jesus might be found. The healer was just another **man!**

ളാ

9
He said '*I am the man*', or, literally translated 'I am'. John thus subtly indicates how the gift of sight has been more than the provision of the use of a sense, but indeed the making of a new creature. Where the old man would use these words of divine self-assertion only blasphemously, now that the man is re-made by the Son, he comes, by sharing in the Son's life, not improperly to echo the language of the Son himself.

11
'*The man called Jesus*': A description meant to emphasize the purely human estimate from which, like all other men, the healed man started.

13 They brought to the Pharisees the man who had formerly been blind. 14 Now it was a sabbath day when Jesus made the clay and opened his eyes. 15 The Pharisees again asked him how he had received his sight. And he said to them, 'He put clay on my eyes, and I washed, and I see.' 16 Some of the Pharisees said, 'This man is not from God, for he does not keep the sabbath.' But others said, 'How can a man who is a sinner do such signs?' There was a division among them. 17 So they again said to the blind man, 'What do you say about him, since he has opened your eyes?' He said, 'He is a prophet.'

At this stage of the story the man who had been so signally healed was taken to the Pharisees, i.e. to the leaders and rulers of God's people. The healing had taken place on the Sabbath, and some interrogation of the healed man was not unnatural. The man repeated his story to the Pharisees, and recounted in simple terms the sequence of events (9^{15}). This produced a division among them. Some saw in Jesus a diabolic influence in the life of God's people: *'This man is not from God, for he does not keep the sabbath'* (9^{16}); though others argued *'How can a man who is a sinner do such signs?'* The motive of the question next addressed to the once blind man cannot be certainly determined, but it was natural enough in the circumstances: *'What do you say about him, since he has opened your eyes?'* (9^{17}). The man, whose vision is clearly represented as not simply a physical affair, because what he has heard has evidently affected his judgement, replies *'He is a prophet'*. Already, and without further 'sight' of Jesus himself, he is prepared, in somewhat high and critical theological company, to affirm more about Jesus than that he was 'just another man'. But the statement that he was a prophet falls short of the confession that the authorities sought, e.g. from John the Baptist (1^{21}), and that the crowd made at the time of the miraculous feeding (6^{14}), and at the time of his great self-affirmation in the temple during the feast of Tabernacles (7^{40}). This confession is simply that Jesus is a man used by God, as any prophet was; it is on a par with the confession of the woman at Sychar (4^{19}), and of the crowds on whose estimate of Jesus the disciples had reported at Caesarea Philippi (Mark 8^{28} //). More insight is to come later in the chapter; but for the moment it is interesting and significant to notice the growing insight of the healed man. The suggestion that Jesus was a *sinner* (9^16) resumes the argument about the rightness of healing on the sabbath day, an argument to which Jesus has already replied by suggesting that thus to state it in his case is to misstate it, for such a mode of questioning avoids the consideration of his status as the Son of God (see notes on chs. 5 and 7 passim).

ରେ

14
This healing doubly broke the sabbath law, which forbade works of healing, and also kneading, which was involved in making clay of spittle and dust.

16
The undisclosed premiss of this verse is probably Deut. 13^2-6, where the sign-worker who leads men away from their inherited worship is deemed worthy of death.

There was a division among them: as also recorded at 7^43 'among the people'. Now even the authorities are divided over Jesus!

17
'*He is a prophet*': Not *the* prophet. Jesus has now been seen as an inspired man.

9^18-23   PHARISEES AND PARENTS

^18 *The Jews did not believe that he had been blind and had received his sight, until they called the parents of the man who had received his sight, ^19 and asked them, 'Is this your son, who you say was born blind? How then does he now see?' ^20 His parents answered, 'We know that this is our son, and that he was born blind; ^21 but how he now sees we do not know, nor do we know who opened his eyes. Ask him; he is of age, he will speak for himself.' ^22 His parents said this because they feared the Jews, for the Jews had already agreed that if any one should confess him to be Christ, he was to be put out of the synagogue. ^23 Therefore his parents said, 'He is of age, ask him.'*

There is no need to search for motive to understand the action of the

Jews (i.e. the Pharisees, here as often in John), for the desire to interview the parents arose from the dilemma which they could not
resolve alone. If such an evidently divine miracle had been wrought,
the agent of it would surely not have performed it on the sabbath.
There must be some error in the reports reaching them, and, very
largely to obviate the need for the division that the reports occasioned,
the authorities decided to interview the parents. The interview did not
assist them much, if at all. It established that the man was indeed the
son of the parents, and that he was born blind. But beyond that the
parents accepted no responsibility. '*He is of age* [i.e. old enough to give
testimony, which meant at least 13], *he will speak for himself.*' The
parents, that is to say, were content to relate the facts, without trying
to assess their significance in terms of the person who was chief agent
in the story. The evangelist reports that this was due to fear, since the
authorities had already *agreed that if any one should confess him to be
Christ, he was to be put out of* [excommunicated from] *the synagogue*
(9^{22}). It is highly doubtful, as learned commentators remark, whether
the authorities had at this stage, or ever during the earthly ministry
of Jesus, decided upon excommunication from the Jewish religion for
any sort of adherence to or confession of Jesus Christ. But it must be
remembered that John is writing from the perspective of the Church,
and the decision to excommunicate Christians is in that perspective
only the logical outcome of the inevitable decisions that had to be taken
during the ministry of Jesus about such an event as this.

ಿಂ

18
The Jews: A term which appears here to be interchangeable with 'the
Pharisees', the idea being that the people as a whole are properly to be
thought of as represented in their leaders.

21
'*he is of age*': If the parents meant that their son was just old enough to
give valid testimony in a court of inquiry, they would be asserting that
he was thirteen. It might seem more natural to suppose that he was not
too far removed from that age than that he was a long way past it;
though certainty is unattainable.

22
*if any one should confess him to be Christ, he was to be put out of the
synagogue:* The phrasing seems undoubtedly to stem from the time
when the Church confessed Jesus to be Messiah and Lord (cf. Acts 2^{36}).

That this would make at any rate part of this scene unhistorical in our modern sense need not cause alarm, for, as has been pointed out before, John writes quite consciously from the perspective of the Church. There is some room for genuine doubt whether in this verse John refers to total or temporary or partial exclusion from the synagogue (the literal translation is that any one confessing Jesus as Christ would be 'extra-synagogue'). A different expression is used in v. 34.

24*So for the second time they called the man who had been blind, and said to him, 'Give God the praise; we know that this man is a sinner.'* 25*He answered, 'Whether he is a sinner, I do not know; one thing I know, that though I was blind, now I see.'* 26*They said to him, 'What did he do to you? How did he open your eyes?'* 27*He answered them, 'I have told you already, and you would not listen. Why do you want to hear it again? Do you want to become his disciples?'* 28*And they reviled him, saying, 'You are his disciple, but we are disciples of Moses.* 29*We know that God has spoken to Moses, but as for this man, we do not know where he comes from.'* 30*The man answered, 'Why, this is a marvel! You do not know where he comes from, and yet he opened my eyes.* 31*We know that God does not listen to sinners, but if any one is a worshipper of God and does his will, God listens to him.* 32*Never since the world began has it been heard that any one opened the eyes of a man born blind.* 33*If this man were not from God, he could do nothing.'* 34*They answered him, 'You were born in utter sin, and would you teach us?' And they cast him out.*

The blind man is recalled for further interrogation. It begins on a different note. The authorities have evidently made up their minds which of the two views that divided them before they will now affirm. It is incontestable, even after inquiry from the man's parents, that Jesus has broken the sabbath law. He must therefore be a sinner. So the first word spoken to the newly seeing man at this second questioning is 'Give God the praise; we know that this man is a sinner' (9^{24}). If the reader turns to the story of Achan (cf. Joshua 7^{19}) he will detect that the phrase 'Give God the praise' really means 'Admit the truth'. The authorities cannot forget that the sabbath has been broken; Jesus is therefore a sinner. But the man cannot forget that he has been healed; Jesus is a prophet. The answer he now gives reflects his inability to overlook the great fact of his being healed; '*Whether he is a sinner, I do not know; one thing I know, that though I was blind, now I see*' (9²⁵). The authorities, who, unlike the man healed, are finding themselves driven further and further away from Jesus, make one last attempt to have the details told so clearly that the issue is settled beyond doubt. '*What did he do to you? How did he open your eyes?*' they ask. The newly seeing man, becoming impatient both with his questioning and his questioners, answers somewhat pertly: '*I have told you already, and you would not listen. Why do you want to hear it again? Do you want to become his disciples?*' (9²⁷). At this the authorities are not surprisingly indignant, and exclaim '*You are his disciple, but we are disciples of Moses*' (9²⁸). In this way they have made clear that the choice with which Jesus confronts the old people of Israel is between the old Moses through whom came the law, and the new 'Moses' through whom grace and truth are come (cf. 1¹⁷; also Matt. 5²¹ᶠ,²⁷ᶠ, etc.). The boast of the representatives of the old Israel continued: '*We know that God has spoken to Moses, but as for this man, we do not know where he comes from*' (9²⁹), though these words formally contradict what the populace had said in 7²⁷ at the feast of Tabernacles, that they knew where Jesus came from. But the contradiction is purely formal. Both sayings are instances of John's irony, being both false and true together. The authorities do know Jesus' birthplace, though they do not know his divine origin; so any statement of ignorance or knowledge about Jesus' origins on their lips will be both true and false. This is the awful fate of those who reject the light that shines to reveal things in their reality.

The man born blind can however say other things. If there be a miracle on that sabbath it is not his receiving sight, it is that the authorities should not know where Jesus *comes from* if he is able to give sight to one born blind, a quite unprecedented healing! Such a man cannot but be 'from God' (9³⁰⁻³³). Such a theological refutation of the official theologians of Israel was inexcusable effrontery; and the man was excommunicated. What the parents had feared, the son endured.

ഇള

24

'we know that this man is a sinner': It was such a claim to certain knowledge and judgement that constituted the basis for Jesus' judgement that the Pharisees claimed to 'see', cf. v. 41.

25

'one thing I know': Belief that is generated by a sign may be in some instances inadequate; indeed even this man's faith can not yet be taken as fully developed; yet it begins from an acceptance of the work that Jesus had done as the one reality that must be recognized unconditionally as such. The 'one work' that Jesus came to accomplish (cf. 4³⁴), to gather in the harvest for the Father, which he does through his being raised up on the cross, is, in the perspective of the Church, the means of Jesus bringing 'sight to the inly blind'; and in this sense Paul's word to the Corinthians 'I decided to know nothing among you except Jesus Christ and him crucified' is an exact parallel to the words of the blind man healed.

28

'You are his disciple, but we are disciples of Moses': This reiterates the substance of previous controversy over sabbath healings (cf. notes on chs. 5 and 7). It serves also to point the contrast made in the prologue (1¹⁷) of Jesus as the source of grace and reality, and Moses as the source of the law.

31

'We know that God does not listen to sinners': This is a notion familiar throughout scripture, and beyond. The Psalmist can say 'If I had cherished iniquity in my heart, the Lord would not have listened' (Psalm 66¹⁸), and James puts the converse truth in writing 'The prayer of a righteous man has great power in its effects' (James 5¹⁶). It is, of course, the unrepentant sinner whom God will not hear; for 'a broken and a contrite heart, O God, thou wilt not despise' (Psalm 51¹⁷).

34

There is room for difference of opinion as to whether the Greek here necessarily implies full excommunication from the synagogue. The present writer thinks that full excommunication is meant, and that, because John is once more writing from the perspective of the Church, it must not be weighed against this interpretation that such a sentence would be unlikely, if not impossible to suppose, at any stage of Christ's ministry before the crucifixion.

³⁵*Jesus heard that they had cast him out, and having found him he said,* *'Do you believe in the Son of man?'ᵃ* ³⁶*He answered, 'And who is he, sir, that I may believe in him?'* ³⁷*Jesus said to him, 'You have seen him, and it is he who speaks to you.'* ³⁸*He said, 'Lord, I believe'; and he worshipped him.*

a Other ancient authorities read *the Son of God*

To be excommunicated was to be put into a position where no true Israelite would have any traffic or communication with the culprit put out. But the one who is and represents the New Israel acts otherwise, and seeks the man who had suffered the severest punishment short of a capital penalty. When Jesus found him, he asked the simple question *'Do you believe in the Son of man?'* (9^{35}). With no aids to help him, the healed, excommunicated man answers with a question: *'And who is he, sir, that I may believe in him?'* (9^{36}). The man is not uncertain as to what the phrase *Son of man* means; he is not asking for information about a figure which was a common element in contemporary Jewish religious expectation. He was asking with what person, if any, the figure might be identified; and the reply of Jesus is electric: *'You have seen him, and it is he who speaks to you'* (9^{37}). It is impossible to say precisely what Jesus and the newly seeing man understood by the term *Son of man* on this occasion, but it is clear from John's use of the term that it always carries two meanings: first, a reference to the heavenly, archetypal man, who can be seen only with the eye of faith; and second, that same figure as he goes, in a human life, to be 'lifted up' on the cross, where his victory will be won. On any showing the words would have extended the spiritual perception of anyone who had seen Jesus in the flesh. Yet in the pause between one sentence and the next, it is almost possible to see the once blind man take a new look at his interrogator, and see precisely the same phenomena as he had seen before, as even his previous questioners had seen as they looked on Jesus – face, hair, clothes, hands, gestures all the same, and like those of any other man – and yet! Yet now, with power of sight given to him by Jesus in a humanity that was a new creation, he can see beyond or through the phenomena that are but signs and symbols to the reality inherent in them, and he confesses 'Lord, I believe'; and he worshipped Jesus. And this is the real miracle of the miracle. As the synoptists had made clear, healing miracles were not unknown among the Jews (cf. Luke 11¹⁹; Matt. 12²⁷); what made the miracle worked on the man born blind unique was in part that for the first time in history sight had been given and not just restored; but in greater part it was that the bestowal of sight by Jesus enabled a man who had only just begun to see to look at the human Jesus and see the heavenly Son of man. Sight had been given with insight. The man had come to do that which cannot be done by man without divine aid – recognize the incarnate Word in the flesh that he assumed.

It is at this point that the question raised by the disciples at the beginning, and its answer by Jesus, may profitably be asked again. Does past wrong-doing, by the sufferer or by another, ever make tolerable to mind and heart the suffering that is 'undeserved'? The answer is 'no' and must remain 'no'; but now that God's work has been done upon the disease and the sufferer, the undeserved suffering has been integrated into something which can be answered with nothing but thanksgiving. The man who had never been able to see has now, because he was so innocent a victim, been given a sight that is profoundest insight as well. He may properly even give thanks for his previous affliction, for otherwise he might have been one of those Jews who though they could 'see Jesus' yet joined together to demand his death. And if that reflection raise, as it does, further questions, the reader must be referred to Paul's treatment of the Jews' opposition to Jesus in Romans 9–11, where he ventures upon some exposition of the eventual rightness of God's apparent 'un-rightness' in his treatment of both Jews and Gentiles. Though he seems to be arbitrary and even 'immoral' in his dealings, in the end all men will come to praise him for the exceeding wisdom of his ways (cf. especially Rom. 11²⁸⁻³⁶).

ಐಐ

35

'*Do you believe in the Son of man?*': Some ancient authorities read 'Son of God' for *Son of man*. The theological difference is not so great as a twentieth-century reader might at first suppose. In the first place the term 'Son of God' had not attained, by the time John was writing his gospel, all the metaphysical character that it acquired in the course of the first four centuries; in the second, the term Son of man in John refers always to the heavenly, the archetypal man, whose destiny lay through being lifted up on the cross to being raised up to the place of authority and power, as the one mediator and judge of men.

36

'*And who is he, sir?*': The word *sir* is the same as that for Lord. The ambiguity is probably often intentional in John, and seems to be so here. The actual course of the historical conversation would give the translation *sir*, but as received in the Church that could share the man's confession, 'Lord' would be more appropriate.

37

'*You have seen him*': In Mark Jesus foretells that the Son of man will be seen – in the future (Mark 13^{26}; 14^{62}). It is characteristic of John to show as present reality what is eschatological expectation in the synoptics.

38

and he worshipped him: This is the proper end of the bestowal of the light that illumines the mind and heart, as physical observation is the end of the quickening of the sense of sight.

9^{39-41} AUTHENTIC SIGHT AND REAL BLINDNESS

[39]*Jesus said,*'*For judgement I came into this world, that those who do not see may see, and that those who see may become blind.*' [40]*Some of the Pharisees near him heard this, and they said to him,* '*Are we also blind?*' [41]*Jesus said to them,* '*If you were blind, you would have no guilt; but now that you say,* "*We see,*" *your guilt remains.*'

The story of the miracle has now been told. Jesus adds a word of explanatory comment. The Pharisees intervene, and Jesus utters a final word of warning.

The sight which Jesus gave to the man born with none is a sight enabling him to recognize Jesus as Son of man – i.e. as a heavenly being who, in his earthly life, must attain his victory by being lifted up on the cross. Once this point has been reached, it is possible for Jesus to indicate once more what the meaning of a 'sign' really is. It is a means by which men may be brought to see him in his reality as the one who by his coming-in-the-flesh, his dying and rising, brings judgement, final judgement into the world; not indeed as a judgement separate from history or beyond it, but taking place within it, as men come to see, or not to see, the reality of what happens when Jesus is 'raised from the earth'. '*For judgement I came into this world, that those who do not see may see*' (and the man born blind is an excellent example) '*and that those who see may become blind*' (9³⁹). This searching saying must not be taken to mean that there is anything automatic about either the 'sight' of the blind man who acknowledges Jesus as the Son of man, or the 'blindness' of the Pharisees who do not. The contrary is indeed emphasized in the brief dialogue that follows. Some of the Pharisees had heard what Jesus said in final comment on the sign; they asked him '*Are we also blind?*' The question picks up the word 'blind' in v. 39, and so means: '*Are we examples of those who "see" but by your judgement are now become blind?*'. Jesus' reply makes it plain that 'seeing' in the sense of 'believing' or being blind in the sense of not believing is a fully voluntary and responsible act of the human person. '*If you were blind, you would have no guilt*' – that is to say, if your inability to confess me as the Son of man along with the healed man were an affliction like physical blindness there could be no possible blame attaching to your unbelief. But that is not the case, for you profess to *know*, to *see*. Therefore your blindness is not an affliction for which you cannot be blamed, but an act of refusal, for which you must accept responsibility. Physically the man born blind could not be blamed for his affliction; spiritually you cannot but be blamed for yours, for you stake a claim to spiritual knowledge and authority. '*Your guilt remains*' (9⁴¹). The word *remain* is normally used in John for Christ or his word or spirit remaining or abiding with men, though not exclusively. Here it is used to emphasize the ineluctable nemesis of refusal to see the light; enduring blindness is the consequence. The synoptic parallel to this 'hard saying' is that about the unforgivable sin (Mark 3²⁹ //).

༄

41

There is a spiritual blindness which is pardonable, and Paul writes of it when he asserts the necessity of law to bring about sin: 'where there is no law there is no transgression' (Rom. 4¹⁵; cf. 5¹³). But the Pharisees, who appeal to the law both to justify themselves and to condemn Jesus, cannot thus be acquitted. Their culpability remains.

John 10$^{1-39}$

The Good Shepherd

Psalm 23
Jeremiah 23[1-8]
Ezekiel 34
Mark 6[34]
Matthew 9[36]
Luke 15[3-9]

The beginning of a new chapter must not be allowed to obscure the formal and material signs that the whole of ch. 10 down to v. 39 continues, completes and crowns the narrative begun at 7[1]. The formal sign consists of the opening words of the chapter: '*Truly, truly*'; for though this distinctively Johannine phrase occurs 25 times in the Gospel it is nowhere used to introduce a new section. Admittedly at 6[26] the phrase is used at the beginning of what Jesus said to the crowds who found him in Capernaum the day after the feeding of the five thousand; but Jesus is there resuming the discourse of yesterday, not beginning some new teaching. Here too the expression marks a resumption and completion of the examination and exposition of the situation following the healing of the man born blind. For though the imagery of the sheep, the shepherd and the brigands is new, the reality which they represent is already under discussion. The beggar who was born blind and comes to believe in Jesus as the Son of man is the sheep who is now said to hear the voice of the shepherd and recognize it; the false shepherds who betray their trust as guardians of the flock are, in an imagery already familiar through the book of Ezekiel, the rulers of Israel, in this context the Pharisees of ch. 9. Moreover, the evangelist now draws together three strands from his previous narrative as he brings ch. 10 to a close: the problem about the person of Jesus as the one who opens the eyes of the blind (10[21]; cf. 9[32, 33] etc.), Jesus' foretelling of his own death (10[11, 15, 17]; cf. 8[28]) and the inability of his opponents to act decisively against him because '*his hour had not yet come*' (10[31-39]; cf. 7[44]; 8[20, 59]).

It is equally evident that ch. 10 is meant to lead on to ch. 11, and to the story of the 'passion' that follows it.* The reference to 'laying

---

* The word 'passion' is used for the convenience of indicating a well-known complex of events recognized under the name; it is enclosed within inverted commas because the term 'passion' is hardly appropriate to the Johannine

393

down his life' and 'taking it again' presents Jesus as the one who has authority over life and death, which is exemplified both in the story of the raising of Lazarus, and in the narrative of his own death and resurrection.

IO$^{1-6}$ THE SHEEP, THE SHEPHERD AND THE BRIGANDS

IO *'Truly, truly, I say to you, he who does not enter the sheepfold by the door but climbs in by another way, that man is a thief and a robber; ²but he who enters by the door is the shepherd of the sheep. ³To him the gate-keeper opens; the sheep hear his voice, and he calls his own sheep by name and leads them out. ⁴When he has brought out all his own, he goes before them, and the sheep follow him, for they know his voice. ⁵A stranger they will not follow, but they will flee from him, for they do not know the voice of strangers.' ⁶This figure Jesus used with them, but they did not understand what he was saying to them.*

The story of the excommunication of the man born blind from the Jewish religious community and his subsequent calling by Jesus has posed for the reader of the Gospel, as well as for Jesus' contemporaries, the question: 'Who is the true leader and ruler of the true people of God? Who has the proper authority to include or exclude a man from the society of God's chosen people?' The 'figure' of the Sheep, the Shepherd and the Brigands begins the answer to such questions. Evidently the tradition did not preserve an authoritative application or interpretation of the figure, and the commentator is left to do his best. The first verse speaks of those who do not enter by the door, but climb in another way, who are thus disclosed to be thieves and robbers. To interpret this obscure saying is hazardous, but some indication of its meaning may be gained from the fact that Judas is called a 'thief' (12⁶) and Barabbas a 'robber' (18⁴⁰). It is therefore possible, perhaps even probable, that such a saying rejects the claims of those who, like Judas, would seek to force a messianic claimant's hand, or, like Barabbas, would turn to armed revolt.

---

narrative, where the emphasis is always on the fact that, even when Jesus dies, he *lays down his life*, is himself acting, and not merely 'being acted upon'.

None such could be true leaders of God's true people. The alternative picture is of the genuine shepherd who enters by the proper door (which may well be a reference by Jesus to his own Davidic descent), calls his own sheep by name (i.e. individually, as he had called the man born blind) and leads them out (i.e. joins them to the New Israel that has to be gathered, at least in part, out of the members of the Old Israel). The picture portrays a fold where several flocks have been lodged for a night, where in the morning the true shepherd can enter and call out his own sheep, who will follow him since they will recognize his voice. The Church is in this sense an *ek-klesia*, a 'called-out' body, called out from among the sheep already gathered in the fold. But the sheep so called out do not constitute the whole flock of the new people of God, for it is to be joined by 'other sheep' (v. 16) to constitute the one flock under the one shepherd.

There may be little certainty about any particular detail of such an exposition of 10¹⁻⁶, but it seems clear that in using the figure Jesus is setting out his claim to be the true shepherd of the real people of God. The true members of God's true people will recognize him for the true leader, the true shepherd he is; they *know his voice*; the plausible authority of *strangers* will not delude them, for they '*do not know the voice of strangers*' (v. 5). True authority among God's true people is not a matter of coercion, but of God's loving care evoking willing response through Jesus Christ.

ಣ

I

The '*sheepfold*' is almost certainly an enclosed courtyard of a house, used as a fold for sheep.

To *climb in by another way* than *by the door* may already mean, in view of what is to come, to seek to exercise an authority other than that which Christ exercises. He has been given to be head over all things to the Church, as Paul puts it in Ephesians 1²².

3

The '*gatekeeper*' in this instance would seem to be an independent person, for the fold is evidently used by more than one flock, the shepherd going outside and calling his own sheep to him (cf. v. 4). The clear meaning of this verse is that each sheep is known by name.

6

That the *figure* was not understood by his hearers is not surprising. Much of what he taught only became clear after the crucifixion and resurrection, even to his own disciples. Certainly the picture of a shepherd who, as the following verses show, lays down his life for his sheep, would not come readily to the mind. The fact would give cogency to the image for the disciples, just as it brought fulfilment to it for Jesus. The word used for *figure* differs from the usual one for 'parable' and probably is meant to indicate that the real meaning is in some measure veiled and symbolic.

⁷*So Jesus again said to them, 'Truly, truly, I say to you, I am the door of the sheep.* ⁸*All who came before me are thieves and robbers; but the sheep did not heed them.* ⁹*I am the door; if any one enters by me, he will be saved, and will go in and out and find pasture.* ¹⁰*The thief comes only to steal and kill and destroy; I came that they may have life, and have it abundantly.* ¹¹*I am the good shepherd. The good shepherd lays down his life for the sheep.* ¹²*He who is a hireling and not a shepherd, whose own the sheep are not, sees the wolf coming and leaves the sheep and flees; and the wolf snatches them and scatters them.* ¹³*He flees because he is a hireling and cares nothing for the sheep.* ¹⁴*I am the good shepherd; I know my own and my own know me,* ¹⁵*as the Father knows me and I know the Father; and I lay down my life for the sheep.* ¹⁶*And I have other sheep, that are not of this fold; I must bring them also, and they will heed my voice. So there shall be one flock, one shepherd.* ¹⁷*For this reason the Father loves me, because I lay down my life, that I may take it again.* ¹⁸*No one takes it from me, but I lay it down of my own accord. I have power to lay it down, and I have power to take it again; this charge I have received from my Father.'*

Before developing the theme of Jesus as the *good shepherd* the evangelist examines a little further the figure of the thieves and robbers in v.1. He begins by taking another part of the whole picture of the sheep, the fold and the shepherd, and using it to indicate what thieves and robbers are. Jesus claims '*I am the door of the sheep*' (v. 7) by which the sheep may pass in and out and find pasture in safety. This contrasts with the activities of the thieves and robbers, who do not facilitate the safe passage of the sheep to proper pastures, but rather steal and kill and destroy the sheep. That is to say the true shepherd exists, and exercises his authority, solely for the good of the sheep, while the thieves and robbers think of the sheep only in terms of what profit they can make for themselves, or how they can best secure their own safety. In terms of the figure of the shepherd as the biblical symbol for the ruler (cf. Ezekiel 34), this passage is seen to be a Johannine equivalent of a synoptic saying such as Mark 10⁴²⁻⁴⁵: 'You know that those who are supposed to exercise authority over the gentiles lord it over them, and their great men exercise authority over them. But it shall not be so among you; but whoever would be great among you must be your servant, and whoever would be first among you must be slave of all. For the Son of Man also came not to be served, but to serve, and to give his life a ransom for many.' To enter by a door other than that by which Jesus enters, i.e. to exercise an authority other than his, is to act as thieves and robbers act, i.e. to force men to service, not win them to glad obedience.

Such a presentation of the figure of sheep, fold and shepherd serves as an admirable introduction to the picture of Jesus as the Good Shepherd. This perhaps best known and most loved figure of Jesus originally meant far more than the usual stained-glass picture of a shepherd with a sheep in his arms can possibly convey to modern man. For one thing, modern man has lost the connexion of the shepherd with the office of ruler, which Ezekiel so forcefully used in his Old Testament prophecy; for another, the simple pastoral presentations of Jesus as the Good Shepherd do not of themselves face the viewer with the profound life-and-death, sacrificial issues that surround the Johannine use of the figure of the Good Shepherd. But vv. 10–15 are very clear as to the profound and ultimate issues that the figure is meant to raise.

In v. 10 the evangelist states unequivocally that the real issue as between the true and the false shepherds of Israel is that of life and death. The false shepherd or ruler is a thief or usurper, and he is that whether he be a foreigner bent on conquest or a Jew who usurps the place that should be reserved for God alone. The false ruler *steals* his kingdom; and his work leads to death. On the contrary the true Shepherd, Jesus Christ himself, governs his people rightly and brings them into proper submission to God, and thus ensures them life, a more abundant life than they can find anywhere else, or under any other rule. Yet the mere figure of the shepherd as a ruler cannot bear the full weight necessary to show Jesus as the Good Shepherd who

governs rightly and brings life; for that can only be done if the figure
is made to convey the fact that Jesus as the Good Shepherd '*Lays down
his life for the sheep*' (v. 11). In a word we are not to think of Jesus as
a shepherd who is the true ruler of his people and who happens to
lay down his life for his sheep, but rather as the true ruler of God's
people only in that and because he lays down his life for the sheep.
His sacrifice is part of his office, and his reign in parts consists in his
self-offering for those he governs. Those who are able to trace in
the story of Hebrew religion the way in which the people of Israel
had been able (or been enabled) to transmute the surrounding pagan
new year rituals of the dying and rising of the king into their own
rigorously spiritual worship can detect here the final fulfilment of the
human conception of a divine king who dies for the life of his people.
Those who remember the language of Second Isaiah concerning the
'servant' whose life is offered as a 'ransom for many' (Isa. 53¹⁰⁻¹²)
will catch the overtones of reference to one who although and because
he is the one true ruler or shepherd of God's people is yet the servant
of all; and as the servant will, like the suffering servant hymned in
Isaiah 53, suffer to liberate his people and give his life for the sins of
many.

Such thoughts are not far from the surface even of the pastoral
image. The evangelist probes this image somewhat farther (v. 12f.).
The distinction between the good shepherd and the bad is that the
good shepherd knows and loves the sheep as his own, while the
bad shepherd does not own the sheep, and has no real concern for
them, but only for his wages. Hence when danger threatens he all too
readily runs away, leaving the sheep at the mercy of the wolf that
attacks. By contrast the good shepherd owns the sheep, and cares
for them; he is known by them, and loved by them, just as the heavenly Father knows and loves the Son and he the Father. So when danger
threatens the good Shepherd is ready to yield up his life for the safety
of his flock. Here is the crown and the highest fulfilment of 'authority'
and 'rule' – that the one who governs should be the one who sacrifices his life.

Yet the figure of the shepherd giving his life for his sheep not only
adds to the simple pastoral relationship of shepherd and sheep, but
itself requires further development if it is to serve as a true picture
of Christ and his flock. For the flock of Christ does not consist
simply of those who are called out of the fold of Israel, but includes

sheep not of that fold, whom Christ must bring, and make into one flock with those called out of Israel under his one shepherding. Such a figure is the very concise Johannine parallel to the Pauline exposition in Romans 9–11 of the way in which God elected Israel-after-the-flesh to be his people, only to have them reject the Messiah when he came, thereby bringing about the gathering in of the Gentiles, so that by their accession to the body of God's people both Jews and Gentiles should be fully brought into one at the last. '*So there shall be one flock, one shepherd*' might well serve as a text for those three chapters in Romans which some have thought to be a sermon on the theme of the unity of God's purpose in history. The Good Shepherd is the saviour of the world.

Finally, the evangelist makes it unmistakably plain that for the Good Shepherd to lay down his life for the sheep is not an inescapable submission to some power or authority that is out of control in God's universe, but a voluntary self-offering in loving fulfilment of the Father's will, in order that the life laid down might be taken up again in a new fulness and victory. The story of the 'passion' in John is not an account of what men did to Jesus, but rather the story of what he did for them. Paradoxically it can be put in the form that where he was most passive (in yielding himself up to death) there he was most active (in bringing eternal life). That Jesus himself initiated the particular chain of events that resulted in his hanging on a cross the readers of the gospel could learn from any one of the synoptics; John makes it clear that not only at the moment of the initiation of these events, but all the way through, even when he hung upon the cross, Jesus was active and in complete control. John would not deny the witness of the synoptists and the writer of Acts that Jesus was crucified according to the determinate purpose of God; he would hardly contest a claim that the cross was for Jesus an inescapable destiny: but he is even more concerned himself to witness to the truth that all through the events of the passion, crucifixion and death of Jesus, the true agent, the true actor remained Jesus himself. His active will turned what might otherwise be a blind fate or an ineluctable destiny into a self-offering and a self-sacrifice. And it all finds its origin and its enactment in the love of the Father for the world which the Son, sharing the Father's love, came to save. Such a figure, such a person is the one who claims to be the Good Shepherd.

7

This is another '*I am*' saying: Christ is the way into the Kingdom, as the synoptists might have put it, as well as the life of the kingdom itself. Cf. 'I am the way' of 14⁶.

8

'*All who came before me*': refers to false messianic claimants who had already appeared, some of them within Jesus' own lifetime, and had misled some Jews into following them. Cf. Acts 5³⁶,³⁷, for a biblical reference to Theudas and Judas.

9

'*I am the door*': The door may be identified with the door that Jews believed to be the entrance to heaven, the same door through which God's messengers to men also pass. If Jesus identifies himself with this door, he is repeating in another form the substance of his assertion to Nathanael that the angels of God would ascend upon the Son of man (see notes ad loc.).

10

'*life . . . abundantly*': The thought is that Jesus brings true, eternal life to men, and a life that is superabundant in its quality. Its 'duration' and its 'quality' are both beyond measure.

11

The '*good*', rather than the normal Johannine 'genuine' or 'real' shepherd, because Jesus does not contrast so much in reality of his rule, but in its character and quality. Others may 'lord it' over men as they govern; he has come to minister and do the office of a servant (cf. the feet-washing of ch. 13).

12

'*hireling*' is now mentioned for the first time, though it discloses the depth of the difference between Jesus as a shepherd who owns his sheep, and cares for them, and will protect them as he will his own life and those who have no such ties of ownership or care for those they govern, and who are thus moved by motives of reward.

14, 15

These verses set out again the parallel between the relation between Jesus and his disciples and that between Jesus and the Father. Mutual knowledge and love, and a life-giving care are the marks of that relationship.

17

'*For this reason the Father loves me*': It is not to be supposed that the

Father only began to love the Son when he had offered himself upon the cross: rather the evangelist is saying that the Father's eternal love for the Son rests upon the Son's eternal sharing of the Father's love for men, which finds expression in the incarnation, and in the incarnation in the self-offering of the cross.

18

It is probable that the true reading in this verse is a past tense of the verb: 'No one *took* it from me'. If so, it but reflects the perspective of the evangelist which, as several passages have shown, is easily inter-changeable with the perspective of the historic occasion. The reason for the change to the present is obvious.

The claim to be able to lay down life and to take it again must not be disconnected either from what precedes, or from what follows. What precedes is the series of affirmations that Jesus is the good shepherd (ruler), that he lays down his life for the sheep, and that the Father loves him because he lays down his life that he might take it again. What follows is the assertion that to lay down his life and take it again has been received as a charge from the Father. This therefore cannot mean that laying down life is made easy or terrorless. The Father loves the Son because in obedience he will lay down his life – the only way by which it may be eventually retained. He must resign his crown to secure it. And that laying down, the resignation, must take place while the Word is in the flesh.

10¹⁹⁻²¹   'WHAT MANNER OF MAN IS THIS?'

¹⁹*There was again a division among the Jews because of these words.* ²⁰*Many of them said, 'He has a demon, and he is mad; why listen to him?'* ²¹*Others said, 'These are not the sayings of one who has a demon. Can a demon open the eyes of the blind?'*

Such high claims understandably caused a division among those Jews who heard them made, just as, according to Mark, the quiet assump-tion of the power to forgive sins (Mark 2⁷) occasioned opposition among the leaders of the Jews. The evangelist uses the phrase *division among the Jews* on three occasions only: here, and at 7⁴³ and 9¹⁶, so that all occur within a section which is taken by the present writer to be a unity, and each recording, as Mark 2⁷, an opposition to a claim that Jesus is of a status greater than that of 'just another rabbi', however learned and respected he be. The division, that is to say (*schism* is the Greek word), is about what theologians call the Person of Christ.

The Jews see two possibilities to explain what Jesus has said: either he is possessed of a demon, and can be discounted as a madman, or he must be possessed of genuine divine powers in order to open the eyes of the blind. This judgement differs somewhat from that reported in the synoptics, where the Pharisees accept the possibility of miracles by demonic power (Mark 3²² //). But John recognizes only that 'the Lord opens the eyes of the blind' (Psalm 146⁸), and his account of the miracle done on the man born blind was intended to make manifest the works of God (9³), and thus be a sign of the presence of the incarnate Word.

৯৫

20
'*He has a demon, and he is mad*': one fact in two perspectives, not two different diseases.

10²²⁻³⁹   THE DEDICATION OF THE TEMPLE

²²*It was the feast of the Dedication at Jerusalem;* ²³*it was winter, and Jesus was walking in the temple, in the portico of Solomon.* ²⁴*So the Jews gathered round him and said to him, 'How long will you keep us in suspense? If you are the Christ, tell us plainly.'* ²⁵*Jesus answered them, 'I told you, and you do not believe. The works that I do in my Father's name, they bear witness to me;* ²⁶*but you do not believe, because you do not belong to my sheep.* ²⁷*My sheep hear my voice, and I know them, and they follow me;* ²⁸*and I give them eternal life, and they shall never perish, and no one shall snatch them out of my hand.* ²⁹*My Father, who has given them to me,ᵃ is greater than all, and no one is able to snatch them out of the Father's hand.* ³⁰*I and the Father are one.'*

³¹*The Jews took up stones again to stone him.* ³²*Jesus answered them, 'I have shown you many good works from the Father; for which of these do you stone me?'* ³³*The Jews answered him, 'We stone you for no good*

work but for blasphemy; because you, being a man, make yourself God.'
^{34}*Jesus answered them, 'Is it not written in your law, "I said, you are gods"?*
^{35}*If he called them gods to whom the word of God came (and scripture cannot
be broken),* ^{36}*do you say of him whom the Father consecrated and sent into
the world, "You are blaspheming," because I said, "I am the Son of God"?*
^{37}*If I am not doing the works of my Father, then do not believe me;* ^{38}*but if
I do them, even though you do not believe me, believe the works, that you may
know and understand that the Father is in me and I am in the Father.'*
^{39}*Again they tried to arrest him, but he escaped from their hands.*

a Other ancient authorities read *What my Father has given to me*

The evangelist writes a simple chronological note: *It was the feast of
the Dedication at Jerusalem; it was winter.* Everything that has taken
place since 7^1 may be presumed to have happened at or about the
feast of Tabernacles. But now the time has advanced some three
months; it is December, and the feast of Dedication or, as it was often
known, 'Tabernacles in December [Kislew]' is taking place. Tabernacles was not only *the* popular feast of Judaism, but also, as was
indicated (p. 108), a prefiguring of the incarnation (the word 'tabernacle' in Greek provides the verb for the 'dwelling' of the Word
among men in his incarnation): so Dedication, with its glad thanksgiving for the restoration of a desecrated sanctuary to its proper use
in 165 B.C., is the prefiguring of the dedication of him who was to
replace the temple, and become the actual restoration of the now outmoded sanctuary on Zion's hill – or Gerizim's! So the simple chronological note turns out to have profound theological significance!

So at the time and in the place where God's people celebrated the
return of their holy place to its rightful use, he who was to become
the new temple, the one meeting place of God and man, is present.
Evidently his presence of itself raised questions of a searching kind in
the minds of the Jews, who asked him to say plainly whether he were
Messiah or not. But there is some difficulty about the translation which
makes the Jews ask *'How long will you keep us in suspense?'* (10^{24}). As
Barrett notes, such a question comes more naturally from not unfriendly
Jews who 'simply wish to find out the truth' (op. cit., p. 316), whereas
the use of the word *Jews* and the hostile thoughts and actions reported
in the context would suggest that *Jews* is being used in its (by now)
almost normative sense of leaders opposed to Jesus. If the element

of hostility in the context does thus lead to an identification of *the Jews* of v. 24 with the hostile leaders, then it is possible to translate the question in another way: 'How long will you vex, trouble, annoy us in this way?' This seems to make better sense of the passage.

In reply Jesus affirms that he has told them plainly enough, and that his works bear witness to him. Although John has recorded one explicit statement of Jesus that he is the Messiah (or Christ) made to the Samaritan woman, it is quite clear from what he has already reported that his claim to messianic status stands. The real difficulty is not that his teaching has been ambiguous, or that his works have not constituted a further powerful claim, but that the response of belief is possible only to the sheep that belong to the Good Shepherd. They know the voice of the true Shepherd of God's flock, and are known of Christ; they follow him, and he gives them eternal life. Their life is permanently secure, and it is impossible for any sheep belonging to the Good Shepherd to be stolen by brigands. To put this in the perspective of the occasion itself, Jesus claims that the Jews will be unable to win back the disciples from their loyalty to him, or to read it in the perspective of the evangelist, the Church claims that Judaism will prove incapable of turning the people of Christ from their allegiance to him. The basis of such an absolute security is in the supreme greatness of the Father, who is *'greater than all'* (v. 29); and since Jesus is one with the Father he shares the Father's insurmountable protection of his own. The saying *'I and the Father are one'* (v. 30) crowns and ends the Lord's reply to his enemies, and helps again to set the scene for the story of the final conflict still to come. To the evangelist and his readers the saying puts into one simple sentence what has been implied so many times in the course of the Lord's teaching so far; but to the Jews it was sheer blasphemy.

Not only did the Jews hear blasphemy, but they reacted violently against it. As once before at 8⁵⁹, they took up stones to stone him (v. 31). In this they arrogate to themselves what should have been left to processes of law, for stoning, as Barrett points out, was not a matter of lynch law. Barrett sees in this 'apparent unfamiliarity with the Jewish practice' some evidence that John was not a Jew who lived in Palestine before A.D. 70. But it is more likely that John records the incident simply to indicate that the issue between Jesus and his opponents, as between differing Jewish opinions about him, was not concerned with the question whether he was demonically inspired or not, still less with the question whether he performed miracles or not, but basically with the question whether he was the Son of God or not. This is brought out in the short dialogue that ensues. Jesus asked his enemies for which of the good works he had done they were proposing to stone him. Their simple answer is that their action is a response to blasphemy. They accuse him of 'making himself God', whereas both the evangelist and his Christian readers know that the real truth is that in Jesus Christ God has made himself man!

Jesus replies to the charge of blasphemy with an appeal to the Old Testament, and thus takes, or the evangelist presents him as taking, the same attitude to scripture as the early Church. The same Old Testament was authoritative for both Judaism and Christianity, though it could be used to produce contradictory judgements, as it did here. Jesus quoted Psalm 82⁶: 'I said, ye are gods', and proceeding on the commonly accepted doctrine of the complete trustworthiness of scripture, argued that if scripture, and he who spoke through scripture, called men 'gods' there could not be an inevitable presumption of blasphemy in his own claim to divine stature. His claim rested on the fact that the Father had 'consecrated' him (here the phrasing may well reflect the religious celebrations at the feast) and sent him into the world; this could not afford a proper basis for a charge of blasphemy. He then appealed once more to his works which, if they were properly understood, witnessed to his divine nature, and spoke to men of his unity with the Father. But the only response he got was a further attempt to place him under arrest.

This incident brings to an end the long section in which John has outlined the swiftly developing crisis between Jesus and the Jews. The evangelist has given the conflict stories of the synoptics a deeper and more revealing interpretation; throughout he has made it clear that the conflict was about a final theological judgement that men have to pass on Jesus: Is he, or is he not, the Son of the Father, sent by him into the world for its salvation? In terms of the world of sense experience all men saw the same phenomena as they faced Jesus – a man of Galilee whose parents were known, as well as his brothers and sisters; but in terms of a gift of God that could and did open the eyes of those who could not see, those who believed saw one whom they could not but confess to be the Son of God, the Messiah. So his coming had inevitably created a division that could only result in the tragedy of his own death, if one looked at that death with eyes of sense, or in the triumph of the divine Son if one looked at the same death with eyes of faith. The following chapters will unfold the story.

❦

22

the feast of the Dedication: In 165 B.C. Judas Maccabaeus had set the temple free once more for its proper usage after its desecration by Antiochus Epiphanes. The feast celebrating this event began on the 25th of Kislew (December) each year, and was a time of great rejoicing, and, as at Tabernacles, of very considerable illumination.

winter may mean 'wintry weather', though at that time of year it would not be unnatural for Jesus to be walking in Solomon's porch.

24

'How long will you keep us in suspense?': Barrett quotes Pallis who quotes Pernot who, in keeping with modern Greek, is able to offer the alternative translation of the commentary. He fortifies his judgement with examples from Sophocles and from Euripides. The context seems to demand such an alternative translation.

25

'The works that I do in my Father's name': Jesus does not simply point to his works, but to those works as necessitating the interpretation of the gospel as the act of the Father in and through the Son.

26

'You do not believe, because you do not belong to my sheep': This reiterates earlier teaching given in Galilee, cf. e.g. 6^{44-46}; 6^{43} ^{65}.

28

'no one shall snatch them out of my hand': The wolf can snatch those who are under the care of the hireling shepherds; but those under the care of the Good Shepherd are safe in the life-giving care and protection that he affords.

29

The Translation of the R.S.V. represents what is perhaps the right answer to a very difficult textual problem. The chief ambiguity arises because the relative pronoun after Father has been preserved in both a masculine and a neuter form. The neuter readings have a considerable weight of authority, but it is difficult to understand the meaning of the saying if one of them is accepted; the translation would read: 'In regard to my Father, what he has given me is greater than all, and no one can snatch them out of my hand'. This may be some sort of Johannine equivalent to Matthew's 'On this rock I will build my Church, and the powers of death shall not prevail against it', but it is a strange form of words for the fourth evangelist to use. Dodd's comment is (op. cit. p. 433 n.1.) 'I think John would never have said it'. If the translation makes the gift of the Father to his Son to be his authority it is, again as Dodd says, hardly appropriate at this point. So the translator seems obliged to accept the masculine relative, and to refer the subordinate clause to the Father. Barrett makes an ingenious suggestion that with the masculine relative pronoun the author wrote a neuter adjective (greater) which has been perhaps accidentally preserved in one manuscript, and which could undoubtedly, as he suggests, have given rise to various attempts to make the grammar somewhat smoother. In any event the text of the R.S.V. translation gives the true sense.

30
The unity of the Father and Son is clearly meant to refer to their unity as they make themselves known to men in revelation. Behind this unity in revelation there lies also a unity in eternal being, which has been stated in the opening of the Prologue. The two thoughts cannot be separated, but it is the revelatory character of the divine unity that is uppermost here.

33
Evidently some stones had been thrown, even if, as Barrett remarks, the force of the verb must be 'conative'.

34
The words exactly quote the Septuagint.

35
Those *to whom the word of God came* may be the prophets, who are often spoken of in this way (cf. Hosea 1^1; Joel 1^1; Jonah 1^1; Micah 1^1; Ezekiel 1^3; Jeremiah 1^2) but are more likely to be the whole people of Israel as they received the word of the Lord at Sinai and were made thereby God's covenanted people.

36
whom the Father consecrated: The word for 'consecrate' is used again in John only at $17^{17, 19}$. Clearly it has profound implications, and its use reinforces the view that the evangelist is intentionally drawing a parallel between the 'consecration' of the Jerusalem temple which was celebrated at the feast of Dedication and the consecration of the Son by the Father to be the new 'temple' in whom alone men could worship aright. The argument has here reached its climax. Scripture, at any

rate as understood in the first century, could speak of the whole people of God as 'gods' because they were made God's people by the word of God mediated to them through Moses at Sinai: there could thus be little objection, on the basis of scripture, to Jesus' claim to be called the 'Son of God' seeing that he had been specially consecrated by the Father and sent into the world. He did not have the word of God come to him; he was the Word of God come to men.

38

'*that you may know and understand*': *That you may know* expresses a Greek subjunctive and implies a beginning of knowing at a certain point of time; *understand* refers to the continuing state of knowing.

39

Jesus' hour had still not yet come. The evangelist reports his escape, as beforehand at 7³⁰; 8²⁰, ⁵⁹, and it was no doubt his intention that his readers should think it a miracle of divine providence again.

John 10^{40–42}

Interlude 5: Across Jordan

40He went away again across the Jordan to the place where John at first baptized, and there he remained. 41And many came to him; and they said, 'John did no sign, but everything that John said about this man was true.' 42And many believed in him there.

If, as may reasonably be supposed, these three verses provide John's presentation of the events summarized in Mark 10^1, then the distinctive features of John's report may well give the key to its interpretation. Mark simply states that Jesus 'went to the region of Judea and beyond the Jordan, and crowds gathered to him again; and again, as his custom was, he taught them'. John's special treatment has therefore been to emphasize the link of the area beyond Jordan with the first activities of the Baptist, and with the people's memory of the Baptist's witness to Jesus.

In a word, the story has come full circle. Jesus is back at the place of his first public appearance, where he was baptized and, as it were, 'ordained' to his ministry, where the Baptist bore unambiguous witness to him as the Lamb of God, and where he began to gather his disciples. Meanwhile, as the evangelist has recounted, Jesus has been rejected by the Galileans, and by the authorities in Judea and Jerusalem. Now he is back at the beginning, at that symbolic place where the entry of the people of God into the true land of promise could be symbolized in action, and part of the meaning of this interlude is a suggestion that the Messiah is now poised at the point where and when he will lead the way into a victorious occupation of the final 'promised land'. The reader will not suppose that the end of the story will come without a tragic climax, for the life of Jesus has been threatened on more than one occasion.

The interlude as John narrates it is focused entirely upon Jesus himself, though it would most probably be wrong to suppose that Jesus was not accompanied by his band of disciples, since they are with Jesus when the next incident is reported in ch. 11. But there is one notable difference between the scene of the earlier visit to 'beyond Jordan' and the present one – John the Baptist is absent. Even with every possible concession made to the notorious difficulties of Gospel chronology, it may safely be said that he was by this time dead. Certainly in any attempt to find parallel points in the synoptic chronology, the Baptist's death has long since taken place; and the fourth evangelist himself seems to presuppose it at 5³³⁻³⁶. But if John himself was absent, his testimony to Jesus lived on, and it is now remembered by the crowd, who recall it as they make a comparison between the Baptist and the Lord.

John 11^{1–53}

Deed and Word: 4
'The Resurrection and the Life'
The Raising of Lazarus
The Sixth Sign
Mark 5$^{22-24, 35-43}$
Luke 7$^{11-17}$
Luke 16$^{19-31}$

This chapter might well be called the *crux interpretationis* of the whole gospel; certainly a great deal of what may be said about other chapters, earlier as well as later, turns upon what is said about the raising of Lazarus. Three general considerations are focused in this chapter. First, John's relation to the synoptics. If he has throughout the gospel been engaged in a deliberate attempt to present synoptic material or themes in the framework of his own theological insights, then the presentation of a miracle of a raising of a dead man to life, particularly on the fourth day, will inevitably provide opportunity for a decisive summary and climax to the whole series of miracle narratives. Second, if John has attempted to fashion his own special order for a gospel, necessitating some quite obtrusive rearrangement of material, then the reasons may perhaps be better discovered at this point than at any other, in view of John's linking of the story with the Jewish decision to accomplish the death of Jesus. Third, even though no synoptic gospel can fail to raise questions of historical veracity for the modern reader, and previous stories in John (e.g. the healing of the man born blind, and the changing of the water into wine) raise similar issues, the story of the raising of Lazarus confronts the reader with the problem of historicity in its acutest forms, historical, philosophical and theological.

The Synoptics and John

Of the six miracles recorded in John as performed by Jesus only one, the story of the feeding of the five thousand, refers indubitably to the same event as is recorded in the synoptic narratives. The exception in the case of the feeding of the five thousand is understandable in view of the eucharistic connexions that John perceives in it, while for the rest it would seem that the evangelist has used a story typical of several in the synoptic gospels in order to present his own story and their similar ones in the light of his own theological commentary (see e.g. the story of the healing of the lame man, John 5$^{2-29}$). It need therefore cause the reader little surprise to find that John has chosen not to reproduce either the story of the raising of Jairus' daughter or that of the widow's son at Nain, but instead has taken a story unmentioned by any of the synoptists, in order to present in his own gospel a narrative whose interpretation may be taken to apply to earlier miraculous restorations to life as well as to the incident now recorded. This is nothing very unusual in this part of his procedure; he is using a miracle narrative of the same general type as the synoptists, even if the particular miracle is a heightened example of its kind, in order to expose for his readers the profound significance that attaches to all miracles done by Jesus Christ, and particularly to any miracle of restoring the dead to life.

Yet the story of the raising of Lazarus is not simply the crown and interpretative medium of the miraculous raisings from the dead found in the synoptic gospels, it is also the crown and interpretative crux of the whole set of Johannine 'signs'. It was indicated in comment on ch. 5 that the healing of the lame man at the pool of Bethzatha was conceived of as far more than the restoration of movement to crippled limbs, as in essence the giving of life to a dying man. And at that time it was also pointed out that this same conception of the true significance of Jesus' miracles had been incorporated into a Marcan story from the beginning of the ministry, viz. in the story of the healing of the man with the withered hand (Mark 3$^{1-6}$), where Jesus asks about his action, just before it takes place, 'Is it lawful on the sabbath to do good or to do harm, to save life or to kill?' It was in ch. 5 that John wrote 'Truly, truly, I say to you, the hour is coming, and now is, when the dead will hear the voice of the Son of God, and those who hear will live' (5^{25}). The story of Lazarus is the fulfilment of the synoptic stories of restoring life to the dead.

The Pattern of the Fourth Gospel

The fourth evangelist makes some remarkable dislocations in the synoptic presentation of events in the life of Jesus (cf. Introduction, pp. 48–56), one of them being the removal of the temple cleansing from the very end to the very beginning of the ministry. Mark's comment on the cleansing is: 'The chief priests and the scribes heard it and sought a way to destroy him; for they feared him, because all the multitude was astonished at his teaching' (Mark 11^{18}). The temple cleansing was for all the synoptics the point at which the decision was made by the authorities to secure Jesus' death. But the removal of this narrative from the end of the ministry to its beginning requires from John some other occasion of the hostile decision being taken. The raising of Lazarus provides this. At a superficial level the two incidents seem to provide the same kind of motivation: Mark tells of the fear activating the leaders, evidently because Jesus' popularity might well lead to political disturbance, dangerous to themselves as to the nation's security: John explicitly states that the authorities were concerned that 'everyone will believe in him, and the Romans will come and destroy both our holy place and our nation' (11^{48}). But both reports demand examination at a deeper level, and again they yield not entirely dissimilar results. The synoptic narrative centres on the restoration of the Jewish temple to its divinely intended use as a house of prayer for all peoples, instead of the restricted use to which Jesus' contemporaries had confined it, with its Court of the Gentiles beyond which no Gentile dare go save on penalty of death, and of which the need to change Roman coinage into Jewish temple currency was an overt symbol. The call for such a restoration was made by the one who was in himself the point of meeting of Jew and Gentile before God; and the choice for Israel-after-the-flesh, as presented by the Temple cleansing, was either to continue the narrow, restrictive use of the Temple and so pass to spiritual national death, or to respond to the call to universal evangelistic responsibility made by Jesus Christ, and so pass to a new life as the newly constituted people of God in the person of his Son. The raising of Lazarus makes plain to the reader of the fourth gospel that Jesus Christ is the resurrection and the life, i.e. the life of God's people, which is mediated through him, through him alone, and through him to all who come to believe. The old Israel must die, and the new Israel be born. Lazarus dies as a member of the old Israel, but he rises by reason of his bond with Jesus Christ, whose word and power of life has authority even beyond death and the tomb. So the dying and raising of Lazarus is a real pointing forward to the death and resurrection of Jesus himself, in which God will offer men the final and most eloquent sign that he will bring his people out of their living death into a new life both abundant and eternal.

The Question of Historicity

Modern man, whether a simple believer inside the Christian church or a sophisticated agnostic or unbeliever outside it, cannot take any report of a miracle for granted. There are four somewhat interlocking reasons for this. First is the widespread conviction that miracles, in the strict sense of actions done against nature, are impossible. This position has been discussed in the Introduction, and it is therefore necessary here only to remark that the Christian believer in the twentieth century cannot accept an assertion of miraculous action without grave searching of his own intellectual honesty and integrity. But, as was observed in the Introduction, the more important question concerns the matter of evidence.

The evidence concerning the raising of Lazarus is confined to the fourth gospel. But the synoptic gospels offer some support of this evidence, not in respect of a person called Lazarus, but in that they tell of Jesus raising the daughter of Jairus (Mark 5$^{21-43}$ //), and of the widow's son at Nain (Luke 7$^{11-17}$). The fact that John does not reproduce either of the synoptic raisings from the dead, but introduces a new, though as usual heightened, incident of the same kind, might be taken as some indication that the stock of such stories in the tradition behind the gospels was not exhausted by the synoptists or himself. And as to the evidence which John includes in his narrative which serves to underline the miraculous character of the resuscitation of Lazarus, this is another, albeit extreme, example of the way in which he has treated other synoptic miracles earlier in the gospel (e.g. the lame man in 5^5 had been paralysed for 38 years; the blind man in ch. 9 had been blind from birth). So it would seem that the evidence for the raising of Lazarus is not worse or better than the evidence for other Johannine miracles. The reader must therefore try to evaluate the evidence for himself, and in particular wrestle with the problem of the precise point that the evangelist wished to establish through his evidence. This was not, in the view of the present writer, the simple fact that Jesus was a quite unusually great thaumaturgist, with powers of reviving the dead to life, but rather that he was the one who, in his own person, linked man and God together in a life that was both abundant and eternal. John is consequently trying to say that the transition from death to life is not to be made at some remote 'last day', nor even at the moment of physical death, but at the point where a man comes to hear the voice of the Son of man and, in obedience to it, comes to eternal life.

The question of the historicity of the story of Lazarus has to be examined from one further standpoint, viz. that created by the use of the study of comparative literature. It is claimed that, on analogy with other literatures, it is possible and indeed probable that John has compiled the story on the basis of the parable of the rich man and Lazarus told by Jesus in Luke 16$^{19-31}$. That there is some connexion between the two passages it is as difficult to deny as it is easy to affirm; but that the fourth evangelist should use a parable ending with the assertion '*If they do not hear Moses and the prophets, neither will they be convinced if some one should rise from the dead*' as the reason of the story of the raising of Lazarus as a basis for believing in Jesus Christ seems to credit the author with a singular insensitivity.

There is thus no easy escape from considering the evidence for the historicity of the story of Lazarus; no valid reason can be advanced for putting it out of court without a hearing. But if it be heard, then it must be heard as one of the miracle stories of the fourth gospel, and judged in the light of the pattern of such stories, which is very different from that of the synoptists. John once more puts the truth about Jesus, that he is the 'Son' of God, the one in whom God and his people are one, into the story of a deed. But the truth that is so put is not that Jesus, as God's Son, is a supremely powerful thaumaturgist, but that he is the one source and giver of true, abundant and eternal life, because he is one with the Father, and the Father one with him. If this be the truth towards which every piece of testimony of the fourth gospel and of the synoptics points, then the question of the actual historicity of such an incident as the raising of Lazarus takes on somewhat different proportions. John can offer no *proof* that the Father was in and with the Son; he can only offer testimony. If the reader accepts the testimony and believes in the oneness of Father and Son, then he may well find his credence more open even to the astounding, impossible-seeming miracle that John reports Jesus as working on his friend Lazarus after he had been dead for four days.

II *Now a certain man was ill, Laz'arus of Bethany, the village of Mary and her sister Martha. ²It was Mary who anointed the Lord with ointment and wiped his feet with her hair, whose brother Laz'arus was ill. ³So the sisters sent to him, saying, 'Lord, he whom you love is ill.' ⁴But when Jesus heard it he said, 'This illness is not unto death; it is for the glory of God, so that the Son of God may be glorified by means of it.'*

⁵Now Jesus loved Martha and her sister and Laz'arus. ⁶So when he heard that he was ill, he stayed two days longer in the place where he was. ⁷Then after this he said to his disciples, 'Let us go into Judea again.' ⁸The disciples said to him, 'Rabbi, the Jews were but now seeking to stone you, and are you going there again?' ⁹Jesus answered, 'Are there not twelve hours in the day? If any one walks in the day, he does not stumble, because he sees the light of the world. ¹⁰But if any one walks in the night, he stumbles, because the light is not in him.' ¹¹Thus he spoke, and then he said to them, 'Our friend Laz'arus has fallen asleep, but I go to awake him out of sleep.' ¹²The disciples said to him, 'Lord, if he has fallen asleep, he will recover.' ¹³Now Jesus had spoken of his death, but they thought that he meant taking rest in sleep. ¹⁴Then Jesus told them plainly, 'Laz'arus is dead; ¹⁵and for your sake I am glad that I was not there, so that you may believe. But let us go to him.' ¹⁶Thomas, called the Twin, said to his fellow disciples, 'Let us also go, that we may die with him.'

¹⁷Now when Jesus came, he found that Laz'arus ᵃ had already been in the tomb four days.

a Greek *he*

The first four verses give the social and theological setting of the story. Lazarus (the name means 'God helps') was ill, and his sisters Mary and Martha sent to Jesus simply to acquaint him with the fact. The evangelist takes pains to identify Mary as the one who, as he reports later in ch. 12, anointed Jesus with ointment, and wiped his feet with her hair, though the reader is under no obligation to follow more modern 'informants' who proceed to identify Mary with the 'woman who was a sinner' in Luke 7³⁷, or with Mary Magdalene (Luke 8²; Mark 15⁴⁰, etc.). Some scholars have proposed, on the basis of the phrase '*Lord, he whom you love*' coming from the pen of the fourth evangelist, to take Lazarus as the 'beloved disciple'; but there can be no certainty about the suggestion, and there seems little, beyond the phrase quoted, to support it. But the great sign is to take place within the circle of those who love Jesus and whom Jesus loves.

The Lord's reaction – it is not a reply to the sisters – is enigmatic, and asks the reader to exercise his judgement. The plain meaning of the words '*This illness is not unto death*' is that the life of Lazarus was not in danger. But it is doubtful whether this was the meaning intended by the evangelist, since, without any further information, Jesus knows, evidently by supernatural means, that Lazarus has died (vv. 11, 14). Thus it may well be that so early in the chapter the evangelist has begun to use language in his accustomed fashion with double meaning, and the phrase may mean much more profoundly that the illness and the course it will run will not take Lazarus out of the sphere of life which comes and flows from Jesus Christ. This interpretation leads much more naturally into the remainder of the Lord's comment on the news of his friend's sickness: [This illness] '*is for the glory of God, so that the Son of God may be glorified by means of it*'. When John uses the word *glory* he has in mind the *glory* of the victory of God which is to be attained through the crucifixion and resurrection of Jesus Christ. On this view the meaning of Jesus' saying is that whatever may happen to Lazarus will not result in his real death, because the issue of his illness will be such as to make manifest the victory that the Father will gain over death in and through the death of the Son. So the illness (as the physical death) of Lazarus will in turn redound to the glory of the Son.

In vv. 5–7 the evangelist again sets the impending miracle in its due setting. First he states the love of Jesus (which is, of course, one with the love of the Father) for the two sisters; whatever is done in what follows flows from such love. Notably John has reserved the statement of Jesus' love for the two women for the place immediately before he reports what might otherwise read as a piece of calculated callousness. When Jesus heard of Lazarus' sickness, he stayed for two days where he was. Two motives may be detected in terms of the later narrative: first, this helps to ensure that the reader will not suppose Jesus simply to have reacted to the news of human suffering, but will be obliged to interpret Christ's whole action as flowing not in reaction to, but in initiatory action upon, the condition of his friend. Second, the evangelist uses the two days to fill out part of the period of four days during which, according to v. 17, Lazarus had been dead when Jesus at last reached Bethany. In any event, it is after this delay that Jesus in his own spontaneity suggests a return to Judea.

The narrative at this point reads as though the disciples had either already forgotten Lazarus, or, if they remembered him, had abandoned any thought of Jesus dealing effectively with his sickness. Presumably, like so many others in the gospel, they took Jesus' saying (in v. 4) literally, and supposed that by now Lazarus would have recovered from his ailment. Certainly their answer to Jesus betrays no thought of Bethany or Lazarus: '*The Jews were but now seeking to stone you* [an incident which took place in Jerusalem], *and are you going there again?*' The response of Jesus to this observation is to deal with it for what it is, and in content it is reminiscent of what he said at the time when he was preparing for the healing of the man born blind (9⁴), for he speaks of the light that the day brings, and affirms the safety of those who walk in it. And since already the reader of the gospel knows that Jesus himself is the light of the world, it is plain that Jesus is saying that to be with him is to be in a place where danger can do no ultimate harm. On the other hand, not to walk 'with him' is to be in the dark, and that is to be in danger, for then neither does the light illuminate the world about, nor shine from within through the light which he bestows.

It is Jesus himself who brings the conversation back to Lazarus, though the digression about light and safety and dark and danger is a proper part of the introduction to the whole story of the miracle, ending, as it does, in a decision to destroy Jesus. Jesus tells his disciples that Lazarus '*our friend*' (i.e. not only a personal friend, but a disciple) '*has fallen asleep*'. The Greek word translated *fallen asleep* is used elsewhere in the New Testament for death, e.g. Acts 13³⁶; 1 Cor. 7³⁹; 11³⁰; 15^{6,18,20}; 1 Thess. 4¹³, a style of language that has fixed itself in the vocabularies of many Christian peoples who speak of dying as 'falling asleep in Jesus'. It is evident that it is in this sense that John gives Jesus' use of the word, and as evident that the disciples are still at the place of misunderstanding. Why should Jesus go to Bethany simply to waken Lazarus out of sleep, even if that sleep be a coma? '*Lord, if he has fallen asleep, he will recover* [from his sickness]'. But the word that the disciples use for *recover* is also a word with a double meaning, and the second meaning is 'to be saved'; so that unwittingly the disciples, even in their misunderstanding, have spoken prophetically: Lazarus will be saved from death when Jesus 'wakens' him. The sleep with which Jesus is about to deal is more than a sleep within life, it is the sleep from life, the sleep of death. Christ can waken men from that.

The last four verses of this brief section are again profound, if enigmatical. John tells the reader that Jesus spoke plainly: *'Lazarus is dead'*. That is plain and understandable enough; but the following saying cannot but puzzle and tax the commentator: *'and for your sake I am glad that I was not there, so that you may believe'* (v. 15). Such a statement cannot, at this stage of the story, be taken to mean that the disciples addressed are in a state of complete unbelief, which will be radically cured by their presence with the Lord when he raises Lazarus from the sleep of death: rather is it to be understood that having already come to believe on Jesus Christ, and to accept his works as signs, they will, in witnessing the last great sign of his power and authority over death, have their belief in him deepened to the point of knowing that he, who is about to die, already possesses authority over death, is the light which will shine to banish all the darkness of death. The disciples seem to understand less than the full depth of the saying, for Thomas says to his fellows: *'Let us also go, that we may die with him.'* This is the ultimate in human loyalty and affection, but not that specifically Christian trust that looks to the Lord not only in life and death, but for the life that lies beyond in the resurrection.

When Jesus reached Bethany he found that Lazarus was already four days dead. We cannot determine with complete certainty whether when Jesus first heard of Lazarus' illness he was still alive or not. The probabilities would suggest that though the sisters would report their brother's sickness while he was still alive, and would have spoken of it with much more urgency had they been in any way apprehensive about his life at the time of sending the messsage to Jesus, nevertheless by the time Jesus heard, Lazarus was already dead. If the journey from Bethany, near Jerusalem, to the place where Jesus was, took the best part of a day's journey, then this conclusion is almost inescapable. If this be so, the two days' delay would not simply ensure that Lazarus would be dead as Jesus arrived, but that he would have reached that state ascribed by the Jews of the time to the dead after three days: the face unrecognizable, the body burst, the soul finally departed. The deed to be done was not the revival of suspended animation; it was real life from real death. Into this place of death and sorrow Jesus comes to manifest the glory of God, the divine victory over death in himself.

☙

1

A certain man: The phrase indicates that the person is not otherwise distinguished. Lazarus and his sisters were ordinary disciples of Christ.

2

The identification of *Mary* with the Mary who anointed Jesus does not carry the reader very far. The point is picked up in ch. 12, but its relation to synoptic passages is impossible to determine. Luke tells of an anointing in the house of Simon the Pharisee, but the incident is recounted of the Galilean period, and is not specifically connected with the Passion. Mark, followed by Matthew, located the incident in the house of Simon the Leper in Bethany, at the time of the Passion, but does not explicitly give the name of the woman. It would not be unreasonable to suppose that the same historical occasion lay behind all four versions, and that John, Luke and Mark had access to slightly different forms of tradition at this point.

3

It would seem to be of some significance that no specific request for help was sent in the message. This may have been because there was no apprehension on the part of the sisters for their brother's life. In any event it shows, as various commentators observe, that Jesus' response is to do all that is asked, and more, indeed whatever is necessary, for those who love him.

'*he whom you love*' almost certainly signifies that the family was one bound in the bonds of discipleship to Jesus.

4

The plain meaning of the Greek is that the sickness will not end in death. The phrase '*for the glory of God*' does not mean 'in order that praise may be given to God' for, as Barrett finely observes 'here as elsewhere the glory of God is not his praise, but his activity'; Jesus will bring the death of Lazarus under the activity of God – and that means life!

5

This verse forewarns the reader that delay does not arise from callousness or indifference, but wholly from the love that Christ bears.

6
he stayed two days longer: It is wholly improbable that John means the reader to understand that Jesus deliberately delayed until Lazarus had died, in order to work a more notable miracle! Nor is it likely that his motive was to come upon the scene only after the final separation of soul from body had occurred. The ground for this waiting must surely lie in the wish of the evangelist to show that here, as always, even when he goes to his death, Jesus acts from his own initiative, not simply in response to stimuli. Moreover, if the evangelist is to present the raising of Lazarus as in any way a rehearsal of the resurrection of the Lord, then the wait of two days is understandable, since it enables Jesus to act as the resurrection and the life on the 'third daẏ'.

7
'Let us go into Judea again': That Jesus speaks of Judea, and not simply of Bethany or of the home of Lazarus, implies that he envisaged this journey as taking him back into the area of sharp hostility where his own life would be imperilled, and his power over death put to the test not only in respect of Lazarus, but of himself.

8
The disciples' reply shows that they have caught the reference to his own danger, but have no inkling of his coming action upon Lazarus.

9
For the Jew the hours of daylight were divided into twelve equal parts. So while the sun shone it was day; similarly while he is in the world, who is the light of the world (cf. 8¹²; 9⁴, ⁵), it is day, and there is no danger of stumbling, for a man can see his way clearly. It is therefore entirely safe for him to return to Judea. The word *stumble* picks up an Old Testament word and shows that the stumbling of men is due to their not walking in the light of Christ. The same point is made in the well quoted saying about the stone of the corner becoming the stone of stumbling (cf. 1 Peter 2⁶⁻⁸; Romans 9³², ³³; 1 Cor. 1²³).

11
'Lazarus has fallen asleep': This is Christ's way of referring to the death of his friend.

14
'Lazarus is dead': This, though spoken by Christ, is the disciples', the human way of referring to the death of Lazarus.

15
'I am glad that I was not there, so that you may believe': Had Jesus been

present, he would doubtless have been asked by Mary and Martha (cf. vv. 21 and 32) to heal Lazarus before he died. And though that miracle, seen in its proper dimensions, would have been nothing less than the gift of life to a dying man (cf. 5$^{21-29}$), it would not have appeared as such to the disciples; but the absence of Jesus now enables him to deal with the situation in such a way that his authority over and beyond death is exemplified beyond question.

16

Thomas: The name means 'twin'. It has been conjectured that Thomas was the twin brother of Jesus himself, and the view appeared e.g. in the Acts of Thomas 1^{31}.

'*that we may die with him*': There is a sense in which, as Barrett says, none can share Christ's death; but there is another sense in which every Christian does, as Paul early and clearly recognized (cf. Rom. 6$^{1-11}$). The evangelist in all probability makes use of both meanings here, showing both how Thomas failed to see the character of the death that Christ was about to die, and yet how unwittingly he prophesied what is the honoured destiny of every Christian man.

II$^{18-27}$ JESUS AND MARTHA

^{18}*Bethany was near Jerusalem, about two miles^a off, ^{19}and many of the Jews had come to Martha and Mary to console them concerning their brother. ^{20}When Martha heard that Jesus was coming, she went and met him, while Mary sat in the house. ^{21}Martha said to Jesus, 'Lord, if you had been here, my brother would not have died. ^{22}And even now I know that whatever you ask from God, God will give you.' ^{23}Jesus said to her, 'Your brother will rise again.' ^{24}Martha said to him, 'I know that he will rise again in the resurrection at the last day.' ^{25}Jesus said to her, 'I am the resurrection and the life;^{b} he who believes in me, though he die, yet shall he live, ^{26}and whoever lives and believes in me shall never die. Do you believe this?' ^{27}She said to him, 'Yes, Lord; I believe that you are the Christ, the Son of God, he who is coming into the world.'*

a Greek *fifteen stadia*
b Other ancient authorities omit *and the life*

While Jesus waited across the Jordan, events at Bethany took their course. Lazarus had died, and his sisters and their friends took all the proper steps for his burial, and for the required mourning. But into that mourning household comes the news that Jesus was coming. Martha, with an energy and practicality the Synoptics have led the gospel reader to expect of her, went out to meet Jesus, and evidently went quite a way (cf.v.30). She met him with a word not indeed of reproach, but of a pathetic regret because, as she put it, *'Lord, if you had been here, my brother would not have died'* (v. 21). That there is no reproach in the plaint is clear from the fact that Martha says *'If you had been here'* not 'If you had come in time'; she accepts both his absence, and his power had he been present. Her statement represents the limited faith of those who cannot but look upon death from the perspective of man's mortality. For men death is either something future for themselves and others, or past for others. Before death something may therefore be done to avoid it; but once it has taken place, nothing can undo it. That is the plain teaching of experience. That Martha can at this point of the story find another word to say indicates how near she has already come to knowing her Lord as the Lord of life. She does not indeed possess the full knowledge of Jesus as the one who holds the keys of life and death, but she can say *'Even now I know that whatever you ask from God, God will give you'* (v. 22). This statement shows that already Martha has perceived that Jesus has a special relationship to the Father, and that no bounds can properly be set upon what that relationship may effect in the world over which God is Lord. Martha has seen a ray of impossible hope!

The reply that Jesus gives is the whole of his answer to dying man *'Your brother will rise again'* – death is not the end. But this statement cannot be separated from the speaker without loss of its specific meaning and power. Apart from Christ the word is an assurance of belief in an ultimate resurrection; in him it is the assurance of resurrection as the actual condition of the believer. But Martha has not yet been able to perceive the full implication of what she had herself said about Jesus and his relationship to God, let alone of the reply which Jesus had just given her. She persists in speaking from that human, historical, mortal perspective in which, outside Christ, man is imprisoned; and she says: *'I know that he will rise again in the resurrection at the last day'* (v. 24). Then Jesus utters what is perhaps the very greatest saying in the Bible, certainly the greatest of the 'I am' sayings that John records: '*I am the resurrection and the life*' (v. 25). In a word Jesus is saying that far from Martha and Mary and Lazarus having to wait until some distant and undefined *last day* for a general resurrection to take place, the real resurrection takes place in and through himself, as men hear him and give themselves to him in trustful obedience. This transference of the future to the present, of the end to the now, is the essence of the Johannine teaching about resurrection and life. It has tremendous implications, which Jesus enunciates: '*he who believes in me, though he die, yet shall he live, and whoever lives and believes in me shall never die*' (vv. 25, 26). If the believer in Christ suffers physical death, as mortal men know it, he will not be subject to that death which is removal from the society of the lovers of Jesus, for in that society he will still be alive, in and through Christ's solidarity with him. And if any man alive believes in Christ he will never die – the same truth put into another form. The believer never really dies, never escapes from the one life that is life indeed, which is to know God and the Son whom he sent into the world. Having made it plain that this is what has to be said about Lazarus four days after his death, Jesus asks Martha '*Do you believe this?*' (v. 26). Martha's reply seems at first sight to be off the mark; but a closer examination shows that it is not. Martha has perceived that what Jesus has said is not a series of two propositions about living and dead men, but rather a statement about himself as the real life of all who love and believe in him. So her answer when it comes is not in the form of assent to the propositions stated, but a confession of her belief in the Lord's special relationship to the Father: '*Yes, Lord;*' she says, '*I believe that you are the Christ, the Son of God, he who is coming into the world*' (v. 27). Martha had been prepared for a right understanding of the last and greatest sign.

ಬಂ

19

many of the Jews had come . . . to console: There is no intention in this mention of the Jews to express their hostility to Jesus. No doubt if Jews came from Jerusalem they would have heard of the recent events in which Jesus' life had been threatened; but they have not come out to Bethany in any expectation of meeting with Jesus, but solely for the proper neighbourly service and duty of sharing in the prescribed mourning. So it is that Jews who had possibly seen the deeds of Jesus in Jerusalem, or would at least have heard about them (the cleansing of the temple, the healing of the man at Bethzatha, the proclamation at the Feast of Tabernacles, the healing of the man born blind, the claim to be the Good Shepherd) are now able to witness the great climax and revelatory end to the whole series of signs. All that they had seen hitherto is now summed up, intensified and expressed; all that they are about to see in the death and resurrection of Jesus is anticipated, prepared for, and prophesied.

20

When Martha heard ... she went and met him: As in Luke 10^{38ff}, she proves herself the practical member of the family.

23

'*Your brother will rise again*': This has all the marks of a saying commonly in use at the time; certainly many Jews held that the resurrection, at least of good men, would take place at the last day. It would be quite in keeping with the evangelist's custom to make Jesus use a conventional saying and charge it with new meaning, as he has already depicted Jesus as giving a new meaning to 'falling asleep' (v. 11).

24

Martha realizes that, in terms of her common Jewish understanding of the saying about rising again, there is little immediate comfort for her or her sister. The last day is a long way off!

25

The reply of Jesus means that the eschatological event, the last day, is present in his person. So his deeds are God's deeds, and so true signs of his glory. It also means that all Christian life has to come to its final inheritance of eternal life through the gate of death as men know death in their mortality. The distinction that the evangelist makes plain is that instead of the transition point being at the moment of the end, it is now at the point where a living trustful relationship is established between Jesus Christ and his disciple. Put in another way it can be said that Jesus constitutes both the source and the substance of eternal life; and that is a far better point at which to understand God's gift of eternal life than any hypothetical 'last time', which is chronological not personal.

27

Martha uses three titles in her reply affirming her belief in Jesus. She calls him '*Messiah*', i.e. the divinely sent restorer of the true life of the true people of God. She calls him '*Son of God*' and thereby not only sees in him the reality of the life of God's people, but also a distinctive relationship to the Father. And she calls him '*he who is coming into the world*', and confesses thereby her conviction that he is the heavenly man coming from heaven for the salvation of the world. He is the head of the new Israel; he is uniquely related to the Father; and he has a special mission to perform. If all this be put together it may not amount to an expectation that Jesus will now cause Lazarus to rise from the dead; but it will certainly not be an attitude that will be astonished into unbelief when the miracle happens! To say, as some commentators do, that Martha's faith still needs a sign is not really to denigrate it; for without the deed actually done there could not be knowledge of Christ's power and authority over death.

²⁸*When she had said this, she went and called her sister Mary, saying quietly, 'The Teacher is here and is calling for you.' ²⁹And when she heard it, she rose quickly and went to him. ³⁰Now Jesus had not yet come to the village, but was still in the place where Martha had met him. ³¹When the Jews who were with her in the house, consoling her, saw Mary rise quickly and go out, they followed her, supposing that she was going to the tomb to weep there. ³²Then Mary, when she came where Jesus was and saw him, fell at his feet, saying to him, 'Lord, if you had been here, my brother would not have died.'*

Although John does not explicitly mention the fact, Jesus evidently asked to see Mary. Why, is a matter of conjecture; and it may be surmised that he wanted to be sure that Mary was as prepared as Martha to accept and understand the last sign before his own death and resurrection. Martha reported to her sister in words that have an overtone of Christian theology in them: she said *'The Teacher is here'* – and in so speaking used in the Greek tongue the verb of the noun *parousia*. It is entirely in keeping with the theology of the fourth gospel that the *parousia* of Jesus Christ should in this way be moved from some date in the future to the present time, and of course in no place would that transposition be more felicitous than in the story of the raising of Lazarus (cf. comment on vv. 24–27). The evangelist says that Martha told her sister of the Lord's wish *quietly*; again, the reasons for any such secretiveness can only be conjectured.

The most likely explanation seems to be that Martha spoke quietly to her sister in order to avoid a large number of Jews being present either when Jesus saw her, or when he proceeded to act the sign; for Jesus was known to them already as a great sign-worker, but as such his work was gravely misunderstood, and the misunderstanding gave rise to danger. Whatever the reason for the secretiveness, Mary rose quickly on hearing the Lord's wish, and went to meet him. As a picture of a disciple in sorrow and loss going out to meet her Lord she is a universal symbol of the distressed disciple.

When the Jews saw Mary leave the house, they supposed that she was going to her brother's tomb to weep there; and they decided to join her in the due pieties of mourning. So Mary and her Jewish friends reached Jesus at about the same time, and both parties were weeping. John tells us two things about Mary as she came into the Lord's presence: she repeated her sister's very words, and she prostrated herself before him. The two actions are not unconnected. To fall at Jesus' feet is to do what the man born blind did when Jesus sought him out and questioned him after his excommunication from the synagogue, viz. to worship him; and in turn that means to accord him those honours which men rightly reserve for God. So in one action Mary has said to Jesus what her sister had come to say in using a threefold title for Jesus – that he would have divine power over whatever enemy had afflicted her brother. This affirmation she makes as a suppliant, and, like her sister, she awaits the answer to her supplication before the faith that quickened it has received the confirmation that brings it to full effect. It is in this situation that the reader must understand the repetition of Martha's words '*If you had been here, my brother would not have died*' (v. 32). Mary is saying that had Jesus been with them, death would not have been able to enter her home and remove her brother, for death could not be in the same place as Jesus, who was worthy of the worship given rightly to God alone.

So, before the great sign of the raising of Lazarus takes place the evangelist has portrayed the chief characters in clear outlines: Lazarus has been dead for four days, but is nevertheless a 'lover of the Lord', a disciple who can still 'hear his voice' and have power to obey: Martha and Mary are both sure that Jesus has power to stop death entering, and recognize that this means ascribing to Jesus absolute divine power and honour, though they are not yet confident what such power can or will do for them in the present situation; the Jews who have come to share in the required rites of mourning stand where the Old Israel generally stood, in patient expectation that at the last day the good would be raised to life: Jesus comes into the situation knowing that his authority runs not only in the world on this side of the grave, but extends beyond it, so that even 'the dead will hear the voice of the Son of God, and those who hear will live' (5²⁵). Yet John gives no ground for thinking that these four parties in the story move about it like puppets. The story unfolds in real and tense human drama, with Jesus as much a partner in the development of the drama as anyone else. The story does not read like a myth or an allegory, but like an actual transcript of something that once happened to real men and women, as the Word-made-flesh moved in the deepest understanding and sympathy among them.

෴

'*The Teacher is here*': The title spoken to Mary seems oddly mundane after the exalted titles used by Martha. Yet Mary Magdalene is to use it at 20¹⁶, and it may well represent the way in which the disciples of Jesus spoke of him when he was not present. If they did, it may represent some reflection of the usage of the sects of the time (cf. the 'Teacher of Righteousness' of the Qumran community).

30
Jesus had not yet come to the village: The reason for this is not stated but it may well be that Jesus knew, either from Martha's reporting it, or from his own acquaintance with the situation of the sisters, that Jews from Jerusalem would be there; if so, it is not unnatural that he should seek to avoid their presence as much as possible.

31
supposing that she was going ... to weep there: The weeping referred to is not quiet or subdued but an unrestrained and loud wailing required by the social customs of the time. It is interesting to note that Mary Magdalene was weeping at the tomb of Jesus (20¹¹, ¹³, ¹⁵).

32
fell at his feet: This is the action that Mark reports both of Jairus and the Syrophoenician woman when they seek the help of Jesus (cf. Mark 5²²; 7⁵²).

³³*When Jesus saw her weeping, and the Jews who came with her also weeping, he was deeply moved in spirit and troubled;* ³⁴*and he said, 'Where have you laid him?' They said to him, 'Lord, come and see.'* ³⁵*Jesus wept.* ³⁶*So the Jews said, 'See how he loved him!'* ³⁷*But some of them said, 'Could not he who opened the eyes of the blind man have kept this man from dying?'*

³⁸*Then Jesus, deeply moved again, came to the tomb; it was a cave, and a stone lay upon it.*

ಬಬಿ

33

This verse sets a difficult problem to translator and commentator. The statement that Jesus was deeply moved in spirit translates a word that undoubtedly has connotations of anger in the Greek language. It seems equally clear from the sentence itself that the cause of Jesus' 'anger' was thought to be the weeping of Mary and of the Jews. But why should this be so? This is the puzzling question that has a good deal to do with the word which a translator uses, and with the comment that an expositor makes. There is no very precise parallel to the use of the word in scripture. It is used in three other places outside this particular narrative, at Mark 1⁴³ and Matt. 9³⁰, where the evangelists employ it to record the stern command with which Jesus urged silence upon someone he had cured; but 'anger' hardly seems the right word for any amount of sternness in such an attitude! The other occasion is when Mark uses it (Mark 14⁵) for the reproach with which some people in the house of Simon the leper met the action of the woman who anointed Jesus with very costly ointment. This usage might more easily embody the sense of 'anger', though 'indignation' might be even there a better word. In this verse, and again in v. 38, the meaning of 'anger' seems quite unsuitable, and some other phrase or word seems called for. In each instance of the word being used in this story it refers to an attitude of the Jews which falls short of what Jesus may rightly have felt they should by now have attained, seeing that many great works had been done before their eyes. Some deeply felt righteous indignation is what the word may well mean, and the rendering 'angry' rather overstates, and 'deeply moved' rather understates what seems to be in mind. Possibly 'deeply resentful in spirit' gets as near to the meaning as is practicable.

The word translated 'troubled' also needs some comment, for it is not simply a passive in the Greek, but carries the suggestion that the troubling was something which arose within and from Jesus himself. 'He troubled himself' would express the thought literally. The evangelist is trying to say that the attitude of the Jews, as those who could do nothing to help Mary and Martha to prepare for the performance of the great and final sign, but could only contain them within the prison of contemporary Judaism, was something quite inexcusable. Such an attitude, that could only result in judgement coming upon the people of God, could not but produce in Jesus a human reaction that would reflect the divine displeasure manifested in the tragic destiny of Judaism. So Jesus was deeply resentful in spirit, and roused himself up.

34

'*Where have you laid him?*': The word behind *laid* is so technical in its flavour that it can well be translated 'buried'. The question is precisely the one that will be asked about Jesus' own body when he is in the tomb (cf. 20², ¹³, ¹⁵).

35

Jesus wept: The word used for Jesus' weeping is different from that used to describe the formal weeping of the Jews. It means 'to shed tears', and shows that Jesus is not outside the sharing of the genuine human emotions of grief and sorrow. This offers contrast to the visiting Jews who do not 'sorrow' but 'professionally mourn' and so in spite of all that they have had opportunity to learn, are unable to mourn save without hope.

36

'*See how he loved him*': This is true; but the Jews, as often, are saying more than they know. For the love of Jesus has not only led him to shed tears in sympathy with his friends, but is about to lead him to deal with the death that is the tragic cause of human grief. '*Could not he . . . have kept this man from dying?*' This is the same remark, in essence, as has already been made by Martha and Mary. The Jews, no less than the rest of mankind, can only rise to a vision of death from the perspective of mortality. Not until the one has acted whose authority extends through death and beyond, will they be able to consider it from any other standpoint, or ask any different kind of question.

38

Jesus, deeply moved again: If the views expressed in the note on v. 33 be right, Jesus is once more deeply resentful at the Jews' inability to do more than suppose that his powers were no greater than those of the ordinary thaumaturgist, operative only before death in the case of any particular individual.

it was a cave, and a stone lay upon it: The use of natural cave forms as tombs was common enough among Jews. The wording does not itself decide whether the cave in question had a stone across the front of it, or over its top. The more likely alternative is that it was in front. Tombs were normally so sealed with a large immovable stone in order to ensure that wild beasts could not gain entrance.

I I $^{39-44}$ JESUS AND LAZARUS: THE SIXTH SIGN

39 *Jesus said, 'Take away the stone.' Martha, the sister of the dead man, said to him, 'Lord, by this time there will be an odour, for he has been dead four days.'* 40 *Jesus said to her, 'Did I not tell you that if you would believe you would see the glory of God?'* 41 *So they took away the stone. And Jesus lifted up his eyes and said, 'Father, I thank thee that thou hast heard me.* 42 *I knew that thou hearest me always, but I have said this on account of the people standing by, that they may believe that thou didst send me.'* 43 *When he had said this, he cried with a loud voice, 'Laz'arus, come out.'* 44 *The dead man came out, his hands and feet bound with bandages, and his face wrapped with a cloth. Jesus said to them, 'Unbind him, and let him go.'*

From this point onwards in the story Jesus takes full command; it is he alone who can bestow life, particularly upon one who, like Lazarus, is dead. The gift of such life comes entirely from the divine initiative. Mary, Martha, the Jews have all had things for which they could have asked earlier before Lazarus died. Now they have no ability to ask any more; but it is precisely now that Jesus brings his unasked, unmerited gift.

The imperative with which this part of the story opens is in the aorist tense; it is the imperative of authority. '*Take away the stone.*' It is evident that even at this point Martha is still unprepared for what is about to happen, for she exclaims '*Lord, by this time there will be an odour, for he has been dead four days*' (v. 39). Martha's apprehension suggests (in some contradistinction to v. 44) that the body of Lazarus had not been embalmed; and that Martha believed that Lazarus was beyond any possibility of restoration to life. The reply of Jesus refers back to a conversation in which the Lord is supposed to have told Martha that if she believed she would see the glory of God (v. 40). No such conversation is reported in the gospel. Yet it would be pedantic to press this point very far. Jesus had spoken about the glory of God in connexion with Lazarus at the time when he and the disciples first heard about the sickness of Martha's brother; and he had told Martha that he was the resurrection and the life, and indicated what that meant for those who believed on him. Moreover it is independently apparent that John has not reported every part of the traditional sayings known to him in this story, for he has not, e.g., passed on the words with which he told Martha that he wished to see Mary (cf. v. 28). More important is it to remember that the glory of God is his action, not his praise. This accounts for the use of the verb *see* in connexion with the glory of God. The word translated *see* is used in connexion with the perception of a spiritual truth. All present will see Jesus' action; yet only those who have faith will *see* it as the manifestation of the glory of God. What is about to be done will not be the action of Jesus alone, but will be the work and act of the Father in and through his Son. It is instructive to recall at this point the verses 5^{19ff}, which speak of the cooperation of Father and Son, and lead directly into the prophecy that the hour is coming when the dead will hear the voice of the Son of God, and those who hear will live.

The stone was taken away. Jesus turned to prayer. *He lifted up his eyes* (v. 41) and so indicated that the source of the deed was not exclusively in him, but that the Father was complicit in it. Jesus' prayer begins with a thanksgiving, in the aorist tense, for some past hearing of prayer, presumably at the time of a miracle. There is only one such occasion in the gospel so far – at the time of the feeding of the five thousand. This is entirely suitable and significant. True the occasion was that of giving thanks for bread, as devout Jews always did before meals; but in each instance, here and there, John uses the same word to express the thanks that Jesus gave – *eucharistein*; and the particular use of the word 'eucharist', with its special reference to the death of Jesus, cannot be far beneath the surface in either passage. It was the miracle of the feeding that led directly to the discourse on the eucharist in ch. 6, in which it is roundly stated that there is no possibility of life save for those who eat the flesh of the Son of man and drink his blood.

Jesus is thus thanking the Father that on the previous occasion

when he had offered prayer there had been effective complicity of
Father with Son, and a sign had been wrought in which those who
had eyes could see not only that bread had been given for the relief of
the body's necessities, but that the true bread that comes down from
heaven had been given for the life of the world. Yet it must not be
supposed that it is only on rare occasions that such accord of Father and
Son is established. On the contrary, dialogue between Father and
Son is always going on, and the Father is always responsive to the
requests of the Son. Prayer such as is offered on a public occasion such
as this is therefore not a special constraint put upon the Father by the
Son, but rather a special admission of others into the area where
Father and Son live together in unbroken communion and dialogue
of word and act. The contrast in the mind of the evangelist is evidently
that between the prayer of Jesus which is always heard because the will
of the Father and the Son are one, and the prayer of ordinary man
who, because he cannot be sure that his prayer is according to the
will of God, cannot be certain that prayer will be 'answered' in the
way that he expects. Yet it is part of the teaching of the fourth gospel
that the Christian disciple can increasingly come to share the prayer
relationship of the Son and the Father.

Prayer ends in action, and Jesus *cried with a loud voice, 'Lazarus,
come out'* (v. 43). It is an unavoidable question as to the precise conditions in which this imperative was spoken to Lazarus. There are
some critics who think that the prayer of Jesus reported in vv. 41-42
was itself the point at which Lazarus had been brought back to life.
This is unconvincing; for the whole point of this and other stories of
the signs of Jesus is that they should be visible signs of the cooperation
of Father and Son. So it is the spoken imperative addressed to the
dead man that must be taken as the moment of restoration to life.
Jesus himself speaks the quickening word; the precedent prayer serves
to establish before men the presence of an unceasing communion of
Father and Son.

There follows what Hoskyns has not infelicitously called 'a miracle
within a miracle', for Lazarus comes out of the tomb, with hands
and feet bound with bandages, and his face wrapped with a cloth.
How could such a figure move in obedience to a call, save by supernatural power imparted by the Word? The wrapping of hands and
feet suggests, though it does not establish, embalmment, while the
wrapping of a cloth round the head may well suggest the burial

of a poor person, according to some Jewish traditions. But the point which the evangelist leaves with his readers is that here is the fulfilment of the prophetic word uttered in 5^{25}: 'The hour is coming, *and now is*, when the dead will hear the voice of the Son of God, and those who hear will live.' Lazarus has heard the voice of the Son, and has come to life. Yet to leave comment there would be to betray the gospel and the evangelist.

The common difficulty perceived in the story of Lazarus is that it is supposed to assert that Jesus brought a man who was dead back to physical life in this world: in that the not unjustifiably sceptical reader senses a difficulty similar to that usually found in the story of the man born blind, in which many readers suppose that Jesus' miracle lay in giving physical sight to a man who had never had it. But, as was urged in comment on the story, the real miracle was that the 'Christ-given' sight enabled the man, when he looked on Jesus, to 'see' that he was the Son of man, worthy of worship. Similarly here, the real miracle is not that Jesus restored Lazarus to physical existence; to think so would be to join the Jews in their materialistic misunderstandings of Jesus' miracles throughout the gospel. The act of bringing Lazarus back to his family and friends was indeed wonderful enough, but it is far more wonderful when he, dead in the tomb, is in that condition brought to the only life that is life indeed, viz. where a man, dead or alive, hears the voice of the Son of God and lives. It is in this sense that the story of Lazarus is the *crux interpretationis* of the whole gospel, for it compels the reader to decide whether he will take John's view of miracle, that it is always in essence the gift of eternal life understood as knowing the one whom God has sent and obeying him, however that be conveyed, in the form of restoration of movement to a limb, sight to an eye, health to a sick body, or life to a dead one; or whether he will take the Jewish view of miracle, that it consists in the actual thaumaturgy of the occasion. It would be the sheerest anti-climax were John to have written his whole gospel only to come in this place to a materialist view of miracle!

Hence, perhaps, the 'miracle within a miracle'. Lazarus obeys the command '*Come out*' while he is still a *dead man*. Yet dead though he be, he has heard the voice of the Son of God and so already lives that life which is life indeed. It is only when that life has been attained and evidenced that Lazarus is restored to his family with the words

'*Unbind him, and let him go*'. It looks as if what has usually been thought of as the miracle, the restoration of Lazarus to the life of his family, is simply the consequence of the real miracle, the life that is given by Jesus Christ to those who believe in him. Of course the two 'lives' cannot really be separated, any more than can the two 'sights' of ch. 9; but they can and should be distinguished, or else John's whole attempt to avoid presenting Jesus as the thaumaturgist par excellence is at least imperilled, if not undermined.

ﬡﬡ

39

Martha . . . said: There has been no report of Martha since she spoke to her sister, but she has by now rejoined the body of mourners. John is still selecting from his source, whatever it be.

41

lifted up his eyes: This is the typical attitude of prayer, and symbolizes the fact that answer to prayer comes from God himself.

'*Father, I thank thee*': Most commentators would think that the verb *thank* even though deriving from *eucharistein* is here used in a quite profane or secular sense. The comment has been written on another supposition.

'*that thou hast heard me*': There is one further possibility of expounding this passage. The O.T. prophet often used the past tense or the future to express the certainty with which he spoke his message about the present. This thanks, ostensibly for an answer to prayer in the past, may therefore be an emphatic way of expressing Christ's certainty that God will answer his prayer on this occasion.

42

'*I have said this on account of the people standing by, that they may believe that thou didst send me*': This is the clearest denial that Jesus is a thaumaturgist. His prayer is offered in public because in this way the crowd will not be tempted to think that Jesus has by his own powers resuscitated Lazarus, but will understand that it is only the work of the Father in, through, and with the Son, that is thus effective. The idea that it is the mission bestowed by the Father that gives Jesus his great authority is a central theme of the fourth gospel.

44

The dead man came out: Literally, he who had died came out. In his death he had heard the voice of the Son of God and had lived. Not that that meant necessarily a return to life in the physical world, which is not of itself life indeed.

45*Many of the Jews therefore, who had come with Mary and had seen what he did, believed in him;* 46*but some of them went to the Pharisees and told them what Jesus had done.* 47*So the chief priests and the Pharisees gathered the council, and said, 'What are we to do? For this man performs many signs.* 48*If we let him go on thus, every one will believe in him, and the Romans will come and destroy both our holy place[a] and our nation.'* 49*But one of them, Ca'iaphas, who was high priest that year, said to them, 'You know nothing at all;* 50*you do not understand that it is expedient for you that one man should die for the people, and that the whole nation should not perish.'* 51*He did not say this of his own accord, but being high priest that year he prophesied that Jesus should die for the nation,* 52*and not for the nation only, but to gather into one the children of God who are scattered abroad.* 53*So from that day on they took counsel how to put him to death.*

a Greek *our place.*

Many Jews had gone to visit Mary in her bereavement, and now, on account of the miracle, came to believe in Jesus. Other Jews however went and laid information about the incident to the Pharisees. In this way John gives his readers a parallel to the act of informing which is presupposed in Mark 11[18]: 'And the chief priests and scribes heard it [the cleansing of the temple] and sought a way to destroy him; for they feared him, because all the multitude was astonished at his teaching.' The particular incident reported to the authorities differs in the fourth gospel from that mentioned in Mark, but the course of the subsequent discussion of the authorities embodies the same substance.

John tells his readers that the authorities called a council (the Sanhedrin) and put the problem officially to it. '*What are we to do?*' they ask; '*this man performs many signs. If we let him go on thus, every one will believe in him, and the Romans will come and destroy both our holy place and our nation.*' The reference to the *signs* is contemptuous, and does not carry the full Johannine meaning of the word. It is note-worthy that at this meeting of the Council there is no word spoken for Jesus by Nicodemus, though he would naturally be at the Council. The argument adduced recognizes not only the fact that Jesus did signs, but that they were having a certain meaning attached to them, which would lead to Jesus becoming a popular leader, provoking action by Rome, inducing the destruction of the Temple and the loss of Jewish nationhood. In the event, of course, the decision to avoid such consequences by disposing of Jesus itself led to the very misfortunes the authorities were seeking to avoid. But one member of the Council, who had the distinction of being High Priest at the time, had a plan to put forward. He agreed that the probable outcome of letting Jesus continue on his course would be the extinction of the Jewish nation; was it not therefore better, more expedient, that Jesus himself should die instead of letting all the people suffer. '*It is expedient for you that one man should die for the people.*' As countless commentators have noticed, never have truer words been spoken, and never with such determination to be rid of an uncomfortable trouble maker. John cannot help adding to his record of the High Priest's advice that this stumbling of Caiaphas upon the truth in such a hostile utterance was due to the prophetic spirit which, as Jews expected, could inspire the speech of the High Priest. And it is not without significance that as he reproduces in his comment what Caiaphas said, he cannot but add a note to incorporate into what Jesus would do not only his work for the Jewish people, but for the whole scattered people of God, Jew and Gentile alike. On such advice, clear-sighted and determined, the Sanhedrin decided to have Jesus put to death.

So once again, in the fourth gospel, a sign has produced two opposite reactions among the Jews: some, who had witnessed the last great sign, believed in Jesus, though it must not be supposed that their belief was any more than that referred to as early as 2²³. Yet it was the raw material of deeper faith. Other Jews, who would seem not to have witnessed the miracle, but presumably had heard about it (for it could hardly have been kept quiet), reported it to the authorities, with an evident intention that the authorities should put a stop at least to the signs, if not to the sign-worker.

ॐ

45

The translation of this verse is not easy, if the true sense is accurately to be reproduced. It is better to translate: 'Many of the Jews, that is, those who had come to Mary, believed in him.' The point is that those who believe at this point are meant to be all those Jews who came to Mary in her mourning. It is not the intention of the Greek that some of those who saw the sign should be thought of as coming to belief and others who saw it failed to do so. Those who went to the Pharisees are thus not of those who saw the sign. Yet it is the sign that is the occasion of the division among the Jews.

46

It is not necessary to suppose that John conceived of the Pharisees as themselves constituting some official court of Judaism, but simply that as leaders of the Jews, they would have power or influence to secure the attention of the regular courts to Jesus and his works.

47

The *council* is evidently the Sanhedrin, the chief court of Judaism.

'*What are we to do?*': This is better translated 'What are we doing?', which clearly invites the answer 'Nothing', and then the argument proceeds 'This man is performing many signs, and if we let him go on unhindered, there will be unpleasant consequences.'

49

Caiaphas, who was high priest that year: This phrase has been used to suggest the extreme ignorance of the author of the fourth gospel of Jewish customs, for the High Priest's office was not an annual one. But it is possible to suppose that the author is drawing attention to the fact that in this auspicious year, when the Saviour of the world gave his life for mankind, Caiaphas was the High Priest.

'*You know nothing at all*': Caiaphas tries to say that there is an answer to the question raised. Something can and shall be done. This one man must die, rather than let the temple and the nation perish.

50

This verse may be said to offer the most forceful example of Johannine irony. Words spoken in opposition against Jesus, and in an attempt to destroy him in order to save the temple and the Jewish nation actually turn out in one sense to be true prophecy: Jesus will indeed die for the people, and not only for the Jewish people, but for all the people of God whom he will gather together. In another sense Caiaphas' statement is the reverse of the truth, for while the death of Jesus was accomplished, that did not secure the safety of the temple, or the continued nationhood of the Jewish people.

51

he prophesied: The Jews believed that their High Priest was invested with some prophetic power in virtue of his office (cf. Exod. 28^{30}; Lev. 8^8; Num. 27^{21}). Luke reports that Zacharias could prophesy as a priest (Luke 1^{67}).

52

but to gather into one the children of God who are scattered abroad: In a purely Jewish document these words would suggest the Jews of the Dispersion, and no one else. But in this Christian writing, particularly in view of John's conception of the Gentile mission, the words can hardly be so confined. Pointing forward as they do to the cross and resurrection they indicate the way in which men of every nation will be drawn into the Church by the death and resurrection of Jesus Christ. Men become children of God, according to the fourth gospel; they are not so by nature. And it is through the death of Christ that the spirit which effects the new birth is released for the lives of men (7^{39}).

443

John 11⁵⁴⁻⁵⁷

John II

⁵⁴*Jesus therefore no longer went about openly among the Jews, but went from there to the country near the wilderness, to a town called E'phraim; and there he stayed with the disciples.*

⁵⁵*Now the Passover of the Jews was at hand, and many went up from the country to Jerusalem before the Passover, to purify themselves.* ⁵⁶*They were looking for Jesus and saying to one another as they stood in the temple, 'What do you think? That he will not come to the feast?'* ⁵⁷*Now the chief priests and the Pharisees had given orders that if any one knew where he was, he should let them know, so that they might arrest him.*

This interlude does not give the reader a picture of Jesus 'on the run', in hurried and desperate flight trying to avoid capture. Clearly, on the other hand, the evangelist makes it clear that Jesus' withdrawal was occasioned by the decision of the authorities to arrest him and put him to death. So Jesus no longer continues a public itinerant ministry among the population of Judea; instead he withdraws to a sparsely inhabited area on the edge of the desert, and takes up residence in a town called Ephraim. 'There,' states John, 'he stayed.' How familiar and significant a word 'stay' is in the fourth gospel. If it be asked why Jesus should decide to discontinue a public ministry because of the decision to seek his death, the answer is not therefore that he was seeking to escape a final confrontation with the authorities; if that had been so, he need never have gone up to the impending Passover. If he had continued his public appearances in an area of relatively thick Jewish population, then the authorities would have been able to arrest him well before the feast. And since it is clear from synoptics as well as John that it was on Jesus' own initiative that he ate the Passover with his disciples in Jerusalem, the reason for the withdrawal to Ephraim near the desert must have been connected with his intention to have his last confrontation with the authorities at the time of the feast.*

* Thus Mark 14¹³⁻¹⁶ clearly implies that before the disciples asked Jesus about the arrangements for the eating of the Passover, he had already made complete provision for it. Mark 10³², recording the last journey to Jerusalem, states that 'Jesus was walking ahead', with the disciples following mystified and anxious in the rear.

The raising of Lazarus had evidently taken place not long before the pilgrims began to go up to Jerusalem for the Passover. John states that they now began to enter the city, so as to give themselves adequate time to undergo all the necessary purificatory rites to render them fit to participate fully in the feast. The reference to purification serves to remind the reader that when Jesus attended the wedding at Cana in Galilee (2^{1-11}) he performed a 'sign' which showed that the purificatory rites of Judaism were inadequate to bring men to God, or to keep them in proper relationship with him. The water symbolizing Jewish purification was replaced by wine which symbolized the Christian means of purification, the self-offering of Jesus Christ in death. Now as the Jews seek to purify themselves to share in God's 'Passover' Jesus is preparing to attend the feast and become the true Passover lamb.

Humanly speaking, of course, it was unlikely that a man whose death had been decided on would make a public appearance in Jerusalem. So the Jews themselves wondered whether Jesus would come. The form of the question implies that there was doubt in the minds of those who put it. To a Jew it must have appeared doubtful, or even highly improbable; but to Jesus it was as certain as any act of loving obedience a son can offer to his father. The doubts that the Jews had rested quite naturally on the fact that orders had been given that if anyone knew where Jesus was, he was to inform the authorities. Would Jesus prove so foolhardy as to come to Jerusalem knowing such orders had been given, for he would be bound to learn of his danger if he came. But Jesus came; not because his decision was determined, positively or negatively, by the order for his arrest, but for profound reasons of his constant love for and obedience to his Father. Certainly it becomes plain, when Jesus returned to Bethany, that his destiny was already clear to him (see notes on 12^{1-8}). He moves freely, though as a free man embracing a high and inescapable destiny.

John 12$^{1-50}$

Rapture, Rupture and Recapitulation

This chapter closes the first great division of the gospel. It is the end of the Book of Signs. But there is a sense in which the death and exaltation of Jesus can be thought of as the seventh sign, but if they are, then they must be seen as together constituting the one reality of which each of the previous six 'wonders' are but signs, the last and mightiest 'wonder' of God in which all the rest find their essential substance and meaning.

The evangelist manifestly takes pains to indicate to his readers on what precise section of the synoptic narrative he offers comment. Before the story of the death and exaltation begins he is concerned that his readers should have a due appreciation of the issues that were involved in the events themselves. To this end he has skilfully woven synoptic and non-synoptic material together in this chapter. Thus he knits together two synoptic traditions of an anointing of Jesus, incorporates material of his own, and adds a reference, impossible for the synoptists, to the raising of Lazarus, and so prepares his readers for what is about to come. Similarly he retells, in his own style, the threefold synoptic narrative of the Triumphal Entry, and follows it with a non-synoptic account of the request by some Greeks for an interview. Once more, the apparently separate pericopes are found to have a single interpretative reference to the drama to follow. Finally, in a section of the chapter which recapitulates the whole, and seeks to show on what issues the final separation between Jesus and the Jews took place, the evangelist uses material from various synoptic places, demonstrating both the profound gravity of the issues that divided Jesus from his contemporaries, and their presence at a much earlier period than a superficial reading of the synoptic narrative might suggest. Thus the chapter falls naturally into three sections, the first (12^{1-11}) dealing with the anointing, the second with the Triumphal Entry (12^{12-26}) and the third with the critical situation when Jesus finally *hid himself* (12^{36b}) from the Jews.

I2 *Six days before the Passover, Jesus came to Bethany, where Laz′arus was, whom Jesus had raised from the dead.* ² *There they made him a supper; Martha served, but Laz′arus was one of those at table with him.* ³ *Mary took a pound of costly ointment of pure nard and anointed the feet of Jesus and wiped his feet with her hair; and the house was filled with the fragrance of the ointment.* ⁴*But Judas Iscariot, one of his disciples (he who was to betray him), said,* ⁵*'Why was the ointment not sold for three hundred denarii^a and given to the poor?'* ⁶*This he said, not that he cared for the poor but because he was a thief, and as he had the money box he used to take what was put into it.* ⁷*Jesus said, 'Let her alone, let her keep it for the day of my burial.* ⁸*The poor you always have with you, but you do not always have me.'*

⁹ *When the great crowd of the Jews learned that he was there, they came, not only on account of Jesus but also to see Laz′arus, whom he had raised from the dead.* ¹⁰*So the chief priests planned to put Laz′arus also to death,* ¹¹*because on account of him many of the Jews were going away and believing in Jesus.*

a The denarius was worth about 9½d., and was thought to be a fair day's wage for a labourer (Matt. 20²ff)

To read this story is to be reminded of a double tradition in the synoptic narratives, the story basically set out in Mark 14³⁻⁹, where, in the house of Simon the Leper at Bethany, an unnamed woman anointed the head of Jesus with costly ointment; and that recorded in Luke 7³⁶⁻⁵⁰, in which a 'woman who was a sinner' anointed the feet of Jesus, wet his feet with her tears, and wiped them with her hair. Whether John is using a separate tradition of his own is perhaps impossible now to determine, but if it can be supposed that he had some acquaintance with the divergent synoptic traditions it is worth while asking why he follows the basic Marcan narrative, with some modifications in the direction of Matthew, and more marked changes towards Luke. In his slight assimilations to Matthew (e.g. omitting the phrase 'whenever you will, you can do good to them [the poor]') John removes some of the characteristic concreteness of the isolated unique historical occasion, and thus enables his reader to come more readily to the theological intention of the story as it was first expounded by St Mark. In the more marked assimilations to Luke the fourth evangelist does two things: he moves the incident from after the Triumphal Entry to before it (though only shortly before it instead of, as in Luke, apparently some time before), and he follows Luke in reporting that the woman who anointed Jesus anointed his feet and not his head. Finally it is important to note that John knits into his narrative a double reference to Lazarus, who appears as a guest at the supper table, and whose death, it is stated, was sought by the authorities since the miracle wrought on him was causing defections from the Jewish faith to Jesus.

In taking Mark's version of this story as his main theme John indicates his intention to interpret it, like Mark, as a foretelling of Jesus' death. And he makes a reference to his own gospel to reinforce this; for in speaking of Lazarus at present, and of the decision of the authorities to put him to death, John is uniting death and resurrection in his own specific fashion. By moving the incident from after the Triumphal Entry to before it, he uses a simple historiographical device to indicate that even before the Entry into Jerusalem there was a context of death and resurrection in terms of which it must be interpreted. And by reporting that Mary anointed Jesus' feet he links the death with the forgiveness of sin (cf. Luke 7^{47}), and also indicates that she has now come to acknowledge that he is the resurrection and the life. In Matthew and Mark Jesus is portrayed as accepting an act of devotion with clear regal and messianic meaning; in Luke the devotion offered is that of a penitent sinner; in John these are skilfully blended into an act which marks Jesus as at once the triumphant Messiah and yet one who is about to die for the sins of men.

Jesus arrives at Bethany on the sabbath before the last Passover in which he was to share, though in John his share in it is to be that of the veritable paschal lamb! His return to the town where Lazarus lived was itself a courageous acceptance of danger, for it was in consequence of his raising of Lazarus that the Jews 'from that day ... took counsel how to put him to death' (11^{53}). When he arrived, he was feasted, though whether at Lazarus' house or that of Simon cannot be decided from John's narrative alone (cf. Mark 14³), nor is the location of particular significance for John. Martha is found as her usual practical self serving at table; but Mary, in accordance with her portrait in Luke (10³⁹), finds a deeper level of relationship to her Lord. She takes a large quantity of expensive ointment and anoints his feet, an action which, in John, is taken as symbolic for an anointing of the whole body (cf. 13⁵⁻¹⁰). It is difficult therefore to resist the conclusion that John intends his readers to see in Mary's action a deliberate attempt to anoint the body of him whom she now believes to be verily 'the resurrection and the life'. By such artistry John emphasizes that Mary had really understood and properly answered the question Jesus addressed to her when her brother was in the tomb: 'I am the resurrection and the life. . . . Do you believe this?' (11²⁵). He who was now already 'the resurrection' could be anointed in the way that other mortals could be anointed only after their death. In Mark's narrative the devotion of a woman in anointing the head of Jesus had been given a reference to his death by his own interpretation; in the fourth gospel the act of Mary is eloquent itself of the faith of one who knows that Jesus 'lives and shall never die', and 'though he die, shall live' (cf. 11²⁵,²⁶).

As in Mark and Matthew the costly devotion of the woman is criticized on the grounds that the money spent on the ointment could have been usefully engaged in poor relief. Whoever made this remark, the 'some' of Mark, the 'disciples' of Matthew, or Judas, as in John, the evident intention of the fourth evangelist is to exhibit the spiritual blindness behind the remark as tantamount to unfaithfulness. If the Son of God had come, he must be paid due honour (cf. the synoptic parable of the Vineyard, Mark 12¹⁻¹¹, especially v. 6), and that honour included the proper treatment of his body at his death and burial. For Mary, who had learnt that Jesus was already the resurrection and the life, it was entirely proper that she should anoint him for his burial. To wish to spend the money on poor relief would involve a lack of recognition of the real nature of Jesus as the Son of God who is the deathless dying one. There is a real place for service to the poor; but the due recognition of the person and stature of the Son of God must also have its place. Not to see this is to lack the basic elements of Christian faith.

❧

1

The *Passover* took place on Friday; so Jesus arrives at Bethany on the previous Saturday.

2

There is little profit in trying to decide at whose house the incident took place. John may be using a different tradition from the synoptics as the source of his story; he may himself have blended the various synoptic trends.

3

The *pound* was of 12 ounces. To anoint the head was a customary act of courtesy to a guest. To anoint the feet was exceptional. For a woman to loosen her hair was considered an act of considerable immodesty. It would appear that John adopts Luke's tradition of the anointing of the feet because of its representation of a penitent believer, and it may well be that Mary is expressing penitence for the unbelief with which she received Jesus when he came at Lazarus' death. She is certainly a picture of sinful, penitent humanity, whose whole hope lies in the worship of him who is the resurrection and the life. A further light on the choice of an anointing of the feet is to be found in the story of Jesus washing the disciples' feet at the Last Supper (13$^{1-11}$, especially v. 10); to have the feet washed is to be washed all over.

pure nard: or, possibly, liquid nard. Barrett suggests that in Mark, where the phrase also occurs, it represents an Aramaic word meaning the pistachio nut, in which case the ointment can be identified as that called *myrobalanum*. But there is no clear guide.

Some commentators have seen in the reference to the smell of the ointment permeating the whole house a piece of Johannine symbolism intended to replace Mark's comment that wherever the gospel is preached the action of the woman would be retold. The 'house' is the Church or even, possibly, the world.

4

In the development, or the variety of the Tradition, Mark reports that there were 'some' who objected to the waste involved in the purchase of the ointment; Matthew says it was the disciples who complained; John identifies Judas as the curmudgeonly complainant. In a previous reference to Judas, the evangelist had indicated that he was 'a devil', in that he was to betray Jesus.

5

This repeats the substance of the complaint recorded in Mark and Matthew.

6

The synoptic narrative leaves the action of Judas quite unexplained. John does not tell his readers anything more about the precise motives that led Judas to *betray* (or, in an equally good rendering, 'deliver up') Jesus, but the information that his was a character which descended to habitual theft of money from his fellows makes the act of betrayal more in keeping.

7

This verse is difficult for the interpreter. The phrase '*Let her alone*' can stand, even though in the Greek of New Testament times the text might well mean simply 'Let her . . . ' as an introduction to the next verb '*keep it*'. It is the suggestion of '*keep it*' which is difficult, and has understandably puzzled commentators. Verse 3 offers a natural suggestion that Mary used all the ointment she had; it would be incongruous to ask that she be allowed to *keep* the ointment after that. It has been suggested that the Greek word *tērein* should be translated 'keep in mind', 'remember'; but the serious doubt about that is that the word does not elsewhere bear that meaning. Barrett notes that in John the word '*tērein*' can mean 'to observe' as well as 'to keep', though he adds that to use that translation does not seem very natural (Barrett, p. 345). The translation on this rendering of the word would go: 'Let her alone; let her observe the last rite now, with a view to the day of my burial.' Is this so unnatural a rendering in the context? The last appearance of Mary in the narrative was when she had said to Jesus as he approached the burial place of Lazarus, 'Lord, if you had been here, my brother would not have died.' At that point she had not yet confessed that Jesus was the resurrection and the life. But to enact upon his living body that process proper only to the corpse is surely intended to symbolize that Mary now realizes that Jesus has a quite unique relationship to life and death, and that therefore it is as natural to anoint his living body, for he is even now the resurrection, as it would be, later on, to anoint his corpse. In this way, it would seem, John provides his readers with his own comment on the story as a proclamation of the 'cross of Christ', which Mark had discerned it to be; though John, in his own characteristic way, introduces even into this acted confession of belief in Jesus not only an acceptance of his death, but an assurance of his resurrection.

8

As in Mark, so here, the one-time death and resurrection of Jesus which demands appropriate response is contrasted with the perpetual opportunities of social service to the poor. To bear witness to the unique significance of the death and resurrection of Jesus in contemporary action is something that must be done now, or not at all. Service to the poor, or any other general care for humanity, is a continuing obligation for Christian people.

9

The appropriateness of a reference to Jesus' raising of Lazarus can well be seen if Mary did in fact testify her belief in the resurrection by her anticipatory anointing of the Lord's body. Jesus is not only one who himself rises from the dead, but also he who can raise others with and in him.

10

Once more the evangelist has seen the indissoluble solidarity of the Messiah with the people of the Messiah, of Jesus with the new people of God created in him. To oppose the one, to seek his destruction, is to oppose and destroy the other.

11

were going away: i.e. leaving the faith of their fathers, and becoming Christian believers.

12$^{12-19}$ 'TRIUMPHAL ENTRY'

Mark 11$^{1-10}$
Matthew 21$^{1-9}$
Luke 19$^{29-38}$
Zechariah 9^{9,10}
1 Maccabees 13^{51}
Psalm 118$^{25, 26}$

^{12}*The next day a great crowd who had come to the feast heard that Jesus was coming to Jerusalem.* ^{13}*So they took branches of palm trees and went out to meet him, crying, 'Hosanna! Blessed be he who comes in the name of the Lord, even the King of Israel!'* ^{14}*And Jesus found a young ass and sat upon it; as it is written,*
^{15}*'Fear not, daughter of Zion;*
  behold thy king is coming,
  sitting on an ass's colt!'
^{16}*His disciples did not understand this at first; but when Jesus was glorified then they remembered that this had been written of him and had been done to him.* ^{17}*The crowd that had been with him when he called Laz'arus out*

of the tomb and raised him from the dead bore witness. 18 *The reason why the crowd went to meet him was that they heard he had done this sign.* 19 *The Pharisees then said to one another, 'You see that you can do nothing; look, the world has gone after him.'*

On the Sunday before he died, Jesus rode into Jerusalem on a donkey. He may well have done this on numerous other occasions, but it is evident from the recital of the story in all four gospels that on this day it was felt, from the start, to have been of special significance. John's account makes it clear that a crowd went out from Jerusalem and met another coming in. Those who came in accompanied him because they had seen the sign of his power at the raising of Lazarus; and those who went out to meet him had heard of the miracle, and acclaimed Jesus as the '*King of Israel*'.

But there were other features of the story which, John says, not even the disciples recognized at the time. Jesus rode into the city on a donkey: but they did not until later realize that this was a fulfilment of a prophecy of Zechariah. At this point of evident popularity, the Pharisees, John reports, acknowledged their impotence to restrain the crowds from following Jesus.

The story is illustrative of many things, not least that it would be pointless to relate it simply in terms of what could be seen and heard, as if some television camera had recorded the incident on 'tape'. The story has point only as it is connected with disciples, with seekers, with Old Testament prophecies in the mind of Jesus and in the conceptions of the crowd. It may also be used to illustrate how John offers some definite comment on the synoptic tradition by the way he makes use of their material and adds some of his own.

It is clear from all four gospels that Jesus himself took the initiative in arranging to ride into the city upon an ass. Mark tells his readers that Jesus sent two disciples to fetch the animal, with full instructions as to what to say and do if they were in any way questioned. Matthew and Luke repeat this information. John omits the mission of the disciples and states simply that *Jesus found a young ass, and sat upon it* (12 14). Mark does not mention the prophecy of Zechariah; it would be difficult to suppose that he did not notice the aptness of the passage, and it may be that he omits it for the reason that John, in the minds of some commentators, seems to offer, viz. that after Jesus had been glorified the disciples *remembered that this had been written of him*.

And in view of John's repeated assertion that the 'lifting up' or 'glorification' of Jesus was a necessary prelude to any full understanding of what had really been 'going on' in the events of his life, it is not surprising that John, following Matthew, associates the prophecy with the story, in the evident belief that this would not misrepresent the mind and intention of Jesus at the time.

And all four gospels bear this out in various ways. Mark tells the story of how Jesus sent for the ass so that he might ride into the city. He goes on to tell how some 'spread their garments in the way' and put their garments on the colt, on which Jesus sat. This is to see the incident from the perspective of the disciples, in terms of the action of the followers of Jehu when he was proclaimed king in Israel (2 Kings 9¹³), as indicating that, like the followers of Jehu, they were ready for martial rebellion and conquest. By contrast Jesus affirmed, in an action that sees the same incident in terms of the prophecy of Zechariah, that his idea was of a king coming in peace, forswearing all weapons of war, and thereby receiving a universal and everlasting kingdom (Zech. 9⁹,¹⁰). So the incident dramatically posed for the participants a radical choice between two possibilities for the perpetuation of the life of Israel as the people of God – by military power, or by the humiliation of peace and the forswearing of war. And when it is realized that even in the synoptics this two-fold perspective is directed to the person of him who is said to be 'Son of God' it is impossible not to treat the incident as having very profound significance.

To the account of the synoptists John adds one significant detail, though he omits much. He states that the crowd that went out to meet Jesus from Jerusalem, because they had heard of the raising of Lazarus, '*took branches of palm trees*' to greet him. If we seek for the meaning of this, we must turn to the account of the entry of Simon Maccabeus into Jerusalem in 1 Maccabees 13⁵¹, when the conquering hero of Judaism, the cleanser of the temple, was received 'with praise, and palm branches, and with harps and with cymbals . . . with hymns and with songs'. John, that is to say, uses a 'power' example much nearer his own day with which to display the meaning of this Sunday entry into the city. The fourth evangelist repeats the synoptic interpretation of Jesus' action in terms of Zechariah's prophecy, though he is careful to say that this meaning was not apparent to the disciples on the day.

But even with such scriptures and types focused upon the incident, it could still be regarded as offering a choice between two 'worldly' alternatives, between, say, a 'militarist' and a 'pacifist' programme for securing the future of Israel. So John takes pains to leave his readers in no doubt as to the real issue. The crowd which came from Bethany and had seen his work on the entombed Lazarus came afterwards to see that the prophecy of Zechariah did apply to the entry. John is trying, by the twin historiographical device of referring to Zechariah and to Lazarus, to show that the real issue that day was between the crowd which hailed Jesus as a Messianic king, and Jesus himself who in action claimed that he was about to receive his kingdom, though the sure future he could secure for it lay beyond the boundaries of terrestrial life. The way of humility, peace and death was the only road to a certain future for the people of God.

It was not until after Jesus was glorified that the full meaning of the Triumphal Entry dawned upon the disciples. Yet there was some germinal discernment of the real issue at the time. *The crowd that had been with him when he called Lazarus out of the tomb and raised him from the dead bore witness*, writes John (12¹⁷). They had some sense that his power over death had something to do with the future of the people of God. They bore witness to him, in a situation where the Pharisees had concluded that because so many people were with him, nothing could be done. In fact the great division had not yet been made. The coming events would do that. The Pharisees, as well as the disciples, were to learn that the issues posed on 'Palm Sunday' were to be acted out in life and death and resurrection.

✵

12

The *crowd* that went to meet Jesus were pilgrims to the feast, and not necessarily the inhabitants of Judea.

13

The *palm* branch is reminiscent of Simon Maccabeus' entry into Jerusalem (1 Macc. 13⁵¹). 'Hosanna' is a direct quotation of the Hebrew word which opens the verse cited from Psalm 118²⁵. This was the last of the 'Hallel' psalms which were sung at the Feast of the Passover (cf. Mark 14²⁶). Thus John applies a liturgical text to Jesus as the new Passover Lamb, which role he is to assume in this gospel. The new Passover, which was to ensure the final 'exodus' of God's people to a new and indestructible life with him was about to take place. 'Hosanna' means

'Save us'. '*The King of Israel*' is a title regarded as Messianic by the Jews. The crowd coming from Jerusalem, like the crowd of which Mark writes (Mark 11^9), hails Jesus as the great military deliverer-to-be.

14, 15
These two verses repeat the report of the dramatic enactment of meaning which Jesus himself put upon his approach to the city. It is in precise opposition to that of the crowd. The future for Israel as God's people will not lie through conquest, but through his own death and resurrection.

16
The story could not be adequately written down in terms of pure 'happening' but only in terms of what was going on in what was happening; and this was not known to the disciples until they could review it from the perspective of the resurrection.

17
The reader must judge what the witness was. It could not have been simply to the fact of the raising of Lazarus, for the crowd from Jerusalem already knew this. It would seem that even here there was some difference about the significance of the raising of Lazarus. Evidently the people from Jerusalem thought that such a display of power endorsed their own views that Jesus would prove an unconquerable deliverer; those who had witnessed the scene in Bethany were evidently more ready to think that the power of Jesus was to be exercised in his authority over death, and not in military might.

19
the world is almost certainly meant to include the Gentile world in the mind of the writer, if not in the thought of the Pharisees; for the evangelist is about to tell the story of the Greeks seeking to interview Jesus. The Pharisees are a symbol of the final impotence of Pharisaic Judaism in face of the gospel.

12$^{20-26}$ JESUS AND THE GREEKS

Mark 11$^{15-17}$

^{20}*Now among those who went up to worship at the feast were some Greeks.* ^{21}*So these came to Philip, who was from Beth-sa'ida in Galilee, and said to him, 'Sir, we wish to see Jesus.'* ^{22}*Philip went and told Andrew; Andrew went with Philip and they told Jesus. ²³And Jesus answered them, 'The hour has come for the Son of man to be glorified. ²⁴Truly, truly, I say to you, unless a grain of wheat falls into the earth and dies, it remains alone; but if it dies, it bears much fruit. ²⁵He who loves his life loses it, and he who hates his life in this world will keep it for eternal life. ²⁶If any one serves me, he must follow me; and where I am, there shall my servant be also; if any one serves me, the Father will honour him.'*

The heart of the synoptic story of the cleansing of the Temple lies in the scripture which Jesus quotes in condemnation of the narrowness of Jewish religion of the time: 'Is it not written, "My house shall be called a house of prayer for all the nations"? But you have made it a den of robbers.' The revealed religion given to Israel through Moses was not intended to be or to become Israel's possession; it could only be kept by the paradox of passing it on. But since the Exile the dominant note had been of national and racial restrictiveness. However understandable the formulation of such policy was in the light of pre-exilic disasters, it was wrong; and Jesus condemned it. The passage in John, telling of the approach of the Greeks, is in the same position in relation to the story of the Triumphal Entry as is the story of the Temple Cleansing in the synoptics. This gives the clue to its meaning, and to the way in which John understood the synoptic narrative in its synoptic place. For it is used to underline the essentially universal character of the Christian faith, but also to assert that the universality which Judaism had lost could not be restored without the death and resurrection of Jesus Christ.

It is not unnatural to suppose that the incident took place within the Temple precincts; the Greeks, like Jesus, had come to worship at the feast. It is again natural to suppose that they made the easiest approach to Jesus, through the most 'Greek' of the disciples, the only two who had Greek names, Philip and Andrew. The reply of Jesus to the request for an interview was to the effect that the universality which he had come to restore to the Temple and to the whole religion and life of God's people was not yet fully inaugurated, but waited upon his own death and resurrection. This does not imply any special restriction upon the approach of Gentiles. The cross is central for the Gospel, whether it be preached to Jews or Gentiles. The real and universal union with Christ is effected for none save through the cross and the resurrection.

Nor is this truth simply a matter of what chanced to happen in the life of Jesus himself. It is rather the reality of the life that God calls his people to live in his Son and for his Son. So John has tried to prevent any readers of the synoptic narrative from supposing that the mere removal of the signs of nationalism from Jewish religion (such as temple coinage and animal sacrifice) would itself achieve the universality which the Temple cleansing prophetically proclaimed. He has not missed the deep meaning of the deceptively simple report in Mark!

ಬಬ

20
It is worth noting that with the coming of the Greeks Jesus has no further dealings with Israel alone. This marks the beginning of the transition to the universality his death and resurrection is to achieve. The Greeks mentioned were not Greek-speaking Jews, but Greeks who had become proselytes (cf. Acts 8²⁷; 17⁴ for other foreign worshippers) and would be permitted within the court of the Gentiles – where the synoptists placed the Temple Cleansing.

21
Philip, like Andrew, had a Greek name, and, in the view of John, came from 'Galilee of the Gentiles', though Bethsaida was really in Gaulonitis.

to see Jesus means to seek an interview with him. Perhaps one of the things John is saying through this narrative is that until Jesus has died and risen again no one can really see him.

23
them: clearly Philip and Andrew; there was apparently no direct meeting with the Greeks. It is noteworthy that, in coming to speak of his death, Jesus uses the term '*Son of man*' rather than 'Messiah' or 'Son of God'. The term characteristically belongs to Jesus' own thought of his triumph through the cross. It is also characteristic for John to refer to the glorification of Jesus, including both death and resurrection in that term.

24–26
It seems as if the parabolic use of the seed which must die to bear fruit is used in three stages. First, the natural truth is stated. Continuation of the species of the seed is only possible if the seed die, i.e. if it ceases to be 'seed'. This is next applied to the life of Israel as God's people; what is true of seed is true of him who has come to offer the continuation of the

life of God's people – he must die (i.e. cease to be the one true human embodiment of the life of God's people) if he is to keep that divine life for ever. But the same truth applies to all his disciples. They must all pass to their own inheritance in the eternal life of God's people, by sharing in the death of their Lord, and subsequently in his resurrection. The disciple must follow his Lord, and that will eventually take him to the place where his Lord finally dwells. So to serve Jesus Christ is to receive the honour of the Father, which is to be made manifest in the glorification of the Son.

12²⁷⁻³⁶ᵃ   THE AGONY OF GLORY

Mark 14³⁴
Luke 22⁴³
Luke 10¹⁸

²⁷*'Now is my soul troubled. And what shall I say, "Father, save me from this hour"? No, for this purpose I have come to this hour.* ²⁸*Father, glorify thy name.' Then a voice came from heaven, 'I have glorified it, and I will glorify it again.'* ²⁹*The crowd standing by heard it and said that it had thundered. Others said, 'An angel had spoken to him.'* ³⁰*Jesus answered, 'This voice has come for your sake, not for mine.* ³¹*Now is the judgement of this world, now shall the ruler of this world be cast out;* ³²*and I, when I am lifted up from the earth, will draw all men to myself.'* ³³*He said this to show by what death he was to die.* ³⁴*The crowd answered him. 'We have heard from the law that the Christ remains for ever. How can you say that the Son of man must be lifted up? Who is this Son of man?'* ³⁵*Jesus said to them, 'The light is with you for a little longer. Walk while you have the light, lest the darkness overtake you; he who walks in the darkness does not know where he goes.* ³⁶*While you have the light, believe in the light, that you may become sons of light.'*

This section of the fourth gospel opens with words which are not only reminiscent but actively evocative of the synoptic story of what has become known as the 'Passion' of Jesus Christ. *'Now is my soul troubled'* sounds very like the synoptic saying 'My soul is sorrowful, even unto death' (Mark 14³⁴ //). Yet John is much more careful

than any of the synoptists to make it clear to his readers that the
troubling of Jesus' soul has nothing at all to do with 'passion' or
uncertainty as to the outcome of the drama about to open. In the
fourth gospel Jesus is 'active' in his 'Passion' all the way through.
*'What shall I say, "Father, save me from this hour"? No, for this purpose
I have come to this hour. Father, glorify thy name'* (12²⁷, ²⁸).

The synoptists were able to convey the ultimate significance of the
events of Christ's dying on the cross by prefacing their story with
an apocalypse which invited their readers to read the subsequent
story of the 'Passion', death and resurrection of Jesus as the embodiment in an actual historical occasion of the quite basic, universal,
all-embracing significance of the eschatology portrayed in their
apocalypse. John associates the eternal and the historical directly in
the actual occasion under review. The glorification of the Son by the
Father, which effects the glory of the Father before men, consists
precisely in the events that the evangelist is to report. Passion is not
to be followed by action; the action is in, indeed is itself, the Passion,
and the Passion itself the action. So John tries to show his readers
that it would be seriously to misunderstand the synoptic narrative to
suppose that it tells of a Passion ending in tragedy, that is afterwards
followed by a new act which achieves triumph; properly understood,
the synoptics themselves assert the triumph in the defeat, the action
in the Passion.

In so doing John does not renounce his sense of historical reality.
For one thing, what is to take place now is really what has been
taking place all along – life is being given for death, the life of the
new Israel is being given in the person of the Word who is exalted
through his cross. Again, for John the obedience unto death which he
now reports is not a matter of easy compliance with a Father's will or
whim, but the testing, trying, obedience of a loving and faithful
son. Obedience demands a soul-shaking sacrifice of Jesus. There is
no 'stage drama' in John's story; here is ineluctable destiny making
supreme demands upon the supreme person.

So John focuses his own narrative upon that section of the synoptic
story familiarly known as the Passion. He uses devices characteristic
of him to show both the true nature of the awful realities Jesus had
to face, which were in fact the only means by which the glory of God
could be ultimately and realistically affirmed in this world. This is the
depth of the Johannine narrative. It is not offered as an alternative

to the narrative of the synoptists, but as a radical exposition of the fundamental meaning of the synoptic story, when that story is taken in its own unity as a combination of eschatology (e.g. Mark 13), realized prophetic history (e.g. Mark 14²⁷) and contemporary occurrence (e.g. Mark 14⁵³).

The first verse of the section is immediately reminiscent of the synoptic account of the agony in Gethsemane (Mark 14³⁴ᶠᶠ). But the next verse provides the characteristic Johannine affirmation: a divine voice answers the submission of the son in his obedience with the words: '*I have glorified* [my name], *and I will glorify it again*'. In other words, ministry and self-offering in death are not two realities, but one; and both are manifestations of the divine glory, which is the divine victory. The crowd could not fully understand what was going on, though there were different levels of insight displayed among them. But Jesus interprets it for them all, and makes it plain that what is about to happen (and so, in view of v. 28, what has happened already too) is that the judgement of the world has come, and the ruler of this world is to be cast out. Jesus says that when he is *lifted up* (an ambiguous term deliberately used to incorporate both the elevation of a body on to a cross, and of Jesus as the Son to the glory of the Father) he will draw all men to himself. Whatever the crowd had thought before, they now realize that Jesus has spoken of his going from the world. '*We have heard from the law that the Christ remains for ever. How can you say that the Son of man must be lifted up? Who is this Son of man?*' (v. 34). The reply of Jesus is couched in terms of the absolute contrast between light and darkness. He, as the true light of the world, will be with his people for only a little longer. Great darkness is about to descend on them as he leaves them. If they do not now walk in the light (i.e. follow him) they will be left in darkness and not know where they are going. The whole possibility of having any knowable future really depends upon their response to him in belief and discipleship.

※

27

John has probably gone independently of the synoptists to Psalm 42 for his quotation from the Septuagint. The quotation shows with what real disquiet Jesus approached the path ahead of him, but it also discloses that for him, as for all the evangelists, what was to take place was something placing even this supreme agony well within the purposes of

God for securing the life of his people. It may well depict the cost to Jesus in his distress: 'My soul is cast down within me ... all thy waves and thy billows have gone over me'; but it also speaks of present help: 'By day the Lord commands his steadfast love, and at night his song is with me'; and it looks to an assured future: 'Hope in God; for I shall again praise him, my help and my God.'

28

In spite of disquiet, the dominant attitude of Jesus is of humble obedience: '*Father, glorify thy name.*' The voice from heaven says that God has already glorified it, and the reference is to the signs that have, in John's theological understanding, revealed God's glory; cf. especially 2^{11}; $5^{41, 44}$; 9^3 (though the word here is 'works' rather than *glory* of God); 11^4. God's glory is deliberately associated with the first sign, in which the evangelist shows how the future of Israel is not in the way of the old rituals and lustrations, but in the new purification achieved in the giving of the blood of the Son of man, which is the manifestation of God's glory. It is in the same way associated with the last 'sign', the raising of Lazarus, where Jesus announces and proves himself to be the true life of the new Israel, bringing to God's people a life over which death has no power. The heavenly voice also says that God will glorify his name again. The cross will be the actual purificatory action which the first sign prefigured; it will be the actual passage of the new Son or Israel of God from this world where his glory can only be seen in ambiguity, to the realm where it can be displayed in its full authority and reality. The cross will actualize in the central event of all history what the sign of Cana and the sign of Bethany have prefigured.

29

Natural man, even the natural man among the people of God, can make of the divine intimation only two things: it can be taken for a natural event pure and simple – some said it thundered: or it can be given a spiritual interpretation, and then it is deemed to be a word spoken to Jesus for his help.

30

Jesus reveals the real purpose of the voice, viz. that the members of the old Israel might be led to recognize both the signs that Jesus had done for what they were, and the sign that he was about to enact for what it would be.

31

The word '*now*' fastens the great crisis of the world on the moment of the crucifixion. At this point the old creation is coming to its end, and the new creation begins to be. The passage from the one to the other is not a simple physical process, but moral and spiritual; hence the need to assert that the moment of crisis is one of judgement. Just as, earlier, Jesus had indicated that the authorities had passed judgement on themselves by their treatment of the man born blind and healed by Jesus, so now he asserts that the world will pass judgement on itself by its killing of him (cf. also 3^{18}: 'He who does not believe is condemned already'). Jesus sees the moment of his elevation on the cross as the moment when he ascends his throne, and so dethrones the usurper who now presumptuously claims command of the world.

32
'*lifted up*' is deliberately ambiguous, referring both to the elevation on the cross and the exaltation to glory.

33
This is also and perhaps inevitably ambiguous. *By what death* may mean the mode of death, i.e. crucifixion, or the sort of death, i.e. one that leads, not to the silence of Sheol, but to the glory to be shared with the Father.

34
'*the law*' is intended to cover the whole of the Jewish scriptures, i.e. the Old Testament. There is no obvious quotation that springs to mind, the passages most cited by commentators being Psalms 110^4; $89^{29, \ 36}$; Isaiah 9^7. It is likely that the general intention is to affirm an expectation which was sensed as scriptural, without claiming precise formulation. In any case the ambiguity of v. 32 continues: if Christ is to remain, i.e. with the Jews of the day, for ever, then he can neither be supposed to be about to die by crucifixion, nor to ascend to the Father, which would also remove him!

35, 36a
Jesus' answer is more satisfactory than it seems. '*The light*' is, of course, himself. His whole ministry on earth is shortly to close. This conveys both the importance of this last appeal to the Jews, and the extreme urgency of the situation. While the light is shining men can see the way, but when the light has gone, there is but darkness, and men must lose their way. So the counsel of Jesus is that they should walk in, believe in the light now, so that they may become '*sons of light*', i.e. come to have light in themselves, and so be able to discern their way (cf. 8^{12}: 'he who follows me will not walk in darkness, but will have the light of life', and – using a different metaphor – 4^{14} 'the water that I shall give him will become in him a spring of water welling up to eternal life').

When Jesus had said this, he departed and hid himself from them.
³⁷*Though he had done so many signs before them, yet they did not believe in him;* ³⁸*it was that the word spoken by the prophet Isaiah might be fulfilled:*

> *'Lord, who has believed our report,*
> *and to whom has the arm of the Lord been revealed?'*

³⁹*Therefore they could not believe. For Isaiah again said,*

> ⁴⁰*'He has blinded their eyes and hardened their heart,*
> *lest they should see with their eyes and perceive with their heart,*
> *and turn for me to heal them.'*

⁴¹*Isaiah said this because he saw his glory and spoke of him.* ⁴²*Nevertheless many even of the authorities believed in him, but for fear of the Pharisees they did not confess it, lest they should be put out of the synagogue:* ⁴³*for they loved the praise of men more than the praise of God.*

⁴⁴*And Jesus cried out and said, 'He who believes in me, believes not in me but in him who sent me.* ⁴⁵*And he who sees me sees him who sent me.* ⁴⁶*I have come as light into the world, that whoever believes in me may not remain in darkness.* ⁴⁷*If any one hears my sayings and does not keep them, I do not judge him; for I did not come to judge the world but to save the world.* ⁴⁸*He who rejects me and does not receive my sayings has a judge; the word that I have spoken will be his judge on the last day.* ⁴⁹*For I have not spoken on my own authority; the Father who sent me has himself given me commandment what to say and what to speak.* ⁵⁰*And I know that his commandment is eternal life. What I say, therefore, I say as the Father has bidden me.'*

The opening sentence of this section is simple and stark: '*When Jesus had said this, he departed and hid himself from them*' (v. 36b). This marks the end of his ministry to his own people; from now on there is no public address to the Jews, but only private teaching of the disciples. Like the synoptists, John tries to help his readers to understand the puzzling fact that the Jews, though apparently so well prepared to receive the revelation through the Word, did not receive it, but rejected it. This tragic rejection, fraught with so many consequences, is not just bitter contingency, but, seen in the light of the story of

God's people, can be recognized as something embraced within the overruling purpose of God.

The synoptists had also been faced with the problem of the rejection of Jesus by the Jews, and had sought a solution very similar to that now offered by John. In Mark 4 the evangelist recorded that Jesus spoke in parables, and that his disciples asked him about them. Jesus' reply was 'To you has been given the secret of the kingdom of God, but for those outside everything is [or better, happens] in parables.' Jesus is saying that just as a parable is a story that can be taken on its own, without any necessity to see any further meaning in it (though then, of course, it ceases to be parable), so with the events of his life: for the disciples there had come the possibility of recognizing that the events of his life were in fact also the arrival of the kingdom of God; but to those outside this privileged community his whole life could be taken at 'surface level' as just another series of events constituting a human biography. The situation in understanding the parable composed of words was parallel to that in understanding the 'parable' composed of events.

The result is that there are some who recognize the meaning of the events of Jesus' life, and they know that his coming means the arrival of the kingdom and the offer of divine forgiveness to men; but those 'outside' are they who can see the same series of events, but not understand them, hear the same words, and not perceive their real meaning. There is nothing particularly difficult about that. The real difficulty comes in the assertion, sounding strange on the lips of Jesus, or on the lips of any Christian who thinks of the gospel as universal, that those outside have not been given the secret of the kingdom precisely in order that they should not attain the insights necessary to discern the real meaning of Jesus' life and ministry. Two things may be said. First, that the language of such purposive elements in the gospels uses an idiom from classical Greek that had lost a good deal of its forcefulness by New Testament times, when it no longer necessarily conveyed the idea, e.g., that outsiders were made insensitive in order to render them incapable of receiving the gospel. Second, that the form of the assertion, that 'they may indeed see but not perceive, and may indeed hear but not understand; lest they should turn again, and be forgiven' (Mark 4^{12}) is a quotation from Isaiah 6$^{9, 10}$, and is intended to mean that the unbelief of the Jews is not something which need cause surprise, since it has been a feature of the

Jewish situation since prophetic times, and was recognized as one of those elements of Israel's history with which God would have to deal fundamentally in the future. So, by focusing upon the situation in the time of Jesus' ministry both the report of contemporary unbelief and the prophetic interpretation and expectation of it from the past, the evangelists were trying to make their readers understand that unbelief was not outside the providential overruling of God. On the contrary, it was a sign that God was about to fulfil his purposes for mankind.

The passage from Mark is repeated in Matthew (13^{15}) and Luke (8^{9,10}), and Mark and Matthew make use of another prophecy of Isaiah to focus meaning upon the unbelief of Jesus' contemporaries, viz. Isaiah 29^{13} (cited at Matthew 15^{8} and Mark 7^{6}). The passage in Luke 11$^{37-52}$ does not cite any such actual quotation, but it does, in similar spirit, make it plain to the reader of the gospel that the whole tragic story of the rejection of Jesus by the Jews is part of the long story of God's dealings with his people. Perhaps the final comment on all these attempts in the gospels is made in Romans 9–11, where it is asserted that Jew and Gentile have alike been involved in unbelief so that all may come at last to believe. The tragedy of man the unbeliever is not lessened: the triumph of God in the believer is made plain. 'God has consigned all men to disobedience, that he may have mercy upon all' (Romans 11^{32}). We are not saved because we believe, but we believe because we are saved.

John records that, even so, there were *many, even of the authorities*, who believed in Jesus, but were afraid to confess it, for fear of the Pharisees. They feared excommunication (cf. 9^{34}), and prized peaceable relationships with their fellows above a proper relationship with God. John has consistently throughout his gospel been willing to speak of those who *believe* in Jesus, and yet believe in some measure deficiently. This kind of observation began at the time of the first ministry in Jerusalem (2$^{23-25}$), and is found now and again stated or implied right through to the story of Lazarus (11^{45}). Israel-after-the-flesh was and remained all through the ministry in an entirely ambiguous position. What belief there was, even among the disciples, even among the Twelve, was not yet fully belief; for the most part belief was in the 'signs'. And 'unbelief' was not fully open rebellion, but something which itself had a place in the economy of divine providence.

In the light of the interpretation of Mark 4^{11}, it is significant that

471

Jesus here gives a parallel statement of the relationship between event and parable. '*He who believes in me, believes not in me but in him who sent me. And he who sees me sees him who sent me*' (vv. 44–5). This is a precise Johannine formulation of the Marcan claim that the life of Jesus is a parable in events.

Then follows a series of statements meant to summarize the situation at the end of the ministry. Jesus has come, he affirms, as light into the world. The light enables some to 'see' and those who thus become believers are not 'in the dark'. To reject the teaching of Jesus is not to incur condemnation from him, for his whole purpose is to bring salvation. But to be faced by Jesus Christ is to be faced with judgement, and what the judgement is becomes known by a man's acceptance or rejection of Christ. In the final issue it is the response of men to the claims of Jesus that will determine their standing. This could not be true if Jesus were to speak and make his claims on his own authority; then he would be but another human claimant on the loyalties of men. But Jesus does not speak on his own authority, but on that of his Father. It is his words that Jesus speaks. So the words of Jesus are, as Peter had said, eternal life. This gift Jesus offers to men at the Father's bidding.

ℵℵ

36b
Jesus leaves his fellow-Jews at the moment when he has confronted them with the ultimate and absolute choice between light and darkness.

37
Jesus had done *so many signs*, although John has recorded but a few. He was aware of more, cf. 20^{30}. John has recorded a certain 'belief' in Jesus occasioned by his signs, though it was not regarded as full or adequate. What he must now explain is how rejection is reconcilable with the divine mission Jesus came to fulfil. The Greek can carry a fully purposive meaning, and if it does the evangelist is stating a quite full doctrine of predestination at this point. But Hellenistic Greek had itself accepted a considerable lessening in the strength of its final clauses, and so drastic an interpretation need not be made. That so rigorous an interpretation was not in John's mind would seem to be indicated by the fact that after explaining unbelief, he goes on to speak of exceptions to it. It would seem safer to conclude that John has set himself the more limited task of enabling his readers to see that the unbelief of the Jews was not something outside the over-all providence of God, but something entirely under control, even if it had its origin in the wills of men.

John, in addition to citing the passage from Isaiah 6^{10} which was

quoted by the synoptists, makes use of the passage at the opening of
Isaiah 53, from the last of the Servant Songs. John is certainly wanting to
indicate that unbelief is within divine providence, but he is also trying
to make clear that it is not just unbelief, but unbelief in the vicarious
suffering of Christ that has, as it were, focused the prophetic perspective
of unbelief upon the events of the life and death of Jesus. It could be
said that John is here trying to say that Jewish unbelief is only superficially a scandal to Christianity; but the suffering and dying of Jesus is a
real scandal to Judaism. Paul echoes this viewpoint when he writes:
'Christ crucified, a stumbling block to Jews and folly to Gentiles'
(1 Cor. 1^{23}).

39
Therefore: Israel in the present, like Israel in the past, found the idea of
God's servant as vicariously suffering a great obstacle to belief.

40
Strictly applied, the text, like so many similar sayings in the Old Testament, means that God has himself hardened hearts and blinded eyes.
But John is probably concerned to do no more than to assure his
Christian readers that Jewish unbelief is no more than a superficial
stumbling block to their own faith. It was something which God had
already seen, foreseen and dealt with in the history of Israel.

41
There is a choice between two readings which make it 'Isaiah said this
when...' or 'Isaiah said this because...'. Either reading probably refers
back to the vision of Isaiah in the temple (Isaiah 6$^{1ff.}$), and what John is
saying in making his readers think back to that occasion is that the
difference between the ordinary worshipper in the temple on the day
when Isaiah had his vision of God in his glory is precisely the same as
the distinction now between those who see Jesus as simply a Galilean
carpenter turned evangelist, and those who see him as the eternal Word
made flesh. The object of the vision that penetrates is the same in each
case. Both Isaiah and the believer see the eternal in and through the
temporal.

42
John is indicating that in the present Israel, as always, there is a remnant
that believes, even if, as previously, the remnant is not of and by itself a
true people of God. That they were not a true people of God is indicated
by the fact that they feared to *be put out of the synagogue,* i.e. excommunicated from the (inadequate) life of the (so-called) people of God.

43
The praise of men was immediate; the praise of God was less so. The

praise of men was evident in social relationships now; the praise of God might not be – might, indeed, lead to dishonour and crucifixion! The dilemma for the believers among the authorities was real – and their solution very human.

44

Jesus cried out: A phrase used by John to introduce pronouncements of special importance and solemnity ($7^{28, 37}$; 1^{15}). There are synoptic parallels of a sort to the saying (Mark 9^{37}; Matthew 10^{40}; Luke 9^{48}; 10^{16}), designed, as this saying, to emphasize the truth that the centre of Christian devotion is not a human figure, but the divine Father. The statement underlines what are the basic issues confronting Judaism as it contemplates the rejection of Jesus, which involves nothing less than the rejection of God.

45

Cf. 1^{18}: God has never been 'seen'; but the only Son has 'made him known'. Cf. also 14^9: 'He who has seen me has seen the Father.'

46

Cf. 8^{12}.

47, 48

This is the Johannine parallel to the synoptic statement found at the end of the Sermon on the Mount about hearing the words of Jesus (Matt. 7^{24-27}). Everything hangs upon a man's acceptance or rejection of what Christ has said.

49

Here the evangelist adds his own comment as to the ground of the ultimacy which his word possesses: he does not speak on his own authority, but with all the authority of the Father. The tense used by Jesus to tell of the Father's commissioning is that perfect which implies that what the Father did in the past still has effect in the present.

50

It seems from such passages as Mark 10^{17}ff (the rich man) and Luke 10^{28} (the lawyer who eventually asked 'Who is my neighbour?') that Jesus accepted the law as that which was intended to bestow eternal life. But it is clear that the fourth evangelist, like the synoptists, believed that without the word of Jesus the law was not complete. In saying that it must also be said that a 'word' is not thought of as a printed letter-form, or a set of vocable sounds, but as a live and quickening reality, which Jesus uttered not only in the words he spoke, but in the deeds he did and the acts he suffered, which were, in the end, more eloquent than any spoken words.

Interchapter

The first part of the evangelist's narrative is now complete. He has told of the fulfilment and recapitulation of the story of the old People of God in the coming-in-the-flesh of the Word. Now in the time of the incarnation, as earlier in the story of Israel, the Word has 'come to his own home' and 'his own people received him not'; yet, as before, 'to all who received him, who believed in his name, he gave power [right] to become children of God'. So the Word has become flesh and 'dwelt among us, full of grace and truth'; and 'we have beheld his glory, glory as of the only Son from the Father'.

So in the fourth gospel as in the synoptics the Son is not a lone theophanic figure. He is not the Word-made-flesh, the Messiah of Israel, save as he is with those for whom he came, who have been given to him, and to whom he gives himself. No Messianic act is done in the synoptics, no sign performed in the fourth gospel until the community of the new people of God, the new Israel, has been gathered together, at least in embryo, in the calling of (some of) the Twelve. And while John is perfectly well aware that the disciples did not fully or really understand what was going on round about them until Jesus had risen from the dead, he is equally certain that what they did after the resurrection was not to project back into the ministry meanings and interpretations which the events did not have at the time of their occurrence, but rather that they then understood those events in their true meaning and perspective for the first time. They had seen his glory.

In the first part of the gospel, now complete, the glory that belongs to the only Son is manifested in the great series of signs. But in the second part, which is now to begin, the glory is to be displayed no longer in signs, but in the reality of what the signs have signified and prefigured – the glorification of the Son of man in his cross, resurrection and ascension. The first sign at Cana had said that no ritual lustrations of Judaism could suffice to make and keep a community worthy to be God's people; only in and through the life and death of the Son could this be effected. The second sign indicated that the real possibility of life-giving communion between God and man lay not in the belief that Jesus could effect miraculous cures, but that he was who he claimed to be. The third sign made it clear that what Jesus had to give in his cures was not mere restoration of physical locomotion, but verily life for death. The fourth sign emphasized that it was Jesus himself in his flesh-and-blood, his human, reality who was the true life of the believer. The fifth sign showed that in the flesh-and-blood reality of Jesus there was more to be known than mere physical appearance could display. The sixth sign at Bethany showed that the life given by Jesus has its bounds outside the area of man's mortality. All that these several signs signified is now unfolded in the story of the evangelist. They become reality by being enacted in that area where the ephemeralities of human history are linked indissolubly with and by the eternal action of God.

So all the past of Israel's history, and all the story of the incarnate Son are focused and fulfilled in this one act or complex of acts which constitute both the humiliation and the glory, the defeat and the victory, the death and the resurrection of the Son of God. This double character of the events now unfolding makes it possible to think of them as constituting the seventh and greatest sign. Not that they share with the previous signs in pointing forward to another event where what they anticipate becomes reality, but that, like the previous signs, they can be seen as a reality of an order quite different from that to which they properly belong. When Jesus spoke of himself as the bread of life, and affirmed that he had come from heaven to do his Father's will (6^{38ff}), the Jews complained unbelievingly 'Is not this Jesus, the son of Joseph, whose father and mother we know?' (6^{42}). They could see the physical reality of the Word-made-flesh, but they could not see his glorious divinity. So now, the Jews and others will see the crucifixion of Jesus of Nazareth for a crime of which he has been found guilty; they will not see it as the transcendent event in which the Son of man gives his life for the salvation of the world, enabling forgiveness of sins to be proclaimed in his name. Here, as throughout the ministry, the reader of the gospel is brought face to face with the ultimate mystery of the act of God himself in the person of the Son.

Yet there is a sense in which even the central realities of the cross, resurrection and ascension point to events beyond themselves, at least in the succession of time. The disciple must 'follow' his Lord. The word 'follow' is used by Jesus in the fourth gospel at the time of the calling of Philip (1^{43}) and at the very end, as the last word to

Peter, when he had received the final command to 'feed Christ's flock' (21²²). The pattern of the dying of the Lord Jesus is to be part of the destiny of his disciples. The fourth gospel gives its own depth to the synoptic theme of the calling of a disciple being 'to be with Jesus'; to be with the Son, who is with the Father, is to be with one who lays down his life. John has his own way of saying that the disciple is not above his Lord, but must take up his cross daily if he is to be Christ's disciple.

As the evangelist recounted the earlier signs he proceeded in a uniform way: first the 'wonder' would be reported, and then would follow a discourse intended to interpret the sign. Now, as the signs give way to the reality which finally embodies them all, the procedure is reversed: The discourse is first stated, and then the 'wonder' is told. This is intelligible for two chief reasons: first, the discourse(s) which precede the narrative of the crucifixion and resurrection are in one sense part of the material already provided, for the precedent 'signs' with their supplementary discourses are but part of the whole 'discourse' intended to precede the story of the cross, and to prepare the reader to understand it when he reaches it. Therefore, as introductory explanatory material the discourses about to be reported belong inevitably here. Second, there is something even more profound. Normally the meaning of an historical event is not discernible until it has receded into the perspectives of the past. And even then to assert a meaning of an event is a hazard of prophecy rather than the certainty of proof. But in the area of God's action there is no question of its reality being in any way dependent upon the possibility of a receding perspective; its reality is known as it happens, at least to the one who is the real actor in it, Jesus Christ himself. The Christian Church is not offering men just another possible way of looking at history; it is affirming just what history is about and what it means. A number of scholars have understandably suggested that the discourses may best be understood as displaced post-resurrection addresses; and the reasons for their suggestions are obvious. But it would seem that John, like the synoptists, is anxious to affirm by the historiographical means at his disposal that he who exercised a ministry in Galilee and Judea was one and the same with the risen Lord who appeared to his disciples after his crucifixion (cf. the story of the transfiguration in the synoptic gospels, which has also been reckoned by some scholars as a displaced post-resurrection appearance!). If we

are to obtain a truly biblical understanding of the events of the crucifixion we shall be going away from it if we suppose that the substance of what is said in the Johannine discourses is nothing but the
fruit of 'hindsight'; we shall be much nearer the biblical witness,
and to the facts of the case, if we affirm that they are the fruit of
'foresight'. Yet the foresight is not just the vision of the future given
to certain erratically inspired men, but rather what belongs by nature
and by right to him who is the Lord of the whole historical process.*

We have said that the story of the Gospel so far has told how the
Word has come to his own home, and how his own people did not
receive him, though he gave the right to those who believed in him to
become children of God, i.e. to become, with him, the beginning of
the new Israel or people of God. What now ensues is the story of how
the Word came to those who had believed, and how, in a somewhat
different way, they too failed to receive him. There is a certain
amount of recapitulation of the earlier story. The feet-washing is in
some ways parallel to the baptism of John offered to the old Israel
at the beginning of the story. The supper at which it takes place leads
to an exposition of Jesus as the real vine, as the feeding of the five
thousand led to the exposition of him as the bread of life. The Passovers of the earlier narrative are summed up in the Passover at which
Jesus himself is sacrificed at the very time of day when the lambs of
the old Passover are being slaughtered in the old Temple. When the
friend of Lazarus is laid in his tomb, he is found to be in himself and
by his own power the resurrection and the life. The end of the gospel
comes when the evangelist affirms in new symbol that 'the whole
world has gone after him' (12^{19}, cf. 21^{11}), and that the fulfilment of
the whole mission of the Son of man gathers into its own suffering
and triumphant destiny the lives of those who believe in him and
seek to serve him.

* See the author's *The Fulness of Time*, pp. 97–107.

John 13¹–17²⁶

Deed and Word: 5 ⎞ *The Cross and*
Rite and Reality: 4 ⎬ *the Glory*
The Seventh Sign ⎠ $13^1 - 20^{31}$

Mark 14^{10-25}
Luke 22^{3-34}
Luke 12^{37-40}
Matthew 10^{24}
Luke 6^{40}
Matthew 10^{40}
Luke 10^{16}
Leviticus 19^{18}
Matthew 5^{44}

1: The Word

13^{1-38} *At the Supper Table*

13^{1-11} *The Feet-washing.* At this point John begins the second part
of his gospel, and it is worth noting how he starts. The synoptic
story lends itself to the familiar division of the Ministry of Jesus into
what preceded the last 'Passion Week' of his life and what came after
it began. Thus it is still liturgically popular to think of the Passion of
the Lord as beginning with Palm Sunday. But the Johannine treatment is different. The Triumphal Entry and the Cleansing of the
Temple belong to that which precedes the final story of the cross
and resurrection. For John the final story begins with a supper; not
indeed the Passover supper, as the synoptic tradition understood,
but a supper preceding the Passover, at which Jesus was entirely
with his own chosen disciples. If there could be a Johannine point
at which we might say the Church was born, it would be most
conveniently put at this point, where Jesus is at table with the Twelve,
including Judas; for, as Augustine observed much later, 'There are
wolves within the fold, and sheep without'.

13 *Now before the feast of the Passover, when Jesus knew that his hour had come to depart out of this world to the Father, having loved his own who were in the world, he loved them to the end.* ²*And during supper, when the devil had already put it into the heart of Judas Iscariot, Simon's son, to betray him,* ³*Jesus, knowing that the Father had given all things into his hands, and that he had come from God and was going to God . . .*

The second half of the gospel begins with a reference to the feast of the Passover, which has not yet taken place. So, as was discussed in the Introduction (pp. 55ff), John dates the Last Supper differently from the synoptics. Yet, as was claimed, both synoptic and Johannine traditions seek to affirm the fulfilment of the Jewish Passover in the events of the crucifixion and resurrection of Jesus. For John the real Passover, of which all the recurring Passovers are but symbols, occurred at the time when the true Lamb of God, Jesus Christ, was offered for the sins of the world upon his cross, at the very time when the now outmoded Passover lambs of Judaism were being offered in sacrifice in the superseded Temple of Jerusalem.

The fulfilment of the old Passover was to take place in the action of Jesus in what Christians have sometimes termed his 'Passion'. He knew that his hour had now come; he knew that he had been given his own to be the first objects of his redemptive love; he loved them to the end, and loved them utterly and incomparably. But, as at the time of the old Passover, there were powers of darkness abroad and the devil had already put it into Judas' heart to deliver Jesus up to the authorities. Knowing all this by means and in measure which transcend normal understanding, Jesus, convinced that his Father had put everything into his hands, and that his story began with the Father and would end with his return to the Father, set in train the series of actions that constitute the glorification of the Son. The paradox is that to human view the first act is one of humility, almost of servility.

❧

1
Jesus knew: What the evangelist intends to convey here is much more

than is normally covered by the word 'premonition', even if that be the nearest human experience for a preliminary understanding. At least he means that Jesus was not taken by surprise by the events that followed, nor yet dismayed at their course. What the experience of omniscience might be mere human beings cannot know. But it seems plain that when omnipotence appears in the world its all-conquering power looks very much like impotence as it hangs upon a cross: it may well be that omniscience as it is embodied in the life of the Word-made-flesh is as real and, to a mere mortal, as unrecognizable as omnipotence!

he loved: This is an aorist tense, the tense for actions and events in history. The event may be the actual foot-washing that is to follow. If so, it will be because it was itself symbolic of the greater act of humble service, the death on the cross.

to the end: The phrase has a double meaning, and probably both were meant, and should be understood. First, to the end, to that moment when the 'eschaton', the 'end', arrived; second, completely, wholly, to the uttermost. His complete love was sufficient to the end for those he loved.

2

during supper: Supper occurs without an article in the Greek, though it would almost certainly have had one had the evangelist wanted to indicate that this was the Passover meal.

the devil had already put it into the heart of Judas Iscariot, Simon's son, to betray him: Barrett (p. 365) argues that this translation presupposes that the name of Judas is in the genitive, which he takes to be a 'simplifying gloss'; the translation he proposes is therefore: 'The devil had already made up his mind that Judas should betray him [Jesus].' He appears to be in the right. But Jesus had already spoken of the diabolic character of one of the twelve whom he had chosen (6⁷⁰).

betray in modern speech has overtones that may be too strong for a true assessment of the narrative here. 'Deliver up' may yield the better sense. The clear implication is that even among the chosen (the elect) there may be devilry at work!

Jesus, knowing that ... he had come from God and was going to God: See note on v.1. for *knowing*. What Jesus knew was the double path of humility. He had come from God – and that was to tread the path of humility (cf. Phil. 2⁵ᶠᶠ); he was to go to God, and that was not less to tread the path of humility, for it involved the cross.

⁴*rose from supper, laid aside his garments, and girded himself with a towel.* ⁵*Then he poured water into a basin, and began to wash the disciples' feet, and to wipe them with the towel with which he was girded.* ⁶*He came to Simon Peter; and Peter said to him, 'Lord, do you wash my feet?'* ⁷*Jesus answered him, 'What I am doing you do not know now, but afterward you will understand.'* ⁸*Peter said to him, 'You shall never wash my feet.' Jesus answered him, 'If I do not wash you, you have no part in me.'* ⁹*Simon Peter said to him, 'Lord, not my feet only but also my hands and my head!'* ¹⁰*Jesus said to him, 'He who has bathed does not need to wash, except for his feet,ᵃ but he is clean all over; and you are clean, but not all of you.'* ¹¹*For he knew who was to betray him; that was why he said, 'You are not all clean.'*

a Other ancient authorities omit *except for his feet*

(a) *In the context of the fourth gospel.* The incident of the washing of the disciples' feet follows immediately after the profound statements about the origin and destiny of the Son. He has come from God, and is going to God; and both journeys involve a voluntary humility. And both receive symbolic representation in the act of humble service now rendered. For the Son to come amongst men as man, for the eternal Word to become flesh is itself a supreme act of humility: it is likewise a startling act of humility for the Lord of the disciples to return to the Father by the way of ignominious death accorded to criminals. Both are pictured in what the Lord now does. He lays aside his own garments, and takes a towel and wraps it round himself instead. Then he poured water into a basin, and began to wash the disciples' feet. The whole setting is symbolic in the extreme. The language of *laying aside* and *taking* echoes that used of the death and resurrection of Jesus. The action was one performed by slaves for their masters (though not by Jewish slaves for theirs), and was in general an office performed always by the inferior for the superior. Jesus reversed the roles.

But the act was evidently not just a lesson in Christian humility, and it is probably only a comparison with the synoptic narrative that has led scholars to think so. What was involved becomes explicit when Jesus attempts to wash the feet of Peter. Peter suggests that the act was not appropriate, and Jesus replies that Peter does not understand it now, though he will later on. This is to put the action in the same category as the cleansing of the Temple and the Triumphal Entry, about both of which it is said that the disciples did not know what was meant until Jesus was glorified. In a word, this action also anticipated his death and resurrection, his return to the Father by the way of his humiliation. Still uncomprehending, Peter protests that he will never suffer the humiliation of having Jesus wash his feet. But when Jesus declares that unless Peter consents he clearly has and will have 'no part' in his Lord, Peter quickly assents, and asks that he shall be completely washed, feet and head and hands! So the act is symbolic not only of the humble death of the Lord of the disciples, but of their incorporation into him, so that they too are brought to share in his triumphant humiliation. The water of the foot-washing, like the water of the wedding at Cana in Galilee, has been made the symbol of the purification wrought by the sacrificial death of Jesus, and by that alone. There is no other way for men to be cleansed so as to appear before God than by their being associated with the Son in his own humble, sacrificial death. In this way the washing of the feet enables the beloved community to understand both the baptism offered to the old community of Israel by John the Baptist, and the water turned into wine at the wedding which took place in the old Israel; for now the real bridegroom of Israel has come to claim his bride, making plain in the symbol of purificatory water with which Jesus ministers to them that it was in and through his death that the new people of God would be purified and kept clean.

But even as he announces the effectiveness of his great act of humble service, offered now in symbol, to be realized later in the deed of the cross, he has to say that not all of the beloved community is clean. One remained beyond the effectiveness of the cleansing, the one who was to 'deliver him up'. And that is the measure of the mystery of iniquity.

(b) *In the context of the four gospels.* That the way of the Lord and the way of his disciples are fundamentally one, is a constant theme of the synoptic gospels. Indeed it could be held that this forms the main idea by which the meaning of the ministry is made known. Mark relates how, on the way up to Jerusalem for the last time, Jesus was approached by James and John asking a favour. It turned out to be a request that they should sit, one at his right hand and one at his left, in his glory. Jesus replied 'You do not know what you are asking. Are you able to drink the cup that I drink, or to be baptized with the baptism with which I am baptized?' – a clear reference to his forthcoming death. When the ten heard of this they were indignant, but Jesus called them to himself and said 'You know that those who are supposed to rule over the Gentiles lord it over them, and their great men exercise authority over them. But it shall not be so among you; but whoever would be great among you must be your servant, and whoever would be first among you must be slave of all. For the Son of man also came not to be served but to serve, and to give his life as a ransom for many' (Mark 10⁴²ff). The humble service of the Son of man was to give his life a ransom for many. The disciples were to be with him in that.

Or again, when Luke recounts the story of Jesus visiting the home of a ruling Pharisee for a meal on the Sabbath, he reports his reaction to the sight of the guests trying to edge their way to the places of honour. Jesus says: 'When you are invited by any one to a marriage feast, do not sit down in a place of honour, lest a more eminent man than you be invited by him; and he who invited you both will come and say to you, "Give place to this man", and then you will begin with shame to take the lowest place. But when you are invited, go and sit in the lowest place, so that when your host comes he may say to you, "Friend, go up higher"; then you will be honoured in the presence of all who sit at table with you. For every one who exalts himself will be humbled, and he who humbles himself will be exalted' (Luke 14⁸ff). It seems quite clear that the last sentence of Jesus is not a general proposition about social etiquette, but rather a plain statement of the proper way to accept an invitation into the Kingdom, where humble service is the way of the Lord.

Or, finally, Luke tells in his story of the Last Supper that even there a dispute broke out among the disciples as to which of them was to be accounted the greatest. Jesus replied in terms very reminiscent of Mark 10⁴⁴f, and said: 'The kings of the Gentiles exercise lordship over them; and those in authority over them are called benefactors. But not so with you; rather let the greatest among you become as the youngest, and the leader as one who serves. For which is the greater, one who sits at table, or one who serves? Is it not the one who sits at table? But I am among you as one who serves' (Luke 22²⁵ff). It is not surprising that some commentators have suggested that this incident from Luke's narrative has formed the basis of the story of the feet-washing in John. It would seem quite natural to suppose that the Johannine source material contained this incident, but that it appeared there, not only because it took place, but because it had the same significance as the saying about humility and service, with its clear overtones of reference to the coming death on the cross.

So we conclude that the washing of the disciples' feet springs from and symbolizes the death and resurrection of Jesus, which both effects the salvation of those whom he loves, and binds them with him in the same humble but victorious destiny. By his death he goes to the Father; by their being made one with him in his death the disciples too can 'go to the Father' and inherit eternal life. Perhaps the best justification for this interpretation of the action lies in the fact that some in the course of the Church's history have regarded the command 'You ought also to wash one another's feet' as an injunction to be sacramentally observed, as the great mass of Christendom has regarded the injunction concerning bread and wine to 'do this, as oft as ye eat (drink) it, in remembrance of me'.

ৰু

4
rose from supper: This indicates that the action was not the normal civility offered to a guest at the beginning of a meal, but a special service which the Lord now undertakes – and invests with his own meaning.

laid aside his garments: for the use of 'laying down' (Greek: *tithenai,* the same word as is used here and translated *'lay aside'*) in connexion with the death of Jesus, cf. the passage about the good shepherd (10¹¹, ¹⁵, ¹⁷f.).

girded himself with a towel: The towel was worn by a (Roman) slave.

5
he poured water into a basin: Jesus provides the element necessary for the cleansing of men.

began to wash the disciples' feet: Began means that he went to each in turn. It has been conjectured that the order in which he visited his disciples might have given rise to the dispute as to precedence (Luke 22²⁴ff.).

6
'Do you wash my feet?': The two pronouns are put together in the

Greek, indicating the forcefulness of the contrast which Peter has perceived.

7

'*afterward you will understand*': Literally 'after these things', i.e. after
the cross and resurrection. Cf. introductory note to this section.

8

'*You shall never wash my feet*': A very strong assertion in the Greek. This
is John's parallel to the protest of Peter which the synoptists record at
the time of the confession at Caesarea Philippi. Peter would not accept
the prediction of the death of his Lord as a fitting end to his ministry.
Similarly here, Peter sees the action symbolizing his humble death as
quite improper for his Lord. He has to be convinced that there is no
other way for the glory to be revealed!

'*If I do not wash you, you have no part in me*': Not unnaturally this has
been interpreted of Christian baptism. In view of all the symbolism by
which baptism has been seen as the 'dying of the believer with Christ'
and his 'rising together with him', this is understandable. What Jesus
has said amounts to an assertion that there is no glory save through the
sharing in the humility and the humiliation. Peter understands and
accepts.

9

'*not my feet only*': A typical Petrine misunderstanding. There can be no
quantitative measurement of the effectiveness of what Christ has done
for his loved ones.

10

This is a difficult verse, not only because the text is uncertain, but because
the meaning is unclear. The longer text, represented by the translation
in R.S.V., states that '*he who has bathed* [taken a complete bath] *does not
need to wash, except for his feet, but he is clean all over*'. This becomes an
intelligible saying in the light of the social custom that a guest should
take a complete bath before going out to a meal, so that all he needed
on arrival at his host's home was to remove the dust from his feet. But
this, though an interpretation of the somewhat better evidenced text,
seems to give far less importance to the feet-washing than do the words
of Jesus in v.8. What Jesus has just done for some, and now offers to do
for Peter, is far more than the removal of slight dust after the real dirt
had been removed by some other washing in a complete bath. So we
may turn to the shorter text, which reads: 'He that is bathed needs not
to wash, but is clean all over.' This text has quite ancient evidence to
support it, and moreover enables the commentator to give full value to

the words of Jesus in v.8. The central factor is the humble service which Jesus offers his disciples, in reality by his dying, symbolically now in the washing of their feet. Peter has mistaken the symbol for the reality (so Hoskyns, p. 439) and Jesus tells him that the action which the feet-washing portrays is actually a complete bath, beyond which no further cleansing is required.

'*and you are clean, but not all*': The church may be pure, even though some of her company are not. Here the mystery of iniquity is at its most impervious point. John attempts no explanation. It suffices that the Lord knows.

13¹²⁻²⁰　　THE IMITATION OF CHRIST

¹²*When he had washed their feet, and taken his garments, and resumed his place, he said to them, 'Do you know what I have done to you?'* ¹³*You call me Teacher and Lord; and you are right, for so I am.* ¹⁴*If I then, your Lord and Teacher, have washed your feet, you also ought to wash one another's feet.* ¹⁵*For I have given you an example, that you also should do as I have done to you.* ¹⁶*Truly, truly, I say to you, a servant^a is not greater than his master; nor is he who is sent greater than he who sent him.* ¹⁷*If you know these things, blessed are you if you do them.* ¹⁸*I am not speaking of you all; I know whom I have chosen; it is that the scripture may be fulfilled, "He who ate my bread has lifted his heel against me."* ¹⁹*I tell you this now, before it takes place, that when it does take place you may believe that I am he.* ²⁰*Truly, truly, I say to you, he who receives any one whom I send receives me; and he who receives me receives him who sent me.'*

a Or *slave*

What Jesus has just done is utterly unique. He and he alone can perform the effective cleansing needed by men to appear before God. Yet there is a sense in which his loved ones are called upon to emulate their Master, and to follow his example of humble service. It is clearly unwise to emphasize the literal act of washing feet as the substance of Christ's command; humble, sacrificial service, particularly when that deals with the wrongs that men do to each other and to Christ's loved ones, is the real imperative laid upon Christian men.

The reversal of traditional roles, where the master becomes the servant, is not to be confined to Jesus in his dying, but must characterize all the living of his followers. That is the one way to real happiness. If the disciples are content to accept the fact that they are not above their master, they will accept this humble but victorious destiny.

Yet the fulfilment of the service carries tragedy within it. There is the one who will deliver Jesus up to those who will kill him; and he comes from the circle of those called by Jesus and loved by him. The wonderful knowledge of this awesome mystery is communicated to the disciples in advance of the event, so that when it takes place they shall not be desolated by it, or come to suppose that its occurrence invalidates anything that Jesus has said. They can still with complete confidence, indeed with greater confidence, set out upon their mission for him. The scripture will be fulfilled in the delivering up. But that will enable him to be with them in their mission for him. In the future any who receives a disciple will receive the Lord of the disciple. It is significant to note that in the Matthean and Lucan versions of this saying, the evangelists place it after a saying about persecution and about judgement respectively. John has not misunderstood his sources.

☒

12
When he had . . . taken his garments, and resumed his place: What he now says to them he says from his accepted and recognized position as Lord.

15
'I have given you an example': This does not really detract from the once-for-allness of the act signified in the feet-washing. On the contrary: it is only those who have been washed and cleansed by the sacrificial death of Jesus who can be asked to enter that reversal of roles which seems in almost every way infelicitous and wrong. Moreover it is in the mutual willingness to serve one another, without reference to orders of superiority, that the disciples' love of the Lord will be manifested.

17
Cf. the Matthean and Lucan forms of the saying printed above. Both forms emphasize that in the proper relationship of teacher and disciple, the disciple grows like his teacher. This is the assumption here. Matthew puts the saying in the 'missionary' charge to the Twelve, and so con-

nects it with the disciples' being sent. Discipleship and mission belong together, inseparably.

'*If you know these things, blessed are you if you do them*': cf. the end of the Sermon on the Mount (Matt. 7²⁴ff).

18

'*I know whom I have chosen: it is that the scripture may be fulfilled*': Inevitably a difficult verse; it is not easy for ordinary men to penetrate into the area where the incarnate Word shares in the omniscience, the omnipotence and the all-inclusive providence of God as he works out the salvation of men. But the issues must be stated. The words can mean either that Jesus has chosen Judas, and knows that, in spite of that election, Judas will betray him; or that Jesus has not really chosen Judas, as he has chosen the other eleven, and so Judas will betray him. In either case the scripture will be fulfilled (see below on v. 26). Variant readings underlie the two interpretations. To the present writer it seems more suitable to the whole context of John's thought to suppose that the former meaning is intended. In the old Israel all were chosen, though many in fact denied and betrayed their calling; in the life of the new Israel there is no more guarantee against infidelity or treachery than in the old. Human nature remains the same. What has changed is the provision offered to those who are in various ways defective in their loyalty. John does not, like Mark, ever state explicitly that all the disciples forsook Jesus and fled on the night of his arrest and trial. But he reports that Peter and the beloved disciple followed him to his trial; and of these two Peter denied Jesus. The beloved disciple is at the cross and is given charge of the Lord's mother. It would seem therefore that puzzling and mysterious as the defection of Judas is, John thought of it as entirely within the bounds of possibility that Jesus had both genuinely chosen him to be one of the Twelve, and that, nevertheless, he knew beforehand that Judas would end up in the fatal disloyalty which yielded Jesus to death. Perhaps Judas is the limiting case of the infidelity of the Christian disciple.

19

'*that I am he*': Again the great name or title given to Yahweh is used by Jesus. See previous notes (especially p. 219), and compare with the interesting parallel in Isaiah 43¹⁰.

20

This verse naturally follows the use of '*I am*' by Jesus in the previous verse. God himself is present with men in Jesus, and he will himself bring the presence of God to his disciples as they go on his errands.

²¹*When Jesus had thus spoken, he was troubled in spirit, and testified,* '*Truly, truly, I say to you, one of you will betray me.*' ²²*The disciples looked at one another, uncertain of whom he spoke.* ²³*One of his disciples, whom Jesus loved, was lying close to the breast of Jesus;* ²⁴*so Simon Peter beckoned to him and said,* '*Tell us who it is of whom he speaks.*' ²⁵*So lying thus, close to the breast of Jesus, he said to him,* '*Lord, who is it?*' ²⁶*Jesus answered,* '*It is he to whom I shall give this morsel when I have dipped it.*' *So when he had dipped the morsel, he gave it to Judas, the son of Simon Iscariot.* ²⁷*Then after the morsel, Satan entered into him. Jesus said to him,* '*What you are going to do, do quickly.*' ²⁸*Now no one at the table knew why he had said this to him.* ²⁹*Some thought that, because Judas had the money box, Jesus was telling him,* '*Buy what we need for the feast*'; *or, that he should give something to the poor.* ³⁰*So, after receiving the morsel, he immediately went out; and it was night.*

Whatever may be the truth about the precise form of the Lord's foreknowledge about the action of Judas, there is no doubt at all about the nature of his own distress. All four evangelists make it plain that the onset of the final conflict was one of great moment for Jesus himself. And none makes it so plain as John. The powers of life and death, of God and Satan *the* adversary are about to engage in final decisive conflict. And the beginning of it, the first move on the part of the evil powers comes from within the circle of friends and disciples whom Jesus has chosen. As he comes to speak of such fatal action, John reports that *he was troubled in spirit* – the same phrase that he used to describe the reaction of Jesus when he saw Mary weeping for grief at the death of her brother (11³³: 'he was deeply moved in spirit *and troubled*'). Out of this depth of emotion he announced: '*Truly, truly, I say to you, one of you will betray me*' (13²¹).

John reports that the reaction of all the disciples was one of complete uncertainty. So had Mark recorded that 'they began to be sorrowful, and to say to him [Jesus] one after another, "Is it I?"' (Mark 14¹⁹). Matthew and Luke confirm, each in his own way (Matt. 26²²; Luke 22²³). It is at this point that the evangelist gives some, though not complete, information as to the arrangements at table. The beloved disciple was on the immediate right of Jesus, *lying* close to his breast. This is one little indication within the general Johannine conviction that the Last Supper was not a Passover, that the meal was a Passover after all, for it was the Passover that was eaten in the reclining position. The place to the right of the host was reserved for an intimate friend, though not for the chief guest, the guest of honour. That place of distinction could not have been occupied by Peter, or he would have been unable to beckon to the beloved disciple to ask him to inquire about the informer from Jesus. Bernard (p. 471) has made the interesting suggestion that the place may have been occupied by Judas, since he was the treasurer of the company. If so, we could understand how the question of the beloved disciple and the words of Jesus to Judas could have been spoken without the whole company hearing every word. It would also explain why there should have been a tradition, explicitly recorded by Luke, that there was argument at the Last Supper as to the order of precedence among the disciples (cf. Luke 22²⁴ff).

In response to the inquiry of the beloved disciple Jesus gave a morsel of bread to Judas, and, after Satan had entered into him, Jesus said to him, *'What you are going to do, do quickly.'* Having received this last token of the intimacy with Jesus, Judas went out to do his business: *and it was night.* Once more, with his almost uncanny eye for the symbolic fact, John reports a profoundly significant natural phenomenon. The supper had probably begun before nightfall; now, as it ended, it was night. Judas went out into the night. Not only into the physical night where the rays of the physical sun could not penetrate, but into that spiritual night where the light of the true sun did not shine. To go from the presence of the Lord was to leave the light and pass into darkness.

ୠୠ

21

troubled in spirit: The same word used at 11³³, when the sight of Mary's grief was, as we say, almost too much for him.

and testified: What is to take place needs 'testimony', 'witness' if it is to be understood. The following words *'Truly, truly'* also indicate that, whatever human judgement may be passed upon Judas, there is a deep soteriological significance attaching to the whole incident. The death of the Lord, in one sense the greatest evil, and in another the greatest blessing, mankind would ever know, was about to take place. And the whole movement begins within the circle of those whom Jesus has called and loved!

23

This is the first mention of *the disciple whom Jesus loved*. It cannot be stated with certainty that he was one of the Twelve, though, in view of the synoptic tradition, that none but the Twelve were present at the supper, it may be assumed that he was. Anything beyond this can be nothing but conjecture.

24

Peter was evidently not so placed at the table as to be able to put the question himself with the reserve the occasion demanded.

26

In v.18 Jesus quotes Psalm 41⁹: *He who ate my bread has lifted his heel against me.* Here Jesus is said to dip a morsel of bread and give it to Judas. In quoting the Psalm John makes some interesting alterations. The word 'ate' is the one he used in ch. 6 to speak of 'eating' the bread of life; and word 'bread' suggests the eucharistic loaf, of which Judas, it must be presumed, partook unworthily. In v.26 the reference to dipping the morsel is another small indication that the meal described was a Passover celebration, for the Passover Haggadah states: 'On all other nights we do not dip even once, but on this night twice.' The total effect of what John states is that from the intimacy of the beloved community Judas will act as the fatal informer. This is a pattern of behaviour not unknown in the community of the old Israel, as the witness of the Psalmist makes plain.

27

Satan entered into him: The name *Satan* (Adversary) is used only here in John. God has an adversary, and his work is being done here. The depth of the mystery is that even such an action is within the redemptive activity of God.

'*What you are going to do, do quickly*': The words convey the Lord's knowledge that Judas was bent on doing what he was to do; and that he now wanted the issue joined and carried through.

29

This verse is in complete consistency with the general Johannine dating of the supper twenty-four hours before the synoptic timing.

30

it was night: The synoptic tradition had spoken of an 'outer darkness' where some sons of the kingdom would go (Matt. 8¹¹ᶠ), and Luke reports Jesus himself as describing the time of his arrest as 'your [the authorities'] hour, and the power of darkness' (Luke 22⁵³).

13 31-35   'GLORY TO GOD IN THE HIGHEST
      AND ON EARTH PEACE, GOODWILL TOWARDS MEN'

³¹*When he had gone out, Jesus said, 'Now is the Son of man glorified, and in him God is glorified;* ³²*if God is glorified in him, God will also glorify him in himself, and glorify him at once.* ³³*Little children, yet a little while I am with you. You will seek me; and as I said to the Jews so now I say to you, "Where I am going you cannot come."* ³⁴*A new commandment I give to you, that you love one another; even as I have loved you, that you also love one another.* ³⁵*By this all men will know that you are my disciples if you have love for one another.'*

For all the heavy tragedy involved in the action of Judas, Jesus can speak quite confidently of the situation once the informer has left the little circle of intimate friends. 'Now is the Son of man glorified, and in him God is glorified . . .' The great act in human history by which God will be glorified, and so vindicated against all false accusations, is now in train. What will happen to Jesus is quite unique, but it will have universal effects throughout the community of his own, and through it, among men. The moment of greatest tension and apparent darkness is at the same time that of the greatest release from tension and of light.

ॐ

31

'Now is the Son of man glorified': This is peculiarly and strongly the Johannine contribution to Christian thought about the death of Jesus. He wants to make it perfectly plain that it was not the case that Jesus died in shame and ignominy and was afterwards restored to honour and glorified, as if the cross were dishonour and shame, and the resurrection for the first time the moment of victory and glory. To John the whole story was the glorification of the Son of man. It begins at the very moment when the Adversary has sent Judas on his fatal errand. And in him God is glorified. What is taking place is not just the settling of a question about the man Jesus, whose death might be seen in a new perspective by a subsequent narrative of his resurrection. The real issue concerns God who has come to man in the form of man in the Person of Jesus Christ. So the real actor in the drama is God himself, and so God will be glorified in the Son, as the Son will glorify the Father.

32

'*at once*': An important part of the Johannine witness about the glory was that it had not been a concept relating to the future, to some near or distant *parousia*. It related to what was happening from the very moment of Judas' defection. God will glorify the Son of man *at once*.

33

'*Little children*': This precise address is not used in the Gospel apart from this instance, though it is used often in the Johannine epistles.

'*Yet a little while I am with you*': The glorification of the Son of man means separation from the disciples. He is about to go where they cannot follow; he will be again at his Father's side, 'in his bosom' (1¹⁸; 13²³). He will resume his status as 'Lord' and no longer be visible as the slave.

'*as I said to the Jews*': In one sense the disciples are not more certain of themselves than were the Jews. If they attain to their true destiny it is not because of themselves, but because of him and what he has done for them.

34

'*A new commandment I give to you*': It has been observed often enough that the injunction to love was not made for the first time by Jesus on the occasion of the Last Supper! The law of Israel had long since required mutual love from the Jews. Leviticus had explicitly stated: 'You shall love your neighbour as yourself.' The newness of the command now given by Jesus is that the love he requires of his disciples is to be of the kind with which he has loved them. In a word, it is to be love of the kind that will 'reverse the roles', and bring the leader to serve as a slave, and the innocent to serve as the guilty, in the love that will bring peace to the world by its sacrificial quality. It will be a love that, like Christ's love for his own, does not ask questions about worthiness, but simply gives itself in humble service. It is much like the love sometimes crudely demanded in a fairy story, where a kiss is demanded for some loathsome creature. For such has been the love of God for men, and the love of Jesus for his own.

35

'*By this all men will know that you are my disciples*': Mutual love is the proof of Christian discipleship.

³⁶*Simon Peter said to him, 'Lord, where are you going?' Jesus answered, 'Where I am going you cannot follow me now; but you shall follow afterward.'* ³⁷*Peter said to him, 'Lord, why cannot I follow you now? I will lay down my life for you.'* ³⁸*Jesus answered, 'Will you lay down your life for me? Truly, truly, I say to you, the cock will not crow, till you have denied me three times.'*

Peter, in fashion typical of all that we learn of him from all four gospels, wants to short-circuit the whole demand of Jesus, and go with him where he is to be. *'Why cannot I follow you now? I will lay down my life for you.'* But Jesus knows Peter better than Peter knows himself, and replies *'The cock will not crow, till you have denied me three times.'* And to make plain that this defection is part of the mystery of the whole coming of the Son, he introduces this forecast with the same phrase with which he spoke of Judas' defection (v. 21), as well as of the great truths of the gospel he enunciated (e.g. 5^{19}; $6^{26,47}$; $8^{34,51,58}$; 10^7). The picture of Peter in his confident self-knowledge faced by Jesus with the divine and compassionate knowledge of Peter is one that reflects something of the relationship of Christ to everyman. It is an accusing picture, but in its accusation everyman has his only real hope.

∞

36
Peter may well have not yet learnt that where Jesus was going was to his death, though what he comes to say next indicates that he realized a real gravity in the situation.

'you shall follow afterward': Follow in both senses (a) of laying down his life for Christ and (b) of going to the Father to be with him in his own eternity.

37
'why cannot I follow you now?': Peter cannot accept the need for any delay. He has not yet learnt that such following as Jesus requires is not just a matter of human wish and will.

'*Truly, truly, I say to you, the cock will not crow, till you have denied me three times*': The prediction of Peter's denial is common, with differences in detail, to all four gospels. Mark and Matthew state that the prediction took place after the supper was over, but Luke shares the Johannine view that it took place at the supper table. It is not without significance that all the evangelists report this incident after they have told of the informer Judas. It is as if they did not wish any member of the Church to suppose that denial was impossible to the ordinary Christian; or that, once denial had taken place, there was no further hope of restoration.

Departure and Return

14$^{1-31}$

Mark 14$^{29-32}$
Luke 22$^{31-34}$

Chapter 13 ended with the story of the Lord's prediction of Peter's denial. The note on v. 38 observed that whereas Mark and Matthew place this prediction after Jesus and the eleven have left the upper room, Luke reports that it was spoken at the supper table. But it is not necessary or even discerning to suppose that John is taking sides with Luke against Matthew and Mark on a point of chronological detail about the last night of Jesus' life; rather, as has been argued in the Introduction (cf. pp. 48–58), is it better to understand this as another of John's historiographical devices for the instructed reader the better to reach a profound theological understanding of the story of the life and death, the resurrection and ascension of the Lord. On this basis there are two things to be said as the reader comes to consider ch. 14. First, Peter (and the same can be said of any other disciple, contemporary with or following after Peter) did not approach, sit through, or depart from the supper in any state of complete perfection. The disintegration of the disciples' community, and of the confidence of Peter himself, did not begin, as Mark's narrative might lead an unwary reader to suppose, only after Jesus had left the upper room and reached the Mount of Olives; on the contrary, the disintegration was there in potentiality and actuality alike, even in the upper room. There is far more than an historical detail involved in this: for the historiographical device is intended to tell the reader that the supper itself, and all the actions and teachings flowing from it, was an act of self-impartation on the part of Jesus to his disciples, an act of sheer grace, on their part unearned and undeserved. Peter, unworthy as every disciple is unworthy, is received into the divine fellowship even while he is unworthy. The displacement of the prediction of the denial from the turmoil of the Mount of Olives to the serenity of the upper room is, as it were, a Johannine way of stating Paul's theological proposition that 'While we were yet sinners Christ died for us' (Romans 5^8). Second, and conversely, by taking the serenity of the supper into the turmoil of the events in the garden, John helps his readers to understand that the power of what was done at the supper, a veritable pre-enactment of the self-giving that was to follow, was not isolated from all that preceded and followed it, but rather took it all up into itself and its own ineluctable victory. The serenity of the upper room did not give way to the turmoil and tragedy of the arrest, the trial and the crucifixion; rather it was saying in action the great triumphant word which crowned the last discourse: 'I have overcome the world' (16^{33}). John has tried to show the theological, rather than the precise historical locus of the events of the last night of the Lord's life.

It is an interesting feature of the three chapters 14, 15 and 16, that each is placed carefully by John at a certain point of the Synoptic narrative; and his pointers to theological meaning are to be found in the body of the chapters as well.

14^{1-3} **THE DESTINY OF THE DISCIPLES**

14 *'Let not your hearts be troubled; believe^a in God, believe also in me.* ²*In my Father's house are many rooms; if it were not so, would I have told you that I go to prepare a place for you?* ³*And when I go and prepare a place for you, I will come again and will take you to myself, that where I am you may be also.*

a Or *you believe*

The situation as the chapter opens is enough to make the bravest heart quail. The disciples have heard that Jesus is about to go to his death (13^{31-33}), that he will be delivered up by one of the Twelve (13^{21}) and that even the outstandingly brave and loyal Peter (cf. 6^{68})

will deny his master three times before the morning cockcrow (13^{38}). To spare the disciples the agony of heart and mind that would otherwise ensue, Jesus now makes plain the nature of his departure and the character of his return.

He begins with an exhortation: '*Let not your hearts be troubled*' (v.1), perhaps a strange word from one who three times recently has been troubled in Spirit – when he saw Mary weeping for the death of her brother Lazarus (11^{33}), when he had to speak of the inevitability of his own death before the Greeks would 'see' him (12^{27}), and when he was about to tell the Twelve that one of them would betray him (13^{21}). On each of these three occasions Jesus had been facing the absolutely critical issue of his own death, in which, it might be said, omnipotence would be manifested in impotence. Moreover, as incarnate in the temporal order, he who was the eternal Word could not but share to some degree in that characteristic of the temporal which always to some extent hides the outcome of events before they occur. For the Lord himself there was thus some understandable ground for a troubled spirit as he approached his final conflict with the Prince of this world. But for the disciples, once his own death had been accomplished, the situation was totally different. They would be able to see beyond the impotence of his dying to the omnipotence really displayed; they would know, after his glorification, that death itself had been surpassed. So the sting of death would have been removed, and they would be able to give thanks to God through their Lord, Jesus Christ.

Jesus follows the exhortation with two imperatives: '*believe in God, believe also in me*' (v.1). The first imperative exhorts the Eleven to take their own religious belief seriously; for to the discerning Jew belief in God was confidence in one who would always find a way to renew the life of his people. He had done so even after the bondage of Egypt; he had done so even after the sack of Jerusalem and the captivity in Babylon: he would do so, even after the death of Jesus the Christ. The second imperative repeats the injunction often found in the body of the fourth gospel, that there are words and deeds of Jesus that warrant belief in him. In putting these two injunctions together at the point where he is speaking of the desolation which might be caused by his death, Jesus is really asserting his own lordship over death, in spite of all the menaces of time and circumstance.

Verses 2 and 3 give a brief rationale of the departure and return of the Lord. He will leave them in order to prepare a place for them in his Father's house, where there are many rooms for permanent accommodation; and if he goes thus to prepare a place for them he will certainly return to take them there, so that the fellowship of disciples and Lord could be finally and irrevocably established. The translation '*many rooms*' hardly does justice to the language of the evangelist, who has chosen a Greek noun (*Mŏnē*) which is formed from the Greek verb meaning 'to abide' (*Mĕnein*). Even so, and quite apart from the difficulties discussed in the note below, the verses require some further elucidation.

In the two other references to '*my Father's house*' in the gospels it is clearly the Temple in Jerusalem which is meant. Many commentators have observed that in the present passage this meaning can only be figuratively accepted, for the real reference is to the eternal dwelling place of God in heaven. But this does not seem to go quite far enough, for already in his gospel John has stated that in the time that is coming and has in fact arrived men will worship God in neither the Temple at Jerusalem nor that at Samaria, but will worship the Father in Spirit and truth (4^{21}). As the commentary claimed in discussing ch. 4, the passage can hardly be understood save as meaning that 'Jesus Christ is the "place" where men of any time or place can at last be free of "place" in their worship of God; he is the substance, the material by which all men are freed from all materialism in their worship, free to worship God at last "in Spirit"' (p. 218). These observations may help the reader to understand why, if there be already many rooms for permanent occupation in the Father's house, Jesus should need to go away to get them ready. If the figure of the Father's house, the temple, is to find its true antitype in himself, then what this statement claims is that by his death he will be able to 'open the kingdom of heaven to all believers'. True universalism in religion is achieved in and through the particularity of the cross. The actual 'preparation' of the permanent dwelling place of the disciples will be done, not after the death on the cross, but in it and by it; it is precisely in his 'going away', his departure, his death, that the preparation is effected.

This understanding may well gain support in an interesting speculation which Hoskyns and Davey consider in their commentary (ad loc.). Does the language about 'preparation' derive from the gospel narratives that at the time of the Last Supper Jesus sent two of his disciples to *prepare* for their last meal together (in the synoptics a Passover meal)? John, with his assignment of a different date to the Last Supper, so that it took place on the day before the Passover, and not on the Passover day itself, could not write of any instruction to the disciples to 'make ready the Passover'. Rather, in the fourth gospel, Jesus himself prepares the 'real', the 'true' Passover, in which he is himself the 'true', the 'real' Paschal Lamb, and the 'place' where the feast is celebrated will not be a room hired temporarily in Jerusalem, but his own person, with risen and glorified life, as the *locus* of the worship of all who come to believe in him. If these speculations are acceptable, and they have much to commend them, then it is all the more fitting to interpret the reference to going away to prepare a place for the disciples as indicating the actual death of the Lord on his cross; for while the Passover lambs of the old Israel were being slain in the Temple of Jerusalem, at that very time, according to St John, Jesus Christ, the true Passover Lamb, was being sacrificed on another altar in the only true temple or meeting place of God and man. What was wrought by that sacrifice was no temporary togetherness of God and man, but an enduring, eternal dwelling together of God and man in and through Jesus Christ, Son of God and saviour of the world.

෴

2

'*many rooms*': *Mŏnē*, the word translated *room* here, has a possible alternative meaning to the one adopted in the notes. It can mean (as it does in Pausanias) a 'stopping place' or a 'station' on a journey. But the evidence of the Church Fathers gives support to the use of it as a permanent abode of the saints in heaven. Jesus has not gone to prepare stopping places on the way to heaven; nor, if verse 3 be any indication, even stopping places within heaven along which the saints may move as they progress in sanctity. He has gone to establish a permanent abiding place for men with the Father.

'*if it were not so, would I have told you that I go to prepare a place for you?*': This is a difficult verse, and none of the usual solutions offered seems wholly intelligible. For example, if we take the translation provided in the R.S.V. (quite a legitimate translation based on a perfectly legitimate text) it has to be observed that in spite of its phrase 'Would I have told you?' Jesus has not yet said anything of the kind to the disciples. It is possible to avoid some embarrassment by noting that John does some-

times record things in this indirect way, e.g. 6[36]; 10[25]; 11[40]. A second
solution to the difficulty is to treat the words 'if it were not so I would
have told you' as a parenthesis; but even so the sense yielded is not good:
'In my Father's house are many rooms – if it were not so I would have
told you – because I am going to prepare a place for you.' Only in the
interpretation adopted in the text, that the many rooms are a figure
for the universality of the salvation wrought by Jesus, does this really
make sense. A third solution is to treat the word translated 'because'
or 'that' as the Greek equivalent to an inverted comma introducing
words actually spoken; this yields the translation: 'In my Father's
house are many rooms. If it were not so, I would have said "I am going
to prepare a place for you".' But this fits the context, especially v.3,
even less aptly than the rest. A final solution is to omit the Greek *hoti*
before the word 'I go', and to insert a full stop after 'told you'. This
leaves a text: 'In my Father's house are many rooms. If it were not so
I would have told you. I am going to prepare a place for you.' But this
seems too neat an escape from a difficulty even though some texts
(including that used by the translators of the A.V.) omit *hoti*, wrongly as
most scholars would now agree.

3
'*I will come again*': The future tense need not imply the absolute
eschatological future. It could equally refer to the return of the Lord
in the resurrection appearances, or to his coming to the individual
disciple beyond those appearances. In view of the general teaching of
the fourth gospel it would be wrong to attempt an exposition of this
word solely in terms of the Second Advent.

14[4-11]   THE WAY TO THE FATHER

[4]'*And you know the way where I am going.*'[a] [5]*Thomas said to him, 'Lord,
we do not know where you are going; how can we know the way?'* [6]*Jesus
said to him, 'I am the way, and the truth, and the life; no one comes to the
Father, but by me.* [7]*If you had known me, you would have known my
Father also; henceforth you know him and have seen him.'*

[8]*Philip said to him, 'Lord, show us the Father, and we shall be satisfied.'*
[9]*Jesus said to him, 'Have I been with you so long, and yet you do not know
me, Philip? He who has seen me has seen the Father; how can you say,
"Show us the Father"?* [10]*Do you not believe that I am in the Father and*

the Father in me? The words that I say to you I do not speak on my own
authority; but the Father who dwells in me does his works. ¹¹*Believe me*
that I am in the Father and the Father in me; or else believe me for the sake
of the works themselves.'

a Other ancient authorities read *where I am going you know, and the*
way you know

Jesus has now made clear what the final destiny of his disciples is: to
be for ever with the Father in him. He now proposes to say more, but
finds it necessary before he can do so to provide further important
explanations. He begins by assuming that the disciples know the way
he is going to prepare permanent dwelling places for them. Thomas
interjects a question which shows how far he (and presumably the
others) was from really understanding what had been said to them.
'*Lord, we do not know where you are going; how can we know the way?*'
(v.5). Evidently the talk of 'going to the Father' and 'preparing a
place' had not been self-evident in meaning to the disciples; this is
perhaps a further reason for thinking that as the words were spoken
they were taken as a symbolic usage of the language of making ready
for the Passover. If Jesus was to prepare a Passover for them, where
(and how) could he do it? But in any case, as for any disciple, where
does Jesus depart to, when he 'goes' from his disciples?

The answer given by Jesus further articulates the high Christology
of the fourth evangelist. It is not the case that Jesus is 'away' from the
Father, and must therefore find and tread the way to him; he is the
way himself: it is not the case that there is a truth about the Father
which Jesus must learn and then pass on; he is the truth himself: it is
not the case that the Father has eternal life which he will give to the
Son when the Son reaches his home, so that the Son can then bestow
life; he is the life himself. And no other approach to the Father can
be made than the one which has been opened in the incarnation of the
eternal Word. And the use of language from the Prologue to the
gospel is at this point far from an infelicity, for the evangelist himself
reminds his readers of what he had said in the Prologue: 'No one has
ever seen God; the only Son, who is in the bosom of the Father, he
has made him known' (1¹⁸). So at the end of the ministry Jesus can
say to Thomas and the ten: '*If you had known me, you would have*
known my Father also; henceforth you know him and have seen him' (v. 7).

By the same words John is also recalling for the reader the story of the man born blind, who in his excommunicated loneliness was sought and found by Jesus, and asked if he believed in the Son of man. To his reply that he did not know who the Son of man was, Jesus answered: 'You have seen him, and it is he who speaks with you' (9^{37}). The force of these words is enhanced if the reading of Codex Sinaiticus and Codex Bezae be accepted, and the translation goes: 'If you know me [as you do], you will also know my Father'. Then the Lord adds the words 'Henceforth [i.e. from now on, in and through and because of my departure in death] you know him and have seen him'. The death and glorification of the Lord is the place and time where the eyes of men can see the Father.

But this, again perhaps understandably, does not suffice. Philip next puts to the Lord a difficulty that many disciples of every age will have felt. He asks for a theophany, with all the authority and self-authentification associated with that given to Moses on Sinai. '*Lord, show us the Father, and we shall be satisfied*' (v. 8). But the same answer has to be given, for the request makes the same sort of presuppositions as Thomas' question: it assumed that the Father was other than the Son, and could not conceive of the unity of Father and Son of which Jesus has spoken so frequently in the Johannine story. What else can the request to be shown the Father mean than that the supplicant has not perceived the bond of unity between Father and Son? Jesus refers to the two dominant themes of the gospel: his word and his works. Neither are done 'on his own'; his words are not spoken on his own authority, but with all the authority of the Father: no theophany could add to their authenticity. His works are not his own doing, but the Father, who dwells in the Son, performs them. So Philip can either believe the words that have been spoken as words from the Father, or he can trust the works that have been done, and all that their doing implies, as works done by the Father (vv. 10–11). So to go to the Father does not mean a departure *from* Jesus; on the contrary, it will mean staying with him, abiding with him for ever. The metaphor of 'departure' must not be pressed to the point of letting any disciple suppose that there is knowledge of the Father to be had beyond Jesus himself. In the Son the Father has been pleased to manifest himself.

4

'*you know the way where I am going*': This is faulty grammar in Greek, but the sense is quite clear. The disciples ought by now to have known whither Jesus was to go. He had said to whom he was going at 7^{33}. Peter had confessed ignorance at 13^{36}, even if that left the disciples in some respects little better informed than the Jews! But now the new community is to learn the secret of the Lord.

6

'*the way*': Jesus is the road by which men come to God. This must not be diluted into saying that the road Jesus now treads must be followed by his disciples. Something much more difficult, and much more profound is being stated than that, though that remains true. It is one way of saying that it is only in union with the Son that any man can come to any kind of union with the Father.

'*the truth*': Not an intellectual proposition or a system of the same, but the embodiment in human life of the true life of the divine Father, revealing the purposes and nature of God himself. Again, the truth is not some statement or theory about Jesus; it is Jesus himself in his divine-human character, making manifest to men the glory of the invisible God.

'*the life*': The life that Jesus is cannot at the same time be something outside himself that he can appropriate and give. He is himself the life. To go to the Father and to have this life is to receive the life of Jesus himself; or, alternatively, Jesus becomes himself the substance of the life of those who believe in him, and love and serve him. Christian theology has still much to explore in expounding the richness of this verse in which Jesus himself is the supreme reality in which all true life shares.

7

'*If you had known me, you would have known my Father also*': This translation derives from the reading of Codex Vaticanus. The reading of Codex Sinaiticus and Codex Bezae yields the other translation referred to in the commentary. Verse 7b suggests that the original reading would have been that of Sinaiticus.

9

'*been with you so long*': The construction with the dative (if the reading of Sinaiticus be again preferred) suggests that Jesus is thinking of the whole period of his ministry.

11

'*Believe me*': Literally this, and not, on this occasion 'Believe in me'. It would be quite correct to drop the word *that* and enclose the words '*I am in the Father and the Father in me*' in inverted commas.

14$^{12-24}$ RENEWAL, RESPONSIBILITY AND RETURN

^{12}'*Truly, truly, I say to you, he who believes in me will also do the works that I do; and greater works than these will he do, because I go to the Father.* ^{13}*Whatever you ask in my name, I will do it, that the Father may be glorified in the Son;* ^{14}*if you ask^a anything in my name, I will do it.*

^{15}'*If you love me, you will keep my commandments.* ^{16}*And I will pray the Father, and he will give you another Counsellor, to be with you for ever,* ^{17}*even the Spirit of truth, whom the world cannot receive, because it neither sees him nor knows him; you know him, for he dwells with you, and will be in you.*

^{18}'*I will not leave you desolate; I will come to you.* ^{19}*Yet a little while, and the world will see me no more, but you will see me; because I live, you will live also.* ^{20}*In that day you will know that I am in my Father, and you in me, and I in you.* ^{21}*He who has my commandments and keeps them, he it is who loves me; and he who loves me will be loved by my Father, and I will love him and manifest myself to him.*' ^{22}*Judas (not Iscariot) said to him, 'Lord, how is it that you will manifest yourself to us, and not to the world?'* ^{23}*Jesus answered him, 'If a man loves me, he will keep my word, and my Father will love him, and we will come to him and make our home with him.* ^{24}*He who does not love me does not keep my words; and the word which you hear is not mine but the Father's who sent me.*

a Other ancient authorities add *me*

Jesus has so far sought to save his friends from despair by speaking to them of the destiny his death (as the true Passover Lamb) will prepare for them, and of the fact that to be with the Father is none other than to abide with the Son. He now claims that so to believe in the Son will enable the disciple to share in the work of the Son, and in one sense to do even greater works than the Son has achieved. To understand this it is important to remember that when Jesus referred in verse 10 to the Father doing his works, he was not referring to what man might call thaumaturgies, but to what the Father was achieving through the thaumaturgies. Thus the 'work of him who sent me' when it was performed on the man born blind (ch. 9) was not simply the gift of physical sight to a man who had never had it; it was much more surely the gift of 'insight' or 'vision' by which, when the newly seeing man was told that he had seen and was talking to the Son of man, he replied 'Lord, I believe' and worshipped Jesus (9^{38}). This work, of bringing men to believe in Jesus Christ as the true Son of man, which had been the work done in his own works, would be continued, in various ways, not necessarily in healings, by his disciples. But in one aspect the work of the disciples would be greater than that of the Lord, for it would be the privilege of the disciple to carry the grace of believing for the acceptance of the Greeks, and all the other Gentiles who as yet knew not the Christ. That they could come to belief at all depended, of course, entirely upon the 'departure', the death of Jesus; if that did not occur, there would be no conversion of the Gentiles: but once it had occurred, the disciples would be able to do what the Lord himself had been unable to do – to proclaim that his death as an historical event had been efficacious in bringing man and God finally together.

The disciples' mission to the world would quicken all sorts of desires in their hearts. There would be many things they would like to receive from their Lord. Jesus assures them that anything they asked in his name, he would do it, though the important qualification is added even to the quite guarded phrase, that if the Lord acts in response to prayer it will be that the Father may be glorified in the Son. So it would be wrong to think that the evangelist has just adopted the words and the meanings of the magic papyri, and that his meaning here is exhausted in the idea that Christian disciples may efficaciously invoke the name of Christ. Rather are the roots of the phrase to be found in the Old Testament idea of the *name* as the real person himself, in his essential nature. In this sense prayer in Christ's name is itself prayer belonging to, and coming from, the essential nature of Christ, who is to dwell in those who both love him and with him seek the glory of the Father.

But such belief and togetherness of Christ and the disciple can and need to be expounded in other terms as well. What binds the disciple to his Lord is not an act of intellectual assent, but rather a bond of love. Love of Christ means seeking the glory of the Father, means accepting the duties of the work of the Son, means, in fact, obedience to the injunctions of the Lord. To those so bound to him Christ addresses a further word. He will ask of the Father that they might have another *Counsellor*. He has himself been their counsellor while he has been with them; now that he is going away their plainest need is for another counsellor of comparable stature. At the prayer of the Son the Father will give the loving disciple the gift of the Spirit of truth, who will remain with the disciples for ever. So his departure will not leave them unsupported and unguided as they might have feared. The coming of the Spirit of truth to stay with them will mark them off from the world; for just as the world cannot see Jesus for the Son he really is, so it cannot discern the presence of the Spirit of truth, for the world cannot *see* him nor *know* him. But the disciples will know him, for he will be dwelling in them.

But just as to go to the Father does not mean for the disciple going beyond or to another than the Son, neither does the advent of the Spirit of truth mean the advent of someone other than the Son. The fear of being left desolate, like orphans, need not trouble the disciples, for the Lord will himself come to them. It will not be long before Jesus is put to death, and so pass out of human sight. But the disciples will see him, for he and they together will enter upon a life with quite new conditions. The evangelist states at this point: '*In that day you will know that I am in my Father, and you in me, and I in you*' (v. 20). *In that day* was almost a technical phrase in Jewish eschatological thinking for the last days when God would finally bring all his purposes to pass. But clearly John is not intending to refer here to the eschatological end, as commonly understood. With his usual facility for compressed statement he has given a subtle reference to the coming of Jesus to the disciples so that they could *see* him, after his resurrection, to his coming to dwell with them in the time of the community of the Church on earth, as also to the final coming at the end of the world. In Jesus' thinking history does not finally lose its meaning when it is superseded by the 'eschaton', the 'end' that lies beyond history; rather does it become possessed of ultimate significance now, because the eschatological fulfilments are to be found within it. In this way it can be seen that what Jesus stated in vv.1–3 was not simply a promise that he would come 'at the last day' to gather his disciples to an eternal as distinct from an historical home; but that his departure and return were to be fulfilled in the one act which would be both crucifixion and glorification, both defeat and victory, both death and everlasting life, both parting from his disciples and his return to them for ever. And the permanent dwelling places are not to be found only when the disciples have died, or when the end of the historical order has come; they are provided even in the time of the earthly pilgrimage, and they endure beyond the bounds of physical death. For, as Paul put it, whether we live or die, we are the Lord's. He is the 'place' where we meet God, to be 'in him' now is to be in him for ever.

Jesus next makes it plain that what he has promised will be available not only to the disciples present, but to anyone who 'has his commandments and keeps them'; for such a one loves him. All through this chapter there is emphasis on the inclusiveness of the Son's labours through the disciples. The man who loves Jesus will be loved by the Father, and Jesus will also love him, and manifest himself to him. This gives rise to the third query of the chapter, put this time by Judas (not Iscariot), which no less than the other two questions is one which cannot but reflect the needs of disciples of every age: *'Lord, how is it that you will manifest yourself to us, and not to the world?'* (v. 22). The coming of the Lord to the believing disciple will confirm the belief he has, and will sustain him in the desperate struggles in which faith is sometimes involved. For such a coming the disciple cannot but be grateful. But is there not a way open to divine omnipotence to make the presence and purpose of God known to the world? Why cannot God manifest himself in some theophany so that even the most secular of men have to confess his reality and power? Jesus meets such reflections with a restatement of what has already been said: *'If a man loves me, he will keep my word, and my Father will love him, and we will come to him and make our home with him'* (v. 23). It is interesting to observe that the word for *make our home with him* reflects the same Greek root as was found in vv. 1–3 at the beginning of the chapter. The eternal dwelling of God with men begins now. Jesus continues that the man who does not love him will not keep his word; so, we may deduce, the Father cannot enter into the same relationships with him as with the loving and obedient disciple. The Lord adds *'the word which you hear is not mine but the Father's who sent me'* (v.24).

In other words, there are some questions that cannot really be answered. Paul deals with something like the same sort of problem in Romans 9–11. There he is trying to understand why God should choose Jacob and not Esau, why he should 'choose' the Jew rather than the Gentile. At one point he answers 'Who are you, a man, to answer back to God?' But to adopt this attitude is not to admit that the whole world order is governed by sheer arbitrariness; for at the end of his review Paul claims that in the end the ways of God, that seem to mortal man to be unjust in their seeming arbitrariness, will be found to justify themselves: 'God ... consigned all men to disobedience, that he may have mercy upon all. O the depth of the riches and wisdom and knowledge of God! How unsearchable are his judgements, and how inscrutable his ways!' (Romans 11[32,33]). Something like that is involved in the presentation by the evangelist at this point of his account of Jesus' comforting of the disciples. God has in fact chosen the way of the Church, i.e. the way of working by the indwelling of himself in the lives and hearts of those who know and love and serve the Son. It would not be possible, indeed, for the Father to dwell in hearts and lives that did not honour the Son. To win an allegiance by some mighty theophany might produce a sullen intellectual assent to the being and power of God: but it would not bring men to a fellowship of love and mutual service. It is well for men to accept the conditions of their historical existence, and to trust God that he has taken the steps proper and open to omnipotence to deal with its tragedies and anomalies.

※

14

This whole verse is omitted from some texts, possibly because it seemed superfluous after v.13. If the verse be retained, it should have the word 'me' inserted after 'ask', as the marginal note in R.S.V. suggests. If genuine, its omission would have occurred because it apparently contradicted 16[23].

15

'*If you love me*': This condition underlies the development of the discourse down to the end of v. 24.

16

Here the Paraclete is given by the Father at the request of the Son. Later (v.26) the Father sends him in Christ's name. But in view of what has to be said about 'in Christ's name' there can be very little difference in meaning between the two statements. Neither is it likely, in view of the close mutuality of nature between Father and Son, that the evangelist intends any profound distinction when he states in later chapters that Christ sends the Spirit from the Father (cf. 15^{26}).

17

'*the Spirit of truth*': Jesus has already declared himself to be the Truth. So naturally the Spirit of Truth will perform his office by bringing to the disciples' remembrance all that Jesus said and did.

18

'*desolate*': The word is 'orphans'. Jesus will not leave his disciples like children without any parents. The same word 'orphans' could be used directly of disciples bereft of their master. John may well have used the term in deliberate ambiguity.

19

'*Yet a little while*': This indicates that the reference to the coming back of Jesus (v.3) is not to a distant parousia, but to some time shortly after the supper, i.e. to the resurrection appearances.

21

'*He who has my commandments*': The man who has really come to understand them.

'*manifest myself to him*': The word *manifest* is peculiar to this chapter of John, but is used in the Old Testament of theophanies. What the evangelist wants his readers to understand is that the 'theophany' of the Old Testament is fulfilled in the very different manifestation of the Father in the coming, the departure and the return of the Son.

22

Judas (not Iscariot): This Judas appears as an apostle only in Luke 6^{16} and Acts 1^{13}. Little more can be said.

'*to us, and not to the world*': The words *to us* and *to the world* are in a position of emphasis and contrast in the Greek.

23

'*keep my word*': The word is the whole teaching of Jesus.

'*we will come to him*': The form of statement indicates that the evangelist is not thinking of the 'second advent' in the ordinary sense of the term. John has his own profound modification of the traditional ways of speaking of the 'coming' of God to man. It is always the coming of the Son, and yet at the same time the coming of the Father. It may refer to the resurrection appearances, in which, though the Son returns to his disciples, the Father comes with him to take up his abode in the disciples; or it may refer to the more familiar return of the Son in power and glory at the *parousia*. There too, the Son does not appear alone, or in distinction from the Father, as if there were two deities. Father and Son are one.

'*and make our home with him*': Here for the second time in the chapter the word *Mŏnē* is used for 'home'. The return of Father and Son will be to a permanent abiding with the loving and obedient disciple.

24

'*the word which you hear*': i.e. what Jesus has had to say about the means by which God has chosen to effect his universal purpose – through the apparently closed and limited fellowship of the Church.

14^{25-31} PEACE AND THE PARACLETE

²⁵'*These things I have spoken to you, while I am still with you. *²⁶*But the Counsellor, the Holy Spirit, whom the Father will send in my name, he will teach you all things, and bring to your remembrance all that I have said to you. *²⁷*Peace I leave with you; my peace I give to you; not as the world gives do I give to you. Let not your hearts be troubled, neither let them be afraid. *²⁸*You heard me say to you, "I go away, and I will come to you." If you loved me, you would have rejoiced, because I go to the Father; for the Father is greater than I. *²⁹*And now I have told you before it takes place, so that when it does take place, you may believe. *³⁰*I will no longer talk much with you, for the ruler of this world is coming. He has no power over me; *³¹*but I do as the Father has commanded me, so that the world may know that I love the Father. Rise, let us go hence.*'

Having given the disciples an account of what 'going' or 'departing' from them really meant, Jesus now begins to take his farewell. So much he has been able to say to them, even if they have not yet fully understood or accepted it. But when he has gone, and the promised Paraclete, the Holy Spirit, has come, then they will be able to understand what he has said. Jesus, as the eternal Word incarnate, can already envisage his own death as something that has already taken place. But the disciples cannot rise to this until the awful deed of the crucifixion has taken place. But once that is behind them, they will be able to enter into what Jesus has already said about it, and to all the fulness of truth that it will reveal to men. But the event is not eloquent in and by itself; it will become and remain eloquent of what Christ has already spoken in so far as it is illuminated by the Holy Spirit. Then, as they remember what Jesus has said, they will understand what he has tried to teach them. His sayings will be lit up with new significance, once the cross and glorification have taken place.

Jesus then speaks the quite colloquial word of farewell, which was the same as that used colloquially for a greeting: 'Shalōm', or 'Peace'. But he is careful to point out that for him to say 'Peace' is something quite different from its utterance by any other person in the world. For his departure is not of the normal kind; it is both more final, and less absolute: more final in that he is to depart in death; less absolute in that he will return as the risen and glorified Lord. So he can repeat now the word with which he began his word of comfort: 'Let not your hearts be troubled', and can add 'neither let them be afraid' (v. 27).

But such an effective utterance of the prayer 'Peace be to you' depends entirely on the Lord's departure in death to the Father, so that he might come again. Had the disciples really understood this, they would have rejoiced at the surpassing wonder and greatness of the news. For to journey to the Father is to journey to the eternal source of power, and had they understood this aright, the disciples would have known that the Lord whom they loved and served could not go from them in final defeat. But, Jesus adds, the forewarning of what is to take place, not as a physical act, but as a religious reality, can now only serve to fortify and renew the disciples in their belief in him.

It has been important to say this much to them. For the final encounter with the 'ruler of this world' is very near, and there is little time for further elaboration. But powerful though he be, he has no power over the Son, for the Son has given himself to complete obedience to the Father; and that brings its own vindication: the world will learn, through the coming events, that Jesus loved the Father. That means that his departure, his going, his death will in the end bring the world to realize that which will make it no longer 'the world', viz. that it is in the love of the Father that true life lies, and that that love has been manifested to the world in Jesus Christ.

The evangelist ends the chapter with words that are also found in the Synoptic tradition of the last night of the Lord's life: 'Rise, let us go hence' (v. 31). The words echo those found in Mark and Matthew at the point of the agony in the garden when the prayer of Jesus is over, and the betrayer was approaching (Mark 14^{42}; Matthew 26^{46}). Again, as has been argued already (p. 48ff), this is not an indication that the evangelist or some editor of his materials has managed to get the narrative in a seriously wrong order, so that the whole of what follows from 15^1 to 17^{26} needs to be transposed to some position before 14^{31}. It is rather another historiographical indication of the theological *locus* of what is being reported. At the time when, in the synoptic narrative, Jesus has faced the issues of life and death without that cooperation from the disciples that he might have expected, at the same moment that Judas comes as a treacherous friend to hand him over to the authorities, then, says John, the reader may best understand the word about the true Vine that is Jesus and the branches that need pruning which are the disciples. At this point the reader can best understand what in the synoptic gospels appears in part in apocalyptic sections, and in part in the missionary charge to the Twelve. So does the fourth evangelist offer a profound theological review of the whole setting of the synoptic story, not to put it right on certain small chronological points, much less to add to confusion by setting material in gross disorder, but rather to show that it is only by its association with and derivation from the death and return of the Lord that any truth of the Christian gospel has final validity.

ಜಜ

25
'These things I have spoken': i.e. the words of comfort and consolation.

26
'the Holy Spirit': Only here in the gospel is the Spirit so described with both adjective and definite article. The Paraclete is identified with the Holy Spirit.

27
'Peace': The word formed the traditional word of greeting and farewell. It is so used at 20$^{19, 21, 26}$. Now that Jesus uses the word after the profound teaching he has given about his own departure, the formal word itself becomes possessed of the profundity of what Jesus has said. And so it has remained in Christian language since.

28
'I go away, and I will come to you': In this short sentence the whole teaching of the chapter can be summarized.

'*If you loved me, you would have rejoiced*': The plain implication is that they had not loved Jesus so.

'*the Father is greater than I*': Understandably this sentence was much debated in the doctrinal development of the Church, particularly between the Arians and their opponents. But the evangelist is not here concerned with the problems of the relationships of the 'persons' of the Godhead, still less with the metaphysical problems about possible distinctions between the 'essences' of Father and Son. Innocent of all that, the evangelist is simply making it plain that the departure of Jesus is his resumption of the omnipotence rightly exercised by the Father, instead of his continuing in the impotence rightly exercised by the omnipotent but incarnate Word.

30
'*I will no longer talk much with you*': These words do not necessitate the conclusion that chs. 15 and 16 as well as 17 should be made to precede 14. See the Introduction, pp. 48ff.

15$^{1-27}$ *The True Israel of God*

Psalm 80$^{8-13}$
Mark 12$^{1-9}$
Matthew 10^{19-25a}
Matthew 24^9
Luke 21$^{12-17}$
Luke 24^{48}

Whatever may be the truth about the proper ordering of chs. 13–17 it would seem inevitable that ch. 15 be taken as relating to the supper table. For it begins with the 'parable' of the vine, the vineyard and the vinedresser, which recalls the familiar Old Testament representation of Israel as God's vine; it continues to expound the meaning of union with Christ in his death, which is so central a thought to the Christian eucharist; and it concludes with a word about witness, which is a notion incorporated into the account of the institution of the Lord's Supper in St Paul's narrative in 1 Corinthians ('... you proclaim the Lord's death until he come' 1 Cor. 11^{26}).

To expound these chapters as a developing unity involves reviewing the situation at this point. The Twelve had come to supper with their Lord, and after supper, and his humble service done for them as a symbol of the even humbler service he was about to render, he identified Judas as the disciple about to deliver him up; and then, for the first time, the embryo Church was alone, without any intrusion of alien elements. To this highly selected company Jesus spoke of what his forthcoming death would mean; it must be thought of not just as departure, but as departure and return. For Jesus was not just 'going away'; he was going to the Father, and his going was but the penultimate step of the divine purpose to come and make a permanent abode with men, in other words, to bring to men the gift of eternal life. The Church, in the persons of the eleven, found this hard and strange doctrine, not least that the manifestation of the Father should be made just to the Church and not to the world. Jesus had replied to their understandable incomprehension that what they were really asked to do was to trust God and do his will. The Father would act so that the world would come to know the Son and his love for the Father.

With this knowledge, John implies by his use of the words from Mark 14⁴², the disciples are properly equipped to face the world. In ch. 15 he thus proceeds to say something to his disciples about the relationship of the divine community, the Church, to the world. He does this first by a reinterpretation of an ancient figure of God's people as a vine which he had planted, and which is watched over by the vinedresser to ensure that it produces fruit; and then by a further analysis of what it means to love another person in Christ. He then makes inescapably plain that the world is inevitably opposed to the Church, and that this will mean suffering and persecution for his disciples. Yet through it all, the disciples must bear witness, i.e. so speak of the events which are about to take place as to show the world that it is not just the death of an itinerant evangelist that has occurred, but the decisive act by which God has redeemed the world.

So John is doing at this point in his gospel what the synoptists did at other points of the tradition. Here is anchored John's missionary charge to the church; it must witness, and it cannot but witness, in the face of hostility and persecution. In the synoptic presentation the 'charge to the disciples' is found in three parts: one at the time of the ministry in Galilee, when the Twelve (or the Seventy) were sent out on their evangelistic campaigns; one in the apocalyptic sections, when Jesus warns his followers of opposition and persecution from the world; and one in the post-resurrection period, where the despondent disciples are brought to a new resolution and receive a new charge to evangelize the world. It is entirely characteristic of John and his theology that he should fashion an historiographical device by which all these three loci of the synoptic charge to the disciples are firmly rooted in the events of the death and resurrection, the departure and the return of Jesus.

15 '*I am the true vine, and my Father is the vinedresser.* ^{2}*Every branch of mine that bears no fruit, he takes away, and every branch that does bear fruit he prunes, that it may bear more fruit.* ^{3}*You are already made clean by the word which I have spoken to you.* ^{4}*Abide in me, and I in you. As the branch cannot bear fruit by itself, unless it abides in the vine, neither can you, unless you abide in me.* ^{5}*I am the vine, you are the branches. He who abides in me, and I in him, he it is that bears much fruit, for apart from me you can do nothing.* ^{6}*If a man does not abide in me, he is cast forth as a branch and withers; and the branches are gathered, thrown into the fire and burned.* ^{7}*If you abide in me, and my words abide in you, ask whatever you will, and it shall be done for you.* ^{8}*By this my Father is glorified, that you bear much fruit, and so prove to be my disciples.* ^{9}*As the Father has loved me, so have I loved you; abide in my love.* ^{10}*If you keep my commandments, you will abide in my love, just as I have kept my Father's commandments and abide in his love.* ^{11}*These things I have spoken to you, that my joy may be in you, and that your joy may be full.*'

There is quite an amount of evidence that the disciples, according to the general early Christian tradition, thought of themselves as in some sense constituting, or about to constitute, the new Israel or people of God (cf. Matt. 19^{28}; 20^{21}; Mark 10^{37}; Luke 22^{30}). That being so, it would have sounded more appropriate to them had Jesus begun this part of his farewell instruction with the words '*We* are the true vine.' For in the Old Testament, where the figure of the vine is a familiar one, it is the nation as a whole that is referred to. Thus it is very important to take with full seriousness a double emphasis and significance which Jesus places upon what he now says. He uses about himself a figure that has hitherto been used of a community; and he uses that figure about himself in one of those exalted self-affirmations that have proved to be of the profoundest importance in the thought and witness of the fourth gospel. '*I am the true vine*' (v. 1).

When the Psalmist sang (Psalm 80[8]): 'Thou didst bring a vine out of Egypt; thou didst drive out the nations and plant it' even the most unpoetic of persons would have known that the 'real vine' of the song was not a horticultural plant that chanced to be removed in some way from Egypt to Palestine, but was rather the people of Israel, whom God had delivered from oppression by the hand of Moses, and had brought them to some security of a new home in the land of Palestine. Yet, as the Psalmist himself and many a prophet knew and testified, Israel had been a 'fruitless' vine. The baptism which John had offered his contemporaries was an open acknowledgement of the fact that Israel had not been a 'true' Israel or people of God; that she had failed to produce in the world the fruits which God sought of her. At the first miracle in Cana it was seen that the purificatory rites by which Israel sought to retain her status as God's people and to dwell with God for ever had been exposed as ineffective, and in prophetic symbolism Jesus had announced that it was only in his own sacrificial offering of himself that God and man could be brought together in the way that God willed.

It has often been observed that the prophetic use of the vine as a figure for Israel always led to a prediction of judgement and disaster. This is sometimes held to be a difficulty in taking the vine here as figuring Israel. But it was surely impossible for the Old Testament prophet to envisage the act of grace and condescension by which God came himself in the person of the Son to become the stock of the new vine, the reality of that human-divine life which is the true life of the people of God. And it was surely just as natural that, as the one in whom was embodied the new beginning of the life of God's people, Jesus should use such an Old Testament figure to make plain to his Israelite contemporaries what his nature and functions were.

'*I am the true* [the real] *vine*' (v.1.). The life of God-with-man, which is the real essence of Israel's proper existence, has now begun. The true, the real vine has been planted. Like all vines, it will have branches, and like all vines, it will need attention. It will need dressing and pruning, and useless branches will have to be cut away and destroyed. But the vine will continue to bear fruit. The relationship of vine and branch conveys to the disciples a real sense of the profound intimacy of their relationship to Jesus Christ. Just as a hand is not a hand unless it be joined to an arm of a living body, and cannot do the work of a hand unless it is so joined, so a vine branch is not a branch unless it is joined to the vinestock, and it cannot bear grapes unless it is so joined. Jesus had spoken already of the intimacy of the disciples being in him and he in them; the figure of the vine is a felicitous illustration of that intimacy.

But it is more, for it includes a reference to the purpose of the intimate relationship which Christ is about to establish by his departure and return. Israel should have borne fruit already by the conversion of the Gentiles. But, as the story of the cleansing of the Temple showed (particularly in its synoptic form), Judaism had come to hoard the spiritual treasures of her revealed religion very much as robbers hoard the spoils of their raids. The true vine would bear fruit; that is to say, the Church would and could and must evangelize. The world must come to know that the Son loves the Father, and the Father the world.

Yet it must not be supposed that the growth of the Church will be a simple horticultural operation! Of course there will need to be dressing and pruning of the vine – i.e. the members of the Church will always live under the judgement of Christ. But even beyond that, the test of fruitfulness, of the prosecution of the Church's mission, has to be faced. And here it is important to interpret v. 7 with due sobriety. If the disciples indeed live in intimate communion with their Lord, and his words (i.e. his words which speak of his death, his departure and return, his humiliation and glorification) abide in them, then they may ask whatever they will, and it will be done. But what does a disciple ask for himself and his work when he has the words of the Lord abiding in him? Certainly not for a straight and easy run of evangelistic success, as a replacement for the difficulties he finds as he confronts the world. For that would be to deny the necessity of the departure of the Lord, to refuse to believe that his suffering and death are an essential part of the ultimate triumph. To bear fruit, then, is not simply to have one's evangelistic efforts succeed; it is to be with the Lord in witness, both in word and in deed, in action and in passion, in suffering and in joy, in defeat and victory, in death and resurrection. This manner of bearing fruit glorifies the Father. This manner of bearing fruit repeats in the life of the members of the new Israel that relationship of love between Father and Son which is the sole reality of the life that is given by the Son. To remain loyal to the words of Jesus in this way is also the one means of attaining the heavenly joy that belongs to the life of Father and Son. And that the disciples should be able to attain that, and, like the Son himself, spend themselves that others might share it, is the whole reason for the Son speaking to them as he has done. And, since he has spoken to them of what he is about to do for them, it is the sole reason for his dying for them.

So word and deed are thought of as one in the exposition of what the community of the new Israel is like. The vine as the basic figure in the exposition has, as already observed, a copious Old Testament usage behind it. But, if in spite of John's different dating of the Last Supper this occasion is rightly understood as charged with Paschal meaning, then the link with what in the synoptic form of the tradition is the institution of the Lord's Supper is equally plain. Nor is it too much to claim that the general structure of the fourth gospel permits, is even favourable to, such a supposition. The first sign Jesus performs at Cana in Galilee began the clear sacramental acts and sayings of Jesus; the miracle of feeding the five thousand is presented in the fourth gospel in an eucharistic context; it is more than likely that ch. 15 is intended to do for the 'fruit of the vine' what ch. 6 did for the bread that was broken. On that assumption the rest of the chapter falls into place quite naturally, for it is concerned with what it means for the Lord himself to lay down his life, and for his disciples to be associated with him in his self-sacrifice. Union with Christ in his death, which is the key to the understanding of the eucharist, is also the theme of the whole of the chapter. The call to love with a love that will lay down its life; the assurance of the propriety of the hatred of the world (for if the world hated the Lord it cannot but hate his disciples), the call to repeat the words and actions of the Lord to the world, and the promise of the Spirit in order that that be done are all of them bound up with the church's eucharist. John has not recorded the institution of a sacramental rite, and on that all must agree; but he has given, in chs. 6 and 15, a carefully worked out and a very profound eucharistic theology, though this interpretation of the two chapters will not be universally accepted.

1

The Old Testament characteristically gives an historical interpretation to the figure of Israel as the vine of God's planting. In later Judaism it became possible to give a mystical interpretation of the metaphor. The appearance of the story of the vineyard in Mark 12$^{1-9}$ suggests that it is right to continue an historical interpretation here in John.

'*my Father is the vinedresser*': He has in his care both the vine itself (Jesus) and the branches (the disciples). The metaphor well sets out the intimacy of the relationship between Christ and his disciples; it must not be counted against it that it cannot, in the nature of things, depict as forcefully the intimacy of the relationship between Father and Son as between them and the disciples.

2

'*Every branch of mine that bears no fruit*': This can be taken to make a primary reference to the Jews as the first unfruitful branch to be cut off. This would be a parallel thought to that of Romans 11^{17}ff, where the rejection of the Jews is brought into Paul's attempt at a theodicy. Cf. also Matt. 15^{13} and 21^{41}. But it seems more evident, in view of the words *of mine*, that the first thought was of apostate Christians.

'*he takes away . . . he prunes*': There is a punning sequence in these two verbs, suggesting that the two operations are not decisively different; both are certainly meant to serve the same end – the rich fruiting of the vine.

3

'*You are already made clean by the word which I have spoken to you*': The mention of cleansing was probably intended to recall the 'cleansing' offered to and accepted by the disciples at the supper when Jesus washed their feet. And though the statement here refers to a word, that could well be the case, for the mere act of lustration, as was noted, is in itself inoperative. Word and deed form a unity, and their final togetherness is in the actual crucifixion and resurrection of the Lord; and the proclamation of both manifests them as the salvation of God.

4

'*Abide in me, and I in you*': It is not felicitous to translate the Greek conjunction in this instance by *and*. Better 'Abide in me, as I abide in you', with the intention of seeking unceasing loyalty from the disciple.

6

Here the movement of metaphor is not an immediate help to clarity. But the disciple who ceases to 'abide in Christ' is in the position of the branch that is no longer on the vinestock. The branch is no longer a branch, but just a piece of wood; and it is treated properly as a piece of wood when it is cast on to the fire. There is no implication of eternal fires of judgement in the verse. A disciple remains a truly human person only as he accepts Christ and remains in him.

9
'*As the Father has loved me, so have I loved you; abide in my love*': The whole sentence, imperative included, is in the aorist tense. The first two clauses are thus made to refer to the finished act of love by which Jesus, in his life, death and glorification, manifested the love of the Father. The imperative in its aorist form makes the injunction specially emphatic.

11
'*that your joy may be full*': 'Complete' is perhaps a better word.

15¹²⁻¹⁷   IN LOVE AND OBEDIENCE

¹²'*This is my commandment, that you love one another as I have loved you.* ¹³*Greater love has no man than this, that a man lay down his life for his friends.* ¹⁴*You are my friends if you do what I command you.* ¹⁵*No longer do I call you servants,^a for the servant^b does not know what his master is doing; but I have called you friends, for all that I have heard from my Father I have made known to you.* ¹⁶*You did not choose me, but I chose you and appointed you that you should go and bear fruit and that your fruit should abide; so that whatever you ask the Father in my name, he may give it to you.* ¹⁷*This I command you, to love one another.*'

a Or *slaves.*
b Or *slave.*

The life of the new Israel has now been disclosed as in essence the historical and ultra-historical existence of the Son, and as the out-flowing of that life into the branches of the true vine. But the love that is of the essence of the life of God's people is not something that flows vertically only, from Father to Son, from Father and Son to the disciples; nor is its movement exhausted when the love of Father and

Son for the disciple is returned in love and obedience. The love that is the real sap of the vine is, as it were, horizontal in movement as well; it must flow between disciples, not exclusively down to them from God and up from them to him. Jesus states this in form of an imperative, and sometimes Christians have wondered whether love can ever be commanded. The answer is found in the very nature of the love that is so enjoined. It had been the fatally easy error of the old Israel to suppose that the descending love of God was for her alone, or at least that it laid no great missionary obligations upon her. If the love came down, was that not sufficient warrant for its reception without any further commitment? So to the new Israel, chosen out of the membership of the old, it is important to make clear at the very start that something more is required than the mere acceptance and acknowledgement of the love of God; it must overflow into neighbourly relationships. This is properly the subject of an injunction. The imperative form of the saying is quite in order.

But immediately the love of God's people has been enjoined as a social obligation, its character is restated with force. The divine love is the greatest of all loves, a love that can bring a man to lay down his life for his friends, as Jesus is about to lay down his life for his friends. Christian love is to be of this kind. Here is John's equivalent to the synoptic demand that the disciple should take up his cross and follow Jesus, knowing that whoever would save his life will lose it, and whoever loses it for the sake of Christ and the gospel will in fact save it (cf. Mark 8³⁴ᶠ and //). If the disciples can understand this, then they will have passed the great divide marking off the life of the new Israel from that of the old, or the world. The disciples had been accustomed to call Jesus 'Rabbi' or 'Lord'; and the proper correlative word for 'Lord' was 'servant' or, even better, 'slave'. But to recognize the truth of what Jesus is now saying, to understand what was involved in his death, this is to enter into a new set of relationships, as indeed the symbol of the feet-washing had emphasized. 'You call me Teacher and Lord; and you are right, for so I am' (13¹³), but this did not prevent Jesus from doing an act quite the reverse of the usual relationship of Lord to slave; and in so doing he transformed the relationship, or perhaps better, exposed it for what it really had been all the time.

Jesus is now accepting the fact that the disciples are those who understand what his death, his departure really means. They are thus part of that intimate fellowship in which there is complete openness between all parties. So has Jesus made known to them what it is the Father is doing in the incarnation, and now especially in the departure and return of the Son. But the disciples must not suppose that the fellowship thus created is of their making; that in some way they have by their own choosing or wisdom placed themselves in the privileged position they occupy. On the contrary it has been entirely on the Lord's initiative that each and all of them has been called into the intimacy and strength of the community of God's new people. Such a choice of the disciples was purposive, and the purpose was that the disciples should 'go' and bear fruit. It is interesting to notice that when Jesus says he has 'appointed' the disciples, he uses the same word as is used of his 'laying down his life', and that when he states that the disciples were appointed to 'go', he uses the same word as is used of his 'going' to the Father. These are certain, if subtle, indications of the identity of destiny and fortune that the disciple shares with his Lord. If the disciples enter upon this life, they will bear fruit, and the fruit, Jesus says, will abide (v. 16). By this is meant that through the costly mission of the church there will be an accession of converts to the faith, who will not fall away but remain loyal and steadfast. Once more, when it has been made clear what the costliness of being in the circle of intimate sacrificial love is, Jesus states that his whole dealing with the disciples was to the end that they might be brought to the point of asking from the Father what they needed. And again it is important to emphasize that this is not an irresponsible invitation to irresponsible petitionary prayer; rather is it a firm placing of the disciple in that context of a life laid down in love that is the strong plea, in action that is passion and passion that is action, that the Father would use the sacrifice for the salvation of the world. The section ends with a repetition of the command: the disciples are to love one another. This is the basis of all their outflowing service.

ဆ

12

'*This is my commandment*': *Commandment*, not commandments. The whole set of injunctions that follow from the words and works of Jesus can be stated in this one implication: Christians owe love to one another. This is not a narrowing from universalism into a Christian, ecclesiastical parochialism; rather it is a binding together of the whole body of disciples in order that their mission to the world might be more effectively undertaken.

13

'*Greater love has no man than this, that a man lay down his life for his friends*': Again, this is not to narrow the range of the love of Christ, or of his disciples. In a gospel which speaks of God's love for the world (3^{16}, etc.) and of Jesus as him who takes away the sin of the world (1^{29}) it is not likely that Christian love would be so restricted. But the love kindled within the Christian fellowship will, like the Saviour's love, work for the saving of the world.

15

'*the servant does not know what his master is doing*': A *master*, or 'Lord', can give orders to his slaves and expect to be obeyed. By the reversal of roles which Jesus had assumed at the supper, he showed that this was not to be his relationship to his disciples. Rather has he come to where they are and obliterated the distinction between master and slave. So he can be nothing other than their 'friend', one who naturally confides his hopes and purposes to those he loves.

16

'*You did not choose me*': This makes it plain, for those at the Last Supper and for every generation of disciples since, that, however much things may appear, and even feel, to the contrary, it is Christ who has chosen them to be disciples, not they themselves. The initiative in Christian life is with the Lord.

'*that you should go and bear fruit*': This saying reflects the imagery of the vine, which in turn reflects the symbolism of the wine at the Eucharist. All the more reason, therefore, to see in the use of *go* a reflection of the fact that the Son is about to 'go' to the Father. The going of the disciples into the world will demand sacrifice too. And it is by sacrifice that fruit is borne; the death of the Son is a pre-requisite of the gospel being preached, and of the Gentiles hearing of the saving acts of God (cf. 12^{20}ff.).

15^{18-27} IN PERSECUTION AND WITNESS

^{18}'*If the world hates you, know that it has hated me before it hated you. ^{19}If you were of the world, the world would love its own; but because you are* *not of the world, but I chose you out of the world, therefore the world hates you. ²⁰Remember the word that I said to you, "A servant^a is not greater than his master." If they persecuted me, they will persecute you; if they kept my word, they will keep yours also. ²¹But all this they will do to you on my account, because they do not know him who sent me. ²²If I had not come and spoken to them, they would not have sin; but now they have no excuse for their sin. ²³He who hates me hates my Father also. ²⁴If I had not done among them the works which no one else did, they would not have sin; but now they have seen and hated both me and my Father. ²⁵It is to fulfil the word that is written in their law, "They hated me without a cause." ²⁶But when the Counsellor comes, whom I shall send to you from the Father, even the Spirit of truth, who proceeds from the Father, he will bear witness to me; ²⁷and you also are witnesses, because you have been with me from the beginning.*

a Or *slave.*

The new people of God, the branches growing from the one true vine, must expect that the processes analogous to pruning must go on for the sake of its own life with its Lord. It must also know that it must be inspired within itself by the grace of a mutual divine love, which will alone be adequate to sustain the members in their sacrificial bearing of fruit in the world. Now, with the words John quoted from Mark ringing even more loudly in the reader's ear, the evangelist proceeds to show how Jesus prepared the new Church for the world's savage encounter with it.

As these sayings are read it will be noticed that they incorporate material very similar indeed to that found in two places in the synoptic gospels. On the one hand John uses language reminiscent of the missionary charge to the Twelve found in Matthew 10, and on the other his language recalls the apocalyptic passages of Mark, Matthew and Luke (Mark 13 //). Again, it is not the case that John is intending to correct any inaccuracy of an historical kind in the earlier gospels or the traditional material that lay behind them; rather is he making clear what the real theological setting of such sayings and of the situation in which they were set really are. Thus in transposing material from a Galilean missionary charge John is claiming that it is only in the light of the crucifixion that the prediction of danger and persecution has any real significance, and as he uses material of a kind suited to the apocalypses of the synoptic material he is saying that whatever transpires at the end of the world will and can do nothing but make plain and universally public what took place when Jesus died.

The new community of the friends of Jesus, the Church, the new Israel of God will find itself hated by the world. This is but the inevitable transfer of the world's hatred of Jesus himself. Neither has the Church any ground for resentment at the world's attitude. Jesus reminds them of what he has said to them already 'A servant is not greater than his master' (13^{16}). On the previous occasion when Jesus said that, he was making plain the nature of what he had done for the disciples in washing their feet (i.e. in laying down his life for them). So here the reference is in all probability to the need for the disciple to be ready to lay down his life, together with his Lord, for the life of the world. It would be erroneous for the Church to suppose that the world's opposition was to itself; it is really opposition to Jesus Christ.* It is on account of him that the disciples will meet hatred, opposition and persecution.

Jesus then analyses the attitude of the world, first to what he has spoken, and second to what he has done. The teaching he has given was sufficient to leave them without excuse for their unbelief. Their resistance to the truth so uttered and made manifest leaves them in a state which can only be characterized as 'sin', or sinful. This is not to equate unbelief and sin, but it is to make it quite plain that some moral conditions in the lives of men may produce such insensitiveness to the truth that when the truth is heard it is rejected. Men can be blinded by prejudice; they can also be blinded by moral delinquency. The unbelief of the Jews who had all the advantages given beforehand by God to enable them to recognize the Messiah when he came reflects a moral and spiritual delinquency which is exposed in all four gospels. It must be said immediately in parenthesis that the Gentiles are in no better plight; their moral defections also produce unbelief (cf. Romans 1^{18-32}; 11^{17-24}). But again, the opposition to Jesus is more than a reaction to an historical person; it is really an opposition to and a rejection of God. This is what unbelief really is – a rejection of God, not of propositions about him: this is the theological exposure of the hatred of the world. The same things have to be

* Luke's narrative of the conversion of St Paul makes the same point in recording the Lord's Question to Saul: 'Saul, Saul, why are you persecuting me?'

said about the works of Jesus. Once more, it must be emphasized that the evangelist is not referring to the works as mere thaumaturgies or 'sheer miracles'; the Jews had their own supply of miracle workers (cf. Luke 11^{19}). The works of Jesus were not offensive to them and rejected by them just because they were in this sense 'miraculous'. What gave offence to the Jews was the claim that the works, like the words, revealed the divine nature of the Son. It was not simply the healing of a man born blind that gave offence, e.g. to the authorities (ch. 9), but the fact that the wonder was wrought on the sabbath day, thus constituting a claim by the wonder worker to be in a position to override the divinely given law. And this core of the offence is endorsed at the end of the story when the newly gifted man sees in Jesus the proper object of that worship which, as a Jew, he knew belonged rightly to God alone. So to reject the works, as to reject the words, is to do more than refuse to believe that Jesus worked miracles; it is to refuse to believe that in his person the eternal Word has become incarnate for the salvation of men.

Jesus sees the rejection of his people as something divinely revealed, and foretold in the Old Testament. He cites a phrase from Psalm 35^{19}: 'They hate me without a cause.' All rebellion against God, all rejection of what he says and does for men, is fundamentally an irrationality. It can have no real justification. This is the great mystery of iniquity, of sin: it can have no real reason assigned to it. Yet, as one of the constant factors in the life of God's people, who have themselves known what it is to expose those who do not believe, the present rejection of Jesus must come both as a reaction already recognized in history, and as the most fateful example of all.

In face of such a rejection, which seems to be so final in its unbelief, the Church may well think that her mission is impossible. It is, or it would be if the members of the Church were left just to their own resources. But, as Jesus now reminds his followers, as they move out to the world that hates and rejects them as it has hated and rejected Jesus himself, there will come to the Church the new Counsellor. He will bear witness to Jesus. That is the major premiss in the missionary motivation and equipment of the Church. Only if that be true (as it is!) can the Church go on to obey the Lord's next injunction – 'and you also are witnesses.' The words remind the reader of the end of Luke's gospel and the beginning of Acts, where it is made clear that the risen Lord commissions his followers to be witnesses to him (Luke 24^{48}), in Jerusalem, in all Judea, in Samaria and to the end of the earth (Acts 1^8). The substance of the witness is to be the suffering and death of Christ and his resurrection; and the forgiveness of sin that is offered to men in his name. John has incorporated this witness in his own profound way in this chapter; it is not insignificant that he should close the chapter with a saying that so closely reminds the reader of the missionary charge to the disciples given by the risen Lord. For it is from that profound theological situation that he wants to present the next chapter.

ಬಿ

18

'*If the world hates you*': There is nothing suppositious about this! The *if* has the same force as it has in another context in Colossians: 'If then you have been raised with Christ' (Col. 3^1) – which does not mean that perhaps a Christian has, and perhaps he has not, been raised with Christ, but rather 'since' or 'because' he has been so raised. It is the same here. 'Because the world hates you, know that it hated me.'

19

'*If you were of the world*': *If* here indicates an unfulfilled condition.

20

'*If they persecuted me . . . if they kept my word*': The words and works of Jesus had produced a double result. On the whole it had been true that the Word had come to his own home and his own people had not received him. But some who saw his works did believe in him (e.g. 2^{23}). The Lord is telling the disciples that their words and works for him will achieve the same double result.

21

'*all this they will do . . . on my account, because they do not know him who sent me*': It is Jesus as the one sent by the Father that his contemporaries found so unacceptable. They thus manifested their ignorance of what God is really like.

22

'*but now they have no excuse*': 'But now' carries with it the implication that the facts are as stated: Jesus has come and spoken to them, and no excuse can properly be offered.

25

'*It is to fulfil the word that is written in their law*': On the general conception of the fulfilment of scripture in John see the Introduction (pp.

19–20, 46). Here the implication is that had the Jews really known their own scripture they would have been able to read their own condemnation in it.

'*They hated me without a cause*': A quotation from Psalm 35^{19} or 69^4. Bernard argues that the citation is really from the latter: 'More in number than the hairs of my head are those who hate me without a cause', on the reasonable grounds that this Psalm was accepted as Messianic. Both Psalms however suit the situation of the discourse on the eve of the arrest and trial.

26

Here alone is it explicitly stated that the Spirit will bear witness, though the real substance of the activity, viz. making plain what the words and works of Jesus really mean, is set out at length in this last discourse.

27

'*and you also are witnesses*': The proximity of the statement about the witness of the disciples and that of the Spirit is probably intended to link the two. If so, the two sayings together echo the thought of the synoptic apocalypse, that the Spirit will give the disciple the right word to say at the right time (cf. Mark 13^{11} //).

'*you have been with me from the beginning*': It is natural, tempting and easy to suggest that this means, and alone can mean, that the disciples have been with Jesus since his ministry began. The thought behind it would parallel that of the writer of Acts as he set out the qualifications required of Judas' successor: 'One of the men who have accompanied us during all the time that the Lord Jesus went in and out among us, beginning from the baptism of John until the day he was taken up from us' (Acts 1^{21f}). But it is more usual for John to use the word *beginning* in a more theological sense, and refer to the beginning of all things. In a sense the disciples, as unborn, could not have been with the Word as the world was created 'in the beginning'; but the idea is not far from Paul's phrase that Christians have been chosen in Christ 'before the foundation of the world' (Eph. 1^4). The only other use of the phrase in John is also ambiguous. It states that the devil has been 'a murderer from the beginning', and that too could mean from the very beginning of time, or from the beginning of whatever active span he has had, i.e. either from his own beginning or the beginning of the order in which he appears. Other uses of the word in a somewhat different phrase are also indeterminate. At 6^{64} the evangelist says that Jesus 'knew from the first [lit. from the beginning] who those were that did not believe, and who it was that should betray him'. It is only if one thinks such a phrase would imply an unacceptable theory of predestination that one would be compelled to translate 'from the first' in an evident attempt to avoid the suggestion that the Lord's knowledge in any way shifted the responsibility of unbelief or betrayal. But such an assumption is not necessary, and in that case a translation 'from the beginning' would be quite possible. In 16^4 the narrative reads: 'I did not say these things to you from the beginnning [a different preposition in the Greek from that used here] because I was with you'. This is a clear reference to the start of the ministry, but for various reasons, chief of which is that another preposition is used, this verse cannot be held to determine the meaning of '*from the beginning*' in 15^{27}.

16$^{1-33}$ *The Mission of the Disciples*

Mark 13$^{9-11}$
Matthew 10$^{17-20}$
Matthew 24^9
Luke 12^{11}
Luke 21$^{12-15}$
Luke 24^{48}
Acts 1^8

Once again John provides his readers with an historical key to the theological significance of the contents of a chapter: he has prefaced ch. 16 with a saying which echoes the words of the risen Jesus to the body of the disciples after his resurrection from the dead (John 15^{27}, cf. Luke 24^{48}). As chapter 16 unfolds the reader discovers material highly reminiscent both of the apocalyptic sections of the synoptic gospels, and of the missionary charges given, in the synoptic tradition, to the disciples while they were still in Galilee (see passages cited above); yet the chapter is the last section of the discourse in which Jesus is trying to make plain to the disciples what his 'going', or death, really means. In ch. 15 Jesus has made clear what the nature of the Church is that God has planted in the world, and how necessary it is that he should care for it as a vinedresser cares for a vinestock, in order that it should bear fruit in the world. He has spoken of the character of the love that must bind the church together, the same self-sacrificing love that he is about to exercise in his own self-giving. He speaks very plainly indeed about the inevitable hostility of the world, but assures the disciples that with the promised gift of the

Paraclete they will be able to be his witnesses. In ch. 16 he proceeds to speak of that witness with a realism that reveals its considerable costliness. For the disciples there is a demand that will be costly to meet; but for the world there is an inescapable and ineluctable judgement. But such judgement is not depicted as it commonly was (and as it still often commonly is) as an event to take place at some time in the future when human history comes to an end: rather is it a continuous separation of church from world, in which all the finality of the traditional eschatology is found. So the mission of the disciples of Jesus Christ, whether undertaken in Galilee before the climax of the Lord's death in Jerusalem, or prosecuted after his resurrection from the dead, or seen as preceding and even producing the final conflict between good and evil that will immediately precede the eschatological end, is always a mission effecting a final separation, a 'last' judgement. But the very possibility of the judgement involved in Christian mission rests on it being a proclamation of the real meaning of the departure and return, the death and glorification of Jesus Christ, the Son of the Father. The mission in Galilee, the discourse at the Last Supper, the continuing missionary work of the Church in history, the final acts of hostility used by the world in the end – these are all relative to and wholly dependent upon the one central reality of the departure and return of Jesus.

So in a sense the discourse, as it comes to its end, provides a forewarning to the disciples, not only of the fact that their Lord is about to give his life for them, but also of the fact that this will eventually involve them in the same costly mission. Yet the evangelist is anchored securely in the actual historical situation, for the chapter ends with Jesus predicting the scattering of the disciples to their homes, while he is left alone (cf. 16³² and Mark 14²⁷ᶠ).

DEPARTURE AND JUDGEMENT

16 ¹*I have said all this to you to keep you from falling away.* ²*They will put you out of the synagogues; indeed, the hour is coming when whoever kills you will think he is offering service to God.* ³*And they will do this because they have not known the Father, nor me.* ⁴*But I have said these things to you, that when their hour comes you may remember that I told you of them.*

'I did not say these things to you from the beginning, because I was with you. ⁵But now I am going to him who sent me; yet none of you asks me, "Where are you going?"⁶But because I have said these things to you, sorrow has filled your hearts. ⁷Nevertheless I tell you the truth: it is to your advantage that I go away, for if I do not go away, the Counsellor will not come to you; but if I go, I will send him to you. ⁸And when he comes, he will convince the world of sin and of righteousness and of judgement: ⁹of sin, because they do not believe in me; ¹⁰of righteousness, because I go to the Father, and you will see me no more; ¹¹of judgement, because the ruler of this world is judged.

¹²'I have yet many things to say to you, but you cannot bear them now. ¹³When the Spirit of truth comes, he will guide you into all the truth; for he will not speak on his own authority, but whatever he hears he will speak, and he will declare to you the things that are to come. ¹⁴He will glorify me, for he will take what is mine and declare it to you. ¹⁵All that the Father has is mine; therefore I said that he will take what is mine and declare it to you.'

Jesus has spoken to the disciples about their future witness for him in almost cruelly realistic terms: they are to experience the hatred and persecution of the world which is about to be focused upon him. Their witness has to be given, if at all, in such a world. Yet his plain speaking has been a task of love, for he has told them such unpalatable truths in order to save them from an even more unpalatable fate – that of 'falling away' from the community of the friends of the Son. The discomforts they suffer as his witnesses, however severe, are infinitely preferable to suffering the condemnation of those who in falling away reject Christ and become part of the world.

With this made plain, Jesus can speak more specifically about some of the consequences of remaining with him. This will involve ex-communication from the synagogue, and possibly the sacrifice of life. Jesus has poise and charity enough to recognize that the opposition his followers meet, though final, will be sincere: the Jews will think that in opposing his followers they are properly serving God. The point was exemplified in the attitude of Paul before his conversion as he himself came to view it: 'I myself was convinced that I ought to do many things in opposing the name of Jesus of Nazareth. And I did so in Jerusalem; I not only shut up many of the saints in prison, by authority from the chief priests, but when they were put to death I cast my vote against them' (Acts 26⁹ᶠ). Paul also illustrates admirably the further point that opposition to Christ's disciples derived from an ignorance of the Father and of Jesus Christ as his Son: once he came to know Jesus for the person he was, he 'was not disobedient to the heavenly vision' (Acts 26^{19}), but himself became a witness, gladly accepting all the cost involved. Thus to be forewarned, says Jesus, is to be forearmed (v. 4). But the equipment of the Christian is more than being warned of what may happen; it is to learn that suffering is transmuted, that tribulation has meaning, and that even death loses its sting and can be faced with confidence, victory and joy.

While he has been with them it has not been necessary for Jesus so to prepare them for the future. The observant reader of the gospels might well ask whether such teaching would have been even credible to the Twelve before this time; the synoptic predictions of the Passion point quite the other way. If the Twelve were mystified and puzzled that their Lord should suffer, they would have been even more bewildered had they been told the details now disclosed to them of their own 'filling out' of the sufferings of their Lord. The central truth involved here is, however, not concerned with the time at which a statement is made, but with the fact that the real defence of the disciple against the ills that befall him is the presence of Christ with him. Until now the disciples have experienced that presence in a bodily reality. The prediction of the Lord's death, bringing the final removal of his bodily presence, has only produced sorrow in the hearts of the eleven. They have not asked Jesus 'Where are you going?': if they had, they would have had a reassuring answer that his 'going' was not just 'going away', but also 'return'. This point has been made to them, not in reply to the question 'Where are you going?' but in reply to a request for information about the way. Not unsurprisingly the profound instruction that his 'going' is also his return has not yet sunk in. So Jesus repeats, in somewhat different form, his assurance that it is for the good of the disciples that he leaves them, and can then send them the Paraclete who will, as promised, abide with them for ever, teach them all things, bring to their remembrance all that Christ has said, and bear witness with them to the nature of the Son and of his service to men.

But the coming of the Paraclete is not only of significance for the disciples, for the church; it has a profound importance also for the world. For he will *convince the world of sin and of righteousness and of judgement* (v. 8). It has already been made clear that the world cannot receive the Spirit (14¹⁷), and what is being stated now is that his coming to the church and his work in it will expose certain facts about the human situation. First, he will be able to expose the world's sin, because the witness of the Church through which the Spirit will operate will bring men to realize (as Saul the Pharisee was brought to realize) that they are sinful beings, and that the death of Jesus occurred because of their sin. The interpreter must be careful not to expound the statement so as to suggest that sin is unbelief; the point is rather that sin is a clouding of the power of spiritual insight which has results in a rejection of Jesus. It is interesting to recall that Luke's story of the coming of the Spirit in Acts is followed by a preaching from Peter that produced precisely this effect of conviction of sin: 'When they heard this they were cut to the heart' (Acts 2³⁷). The sin of the world is as it were concentrated in and focused on the rejection of Jesus, culminating in his crucifixion. The Spirit's witness in and through the Church will bring this home to the world.

Second, the Paraclete will expose to the world the righteousness of God. The same witness that will bring the world to feel 'cut to the heart' for its sin will also bring it to recognize that God's purpose for his people, as it was incorporated in his Son, has in fact been accomplished, and that the death of Christ was not his passage into nothingness or into an ineffective life in Sheol, but a journey to the Father and a return to his own, so as to bring to ultimate fulfilment the inclusive salvation of God. No doubt such salvation has some connexion with *righteousness* as usually understood; but the use of the word in this verse (the only one in which it is used in the fourth gospel) approximates much more closely to its meaning in Second Isaiah. In the earlier English versions (A.V. and R.V.) Isa. 51⁵ was translated 'My righteousness is near, my salvation is gone forth'. In the R.S.V. this has become 'My deliverance draws near speedily, my salvation has gone forth'. For the prophet of the exile righteousness was thus not so much a certain moral quality as the securing of a victory for a specific cause; this is the meaning of the evangelist here. The witness of the Church in and through the Spirit will convince men that in the death of Jesus God's purpose has triumphed; his *righteousness* has been effectively demonstrated in that the mission of Jesus has not been frustrated by death, but rather for the first time brought to the point of accomplishment. Another word of Isaiah will find fulfilment: 'All the ends of the earth shall see the salvation of our God' (Isa. 52^{10}).

Third, the Paraclete will expose to the world the judgement, the final verdict passed upon it. For the same witness to the real meaning of the death of Jesus will inescapably make plain that part of the story will have to be that of the defeat of Christ's adversary in and through the events of his death. A superficial review of Christ's end will suggest that he suffered defeat; but a review under the instruction and witness of the Spirit will show that he really achieved a victory in and through defeat. It is important to remember that the Greek perfect tense is used here: 'The prince of this world has been judged already' (v. 11). From what vantage point is this judgement made? Is the suggestion correct that it is fashioned from the evangelist's not uncommon 'perspective of the Church'? Not necessarily so; for it is quite possible and reasonable to claim that the perspective is that of the Last Supper itself. The synoptists report sayings which leave it clear that Jesus thought of his own death as a 'baptism'. When the sons of Zebedee ask him for seats of splendour at his coming in his glory, Jesus asked them 'Are you able to drink the cup that I drink, or to be baptized with the baptism with which I am baptized?' (Mark 10^{38}). Luke records another saying: 'I have a baptism to be baptized with; and how I am constrained until it is accomplished!' (Luke 12^{50}). There is thus a sense in which the baptism at the end of his life (his crucifixion) has already been enacted, though enacted to await fulfilment, as was the baptism at the beginning of his ministry. That baptism was followed in the synoptic tradition by the story of the struggle with the devil in the wilderness, from which, in all the synoptics, Jesus emerges victorious. That does not of course rob the final encounter of its reality or its agony; but it does mean that however real the encounter the outcome is assured, at least to him who accepts the assurance. Jesus was confident of the outcome of this last encounter; his adversary, the prince of this world, would certainly be defeated, because he had already suffered defeat. Christian disciples can have no ground for query or complaint as they encounter the same adversary, for the conditions in which they meet him are no different from those in which their Lord faced him at the cross: 'The ruler of this world has been judged' (v. 11).

Next follows a brief summary of what the departure of the Lord will involve. It means that he is unable to say many things at this particular time, because the disciples are unable to bear them before he leaves (v. 12). But when the Spirit of truth comes he will guide the company of God's people into all the truth (or, with the reading 'in' instead of 'into', in the whole realm of the truth). The language used is reminiscent of the Psalmist's descriptions of God leading his people across the wilderness (Psalms 77^{20}; 78^{72}). The Spirit will not bring any new truth, as if he were a source of truth independent of the Son. He is not an independent authority, but speaks only what he learns. He will declare to the disciples *things to come*. Three possibilities of exposition are open: first, the *things to come* could be the matters attendant upon the 'last day', the eschatological end of the world; but in view of the whole trend of this gospel, particularly of this section and context, this seems the least likely. Second, a general promise of prophetic ability to 'foretell' events, in the way, e.g., that Agabus foretold a world-wide famine in the days of Claudius (Acts 11^{27ff}). But this seems uncoordinated with this context, and should probably be rejected. This leaves the third meaning as the most probable. It involves taking the words as having the perspective of the Last Supper, and so thinking of the cross as something future. On this interpretation the promise is simply another in the series that Jesus repeats from an earlier part of the discourse, and means that the Spirit will bring to the disciples the true meaning of his crucifixion. Without the Spirit's illumination Christ's death would be complete tragedy; under his instruction it will be the great victory of the Lord over the adversary, the decisive moment in the salvation of the world.

This interpretation finds confirmation in the way the passage continues: '*He will glorify me, for he will take what is mine and declare it to you*' (v. 14). To glorify is precisely to make plain that the humiliation of apparent defeat is nothing else than the triumph of real victory: the Spirit accepts the victory for what it really is, and makes its true character plain to the disciples. And if it be objected that such glory is always eschatological, then it must be remembered that John's distinctive contribution is to affirm that this same eschatological glory has in fact been displayed and manifested in history at the crucifixion of Jesus. And this fact can be known, under his instruction, by Christ's disciples, even in this world.

But it is not just the fact of a killing by crucifixion that the Spirit will make known. The disciples could learn about that by the simple process of observation or hearsay. They are to learn that the death on the cross is only part of what they must know and can learn about Jesus from the death he undergoes. To set forth Christ's glory as the victory on the cross will mean letting the disciples know '*what is his*'; and, as the Lord goes on to say '*All that the Father has is mine*' (v. 15). So to understand the apparently simple fact that Jesus dies upon a cross the disciple must learn, under the instruction of the Spirit, the depths of the relationship between Father and Son in the Godhead.

രു

1

'*I have said all this to you*': *All*, i.e., that had been concerned with the hostility of the world for Jesus and for them.

'*to keep you from falling away*': In Mark's account of the Passion, when Jesus foretold the desertion of the disciples, Peter exploded 'Even though they all fall away, I will not' (Mark 14^{29}). This saying would have a particular significance in the perspective of the Church – to fall away was to become apostate.

2

'*They will put you out of the synagogues*': No doubt this saying also had special significance in the early days of the Church, when many of its converts came from Judaism. Excommunication could be imposed in three degrees, for seven days, for thirty days, and indefinitely. (It is worth recording, in view of the story of the man born blind, and his pertness during his second interview by the authorities, that the seven-day ban was largely used for insult offered to religious authority!)

'*indeed, the hour is coming*': This is a clear reference to a chronological future. But what is theologically important is that the future persecution of Christians flows from, and is one with, the hostility to Jesus which will, in the next hours, bring him to death. Their future persecution, in a real sense, begins when the world attacks Christ.

4

'*when their hour comes*': Jesus will have his hour, and it will appear to be tragedy and disaster, though it will in fact be triumph; his enemies will have their hour (chronologically indistinguishable from his!) which will seem to be victory, though it will in fact be eschatologically as well as temporally defeat.

'*from the beginning*': cf. note to 15^{27}.

5

'*none of you asks me, "Where are you going?"*': The present tense is important, and might be better translated: 'None of you is asking me ...' The statement formally contradicts 13^{36} (and possibly 14^5). Jesus is speaking of the reaction of the eleven to the statement he has just made: the more he repeats that he will be going away, the more their human sorrow prevents them from probing the depth of his announcement.

7

'*it is to your advantage that I go away*': The only other times when John uses this expression is when Caiaphas speaks of the benefit to the Jewish nation that this one man should die for it! (11^{50}; 18^{14}). These are fine examples of Johannine irony.

9

'*of sin, because they do not believe in me*': The phrase to 'convict of sin' has already been used at 8^{46}, and, as Barrett observes, that example is probably sufficient for rejecting the suggestion that the same Greek phrase should here be translated 'Convince in regard to sin' meaning 'convince the world of its error about sin, making it plain that sin consists in not believing in me'. Of the other alternatives it seems right to reject the translation which treats the Greek *Hoti* as meaning 'in that', which would make unbelief the sin. So the remaining possibility is to be accepted and the phrase understood to mean: 'convince the world of sin because sin reached its real height of offence when men failed to believe in Jesus Christ'. John, as Barrett observes, seems to be giving the fundamental ground of conviction of sin (and righteousness and judgement) rather than stating their content. The Spirit can convict the world of its sin because sin is focused in the rejection and killing of Jesus.

10

'*because I go to the Father, and you will see me no more*': The two are ingredients in the one event which is to embody the ineluctable purpose of God. The world will learn of what God's righteousness is when the story of the 'going' is complete.

11

'*because the ruler of this world is judged*': the final outcome of the 'going' of the Lord in death will be the complete reversal of the 'judgement' that the world will have passed on him. They will have judged him worthy of death, and committed (judged) him to the death penalty.

But in fact he will rise to eternal life, and it is his enemies that must then face a death that is more than physical cessation.

13
'*he will not speak on his own authority*': Any more than Jesus himself, who only spoke what he heard from the Father (12⁴⁹).
'*the things that are to come*': This is a phrase whose application ought to be made as from the last supper. The Spirit will show the disciples what is to happen, i.e. what the real meaning of the events is, when Jesus is arrested, tried, condemned to death and crucified. The disciples, at the time that the gospel was written, were already living in the age of the 'things that were to come', in the time of 'realized' eschatology.

14
It seems necessary to emphasize that when the Spirit glorifies Christ he is doing more than 'anticipate' Christ's eschatological functions (Barrett). For the eschatological functions of Christ have at least in part been performed by his death, resurrection and glorification. This part of Johannine eschatology is properly described as 'realized'.

16¹⁶⁻³³ THE FUTURE, PROXIMATE AND ULTIMATE

¹⁶'*A little while, and you will see me no more; again a little while, and you will see me.*' ¹⁷*Some of his disciples said to one another, 'What is this that he says to us, "A little while, and you will not see me, and again a little while, and you will see me"; and, "because I go to the Father"?' ¹⁸They said, 'What does he mean by "a little while"? We do not know what he means.' ¹⁹Jesus knew that they wanted to ask him; so he said to them, 'Is this what you are asking yourselves, what I meant by saying, "A little while, and you will not see me, and again a little while, and you will see me"? ²⁰Truly, truly, I say to you, you will weep and lament, but the world will rejoice; you will be sorrowful, but your sorrow will turn into joy. ²¹When a woman is in travail she has sorrow, because her hour has come; but when she is delivered of the child, she no longer remembers the anguish, for joy that a childᵃ is born into the world. ²²So you have sorrow now, but I will see you again and your hearts will rejoice, and no one will take your joy from you. ²³In that day you will ask me no questions. Truly, truly, I say to you, if you ask anything of the Father, he will give it to you in my*

name. ²⁴Hitherto you have asked nothing in my name; ask, and you will receive, that your joy may be full.

²⁵'I have said this to you in figures; the hour is coming when I shall no longer speak to you in figures but tell you plainly of the Father. ²⁶In that day you will ask in my name; and I do not say to you that I shall pray the Father for you; ²⁷for the Father himself loves you, because you have loved me and have believed that I came from the Father. ²⁸I came from the Father and have come into the world; again, I am leaving the world and going to the Father.'

²⁹His disciples said, 'Ah, now you are speaking plainly, not in any figure! ³⁰Now we know that you know all things, and need none to question you; by this we believe that you came from God.' ³¹ Jesus answered them, 'Do you now believe? ³²The hour is coming, indeed it has come, when you will be scattered, every man to his home, and will leave me alone; yet I am not alone, for the Father is with me. ³³I have said this to you, that in me you may have peace. In the world you have tribulation; but be of good cheer, I have overcome the world.'

a Greek a human being

At this point of the discourse Jesus comes down quite unambiguously into the present situation of the disciples at the supper table. 'A little while, and you will see me no more; again a little while, and you will see me' (v. 16). Within a few hours he will be taken from them in death, and they will see him no more 'after the flesh'. But equally truly, in a little while, they will see him again, in his resurrection appearances which John records. The commentators are not slow to point out the ambiguity of this unambiguous descent into the concrete historical situation: the language a little while and you will not see me; and again a little while and you will is applicable, they indicate, not only to the period between the burial and the resurrection appearances, but also to the interval between the ascension and the parousia, the 'second coming'. But such ambiguous unambiguity is wholly characteristic of John and of the things he is trying to say: the parousia, the final 'coming', of Jesus is not dissociated from his coming in the flesh, nor from his coming as the risen and glorified Lord to visit his disciples. John has used this method of writing in order to make his point that history and eschatology cannot, in any deep understanding of the Christian faith, be separated, at least to the extent of holding that historical time has been charged with eschatological significance by the life and death and glorification of the Son.

The disciples, no less than later commentators, were puzzled. And, like their successors, they fastened on the more tantalizing, if less profound, aspect of the puzzle. Jesus had spoken at an earlier stage of 'going to the Father'; now he was speaking of 'just a little while'. It was the apparently simpler chronological puzzle that held their attention, and Jesus noticed this. He sought to use that focus of attention to lead them to reflect on the other aspect which puzzled them. He began by contrasting their mourners' sorrow with the delight of the world that he would be put out of the way. He then stated firmly the complete reversal that would take place 'in the little while' of which he had spoken: *'Your sorrow will turn into joy'* (v. 20). He then associates their change of mood with that of a woman in childbirth who from suffering the pangs of labour passes to the delight of knowing that she has brought a child into the world. This figure had been used in the Old Testament to depict the coming of the Messianic community; e.g. in Isaiah 26^17-19: 'Like a woman with child, who writhes and cries out in her pangs, when she is near her time, so were we because of thee, O Lord; we were with child, we writhed, we have as it were brought forth wind. We have wrought no deliverance in the earth, and the inhabitants of the world have not fallen. The dead shall live, their bodies shall rise. O dwellers in the dust, awake and sing for joy! For thy dew is a dew of light, and on the land of the shades thou wilt let it fall.' The pangs that they will suffer for a little while are comparable to the pangs of a woman, to the pangs of Israel who through tribulation may bring a new people to birth. And though the birth of a new community of God's people was not an historical reality or possibility to Israel-after-the-flesh, it would now be possibility and actuality through the resurrection of the Son, through his 'departure' to the Father which is also his 'return'.

When the day comes that the new people of God is born, says Jesus, you will ask me no questions. The surpassing character of the reality will in itself demonstrate the justification of all that has preceded it. The coming of this new era is indicated by the stock eschatological phrase 'in that day', which is yet another indication of the way in which John seeks to impress upon his readers the eschatological character of human history as it has now been entered into by the eternal Word, and taken by him into the life of the eternal Godhead. When he returns to his own, human society will know within the bounds and the experiences of human history what the ultimate fellowship between God and man will be. And the end will show itself to have justified all the means that had to be employed, however difficult to understand and sorrowful to endure.

But in that day, when the Lord has returned to his own, they are encouraged to ask anything in the name of the Son; and the Father will give it. It is important again to note the setting of this promise, which cannot be used to justify any petitionary irresponsibility, as if once the resurrection were over Christian disciples could have things just as they wanted! On the contrary, once the resurrection is over, Christian disciples will know the joy of pain, the victory of defeat and the life that is in death. It is only then that they can be rightly invited to ask anything of the Father, knowing that it will be given in the name of the Son. So far they have not made petitions in Christ's name; after the resurrection that will be spiritually feasible. It is not unimportant that John here incorporates into the discourse words that are reminiscent of a saying from the Sermon on the Mount: 'Ask and you will receive' (v. 24, cf. Matt. 7^7: 'Ask and it shall be given you'). Even the Sermon on the Mount cannot really be understood save in the context of the crucifixion and resurrection of the Son of God. If disciples really ask in the name of Christ, then their petitions will be granted and their joy will be full, or complete.

Jesus has been trying throughout the discourse to convey to the disciples the real significance of the fact that he is about to die. To do so he has had to use veiled language of different kinds – to talk about the good shepherd (before the Last Supper), the vine and the branches, and the woman in labour being delivered of a child. But now the hour is coming when he will no longer have to speak in figurative or allusive language, but will be able to speak directly of the Father. This is another saying that can best be understood in the perspective of the Last Supper. The time when Jesus will be able to talk without mystery or puzzlement to the disciples about his death will be when it is passed and crowned with his glorification. Then, in the person of the Spirit, he will be able to speak directly of what 'going to the Father' has meant.

It is in this same eschatological time that will supervene upon the crucifixion that the disciples will themselves be able to direct petitions to the Father in a new and valid way. When Jesus adds that '*I do not say to you that I shall pray the Father for you*' (v. 26) he is indicating to the disciples that his office is not that of a less stern intermediary than the Father himself, as if Jesus would grant petitions which the Father would not. The basic theological reason for this is that the Father himself loves and has loved the disciples in their love of the Son and their belief in him. The discourse closes with an apt and pregnant summary: '*I came from the Father and have come into the world; again, I am leaving the world and going to the Father*' (v. 28). These are the two movements in the one 'coming' of the Son. Neither can properly be stated without the other. If Christianity is a religion of incarnation, as it is, it can nevertheless be grossly misunderstood unless it be also envisaged as a religion of the resurrection. And as a religion of resurrection it is not a religion with its saviour absent, but with its saviour present.

When Jesus said '*the hour is coming when I shall no longer speak to you in figures*' he did not add, as he had done at other times when he had used the phrase *the hour is coming*, the additional words 'and now is'. But the disciples seem to have thought that, even if he had not used the words, he had meant them. For now they seem to have found something intelligible to lay hold of. They at once respond to his statement of coming from and going to the Father by an expression of relief that he seemed to have forsaken enigma at last! '*Now you are speaking plainly, not in any figure*' (v. 29). But what they had forgotten was that this speech is itself still figurative; Jesus had left it quite plain that his 'journey' was not one that could be undertaken by any who wanted to 'go that way' (cf. 13³⁶); the language of a journey undertaken to God was inevitably figurative, covering the mystery of the death, resurrection and glorification of Jesus Christ. Yet in their understanding of his language the disciples had the confidence that he knew everything, and that questions were quite beside the point. No need any longer to pursue the query as to what he meant by *a little while*. Because he had at last spoken so directly of what he was about to do they confessed: '*By this we believe that you came from God*' (v. 30). Of course the assertion is deficient in that it picks up only one half of what Jesus had said about himself: his coming from the Father. Jesus does not point this out to them, but proceeds to tell them of what will follow in their (unrecognized) deficiency of understanding: '*The hour is coming, indeed it has come* [the phrase of present identification appears ominously at this point], *when you will be scattered, every man to his home, and will leave me alone; and yet I am not alone, for the Father is with me'* (v. 32). This statement of foreboding is a strong reminder of the synoptic narrative at the point when the company of Jesus and his disciples had reached the Mount of Olives, and Jesus, quoting Zechariah, said: 'You will all fall away [cf. John16¹:" *I have said all this to you to keep you from falling away*"]; for it is written, "I will strike the shepherd, and the sheep will be scattered". But after I am raised up, I will go before you to Galilee' (Mark $14^{27f.}$). John can state the foreboding as clearly as the synoptists; they can express the hope as clearly as John. But John has his own way of stating the hope, and the ground for it. The scattering of the disciples will leave him alone; but that is precisely what he will not be, for the Father will be with him, as he always is. Thus though the disciples will leave him alone, and in their eyes and the eyes of all men he will appear completely deserted, he has with him one who is more than all that are or will ever be against him – the Father in his power and mercy and glory. So the disciples have been 'forewarned'. It has all been done that the greeting '*Shalōm*' which he will use as he leaves them, may be a real and not a formal word. In spite of the turmoil of the time they will come to know his peace, which derives from the presence of the Father. They will continue in the world in which he has come, and come to die. They need not, they must not, be despondent. On the contrary they may be really full of good cheer. For already Jesus has overcome the world. He cannot be who he is and not be conqueror.

ॐ

16

'*and you will see me*': This evidently could mean 'in two or three days' time, after the resurrection'. But it could equally well refer to an eschatological event expected in the near future when the Parousia of the Lord would take place. It could also, as Barrett argues, be taken to include within it, as part of its meaning (cf. a similar use of 'coming' by the Father and the Son in 14^{23}), some sense of a vision of God realized by the Christian in his daily life.

Some manuscripts add to verse 16 the words: 'because I go to the Father', evidently to prepare for the latter part of the question in v.17; even if the reading be rejected, it is only necessary for the reader to refer back to an earlier passage of the discourse, in which two things have remained to puzzle the disciples – the point of chronology, and the point of theology. See the commentary.

20

'you will weep and lament': Words that are associated with death, especially *weep*, which is reserved for that purpose. Jesus is talking about his death.

21

The Old Testament passages which lie behind this verse make it plain that the evangelist is once again treating the historical event of the death of Jesus as at the same time an eschatological reality.

22

'but I will see you': A significant change from the promise of v. 16 that 'in a little while' the disciples will see him. It is not that the words are intended to guard against any hallucination on the part of the disciples, but rather that the effective reality of the new situation will not be that they see him, but that he will see them. To have the divine being *see* one is to have life.

23

'you will ask me no questions': The Greek word for 'question' can mean *ask* in both of its senses – to question and to make a request. The context must always decide. It seems inevitable that here it means 'question'. The questions which they will 'in that day' (see commentary) cease to ask are those about such puzzles as the meaning of 'a little while' (v.16) and any questions that arise from doubts as to the rightness, the wisdom or the justice of allowing the Son to die.

'if you ask anything of the Father': The Greek word here, different from that in the first part of the verse, can also have the same double range of meaning; once more the context seems to make it perfectly plain that here the meaning is 'petition'.

25

'I have said this to you in figures': The only other use of the word *figure* in John is in 10⁶ to describe the teaching about the Good Shepherd. Jesus knows that what he has said cannot but be enigmatic to the disciples. But once the death has occurred and the glorification of the Son has taken place, the enigmatic character of speech about his death will have gone. John is probably truer to the facts than Mark in suggesting that right to the very end the disciples did not fully understand the teaching of Jesus, but found it puzzling. (Contrast Mark's phrase: 'To you [the disciples] has been given the secret of the kingdom of God, but for those outside everything is in parables.') The life of Jesus is like a parable; it can be told as a life, and as such can be quite intelligible. That is how the outside knows it. But to those 'inside' the life story is

like a parable: there is a meaning behind the story more important than the story itself, because it consists of what the story is really trying to say. But even on Mark's own showing, the disciples did not understand the Lord's teaching about the cross (cf. Mark 8³³; 9³²).

27, 28

'*the Father himself loves you*': i.e. he needs no mediatorial prompting from me. The Godhead is not divided against itself!!

'*because you have loved me and have believed*': This does not mean that the love of God is narrow, or even contingent upon a man coming to love the Son. The reader must not forget that this is the gospel which says 'God so loved the world ...' What Jesus is doing here is to assure the disciples that as they live within the love of the Father for the Son and share in it, they can be perfectly certain that their proper requests 'in the name of the Son' will be granted. There is no reluctance to be overcome.

'*that I came from the Father*': In some manuscripts the words *I came from the Father* in v.28 are omitted. This would leave a sentence which declared that the disciples believed that Jesus came from the Father and had come into the world. Jesus adds, in either case, that he is to leave the world and go to the Father.

30

'*Now we know that you know all things ... we believe that you came from God*': The disciples have assumed, on the basis of either the longer or the shorter text, that Jesus has confirmed them in having a full and orthodox faith. They have not perceived that in repeating their faith in brief compass they have omitted that part of Jesus' own statement which spoke of his going to the Father. Jesus does not enter into theological argument. He simply brings them to the point of facing the crisis awaiting them with an as yet inadequate faith. But not even that spells disaster for them. Their hope cannot be in themselves, or their own self-confidence; it can be only in the one triumphant thing – the fact that he has overcome the world.

32

'*the Father is with me*': There may well have been a temptation to understand from the 'cry of dereliction', so-called, in the synoptic tradition, that God did actually forsake Jesus. John makes it clear that this was not so.

33

'*I have said this to you*': Lit. 'these things', which may refer simply to the word about the Father being with him, so that, in any remorse they may feel after they forsake him, they might have some comfort; or the reference may be to the whole discourse, which has been an attempt to prepare them to face his 'departure' with some measure of insight that will grow deeper as the reality occurs and is completed.

'*In the world you have tribulation*': The word *tribulation* is characteristic of apocalyptic. John is again showing how this one act in history focuses into itself the apocalyptic and the eschatological as well as the fulfilment of all the historical.

'*I have overcome the world*': What is it for Jesus to overcome the world? There must be some element of hostile meaning for the word *overcome* to have been used. The phrase seems to include the overcoming, the destruction, of all that is evil in the world, i.e. in the world of human life organized against God and against Jesus Christ. Yet it has been envisaged that the world will come to know that the Father loved the Son; and it is probable that this is also part of 'overcoming the world'. In any event there can be no room for ultimate despair or incurable remorse on the part of the disciples. Jesus Christ is the absolute victor over all the powers that opposed him.

17^{1-26} *The Lord's Prayer* Matthew 6^{8-13}
Matthew 9^6
Matthew 28^{18}

The reverence which properly becomes any commentator on this chapter of John's gospel must not be used as an excuse for avoiding discussion of the various historical and critical issues that have been raised about it. Although the synoptic gospels report more freely than does the fourth a number of occasions on which Jesus engaged in prayer (Mark 1^{35}; 6^{46}; Luke 3^{21}; 5^{16}, etc.), some of which were long periods of prayer (e.g. Mark 1^{35}: 'A great while before day he went out to a lonely place, and there he prayed'; Luke 6^{12}: 'and all night he continued in prayer to God'), this is the only time in all four gospels when an evangelist presents his readers with the content of a long prayer. How much can the reader take as historically reliable?

This question comes the more forcibly to one who has already become familiar with the synoptic tradition of the 'passion'; for in it the prayer that the Lord offers on the night of his betrayal is recorded, though it is a shorter – much shorter – prayer, and its content and tone are markedly different from the prayer recorded in John. Can the intelligent reader suppose that both forms of prayer were in fact offered – one, say, in the upper room, and one in the garden – or is he bound to think that not both the two forms of prayer would have been offered by Jesus on that last night? The answer to this particular question cannot be given without reference to the general answer given to the whole question about the nature of the historical value of the fourth gospel (see Introduction, pp. 48ff). If that be taken into consideration the reader will observe that the point at which John inserts his prayer into the narrative is parallel to the point in the synoptic story when Jesus and the eleven had gone to the Mount of Olives, and Jesus had foretold the desertion of the disciples. John's placing of the prayer is thus to be taken as indicating what the real significance of that desertion was. What is conveyed in this way is that (a) Jesus, though deserted by the disciples, is not alone (cf. 16^{32}) but can still enjoy the communion with God which is the high prerogative of the Son (17$^{1-5}$); (b) that though the disciples have deserted their master, they are not permanently lost, but will in fact be restored as his witnesses, in whom and through whom both he and the Father will work their unitary purpose and will (17$^{6-20}$); and (c) that in spite of their desertion their return to him and to the work of witness will be the foundation of the life of the continuing community of those who believe on his name.

But such observations do not wholly relieve the commentator from asking whether Jesus actually offered a prayer such as this on the night of his betrayal, or whether he also or instead prayed another sort of prayer, such as the synoptists describe (e.g. Mark 14^{35,36}). It is not impossible to suppose that after the solemnities of the last supper, whatever they were, with so evident a premonition of his coming death, Jesus should have offered the sort of prayer which John here records. It would be foolish to claim that the words of the prayer found in John are the *ipsissima verba* of Jesus as he offered prayer after supper in the presence of the eleven. Even had a scribe been present with the tools of his trade it is improbable that he would have taken down, or even tried to take down, the words of a prayer like this. But if such a prayer were offered, it would naturally impress itself deeply on the minds and memories of the disciples, and it might not be difficult to remember the substance, even some of the phrasing of it.

It could be that in the words given to the reader in St John, there is such an honest if approximate remembering of a prayer offered by the Lord. Yet it must not be forgotten that the literary conventions of the time would not have condemned as unhistorical a prayer that the evangelist 'composed'.

As to the manifestly different tone of this prayer from that recorded in Mark 14^{36}, it can be said that such a prayer of relative detachment would not be as impossible as many critics have supposed, particularly if the reader reminds himself of the person and the stature of the one who is offering the prayer. Nor need the intelligent sensitive reader of the fourth gospel hesitate to think that Jesus asked in the garden that, if it were possible, this cup might pass from him; for in the fourth gospel itself the evangelist tells his readers that Jesus was on three occasions 'troubled in spirit', i.e. deeply disturbed, and on each occasion it was in consequence of his facing the fact of the ineluctable laying down of his life which was ahead of him (11^{33}; 12^{27}; 13^{21}). The synoptic prayer is a narrative form of the same statement. So without too much special pleading the conclusion may be drawn that the prayer recorded by John is not an entirely improbable prayer to come from Jesus; and that the prayer reported by the synoptists is not a Johannine 'impossibility' unsuited to the time and place given it in the synoptics. All that need be claimed, viz. that what is recorded in either place enables the reader to understand more clearly the meaning of what took place when Jesus was 'delivered up', is within the bounds of possibility and integrity.

But since many scholars accept alternative explanations of the origin and formation of the prayer in John, some other views merit discussion. The fourth evangelist may well have composed the prayer with the aid of his own sanctified imagination, as he may well be presumed to have compiled at least part of the discourses in the gospel. This is certainly not an impossible or even an improbable theory; and it is well within the literary conventions of the time. If the reader comes to think that the prayer here recorded matches extremely well the occasion of its utterance, that is explained satisfactorily either by assuming that the evangelist has drawn upon his memory or an accessible tradition of what the Lord said in a prayer, or by seeing in the relevance to the occasion yet another example of his deep spiritual sensitivity. Again, the suggestion has been made that the prayer in ch. 17 was composed by some Christian prophet as a eucharistic prayer for use in his church. Again, this is by no means an improbable suggestion, though it might be expected that a eucharistic prayer in the fourth gospel would have echoes in it of the teaching of 6$^{32ff,\ 48-58}$. Yet, attractive though this suggestion is, it cannot wholly displace the possibility that some tradition of a prayer offered on this occasion lies behind the present form (see Bernard, pp. 557f). Another view, that the prayer has been influenced by the desire to show that Christianity fulfils what the mystery religions know imperfectly of the death and resurrection of the deity, is a less feasible hypothesis; if it were so, then the influence of the mystery religions has been very much subordinated to the need to be relevant to the situation in the upper room. It is thus possible to hold that one possible view of the genesis of the prayer of ch. 17 is that it derives from some prayer actually offered by Jesus on the night in which he was delivered up.

If this view be adopted it must be added that this chapter represents only one tradition of what took place on the night described. Yet this tradition, like others, presents its material in order that what is reported should illuminate and explain the worship and liturgy of the church, and not vice versa. There is of course a very real sense in which the Christian experience of the Eucharist throws light upon what took place in the upper room, on Calvary, at the tomb on Easter morning: but in the end this can only be derivative from the light thrown upon the Eucharist by what took place when the last supper was first held.

The prayer here recorded has often been called 'The High-Priestly Prayer' or 'The Prayer of Consecration'. The titles are useful so long as they do not impair the prayer as a prayer, i.e. as a vehicle of real communion between man and God. The prayer teaches the Christian much, but it was not offered for that reason. And even if the prayer be a free composition, it is a free composition of a prayer, and not of another discourse! It seems therefore right to expound the prayer as a prayer, and not as a liturgical form of a didactic discourse. This does not of course exclude that possibility and indeed the propriety, once the prayer is received as such, of noting theological implications which it contains. Perhaps the theological points are not properly seen unless they arise from an exposition of the passage as a prayer, whether an 'original' prayer of Jesus, or one put on to his lips by the evangelist or his tradition.

Neither 'High Priestly Prayer' nor 'Prayer of Consecration'

misleads. Both titles derive from the situation of the upper room, where Jesus offered high-priestly prayer for his disciples, and consecrated himself (and them) to the sacrifice that was to be required. But what stands out in that specific situation is not simply the High-Priestly or consecratory aspect of the situation, but the intimacy of Father and Son within which the prayer as it is offered becomes a possibility. So for purposes of indicating the inward character of the prayer the present writer has thought it fit to use a more familiar if borrowed title, 'The Lord's Prayer'. Here the Lord of all disciples communes with his Father in prayer.

It is probably neither sheer coincidence nor the result of literary contriving that the great prayer of ch. 17 echoes much of what has become known throughout Christendom as 'The Lord's Prayer'. 'Our Father', with which the synoptic prayer starts, is echoed in various forms in John, and is the basic relationship out of which the whole prayer grows (vv. 1, 5, 11, 21, 24, 25). 'Hallowed be thy name' finds expression in vv. 6, 11, 12, 26; 'Thy kingdom come' is probably the synoptic form of the Johannine 'glorify the Son' in vv. 1, 5, 11, 23; 'Give us this day our daily bread' finds an echo in the Johannine teaching of the necessity of feeding on Jesus Christ as the bread of life; 'lead us not into temptation' finds some form of expression in v. 12; and 'that thou shouldst keep them from the evil one' almost reproduces the synoptic petition 'Deliver us from evil [or, the evil one]'.

The prayer well nigh analyses itself into three parts, each of the first two being the necessary basis and starting point for the next. Verses 1–5 form that part which particularly springs out of the relationship of Father and Son; verses 6–19 are those which arise especially from the relationship of the Son to the disciples; and verses 20–26 derive from the relationship of the disciples to future believers.

17$^{1-5}$ THE LORD'S PRAYER: FATHER AND SON

17 When Jesus had spoken these words, he lifted up his eyes to heaven and said, 'Father, the hour has come; glorify thy Son that the Son may glorify thee, ²since thou hast given him power over all flesh, to give eternal *life to all whom thou hast given him. ³And this is eternal life, that they know thee the only true God, and Jesus Christ whom thou hast sent. ⁴I glorified thee on earth, having accomplished the work which thou gavest me to do; ⁵and now, Father, glorify thou me in thy own presence with the glory which I had with thee before the world was made.'*

John carefully draws attention to the place in which he reports the content of the Lord's prayer in his gospel: *When Jesus had spoken these words* (v. 1). The words referred to were, as has been noticed, his own equivalent to the synoptic part of the narrative of the 'Passion' where Jesus predicts that every one of the eleven who have accompanied him to the Mount of Olives will 'fall away; for it is written, "I will smite the shepherd and the sheep will be scattered"' (Mark 14²⁷, cf. 16³²). John immediately makes it plain that this prediction is not something that, if fulfilled, will lead to tragedy and defeat, for Jesus at once adds, in the fourth gospel, 'In the world you have tribulation; but be of good cheer, I have overcome the world' (16³³). In placing the Lord's prayer here John is inviting his readers to understand that whatever may happen in fulfilment of what seems to be in its utterance a tragic prediction is not actually defeat, nor does it take place because of any failure on the part of the Father or the Son, but rather that all that happens from now on in the Johannine account of the death of Jesus is to be understood in terms of the Father's glorification of the Son, the Son's glorification of the Father throughout creation, and this double fact as deriving from and revealing the glory which belongs to the Father and the Son together in the eternal life of the Godhead.

This puts the whole Christian story of the crucifixion in its proper theological setting. Unless this profound understanding of the unitary glory of Father and Son be the means of interpreting the historic events now to be recorded, they might well be thought merely to set forth a dramatic conflict between opposing divine and satanic forces. But in fact the dramatic conflict itself reveals that it has a much deeper basis, viz. the life of the eternal Godhead where Father and Son share an eternal glory. It is this eternal reality which underlies and alone can render meaningful the events of the hour that has now come. The dramatic conflict takes place because the Father and Son have a relationship of mutual glorification, because the Father has given the Son who has become incarnate in the world of creatures authority over all living things, and because the incarnate son is now to complete the work which had been given him to do.

To be able in any way to make such mutual glorification real in the world of time and sense, in the area of human life and its history, cannot but demand that communion be established and maintained between the eternal Father and the incarnate Son. The Lord's Prayer in John's gospel exhibits this communion as the basis of the action which the Lord is about to perform and by which he will finally assert his Father-given authority over all flesh. Father and Son cannot share a divine glory if they are not in communion with each other; if, for whatever reason, they are separated from one another and unable to have communion or communicate. It is entirely right and fitting therefore that the prayer about the glorification of the Father in and through the events that are about to happen should begin with an act of intimate communion between the Son and the Father. For that bond underlies and alone renders intelligible the otherwise impenetrable darkness of the deed.

ಬಿಬಿ

1

When Jesus had spoken these words: i.e. the words about the scattering of the disciples, his subsequent solitude that would be divine company, and his already achieved victory over the world.

he lifted up his eyes to heaven: cf. 11⁴¹ for a similar use of the phrase. It does not necessarily imply that Jesus was out of doors!

'Father, the hour has come': *Father* is the word that Jesus began to use for his communion with God and for that of his disciples; it comes from the intimate language of the family circle. Here the term is used without precedent adjective (contrast vv.11 and 25), for it is the vehicle of communion between Jesus and the Father, not the basis of a petition as such.

That the hour has come means the whole complex of events that includes the hour of the death of the Son, but also the hour of his ultimate victory. It is an hour whose coming has been anticipated many times in the course of the gospel (e.g. 2⁴; 4^{21, 23}; 5^{25, 28}; 7³⁰; 8²⁰) and one which has been asserted in some sense to have come already in the presence of the work or deeds of the Son (4²³; 5²⁵; 12²³).

'glorify thy Son': The basic movement, even in the self-offering of the Son, is, as ever, from the Father to the Son, from heaven to earth; else the death of the Son could be another, even if an unique, martyrdom.

But what the Father does for the Son to glorify him makes this utterly different.

'*that the Son may glorify thee*': What the Father will do to glorify the Son will in fact make the death and the sacrifice and the tragedy the means of the salvation of the world.

2

'*since thou hast given him power over all flesh*': The word translated *power* (*exousia*) denotes 'authority', 'right' rather than crude power. The same word is used at 1^{12} (cf. note), 5^{27}, 10^{18}, and the same idea of place for the rightful exercise of dominion in passages like Eph. 1^{22}. The phrase *over all flesh* occurs only here in John, but is a common O.T. term for human nature in all its weaknesses. But *all flesh* is also used in the O.T. to refer to the whole animate order, e.g. Gen. 6^{19}; Psalm 136^{25}. It seems as if the evangelist is finding in the person of Jesus the one example of ' man' who, according to Psalm 84^{-8}, has been given dominion over 'all sheep and oxen, and also the beasts of the field, the birds of the air, and the fish of the sea'. There are traces of this same thought in the synoptic tradition, e.g. when Mark reports that Jesus was 'with the wild beasts' in the wilderness during the forty days of his temptation (Mark 1^{13}). So the words of the prayer give expression to a conception of the status and function of the Son of man which in its universality condemns all Jewish exclusiveness (the Son is the proper authority over all mankind, Gentiles as well as Jews) and all anthropologies that fail to see man in organic unity with the rest of creation. The Son is the redemptive link between the Father and the whole of his creation, not just the saviour of the human race or the Jewish people. What is about to take place will therefore affect the life of the whole creation, and will not simply be an incident in Jewish history.

'*to give eternal life to all whom thou hast given him*': It is difficult to find a felicitous translation to bring out the full force of the Greek. A literal translation might read 'in order that the "lot" [or "the whole"] thou hast given him, to these he might give eternal life'. There are three points to make: first, the authority, right, dominion of the Son consists in his bestowal of eternal life; second, that the Son has received his authority, right, dominion in order to bestow eternal life; third, those to whom eternal life is given are thought of most emphatically in their unity ('the lot'), although their unity is not such as to destroy their individuality ('to these he might give eternal life'). In this early verse of the chapter the theme of unity is strongly stated.

3

'*And this is eternal life*': Most modern commentators not unnaturally

find this verse difficult to understand unless it be regarded as a footnote
to the text of v. 2, inserted by the evangelist into the text of the Lord's
Prayer, because the useful technique of writing a footnote at the bottom
of the page had not then been developed. As Bernard observes (ii, 561)
'To suppose that he [St John] means to represent Jesus as introducing a
definition of "eternal life" into His prayer, and as calling Himself
"Jesus Christ" when speaking to His Father, is not a probable hypothesis'. Quite so: and yet ... If this part of the prayer represents in words
some communion between Father and Son in their intrinsic and eternal
relationship, this form of words may not seem so improbable. If the
Lord's Prayer has been rightly divided into three sections, and the
first section is rightly thought of as flowing out of the Father–Son
relationship in its eternal aspect, then we have to try to think what would
be natural in that quite unusual, indeed unique, situation and relationship. In the eternal side of the relationship it would not be in terms of
'Jesus the Messiah' that the Son would conceive of his relationship.
Jesus the Messiah is the figure that appears in human history; and there
may be something utterly right in this sensitive awareness that as the
Son communes with the Father in the eternal side of their relationship
(the phrase is clumsy, but it may serve to indicate an elusive concept)
the mission he has on earth should be naturally defined as giving men
eternal life, which consists in knowing 'thee and Jesus Christ whom
thou hast sent'. The effect of this note is really to say that it is difficult for
ordinary mortals to say what is truly 'probable' or 'improbable' in the
language of communion between the incarnate Son and the heavenly
Father.

'that they know thee': The exercise of the universal authority of the
Son is to be realized in imparting knowledge of the one true God.
This is a Johannine form of a strong element in Old Testament prophecy:
e.g. Hab. 2¹⁴: 'For the earth will be filled with the knowledge of the
glory of the Lord, as the waters cover the sea.' Amos saw the profound
connexion between knowing God and having life: 'Seek me, and live.
... Seek the Lord and live. ... Seek good, and not evil, that you may
live' (Amos 5^{4, 6, 14}). As will become plain as this verse is further
examined, the use of the verb 'to know' does not imply any form of
Gnosticism, though it is in character with Jewish 'Wisdom' usages.

'the only true God': These two adjectives together represent an indispensable basis of monotheism. The Greeks were popularly polytheistic
and the Jews, while monotheists, were involved in idolatries of one
kind and another, as the prophets had often pointed out. The phrase
finds verbal parallel in Athenaeus (vi, p. 523c, quoted by Bernard from
Wetstein), but the linking of it here with the coordinate phrase 'and

Jesus Christ whom thou hast sent' removes it from any possible pagan usage. The Father with whom Jesus is communing is the only God, because he is the real (true) God, and the true God because he is the only deity.

'*and Jesus Christ whom thou hast sent*': This is strictly a coordinate phrase, and must be interpreted so that the act of knowing God is one act, bringing the twin knowledge of both Father and Son. If the phrasing of the Greek be parallel in this phrase to that preceding, it should be translated: 'that they should know thee, the only true God, and him whom thou hast sent, Jesus Christ'. It is failure here that now prevents the Jews from recognizing the one true God. The 'truth' or 'reality' of God is known to men precisely in the appearance in historical reality of the incarnate Son, Jesus the Messiah. The Christian God is not a 'concept'; he is a real God who acts, and has acted in history.

4

'*I glorified thee on earth*': A simple exegesis of this statement is possible if it be held that the prayer is a composition from the time of the Church, looking back from its perspective. Alternatively, and to the present writer more profoundly, it can be held that it goes back to and resumes the thought of v.1. The aorist tense of completed historical action is evidently intended to be applicable in more than one way. There is a sense in which, by establishing already a community of disciples now with him in the upper room, men who believe in the one true God and in Jesus the Christ who had been sent, the task of glorification can even now be spoken of as already accomplished. There is another sense, familiar to the Hebrew mind, in which the certain event of the future can be spoken of by the prophet as having already occurred, and when it is so spoken of, its inevitability is sure. So now, Jesus speaks of the glorification that will follow his own death, by which the Gospel will reach to Jews and Gentiles alike. There is another sense, from the perspective of the Church and of the author, in which Christians look back on the death, resurrection and glorification of Jesus Christ as finished events. All three meanings are embodied in the text here, and all three point to the fourth perspective of the saying, viz. the eschatological, when, from the contemplated end of history, the Christian with his Lord looks back on a work that is finished, as it was finished in the glorification of the crucifixion and resurrection.

'*having accomplished the work which thou gavest me to do*': The word used for *accomplished* means 'perfected' or 'finished completely'. This same word is used in John at 4^{34}, 5^{36} and, on the cross, at 19^{30}.

5

'*and now, Father, glorify thou me in thy own presence*': This is surely intended to be in contrasting parallelism with v.4: 'I have glorified thee on earth' – now paralleled with what means 'Now glorify me in heaven'. This is a further indication of the relationship of earthly events to the heavenly purposes of God. Apart from what God would be doing in the things about to happen they would simply constitute the historical factors in another human sacrifice and martyrdom; but when the Father acted to glorify the Son, and he had to act in the 'heavenly places' which were his abode, then those same events were transformed into the victory of the Son and the salvation of the world.

'*with the glory which I had with thee before the world was made*': This is an expression which indicates that the events which will turn out by the action of the Father to be the glorification of the Son will not be exhausted simply in the dimension of human history, as if the sole element of glory was the vindication of Jesus the Messiah as the true Son of the Father manifested in history in incarnate form. On the contrary they will end in a revelation of that unitary glory that the Son shares eternally with the Father, a restoration, if we are to use language of time for the great mysteries of eternity, of the pre-mundane glory of the Son which was his before the world was made and historical time began.

Finally, it is wise to append a repetitive note to the whole exposition of this first part of the Lord's Prayer and state once again that what the evangelist has provided here is not a crude attempt to use prayer, rightly and properly directed to God the Father, as a means of imparting theological or any other sort of truth, nor yet to set a pattern or give an example of prayer or the uses of prayer: what he provides, and what makes the exposition of the passage an impossibility to the commentator, is the record, by one who heard (first or second-hand), of the Lord communing with his Father at the time of his approaching death. It cannot but be baffling to the human mind when (to adapt Wesley's phrase) the immortal prepares to die.

17^{6-19} THE LORD'S PRAYER:
THE SON AND THE DISCIPLES

⁶'*I have manifested thy name to the men whom thou gavest me out of the world; thine they were, and thou gavest them to me, and they have kept thy*

word. 7*Now they know that everything that thou hast given me is from thee; 8for I have given them the words which thou gavest me, and they have received them and know in truth that I came from thee; and they have believed that thou didst send me. 9I am praying for them; I am not praying for the world but for those whom thou hast given me, for they are thine; 10all mine are thine, and thine are mine, and I am glorified in them. 11And now I am no more in the world, but they are in the world, and I am coming to thee. Holy Father, keep them in thy name which thou hast given me, that they may be one, even as we are one. 12While I was with them, I kept them in thy name which thou hast given me; I have guarded them, and none of them is lost but the son of perdition, that the scripture might be fulfilled. 13But now I am coming to thee; and these things I speak in the world, that they may have my joy fulfilled in themselves. 14I have given them thy word; and the world has hated them because they are not of the world, even as I am not of the world. 15I do not pray that thou shouldst take them out of the world, but that thou shouldst keep them from the evil one.ᵃ 16 They are not of the world, even as I am not of the world. 17Sanctify them in the truth; thy word is truth. 18As thou didst send me into the world, so I have sent them into the world. 19And for their sake I consecrate myself, that they also may be consecrated in truth.'*

a Or from evil

The first section of the Lord's Prayer has painted a picture of Jesus preparing himself, rather already prepared, for his death. He has accepted its necessity, its inevitability, and he knows it for what it is: the actual historical means by which the eternal glory of Father and Son will be displayed. But 'display' is not self-display, no mere proud showing off of the powers of deity. For the acts by which glorification is manifested are done from compassion and love, so that the whole created order may come to share in the glorious life that is the eternal felicity of the Godhead. But already, even on the night when Jesus was delivered up, there was a circle of those who had already glimpsed the glory that was to be fully manifested, and the little Church, purged by the word of the Lord, cleansed by his washing, purified by the exit of Judas to do his errands, was with the Lord in this moment of his self-preparation, self-dedication and self-consecration.

So now, having reached the point of profoundest communion with the Father, the glory which belongs to both Father and Son beyond all temporalities, Jesus remembers the little Church that is with him, and brings them into the orbit of a prayer in which the Son communes with the Father in glory. This part of the prayer begins with a recitation of what has so far happened to them. Jesus has manifested the Father's name (nature) to them. He has accepted them as the Father's gift to himself, and has therefore given them the Father's word. They have kept that word. By it they have learnt that everything about their Lord is more-than-human, is from God; he does not belong simply to the area of human magnitudes, but to that of the divine. They have come to believe that the Father has sent the Son (cf. 16^{29}). And though their understanding of this basic truth be inadequate, it is the point from which real growth is possible. For this truth marks off the area of belief from that of unbelief, the believer from the unbeliever, the Christian from every other religious man.

The group of men so marked off is with Jesus at the supper table. And it is through such a group of men that the Father has chosen to work his glory, which is but another way of saying that he has chosen to manifest his glory in history. So, in complete distinction from a manifestation of glory by sheer power, as is the way of men, God will manifest his glory through the testimony, the service, the sacrifice of the Son and of those who believe in his name. So it is for such a circle of believers, the cleansed and purified Church of the upper room, that the Lord now prays. It is still a prayer for the glory of the Father, for this is the one way by which, in history, that divine glory can be manifested.

The disciples have become the Father's own possession in becoming Christ's. And in their acknowledgement that the Son has come from the Father the Son himself is glorified, for it is the Son's peculiar glory to make known to men the glory of the Father. But at the very time when they have come openly to acknowledge his divine origin, the Son is about to leave the world where the Father has chosen to reveal his glory. So the Son appeals to the 'Holy Father' to keep this body of men in his name. The word Holy has apt relevance here, for it is the word which emphasizes the divine 'separation' from the world, and if the disciples are to remain in the true faith they will inevitably be in separation from the world, and remain 'in God', or, in the word of the evangelist, 'in the name', the very being, of God. Such a relationship to the Father will be the constitutive fact of the unity of the disciples. Their unity will not consist of any common human interest they may have in any part of human life or thought; it will consist solely in their sharing the one relationship to the one divine life and glory of Father and Son.

This is the time of the Lord's departure, and Jesus recalls that while he has been with the men given to him, he has been able to hold them all within the unity of which he now speaks – all, that is, except the 'son of perdition'. His appearance only testifies to the truth of the insights of the holy scriptures upon which the Lord and his disciples have been fed during the years. But will the Eleven be held in the absence of the Lord as they have been held in his presence? The answer to that is contained in the very fact that the Lord is now praying for them, for that will secure their coming to share the Lord's own joy themselves, the joy of bringing others to know, and to remain in, the knowledge of the one true God, and Jesus Christ whom he has sent. As in Luke's narrative of the Last Supper Jesus is said to have prayed for Peter, and later events show that his prayer was effective, so now Jesus prays for the whole body of the disciples, and later events show that his prayer was not unrealized. It is the prayer of the Lord that is the security of the Church, and its pledge of an inheritance in the divine joy at the end.

But even though the ultimate issue be thus secured in the prayer of the Lord, the problem of proximate trials has to be faced. The Lord is aware of this, as his prayer makes clear. To pray that the band of disciples may find his own joy fulfilled in themselves is not to ask that they may escape from the tribulations of this earthly pilgrimage (cf. 16^{33}), and the Lord had not sought that even for himself. To do that would be to ask for them to be taken out of the world. The Lord's Prayer for his disciples is thus rather a request that they be kept from the evil one, remain in the possession and power of the Father. To be '*not of the world*' just as Christ is means precisely to be with the Father, to belong to him. So the prayer passes into the request that the disciples be sanctified in the truth. The word 'sanctify' is not the same as 'purify'; the disciples have already been declared 'clean' (13^{10}; 15^{3}). To be sanctified is to be made ready for a specific task, and the prayer seeks the endowment of the disciples for their apostolic mission. The word has no necessary connexion with the idea of sacrifice in death, though it gains something of that significance by its context here where the Lord goes on immediately to speak of his own 'sanctifying' of himself, his own task for his disciples, viz. that of dying for them.

The disciples are to be sanctified, equipped for their task in the truth, meaning by truth the Father's word. 'In the truth' is more than 'in reality', such is the force of the definite article before *'truth'*. *The* truth is the whole message of God's love and glory as it is contained in the life and work and words of Jesus; it is, in one sense and in one use of the word, Jesus himself (14⁶). So it is Jesus himself who sends them into the world on their mission, just as the Father had sent him into the world on his mission. But for that mission and this prayer to become effective something else is now offered: Jesus will sanctify himself, consecrate himself (the Greek word is the same as that used in v. 17 of the disciples) for his followers, and that will enable them to be sanctified, equipped for their task, in truth, i.e. fully and completely and really. They must conquer by his submission, and live by his death.

ॐ

6

'I have manifested thy name to the men whom thou gavest me out of the world': To manifest the name is not quite the same thing as to glorify the Father, for the true glory of the Father is distinctively shown in the shame and humiliation plus the triumph and victory of the cross. But Jesus has already manifested the name of God to the disciples in both his teaching and his presence; the apostolic band has been privileged to 'see the Father', to learn something of the very nature of God himself.

The disciples are regarded as God's gift to Jesus; they were his, and so the Father could give them to the Son. Again, this emphasizes that the response of the disciple to the call of the Lord is not a matter simply of a movement inside a human mind, heart and will; it is in fact at the same time, and much more profoundly and really, an act that God performs.

'they have kept thy word': If the singular *word* has special force here as over against a possible plural 'words' it conveys the idea that the disciples have kept the divine message of Jesus taken as a whole, instead of having observed various precepts that the Master had given to his followers. Such a perception of the meaning of the words and works of Jesus seen as a whole was recorded, for all its inadequacy, at 16³⁰: 'By this we believe that you came from God.'

7

'Now they know that everything that thou hast given me is from thee': This

is from the perspective of the Last Supper, where the oncoming death of the Lord has had to be accepted; and so it is also from the perspective of the cross as both disaster and triumph together; and it is from the perspective of the 'end' when past all tribulation the joy of the Lord will be full.

8

'*I have given them the words which thou gavest me*': The 'word' of the Lord must be communicated in a number of *words* or 'sayings'. But the sayings of Jesus, as the evangelist has made plain, are not his own, but the Father's (cf. 7^{16}; 12^{49}).

'*and they have received them*': cf. 1^{12}: 'To all who received him, he gave power [authority] to become children of God'; 13^{20}: 'He who receives me receives him who sent me.'

'*know in truth*': really know, truly know, know for sure.

'*know ... have believed*': It is not really possible to play off these two against each other in this context. The substance is clearly identical even if the words be different. The tense used is aorist, of an action that is historical and complete.

9

'*I am praying for them*': Jesus now passes to the actual intercession which he can offer for his disciples at the moment of his own departure by death.

'*I am not praying for the world*': It would be wrong to conclude from this phrase that Jesus had no care for the world, or that he never prayed for others than his own friends. The synoptists treasure a tradition that he both taught prayer for one's enemies (Matt. 5^{44}) and practised it at the most tragic moment of his life (Luke 23^{34}). In this gospel it is made quite clear that, though the world is hostile to God (1^{10}, etc.), yet God loved it (3^{16}), and that through the mission of the Son passed on to the disciples, the world was to be reconciled to the Father at the last (v.21).

10

'*all mine are thine, and thine are mine, and I am glorified in them*': *All mine* is neuter plural – see note on v.2 – more than the area of human life is meant to be included here, even though it is through the response of men that the glorification of the Father in creation can become manifest.

11

'*I am no more in the world*': The future state as a present fact, as so often in Hebrew thinking. This is the basis of the intercession for the disciples;

he will no longer be constantly with them to shield them from the attacks of the evil one.

'*but they are in the world*': They, like Jesus himself, are liable to all the hostility that the world inevitably displays against God. Their being 'in God' does not free them from that, any more than it would prevent Jesus from undergoing arrest, trial and death.

'*I am coming to thee*': '*Coming*' is the right word for this intimate dialogue between Father and Son. Elsewhere, of course, the typical word is 'go' to the Father.

'*Holy Father*': A characteristically Jewish mode of address to God, which recognizes his 'apartness' from the world. Since it is the 'apartness' of the disciples, their being able to be *in the world* and not 'of it', that is to be the subject of prayer, this attribute of God is rightly invoked here.

'*keep them in thy name*': The *name* was the whole being of a person or thing in its essential features. It was not an abstraction, but the living power of a person, a point which can become clear in citing Psalm 20^1: 'The name of the God of Jacob protect you.'

'*thy name which thou hast given me*': *Name* in precisely the sense just described – the active and purposeful being of God. This had become the entire life and work of the incarnate Son.

'*that they may be one, even as we are one*': This text is manifestly not directed to the uniting of separated Christian bodies or churches. It is a prayer that the disciples should find and keep their unity in that one thing which the Father and the Son would do with and through and for them – make manifest the eternal glory of the Godhead. The ecumenists of the twentieth century are basically right, however, in supposing that a disunited body of disciples could not possibly be thought of as in full possession of the benefits of the intercession of the Lord!

12

'*While I was with them, I kept them in thy name*': It was not only that the disciples held together as a body (there are a number of signs in the gospels that there were sometimes acute tensions among them!) by the presence of Jesus, but, more fundamentally, that they were held together spiritually by the grace of Jesus Christ. To continue in the fellowship of the Twelve at all was a result of a daily renewed act of forgiveness and renewal of the disciple on the part of the Lord.

'*I have guarded them*': A figure with a somewhat stronger flavour. It comes from the area of war, and suggests that Jesus was the effective guard who watched for and warded off, by his own prowess, the threatened attacks of the enemy.

'*and none of them is lost but the son of perdition*': A clear reference to Judas. *Son of perdition* sounds bad in modern English, and indeed the judgement behind the words is 'bad'; yet it would more precisely convey the meaning of the Greek, which represents a Hebrew idiom, were the translation to read 'but the lost man'. The word *lost* represents a play on words in the Greek, and suits the context well. It may be, as has been suggested, that the description of Judas as the 'loss', or 'lost' man, derives from the incident reported in Mark 14⁴ when some complained of the 'waste' or 'loss' or 'lostness' of the ointment.

'*that the scripture might be fulfilled*': To suppose that the evangelist imagined that some odd word of scripture coerced Judas, albeit unconsciously, into his action, is highly improbable. The fulfilment of scripture was appealed to on many occasions because such an appeal would establish that what was being asserted as an act of God was not something utterly new and unheard of, but wholly within the plan of God's actions as Holy Scripture had already revealed them. What the evangelist is trying to say then is something like this: 'Tragic and mysterious though this action of Judas may be, and however difficult men may find it to reconcile with the nature of God as Jesus Christ has revealed him, nevertheless such an action is not unknown, but has been part of the pattern of divine action in history as the sacred writers of scripture have borne witness.'

13

'*and these things I speak in the world, that they may have my joy fulfilled in themselves*': Again, this verse may be seen as indication of a post-crucifixion authorship. But it is also from this verse that some commentators have deduced that Jesus offered his prayer out loud in the hearing of his disciples so that they might be encouraged by it. But there is no necessary implication of that sort. What Jesus is saying is that prayer like this has to be made 'while he is in the world', not while he is within earshot of his disciples! And such prayer must be offered in the world because it is from the perspective of this world that alone it is real to offer it. The end of the prayer that is thus discerningly offered for the disciples who are to be bereft of their Lord will have the effect of bringing them to share in the joy of their Lord.

'*that they may have my joy fulfilled in themselves*': The joy of the Lord is to do his Father's will, to see the glory of the Father made manifest, even at the cost of self-sacrifice. This is to be the happy destiny of the disciples.

14

'*I have given them thy word; and the world has hated them*': There are two tenses in the Greek, the perfect in *I have given*, implying that Jesus had continually given the disciples the word of the Father, and was still giving it; the aorist in *the world has hated* to refer to the opposition of the world in that single, terrible act of hatred which opposes both them and their Lord. But the act of hatred can be seen as terminable; the gift of God never ceases to be made.

'*I am not of the world*': This phrase summarizes a good deal of the gospel's teaching about Jesus. He is 'from above'; he has 'other food to eat'; he speaks other than earthly words; he gives other than earthly gifts.

'*they are not of the world*': The disciples share in the 'otherness' of their Lord. They have been begotten 'from above' (cf. 1¹³; 3³⁻⁸ etc.); they have been given 'bread from heaven', and a life that is not 'of this world', but eternal life.

15

'*I do not pray that thou shouldst take them out of the world*': It is the lot of the Christian disciple to be and remain in the world. There is really no retreat from it. The temptations of the world can even enter into the places of spiritual seclusion that men build for themselves.

'*but that thou shouldst keep them from the evil one*': The saying could be about *the evil one* or just 'evil'. The suggestion of the other uses of the phrase in the gospel (3¹⁹; 7⁷) and even more in the epistles (1 John 2¹³, ¹⁴; 3¹²; 5¹⁸f.) is that the reference is to the evil one, the 'prince of this world'.

17

'*Sanctify them in the truth*': The word *sanctify* in these verses can hardly be different in meaning from that which it has in v.19, where the R.S.V. translates with the word 'consecrate'. In 10³⁶ God is said to have consecrated the Son and sent him into the world. That is, the sanctification or consecration is almost identified with the commissioning of the agent to do a specific task. This must at least be the meaning here, that Jesus prays that the Father should sanctify the disciples as he has already consecrated the Son, and as the Son now commissions himself for the task set him – to give his life for his friends. It is the appearance of the word in the context of the supper where the mission of the Son is so clearly seen as glorifying the Father in the laying down of his life that gives both uses of the word a somewhat deeper meaning than mere 'commission' or 'appoint'. Of itself the saying about the disciples does not carry the implication that a Christian disciple must either lay down his life, or not be a disciple; but it does mean, in this context, that the disciple cannot offer less to God than a dedication that is willing to lay down life, if that be asked for.

'in the truth': See the notes in the commentary.

18

'As thou didst send me into the world, so I have sent them into the world': Again the text poses a problem of perspectives to the commentator. It may be that in the prayer Jesus was using the language of a super-temporal perspective, and so can speak of his having already sent the disciples on their mission. If so, the implication is that the mission on which the disciples were sent in Galilee, according to the synoptic tradition, could not be other than a mission of the Lord who was even then 'the Lamb slain before the foundation of the world'. It may properly be claimed that by sending the disciples into the world to do the work of Father and Son Jesus is elevating them to the status of those 'who are born not of blood, nor of the will of the flesh nor of the will of man, but of God'.

19

'And for their sake I consecrate myself': *For their sake* is a phrase which lends a very sacrificial colour to this phrase. It comes in the phrase quoted in Mark from Isaiah when Jesus speaks of 'giving his life as a ransom for the sake of many' (Mark 10⁴⁵). The idea behind the phrase is that of the figure of the suffering servant in 2 Isaiah.

'that they also may be consecrated in truth': The sanctification of the disciples, their equipment to undertake the mission of the Son for the Father, depends wholly upon the fact that Jesus will lay down his life. As the evangelist has made plain, there is no good news to preach until the Son of man is glorified, i.e. until cross, resurrection and ascension have taken place. Such a preparation will be one that takes place in reality, in history; they will really be equipped when these events have taken place.

THE LORD'S PRAYER:
THE DISCIPLES AND THE CHURCH TO COME

²⁰'*I do not pray for these only, but also for those who are to believe in me through their word, ²¹that they may all be one; even as thou, Father, art in me, and I in thee, that they also may be in us, so that the world may believe that thou hast sent me. ²²The glory which thou hast given me I have given to them, that they may be one even as we are one, ²³I in them and thou in me, that they may become perfectly one, so that the world may know that thou hast sent me and hast loved them even as thou hast loved me. ²⁴Father, I desire that they also, whom thou hast given me, may be with me where I am, to behold my glory which thou hast given me in thy love for me before the foundation of the world. ²⁵O righteous Father, the world has not known thee, but I have known thee; and these know that thou hast sent me. ²⁶I made known to them thy name, and I will make it known, that the love with which thou hast loved me may be in them, and I in them.'*

The prayer of the Lord began with a communing of the Son with the Father within the indivisible unity of the Godhead. When that communing was brought to contemplate the Eleven who were with Jesus in the place of the supper, it became a prayer that they should come to share in the glory and unity of the Father and the Son (vv. 10, 11). Now the communing between the Son and the Father takes into itself those people who would come to believe on the Son through the work and witness of the Eleven, that is to say, the Church that is to come. The prayer remains in substance the same: that all who believe might share in the same unity and the same glory that characterize the Godhead in the unity of Father and Son. Such a participation in the perfect unity of the Godhead will be both an historical and an eschatological privilege of the Church.

The Lord's Prayer is throughout firmly anchored in the unity that binds Father and Son together in the Godhead. As men come to share that unity, and the glory inseparable from it, during their earthly life, they will be able themselves to recognize the divine origin and quality of the life of the Church; and by the same token, other men will be able to share their recognition. Christians are those who recognize that the Son has been sent by the Father, for the

Son has revealed the Father in his love and glory. Such a work of revelation and witness the Son will continue until the love of the Father for the Son which is fully perfected as the love of God for the world is known by men and answered by them in a terrestrial love that, in its apprehension of divine love, is incorporated by it and transformed from glory to glory.

ဘ

20

'for these only': John never states categorically that those with Jesus at this time were the Eleven; but Christian tradition has with due propriety and real probability generally assumed so.

'to believe in me through their word': The order of the words in Greek is: 'To believe through their word – or testimony – to me'. Either translation leaves it clear that in the Johannine tradition it was believed that Jesus himself intended and envisaged that a community of disciples, a Church, should continue the ministry he had begun.

21

'that they may all be one': This is the purpose and content of the prayer, as it had been the purpose and the actuality of the incarnation. As at v.11 the petition cannot be directly applied to the situation of a divided Christendom, though it cannot but be a condemnation of any division in the Church that destroys and hinders a true unity, or establishes or encourages a false one.

'even as thou, Father, art in me, and I in thee': This is the only proper criterion for the unity of the Church. The Father is in the Son, and works in the Son. The Son does the Father's will, and is one with him in all the operations and life of the Godhead. Likewise the Church is to be the vehicle for the life of God to be lived in the world; the Father and Son in their unity will work their works in her, and she will be one with them in doing their will, and in all the operations and life of the Godhead. The Church, because of the indwelling of God, will be both one and many – one God in her and through her, and many members sharing the one life.

'so that the world may believe that thou hast sent me': This is both the Lord's prayer for his Church, and also his prayer for the world. Indeed it is impossible to pray for the Church with any sort of integrity without in this sense praying for the world. For the Church has no reason at all for her existence unless she continues the work and mission

of her Lord – to make known and effectual the love of the Father for the world (3¹⁶). But it is the unity of believers in the Church that will be the effective testimony to the love of the Father for the world, assured to men in the mission of Jesus the Christ. For such a unified community to exist at all is an eloquent testimony to its supernatural origin (cf. the point made more than once by Paul that Christian fellowship had brought impossible diversities together: Jews and Greeks, slaves and freemen, barbarians and men of high culture, cf. 1 Cor. 12¹³; Gal. 3²⁸; Col. 3¹¹). There seems to be little room for doubt that what is envisaged in this prayer is that the 'world' should come to believe, and so to be saved. It would seem that John has not attempted to reconcile two convictions, perhaps not even seen a possible contradiction between them – that in the world, i.e. in history, Christians will have tribulation (16³³) and that, nevertheless, the world will come to believe.

22

'*The glory which thou hast given me I have given to them*': The glory given to the Son is manifested in weakness and humility, in defeat and death. The Church is called to this same destiny along the same path of glory. Cf. 2 Tim. 2¹²: 'If we endure, we shall also reign with him'.

'*that they may be one even as we are one*': To be made one with God does not mean removal from the tribulations of the world; that is clear from what lies immediately ahead of the Son. On the other hand the only unity possible between heavenly Father and incarnate Son is that between one who suffers and one who is all-glorious. This unity the Church is to share.

23

'*I in them and thou in me*': The complete reciprocity of relationship between Father and Son is to be reflected in the relationship of the Godhead and the Church.

'*that they may become perfectly one*': Lit. 'That they may be perfected into one.' John uses the word 'perfect' for the completion or carrying out of some specific task. The Church is 'perfected', she 'completes her task', when she is one. This does not mean to say that she cannot embody her unity in her historical manifestation; on the other hand, as an eschatological reality in history she should manifest the divine unity in her own life. That is precisely the point of the Lord's prayer: that, by manifesting her supernatural unity, the world might be brought to believe.

'*that the world may know that thou hast sent me and hast loved them even as thou hast loved me*': For the first part of this phrase see note on v. 21.

The second part needs to be given its full weight. The love of the Father for the Son can hardly be over-emphasized. Yet the evangelist wants his readers to be quite clear that in the mind of the Lord as he prays for the last time to his Father while he is in the world, he recognizes, beyond all the bitter opposition of the world that he is about to experience, that God loves that same world as he loves his own Son.

24

With this verse the thought of the prayer moves, understandably in view of the last petition, from the historical to the eschatological and the eternal. The Lord seeks for the Eleven and the Church that follows them a share in the heavenly life which he already shares with the Father in the glory that, if temporal language is to be used at all, has to be spoken of as the glory which Father and Son shared before the foundation of the world.

'*Father, I desire*': In this petition Jesus does not use the word of previous requests (e.g. v. 20: 'pray') but the word 'wish' or 'desire'. The explanation is almost certainly not that Jesus has now come to some matter improper for petitionary prayer, and so tells the Father what his desire is; but rather that not even here in so exalted a conception of the Church's destiny can it be supposed that there is any difference between the 'wish' or 'desire' of the Son and that of the Father.

'*may be with me where I am*': In terms of historical temporal sequence Jesus is not yet united with the Father in the glory which they shared before the cosmic process started. But in another sense he has never ceased to share that glory. It is possible to claim that this prayer is properly offered both from the perspective of the present (since the Lord who is about to suffer *is* the Lord who comes from and goes to the eternal glory without losing it, even though it be veiled) and from the perspective of the end, when the relationship of the suffering to the glory will become fully exposed to the vision of the disciples.

25

'*O righteous Father*': The word *righteous* refers both to the deliverance that God brings, and the ineluctability of it. God's righteousness consists both in his deliverance and in the consistency and certainty with which he accomplishes it. It is an appropriate epithet here, when before the final summing up of all things in the pre-mundane glory of the deity, the agony of the crucifixion has to be faced.

'*but I have known thee; and these know that thou hast sent me*': This is the means by which Father and Son will, indeed already have, 'overcome the world'. Cf. 16^{30}, and note that it is on the basis of an as yet inadequate acknowledgement of the Son that the Lord is willing to trust the future, and it is in this confidence that he now makes his last prayer.

26

'I made known to them my name': In words and deeds, and the whole of the incarnate life.

'and I will make it known': In part, certainly, through the gift of the Paraclete; but in part also through the new personal union which this prayer has contemplated: 'I in them, and thou in me . . .' (v. 23).

'that the love with which thou hast loved me may be in them, and I in them': First, it is important to underline the thought that it is the very love of the Father for the Son that is to be in the Church. It is an all-sufficient love; not one that will remove them from all discomfort and tribulation, for it has not done that for the Son; but a love that, in and through whatever happens, will be sufficient stay and illumination to render fidelity and obedience the deepest satisfaction and joy, be the tribulation what it will. Second, it is important to make plain that the love of God is not an emotion confined to the breast of the Godhead! Rather it is always an active caring for the object loved. Hence, third, it must be shown that when the love of the Father is in the Church, the love that gave his Son for the world, then the Son cannot but be in the Church too. For he is the love of the Father in its saving historical action. Nothing could more appropriately be appended to this final prayer than the great words spoken in the discourse to Nicodemus: 'For God so loved the world that he gave his only Son, that whoever believes in him should not perish but have eternal life' (3^{16}).

John 18:1–20:31

Deed and Word: 5
Rite and Reality: 4
The Seventh Sign

2: The Deed

With the majestic phrases which close the Lord's Prayer of the fourth
gospel the evangelist has concluded what may well be thought of as
the 'discourse' attached to the last and seventh sign. Not that the
last sign can be so called in precisely the same terms as the other six
in the gospel; it is, on the contrary, the reality, the concrete historical
event, to which they all point forward. Yet even in its historical
happening the reality of what God has done in and through the incarnate Word is but symbolized: what the eye can see and the ear
hear are but the data in and through which some see only a person
crucified and some of his followers re-inspired, while others believe
themselves to behold the glory of the only-begotten Son of God.

As the reader passes from the 'discourse' about the sign to the
event which is the sign enacted in an historical occasion he will do
well to remember that the meaning of the narrative upon which the
evangelist now embarks has already been stated in the previous
section from 13^1 to 17^{26}, just as, for example, the meaning of the
action in 5^{2-9} is stated in the attached discourse of 5^{10-47}. In brief this
means that John helps his readers to approach the story of the crucifixion and resurrection knowing that in this single event which constitutes the glorification of the Son of man, there is rooted the new
constitution of the Israel of God (15^{1-27}), the unity (17^{1-26}) and the
mission (16^{1-33}) of the Church, the departure and return of the Lord
(14^{1-31}) and the transformation of an old ritual into a new reality of
a destiny at once humiliating and victorious (13^{1-35}). The story of the
glorification does not stand on its own; it requires its own discourse, as
much as any of the Johannine signs.

John is not alone in prefacing his account of the death and resurrection with explanatory material. Each synoptist has used some
apocalyptic material in this way (Mark 13; Matt. 24, 25; Luke 21),

and has incorporated into his report of the crucifixion some character-istically apocalyptic elements, such as the darkening of the sun (Mark 15^{33}; Matt. 27^{45}; Luke 23^{44}), the eruption of an earthquake (Matt. 27^{51}) and the raising of the dead (Matt. 27$^{52, 53}$). The end of Judaism and its replacement by Christianity is figured in the rending of the temple curtain (Mark 15^{38}; Matt. 27^{51}). This does not mean that John does not believe with the synoptists that at the crucifixion the old world came to an end and a new one was born; on the contrary, he has made it transparently clear from the very commencement of his gospel that in Jesus Christ the whole universe is made anew. At this point of the gospel the reader has been told something of the nature of the new order that is to be. Jesus has spoken of a new com-mandment, a new world where his followers will do greater works than he has achieved himself, a world where God will finally and lastingly dwell with his people and be their God. He speaks, like the synoptists, of a coming persecution of his followers as evidence of the finality (eschatology) of the conflict between himself and the world. He speaks of his going and returning, and prays that the unity between himself and his followers, between them and the Father, between each of them shall be like that between Father and Son, eternally changeless and sure. And all this is more than hope, more even than apocalyptic hope; it becomes realized hope, realized eschatology in the eternal-historical victory of the cross and re-surrection which constitute the glorification of the Son of man.

Something of the peculiar Johannine presentation of the story of the crucifixion and resurrection derives then from the different eschatology with which the evangelist works. John's 'realized' eschatology attempts to make clear that in and through the drama he reports a new relationship was wrought between God and the world. So the story is told in such a way as to leave it indubitably clear that this was wholly a divine action, even though the divine action could use human and even sinful action within its own opera-tion. The story is thus unfolded to show that he who might in normal human terms be called 'the victim' was really the initiator and even the author and actor of the whole historical drama. He was in many ways 'passive', and can be said to have had a 'passion'; yet the far deeper and important truth is that even in his passivity, his passion, he was agent and actor. Such thoughts are suggested to the reader in the 'discourse' preceding the sign. The 'discourse' speaks of one who will humble himself for his servants (13$^{1-17}$); who will set in train the action of the betrayer (13$^{21-30}$); who sees what is about to happen as a deliberate 'going' and 'returning' (14$^{1-31}$); who recognizes that his own passion will produce a like passion for his followers (15$^{1-27}$); who sees his own and his followers' passion as the brief prelude to the birth of a new world order (16$^{16-33}$); who prays for his followers to be held in the divine unity that binds Father and Son indissolubly together (17$^{1-26}$). Little wonder that such an author selects his material and makes his characteristic emphases as he selects his material and presents it to his readers.

John thus omits the story of the agony in the garden (Mark 14$^{32-42}$); the information that Simon of Cyrene carried Jesus' cross (Mark 15^{21}); the darkness that lasted from the sixth to the ninth hour (Mark 15^{33}); and the rending of the temple curtain from top to bottom. He introduces the retreat of the guard sent to arrest Jesus (18^6); the dialogue between Pilate and Jesus (18^{33}–19^{11}); the concern of the dying Lord for his mother, his dying thirst and final cry of victory (19$^{25-30}$); and the story of the blood and water flowing from the Lord's pierced side (19$^{31-37}$). In such ways does the evangelist seek to convey his deep insights to his readers.

Yet for all John's awareness of the divine initiative throughout the story he tells, he is as insistent as any synoptist, perhaps more so, upon the guilt of men in their complicity in Christ's death. He is certainly more outspoken about Judas than the three other evangelists. In ch. 6 he has already reported Jesus as saying that Judas was a devil (6^{70}); he portrays him as the disciple who complained about the waste of money spent upon Mary's anointing of Jesus (12^4); twice in his account of the Last Supper he tells of the devil's entry into Judas (13$^{2,\ 27}$). By contrast the synoptists simply state in their list of the Twelve that Judas 'betrayed' Jesus, or, in the case of Luke, 'became a traitor' (Luke 6^{16}). Matthew relates what happened to Judas when he realized that he had betrayed 'innocent blood' (Matt. 27$^{3-10}$); but neither he nor Luke (Acts 1$^{15-20}$) ventures upon such strong theological condemnation as John. Similarly John is perhaps more concerned than the synoptists to expose the heavy burden of guilt resting upon *the Jews*, by which he means primarily the chief priests and scribes. And in reporting the part played by Pilate he is careful to leave it quite clear that though it is a divine concession which enables Pilate to have and to exercise an authority that can put Jesus to death, and though other persons and groups are complicit with him and perhaps share more guilt than he, yet he is responsible for his decisions and the consequences that flow from them. The sovereignty and acts of God in no way diminish the sin and guilt of men.

In the synoptic gospels the Lord's teaching, largely confined to the Galilean ministry, is very much occupied with the theme of the Kingdom of God, and of the Lord's own relationship to it. But the theme of *kingship* receives little emphasis in the passion narrative as such. In the fourth gospel this situation is largely reversed. There is little direct teaching about the Kingdom of God in the story up to the time of the 'passion', and little enough action connected with the idea (the attempt to make Jesus king in 6¹⁵ is the only example); but the whole presentation of the glorification of the Son of man in cross and resurrection can be understood as cast in the mould of his kingship. More than any other evangelist John gives the poet the occasion to sing that Christ reigns from the tree.

In giving such a regal description of the humiliating death of the Lord, John is clearly setting the event of the crucifixion in his own characteristic perspective. Yet it is important to observe that he cannot easily be charged either with replacing the synoptic story, if he knew it, with one of his own, or with telling a quite different story, if he were unacquainted with the other traditions; the only adequate solution is that John is deliberately putting the traditional story of the crucifixion into a wider and profounder perspective. It can roughly be said that instead of seeing the resurrection as the dramatically victorious reversal of a defeat suffered on the cross he regards the cross itself as the place and time of Christ's victory, a victory which has been foreseen by the Lord, even though it were a victory through much humiliation. The anticipated humiliation is quite apparent at the Last Supper, as he washes the disciples' feet (13¹⁻²⁰); the victory in the humiliation is evident in the first remark that followed Judas' exit to accomplish his mission: Jesus said: 'Now is the Son of man glorified, and in him God is glorified; if God is glorified in him, God will also glorify him in himself, and glorify him at once' (13³¹,³²). However difficult twentieth-century men may find the idea, John seems to have believed that theology was not something which could be used to read a meaning into events, but rather something that was to be discovered in them. His story is what it is because his theology is what it is; but his theology is what it is because the story happened so.

18 *When Jesus had spoken these words, he went forth with his disciples across the Kidron valley, where there was a garden, which he and his disciples entered.* ²*Now Judas, who betrayed him, also knew the place; for Jesus often met there with his disciples.* ³*So Judas, procuring a band of soldiers and some officers from the chief priests and the Pharisees, went there with lanterns and torches and weapons.* ⁴*Then Jesus, knowing all that was to befall him, came forward and said to them, 'Whom do you seek?'* ⁵*They answered him, 'Jesus of Nazareth.' Jesus said to them, 'I am he.' Judas, who betrayed him, was standing with them.* ⁶*When he said to them, 'I am he,' they drew back and fell to the ground.* ⁷*Again he asked them, 'Whom do you seek?' And they said, 'Jesus of Nazareth.'* ⁸*Jesus answered, 'I told you that I am he; so, if you seek me, let these men go.'* ⁹*This was to fulfil the word which he had spoken. 'Of those whom thou gavest me I lost not one.'* ¹⁰*Then Simon Peter, having a sword, drew it and struck the high priest's slave and cut off his right ear. The slave's name was Malchus.* ¹¹*Jesus said to Peter, 'Put your sword into its sheath; shall I not drink the cup which the Father has given me?'*

¹²*So the band of soldiers and their captain and the officers of the Jews seized and bound him.* ¹³*First they led him to Annas; for he was the father-in-law of Ca'iaphas, who was high priest that year.* ¹⁴*It was Ca'iaphas who had given counsel to the Jews that it was expedient that one man should die for the people.*

In the story of the arrest of Jesus and his primary confrontation with the Jewish authorities John uses several devices to indicate his own profound and important conviction that the initiative lay throughout with Jesus. Thus Jesus 'goes out' from the house and the city to the garden. From the shelter of the garden he 'goes out' to reveal himself to his enemies. With his enemies he bargains for the safety of his followers before yielding himself to be bound as a prisoner. Where John's treatment of the story brings his account into conflict with the synoptic traditions it is probably impossible to determine which of the traditions is historically correct; but where the theological basis and intention of John's narrative can be discerned the reader of John can accept the Johannine account for its theological point whatever he may think of its narrative accuracy. It may well be, of course, that John has both theological and historical truth together in his narrative, or parts of it; but even that does not detract from the primacy of the theological significance of the things that happened on the night when Jesus was delivered up.

After the Lord's prayer Jesus led his disciples out of the house where they were, out of the city, across the Kidron stream to a walled garden they were accustomed to make use of, and entered it.

Meanwhile, Judas had been active, and had gathered a sizeable company of men to arrest Jesus. Some were Roman soldiers, and some officers and men of the Temple Guard; so that from the beginning 'Church and State' moved together against Jesus. It was the season of the Passover full moon, yet Judas' company went out provided with torches and lanterns: as John had said in reporting Judas' exit from the Last Supper: 'it was night', and in that night nothing but the light of the world could bring effective light to bear on what was taking place. No torch or lantern, not even the light of the moon which so clearly lit up the landscape, could suffice to relieve the utter darkness of the time when men extinguished the light of the world.

Jesus did not wait for Judas in any way or by any means to come forward and identify him. He went out of the walled enclosure of the garden and asked whom they were seeking. When they answered '*Jesus of Nazareth*' the Lord answered with a phrase that has special significance for St John: '*I am he*', or '*I am*'. This is the phrase by which Yahweh in the Old Testament had revealed himself to men, and ordinary men had found this revelation unbearable. So now, as the Lord discloses himself with words having so divine an overtone, his enemies are driven back, and fall to the ground. Jesus repeated his question as to whom they were seeking, and upon receiving their answer bargained for the free passage of his disciples. He is to face the last crisis alone. In another way than the synoptists John has stated that the shepherd will be struck and the sheep scattered (cf. Mark 14²⁷; Zech. 13⁷), and it is not without significance that so plain an

Old Testament reference should be omitted and replaced by an action and saying of Jesus, particularly when the word he spoke was the 'I am' so sacred to the Old Testament as a divine name. John himself tells his readers that this bargain with his captors was struck to fulfil Christ's word that he would lose none of those whom the Father had given him.

John next relates the story of the cutting off of the ear of the high priest's servant. The incident is recounted in all four gospels. Mark simply states that 'one of those who stood by drew his sword and struck the slave of the high priest and cut off his ear' (Mark 14⁴⁷). Matthew adds that the intervention was made by 'one of those who were with Jesus' (Matt. 26⁵¹); and that Jesus rebuked him. Luke (22⁵⁰) makes the further addition that Jesus exclaimed, 'No more of this', and touched the ear of the wounded man and healed him. John, as is at once clear from the narrative, has provided circumstantial additions to the story. It was Peter who drew the sword and cut off the right ear of Malchus the high priest's slave, he reports. Jesus goes on to tell Peter to sheath his sword, and asks *Shall I not drink the cup which the Father has given me?* As many commentators have observed, it is not unusual, but entirely ordinary, that a later author should find his version of a tradition filled out with individual names in particular incidents. But is that all that can, or ought to, be said about John's particular additions here? The names, admittedly, may have come to him in the normal accretions that come to narratives in the course of time. But it is by no means impossible to imagine why John makes use of them at this point of his narrative. First, he indicates that the issues between Jesus Christ and his enemies bring his own followers *as individuals* into new areas of conflict and stress. To be joined to him is to be brought as an individual face to face with other individuals who are not joined to him, and to find opposition and conflict inescapable. Second, John indicates that no conflict between followers on either side can in any way detract from, or substitute for, Jesus' own conflict with the powers arrayed against him. Peter as chief of the apostles cannot really fight his Lord's battle; rather must the Lord fight Peter's battle for him. And so third, the issue of the conflict is one which Jesus must secure for himself in his own humiliation. It is not without significance that at this point of the gospel John uses a saying about drinking the cup which echoes the synoptic tradition as it is found at two points: first, when James and John have asked for the chief places in the glory to come, to which Jesus replies with a question whether they can drink the cup which he must drink; and second, when Jesus offers agonized prayer in Gethsemane that *'if it be possible'* the cup might pass from him; yet beyond that prays that the Father's will be done.

The combined Roman and Jewish force then took Jesus and bound him as their prisoner. In the synoptic tradition Jesus is not bound until the end of the trial before the high priest, before he was taken away to Pilate. But in John the verdict of the Jews has already been given, and the rejection of Christ's claims made quite explicit (cf. 11^{47ff}; 12^{37ff}). The theological point is thus marked with complete 'synoptic' accuracy by John. The Jews, having rejected Jesus, join with the civil power of Rome to destroy him.

But there is another and purely Jewish feature of John's narrative which links with the previous rejection of Jesus by the Jews. The synoptic tradition as preserved in Mark tells of two trial scenes before the Jews, at one of which Jesus is interrogated by the high priest, who claims that Jesus' confession that he is the Christ, the Son of the Blessed, is open blasphemy; and at the other the Sanhedrin decide to send their prisoner to Pilate. Matthew follows Mark, but Luke abbreviates the story, reporting only a hearing before the Sanhedrin at which there is an interrogation very much akin to that in Matthew and Mark. John tells of only one interrogation by the Jews, conducted by Caiaphas (referred to as *the high priest*) in the house of Annas, his father-in-law, though it is a very different questioning from that described in the synoptics. It is probably impossible to reconstruct the precise order in which the events took place; what can be said is that for the writer of the fourth gospel the issue about Jesus' claims to divine status have at this point already been heard and rejected, particularly in chs. 7–10. This enables him to omit reference to one interrogation by the Jewish authorities (if that indeed be what he has done!) and to avoid the particular apocalyptic references which the synoptic record introduces through the confession of Jesus that he is the 'Christ, the Son of the Blessed'.

☙☙

1

Jesus . . . went forth: Almost certainly meant to indicate his leaving the house in which they had supped.

across the Kidron valley: A *wadi* which is an actual water-course only in wild weather. The name may well mean 'Dark'; if so, it adds to the general 'real metaphor' of darkness which John detects at several points in his narrative of the night's doings (cf. 13³⁰; 18⁴).

where there was a garden: The synoptists say 'the place'. For John it seems important to record that the place of the arrest, as of the crucifixion and resurrection, should be in or hard by a garden. It is natural to think of the garden of Eden, and of the reversal of man's consequential lot by the events of the crucifixion and resurrection. It is perhaps fair to suggest that the same location for the three events in the same way indicates their theological identity: they belong inseparably together, historically as well as theologically; theologically as well as historically.

which he and his disciples entered: The shape of this sentence means that in all probability the garden was walled round.

2

Judas . . . also knew the place: This suggests that there was no inevitability, but only a presumption, that Jesus would be there on this particular night; and that Judas had been told that the little company would in fact go to the garden on this occasion.

3

procuring a band of soldiers: How likely or unlikely this was is difficult to say. With backing from Jewish authorities it is perhaps quite conceivable; though had Roman soldiers been involved in the act of arrest it would be more likely that the prisoner would be taken directly to a Roman official. The size of the detachment in any case seems large for the task. A *band* was a company of some 600 men (a cohort), though it might be taken to refer to one of 200 (a maniple). But, at the time of the Passover, with thousands of pilgrims available for incitement, and some prima facie evidence (the 'Triumphal Entry') that Jesus was likely to stir up trouble, even 600 might not be thought an impossible number.

went there with lanterns and torches and weapons: The need for light may have been due to a dark, overclouded night; to the fear that Jesus might have sought cover in the shrubbery on the hillside; or it may be another of John's 'symbolic' incidents in which he sees the futility of any man looking for him who is the light of the world with a mere lantern! Without the light of the world, as these men are, their world is dark indeed!

4

Jesus, knowing all that was to befall him, came forward: In recording this initiative of Jesus, John offers an alternative account to that of the synoptists, who state that Judas came to Jesus and kissed him as a sign of identification. Jesus is not exposed, even to his enemies, by any other than himself; his self-disclosure follows, and in words that are recognizably authentic of his divine self-knowledge as set forth in John. The verb *came forward* means, literally, 'came out'. If he had to 'go into' the garden and also 'come out' of it, the suggestion that it was a walled area is much strengthened.

5

Judas, who betrayed him: This could be translated: 'Judas, who was in the act of betraying him (or delivering him up)'.

Jesus said to them, 'I am he': Even if these are a correct record of words used by Jesus at his arrest, they are not meant to indicate that those to whom they were addressed recognized them for the profound statement that the Christian church can discern them to be. In the actual context they could mean for the men who had come to arrest Jesus simply 'I am Jesus of Nazareth'. Yet it seems quite clear that John intends his readers to observe the deeper meaning, and to connect the reaction of the arresting forces with it. The one who uses these exalted words, used in the Old Testament as a name of God, is himself of that same divine status. Hence when men drew near to him it is not impossible that they should find the presence unbearable as the people of God had done in times past.

6

they drew back and fell to the ground: They could not acknowledge the real status of the man they had come to arrest; but they were brought to such acknowledgement entirely unconsciously by the sheer power of the presence in which they sought to stand.

8

Jesus answered ... 'let these men go': The picture is one of the disciples outside the entrance to the garden, behind their master, who pleads for them. They are thus able to learn by observation what it is to drink the cup which the Father has prepared for his children. Jesus' death buys their life.

9

This was to fulfil the word which he had spoken: The words referred to are in 6^{39} and 17^{12}. It would not be right to think that John's meaning was simply that by this device Jesus had enabled his followers to avoid death at that particular Passover. Rather must it mean that unless they had been free to see and ponder his own death for them, they would never have been able to share with him in the drinking of the Father's cup.

10

Simon Peter, having a sword: Bearing of swords was forbidden at Passover time, and this detail therefore accords with John's dating of the Last Supper as taking place the day before Passover. *Sword* is perhaps too strong a word, which could be better replaced by 'dagger' or 'knife'.

drew it and struck the high priest's slave: The Greek at least suggests that the slave was some special servant of the high priest; this would lend additional support to the view in the text above, where the struggle between followers of Jesus and of the high priest would be more evenly balanced if Peter, the chief of the apostles, were matched by one who had some outstanding office in the retinue of the high priest.

13

First they led him to Annas: Annas had been high priest from A.D. 6 to A.D. 15. He still had and exercised much influence, and it was for this reason that Jesus was taken first to his house. If John be read as a narrative in its own right, it must be assumed that Caiaphas, who was high priest, went to Annas' house, and was there to conduct the interrogation (18¹⁹ff).

It is interesting to note that in an attempt to harmonize the text at this point, one ancient text, the Syrian Sinaiticus, inserts 18²⁴ after 18¹³.

18¹⁵⁻¹⁸   PETER'S TRIAL

Mark 14⁵⁴, ⁶⁶⁻⁶⁸

¹⁵*Simon Peter followed Jesus, and so did another disciple. As this disciple was known to the high priest, he entered the court of the high priest along with Jesus,* ¹⁶*while Peter stood outside at the door. So the other disciple, who was known to the high priest, went out and spoke to the maid who kept the door, and brought Peter in.* ¹⁷*The maid who kept the door said to Peter, 'Are not you also one of this man's disciples?' He said, 'I am not.'* ¹⁸*Now the servants[a] and officers had made a charcoal fire, because it was cold, and they were standing and warming themselves; Peter also was with them, standing and warming himself.*

a Or *slaves*

Each of the four evangelists records the threefold denial of Peter. John is alone in separating one denial from the remaining two. It would seem as if he wishes to remind his reader that there is not only one trial going on during this night, but two. In the one men have judged the divine claims of Jesus falsely, and he is put to death for blasphemy and rebellion of which he was not guilty. In the other Peter is rightly judged to be a follower of Jesus, and in his denial of that fact Peter proves himself to be as frail and untrustworthy as any of the Eleven. It is Christ alone, not Peter or any other disciple, who can rightly claim to be superhuman.

John has some characteristic details to add to the synoptic tradition. Peter followed Jesus to Annas' house; so, said John, did another disciple. It has often been suggested that this person was no other than the beloved disciple. If so, he was one known to the high priest, and so was able to penetrate further than Peter, and actually enter the court of Annas' house. This acquaintance with the high priest gives little help in identifying the person of the beloved disciple (if he were the companion of Peter on this occasion) though it restricts possibilities to some extent. The phrase probably implies considerable familiarity, and could indicate that the other person was a member of the Sanhedrin, for it is on record that Jesus had followers there (12⁴²). If the beloved disciple were John, the son of Zebedee, then he had priestly connexions through his mother's connexions with Elizabeth, who was one of the 'daughters of Aaron' (Luke 1⁵). If some other than the beloved disciple is to be named, Nicodemus and Joseph of Arimathea come to mind. Little more can be said, save to observe that the disciple who ran with Peter to the tomb on Easter morning is identified as the beloved disciple; which seems to suggest that he is intended to be Peter's companion here, as a joint witness both of the arrest-and-crucifixion and of the resurrection.

Whoever the other disciple was, it was through his agency that Peter was brought inside the court by the doormaid. She asked Peter: 'Are not you also one of this man's disciples?' – a question indicating scorn rather than pity for the prisoner. Peter denied the association. Peter, John observes along with the synoptists, was inside the court, enjoying the comfort of a fire. Perhaps John is giving rein to his power of irony even here; for, in any strictly Christian definition of what a 'disciple' is, Peter failed to qualify because of his denial. But Peter by the fire is not a completely unique figure; confession of Christ is often avoided by 'disciples' because of the possible loss of some social or physical comfort.

16

and brought Peter in: It is equally possible to translate 'and she brought Peter in', and this would seem to be the natural way to translate the sentence, and to secure the best continuity for the story. That the maid kept the door confirms John's statement that the hearing took place in a private house. Peter would be admitted to the atrium or court. It is interesting to speculate what occupied Peter's mind as he waited outside at the start. Was he just waiting to see what the result of the hearing was? Did he half hope for, or even expect, some dramatic divine intervention? Why did he go inside? Because, once asked, it was difficult to refuse? Because he really wanted to be a witness to what happened to his Lord? In any event Peter shows the inevitable consequence of coming nearer to Christ in any way – the one who draws near has to declare himself sooner or later.

17

'Are not you also one of this man's disciples?': Without the word *also* this question would have anticipated the answer 'No'. With it, however, it evidently expects the reply 'Yes'. Apparently the 'other disciple' was known as such, and the maidservant did no more than ask Peter if he were a disciple like his sponsor for admittance. Peter was too frail to acknowledge his discipleship.

'I am not': It must be admitted that it is all too easy to read too much into the delicate and intricate structure of John's gospel. But it is hard not to remark on the fact that Peter's denial is couched in a phrase which is the direct negative of his Lord's 'I am' in v.5. So he is divine; Peter is all too human.

18

it was cold, and ... Peter was warming himself: These are two little details provided only by John. They may well indicate that he is dependent upon (his own?) eyewitness, and they may also underline the theological point that so far Peter 'sides with men' rather than with his Lord (cf. Mark 8³³: 'Get behind me, Satan! For you are not on the side of God, but of men' – addressed to Peter when Peter objected to the tragic destiny Jesus foretold for himself).

18 19-24   THE HIGH PRIEST'S INTERROGATION
Mark 14 53-65

¹⁹ *The high priest then questioned Jesus about his disciples and his teaching.*

²⁰*Jesus answered him, 'I have spoken openly to the world; I have always taught in synagogues and in the temple, where all Jews come together; I have said nothing secretly. *²¹*Why do you ask me? Ask those who have heard me what I said to them; they know what I said.' *²²*When he had said this, one of the officers standing by struck Jesus with his hand, saying, 'Is that how you answer the high priest?' *²³*Jesus answered him, 'If I have spoken wrongly, bear witness to the wrong; but if I have spoken rightly, why do you strike me?' *²⁴*Annas then sent him bound to Ca'iaphas the high priest.*

At this point in the Johannine record there is considerable divergence from the synoptic tradition in all its forms. There is little profit in trying to harmonize the differing accounts, so far as John is concerned, because the differences are not chronological–historical in essence, but basically theological. Having already given at some length the nature of Christ's controversy with the Jews, and the nature of the decision which the authorities took, John has no need to set it all out again, particularly when to do so with the synoptic material as a basis would introduce apocalyptic elements which he wishes to avoid.

John states very baldly that the high priest questioned Jesus about his disciples and his teaching. Tantalizingly the evangelist does not tell us who is meant by 'high priest'. If the term is accurately used, it must mean Caiaphas. If, as some think, this would leave the holding of the interrogation in Annas' house unexplained, then the title might be loosely used of Annas, who was nothing if not the influential leader of the authorities. But it is not impossible to suppose that Jesus was taken to Annas' house because an informal interrogation such as this could more easily take place at the 'headquarters' of the opposition to Jesus; and if that be so, then it is not impossible or indeed improbable that Caiaphas conducted the questioning. The questioning, John reports, was about Jesus' disciples, and about his teaching. In view of what is said later when Jesus is before Pilate (e.g. 18³³ and 19¹²) the questioning could well have concerned the role of Jesus' disciples in any possible insurrection, and the nature of any teaching he may have given about himself as a messianic king. But Jesus does not propose to condemn himself at the trial. Indeed to have contrived that he should do so was strictly against the law. So he simply states that he has done everything in public, and witnesses could be found to establish what it is that he has said and done. This was to make a perfectly proper point, though one of the officers detected what he took to be impertinence to the high priest in Jesus' answer, and struck him with his hand. Jesus, in full control of the situation, appeals to what he has said; nothing has been out of place, he has made a perfectly proper legal point. It is worth noting that such an action by an officer could hardly have taken place at a regular session of a Jewish court.

It is at this stage that a final review has to be taken of the possibilities of the person of the interrogator. For now John reports that Annas sent Jesus bound to the high priest. If Annas had been the interrogator under a loosely applied title of high priest, then the narrative is in order. All that is envisaged is that Jesus is securely bound up before he is moved either to another house, or to another part of the same house, for further questioning by Caiaphas. Or we may decide that the ancient manuscript Syrian Sinaiticus (see above, p. 587) has in fact preserved the right order of events, and that v. 24 ought to follow v. 13. But if Caiaphas has been the interrogator so far, then either v. 24 has to be regarded as displaced, or after some interrogation by Caiaphas at Annas' house, and under his general supervision, Jesus was sent upon Annas' instructions to an official hearing at the house of Caiaphas. The various possibilities are intriguing; yet it remains true that the centre for John is not in the precise chronological historical order, but in the theological significance of the events he records. As long as that is preserved an historical decision can be made which best accords with the requirements of historical consistency. None is entirely free from difficulty, though the choice seems to lie between a first questioning by Annas, loosely being called 'high priest', and a first interrogation by Caiaphas at Annas' house, before a more formal questioning at the residence of the high priest. The latter seems to require the least adjustment of the Johannine narrative.

❧

19
about his disciples: The synoptic record, as well as 19¹², suggests that the possibility of an armed rising was envisaged.

and his teaching: Mark records an explicit question about what Jesus had to say concerning his messianic office.

20

'*I have spoken openly to the world*': *Openly* means publicly as opposed to privately. The *I* is emphatic in the sentence. It reflects his own awareness that it is his person and his teaching that is in question, and perhaps a contrasting judgement that those who have opposed him have worked in secret. Cf. Isaiah 48¹⁶: 'From the beginning I have not spoken in secret.' *The world* indicates that even now John conceives his story as linked with the whole world; and this has been in the mind of Jesus always.

21

'*Why do you ask me?*': Rabbinic law held that it was improper to try to secure evidence from an accused person to incriminate himself. Jesus is pointing this out.

22

one of the officers: i.e. one of the temple guard, struck Jesus with his hand: cf. 19³; Mark 14⁶⁵. These are blows on the cheek delivered with the flat of the hand, more to convey an insult than to cause hurt or injury.

'*Is that how you answer the high priest?*': There is a real concern for the dignity of the high priest, but the zealous officer has not seen the validity of the Lord's reproof.

23

'*If I have spoken wrongly*': said anything which is inadmissible in court.

'*bear witness to the wrong*': i.e. give your evidence, as I mine, in good legal form.

PETER'S TRIAL (*concluded*)

Mark 14⁶⁹⁻⁷²

²⁵Now Simon Peter was standing and warming himself. They said to him, '*Are you not also one of his disciples?*' He denied it and said, '*I am not.*' ²⁶One of the servants*ᵃ* of the high priest, a kinsman of the man whose ear Peter had cut off, asked, '*Did I not see you in the garden with him?*' ²⁷Peter again denied it; and at once the cock crowed.

a Or *slaves*

Jesus has stood his ground with dignity and calm; but Peter, though within range of his Lord, finds the ground slipping from under his feet. He cannot stand where earlier in the evening he thought he could stand, and lay down his life for his Lord (13³⁷), but finds himself utterly lost in miserable denial. The group round the charcoal fire asked Peter whether he were not one of Christ's disciples. He denied it, with the same 'I am not' that he had used to the serving maid. Finally a relative of Malchus whose ear Peter had severed claimed to recognize Peter as present in the garden with Jesus. In spite of all the circumstantial strength of the evidence against him, Peter denied it again.

And the cock crowed. Cf. the words of Jesus in 13³⁸: *And Jesus answered, 'Will you lay down your life for me? Truly, truly, I say to you, the cock will not crow, till you have denied me three times.'* The artistry and theological power of John's narrative in 18²⁷ is to stop precisely where he does.

18²⁸–19¹⁶   Pilate, Jesus and the Jews

Mark 15¹⁻¹⁵

John is completely silent as to what happened at the house of Caiaphas. But his account of what took place before the Roman governor gives the reader some clues as to what went on. Strangely enough, there seems to have been no specific charge laid before Pilate by the Jewish authorities. There are three stages in the trial: First in answer to Pilate the Jews say that Jesus has been handed over as an evildoer; Pilate replies by offering to hand Jesus back for punishment in accordance with Jewish law. But the authorities want none of that, since, they say, it is not possible for them to inflict capital punishment. Second, Pilate questions Jesus in connexion with an evident charge that he has claimed to be king. There is no indication whence Pilate gained the information underlying his interrogation, though it must surely have been supplied in some fashion by the Jewish authorities. It is during this interrogation that Pilate is confronted with the calm and majestic claims of Jesus to a kingship that is not of this world. Again, on this accusation, Pilate is reluctant to sentence Jesus, and proposes that he be released in accordance with a Passover custom. But the Jews demand the release of a brigand Barabbas instead. Third, Pilate asks Jesus a question with a very specific and profound meaning in the fourth gospel: '*Where are you from?*' Once more Pilate sought to effect Jesus' release, but was unsuccessful. He eventually handed Jesus over for crucifixion.

The story is told with immense restraint. No doubt a good deal of concentrated imagination has gone into the production of the narrative; but it is a construction that no Christian would want to be without. And whether it be 'historically true' or not, it does set out in sharp and clear relief the precise, great and profound theological issues calling for judgement from Pilate, from the Jews and from the disciples on that night of nights, issues that still demand judgement from every man who hears the story as John tells it.

18²⁸⁻³²   JESUS ACCUSED TO PILATE

²⁸ *Then they led Jesus from the house of Ca'iaphas to the praetorium. It was early. They themselves did not enter the praetorium, so that they might not be defiled, but might eat the passover.* ²⁹ *So Pilate went out to them and said, 'What accusation do you bring against this man?'* ³⁰ *They answered him, 'If this man were not an evildoer, we would not have handed him over.'* ³¹ *Pilate said to them, 'Take him yourselves and judge him by your own law.' The Jews said to him, 'It is not lawful for us to put any man to death.'* ³² *This was to fulfil the word which Jesus had spoken to show by what death he was to die.*

Jesus was taken, as all the synoptists agree, to the official Jerusalem residence of the Roman procurator. Normally Pilate lived in Caesarea, but at times like the Passover, when riots might assume disturbing proportions, the precaution was taken of residing in the Praetorium in Jerusalem. Hither the Jews brought Jesus, though they only went to, not into the official residence. Jesus passes inside, and is now cut off from 'his own people' until he faces them again and hears their demand for his death.

The non-entry of the Jews is stated to have been because they did not want to suffer defilement and so be unable to eat the Passover. In view of the fact that such defilement could have been washed away in a bath taken at sunset, it is hard to know what the precise point is.

All the synoptists mention the proceedings in the Praetorium, though without John's narrative the reader would suppose that Jesus, crowd and Jewish leaders alike were inside. The one thing that remains clear in the Johannine story is the irony of the evangelist who shows that the very men who can plot the crucifixion of the Son of God are at the same time scrupulous to the extreme about their own religious observances. There is, of course, nothing specially Jewish about that!

Once in the Praetorium, and presumably after some quiet pre-liminary word either with the prisoner or his Roman guard or both, Pilate goes outside his residence and asks for the formal accusation against Jesus. He receives the reply that Jesus is '*an evildoer*', i.e. a malefactor – an habitual criminal in twentieth-century phrase. To this accusation Pilate seems happy to make the reply that it would be quite proper for the accusers to take Jesus back and try him by their own law. The Jews reply that it is not lawful for them to put any man to death. This is a statement which merits special consideration. It could be that this was the first indication Pilate had had of the nature of the trial upon which he was about to embark. If so, what the Jew's answer had done for him was to let him know that the crime for which he had been delivered up to Rome was one which merited the death penalty, and was outside the particular province of the Jews to deal with in that way. That is to say, the Jew's reply could be taken as being tantamount to an accusation of political insurrection.

※

28
It was early: The last two watches of the night were 'cockcrow' and 'early'. The proceedings before Pilate must be thought of as being conducted before 6 a.m. on the day on which the Passover began.

They themselves did not enter the praetorium: The law did not permit them to enter a Gentile dwelling without incurring defilement; but it would be quite possible for them to be in a colonnade surrounding the interior, or in a court outside the house.

but might eat the passover: small but significant addition to the indications in John that the Last Supper was not the Passover meal.

29

So Pilate went out to them: Perhaps unusual, but not impossible to conceive, granted the conditions John reports. A prisoner has been delivered to Pilate, and his accusers cannot appear before him inside the house; so he must either avoid action now by refusing or postponing a hearing, which would have looked and been both dangerous and irresponsible, or go outside where he knew the accusers were waiting.

'What accusation do you bring against this man?': Pilate proposes to have everything in due and proper order.

30

'If this man were not an evildoer, we would not have handed him over': A highly unspecific charge! Similar charges were often made against members of the early church. It is not necessary to assume that there is any insolence in the reply of the Jews. Clearly any charge against Jesus is going to be hard to bring home (as was recognized also in the synoptic gospels) and if a general accusation of wrongdoing would suffice, so much the better.

31

'Take him yourselves': Pilate's reply is that if the charge is one of general criminality, Jewish law could perfectly well dispose of the case. This was as unacceptable to the Jews as it would have proved inadequate to Christians to discern the true nature of the conflict between Jesus and his own people, and between Jesus and the representative of Rome. The issues at stake are far deeper than general law-breaking.

'It is not lawful for us to put any man to death': Here for the first time Pilate learns of the true magnitude of the issues between Jesus and the Jews. The Jews did not think that these could be settled by any sort of penalty they could inflict for general wrongdoing, however severe a sentence they might pass. The only way to deal with Jesus was to put him to death.

It seems very doubtful whether John's statement concerning the ability of a Jewish court to order capital punishment is true. There is some evidence in support of it, e.g. in Y. Sanhedrin 1¹⁸ᵃ, ³⁴; 7²⁴ᵇ, ⁴¹, where it is asserted that the right to pass a death sentence was taken from the Jews forty years before the destruction of the temple. This would cover the time of the trial before Pilate. But even this evidence has to be questioned: Luke reports a death sentence as being passed by a Jewish court on Stephen (Acts 6¹²f; 7⁵⁷ff). Paul seeks to avoid trial for his life before a Jewish court, and appeals to Caesar (Acts 25¹¹). It is pertinent to add one historical and one theological comment. Historically it may

well have been the case that the authorities were very sceptical about
the possibility of being able to execute Jesus themselves, in view of the
highly successful popular welcome given by him at his 'triumphal
entry'; and even if execution had been possible, perhaps the price
needing to be paid would have appeared too great, their own loss of
popular esteem too much, to have made the risks worth taking. So a
charge had to be laid against Jesus in a Roman court for which a Roman
sentence of death could be passed. The Jews seek to gain such a sentence
from Pilate at the lowest accusation possible. And this leads directly to
the theological comment, for it proves to be impossible to secure a
death sentence from Rome unless a charge is made which brings out
much more fully the nature of the issues between Jesus and the Jews,
and between Jesus and all worldly authority. No one who has read the
fourth gospel with care can be in any doubt that the issues which the
coming of the Word into the world raises are those of life and death.
The fourth evangelist tries to show, in his handling of the narrative of
the trial, as throughout his gospel, that at every point witness is borne to
the issues of life and death which the coming in the flesh of the eternal
Word raises for men, Jews and Gentiles alike.

32

by what death he was to die: The reference is to 12³², and possibly
earlier sayings, e.g. 3¹⁴; 8²⁸. All the four gospels indicate that Jesus fore-
saw death by crucifixion. Whether such foresight was an historical fact
is much debated. But if Jesus were able to recognize the sharpness of the
conflict between himself and his opponents, and if he could further see
that only by a coalition of Jews and Gentiles could his opponents be
rid of him, the evangelists may well be right in general, if not in every
part of their record of the fact. Moreover some weight must surely be
given to the varying sensitivity of different people to the events yet in the
future. Jesus may well have been sensitive, as he would surely be
aware of the radical character of the issues his coming and his ministry
raised.

If it be allowed that a Jewish court could condemn to death for
certain offences, then the charge of blasphemy is clearly not thought to
be a possible basis for a sentence by Pilate. This is not to say that Jesus
did not believe himself to be the one of whom John writes so exaltedly,
but simply that he did not imagine that such a charge could be made to
stick in a properly conducted court, or, alternatively, that it would be
thought inexpedient to have him executed by Jews inflicting the penalty
of stoning. Jesus may well have expected that the authorities would have
to pass him over to Rome, where the death penalty was crucifixion and
the charge for it would be rebellion.

³³*Pilate entered the praetorium again and called Jesus, and said to him, 'Are you the King of the Jews?'* ³⁴*Jesus answered, 'Do you say this of your own accord, or did others say it to you about me?'* ³⁵*Pilate answered, 'Am I a Jew? Your own nation and the chief priests have handed you over to me; what have you done?'* ³⁶*Jesus answered, 'My kingship is not of this world; if my kingship were of this world, my servants would fight, that I might not be handed over to the Jews; but my kingship is not from the world.'* ³⁷*Pilate said to him, 'So you are a king?' Jesus answered, 'You say that I am a king. For this I was born, and for this I have come into the world, to bear witness to the truth. Every one who is of the truth hears my voice.'* ³⁸*Pilate said to him, 'What is truth?'*

After he had said this, he went out to the Jews again, and told them, 'I find no crime in him. ³⁹*But you have a custom that I should release one man for you at the Passover; will you have me release for you the King of the Jews?'* ⁴⁰*They cried out again, 'Not this man, but Barab'bas!' Now Barab'bas was a robber.*

In the body of his gospel John has given a much longer and more precise account of the nature of the issues at stake between Jesus and the religious leaders of his own people. He now proceeds to give a much more precise account of the nature of the issues between Jesus and the lawfully established political authority as focused in the person of Pontius Pilate. There are many things which a modern historian would like to know, which John does not tell, e.g. how Pilate learnt that the question to put to Jesus was whether he were King of the Jews. But what John does in this first interview between Pilate and his prisoner is to link the kingship claimed by Jesus not only with the apocalyptic hopes of Judaism, as the synoptists had done in their account of the hearing before the high priest, but also with the imperial dominion of Rome. There are signs that Pilate was more impressed by his prisoner than he dare admit, to Jesus, to the waiting Jews, or even to himself.

Pilate's own deep and tragic dilemma is evidenced by the way in which he approaches the Jews at the end of his first interrogation. He declares Jesus innocent; offers to set him free, and yet makes what could only have been a provocative reference to him as 'King of the Jews'. It seems strange that Pilate should offer to set Jesus free while he was still uncondemned, particularly as the alternative subject of the proposed amnesty was a convicted criminal. Yet if the record does not make its historical facts as precise as a modern reader would like, the theological points are made precisely and powerfully. The real King of men confronts the rulers who would try him. The story cannot be read without realizing how profoundly the roles of judge and prisoner are really reversed.

When Pilate returns to Jesus inside the Praetorium he has a question to put to Jesus which breaks new ground in the Johannine narrative; for he asks: *'Are you the king of the Jews?'* Jesus does not know how Pilate has heard of this accusation, and he asks the governor how he has come by it – by his own sensitive observation or by the accusation of 'others', i.e. his Jewish adversaries. Pilate's reply is completely self-disclosing: *'Am I a Jew? Your own nation and the chief priests have handed you over to me; what have you done?'* In a word, the whole matter is a Jewish charge, and as such means nothing to Pilate. All that the governor wants to know is what Jesus has done to engender such hostility!

Pilate receives an answer which is both related to the particular situation and as independent of it as it is possible to be. It is independent of it in that Jesus does not descend into the area of 'what he has done' to deserve his people's hostility: it is closely related to the situation in that Jesus points out that if his claims to kingship were of the kind which the governor must properly resist, his own 'officers and men' would have at least resisted arrest a short time ago. *'My kingship is not of this world'.* The sovereignty I exercise, Jesus is saying, is not in the realm of the world's political struggles, but in the realm where men are set in hostility against God.

Pilate, practical Roman administrator, trying to catch some piece of concrete evidence, takes up Jesus' word about his kingship and says: *'So you are a king?'* Jesus replies *'You say that I am a king'*, i.e. 'Those are your words, not mine'. At this point Jesus turns the conversation to something which lies at the basis of his own kingship: *'For this was I born, and for this have I come into the world, to bear witness to the truth'.* The true kingship which Jesus exercises is not a matter of political power, but one of hearing and believing the truth. *'Every*

599

one who is of the truth', says Jesus, '*hears my voice*', i.e. knows that I speak, and bring, and am, the truth, and receives it from me with gladness and obedience. The trial was not going as Pilate had anticipated. He can only muster a confused and speculative '*What is truth?*'

Significantly at this point, when Jesus has said so little and yet so much about his kingship, Pilate goes out to the Jews and makes a direct bid to get Jesus released. He appeals to a custom, unknown save for the Christian gospels, that the governor should at Passover time grant a full pardon to some one prisoner. He proposes that Jesus be made the subject of this amnesty, but his proposal is not accepted. It may be but another play of Johannine irony that in his account of this incident the evangelist contents himself with the brief report that the crowd cried out '*Not this man* [for amnesty] *but Barabbas*', a name which means 'Son of the Father'; and Pilate is about to learn that Jesus had claimed to be the Son of God. It may be equally a touch of his irony that he adds the antithetical information about Barabbas that he was a *robber* – a brigand or insurrectionist, which Jesus certainly was not.

꩜

33
'*Are you the King of the Jews?*': The *you* seems emphatic in the Greek; but with what sort of emphasis? It would seem to call attention to the condition of one who claimed to be the Jews' king, either in commiseration or in some measure of contempt. There is no clue given in John as to how Pilate came to have this question to put to his prisoner. He could, as suggested above, have heard of Jesus' claim when he had gone outside to talk with the authorities. He could have been told of the possibilities of such a charge before the arrival of the party, for it would seem inevitable that Pilate was roused from his bed in order to deal so early in the morning with such a prisoner. The question may, on the other hand, be itself a Johannine instrument for theological probing, rather than for 'accurate historical statement'.

34
'*Do you say this of your own accord?*': Jesus needs to know the answer to this. If the question has come solely from his Jewish accusers he knows that it will have one meaning, and one meaning only for Pilate – he will be regarded as at least a potential rebel. If it has come from some insight

granted to him as he is confronted by the Lord, then some other outcome may be expected.

35

'*Am I a Jew?*': It is highly significant that Pilate does not give a direct
answer to Jesus' question. Perhaps he hardly dared! In any event the
Johannine record shows Pilate as very ready to secure Jesus' release, if
at all possible, and it is not unlikely that the demeanour of the prisoner
made more than a passing impression on the governor. But he does not
regard any such impression as a valid basis of judgement or action in a
Roman court; so he answers Jesus on the first part of his question
somewhat evasively, and on the second with a brief statement that the
chief priests have handed Jesus over for trial and sentence. The conclusion
is inevitable: Pilate has from the Jews enough information to proceed
with the trial.

36

'*My kingship is not of this world*': This does not answer Pilate's question,
any more than Pilate's reply answered Jesus' question. But Jesus,
perhaps sensing that Pilate really understood more about him than could
be given by any information laid by his accusers, proceeds both to
admit his kingship, and to remove it by definition from the area where a
charge of sedition could be validly made.

John's story at this point is considerably different from that of the
synoptists. They all state that in reply to the question '*Are you the king
of the Jews?*' Jesus replied 'You say so', or 'Those are the words you
have used' – which is about as non-committal as can be. But also in the
synoptic story, at the hearing before the high priest, Jesus is asked
about his messianic claims: 'Are you the Christ, the Son of the Blessed?'
(Mark 14⁶¹): to this Jesus replies; 'I am; and you will see the Son of
man sitting at the right hand of Power, and coming with the clouds of
heaven' (Mark 14⁶²). In other words the synoptists, like John, have
affirmed very clearly that Jesus' kingship is not of this world, and have
described it in terms of current Jewish apocalyptic hope. John has not
reported that particular piece of interrogation before the high priest,
but focuses the statement about Christ's kingship on to this point of the
trial before Pilate. The synoptists must be taken with full seriousness in
their quite drastic re-interpretation of Jewish eschatology into Christian
terms; for what is meant by the quotation from Daniel (7¹³) is that upon
his death Jesus will, like the Son of man in Daniel, appear before the
'ancient of days' and receive from him an imperishable and universal
kingdom. In John this conception is deliberately set over against the
normal political conception of a kingdom as understood by Rome, and

by every human political authority before or since. Jesus is saying that his imperishable and universal kingdom is not in the order of political magnitudes. If it were, then his own followers would have acted in the normal 'political' way, and fought on that very evening to prevent his arrest and appearance before the Jews. In a word, there is nothing seditious in his claim to be a king.

37

'*So you are a king?*': Once more the *you* is emphatic – with all the emphasis of bewildered incredulity. The *so* demands a straight answer, which, however, Jesus still fails to give.

'*You say that I am a king*': Still Jesus does not admit to the truth of Pilate's phrase. On his lips the words mean something other than on the lips of Jesus. 'Those are words that you use' is thus a very proper comment on the course of the dialogue.

'*For this I was born, and for this I have come into the world, to bear witness to the truth*': The reference to his birth is to indicate that the whole of his life has to be understood in terms of its final aims; the reference to his coming into the world, to the 'incarnation' as distinct from the 'nativity', must be interpreted to mean that the life itself, in its completeness, is part of a wider purpose which belongs to him as the king with an eternal and universal kingdom. Jesus had not come to establish a political sovereignty, but to bear witness to the truth, the truth of God's sole sovereignty, eternal and universal in distinction from that of man's temporal and finite, partial and competitive sovereignties.

'*Every one who is of the truth hears my voice*': This may well be a last silent appeal to Pilate to listen to the inward voice that has evidently made itself heard in Pilate's consciousness. For an understanding of what it is to *hear his voice* the reader is referred to 10³, 16²⁷ where the figure is used under the metaphor of Jesus as the good shepherd; and the good shepherd is the good king. (See notes above.)

38

'*What is truth?*': What immense issues can be dismissed from the area of proper responsibility by so profound and unanswerable a question! Confronted with him who is 'the Truth' (14⁶), and having been profoundly moved by his response under interrogation, Pilate stifles any incipient response he may have thought it possible to make, by turning from the personal to the abstract, and asks '*What is truth?*'. Reluctant but inadequate sympathy had signally failed. For all his efforts Pilate was now bound to pass the death sentence upon his prisoner. He has reached and passed the point of no return. Pilate has tried to take neither the side of the accusers, nor that of the accused; but that does not work. Any man is either 'for him' or 'against him'. Neutrality is impossible; and Pilate has to recognize this in action, if not in word.

'*I find no crime in him*': Pilate has evidently been convinced by the conversation with Jesus that there is nothing insurrectionist about the kind of kingship Jesus claims. So he announces to the Jews that he can find nothing to sustain a criminal charge.

39

'*But you have a custom that I should release one man for you at the Passover*': Such a custom is not known outside the evidence of the four gospels; though individual instances of releasing a prisoner were not unknown. Pilate might have offered to release Jesus of Nazareth, or Jesus King of the Jews, and the crowd have clamoured for the release of Barabbas, whose name in some manuscripts of Matthew is said to be Jesus Barabbas (the son of the father!).

'*will you have me release for you the King of the Jews?*': The use of the title by Pilate at this point displays the weakness that tradition has rightly seen in his character. He must have known that it would offend the Jews gathered outside. Was he somewhat fearful of riotous action if he made too plain his conviction of the prisoner's innocence? Whatever be the truth about Pilate, his proposal provided some sort of honourable escape all round. Had Jesus been released at this point, no-one could have complained of improper legal proceedings.

40

They cried out again: There is no report of a previous crying out in John. He is evidently using material from a source that tells the story in more detail. The verb for 'cry out' is a strong word, and indicates considerable force in the outcry.

'*Not this man, but Barabbas*': Mark tells his readers that the high priests suggested this action to the crowd, while Matthew is alone in recording that Pilate offered them the choice between Jesus and Barabbas. Neither statement is inconsistent with the other, or with John's narrative here. Barabbas is variously described in the gospels: Mark says he had committed murder in the insurrection (Mark 15⁷); Matthew simply states that he was 'a notorious prisoner' (Matthew 27¹⁶); Luke says that he had been thrown into prison for an insurrection started in the city, and for murder (Luke 23¹⁹, ²⁵). John's statement that he was a *robber* is thus somewhat mild. The one clue which John gave that he shares the synoptists' view of Barabbas' notoriety is that he uses the definite article before his name: 'Not this man, but the Barabbas'.

Barabbas: In Matthew 27¹⁷ one variant reading gives the name as 'Jesus Barabbas'! So the crowd must choose between Jesus the son of the father, and Jesus the Son of the Father!

19¹⁻¹⁶   PILATE AND THE JEWS

19 *Then Pilate took Jesus and scourged him.* ²*And the soldiers plaited a crown of thorns, and put it on his head, and arrayed him in a purple robe;* ³*they came up to him, saying, 'Hail, King of the Jews!' and struck him with their hands.* ⁴*Pilate went out again, and said to them, 'Behold, I am bringing him out to you, that you may know that I find no crime in him.'* ⁵*So Jesus came out, wearing the crown of thorns and the purple robe. Pilate said to them, 'Here is the man!'* ⁶*When the chief priests and the officers saw him, they cried out, 'Crucify him, crucify him!' Pilate said to them, 'Take him yourselves and crucify him, for I find no crime in him.'* ⁷*The Jews answered him, 'We have a law, and by that law he ought to die, because he has made himself the Son of God.'* ⁸*When Pilate heard these words, he was the more afraid;* ⁹*he entered the praetorium again and said to Jesus, 'Where are you from?' But Jesus gave no answer.* ¹⁰*Pilate therefore said to him, 'You will not speak to me? Do you not know that I have power to release you, and power to crucify you?'* ¹¹*Jesus answered him, 'You would have no power over me unless it had been given you from above; therefore he who delivered me to you has the greater sin.'*

¹²*Upon this Pilate sought to release him, but the Jews cried out, 'If you release this man, you are not Caesar's friend; every one who makes himself a king sets himself against Caesar.'* ¹³*When Pilate heard these words, he brought Jesus out and sat down on the judgement seat at a place called The Pavement, and in Hebrew, Gab'batha.* ¹⁴*Now it was the day of Preparation for the Passover; it was about the sixth hour. He said to the Jews, 'Here is your King!'* ¹⁵*They cried out, 'Away with him, away with him, crucify him!' Pilate said to them, 'Shall I crucify your King?' The chief priests answered, 'We have no king but Caesar.'* ¹⁶*Then he handed him over to them to be crucified.*

In this section of the hearing before Pilate John directs his attention more to Pilate's dealings with the Jewish authorities. His decision to scourge Jesus before sentence had been passed is unusual and irregular; it looks as if he were trying to help Jesus by presenting a quite impossible object of humanity to the Jews to recognize as their 'king'. Certainly by the time Pilate took Jesus out to the Jews, scourged and with a crown of thorns upon his head, he would have looked far from kingly! The immediate reply at the sight of Jesus *'Crucify him!'* may well indicate that the Jews took a view of the claim to kingship very different from Pilate's, or at least that they wanted Pilate to take a very different one from that which he had evidently so far taken. The demand for crucifixion could only be made upon a basis of an offence against Roman law; and it therefore seems that the demand for crucifixion was an insistence that the claim to kingship was really seditious and revolutionary.

Pilate is still unconvinced on the point, but is content to hand him back to the Jews. But they insist that he has been guilty of a capital crime: they mention a blasphemous claim to be the Son of God. Now the penalty for blasphemy in Jewish law was stoning. If it is permissible to refer to the synoptic stories at this point, it may be recalled that the Jews found it difficult to get witnesses to agree about this charge, a highly inconvenient thing, since the witnesses to the crime had to begin the process of stoning! There may well have been reason for pressing Pilate to pronounce sentence, for then his soldiers could carry out the execution. But if blasphemy were the accusation made here, then it could not be made for purposes of strict legal action. Two points can be made: first, that by adding the charge of blasphemy to that of kingship, the Jews might well have thought themselves able to convince Pilate that Jesus was a danger to public peace: such messianic insurrection had been known before. Second, the introduction of such a supernatural claim might upset the judgement of a man given to superstition, and the Jews might well have known Pilate was easy prey for such a move. But whatever the reasons, the move was effective, and Pilate returned to the Praetorium to question Jesus further.

The question he puts to Jesus comes from the heart of the fourth gospel, and from the heart of the issues as between Jesus and the Jews (cf. 7$^{27ff, 40-43}$; 8$^{14-16, 52}$; 9$^{29, 33}$). At this point Jesus is silent. Whatever he says will be misconstrued, and silence is the only refuge. When Pilate reminds Jesus of the life and death power he exercises as the Roman governor of the province, Jesus reminds him of the derived character of all human authority, and indicates that Pilate's share of guilt is lessened because he has to act upon an authority properly committed to him.

At this stage it would seem that Pilate once more went out of the Praetorium and tried to persuade the Jews to let him release Jesus. He was met with an unanswerable argument when directed to a Roman governor: he must not in any way support sedition. So he presents the Jews for the last time with their king, is met with a renewed demand for crucifixion, which even then he tries to circumvent. But when the Jews declare that they have no king but Caesar, he hands Jesus over to be crucified.

It would not be fair to the Jews concerned to close this review of the legal proceedings without observing that there was some real substance in the case they laid before Pilate. Jesus had been given a tremendous and spontaneous welcome as he entered Jerusalem at the 'triumphal entry' just before the Passover. This would have filled the official mind with very considerable foreboding as to the possible consequences should Jesus declare himself as the divine messiah of Israel during the days of the feast. To avoid any such development it might suffice simply to have Jesus arrested and put into prison; but it could equally well be argued that such measures were inadequate, for the crowd supporting Jesus could well have started a riot to effect his release once he were known to be in prison. It could well be that sensible prudence came to a very reluctant conclusion that execution at this very time was the only wise course. There is some difficulty in deciding simply from John's narrative whether the Jews ever thought of promoting a capital sentence themselves; but from the synoptists it would appear that there was difficulty in securing agreement between the witnesses who were prepared to swear to an accusation of blasphemy. In any event the death penalty was sought from Pilate. There is evident reluctance on the part of the Jewish authorities to lay any charge more serious than proved minimally adequate to have Jesus executed. In short what the story shows is that the crucifixion of Jesus Christ was not the result of an alliance between men motivated wholly by vicious inclinations; it is rather that good men are driven to evil sometimes by the very soundness of their good intentions. That is a measure of the grip of evil upon man!

1

Pilate took Jesus and scourged him: It seems that it is at this point that Pilate accepts responsibility for the treatment of his prisoner. He took him. The act of scourging was really part of the capital sentence, and appears so in Mark (15¹⁵). In John it appears that Pilate uses this punishment in order to seek the release of Jesus (cf. v.4).

2

the soldiers plaited a crown of thorns ... and arrayed him in a purple robe: This is all a mocking parody of kingly splendour, though the keen eye of John sees an immense pathos in such homage to the real king.

3

they came up to him, saying, 'Hail, King of the Jews': The verb 'to come up to' indicates a mocking advance of a subject to a sovereign. The soldiers 'played' at a royal reception.

struck him with their hands: cf. 18²², and note.

4

Pilate went out again: To prepare the Jews for the sight of Jesus after his scourging.

'that you may know that I find no crime in him': This is not only a reaffirmation of the innocence asserted at 18³⁸, but an invitation to share with Pilate in a verdict of 'not guilty'.

5

Jesus came out, wearing the crown of thorns and the purple robe: Such mock-majesty might have produced leniency in the hearts of men, and it can only be supposed that the results of yielding to leniency were such as no responsible Jewish official could entertain. There were real grounds for Jewish fears.

'Here is the man': This is one of the phrases which Johannine irony has most filled. The dressed king is announced as a man; the claimant to divine status is announced as a man; and yet, as both author and reader know, this man despised by both Pilate and his accusers is, in a very real sense, 'the man', the 'proper man', as Luther called him.

There may well be some reference in the Johannine vocabulary at this point to the myth of primal man, to whom, all unwittingly, Pilate now points.

6

'Take him yourselves and crucify him': As Pilate well knew, the Jews could not do this. The words cannot but be a taunt, uttered by Pilate

in the heat of exasperation at the Jewish refusal to allow Jesus to be acquitted.

7

'*We have a law*': i.e. one of our laws, a particular statute.

'*because he has made himself the Son of God*': The penalty for blasphemy was stoning (Lev. 24^{16}). The point of the rejoinder could not therefore be that this charge could be pressed as a ground of crucifixion; rather, as the next verse bears out, it was spoken in order to play upon Pilate's superstitious fears.

8

When Pilate heard these words, he was the more afraid: Not 'more afraid than he had been before', but, in an idiom well-known at the time, more means 'very'. 'Pilate was very much afraid' or 'very frightened indeed'.

9

he entered the praetorium again: evidently taking Jesus with him.

'*Where are you from?*': see notes above. It is pointless for Jesus to make any answer.

10

Pilate therefore said to him ... 'Do you not know that I have power to release you, and power to crucify you?': Pilate talks of the *potestas* belonging to the governor, and, so regarded, his comment is entirely accurate. But considering that already he has twice tried to have Jesus released, the assertion may not have come to Jesus with any sort of conviction. And from the way in which the Jews had demanded his crucifixion he may well have doubted Pilate's power to resist their plea.

11

'*You would have no power over me unless it had been given you from above*': Jesus is enunciating substantially the same principle as is advanced by Paul in Romans 13^1: 'There is no authority except from God'. For the well-being of men and their societies God has ordained that certain authority be vested in certain offices and officers. Those who occupy such offices cannot avoid their responsibility to God.

'*therefore he who delivered me to you has the greater sin*': These are manifestly enigmatic words for any commentator. They would seem to be an attempt to say to Pilate that, as an official who has to perform his duties in fulfilment of the responsibilities of his office, he is, in this particular case, far less culpable than the one who, without any requirement of office, delivered Jesus up for judgement to the Roman governor. Once Pilate has been appealed to, he has to act in order to fulfil his office; but the situation is very different for the one who had no need to act by yielding Jesus into Pilate's hands. Jesus is to die, and Pilate cannot escape some real complicity in his death; but the one who gave him into Pilate's judgement is more guilty than Pilate.

But who is *he who delivered* Jesus to Pilate? Not, presumably, Judas, for he gave Jesus into the hands of the Jews. The high priest? Or the Jewish authorities viewed as a single whole? One of these is probably the meaning, and Jesus is stating that his own people are inevitably more involved in his death than is the Roman governor, who, in spite of quite severe imperfections in his conduct of the proceedings, cannot but take action when a case is brought to his notice, and so pressed as this case against Jesus has been pressed.

12

Upon this Pilate sought to release him: An example of Pilate's vacillation. He would have had to go out to the Jews again, and put his plea for Jesus' release to the crowd outside.

'*If you release this man, you are not Caesar's friend*': *Caesar's friend* was a term that later had an official significance in the time of Vespasian. But at this point of the trial it means no more than 'loyal to Caesar'.

'*every one who makes himself a king sets himself against Caesar*': With these words it is made quite clear to Pilate that the charge against Jesus is not, in the eyes of the authorities, simply a matter internal to the Jewish religion, but a situation rightly calling for the consideration of the governor. A Jewish king cannot but be involved in insurrection. Pilate cannot but take swift steps to stamp out any incipient revolt at this festival time.

13

Pilate . . . brought Jesus out and sat down on the judgement seat at a place called The Pavement, and in Hebrew, Gabbatha: Pilate has come to the end of his ability to delay sentence. So he calls for Jesus to be brought out, and then proceeds to make the formal arrangements for giving the verdict and sentence.

The judgement seat was the tribunal of a magistrate. Josephus tells of such a tribunal or judgement seat being set up out of doors (Wars, 2⁹·³). Some commentators have raised the question whether the verb *sat down* be transitive or intransitive, i.e. whether Pilate himself sat on the seat, or whether he sat Jesus on it in a last piece of mockery. Either sense is grammatically permissible, but it would seem quite alien to the occasion for Pilate actually to pronounce sentence while staging a mockery, however much he had done so before. The justice of Rome could hardly be treated with that levity!

at a place called The Pavement: Governors sometimes carried about for their tribunals a portable mosaic paving, and this may be indicated here. But Josephus reports that this part of the fortress of Antonia was covered with a tessellated pavement. No final accuracy seems attainable.

Gabbatha: This is a word whose meaning cannot be determined with any sort of precision, neither can its location be accurately determined. John does not say that the Hebrew word translates the Greek, as he does e.g. at 1³⁸.

14
Now it was the day of Preparation for the Passover: i.e. the eve of the Passover, Nisan 14. This date conflicts with the synoptic chronology (see Introduction, p. 55ff).

it was about the sixth hour: Mark states that 'it was the third hour when they crucified him' (Mark 15²⁵). John is concerned to use a chronology that will disclose Jesus being slain upon the cross at the same time that the passover lambs were being slain in the temple for the festival meal. John's hour for the crucifixion in inherently more likely.

'Here is your King': Another touch of Johannine irony. Pilate spoke more truly than he knew.

15
'Shall I crucify your King?': This could as well be translated: 'Must I crucify your King?', which would add to the drama of the occasion.

'We have no king but Caesar': Thus do the representatives of Judaism tacitly deny their fundamental religious conviction that Yahweh is king. To deny the son of God brings religion and politics alike into gross distortion.

16
he handed him over to them to be crucified: The nearest that John comes to reporting a sentence. Of course John does not mean that the Jews were to carry out the execution; he is simply underlining the fact that Pilate has at last yielded to the will of the Jews and consented to the death penalty they have sought.

'THEY WILL KILL HIM'

Mark 15^{16-41}
Exodus 28^{32}
Psalm 22^{18}
Psalm 69^{21}
Psalm 22^{15}

¹⁷*So they took Jesus, and he went out, bearing his own cross, to the place called the place of a skull, which is called in Hebrew Gol'gotha.* ¹⁸*There they crucified him, and with him two others, one on either side, and Jesus between them.* ¹⁹*Pilate also wrote a title and put it on the cross; it read, 'Jesus of Nazareth, the King of the Jews.'* ²⁰*Many of the Jews read this title, for the place where Jesus was crucified was near the city; and it was written in Hebrew, in Latin, and in Greek.* ²¹*The chief priests of the Jews then said to Pilate, 'Do not write, "The King of the Jews," but, "This man said, I am King of the Jews."'* ²²*Pilate answered, 'What I have written I have written.'*

²³*When the soldiers had crucified Jesus they took his garments and made four parts, one for each soldier. But his tunic was without seam, woven from top to bottom;* ²⁴*so they said to one another, 'Let us not tear it, but cast lots for it to see whose it shall be.' This was to fulfil the scripture.*

'They parted my garments among them,
and for my clothing they cast lots.'

²⁵*So the soldiers did this; but standing by the cross of Jesus were his mother, and his mother's sister, Mary the wife of Clopas, and Mary of Mag'dalene.* ²⁶*When Jesus saw his mother, and the disciple whom he loved standing near, he said to his mother, 'Woman, behold your son!'* ²⁷*Then he said to the disciple, 'Behold your mother!' And from that hour the disciple took her to his own home.*

²⁸*After this Jesus, knowing that all was now finished, said (to fulfil the scripture), 'I thirst.'* ²⁹*A bowl full of vinegar stood there; so they put a sponge full of the vinegar on hyssop and held it to his mouth.* ³⁰*When Jesus had received the vinegar, he said, 'It is finished'; and he bowed his head and gave up his spirit.*

John takes little space to tell his reader what he believes to be necessary for them to know about the crucifixion of the Lord. It is done in two, or at the most three verses (19^{17, 18} and, possibly, ³⁰). He finds it unnecessary to include some of the synoptists' material, notably the story of Simon of Cyrene carrying Christ's cross, and the darkness that came over the land. He thinks it important to embellish the tradition with the story of the soldiers at the cross, with the record of the Lord's concern for his mother, and with an account of the dying thirst of Jesus and his final proclamation of victory. Into such a distinctive narrative he brings the figure of the one who had been rejected by the Jews, tried before Pilate, and sent to his death clad in the mockery of kingly raiment, and yet, for all the satisfaction that may have given to some, clad appropriately for all those who saw and who have since come to see the validity of his claim to be king.

If John has deliberately omitted the story of Simon of Cyrene the reason is not difficult to surmise: he wants his readers to be quite clear that Jesus goes to his death entirely reliant upon his own more than adequate resources. For this reason there need be no attempt to effect an historical harmonization between the synoptists and John, such as the suggestion that Jesus carried his own cross for some distance, and then handed it over to Simon. That would be to subject John's profound theological narrative to a quite superficial historical examination.

The story of Pilate and the wording of the *titlon* that was placed upon the cross is also of importance for John. The protest of the chief priests can hardly have come from their recently pronounced conviction that their only king was Caesar! Rather does it recoil upon their own heads as a way of stating the truth which they can no longer consistently combat.

With his eye for the symbolic occasion it is not surprising that John should see in the action of the soldiers on duty at the cross an actual incident that was eloquent of the messianic character of the crucified man upon the central cross.

Finally John tells of three 'words from the cross'. One is linked with the whole expectation that scripture has given to the Christian; the other two may be seen as incorporating some important strands which John has skilfully woven into his narrative, the final word particularly bringing to suitable climax the whole story that he has told.

୪୨

17
they took Jesus: The word used here is the same as the evangelist used

in the Prologue to state that when the Word came to his own, his own did not receive him. There is dramatic irony that at this point of the story, his own people do receive the incarnate word – but to crucify him!

he went out, bearing his own cross: John would have his readers think of the complete sufficiency of the resources of Jesus to face all that his dying might mean, even to the physical burden of carrying the cross. His physical sufficiency was parabolic of his spiritual sufficiency to offer himself in death. The usual picture of Jesus carrying a cross composed of two pieces of wood at right angles to each other is possibly not accurate; the criminal would most probably be required to carry the cross beam upon which his arms were to be stretched.

the place of a skull: There is no evidence in John, or indeed in the synoptics, why the place is called 'the skull'. Possibly it was because it was a place of execution; less probably because the hill has itself a skull-like shape.

18

There they crucified him, and with him two others, one on either side, and Jesus between them: Nothing is said in the fourth gospel about the crimes of the other condemned men. It appears that Jesus, crowned as king, is given the 'place of honour' in the centre of the group. Again, John's sense of irony detects that even so unwillingly the executioners bear testimony to the truth.

19

Pilate also wrote a title: Title was a technical term for such a note of the crime for which a man was condemned. That it was put upon the cross suggests that the type of cross on which Jesus was crucified has been correctly represented in traditional Christian art (Matt. 27^{37} confirms this when he says that the *titulus* was placed 'over his head'). The phrase in this verse is not to be taken to mean that Pilate wrote the *titulus* himself, but more probably that he caused it to be written. The *titulus* could state both the name of the criminal and the offence for which he was suffering. That provided for Jesus did both. John alone gives this wording thus. Though the synoptists differ among themselves none of them uses the description *of Nazareth*. The naming of his habitual residence may well pick up various strands in the gospel, the confident assertion e.g. that the Jews 'knew his father and mother' and that he therefore could not have come down from heaven (6$^{41ff.}$), as well as answer the question which Pilate put to Jesus for the last time in his life: 'Where are you from?' (18^9). John's irony is still at work. So much is stated by those who do not even know the real force of what they are saying!

20

it was written in Hebrew, in Latin, and in Greek: The three languages are clearly intended by the evangelist to depict the way in which even the executioners bore universal testimony to him whom they were crucifying.

21

The chief priests . . . then said to Pilate, 'Do not write, "The King of the Jews"': Pilate evidently made the priests feel insulted by the form of words. But had they thought that they had no king but Caesar they would surely have been able to regard such a description of Jesus with the same belittling scorn as Pilate himself.

22

'What I have written I have written': The statement means what the tense of the verb implies, that something has been written down once and for all. Pilate will not go back upon it. It must stand. So by the strange irony of events Jesus dies with a true statement of his nature proclaimed upon his cross by a Roman official who did not believe in him. It is not unimportant for John that Pilate should be thus unwittingly a witness to the Jews that Jesus was their king. For the Lord's claim to a wider kingship than that of the Jews did at any rate start there. It was only by coming to his own that he could come at all to claim a universal kingship; for that was the way foreseen by prophets of old, that the universal dominion of Yahweh would be brought about through the exercise of dominion by his chosen people. Here, where the kingship of Christ is asserted in the deed of the crucifixion, the evangelist has combined the particular (*King of the Jews*) and the universal (Hebrew and Latin and Greek) in one act of testimony to Israel and to the world. The King of Israel, and of the world, hung upon the cross.

23

made four parts, one for each soldier: There would seem to be one quaternion of men on duty at each cross – quite a contrast to the 600 sent out to arrest Jesus the previous night. But now that Jesus had been condemned to death for a political offence against Rome, the danger of a Jewish messianic rising instigated by him had gone. Normal 'execution duty' now sufficed.

Roman law provided that a prisoner's garments, removed before crucifixion, became the property of the soldiers on guard. All the synoptists record the division of the garments by lottery; it is a special refinement of the Johannine narrative that tells of an easy division of the clothes into four parts, with the lottery being made for the tunic alone. *This* comments John *was to fulfil the scripture* and he goes on to quote Psalm 22¹⁸. It may well be that the particular specification of a double division of the distribution of garments in John is due to the somewhat prosaic interpretation of the Psalm which was really poetry. Hebrew poetry accumulates synonymous phrases, and there is little doubt that originally *garments* and *clothing* in the verse quoted were meant to be identical terms. But John, like Matthew in dealing with Zechariah 9⁹ (Matt. 21⁷), is so anxious to ensure that the readers will not be able to escape the rightness of the application of the prophecy that he itemizes the raiment in detail. Two possibilities thereupon open out: first, it may be taken as a signal illustration of the messianic character of the death of Jesus. For Psalm 22 was regarded as a messianic psalm, and John uses it here to indicate that, again quite unconsciously, even the soldiers on duty at the cross are caught up in the messianic complex of events. Second, the actual division may well be significant. The tunic was an undergarment, and this one was, like that of the high priest according to Josephus, woven in one piece (cf. also Leviticus 16⁴, where Aaron is directed to come to the holy place of sacrifice having put on 'the holy linen tunic'). The symbolism of the one piece was quickly noticed by both Jews and Christians and it may well be that at this point John is trying to show that the death of Jesus will not destroy the unity of the people whom he has gathered together.

25

standing by the cross of Jesus were his mother, and his mother's sister, Mary the wife of Clopas, and Mary of Magdalene: The Greek is not unambiguous, and could imply any number of women between two and four. If two be the number intended, then *Mary the wife of Clopas* must be translated, as it certainly can, 'Mary the daughter, or sister, of Clopas'. The text would then be saying that Jesus' mother, the daughter or sister of Clopas, was at the cross along with her sister Mary Magdalene. Three could equally well be intended, and if so they would be Mary, the mother of Jesus, and her sister Mary the daughter, sister or wife of Clopas, and Mary Magdalene. Or again, four women may be intended, Mary the mother of Jesus, and her sister, and Mary the daughter or sister or wife of Clopas, and Mary Magdalene. The synoptists do not greatly help in these identifications. Mark reports that among a number of women who watched from afar were Mary Magdalene, Mary the mother of James the younger and Joseph, and Salome. Matthew reports the two Marys with Mark, and adds that the mother of the sons of Zebedee was also present; which may mean that she was called Salome. If this latter identification holds, and if the beloved disciple is John the son of

Zebedee, then since Salome was the sister of Jesus' mother, Jesus was putting his mother into the care of her nephew. He was a disciple, and the Lord's brothers were not. Whether or not Mary was herself a 'believer' or not cannot be stated for certain. What evidence there is seems to be against it. The synoptists all report an incident in which Jesus' mother and his brothers asked to see him, and he replied by saying 'Here are my mother and my brothers! Whoever does the will of God is my brother, and sister, and mother' (Mark 3³⁴ᶠ). Again, it would seem the only inference to be drawn from Jesus' remark upon his rejection in the synagogue at Nazareth: 'A prophet is not without honour, except in his own country, and among his own kin, and in his own house' (Mark 6⁴).

26

Jesus . . . said to his mother, 'Woman, behold your son': The seeming harsh word *woman* is not really indicative of any disrespect. It was used, the reader will remember, at the wedding feast in Cana (2⁴), and it may well represent in John the sense of a loving relationship transcending even that of the family, which the quotation from Mark expresses in a characteristically different way (cf. above quotation from Mark 3³⁴ᶠ). The phrase *behold your son* deserves further comment. It stands as a simple yet thoughtful attempt on the part of Jesus to provide some future shelter for his mother within the company of those who, like the sons of Zebedee (or the beloved disciple), had come to believe in Jesus Christ. But more profoundly it can well be taken to mean that that which has come out of the root of Judaism, God's people after the flesh, must henceforth find its proper home with that which has come out of the ministry of Jesus, the Christian church. John may well be indicating in this symbolic way that the true destiny of Israel is to be found in belief in Jesus Christ and in the fellowship of the Church.

27

Then he said to the disciple, 'Behold your mother!': This saying is similarly patent of interpretation at two levels. It undoubtedly constitutes the concern of Jesus for the future of his beloved disciple; the true love which can nourish and sustain his faith is to be found in and from her who bore him. Similarly it may well represent a word to the young Christian church not to forget the Judaism from which it sprang. The same point is made, in a vastly different way, by the apostle Paul in Romans, where it appears quite clear that without the contribution that Israel can give, the whole Christian church will be infinitely the poorer.

If these reflections approximate in any way to the truth, then it must remain as one of the greatest tragedies of history that within a few years

of Jesus' death the rift between Church and synagogue should have
become humanly speaking quite unbridgeable. Yet it was the deep
insight of the fourth evangelist to see that these two great religions are
incomplete, the one without the other.

28

Jesus, knowing that all was now finished, said (to fulfil the scripture), 'I
thirst': John says that this saying from the cross was 'after' the previous
word to his mother and the beloved disciple. There is no suggestion
that it was immediately after; and it is highly likely that some considerable interval of time took place (cf. the three hours recorded by Mark
[Mark 15²⁵: the third hour; 15³³: darkness until the ninth hour]). The
statement that Jesus knew that all was now finished indicates, as the
same kind of language at 13¹, that he was really in control; not waiting
upon events to discover when the end should come, but knowing that
it was due. What is finished is not just the physical life, not even the
human ministry, but the whole work of the incarnate Word. Knowing
that victory was about to be completed, he said, according to John, 'I
thirst'. John adds that this was to fulfil the scripture. We should
misinterpret John and indeed the whole biblical story were we to think
that at this moment of his life Jesus was trying to think of what he had
to do in order to make his actions conform to the predictions (so-called)
of scripture. John is not so naïve as that. What he is trying to say is that
if this cry of thirst is properly understood, it will be seen to reflect the
situation envisaged in the scripture to which he refers; and that to
carry the appropriate scripture to what Jesus now says is to see it in its
true meaning and perspective. The scripture reference seems to be
twofold, to Psalm 22¹⁵ and to Psalm 69³ and especially 69²¹ᵇ. Again the
point is not so much in the apparent foretelling of Christ's thirst and the
rough attempt to quench it with vinegar: that is a far too trivial
conception of the relevance of scripture for a profound thinker like
John. Rather it is again a sense that in this moment of weakness Jesus
knew that the uttermost point of his 'descent' was upon him, and that
this meant that at the same time and by the same token, the topmost
point of his uplifting was upon him. The two messianic psalms are
eloquent of this. The tragic verses of Psalm 22, with their uncanny closeness to the events of the crucifixion, end in triumph: 'Yea, to him shall
all the proud of the earth bow down; before him shall bow all who go
down to the dust, and he who cannot keep himself alive. Posterity shall
serve him; men shall tell of the Lord to the coming generation, and proclaim his deliverance to a people yet unborn, that he has wrought it'
(Psalm 22²⁹⁻³¹). Psalm 69, where again the sufferings depicted are fierce
and many, ends in a note of triumph: 'I will praise the name of God with

a song; I will magnify him with thanksgiving . . . For the Lord hears the needy, and does not despise his own that are in bonds . . . For God will save Zion, and rebuild the cities of Judah, and his servants shall dwell there and possess it; the children of his servants shall inherit it, and those who love his name shall dwell in it' (Psalm 69³⁰⁻³⁶ selections).

29

so they put a sponge full of vinegar on hyssop and held it to his mouth: This is the incident depicted so strangely in Psalm 69²¹ᵇ 'for my thirst they gave me vinegar to drink'. The reporting of it reflects John's eye for the symbolic again.

hyssop is not a very useful implement for holding a sponge. Yet it seems too opportune an alternative when a late reading provides the reader with the word to be translated 'javelin', by the mere dropping of one syllable from the Greek word. Hyssop is manifestly the original reading, and while somewhat inappropriate for the purpose of carrying a sponge, it is worth remembering that it did not have to raise the sponge very high (the heads of the crucified were not greatly above ordinary level), and that it is eminently suitable for association with the Passover, perhaps especially with the death of him who was called at the very beginning of the gospel 'the lamb of God', and who is now dying on the cross at the very time that the Passover lambs are being slain in the temple, not very far away. Once again it is important to remember that for John, history is written in order to indicate the theological meaning he was convinced it really had.

30

Jesus . . . said, 'It is finished': This is by no means just an indication of a terminus being reached, as if Jesus were saying 'The end has come'. The word used conveys a note of triumphant accomplishment, as if he had cried out exultingly 'It's done!'. In one sense these words can be taken as the very centre and heart of John's gospel, for they state the triumphant story he has to tell in three significant words (one only in the Greek). It cannot be too strongly emphasized that for John the cross is the instrument and point of victory, not the point of defeat which has to be reversed on Easter morning. Here, as the Lord dies, he conquers. Here, submitting to death, he vanquishes it.

and he bowed his head and gave up his spirit: Even at the moment of dying John uses active verbs. There is no 'passion' in John; even death is an act for Jesus. In this he is companion with all the synoptists, who also state the event of his death in active verbs (he breathed his last, or yielded up his spirit). But it appears that John's account can be both nearer to the actual facts of death by crucifixion as well as more noticeably indicative of Jesus' initiative. It appears that in crucifixion the condemned person found that as his body tired he was increasingly unable to keep his chest in a position in which breathing was easy and effective. The tendency was to become increasingly unable to press upwards from the feet, so as to keep the chest in a position where, by holding the head upright, breathing could be properly carried on. It was possibly for these reasons that the legs of criminals crucified were broken: once that were done the crucified could no longer press upward from his feet, and his body would sink down and make breathing impossible. What John's account seems to indicate is that Jesus did not succumb passively to death by crucifixion, but rather deliberately chose the moment of his death by bowing his head, thus restricting his breathing, and causing life to become extinct. So even in his physical death he was an agent, as he certainly is set forth as the agent of his death in a wider sense and frame of reference. Again, if this be a feasible comment, the reader has benefited from John's uncanny eye for the symbolic incident to light up an historical occasion with its proper meaning.

19³¹⁻⁴²   'DEAD AND BURIED'

Mark 15⁴²⁻⁴⁷
Exodus 12¹⁶
Deuteronomy 21²³
Exodus 12⁴⁶
Zechariah 12¹⁰

³¹*Since it was the day of Preparation, in order to prevent the bodies from remaining on the cross on the sabbath (for that sabbath was a high day), the Jews asked Pilate that their legs might be broken, and that they might be taken away.* ³²*So the soldiers came and broke the legs of the first, and of the other who had been crucified with him;* ³³*but when they came to Jesus and saw that he was already dead, they did not break his legs.* ³⁴*But one of the soldiers pierced his side with a spear, and at once there came out blood and water.* ³⁵*He who saw it has borne witness – his testimony is true, and he knows that he tells the truth – that you also may believe.* ³⁶*For these things took place that the scripture might be fulfilled, 'Not a bone of him shall be broken.'* ³⁷*And again another scripture says, 'They shall look on him whom they have pierced.'*

³⁸*After this Joseph of Arimathe'a, who was a disciple of Jesus, but secretly,*

for fear of the Jews, asked Pilate that he might take away the body of Jesus, and Pilate gave him leave. So he came and took away his body. ³⁹Nicode'-mus also, who had at first come to him by night, came bringing a mixture of myrrh and aloes, about a hundred pounds' weight. ⁴⁰They took the body of Jesus, and bound it in linen cloths with the spices, as is the burial custom of the Jews. ⁴¹Now in the place where he was crucified there was a garden, and in the garden a new tomb where no one had ever been laid. ⁴²So because of the Jewish day of Preparation, as the tomb was close at hand, they laid Jesus there.

In this section of the record of the great seventh sign, which includes both the death and the resurrection of the Lord, John is anxious among other things to leave his readers in no doubt at all that Jesus really and truly died, and that his death was wholly within God's purpose and design. He makes his points, as often, through certain incidents, some peculiar to his own narrative.

For John it was doubly important that the bodies of the crucified men should not be permitted to hang on the cross beyond the end of the day, since the day of crucifixion was a Friday, and the next day was not only a sabbath, but also, this year, the first day of the feast of unleavened bread. The Jews therefore asked Pilate for the men's legs to be broken, to ensure their death in time for removing their bodies before the sabbath began. (For one possible explanation of the request for the breaking of the legs to ensure death, see the immediately preceding note.)

Pilate readily complied with the Jewish request, and the soldiers were sent upon their errand. But when they came to Jesus they found that he was already dead. His legs were therefore not broken. But, to be certain of the death of Jesus (evidently it had occurred 'too soon' for normal expectation), one soldier pierced the side of Jesus with a spear, and the report of an eye-witness, strongly emphasized at this point, is that blood and water issued from the wound. The evangelist expresses his conviction that the incident, like others at the crucifixion itself, could be seen as fulfilment of scripture.

The last scene of the dying of the Lord Jesus came when Joseph of Arimathea sought permission from Pilate to bury the body of Jesus. Permission was given, and Joseph and Nicodemus put his body in a tomb in the garden near to the place of execution, using a large quantity of spices in so doing. It was their evident intention that after the sabbath they would move the Lord's body to some permanent grave.

The narrative is a strange mixture of the credible and the incredible. There is nothing to excite modern comment in the request of the Jews that care be taken to ensure that the crucified men were dead before the sabbath began. There is nothing particularly requiring comment in the fact that Jesus was found to be dead, while the two others were not. This may be accounted for in a variety of ways, and need not elicit comment here. But what is incredible is that blood and water should have come out of a pierced side. The assertion has received a good deal of expert medical attention, and opinion is divided among experts. It is by no means clear that John is chiefly concerned that his readers should learn that blood and water came from Christ's pierced side. The fact – if it be a fact – might well be subordinated, as often in John, to the assertion of some point of theological interpretation or meaning. And as to what that was, he has provided some clues. He applies two Old Testament passages to the incident: one from Exodus concerning the Passover lamb, that its bones must not be broken; and one from Zechariah, that God will pour out his spirit upon the house of David and the inhabitants of Jerusalem that when they look on him whom they have pierced, they shall mourn for him as one mourns for an only child. If these two are applied to the emphasized action of the soldier in (a) not breaking the legs of Jesus and (b) piercing his side, it becomes fairly clear what the evangelist is trying to state. In the case of the first 'prophecy' he is saying that Jesus Christ may be considered as the true Passover lamb, slain at the proper time for Passover lambs to be slain, and, like a proper lamb for the feast, without broken bones. In the case of the second 'prophecy' the evangelist is predicting that the Jews will come to mourn the death and the killing of Jesus, which is to say that he envisages the final triumph of Jesus in the conversion of the Jews to the Christian church.

The residual problem is then the meaning of the assertion that when he was pierced, blood and water issued from the wound. It would seem that in any case this is the lesser detail, but the two words blood and water are not without meaning for the reader of the gospel. Blood stands for the life of the Lord given in sacrifice for men as that is symbolized also in the eucharist, and water for the gift of the spirit, or for the rite of baptism.

Further comment will be found in the notes.

Joseph of Arimathea is evidently one of those leaders of the Jews who are reported by John to have followed Jesus, yet without open acknowledgement of the fact. But now it becomes possible to express the attachment without fear, for is not the whole story over? So he approaches Pilate with the request for the body. It is granted. Haste must have been the order of the day. The body had to be taken from the cross, decently wrapped up and anointed, and buried in some tomb before the sabbath began at 6 in the evening. Happily there was a tomb available and handy in the garden where the crucifixion had taken place. This was used as a temporary burial place for the master. Little did either Joseph or Nicodemus know how temporary it would be!

ನಾಣ

31

the day of Preparation: i.e. Friday. Jesus died on Friday afternoon. The sabbath would begin at 6 p.m. on that day. Much had to be done in a short time.

34

one of the soldiers pierced his side with a spear: Some early texts of the gospel of Matthew insert this incident at the end of 27^{49}, i.e. while Jesus is still alive. This will not suit the Johannine intentions at all. The weapon used was a lance, spear or javelin, and it is not clear from the word used whether the wound inflicted was something of a prick, just to see if the person were really dead, or whether it were of such a nature as to ensure death, if by any chance he were still alive. The story told in 20^{27} seems to indicate that a large wound was made, and that is probably more consistent with the testimony that blood and water were seen to flow from it.

What is the purpose of John in telling this incident? It seems quite clear that one reason is to leave his readers in no doubt at all that Jesus' death was quite real. If it happened as he said, and he claims to be an eye-witness, then he has a double piece of symbolism in the actual event, as has been argued above. Yet it is hard to escape the conclusion that the spear thrust could do very little were Jesus already dead, save, in the absence of any bodily reaction, to indicate that unconsciousness was complete. Whatever be the answer, it is quite plain that John is once more using a symbolic element in what he takes to be an historical occasion to drive home a theological truth. John is engaged in a piece of anti-docetic statement, an assertion that the humanity of Jesus had been truly a physical humanity in the fullest sense. He had lived as a man, and had died as a man. The son of God had really *come in the flesh*. But his death was not an event on its own, but one into which other men could enter through the sacraments of blood and water. So from the side of him who lived and died there flowed the twin streams of the life-giving sacraments of the church in which Christ dwells.

35

and he knows that he tells the truth: The words in parenthesis are those of the evangelist, and they are his own support of the evidence given by the eye-witness who saw the piercing of the side.

36

'*Not a bone of him shall be broken*': The Passover lamb had to be a perfect specimen. This Jesus was. The language is like that used by Paul in 1 Corinthians 5⁷: 'Christ, our paschal lamb, has been sacrificed'.

37

'*They shall look on him whom they have pierced*': Here John makes his own translation of the Hebrew text of the Old Testament. The Septuagint has completely mistranslated the Hebrew as 'dance insultingly'.

38

Joseph of Arimathea: Arimathea is some 60 miles from Jerusalem and 13 miles east-north-east of Lydda. Joseph was a member of the Sanhedrin (Mark 15⁴³), and presumably one of Jesus' secret disciples (12⁴²).

39

Nicodemus is already known to the reader. Probably he had become, like Joseph, a 'secret disciple'.

a mixture of myrrh and aloes: This was the normal means for preparing a body for burial. The extraordinary thing is the quite enormous quantity provided; 'lavish' is not too strong a word.

40

bound it in linen cloths: A detail peculiar to John. Jesus' body is thus treated in the same way as that of his friend Lazarus (11⁴⁴). The linen cloths provided a kind of bandage which was wrapped round the corpse, the spices being laid between the layers.

41

there was a garden: Another detail peculiar to John. Where the Lord dies, is buried and is to rise is the new Paradise, the true 'garden of Eden [i.e. delight]'. The language suggests a sizeable plot, an orchard or plantation.

a new tomb: New in not having been used before. All this careful specification of the burial recalls the substance of the picture of the Servant in Isaiah 53⁹: 'They made his grave . . . with a rich man in his death'. More than abundant spices, a private garden and an unused tomb, this was lavish burial indeed. The garden and the tomb would probably belong to Joseph or Nicodemus or one of their friends.

42

because of the Jewish day of Preparation, as the tomb was close at hand, they laid Jesus there: The language certainly suggests that the arrangements were only temporary. The mission of the women on Easter morning is thus understandable. 'Day of Preparation' usually means Friday, though the qualification 'Jewish' probably indicates Passover, since John is accustomed to speak of the Passover of the Jews.

20$^{1-18}$ EASTER MORNING
                                            Mark 16$^{1-8}$

20 *Now on the first day of the week Mary Mag'dalene came to the tomb early, while it was still dark, and saw that the stone had been taken away from the tomb.* ²*So she ran, and went to Simon Peter and the other disciple, the one whom Jesus loved, and said to them, 'They have taken the Lord out of the tomb, and we do not know where they have laid him.'* ³*Peter then came out with the other disciple, and they went towards the tomb.* ⁴*They both ran, but the other disciple outran Peter and reached the tomb first;* ⁵*and stooping to look in, he saw the linen cloths lying there, but he did not go in.* ⁶*Then Simon Peter came, following him, and he went into the tomb; he saw the linen cloths lying,* ⁷*and the napkin, which had been on his head, not lying with the linen cloths but rolled up in a place by itself.* ⁸*Then the other disciple, who reached the tomb first, also went in, and he saw and believed;* ⁹*for as yet they did not know the scripture, that he must rise from the dead.* ¹⁰*Then the disciples went back to their homes.*

¹¹*But Mary stood weeping outside the tomb, and as she wept she stooped to look into the tomb;* ¹²*and she saw two angels in white, sitting where the body of Jesus had lain, one at the head and one at the feet.* ¹³*They said to her, 'Woman, why are you weeping?' She said to them, 'Because they have taken away my Lord, and I do not know where they have laid him.'* ¹⁴*Saying this, she turned round and saw Jesus standing, but she did not*

know that it was Jesus. ^{15}*Jesus said to her, 'Woman, why are you weeping?*
Whom do you seek?' Supposing him to be the gardener, she said to him,
'Sir, if you have carried him away, tell me where you have laid him, and I
will take him away.' ^{16}*Jesus said to her, 'Mary.' She turned and said to him*
in Hebrew, 'Rab-bo'ni!' (which means Teacher). ^{17}*Jesus said to her, 'Do*
not hold me, for I have not yet ascended to the Father; but go to my brethren
and say to them, I am ascending to my Father and your Father, to my God
and your God.' ^{18}*Mary Mag'dalene went and said to the disciples, 'I have*
seen the Lord'; and she told them that he had said these things to her.

Throughout his gospel John has had in mind the difficult yet important problem of the relationship of 'seeing' to 'believing'. It receives
some statement in the Prologue: 'The Word became flesh ... we
have beheld his glory' (1^{14}); 'No one has ever seen God; the only
Son, who is in the bosom of the Father, he has made him known' (1^{18}).
The Baptist's testimony to Jesus closes with the words: 'I have seen
and have borne witness that this is the Son of God' (1^{34}). To the
sceptical question of Nathanael, whether anything good could come
out of Nazareth, Philip replied: 'Come and see' (1^{46}). There are
times, of course, in the gospel when sight is by no means the only
sense involved in the mysterious relationship to faith, but it remains
the characteristic sense both for the gospel and for succeeding generations of Christian men. It was more than sight which was involved in
the discernment of the sign at the wedding feast in Cana, though the
'manifestation of glory' (2^{11}) was even there in part conveyed
through sight. The woman of Samaria asks her fellow Samaritans
to 'come and see' a man who had told her all that she ever did.
   The six great signs which Jesus wrought all made demands upon
the sight of men; and what they saw differed considerably. Some
would see an event within the framework of space and time, of
ordinary human experience, and even (and indeed inevitably) recognize it as miraculous, and yet never see the reality of what went on.
So it is that on the day after the feeding of the five thousand Jesus
said to the crowds who found him: 'You seek me, not because you
saw signs, but because you ate your fill of the loaves' (6^{26}). All the
signs posed this sort of issue to the human spirit – and they still do.
But there is a real sense, indeed the most profound one, in which the
relationship between seeing and believing is centred in the sight of
Jesus himself. This receives special treatment in the story of the fifth

sign, where the man born blind, and who therefore has no sight, is given his power to see not by natural processes, but wholly by Jesus Christ. The visual powers that then come to him enable him to know that Jesus is a man (9^{11}), to perceive later that this man was a prophet (9^{17}), and finally, when Jesus disclosed himself to his newly given sight in person, to worship and adore (9^{38}).

The point is put very fully by Matthew in his report of how Jesus preached in the synagogue of his own town. The congregation was astonished and said: 'Where did this man get this wisdom and these mighty works? Is not this the carpenter's son? Is not his mother called Mary? Are not his brothers James and Joseph and Simon and Judas? And are not all his sisters with us?' (Matt. 13^{54-56}). John has preserved a similarly obtuse rejection of Christ's claims, coincidentally located in the synagogue at Capernaum. The Jews, John reports, murmured because Jesus claimed to be 'the bread which came down from heaven' (6^{41}); and their difficulties were admirably and forcefully put in the words: 'Is not this Jesus, the son of Joseph, whose father and mother we know? How does he now say, "I have come down from heaven"?' (6^{42}). The crux is indeed here in these two stories. Both the Jerusalem man born blind and the congregation in the synagogue at Capernaum *saw* the same 'phenomena', if that neutral word can for a moment be admitted. They saw in common a certain face and hands and body; they saw alike the same raiment and the same gait; they heard the same voice and caught the same glance of the eye. Yet one saw something to worship; the others saw a purely 'natural' man.

John, of course, has his own views as to the difference. Those who 'see and believe' have been 'drawn by the Father' (6^{44}). In his prayer after the Last Supper Jesus acknowledges that all those who believe on him have been given to him by the Father ($17^{6,9,24}$). In the end to know Jesus Christ as the Son is really to know the Father in the Son (8^{19}; $14^{7,9-11}$). The Father cannot be 'seen'; there is a sense in which the Son cannot be 'seen' either, though there is another in which it is quite plain that he can. It is a constant theme of the fourth gospel to make the relationships plain.

But the problem extends throughout the gospel. It did not cease at the time when Jesus was laid in the tomb. Neither was it absent in those days, to which the evangelist bears witness, when the disciples were visited by the risen and glorified Lord. Neither is it absent for Christians of any century, for the Christian life has still to be lived in a world of sense, of sight and sound and touch and taste and smell. It is easy for any reader to see the problem raised by John concerning the earthly ministry of Jesus of Nazareth. How can it be held that Jesus can be 'seen' and yet 'not be seen'? It is easy to see the problem which John raises at this point of his narrative as he writes of the visitation of the disciples by the glorified Lord: how can he be 'seen' and yet 'not seen'? It is surely not difficult for any Christian to recognize the problem which John raises for men of his own and of all times: how can Jesus Christ be 'seen', if at all, at the present time; and, if he cannot, how can a man 'believe' in him? The great merit of the fourth gospel and its value for contemporary man is that it faces these problems quite honestly, and offers him an answer which brings all three phases of the problem together in the light of a single and final diagnosis.

The importance of John's contribution is that he shows how the need for seeing Jesus during the days of his earthly ministry is linked with the impossibility of seeing him today, and does this in such a way as to show that belief is really identical throughout. The link between belief with sight and belief without it is found in the narratives of the appearances of the glorified Lord to his disciples. During the earthly ministry belief in Jesus was dependent upon seeing him, and was focused in that experience. John the Baptist ($1^{29,36}$), Philip (1^{46}), the Samaritan woman (4^{29}), and even Jesus himself (1^{39}; 14^{9}) testify to this fact. Yet to see Jesus, however necessary an element in coming to believe in him, was even then certainly not identical with believing in him. A Johannine revision of the phrase 'Many are called, but few chosen' could well take the form: 'Many see, but few believe'. Certainly many saw him, the chief priests, the scribes and pharisees, the crowds in Jerusalem, congregations in synagogues and in the temple, guests at a wedding in Galilee and mourners at a funeral in Judea; but belief was by no means the inevitable result of sight. Sight could certainly yield incontrovertible evidence that Jesus of Nazareth had a temporal, historical existence, and this fact is included in any true Christian belief; but the historical existence of Jesus is not the real issue of belief, and it is equally testified by both believers and unbelievers, by the disciples and by those who opposed him. To believe in him was to believe something about him, viz. that even in his historical existence he was the Son of God and the saviour of the world.

Before this point is looked at again in the setting of the resurrection narratives it is worth reviewing the story of the Greeks who came to Jerusalem at the last Passover, and asked to see Jesus. Their request was conveyed to Jesus by Philip; and the Lord's reply was, in the context of the present discussion, highly significant. For he said: 'The hour has come for the Son of man to be glorified. Truly, truly I say to you, unless a grain of wheat falls into the earth and dies, it remains alone; but if it dies, it bears much fruit' (12^{23,24}). The Greeks evidently did not see Jesus. And the point of his at first sight somewhat elusive remark that the hour had come for his glorification? Surely that 'seeing' him in the flesh was not to 'see' him in the deeper sense of 'seeing who and what he was'; that could be seen only after he had been glorified; and the glorification, as he knew, would take place at the time of the Passover, which was about to begin. When that was over, Greeks and Jews alike would be able to 'see' him in a new way.

Or would it be a new way? When Jesus replied to Philip's request at the last supper table for the Lord to show his disciples the Father, he stated quite categorically 'He who has seen me has seen the Father' (14^9). To look on Jesus was to look on more than one human being in his historical situation, though it was at least that; it was also to see the Father, to see God, at his work of redemption. It would not be wholly improper, though it might be for some reasons confusing, to speak of 'first sight' which enables a man to see Jesus as an historical person, and of 'second sight' which enables him to see Jesus as the one in whom God dwells, and through whom he acts in history. Second sight is never found isolated from first sight, though first sight is often found without the second. The transition from having first sight only to the possession of second sight as well is, according to John, the work and the gift of God, and specifically the work of the Spirit in the days after Christ's glorification.

It is against such considerations that the story of Easter day with which John closes his gospel must be read. For what friends and enemies alike knew (and neither party ever had grounds for revising their judgements) was that the crucifixion had removed Jesus from the realm of visible historical persons. Without seeing him, his enemies thought, there would be a stop to belief in him. How could the preposterous beliefs which he sought to engender survive the cessation of his visibility? It is not clear that the disciples themselves thought very differently at the time of the crucifixion and burial. What, then, did Easter do? What part did the empty tomb and the appearances of the glorified Lord play in the final formation and perpetuation of Christian belief in Jesus Christ as Son of God and saviour?

The answer is not that the empty tomb confirmed his removal from the visible world of historical persons, and that, nevertheless, the resurrection appearances restored him to that world. It is rather that they provided a very limited period of transition between complete historical visibility and complete historical invisibility, during which it became possible for the apostles to learn that though their Lord had been removed from visibility he was not removed from them. Belief in him, which had never been identical with visible experience of his physical presence, was made possible in a new way at a time when visual experience of his historical person had ceased to be possible. The function of the visual experiences of the appearances of the glorified Lord to his disciples was to enable them to identify the new set of experiences of his fellowship with them with the old set of experiences when he was visible. Once the identity had been recognized between the Jesus of the earthly ministry and the glorified Lord of the Church's life, then the particular set of resurrection appearances could and did cease. And the Church has been able to pass on a valid and genuine 'experience' of Jesus Christ, because its fellowship is rooted in the normative and creative experience of the first apostles. So Christianity is not a religion of some quite generally mystical and universal 'communion with the divine'. It might well have grown into that (or ceased altogether) had not the resurrection appearances taken place. It is still communion with the Father through the Son, through him, that is to say, who was once an historical person born, living, acting, dying, and now triumphant over death, and still the one in whom and through whom men come to believe in God. And men come to such belief not by the light of nature, but by the testimony of God, the testimony of the Holy Spirit within them. If Christianity remains in this profound sense an historical religion, it is because it is anchored in those events which John relates at the end of his gospel as the final act of the seventh sign.

A good deal of the material of ch. 20 is peculiar to John. Yet it would not be right to conclude that the evangelist is really saying anything different from what the synoptists say, or is trying to report different events. In spite of considerable differences between the narratives of the four gospels as they relate the resurrection, there is a quite remarkable unanimity of testimony to the central events that happened and as to the persons concerned in them. But John, as always, is not here concerned simply to repeat the synoptic tradition, but rather to present it in his own perspective. His chief concern in writing of this last sign is to assure Christians of the future, who were unable to be present with Jesus and the apostles at the time of its enactment, that they are nevertheless fully able to share in it in the only way that matters, indeed in the veritable apostolic manner – as those who believe in Jesus as the Christ, the Son of God.

Chapter 20, and therewith the gospel, closes with a reference to the book the author has written. The fact that Christianity is thus a religion of a book is very much bound up with all that has been written in this introduction to ch. 20. For the story of Jesus and his ministry are the 'eyes' with which men of every age can look at the historical character whom some believe to be the Son of God. So the printed page of the Bible takes upon itself something of the character of those events which John records, and can be taken in two ways: either as an interesting document out of the vast literature of the history of religions, or as the one decisive word which God has spoken to men. Sound commentary must therefore be both 'scientific' and devout.

Neither John nor any other evangelist gives any account of the Jewish Passover. It was indeed superfluous; the new Passover had been instituted, the new Passover lamb slain. The readers of the gospel in the early, as in the later church, would know how they could for ever 'eat' the flesh of the new-slain lamb in the eucharist (cf. 6^{51ff}). Instead all four evangelists pass immediately to the events that took place approximately forty-eight hours later, beginning with what happened when certain women went to the tomb where Jesus had been buried. Mark tells of three women who went with spices to anoint Jesus; Matthew that two went to see the sepulchre; Luke does not specify the number of women who went to the tomb with spices. John mentions only one by name – Mary Magdalene, though it is clear from her statement in v.2 that she did not go alone. It is possible that her little company took spices with them, particularly if, as Bernard thinks, Mary herself is to be identified with Mary of Bethany who had brought Jesus a gift of ointment which he asked that she might keep for the day of his burial (12⁷).

What they came upon when they reached the garden was the disturbing sight of the stone having been rolled away from the mouth of the tomb. It was 'early', John says, i.e. that part of the night after cockcrow and before dawn; but there could not be any mistake as to whether a stone at the entrance to a tomb were in place or not. Mary seems to have taken the initiative and run to the house of Peter, and of the beloved disciple (with whom, of course, Mary the mother of Jesus would be staying). She told them: '*They have taken the Lord out of the tomb, and we do not know where they have laid him.*' This would seem to imply that Mary had made some even cursory inspection of the tomb before she set out for Peter's house. If so, she was the first witness to the empty tomb.

John now tells how Peter and the beloved disciple come and witness the fact of the empty tomb. He is concerned to have witness and testimony that could be regarded as adequate in the courts of men – two adult male witnesses. Both disciples run to the tomb; it is disturbing news they have heard; even later in the day they were still in fear of the Jews! The beloved disciple reached the tomb first, stooped to peep in (such is the force of the Greek word) but did not go inside. Peter however did go in, and found the strange setting of the linen cloths lying without the body in them, and the napkin used for wrapping the head neatly rolled up and by itself. Evidently Peter came to no conclusions from what he saw. But the beloved disciple, perhaps encouraged by Peter's example, joined Peter inside the tomb. He saw the self-same arrangement of the contents, but reacted quite differently: he saw *and believed*. There can be no doubt that what John means his readers to understand is that this was the point at which the beloved disciple really came to believe in Jesus as the Christ, the Son of God. What John is trying to leave clear is that the beloved disciple did not jump to the conclusion that some astoundingly unique miracle had been performed; that did not constitute 'belief'. He had come to believe that the one who could thus be free from death must be what he had been claiming to be, the very Son of God.

It seems, at first sight, that John makes it difficult to hold any such view, for he goes on to say *for as yet they did not know the scripture, that he must rise from the dead*. John does not say what particular scripture he has in mind; but the point would not be clearer, even if he had. To have been aware, at the moment of discovery of the empty tomb, of the scripture which told of Christ's rising from the dead would have enabled the disciples to have understood the resurrection in a full Christian sense. It would not have left them with an apparent obligation simply to boggle at the quite unparalleled miracle that had been wrought. It would rather have permitted them, in conceiving of the possibility of such a miracle having been wrought, to have seen it in the perspective of God's great purpose of the world which spans it all, as scripture witnesses, from creation to consummation. To have known the scripture, then, would have enabled Peter and the beloved disciple to have seen the resurrection as the resurrection by which God fulfilled his own plan for his Son and for his sons in his own promised way. Without such knowledge of scripture the sensitive insight of the beloved disciple stands out remarkably clearly. Peter and his companion then went back home. John does not tell his reader what report they took.

The story now returns to Mary. She has been the first witness of the empty tomb; now she is to be the first human being to whom the risen Lord appears. Thus she combines in her own experience (the first to do so) the twin facets of what the Church has taken to be the basic experience of the resurrection. The tradition contained both an assertion of an empty tomb, and a recollection of a number of appearances of the risen Lord to his disciples. There seems to be something remarkably discerning in that a woman was made the first recipient of both these elements of the Church's faith, entirely consistent with the lowliness and humility of its Lord, and with the profound insight e.g. of Paul who observed that 'not many wise, not many powerful, not many of noble birth' were among those called by God into the Church.

Mary returned to the garden, and stood crying outside the tomb. Then, like the beloved disciple, she peeped in. What she saw was something not displayed to either of the two men: she saw two angels in white, sitting at the place where the feet and the head of Jesus had been. They asked her why she was crying, and she told them what she had told Peter and the beloved disciple. She turned away from the tomb and saw Jesus standing there. She did not recognize him. He asked her why she was crying, and whom she sought. She thought that he might well be the gardener, in charge of the small estate in which the tomb was situated. Apparently she supposed that he might have removed the body, for she asked him if he had, undertaking to remove it if he told her where it was. This remark reinforces the supposition made in ch. 19 that the burial of the Lord's body was designedly quite temporary. Mary seems to be offering to take over responsibility for the body which she supposes even the gardener knew was only temporarily laid to rest in the garden. Jesus replied with one word: '*Mary*'. Then, a sheep that knows her shepherd's voice, Mary recognizes the Lord and she exclaims to him '*Rabboni!*' The word, as John remarks, means 'teacher'; but, as John does not tell his readers, it was a form of the word 'Rabbi' which was used almost exclusively in address to God. Mary is thus doing more than recognize some quasi-physical identity between the earthly Jesus and the risen Lord; she is giving expression to a new attitude in which Jesus is worshipped as God. The sign has once more been perceived for what it is: not a miracle as such and on its own, but the final act of God in the Word-made-flesh, in the drama of the divine redemption of the world. Jesus said to Mary, 'Cease holding me' (see the notes below for the grounds for this translation), adding that he was not yet ascended (better, perhaps, 'gone up') to the Father. He then gave her a message to those whom, for the only time in the gospel, he calls his 'brethren'. She is to tell them that he is going up to his Father and their Father, to his God and their God, thus indicating, in a delicate subtlety of language, that their standing with the Father as sons in the divine household was due to his own act as the Son come in the flesh, crucified and risen. Mary went and exclaimed to the disciples: '*I have seen the Lord.*' The picture is vividly and realistically drawn. It is only when this has exploded from her lips and her heart that she can deliver the message to the disciples.

וֹשֵע

I
Mary . . . came to the tomb early: The last time the word *early* was used in the gospel was at the time when Jesus was being led to the Praetorium forty-eight hours earlier. So swiftly does the new era begin.

saw that the stone had been taken away from the tomb: All four gospels record that the stone was rolled away before the women came. Matthew tells his readers that an angel moved it (Matt. 28$^{2ff.}$). The tradition was evidently thought important by the evangelists, though it finds no place in the traditions about the resurrection in the epistles. Whatever else the tradition has done, it has kept Christians from any temptation to seek communion with their Lord through physical 'relics' of his body. This is entirely in keeping with the theology of the fourth gospel.

Furthermore it has given to earlier ages perhaps more than the present a basis for understanding the apparent physical resemblance of the risen Lord to the Jesus who was crucified.

2

she . . . went to Simon Peter and the other disciple, the one whom Jesus loved: It is possible, as some commentators have suggested, that the double object of the verb here implies that Peter was staying with the beloved disciple. This is not an impossible suggestion; Mary was certainly thought to be there by the author.

'They have taken the Lord out of the tomb': This is an equivalent to a passive form of the verb and so possibly meant to ascribe the action to God. It seems to express, when read with the following sentences, simply the conviction that the body of Jesus had already been moved to its final resting-place, and that Mary did not know where it had been taken, or by whom it had been removed.

3

Peter then came out with the other disciple, and they went towards the tomb: Mary had evidently expected that someone at the house would have known about the removal of the body. But no one did; hence Peter and the beloved disciple set out to investigate.

5

and stooping to look in: It would seem that though the tomb could be entered easily, it was not possible to survey the contents without stooping down. The entrance would not be very high.

6

he saw the linen cloths lying, [7] *and the napkin, which had been on his head, not lying with the linen cloths but rolled up in a place by itself:* When Lazarus was raised, he came from the tomb swathed in his cloths. The fact that the cloths were left lying seems to suggest that the Lord left the tomb in a manner different from that of Lazarus' resuscitated body. Resuscitation is not resurrection!

8

he saw and believed: This can hardly be read save in the light of what John has to say about the word of the Lord to Thomas later in the chapter. The beloved disciple saw the empty tomb and the abandoned cloth lying in it. On that sight, he believed. So does the evangelist begin to make it clear that it is not by seeing the earthly Jesus that one 'sees' the Lord. He can be 'seen' in this profounder sense through the witness of an empty grave.

9

for as yet they did not know the scripture, that he must rise from the dead: John does not specify what scripture he had in mind. The most necessary comment on that has been made above (p. 631). But it may also be noted that the process of understanding all that Jesus Christ was and did sets the Christian out upon an unending adventure in coming to know more and more of the fulness of God's purpose as revealed in scripture.

11

But Mary stood weeping outside the tomb: This would suggest that she had run back with, or more probably behind, Peter and the beloved disciple.

12

she saw two angels in white: The angels are, as it were, the 'halo' round the event to mark it out as the action of God. Angels were thought to be garbed in white, and to perform services for God. They were introduced into Jewish theology under Persian influence, and offered to the austere monotheism of Judaism a way of establishing the possibility of communication between Yahweh and his people on earth. They appear at several points of the gospel narrative (e.g. to Joseph [Matthew 1^{20}], to Zechariah [Luke 1^{11}], to Mary [Luke 1^{26}], to the shepherds [Luke 2$^{9, 13}$]). Their presence is not reported otherwise than here in the fourth gospel, though their ministry is envisaged as the means for the sustenance of the Son of man. Thus Jesus promises Nathanael that he shall 'see the heavens opened, and the angels of God ascending and descending upon the Son of man' (1^{51}). Matthew relates that it was an angel that came down and moved the stone from the tomb (Matt. 28^2). Mark does not use the word *angel* but states that when the women entered the tomb on Easter morning 'they saw a young man sitting on the right side, dressed in a white robe; and they were amazed', the word 'amazed' being the technical term for awe inspired by the supernatural. Luke tells of two witnesses at the tomb, 'two men in dazzling apparel', and it is clear from what he tells later that the women who saw them held them to be angels (Luke 24$^{4, 23}$). Their function here is, as in the birth stories of Luke, to make it plain that an otherwise wholly terrestrial happening is really a divine action. The shepherds who went to the manger actually 'saw' no more than the innkeeper or the oxen; yet they did in fact 'see' ineffable things in the stable, and saw them only because of the angels' preparation. That is to say, it is only the eye that has been illuminated by faith that can penetrate to the reality of what the visible world displays. So here at the tomb. All that can be seen is emptiness and an abandoned shroud; but when angels attend, the eyes of the visitors are opened; as Mary's were.

13

'Because they have taken away my Lord, and I do not know where they have laid him': Once more Mary uses the word *Lord*; and it has not been used in this way until this point in the gospel! Mary is still ready to suppose that all that has happened is that someone has anticipated her own proposed service, and moved the Lord's body to its final resting place. She may not even dare to hope for more than that, even in the evidently exalted setting in which she moves.

14

she turned round and saw Jesus standing, but she did not know that it was Jesus: She turned away from the angels and the tomb, probably to leave it and the garden for the last time. She is confronted by Jesus, though she does not recognize him. Matthew (28^{17}) and Luke ($24^{13ff,36}$) also state that Jesus was not immediately recognizable by those who had known him. There is certainly an intention to establish complete identity between the one who was crucified and the one who returned after the resurrection; but there is also a concern to indicate that there was change. The situation of Mary is interesting indeed. In the body of the gospel men have often failed to understand the meaning of a metaphor, or of a sign; Mary now, momentarily at least, fails to identify the Lord himself.

15

Jesus said to her, 'Woman, why are you weeping? Whom do you seek?': *Woman* is the word Jesus used to address his mother at the feast of Cana, and from the cross. The bonds of family kinship are transcended in the life of the Christian fellowship. The addition of the words *Whom do you seek?* to the question of the angels is significant. They presuppose that it is a living person, as indeed it is, that Mary is looking for. But the nuance escapes Mary; and, thinking that Jesus may be the gardener, she asks him if he has been responsible for the removal of the Lord's body (as indeed he had!) to its final resting place. The question repeats for the last time Mary's intention to discover where the body of her Lord may be. Jesus answered her by one word: *Mary.* It was enough. The sheep knew the sound of the shepherd's voice, and all was well.

16

She turned and said to him . . . 'Rabboni': She turned: evidently her last recital of her fears had led her to go away from the gardener, the garden and the tomb altogether; for she had been facing Jesus before this point (v.14). The calling of her name as she went away brought her swiftly round, and back to her Lord to embrace him in a clinging embrace, with the word *Rabboni*. This was a moment highly charged with feeling, but the word she used indicates the nature of it, for it is a word used characteristically for the deity. Imagination can picture her clasping the feet of Christ in humble adoration.

17

Jesus said to her, 'Do not hold me': The Greek here uses a present imperative with a particular form of the negative, and the use indicates that an action already in progress is to be stopped. The best way to render the imperative in English therefore is to say 'Cease from clinging to me'. Bernard has detected the possibility of another text to relieve the interpreter from the difficulty of expounding this imperative in its obvious connexion with the following sentence. He suggests that the original text may have been one which can be translated 'Do not be afraid' (*Me ptou* instead of *Me aptou*). If this were thought to be the right reading, it would have the twofold advantage of conforming the injunction with the one given in other gospels 'Do not be afraid' (Matthew 28^{5, 10}; Luke 24^{37, 38}), and making it much easier for the saying to be related to the following words.

'for I have not yet ascended to the Father': The word *ascend* is the same one used earlier in the gospel to speak of Jesus being 'lifted up' and, as was noted on p. 310, Dr Dodd has thought it probable that for the writer of the fourth gospel even in this use of the word there was some overtone of reference to the 'going up' or ascending of the Son of man. Jesus 'goes up' to Jerusalem to die. He is 'lifted up' upon the cross. What really constitutes his 'going up', his ascension? The Johannine answer is that the ascension is more realistically described as the 'return to the Father', and in the normal way it would be natural to think that Jesus returned to the Father at the moment of his death. He came from the Father into the world, presumably at the moment of his birth, if any moment can be specified. Similarly, if any moment may be specified for his return to the Father it would be the moment of his death. But Jesus is saying on this day of resurrection that he has not yet ascended, i.e., in Johannine language, not yet returned to the Father. This cannot but mean that there has been purposeful delay. And it would seem that the delay has been undertaken for the sake of establishing the necessary continuity between the earthly Jesus and the glorified Christ. What Jesus is doing and saying to Mary can be summed up thus: She is to cease from holding him, because the new

relationship between Lord and worshipper will not be one of physical contact, though it will be a real personal relationship. He has appeared to her in a form that while it was evidently different from that in which he had been known in the days of his flesh had sufficient elements in it to enable Mary to satisfy herself, and persuade others, of the identity of the Jesus who was, with the Lord who would for evermore be. The meeting with Mary is at this precise point of transition. More, it is difficult to say; certainly a twentieth-century commentator would be wrong to try to 'spatialize' his solution of the problem of 'ascension'. It is worth noting that only Luke tells of an ascent which was a visible spatial event. It is much more to the Johannine point to remember that one of the most puzzling uses of the word 'ascend' in the fourth gospel was after the great discourse on Jesus as the bread of life. As a response to the discourse many disciples expressed their difficulties. Jesus said: 'Do you take offence at this? Then what if you were to see the Son of man ascending where he was before?' (6^{62}). It is far from fancy to think that John may well be making clear to Christians that it is with the risen and ascended, the glorified Christ that they have communion, on whom they feed, in the eucharist.

18

Mary Magdalene went and said to the disciples, 'I have seen the Lord': Not only is this consummate artistry and acute personal observation on the part of the historian, for this is just what Mary would be so likely to do, but it puts things theologically right. Before she can give the Lord's message to the disciples with any hope of acceptance she has to tell them that she has seen him. Seen him, and, by every inference, believed.

20$^{19-23}$ EASTER EVENING

^{19}*On the evening of that day, the first day of the week, the doors being shut where the disciples were, for fear of the Jews, Jesus came and stood among them and said to them, 'Peace be with you.'* ^{20}*When he had said this, he showed them his hands and his side. Then the disciples were glad when they saw the Lord.* ^{21}*Jesus said to them again, 'Peace be with you. As the Father has sent me, even so I send you.'* ^{22}*And when he had said this, he breathed on them, and said to them 'Receive the Holy Spirit.* ^{23}*If you forgive the sins of any, they are forgiven; if you retain the sins of any, they are retained.'*

The incident which John reports as taking place on the evening of

Easter Day is peculiar to him. It seems wrong (cf. Introduction, pp. 49ff) to try to construct some 'harmony' of the four evangelists' testimony about the resurrection from their four narratives, for each has his own particular points to make in selecting as well as in telling his stories. John is concerned, as has been said, with establishing the identity of the person of Jesus who was crucified with that of the one who is the ever-present Lord of the Church, and to point out to the Church what the nature of belief in such a Lord may be. The present story helps to lay the foundation for the final stage of his disclosure about belief.

On Easter evening the disciples had met together behind locked doors. They were fearful of what the Jews might do to them now that the Passover was almost over. Into the midst of this assembly of fearful men, Jesus came, without door being opened or knock being heard. He greeted them with the conventional Jewish greeting 'Peace to you'. But with his coming in this way the greeting was more than conventional. It was as if he had come to a group of English disciples on such a day, and said 'Good evening', and the Englishmen would at once have known that the words could never have the same merely conventional meaning again. So the greeting 'Peace' came to be part of Christian social life, as well as a permanent part of its liturgical practice. Upon saying the greeting Jesus showed the disciples his hands, presumably with the wound prints, and his side, with the spear wound visible. So was his unquestioned and unquestionable identity established; and it was an occasion of great joy. Then Jesus began to speak once more. Again he said to them, surely now in much more than a formal greeting: 'Peace to you.' Then he gave them a commission such as they had not had before, and which left it quite plain that their mission in the world was now to be his, and his theirs.

'Receive the Holy Spirit', he began. John has prepared his reader well for this. He had said that the Spirit was not given previously because Jesus had not been glorified (7^{39}). But now the Spirit is given; therefore Jesus is now glorified. He is no longer, as in the morning, 'not yet ascended'; he has now 'gone to the Father', he has finally received from the Father the glory which was his with the Father from the foundation of the world. He can now bestow the Spirit, and does. It is a vain operation to try to harmonize this account with the report Luke gives in Acts of the Day of Pentecost, or Whitsun. Both authors set the gift of the Spirit in a certain historiographical scheme, and it is to miss the points of their respective narratives to debase them into simple chronological puzzles. John is trying to say that the Holy Spirit speaks to the minds and hearts of men about God, but only in terms of the whole life and work, the death, resurrection and return to the Father of him who was the Son of the Father incarnate – Jesus of Nazareth. Naturally the Spirit is given as soon as Jesus returns to the Father; and when John reports that the Spirit is given, it is perverse to suppose, as Bernard (I.C.C.) does, that what he calls 'the ascension' did not happen for at least a week after the resurrection. All that Jesus said to the disciples on the first Easter evening, according to John's narrative, presupposes that he has returned to the Father, to share his pristine glory.

Pristine glory: the gift of the Spirit. These two things are closely linked in the scriptures of the Old Testament. It was the Spirit that first brooded on the face of the waters before creation began (Gen. 1^2); and it was through the breathing of the Spirit (breath) in man's nostrils that man was made 'a living being' (Gen. 2^7). Jesus does more than simply announce that the Spirit is given, he actually dispenses it by breathing on the disciples, as God breathed upon the first man. So the new creation has begun, and the very possibility of its beginning has lain in the readiness of the only begotten Son to become incarnate and to live, suffer and die for the sins of men.

Jesus went on to say: 'As the Father has sent me, even so I send you'. After the new Adam has been corporately created, he takes over the work of the new Adam who had come in the flesh and died upon the cross. Here in John is the great commissioning of the Church, parallel to the great commission in Matthew 28^{19}: 'Go therefore and make disciples of all nations, baptizing them in the name of the Father and of the Son and of the Holy Spirit, teaching them to observe all that I have commanded you; and lo, I am with you always, to the close of the age.'

Jesus next says: '*If you forgive the sins of any, they are forgiven; if you retain the sins of any, they are retained.*' There are five comments to be made on this strange and profound saying. First, that it does not, and surely cannot, take away from the fact that it is God alone who can forgive sins. That remains his prerogative. Hence it must be pointed out with some emphasis that the authority to act in the forgiveness of sins is governed by and conditional upon the gift of the Spirit, and the acceptance of the Lord's commission to share his mission. Only those who have received the Spirit and accepted the mission from the glorified Lord have this privilege and authority given to them. Second, the authority to forgive sins is made to whatever company was assembled that night. Thomas is a known absentee; no one can know who was present or absent apart from that. The use of the word 'disciples' suggests that there were more there than the members of the 'Twelve', but even that point, though probable, could not be pressed with any certainty. Perhaps the best service the commentator can render at this point is to remind those who would use it for supporting certain claims in the realm of church order and discipline that, whatever the merits of certain church orders, they cannot be supported by an appeal to this text. It is as precarious to argue that it limits power to forgive sins to the apostles as to argue that it must extend it to the whole Church. Jesus is said to have given this power to those present on Easter evening. More than that it is hard to say.

Third, it is useful and important to observe that though this particular saying of the risen Lord is confined to John's narrative, there are other sayings in other gospels before and after the resurrection which are not unlike it. Luke states that Jesus told a mixed company of the Eleven and others, together with the two who met him on the way to Emmaus: 'Thus it is written that the Christ should suffer and on the third day rise from the dead, and that repentance and forgiveness of sins should be preached in his name to all nations' (Luke 24$^{46, 47}$). Mark's gospel, in the longer ending, has the passage: 'Go into all the world and preach the gospel to the whole creation. He who believes and is baptized will be saved; but he who does not believe will be condemned' (Mark 16$^{15, 16}$). Matthew echoes one part of Mark's injunction: 'Go therefore and make disciples of all nations, baptizing them' (Matt. 28^{19}). But Matthew gives a saying very similar to this in the story of the earthly ministry, in two contexts. In one it is addressed to Peter alone: 'I will give you the keys of the kingdom of heaven, and whatever you bind on earth shall be bound in heaven, and whatever you loose on earth shall be loosed in heaven' (Matt. 16^{19}); in the other it is spoken to 'the disciples': 'Truly I say to you, whatever you bind on earth shall be bound in heaven, and whatever you loose on earth shall be loosed in heaven' (Matt. 18^{18}). There is no doubt from the context that the reference is to forgiving sins, or withholding forgiveness. But though this sounds stern and harsh, it is simply the result of the preaching of the gospel, which either brings men to repent as they hear of the ready and costly forgiveness of God, or leaves them unresponsive to the offer of forgiveness which is the gospel, and so they are left in their sins.

Fourth, the exercise of this authority is really carrying on the same work that Jesus himself had had to do. He could give sight to the man born blind, and bring him to the point of offering worship where worship was due; but he could not perform that same office for those Jews who questioned his claims and excommunicated the man who had been blind. Such persons heard the final word 'If you were blind, you would have no guilt; but now that you say "We see", your guilt remains' (9^{41}). It is the essence of love that it can be rejected; and if God is to love sinners into repentance so that they receive his forgiveness prepared for them, it must be that they are free to reject the divine offer. That is the mystery of man's freedom, and God's free pardon and love.

Fifth, since the authority to forgive sins is given under the gift of the Spirit, it is instructive to refer back to the functions of the Spirit as Jesus had earlier described them. He said: 'When he comes he will convince the world of sin, and of righteousness and of judgement' (16^{8ff}.). It will be seen, in reference to the note on the passage (p. 536), what this means for the present text. The sin which the Spirit brings home to men is that disposition of the human heart which found its terrible climax in the crucifixion of the Son of man. Sin is not the committing of social or even religious peccadilloes, but the sharing in such a life as leads to the rejection and the crucifixion of the Son of man. Man can be authoritatively assured that God will offer effectual forgiveness of such sin. If men accept, pardon is theirs; but if they refuse, clearly their sin remains.

It is worth asking one futile question: Is John right in telling his readers that on the very evening of Easter Day there took place the act which initiated, at any rate in one sense, the new creation; the gift of the Spirit which Luke, in Acts, states came fifty days later; the great commissioning of the Church to continue the mission of its Lord, which Matthew reports in a way which makes it quite certainly not take place on the evening of Easter Day? The answer to the question is precisely that it is futile. John has used his own historiographical tools to indicate what the gift of the Spirit, the fact of the new creation, and the mission of the Church really are, and what they properly mean. He is not engaged in making corrective chronological notes upon false chronology in other forms of the Christian tradition. He is working out, in his own way, the locations of events that bring to them their fulness of meaning. It is impossible to know what John himself would say to such a question as has been put; but the signs are that he would think it a quite improper and a quite misleading one. Were he asked what he meant by placing the great commission, the new creation and the gift of the Spirit together with the pardoning authority of the Church all on the evening of Easter Day, he would in all probability say that each was so inextricably bound up with the moment of the glorification of the Lord that no other place could possibly display their meaning half so well. And if we think in terms of his own writing, that remains unanswerably true.

৩৯

19

On the evening of that day: By Jewish reckoning the second day of the week has started by this time. John is thus not using the Jewish demarcation of the day, which went from 6 p.m. to 6 p.m.

the doors being shut: This makes it quite plain that the entry of Jesus was abnormal and miraculous. It is a safe assumption that the disciples were discussing the events of the day, as reported by Peter, the beloved disciple and Mary Magdalene.

'Peace be with you': This greeting came with triple force: It was the ordinary greeting, which could now be resumed between Jesus and his friends. It was one of the last words spoken by Jesus before the crucifixion (14²⁷). And now it came to frightened disciples from the one who had himself conquered the death they still feared.

20

he showed them his hands and his side: John reveals no knowledge of any wounds on the feet, though Luke does (Luke 24³⁹). Crucifixion could be carried out by tying the feet to the cross, or nailing them there.

'As the Father has sent me, even so I send you': Even so may not convey with full emphasis the closeness of the similarity of the 'sending' of the disciples by Jesus and the 'sending' of Jesus by the Father. Henceforth their mission would be 'from above', however much it had to be 'down below' on the earth, showing all the signs of a human devising.

22

he breathed on them: As Yahweh had *breathed* into the nostrils of man at his first creation to make him a 'living soul'. Paul's word to the Christians in Corinth is relevant here: 'The first Adam became a living being, the last Adam became a life-giving Spirit' (1 Cor. 15⁴⁵). The very same verb used here for 'breathe' is used in Genesis 2⁷ in the Greek translation of the Hebrew text (Septuagint). So John's gospel ends with an announcement of the new creation, as it also began.

'Receive the Holy Spirit': One small indication that John may have had the eucharist in mind as he wrote this section is that the word used for 'receive' is the same word translated 'take' in the account of the Last Supper and the institution of the eucharist (Mark 14²²; Matt. 26²⁶; Luke 22¹⁷).

²⁴*Now Thomas, one of the twelve, called the Twin, was not with them when Jesus came.* ²⁵*So the other disciples told him, 'We have seen the Lord.' But he said to them, 'Unless I see in his hands the print of the nails, and place my finger in the mark of the nails, and place my hand in his side, I will not believe.'*
²⁶*Eight days later, his disciples were again in the house, and Thomas was with them. The doors were shut, but Jesus came and stood among them, and said, 'Peace be with you.'* ²⁷*Then he said to Thomas, 'Put your finger here, and see my hands; and put out your hand, and place it in my side; do not be faithless, but believing.'* ²⁸*Thomas answered him, 'My Lord and my God!'* ²⁹*Jesus said to him, 'Have you believed because you have seen me? Blessed are those who have not seen and yet believe.'*

The story with which John concludes his account of the last and greatest 'sign' in the gospel is rightly conceived as part of the sign. A sign is never sheer miracle standing on its own, to be judged miraculous or not according to man's changing powers of explaining occurrences in his world: it is always a demonstration of the loving, saving, merciful yet judging concern of God for his children, itself incomplete unless and until it wins the appropriate response from men. The resurrection might stand as a miracle about which men could argue fiercely as to its possibility, even were it not reported as a 'sign'; and it is as such a 'de-signified' reality that much discussion of it has taken place. John is never in danger of falling into this mistake, and those who read his gospel must be careful to understand the nature and consequences of his testimony!

It is worth recalling that when Luke speaks of the 'sign' to be displayed at the birth of Christ, he does so as he describes how angels (supernatural insights) say to the Bethlehem shepherds: 'This will be a sign for you: you will find a babe wrapped in swaddling cloths and lying in a manger' (Luke 2¹²). Yet his story of the 'sign' does not end with the shepherds simply 'seeing' the sign with the natural eye, but in their own acceptance of what they saw as a sign that a saviour had been born. It can be stated that the spreading of the news of the birth of the saviour was, and remains, part of the sign, part of the event that constitutes Christmas. Similarly with John's account of Easter. The 'sign' of the empty tomb and of the appearance of the glorified Lord to his disciples are not simple statements of miracle that can be properly discussed quite objectively. The glorification of the Lord is not something which just happens to him; the whole of the Lord's Prayer in John has made it abundantly clear that the Lord's glory in large measure consists in the effective testimony of men to his great nature and saving work. The story of Thomas, which John now unfolds, deals with the perpetual situation in which the Church must find herself as she bears witness to the great sign in which Jesus of Nazareth was both crucified and glorified.

The evangelist provides a necessary and important introduction to the story. Thomas was not present when the glorified Lord appeared to the disciples on Easter evening. Neither, of course, were the first readers of the gospel; nor the readers of this commentary! In this way John indicates that his story is for every one who was not present, as well as for those who were present when Jesus first returned after his glorification to visit his own. When Thomas heard the testimony of his fellow-disciples he replied with understandable scepticism and pardonable candour: '*Unless I see in his hands the print of the nails, and place my finger in the mark of the nails, and place my hand in his side, I will not believe.*' No modern critic or sceptic could have made a sceptical comment more successfully. Yet with John it is necessary to see that nothing less than such a critique can possibly afford an adequate starting place for the Church if it is to meet each generation of men with a convincing word about the story of Jesus.

Eight days after Easter Day, i.e. on the Sunday after Easter, the disciples had gathered together again, Thomas being present. It is interesting to recall what John has already told his readers about Thomas. It was Thomas who, when the disciples generally were trying to persuade Jesus not to return to Bethany at the time of Lazarus' fatal sickness, exclaimed with perhaps more impulsiveness than prudence: 'Let us also go with him, that we may die with him' (11¹⁶). It was Thomas also who, at the Last Supper, interrupted the discourse given by the Lord to say to him: 'Lord, we do not know where you are going; how can we know the way?' His was a nature evidently impulsive, loyal, discerning, yet not capable of much sustained thought. When Jesus appeared to the disciples on this second occasion, he seemed to have come primarily to meet Thomas, and to meet him (as in ch. 21 he meets Peter) in the full presence of his fellow-disciples. The Lord met the company with his new-old greeting: '*Peace be with you*', and then turned specifically to Thomas. '*Put your finger here, and see my hands; and put out your hand, and place it in my side; do not be faithless, but believing.*' So at last Thomas was able to have all the proofs he had desired. Now was his chance to demonstrate that 'seeing was believing'. Yet he did not take it. To the almost impossibly generous invitation to the good sceptical mind he responded with something as far removed from scepticism as anything in scripture, with the words: '*My Lord and my God.*' The words *My Lord* would have sufficed to show that Thomas was now as satisfied as any other of the disciples that Jesus had returned to them; in adding the words *and my God* he is taking a step beyond the intra-human relationship between disciple and Rabbi into a new one where a man is brought into the presence of his God. And this, of course, is the crown of the Johannine gospel.

It is quite plain from John's narrative that Thomas did not accept the invitation to touch the Lord's hands or feel his side. He had learnt in the mere 'seeing' of the glorified Lord that sense and sight were not the sufficient things he had supposed. In a strangely paradoxical way he had found through seeing that seeing was not believing. And this makes Thomas the link, as it were, between the first apostolic belief in and confession of Jesus Christ as Son of God and the believer of every age who makes the same confession of faith. The modern believer, like Thomas, may well at times think: 'If only I could touch the wound prints on his hands, or see the spear mark in his side, then I could know for sure.' But were he to be put into a situation where these physical experiences became possible, he would know at once that all his sophistication would rise to make him as sceptical about sight and touch as about sheer belief. Belief, that is to say, is not the inevitable concomitant of sight as such; it is, as John and the whole New Testament make plain, always the work of the Holy Spirit.

The comment of Jesus upon Thomas' confession makes all this plain. '*Have you believed because you have seen me? Blessed are those who have not seen and yet believe*'. Did Thomas believe because he had *seen* Jesus, even Jesus in his glorified appearance? It is doubtful whether Thomas himself drew so hard a distinction between touch and sight as to warrant an affirmative answer to the question. But even if an affirmative answer be given, the further question must be asked as to what constitutes belief, particularly in the distinctive Johannine sense. It is not simple 'belief that Jesus who was crucified had been raised from the dead and could therefore visit his disciples again'. That would be belief in a miracle of resuscitation, or even of resurrection; it would not of itself constitute belief in Jesus Christ as he who is one with the Father. It would justify Thomas saying 'My Lord', but it could hardly justify him in saying '*My God*'. Jesus had said 'He who sees me sees him who sent me' and it is this paradoxical vision that underlies the conception of sight here. Physical sight is of physical objects; and even were the resurrection experiences to be classified as visions, they would still for this purpose count as physical, i.e. seen with or through the physical eye located in the physical body. But the eye with which a man 'sees' the one who sent Jesus Christ into the world is not located in any physical body as a sense organ, and its functioning can therefore take place both in association with physical seeing, as in the case of the beloved disciple, Mary Magdalene, the disciples on Easter evening and now Thomas on the octave of Easter; but it can also, even there, be recognized as distinct from physical sight, and this is made clear in the story of Thomas, who stands for all ages as the link between the experience of the apostles and that of the later Church, making plain to all believers that there was no advantage to the apostles in 'seeing'; not really, because physical seeing can be as seriously questioned as any other experience of sense; not really, because the vision of Jesus as the Word of God incarnate is the gift of the Spirit both to those who 'see' certain things, and to those who do not. The blessedness of belief is thus really to those who believe, not to those who see. This is the universal beatitude with which John closes his gospel. It includes Thomas as well as contemporary man; and contemporary man as well as Thomas.

❦

24

Thomas, one of the twelve: A title used at 6⁷¹. It may still serve, even after the defection of Judas, to refer to the intimate apostolic band.

25

'We have seen the Lord': The same phrase (though in the plural) as Mary Magdalene had used. All the gospels report some measure of scepticism about the resurrection (Mark 16¹³; Matt. 28¹⁷; Luke 24^{22ff, 38, 41}). John has his own way of meeting the inevitable scepticism of human nature, so dependent upon knowledge through the senses.

'place my hand in his side': Some commentators have supposed that this implies that Thomas was present at the crucifixion, or at least at the fraction of the legs that followed it. But no such inference is inevitable, even should it be (undemonstrably) true! Thomas could have heard of the incident from an eyewitness, certainly by the time that the disciples told him of their visitation from the glorified Lord.

26

Eight days later: This indicates that the disciples stayed in Jerusalem for the whole of the Passover at which Jesus died.

27

he said to Thomas: It is this phrase which makes the narrative sound as if Jesus came specifically to manifest himself to Thomas, and to put right, once and for all, the issue as between sight (and other senses) and belief.

'do not be faithless, but believing': This could well be rendered: 'Don't become an unbeliever, but become a believer.'

28

'My Lord and my God': With these words the evangelist has brought his gospel full circle. In the beginning the divine Word had been proclaimed as God (1¹); now that profound truth is confessed as the only possible word to be uttered about him who had been incarnate and humbled, but now is risen and glorified. And the word is uttered by Thomas: *'My Lord and my God'*. Christianity is fact, not metaphysic.

29

'Have you believed because you have seen me?': The word *believe*, thus used absolutely, cannot but mean full belief in Jesus as Christ and Son of God (20³¹). That belief, as Thomas was bound to see, could not be

guaranteed even by the sight of the Lord's glorified body, but only by the operation of the promised Spirit in the heart. Thomas, as has been claimed above, is the link between the apostles and the present-day believer. He belongs to both groups, for belief has the same real basis for both.

20^{30, 31}   CONCLUSION

³⁰*Now Jesus did many other signs in the presence of the disciples, which are not written in this book;* ³¹*but these are written that you may believe that Jesus is the Christ, the Son of God, and that believing you may have life in his name.*

Having come to the end of his gospel, John adds a final word as to its scope and purpose. There were many other signs, he states, which Jesus did, thereby indicating that in the immediately preceding narrative he has been recounting one of the Lord's signs. But John has had to make a selection, and tells his readers the basis of his choice of material. It is highly probable that John knew of the existence of some of the synoptic gospels, and almost certainly that he knew of a 'synoptic-like source'; he may well, as Professor Dodd has argued, have had a special source of his own. He has selected his material to help the reader to come to the point at which his closing story found Thomas – to a confession that Jesus is the Christ, the Son of God. That, as his gospel has insisted many times, is the true attainment of eternal life. To believe is, John puts it, *to have life in his name*. The phrase is new, but its meaning is clear. John has spoken of 'praying in his name', which means more than ending a prayer with the words 'through Jesus Christ our Lord'; it means offering prayer in Jesus Christ, as if the believer were his Lord, and his prayer the prayer of his Lord. Name is person, and to pray in the Lord's name is to pray in his person. Likewise to have life in his name is to have or to share his life, to become identified with him so that his eternal life becomes the reality of the believer's own life. John is not concerned just to offer a characterless immortality. He has a gospel of resurrection, of glorification, to proclaim, in which immortality is blessed because it is precisely a sharing of the life of God, in his eternal felicity and bliss.

John 21¹⁻²⁵

The Epilogue

If there had never been a copy or manuscript of the fourth gospel that contained ch. 21, it would be hard, even for the most inventive and imaginative scholar, to claim that some final chapter was manifestly missing. For in every way, save for the presence of ch. 21, John ends at 20³¹. Any impartial review of 1–20 makes ch. 21 seem somewhat superfluous, and yet, save for one Syriac manuscript, the gospel has always included ch. 21 as part of its text.

It is thus difficult to dispute the claims of ch. 21 to be a part of what in modern terms might be called the 'first edition'. Short of that, however, many questions can be asked. Was ch. 21 written by the author of 1–20? Or by another person? If by another person, was he the editor of 1–20, or a different editorial hand? And what, in any case, did the person responsible for including ch. 21 think that it added to the main body of the gospel? On all these questions opinions have been, and still are, very understandably divided.

For example, some have argued that the presence in this relatively short chapter of 25 verses of 28 Greek words not to be found in the rest of the gospel indicates that it comes from the pen of some other person than the writer of 1–20. But such a conclusion must not be hastily drawn; for, as others point out, some of the 28 words new in ch. 21 (e.g. those translated *net* [v. 6], *fishing* [v. 3], *beach* [v. 4], *dragging* [v. 8] and possibly *clothes* and *naked* [both v. 7]) are words naturally confined to a fishing incident, and no such incident is recorded in 1–20.

Similarly certain differences in literary style between 21 and the rest of the gospel suggest that they are by different authors. Thus Jesus calls the disciples 'children' (v. 5); Christians seem to be identifiable by the term 'brethren' (v. 23); the phrase 'dare to ask' contains two verbs in Greek peculiar to 21, and indicative of a distinctive style; 'not far' (v. 8) would almost certainly be rendered 'near' in the earlier chapters. Such a list could be, and has been, extended. Yet there are quite contrary stylistic indications: John's characteristic particle *oun* 'therefore' is found seven times in the first 23 verses of 21. The word used for *revealed* (v. 1) is a typical Johannine term (found at 1³¹; 2¹¹; 7⁴; 17⁶); and Dr Plummer (c.g.t. p. 348) finds a total of 25 distinct stylistic marks 'tending to show that ch. XXI is by S. John'.

No simple, clear, incontestable conclusion can be drawn. Yet even if it be admitted that the onus of proof lies with those who deny the chapter to the writer of 1–20, and that the case for such denial cannot be made with anything like certainty, it must also be admitted that to accept 21 as Johannine, as by the same author as 1–20, or as added by him to 1–20, is hardly less difficult. For in addition to the stylistic points noted, the 'traditional' view has some puzzling editorial considerations to dispose of. Some are historical: e.g. would the author of ch. 20 himself write or include a statement about an appearance of Jesus to the disciples after that on the evening of Easter octave, one which was described as '*the third time that Jesus was revealed to the disciples after he was raised from the dead*' (21^{14})? According to ch. 20 Jesus had already appeared three times after his resurrection – to Mary Magdalene (20^{14ff}), to the disciples on Easter Day (20^{19ff}), and a week later (20^{26ff}). And if it be pleaded that the appearance to Mary was not an appearance 'to the disciples', then attention has to be drawn to points of the narrative in 21 which suggest that its writer thought of it as the first appearance of Jesus after his resurrection. Thus the disciples fail to recognize Jesus from the boat, which seems strange if they had seen him twice already! And when they reach the shore no disciple dared ask Jesus who he was, even though they knew it was the Lord (21^{12}). This is hardly the reaction at a third, but much more at a first, encounter with the risen Jesus. It also seems strange that the rehabilitation of Peter as a chief (or the chief) apostle should wait until the third time Jesus saw him after the glorification.

It is therefore understandable that it is in the realm of theological rather than historical considerations that more satisfying answers may be found as to why 21 was included even in the earliest manuscripts of the gospel. The literary unity of 1–20, and the almost* entire appropriateness of the ending of the gospel at 20^{31} must be conceded. Ch. 21 is an addition, and its addition was made without that careful attention to the integration of the material with the rest of the gospel which would have been necessary had it been more than an appendix. Some sort of hurried editorial work is probably the best explanation both of the somewhat conflicting stylistic features of 21, and of the

---

* 'Almost', because, as will appear, it is possible to hold that 21 is an indispensable part of the gospel, which would be seriously, if almost indetectably, incomplete without it.

evident inconsistencies between 21 and the earlier chapters of the gospel. The question remains: What can account for the author's (or editor's) desire to add 21 to the gospel, already a satisfactory whole?

One attractive suggestion is that ch. 21 deals, by dominical authority, with a problem of some importance for the early Church, perhaps for the particular local church at Ephesus, the problem of the relationship of Peter and the beloved disciple. The gospel, it is suggested, was written after both men had died, in order to assure the Church at large, as well as the Ephesian congregation in particular, that neither of these two great men should be exalted above the other. John's gospel is traditionally associated with Ephesus; Peter addressed a letter to the churches of Asia (cf. 1 Peter 1^1 – a letter written by Peter or by one claiming his status and dignity); it is not impossible to suppose that the relative authority and merit of the two men caused trouble in the churches, much in the way that produced rival parties labelled 'Pauline', 'Petrine' and 'Apollonian' in Corinth (cf. 1 Cor. 1^{12}). To bring to the notice of the Church some relevant material from what was evidently a vast store (21^{25}), and to include it without meticulous care for its literary adaptation, would be both understandable and excusable if thereby schism and misunderstanding were to be prevented in the Church.

Another suggestion is that the author or editor is trying to indicate to his readers that what took place at and after the resurrection of Jesus left no expectation unfulfilled. This appearance by the Galilean lake is intended, so it is supposed, to fulfil the promise made by Jesus to meet the disciples in Galilee (Mark 16^7; Matt. 28^7). John does not himself report any such arranging of a meeting in Galilee; but it is thought that he knew of a tradition which did report it, and that he wanted his gospel, like those of the synoptists, to let the world know that such a meeting had taken place. If this be taken as even part of the answer to the question as to why ch. 21 was added to the apparently complete gospel, it must be recognized as both an historical and a theological answer. The evangelist is trying to say not only that Jesus kept his appointment as a matter of fact, but also that he kept it because the whole faithfulness of God was involved in the tryst.

There are some indications of more strictly theological intentions of the author/editor. It might be held, for example, that ch. 21 is but the final review of a question first posed in ch. 1 as to the nature of discipleship, or the 'following' of Jesus. It is not difficult to see similarities between the account of the miraculous draught of fishes in Luke 5$^{1-11}$ and the story of the haul of 153 fish when Jesus came to the disciples after the resurrection. In Luke's gospel the evangelist gives the reader his own parallel to Mark 1$^{16-20}$, which tells of the call of Simon and Andrew, and of the sons of Zebedee, James and John. Mark had related how all four were at their fisherman's tasks, but at the summons of Jesus and his promise to make them 'fishers of men' they had 'left their nets and followed him'. Luke provides an interesting alternative to this account. Jesus, says Luke, was pressed by a crowd wanting to hear him; he got into a fisherman's boat. This chanced to be Peter's, while Peter was washing his nets. When Jesus came to the end of his teaching, he told Peter to 'put out into the deep, and let down [his] nets for a catch'. Peter answered that they had toiled all night and caught nothing, but consented to do as he was charged. On letting down their nets they caught a great shoal of fish, almost breaking their nets. They called on their partners for help, but even with two boats the catch was still threatening to sink them. At this point Peter fell at the knees of Jesus and said 'Depart from me; for I am a sinful man, O Lord.' Jesus answered Peter 'Do not be afraid: henceforth you will be catching men.' This is clearly the 'calling' of Peter, according to Luke.

Luke's story stands midway between the narrative of Mark 1$^{16-20}$ and the present narrative in John. By one of his characteristic 'dislocations' Luke has tried to show that when Jesus called Peter he had already made plain his claim to fulfil the scriptures of the Old Testament (Luke 4$^{16-21}$ as parallel to Mark 6$^{1-6}$), and that at the call of Peter there was much more than any chance exercise of personal magnetism might explain. For Luke makes it clear that Peter experienced something which in modern language would be called 'numinous' about the person of Jesus; 'depart from me, for I am a sinful man' is his immediate reaction to the Lord's fruitful advice about the casting of the fisherman's net. It is only after this perception of the supernatural character of Jesus that Luke records the Lord's call and the fisherman's responses.

When a comparison is made between Luke and John two significant similarities appear: in both there is a miraculous catch of fish, and in both Peter is the one named disciple. These two similarities suffice to raise the question whether they are not either identical or closely related elements in the early traditions about Jesus, and to suggest that they are really variant accounts of one actual occasion. But if they are, or even if they are not, why does John place his story at the end of his gospel, and Luke his version near the beginning of his narrative? The answer turns upon that to another question: when is a man appointed to be a disciple, a member of the Twelve? To the present writer it appears right to believe that John was aware of the tradition now preserved in the synoptics, that the disciples were called to be such, and appointed to be apostles quite early in the historic ministry of Jesus: indeed the fourth gospel itself incorporates some of these traditions, and the convictions underlying them (cf. 1^{35-51}). But just as John is careful to show about Jesus that he did not advance from human status to the divine at some point like his baptism, transfiguration or crucifixion, but was of divine status and nature throughout, and made this plain by the interesting historiographical device of some quite un-synoptic sayings in ch. 1 (see notes ad loc.), so here he is careful to show that however true it may be to say that disciples and apostles were appointed in Jesus' earthly ministry, it must nevertheless be equally true that the only 'time' that any man can be called and appointed to discipleship and apostleship is when the son of man has been crucified and glorified. The appointment of a disciple or an apostle is no more to be precisely located on a chronological time-scale than is the possession of a divine nature by the man Jesus of Nazareth. And if the former truth about Jesus can be brought home in this gospel by using some synoptic 'last' material 'first' (e.g. the use of 'Lamb of God' in $1^{29,36}$, or of 'Messiah' in 1^{41}) the latter truth may equally be testified by the use of 'first' material 'last' (as here, where the early synoptic phrase *Follow me* is used at the end of John, as well as at the beginning [21^{19} and 1^{43}]).

If this be a valid way of reading ch. 21 it appears to be much more than a pamphlet addressed to a particular situation in the Church at Ephesus, or in the churches generally, where excessive partiality for Peter and John threatened to bring schism into the Christian community: it is a quite independent, fundamental and universal exposition of the nature of Christian discipleship and apostleship, of what it means in the end to 'follow Christ'.

But there are more theological clues in ch. 21; clues which relate to the whole development of chs. 1–20. As ch. 20 was expounded it was seen to be the author's intention to use the experiences of the disciples who saw the glorified Lord as a link between the communion they had had with him in the days of his flesh, and the communion which they, and all other Christians, were to have with him throughout time. But had the fourth gospel finished without ch. 21, it might well be held against it that it really failed to provide such a link, which is provided only by ch. 21 itself. The argument might run thus: ch. 20 is a record of what took place within the octave of the Passover during which the true Paschal lamb, Jesus Christ, died. However miraculous the resurrection appearances there recorded were, they occurred only during that Passover, and offer no sort of guarantee that they have any validity or even promise outside the feast. Is it possible that the evangelist was aware of this, and that ch. 21 affords, at least for him, the link between that Passover and the subsequent life of all Christian men? If that be so, then some narrative like 21$^{1-14}$ is a necessity for him, as for every succeeding Christian, for here is the connexion between the one 'real' Passover, and the rest of human history, the 'secular' life of ordinary disciples.

The story of ch. 21 begins when Peter says (21^3): '*I am going fishing.*' This is really to say, in effect, 'The whole episode of our discipleship, our "following" of Jesus of Nazareth, is over. We had better go back to our fishing.' It is perhaps not too fanciful to think that the evangelist might be inviting some observation that just as Jesus had seen, quite truly, that his own life had been somewhat circular – a coming from God and a going back to God (13^3) – so Peter now thought that their life had been in a sort of secular circularity – going from fishing and now going back to fishing: there was nothing else to do, now that Jesus had 'returned to the Father'. The importance of the appearances recorded in ch. 21 is that it brings Jesus to the disciples when they have returned to their secular, everyday jobs. So the link between the Easter appearances and the contemporary presence of Christ to his people throughout the ages is established in ch. 21.

Finally, it may be held that ch. 21 brings to full and final expression all that the gospel wants the Christian to understand about the nature of discipleship. When Luke tells of Peter's call to be a follower of Jesus, he relates that, after the miraculous catch of fish, Peter falls to Jesus' knees, and says 'Depart from me, for I am a sinful man, O Lord' (Luke 5^8). Jesus meets this request with words which bind Peter to him for good, words which in Matthew and Mark are also addressed to Andrew: 'Henceforth you will be catching men' (Luke 5^{10}; Mark 1^{17}; Matt. 4^{19}). It would not be difficult to suppose that Mark and Matthew believed the same words were used as invitation and promise to James and John. In John 21, as Peter makes a threefold confession of his lack of self-confidence in asserting his love for his Lord, thus matching his threefold denial at the time of the trial, he receives a threefold charge to tend and feed Christ's flock. Next he obtains a clear indication that he would suffer martyrdom: and only then does he hear the command which was addressed to Philip in 1⁴³: 'Follow me.' And only here is all the material readily available for the ordinary reader to plumb that brief imperative to its depth. Clearly here it means more than to walk behind Jesus spatially; it means to follow him in laying down one's life, in really accepting the destiny of the cross in utter trust in God's power to raise from the dead.

This scene in ch. 21 is remarkably like that recorded by Luke in Luke 5, where at Jesus' command the disciples take action resulting in a catch of fish that is miraculous. In John 21 the catch is not only miraculous, but also symbolic in its number (see note ad loc.) of the totality of mankind that the divinely instructed and commissioned fishermen will 'catch'. Thus John makes the incident equivalent, though with a quite different historiographical device, to the great missionary charge in Matthew 28^{18f} (cf. Mark 16¹⁵). So to be a disciple is not just 'following Jesus'; it is to be his 'fisherman', to share in his own gathering of the messianic community; it is to suffer with the Messiah in the all-decisive messianic woes; it is to witness, by life and by death, to the victory of the crucified. To follow him is to be with him in all that he suffered, and therefore to be with him in his glory. John may thus be said to seek to establish once and for all that the world-wide mission of the Church derives from none other than the Lord himself. And, what is as important, that at whatever temporal point a disciple be called, an apostle appointed, or a mission begun, the real occasion was with the one Lord, incarnate, suffering, dying, rising, entering into his glory and reigning, sharing with the Father the glory which was his from the foundation of the world.

Finally, in the light of such comments it is worth while asking once again to what extent ch. 21 is a mere appendix, added for some specific situation, or whether, even if it were so added, it is not also provided for the general reader as an essential epilogue to the whole gospel, much as the prologue is an essential preface to the gospel. From 1¹⁹ to 20³¹ the evangelist gives his readers his own profound version of the life of Jesus, drawing upon a rich tradition in such a way as to complement and theologically deepen the synoptic presentation of material from identical and similar sources. But where Mark takes the story back to Hebrew prophets, Matthew to Abraham, Luke to Adam, John takes it back to the creative action of God himself, in the Word or purpose which established the world and speaks of God's nature and purpose to men. So at the end of the gospel, where Mark ends his story with the awesome wonder of those who had heard that the crucified one had been raised on the third day; where Matthew speaks of a worldwide commission for a Lord who would be with his people to the end of the age; where Luke tells of a final blessing from the risen Lord as he parted from his disciples, John portrays in his own characteristic and powerful symbolism how the risen Lord would find his disciples in their resumption of life in the secular world, and would there empower them to complete his universal mission, in the mystery and power of that laying down of life which had seemed to men the shame and defeat of the cross, but which to the Lord and his community was the manifestation of the glory of the eternal God. Such a chapter is more than a mere appendix; it is not less than epilogue and crown.

21 $^{1-3}$ THE RETURN OF THE FISHERMEN

Mark 1 $^{16-20}$

John 1 ^{45}

2 1 *After this Jesus revealed himself again to the disciples by the Sea of Tibe'ri-as; and he revealed himself in this way.* [2]*Simon Peter, Thomas called the Twin, Nathan'a-el of Cana in Galilee, the sons of Zeb'edee, and two others of his disciples were together.* [3]*Simon Peter said to them, 'I am going fishing.' They said to him, 'We will go with you.' They went out and got into the boat; but that night they caught nothing.*

In this short section the evangelist (or so we propose to refer to whoever it was designed this chapter and/or added it to the body of the gospel) deliberately reconstitutes a situation such as is typically described in the synoptic tradition as occurring at the very beginning of the ministry, with one touch to take his readers back to his own

narrative of the first appearance of the Lord to his disciples in Galilee
(1^{45}), when his first sign was done (2$^{1-11}$). But only seven of the
Twelve were present when Peter declares '*I am going fishing*'. The
number seven is not likely to be meant as the 'perfect' number, in
view of the impending apostasy of the seven, who seem ready enough
to agree with Peter's decision to return to their old trade. It is precisely
in the doing of a 'secular' job, even at a time of desertion and apostasy,
that the glorified Lord will make himself known. This is the great
link between the Christian of every age and the apostles who saw
Christ in the flesh and in his body of glory.

ᛙᛈᛈ

1

After this: The preposition should not be pressed. It need be no more
than a general introduction to one pericope in the tradition accessible
to John, not necessarily connected, therefore, in historical continuity,
with the events last recorded in ch. 20.

again: Once more, the temporal reference should not be pressed, as if
it necessarily implied that *again* meant specifically after the two (or
three) appearances recorded in ch. 20.

to the disciples: There is no clue as to number in this phrase by itself.
Presumably to no more than the seven mentioned in v.2, though *disciples*
as a word could be used more widely than even for the Twelve (cf. 2^2).

the Sea of Tiberias: By this means John incorporates into his gospel an
account of an appearance of the glorified Lord in Galilee – Galilee of the
Gentiles, as it was called.

2

Simon Peter: He was a fisherman, as were the sons of Zebedee; the
beloved disciple was also with Peter, though we know nothing of his
secular interests. Thomas and Nathanael bring the number to six, and
the seventh may have been Andrew (as Pseudo-Peter claims) or Philip,
who came from Bethsaida.

the sons of Zebedee: This is a synoptic way of referring to James and
John, not previously used in the fourth gospel. This may well indicate
the author's use of another source for this chapter.

were together: The phrase suggests that the seven men had gone into
partnership to trade as fishermen.

3

Simon Peter said: Characteristically Peter takes the lead. This is one of the points upon which Jesus causes Peter to reflect later (v. 15).

'I am going fishing': It is not, as some commentators suppose, unthinkable that after the events of ch. 20 Peter should give way to such apostasy. On the contrary it may well have appeared that now the Passover time was over, and Jesus dead, even though he had appeared to them in Jerusalem, the only thing left now they were back in Galilee was to resume their normal tasks. It is possible that we have here another instance of John's irony, for though Peter thinks he is to return to the catching of fish, he is to learn all over again what he had been told at the beginning of his discipleship, as the synoptists record it, that he was to become, as Christ's disciple, a 'fisher of men'.

that night they caught nothing: The night was the best time for fishing, but on their own, without their Lord, nothing could be made even of the best opportunities.

21⁴⁻⁸   2. THE GREAT CATCH – A PARABLE
                                               Luke 5¹⁻¹¹

⁴*Just as day was breaking, Jesus stood on the beach; yet the disciples did not know that it was Jesus.* ⁵*Jesus said to them, 'Children, have you any fish?' They answered him, 'No.'* ⁶*He said to them, 'Cast the net on the right side of the boat, and you will find some.' So they cast it, and now they were not able to haul it in, for the quantity of fish.* ⁷*That disciple whom Jesus loved said to Peter, 'It is the Lord!' When Simon Peter heard that it was the Lord, he put on his clothes, for he was stripped for work, and sprang into the sea.* ⁸*But the other disciples came in the boat, dragging the net full of fish, for they were not far from the land, but about a hundred yards⁰ off.*

a Greek *two hundred cubits*

The story of how Jesus manifested himself to the seven who had joined in a return to secular occupation reminds the reader at several points of the earlier part of the gospel. This is a 'resurrection' story, and, like the narratives in ch. 20 as well as in the synoptics, it begins very early in the day – *as day was breaking* (v. 4). Jesus stood on the beach, unrecognized. He asked the seven whether they had caught any fish, and was told 'No'. He then told them to cast on the right side of the boat, and on doing so they made a very large catch, and were unable to haul it in. The beloved disciple sensed that the stranger on the shore was Jesus, and told Peter of his conviction. Peter, impetuous as he was, put on his clothes and sprang into the water. The disciples left in the boat brought the vessel and the catch to shore.

Here are found some of the usual elements of an 'Easter Day' appearance of the Lord. It takes place early; there is a lack of recognition. The beloved disciple and Peter play the accustomed roles that have been noted in the story of the passion and resurrection.

There is also, as was noted above, a considerable likeness to the story of the miraculous draught of fishes in Luke 5. It seems neither impossible nor improbable to see in these phenomena an interesting example of Johannine historiography. A Mark may tell how at the very beginning of the ministry Peter was called to become a 'fisher of men' (Mark 1^{17f}); a Luke may give the same information, spelling it out with the story of a miraculous catch of fish under instruction from Jesus, to show how marvellously the fisher of men would practise his new trade under guidance of his new Lord. But John, putting these elements of the story at the time when the glorified Lord was making himself manifest to his disciples, at a time when they had decided to return to their old trade, makes it quite plain that the call to Christian discipleship is not really fulfilled until the Lord is crucified and glorified; and that when the call proceeds from this point, it is finally and completely effective in the world.

☙❧

4
Just as day was breaking: The Greek word used in this phrase is in a form not found in the body of the gospel, suggesting that a different source is being used, or a different author or editor at work.

yet the disciples did not know that it was Jesus: Such inability to recognize Jesus was not unknown on similar recorded occasions (see the note on 20¹⁴).

5
'have you any fish?': The form of question in the Greek expects the answer 'No'. The verb *have* in the setting of a fisherman's life could well be rendered 'Have you caught'. *Fish* is a word used in the Greek

for other foods, which could serve as a relish for eating with bread. Here the question refers to the possibility of the disciples having caught some fish for use at a meal with bread.

6

'*Cast the net on the right side*': The right side was thought to be the lucky side. But John is fundamentally concerned with the different results to be obtained with and without the advice and help of the Lord.

they were not able to haul it in: The word for *haul* is the same as that used in 6⁴⁴: 'No one can come to me unless the Father who sent me "draws" him.' This fact lends some plausibility to the view that John was not unaware of the parabolic nature of the incident he was recording.

7

That disciple whom Jesus loved said to Peter, 'It is the Lord': The two disciples play their accustomed roles. The beloved disciple is the first to recognize Jesus, and Peter the first to act upon the recognition.

put on his clothes, for he was stripped for work: The translation is not inaccurate though it probably does not convey precisely the information the evangelist is able to impart. Peter had evidently taken off his workman's 'frock' or 'smock' and was thus in his working clothes, somewhat stripped – without coat or waistcoat might be the modern equivalent. When he decided to make his own way to Jesus ahead of the others he put on his 'smock', tucked it into his belt to keep it dry from the sea and waded ashore. The suggestion that he waded for one hundred yards is improbable, but so is the suggestion that he put on his smock before taking to the water. If it is thought to be important to get events in possible sequence, then Peter would have put on his smock while the boat was travelling part of the hundred yards to the shore, and left it at the point when he could reasonably get to the beach by wading.

21⁹⁻¹⁴   LOAVES AND FISHES AGAIN

9 *When they got out on land, they saw a charcoal fire there, with fish lying on it, and bread.* 10 *Jesus said to them, 'Bring some of the fish that you have just caught.'* 11 *So Simon Peter went aboard and hauled the net ashore, full of large fish, a hundred and fifty-three of them; and although there were so many, the net was not torn.* 12 *Jesus said to them, 'Come and have breakfast.'*

Now none of the disciples dared ask him, 'Who are you?' They knew it
was the Lord. ¹³*Jesus came and took the bread and gave it to them, and so*
with the fish. ¹⁴*This was now the third time that Jesus was revealed to the*
disciples after he was raised from the dead.

One of the stranger details of the whole story of this third manifestation of the glorified Lord is that when the disciples come to land with
their miraculous draught of fishes, there is already a provision of both
bread and fish for the meal which the Lord has prepared himself,
without their help. He can feed them without their aid; they cannot
fish without his. The parabolic strain surely continues!

Jesus asks for some of the fish that had been just caught. It is not
stated that any were eaten at the time, though the evangelist is
careful to state the precise number of fish caught. This is in some
contrast to the story in Luke, where the evangelist gives the impression
of miracle by stating that the catch of fish was enough to set two boats
sinking. Why does John report a precise number? In all probability
because the number was significant, though what its significance was
is hard now to determine. Speculation has been rife and inventive
down the ages. It is 'the sum of the first 17 of the natural numbers'
(Hoskyns and Davey ad loc.). But, though interesting, this suggests no
special significance. Or 7 and 10 are both perfect numbers, and the
two together thus indicate the full perfection of the Church – but that
seems far-fetched. Or again, it is, in Origen's understanding (cf.
Hoskyns and Davey ad loc.), the blessed Trinity: fifty (but why fifty?)
multiplied by three, plus three. Or finally, it was seen as 'one hundred
heathen, fifty Jews, and the Trinity (Severus, cf. Hoskyns and Davey
ad loc.). It seems much more likely that the number was recognized
as that representing the total number of species of fish (cited from
Jerome in Hoskyns and Davey ad loc.) and the catch was parabolic of
the successful universal mission of the Church.

When the universality of the Church's mission had thus been
dramatically demonstrated, Jesus asked the disciples to '*come and have*
breakfast'. Presumably they ate of the meal Jesus had prepared; and
that consisted of bread and fish, as had the meal when the five thousand were fed in Galilee at a previous Passover time. But now the food
was not provided by a young lad, but entirely by Jesus. He is now the
bread of life, and he gives his self-provided and self-offered bread to
them. 'And so with the fish', adds John. In some early pictorial

representations of the eucharist in Christian art, the bread of the sacrament is accompanied by fish, and not by wine.

If the attempt be made to discover what sort of historiographical inference may be drawn from this part of the narrative, it would seem likely that John is saying that, just as the calling of the disciples recorded earlier in the ministry really stems only from the crucifixion and glorification of the Son of God, so does the eucharist itself. The meal on the Galilean hillside may have been a eucharist of anticipation; but this meal by the lakeside was one of fulfilment. Part of the elements Jesus himself provided, but part would be brought by the Church and through its mission. 'Would be brought' because it seems that the catch of fish was not used by Jesus at this time. The catch was but parabolic of the catch that would come. It would come only when the disciples now sharing the sacred meal with their glorified Lord had themselves shared in the cup which he had had to drink, as indeed Jesus is going on to say to Peter later in the chapter. Here for the moment the nucleus of the Church learns that if it obeys its Lord its mission will be miraculously successful, and that it can maintain fellowship with him and receive sustenance from him, for even if they should be unfaithful and apostate, he will still come to them and call them back to his service.

ॐ

9
When they got out on land: The only other time the Greek word used here is found in the N.T. is at Luke 5² !

with fish lying on it: The word for *fish* here was used at 6⁹ in the story of the feeding of the five thousand. Surely a gentle reminder by the evangelist that what was anticipated there is fulfilled here. Dr Barrett thinks that because the fish on the fire did not come from the catch, it is probable that two stories are being conflated. But it seems equally possible to suppose, as in this exposition, that there is a proper theological, historiographical significance in the two sources of fish.

10
'Bring some of the fish you have just caught': Nothing is said further, save to relate the number of the fish (see above). Can it be that the fish already provided represent the Jews, to whom the Lord came, and whom he still represents; and that the fish caught represent the Gentiles, thus bringing in the whole of mankind?

11

the net was not torn: If the story be at all parabolic, as well as historical, then the net may represent the Church which undertakes to capture men for Christ.

12

'Come and have breakfast': The first meal of the day, and the first new meal or eucharist of the new *day* that had dawned with the resurrection of the Lord. They had spent a night without catching any food; now they were to be fed from his supply. They had gone through the dark night of despair, had thought the whole thing was over, and that they must return to secular life again; but now they were to learn that a new day had dawned and new power would come to make them, in Paul's words 'more than conquerors'.

none of the disciples dared ask him, 'Who are you?': The Jews had been ready enough to put precisely this question to him before (8^{25}), but now, in his risen and glorified appearance, he renders all such questionings superfluous. This was not to be a social meal of simple bonhomie; it was a sacramental occasion (see below on v. 13).

13

Jesus came and took the bread and gave it to them: Codex Bezae has the actual words 'gave thanks and gave it to them', thus filling out what already in the received text seems a clear eucharistic reference.

and so with the fish: Reminiscent of the feeding of the five thousand. See above.

14

This was now the third time that Jesus was revealed to the disciples: It would be wrong to suppose that in making this statement the author was doing any more than referring to what had already been said in ch. 20. He is not, in all probability, making any attempt to comment on the synoptic gospels as such.

21^{15-19} THE CHARGE TO PETER

Luke 5^{8-11}

[15]*When they had finished breakfast, Jesus said to Simon Peter, 'Simon, son of John, do you love me more than these?' He said to him, 'Yes, Lord; you know that I love you.' He said to him, 'Feed my lambs.'* [16]*A second*

time he said to him, 'Simon, son of John, do you love me?' He said to him,
'Yes, Lord; you know that I love you.' He said to him, 'Tend my sheep.'
¹⁷He said to him the third time, 'Simon, son of John, do you love me?' Peter
was grieved because he said to him the third time, 'Do you love me?' And he
said to him, 'Lord, you know everything; you know that I love you.' Jesus
said to him, 'Feed my sheep. ¹⁸Truly, truly, I say to you, when you were
young, you girded yourself and walked where you would; but when you are
old, you will stretch out your hands, and another will gird you and carry you
where you do not wish to go.' ¹⁹(This he said to show by what death he was to
glorify God.) And after this he said to him, 'Follow me.'

In the synoptic gospels the appointment of a disciple at the very
beginning of the ministry was accompanied with the words with
which Jesus now ends his searching examination of Peter: *'Follow me.'*
It is hard to resist the conclusion that John is trying to make a profound point by this historiographical device, viz. that true discipleship flows from the death and glorification of the Lord. Here is
enacted the reality of what was really but promise in the earlier 'call'.
The scene is solemn. The seven disciples who had gone back to their
jobs had found that the glorified Lord came to them even there, and
fed them with the bread and fish that had been the symbol of the
'bread of life', which was himself, on the Galilean hillside (6⁹). After
the solemn sacramental meal was over Jesus began a searching questioning of Peter. The reader will already be aware that the knowledge
Jesus had of Peter on the night of the trial was much truer than that
which Peter had of himself. Now Peter's replies to the Lord's questioning show that he has realized this for himself.

One of the points upon which the commentator has to make up
his mind is whether there is any significance in the fact that John uses
two Greek words for *love* in the cross-examination of Peter. There was
a time when this could be done without much reflection, but recently
scholars have pointed out how very much John is given to the use of
synonyms, and that has made it very unfashionable to interpret the
passage as if the two words were other than synonyms. Yet it would
seem fair comment to say that, unless there are special reasons to the
contrary, it must be the nature of the context which must determine
whether an author is in fact using two words quite synonymously
or not, with the added test that a reasonable improvement in exposition would be a natural consequence of such an assumption. It is the

view adopted in the following exposition that the two words for *love* are not synonymous in this passage, whatever may be true of them elsewhere in the gospel. It seems quite clear that John has it in mind to show that the threefold denial which Peter made on the night of the trial is now matched by a threefold confession. In that situation the progression from the strong word for love (*agapao*) to a weaker one (*phileo*) when Jesus goes from his second to his third question to Peter gives an intelligible and intelligent reason for the use of two distinct meanings. The course of the examination may therefore be set out thus: Jesus puts his question for the first time, addressing it to Peter under his name of Simon, i.e. not the name that Jesus had given him, but as he was when Jesus first called him. He asks him a question which reflects that Peter had always been the disciple who was first with his protestations of love and loyalty, and first also in insight (cf. e.g. Mark 8²⁹; 9⁵; 14²⁹) as well as the one who had also failed perhaps beyond others (e.g. cf. Mark 8³²; 8³³; 14⁵³, ⁵⁴; 14⁶⁶⁻⁷²). 'Simon . . .' said Jesus, '*do you love me more than these?*' Peter, who would on some occasions undoubtedly have answered with a confident 'Yes', now knows that he can make no such claim. The events of the night of the trial have proved beyond question that his loyalty was at least no better, and at most a good deal worse, than that of the others, Judas alone excepted. So Peter declined to answer with any reference to the comparison which he must have felt to be quite humbling, and simply said: '*Yes, Lord; you know that I love you.*' But if the commentator may take note of the difference in the two words John uses for *love* in telling this story, Peter says a little more, by saying a little less than that. If the two words are not synonyms then Peter's reply can be translated: 'Yes, Lord, you know that I care for you.' It seems as if when he is faced with so searching a question about his own love and loyalty to Christ in comparison with that of his fellow-disciples, he feels unable to use the word, the distinctively Christian word for love, that implied a deep and final commitment. *Love* in this profound sense is that commitment which Christ makes possible for a man, both in his relationship to God, and in his relationships with other human beings. Peter knows that he cannot rightly lay claim to such a word; so he uses one normally associated with human temperament and disposition, not so divinely conditioned, so sure or so secure. The reply of Jesus to so sensitive an awareness of weakness seems astounding: '*Feed my lambs*'. Yet this reply embodies the whole gospel of divine grace. First, it makes plain that not until a man has come to realize that his sufficiency is not in himself or in his knowledge of himself, but in his Lord and in his Lord's knowledge of him, can he either know or communicate what real discipleship means. Second, it is significant that it is precisely to Peter who has denied, forsaken, and even tried to divert his Lord, that the great divine commission comes. Christ does not wait upon a man's attainment of perfection before admitting him to discipleship or appointing him to apostleship: both offices alike are his gift to sinful men.

In his second question to Peter Jesus omitted the reference to the other disciples. It is as if he said: 'Very well. It is perhaps quite understandable that you should not now want to claim any precedence in love and loyalty. So forget about the others. Think simply of your own relationship to me. Do you love me?' In the setting of the three questions this seems to be implied by the second formulation. Peter's reply was no different. Whether he judged himself in comparison with others, or whether he tried to assess himself entirely alone, the same confession had to be made. He would not and could not deny his *love*; but he would not and could not affirm it. He answered again: 'Yes, Lord; you know that I care for you.' Jesus replied with a second commission: *'Tend my sheep.'*

The third question is perhaps the crucial one for the interpreter. For when Jesus questioned Peter for the third time he said (to continue to treat the two words for love as not synonymous): 'Simon son of John, do you care for me?' The words with which John follows this question: 'Peter was grieved because he said to him the third time "Do you care for me?"' seem to confirm the view that the two words are not synonymous. It is indeed understandable why Peter should have been grieved had the narrative been using two synonymous words for love. But to treat them as not synonymous brings an immediately heightened tension and drama into the narrative. Twice Jesus had used the strong, new, typically Christian word for love; and twice Peter had deliberately avoided using it in his reply. Now, in his third question, that must have brought to Peter's mind the bitter memory of his three denials, Jesus used the very word by which he had hoped to escape the worst of the probing. 'Simon, son of John, do you really care for me? Are you sure even of that?' seems to be the dramatic question Jesus now puts. And Peter cannot and knows he cannot lay claim even to this. All his self-knowledge and all his self-confidence have gone; the only thing he can trust is his Lord's knowledge of him that has, even at this moment, twice recommissioned him, and he says: 'Lord you know everything; you know that I care for you.' So at last Peter is brought to the point of being completely broken; and at that point he is completely remade in the reception anew of his divine commission: '*Feed my sheep.*'

But more still was to come to the newly humble and therefore newly strong Peter. Jesus tells him how in the future he will come to die, to 'drink the cup' that the Father had prepared for his Son (18¹¹; Mark 10³⁸; 14³⁶). The prediction is in the form of a contrast between Peter's freedom when he was young (he would seem to have been middle aged and certainly married at this time of his life) and the constraint under which he would be as the Lord's apostle, a constraint which others would exercise upon him by stretching out his hands upon a cross. It was only after all this was completed that Jesus said to Peter, in the Johannine presentation of the story: '*Follow me.*' While this seems in some ways to belie the synoptic narrative, John is not putting any un-synoptic interpretation upon what 'following Jesus' means (cf. e.g. Matt. 8¹⁹ᶠ; 10³⁸; 16²⁴; 19²¹; Mark 8³⁴; 10²¹). But what the reservation of this injunction to the very end of Peter's time with his Lord makes plain is that following can be in no way valid unless it flows from the cross, and leads to it. This story puts in graphic form the theologically phrased conviction of Paul that 'we are crucified with him'.

&

15

When they had finished breakfast: That is to say, when the sacramental experience was over. It is interesting to recall that in Luke's story of the Last Supper there was quarrelling as to who should be greatest among the disciples (Luke 22²⁴). At this meal Jesus takes the initiative by dealing with Peter.

'*Simon, son of John*': The Lord does not use his 'Christian' name. It is to Peter as a member of manhood-after-the-flesh that he speaks. This Peter is the puzzling, heroic, yet craven disciple who can make great affirmations, and yet bend almost treacherously to circumstance.

'*do you love me*': There is an extensive note in the I.C.C. (Bernard) which demonstrates that both words used here for *love* can be used in very much the same variety of meanings, so that 'it would be precarious to lay stress on the change' which has been noted (Bernard II, 703). But the point must still be made that though such lexical evidence as Bernard produces proves the general point of rough synonymity, it does not prove that the words are used synonymously here, even though synonymity may be admitted elsewhere in John.

'*more than these*': It is possible that *these* refer to the nets and boats round the group, though it is wholly less likely. It is only at Matt. 26^{33} and Mark 14^{29} that Peter makes any actual claim of superiority, but from all the four gospels it appears that he was the one who took the lead. He should have been the least likely to fail his Lord.

'*Yes, Lord; you know that I love you*': The *yes* cannot be stated alone, but must be qualified by the knowledge which Peter now knows Jesus has of the disciple's heart (cf. 13^{38}).

'*Feed my lambs*': This seems almost to mix the metaphors of the passage. But the metaphor of the net which catches the whole range of men, the Church, i.e. which succeeds in its mission to the whole of mankind, will not sustain all the duties that befall one who is to be 'the greatest fisherman' for Christ. His duties will include tasks which are more like that of the shepherd. He must guide and feed the flock of Christ, and become an 'under-shepherd' to Christ the great Shepherd of the sheep. Moreover, the figure of the shepherd more easily leads on to the thought of the good shepherd who 'lays down his life for the sheep' (10^{11}), as Peter will be told he must do later on.

16

'*Simon . . . do you love me?*': On this occasion the reference to the other disciples is dropped.

'*Tend my sheep*': The word used for *tend* includes all the duties of the shepherd, not simply that of providing them with pasture, though this distinction, as that between *sheep* and 'lambs', should not be pressed too far.

17

Peter was grieved because he said to him the third time 'Do you love [care for] me?': It may suffice to quote Barrett on this verse: 'Peter was grieved because the question was asked three times, not because [another word] was used' (Barrett, p. 487). There seems to be no argument to bring the reader's judgement to Barrett's point of view.

'*Lord, you know everything . . .*': To this third question Peter does not reply 'Yes'. Not that he could not do so, but because he wants to make (or the evangelist wants to make) it absolutely clear that what he (Peter) is certain of is not even his 'caring for' his Lord, but his Lord's knowledge of him. How different this was from the Peter of the trial night!

18

'*Truly, truly, I say to you*': A very common, and very characteristic Johannine phrase, and if it be other than the imitation of some other author, it indicates, in all probability, a new departure in the discourse, and some specially significant statement.

'*when you were young*': Literally 'younger', though the comparative did not always have comparative force.

'*you girded yourself and walked where you would*': This is a simple statement of the physical freedom enjoyed by the young man, who can easily clothe himself, or put on his armour, and walk where he pleases.

'*but when you are old, you will stretch out your hands, and another will gird you and carry you where you do not wish to go*': This could be a simple statement of the physical dependence of the aged. The really old man cannot put his own clothes or armour on, but must hold out his arms while some other person puts his garments on him. He cannot go where he pleases, for he has to be taken by someone else. So his freedom and independence are severely curtailed. But the phrase *stretch out your hands* has been regarded by a number of ancient authors as descriptive of death by crucifixion. If this is in the mind of the author here, then the passage becomes a subtle prophecy of the martyrdom of Peter, probably already a past event at the time the gospel was written and published. The whole second phrase of the sentence then takes on a new meaning.

19

(*This he said to show by what death he was to glorify God*): At 12^{33} the evangelist records that the Lord showed 'by what death he was to die'. Here the same prophetic anticipation is made of Peter's death. The phrase which speaks of glorifying God is found also at 1 Peter 4^{16}: 'If one suffers as a Christian, let him not be ashamed, but under that name let him glorify God.'

after this he said to him, 'Follow me': In this way the treatment of discipleship was brought full cycle both for the gospel of John, where the command was used by Jesus to Philip at 1^{43}, and for the synoptic tradition, where *Follow me* is the call given to Simon and Andrew, to James and John and Levi. As in the earlier instances, there is a quite literal side to the injunction which cannot be dispensed with. Philip had to 'follow' Jesus to Galilee; the disciples in the synoptic story had to leave their nets or their tax office and 'follow' Jesus. Yet it is very plain that at this point of the gospel more is meant than that Peter should accompany the beloved disciple and others in walking with or behind Jesus away from the lake. *After this* Jesus said *'Follow me'* means that the reader must now understand that to follow Christ is to be taken by divine destiny to the point where the disciple, like his Lord, glorifies God.

21²⁰⁻²³ THE DESTINY OF THE BELOVED DISCIPLE

²⁰*Peter turned and saw following them the disciple whom Jesus loved, who had lain close to his breast at the supper and had said, 'Lord, who is it that is going to betray you?'* ²¹*When Peter saw him, he said to Jesus, 'Lord, what about this man?'* ²²*Jesus said to him, 'If it is my will tha' he remain until I come, what is that to you? Follow me!'* ²³*The saying spread abroad among the brethren that this disciple was not to die; yet Jesus did not say to him that he was not to die, but, 'If it is my will that he remain until I come, what is that to you?'*

In these few verses some commentators find the key to the problem as to why the author added ch. 21 as an appendix to the gospel. It seems an inadequate theory, as has been argued; but in these verses the author is concerned to clear up some misunderstandings in the Church.

After Peter had been questioned it seems as if the company left the sea – for good? Peter was evidently walking with Jesus, and chanced to turn round and saw the beloved disciple following them. If the exposition of the chapter so far is right, it does not require much imagination to understand why Peter should ask Jesus: 'Lord, what about this man?' He too was a disciple. He had behaved very differently on the night of the trial and the day of the crucifixion. He had been with Peter at the grave on Easter Sunday morning. He was now 'following' Jesus. But would 'following' in his case also mean a tragic destiny? It may well be that there was some uncertainty in Peter's own mind about his position *vis-à-vis* the beloved disciple, even after the clear charge he had just received to 'tend the flock'. The beloved disciple was also clearly a 'special' case. What would the discipleship involve for him? 'Lord what about this man?'

The Lord's reply is at the least enigmatic, and may at the most be thought to constitute a rebuke to Peter. Had he not yet learnt that any sort of comparison was wrong? So Jesus answered Peter: *'If it is my will that he remain until I come, what is that to you? Follow me!'* In other words, the command to *follow* is individual and must be accepted as such. The Lord must be Lord, and the destiny of his disciples can be safely left in his hands. The evangelist adds what is clearly a note to clear up some misunderstanding in the early Church. Evidently on the basis of this saying it had been assumed that the beloved disciple would not die. The author is careful to point out that this was not stated by Jesus at all. The inference seems plain. Just as the Lord's word to Peter ended with the injunction *'Follow me'*, so must each Christian and each reader of the gospel repeat that command to himself, and embrace it for his own life and destiny. Discipleship is not fulfilled or exercised in inquiry as to the destiny of other people. It is properly exercised only in a humble acceptance of whatever destiny the Lord has laid up for each disciple who loves him.

૨૦૨

20

who had lain close to his breast at the supper . . .: This additional information, surely superfluous at this point of the gospel, indicates that the author has incorporated material from some independent tradition.

21

'Lord, what about this man?': Literally 'This man, what?' Peter is still thinking about his own destiny as it has been anticipated by the Lord. What will that of the beloved disciple be?

22

'If it is my will that he remain until I come, what is that to you?': This is evidently the saying that has given rise to the misunderstanding which the evangelist sets out to correct. It is therefore mistaken to argue, as Lightfoot does (p. 343) that 'if the word [tarry] carried this meaning [spiritual=abide] here, the misunderstanding mentioned in 21²³ could not have arisen'. It would not be impossible for a saying to be given an eschatological instead of a 'spiritual' meaning, any more than it would for an eschatological saying as such to be misapplied. Possibly Dr Plummer's verdict is still correct: 'He [Jesus] is not giving an answer [to Peter] but refusing one.' If that be so, then Bernard will be right in holding (I.C.C., p. 711) that 'the emphasis is on "If I will" . . . Jesus is

not represented as saying that it *is* His will that the Beloved Disciple would survive; but that if that *were* His will, it was no concern of Peter's'.

It seems quite clear that the current misunderstanding which the evangelist is trying to correct took the saying to mean that the beloved disciple would survive until the Parousia; he does so by pointing out that Jesus never said that the beloved disciple would not die. Two problems remain: does this language imply that the beloved disciple was by this time dead? And what are readers to think was the original meaning of the saying?

Verse 23 seems more consistent with a situation obtaining after the death of the beloved disciple, which would need explaining in view of the 'misunderstood' saying of the Lord. Yet v. 24 on the face of it seems to imply that the beloved disciple is very much alive, and indeed the author who is writing. But it can be held that another writer may be saying that the testimony of the beloved disciple, which has been committed to writing, is known to be true by the current writer: *we know that his testimony is true*. So that, unless it be held that the beloved disciple is the author of the gospel, there is no need to think that v. 23 does not imply that he is already dead. And that fact would give proper ground for the questions about his death which the evangelist is evidently concerned to deal with.

But what was the original meaning of the saying? A literal translation of the Greek would run: 'If it is my will that he should abide while I am coming, what is that to you?' In Johannine language, this context apart, that statement could well be taken to mean: 'If it is my will that he should be my disciple', for the term 'remain' or 'abide' is one that finds its crown in the phrase 'to abide in Christ', and to speak of the Lord's will that he should 'abide in Christ' while he is coming, seems quite possible to understand as 'abiding in Christ until his life's end', for the Lord will not cease to come to his own, as the coming by the lakeside has shown. The present writer would think this a quite permissible and possibly the correct view. But it is perfectly clear that if that were the original meaning of the phrase, it very soon suffered misunderstanding. If so, it was not alone. And it is highly probable that the whole range of eschatological terms used by Jesus was misunderstood by Jews and Christians alike, the more so as Jesus injected them with new meanings associated with his own 'coming'.

Yet it must be at once admitted that to use the verb *remain* in the sense of 'tarry' or 'remain alive' is not unknown in the N.T., e.g. at 1 Corinthians 15⁶ where the R.S.V. translates 'still alive'. Further it must be admitted that '*while I am coming*' can be otherwise rendered, as it is and ought to be rendered at 1 Timothy 4¹³, where the R.S.V. translates: 'Till I come attend to the public reading of scripture, etc.' The argument for the traditional view is thus quite strong.

What is clear is that on the basis of the saying the brethren had framed a belief that the beloved disciple would not die. It seems inevitable that their understanding of the saying was to think that it meant that he would survive until the Parousia. But did their misunderstanding extend so far? – or was it confined simply to not noting that the whole saying about remaining alive until Christ came was the consequence of a conditional clause: '*If it is my will that* . . .'? These are the imponderables in the problem, and they prevent finality being claimed on one side or another. It is just conceivable that the misunderstanding was one which began when a term of what C. H. Dodd might call 'realized eschatology' was transmuted into one of a futurist eschatology. If so then the first interpretation offered would be possible. Possible, but not, in all probability, popular with the world of scholars.

21²⁴, ²⁵   THE AUTHOR'S FINAL POSTSCRIPT

John 20³⁰, ³¹
John 19³⁵

²⁴*This is the disciple who is bearing witness to these things, and who has written these things; and we know that his testimony is true.*

²⁵*But there are also many other things which Jesus did; were every one of them to be written, I suppose that the world itself could not contain the books that would be written.*

In this final appendix to the gospel there is an identification of the beloved disciple as the one upon whose testimony the gospel rests. The identification and authentification which follow are important, since they bring the gospel into conformity with the requirements for reliable evidence which are stated in the gospel itself (5³¹, ³²; 8¹³, ¹⁴). The witness does not bear witness alone (5³¹) but has the witness of another (5³²), and the confirmation of the evidence by the *we* of the verse will suffice even to satisfy the demands of the Pharisees (8¹³), for they are not bearing witness to themselves, any more than the beloved disciple is.

Verse 24 begins by identifying the disciple spoken of in v. 23 with the one whose witness underlies the rest of the narrative. It goes on to say that he *has written these things*. It need not be assumed that what is stated necessarily implied that the beloved disciple wrote the gospel itself, or even whatever traditional material the evangelist himself used, any more than the phrase 'Pilate also wrote a title' means that Pilate himself wrote the title nailed to the cross. The beloved disciple need have done no more than 'caused to be written' or 'dictated to a secretary'.

The transition to the first person plural in the second part of the verse probably indicates, as the great majority of scholars would hold, that the elders of the Church in Ephesus add their testimony to the work of the author as he makes available to the world the profound witness of the beloved disciple.

The final verse underlines the highly selective character of John's own gospel – and also, by implication, the highly selective character of any gospel? – which has been written for a quite definite purpose of witness, stated in v. 24, and made articulate as to its objective in 20³¹. In spite of some critics, this need not be taken as a weak ending. It is tantamount to saying that there is a great deal more that can be known about Jesus, but nothing more need be known. John has, in some ways, told less about the 'life' of Jesus than his synoptic colleagues whose work is bound together with his in the New Testament. But he has said enough to guide the reader both of his own gospel and of the synoptics to a discerning understanding of the narrative that will see beyond the printed word the reality of him who is the living Word, once made flesh, now glorified and victorious, yet the life of those who trust in him.

John 7⁵³-8¹¹

The Woman Taken in Adultery

Luke 7³⁶⁻⁵⁰
Matthew 21²⁸⁻³¹

7 ⁵³ *They went each to his own house,* **8** ¹*but Jesus went to the Mount of Olives.* ²*Early in the morning he came again to the temple; all the people came to him, and he sat down and taught them.* ³ *The scribes and the Pharisees brought a woman who had been caught in adultery, and placing her in the midst* ⁴*they said to him, 'Teacher, this woman has been caught in the act of adultery.* ⁵*Now in the law Moses commanded us to stone such. What do you say about her?'* ⁶*This they said to test him, that they might have some charge to bring against him. Jesus bent down and wrote with his finger on the ground.* ⁷*And as they continued to ask him, he stood up and said to them, 'Let him who is without sin among you be the first to throw a stone at her.'* ⁸*And once more he bent down and wrote with his finger on the ground.* ⁹*But when they heard it, they went away, one by one, beginning with the eldest, and Jesus was left alone with the woman standing before him.* ¹⁰*Jesus looked up and said to her, 'Woman, where are they? Has no one condemned you?'* ¹¹*She said, 'No one, Lord.' And Jesus said, 'Neither do I condemn you; go, and do not sin again.'*

The Authorized Version of the English Bible contained this passage in the text of St John. It thus became well known to generations of Christian people, and is still made familiar to them through the continued use of the Authorized Version. But more modern versions make it clear that on grounds of scholarly integrity the section cannot be regarded as part of the original text of the gospel. Some, like the Revised Version print the story within brackets, adding a note that it cannot be yielded the authenticity of the rest of the text; others, like the Revised Standard Version, remove it from the text and print it in a footnote, or in a separate section at the end of the gospel. The commentator must therefore indicate why modern scholars have come to regard the section as an intrusion into the gospel; and why, not being part of the original text, it has been inserted, and inserted at precisely the point where it was for so long printed.

The evidence for the exclusion of the passage from the gospel proper may be briefly summarized thus: the whole passage is omitted by all but one of the early Greek uncial manuscripts, the chief being three fourth-century (Sinaiticus, Vaticanus and Freerianus) and one ninth-century manuscript (Koridethian). One eighth-century and one ninth-century uncial omit it, but leave a space where it might have been inserted, indicating that even then it was deemed unauthentic. Further, a number of cursive manuscripts omit it, while the Ferrar cursives place it in Luke between the apocalyptic discourse of ch. 21 and the opening of the 'Passion story' in ch. 22. Another cursive places it at the end of John, and another after John 7³⁶.

It is perhaps as significant that for the first thousand years of the Christian era no Greek commentator expounds the section at all. indeed it is Latin and western evidence that gives the section any kind of support. The earliest and chief of the early manuscripts which give the passage is the fifth-century Codex Bezae. It is thereafter to be found in a great number of later uncials and cursives, though many of these mark it with a distinguishing mark suggesting its doubtful authenticity. Latin texts are much more favourable to it, and it appears in Jerome's Vulgate. Some Latin fathers refer to it, e.g. Ambrose, Augustine and Jerome.

Apart from the evidence of manuscripts the style of the section is strongly suggestive of another writer than that of the gospel. The Greek particle *de* appears in this short section ten times; it is not a word characteristic of John (it occurs only 202 times in the rest of the gospel), who uses *oun* almost as frequently (195 times). John uses the word *ochlos* for 'crowd'; but in this section the word used is *laos*. The scribes are mentioned in this passage, but not in the rest of the gospel, where the Lord's opponents are called simply 'the Jews'. The Greek word for 'early' in this section (*orthrou*) is not the one otherwise used by John (18²⁸; 20¹; 21⁴) where the word is *proi*. These are the chief stylistic indications that sufficiently indicate, in what is after all a very short passage, that the writer is not the same as he who wrote the gospel.

But if it be not part of the original text of the gospel, whence did it come, and why was it inserted at this point in John? There can be no certainty about an answer to either of these two questions. But the story is mentioned for the first time in the Apostolic Constitutions, a third- or fourth-century product, though it is not there ascribed to the fourth gospel. This may well mean that the story was in circulation in the third and fourth centuries, and was first adopted by the Latin Church at that time. Eusebius reports that Papias related 'another story of a woman who was accused of many sins before the Lord which is contained in the Gospel according to the Hebrews' (Eus. *Eccles. Hist.*, III, 39). None of this evidence is proof of the origin of the story in John 7⁵³–8¹¹; but it does indicate that a story at least similar to it was current at the time when it first found its way into the text of the fourth gospel.

The story as it stands is not unlike some other stories of Jesus told in the synoptics; it is worth comparing it with the two passages printed at the head of this section, for the present narrative seems to combine the tenderness of the one with the lack of any reference to repentance in the other. As to why it should have been selected for insertion into the gospel, a reasonable conjecture is that it was thought to offer some dominical example of lenient treatment of a sinner to bishops who were inclined to be too severe in their treatment of offences. Severity in the treatment of adultery may well have been thought universally to be necessary in earlier days, while Christians were struggling to make clear the lines of demarcation in conduct between themselves and the pagan world. But when the new Christian morality had become established and recognized, it would be possible to take a more lenient view of offences. At that time a story such as that of the woman taken in adultery would have been an admirable help to the protagonists of leniency. As Bernard says (I.C.C. vol. II, p. 176): 'It was but a short step from quoting the story as edifying to treating it as suitable for reading in Church. It would thus get into lectionaries. . . .'

Why then has it been placed between 7⁵² and 8¹²? Once more certainty cannot be claimed; but reasonable conjecture can offer a satisfying explanation. The story may well have been thought to offer a satisfying comment on the saying of 8¹⁵ '*I judge* [or condemn] *no one*'. At a time when greater leniency in the treatment of matrimonial offences was being sought, this may have given the discerning editor the right sort of dominical saying on which to append a pericope of the sort which is found here. If this be anything like a satisfactory explanation, it echoes a number of sayings in John, from 3¹⁷ to 12⁴⁷. This pericope puts into narrative form the theological truth that the Son did not come into the world to condemn it, but to save it.

The pericope begins by placing the incident at a time in the ministry when Jesus went to the Mount of Olives and then resorted to the temple. This exactly fits the situation of Mark 11¹¹, and the last week of the Lord's life, when he appears to have been in Jerusalem during the day, and on the Mount of Olives (or Bethany, beyond the Mount of Olives) during the night. If there be any significance in this, it is theological rather than simply chronological. In a word, John wants his readers to understand that the claim not to condemn is made about the meaning of the crucifixion, rather than about a general attitude of Jesus. The incident is placed in the temple, the place where Judaism is thought to be preserved in its purity, and where the one who is to transcend it and the temple at Samaria now returns. As the one who is the source of the new religion of Israel is teaching his people, the authorities of the old Israel bring to him a woman caught in the very act of adultery, and ask Jesus to say what should be done to her. They remind him of the penalty demanded in the Mosaic law for such an offence, and seek his own judgement. The trap which was thus set for Jesus consisted in this: either he must answer that the woman must be stoned, as the law of Moses required, when he would appear to be much stricter than the then contemporary attitudes required; or he would reply that the woman should be freed from the death which the Mosaic law demanded, in which case Jesus would be exhibited as a Rabbi not faithful to the Mosaic law.

But Jesus was not so easily to be caught in the trap set for him. He spent some time in writing in the sand, and then stood up, and invited anyone who was quite guiltless to cast the first stone in executing the Mosaic sentence. But this proved too much for those who had thought to entrap Jesus, and one by one they left the scene, until at last Jesus was left alone with the adulteress. He asked her what had happened to her accusers. She replied that no one remained to act as an accuser. Jesus then replied: '*Neither do I condemn you*; *go, and do not sin again.*'

The story thus told has all the colour, drama and realism of a synoptic incident; it has all the marks to make it a proper item for inclusion in a synoptic or synoptic-like record. If John uses it here it is in all probability because in such a story he can best bring home the very general assertion '*I judge no one*' which is shortly to follow. If it be a later editor who has inserted the story into the Johannine text, it will have been inserted as an illustration of the kind of leniency that the dominical saying entailed in the area of matrimonial offences.

෴

7⁵³; 8¹

They went each to his own house, but Jesus went to the Mount of Olives: This suggests the situation described in Mark 11¹¹ff., when, during the last week of his life, it seems that Jesus left the city of Jerusalem each night, while, presumably, the Passover crowd stayed for the most part in the city. But the point is made not for chronological reasons alone, but for theological reasons chiefly, so that what follows might be interpreted as what the 'preaching of the cross' might mean for sinful men and women. It brings a word of forgiveness rather than of condemnation; and of condemnation only because it is primarily a word of forgiveness.

The Mount of Olives is a typically synoptic term, not found elsewhere in John.

2

Early is a translation of a Greek word used in the synoptics, but not in John.

all the people: The Greek word for 'people' here is the synoptic *laos* rather than the usual Johannine *ochlos*.

he sat down and taught them: In Matthew's account of the arrest of Jesus, it is reported that Jesus said to the crowds '. . . Day after day I sat in the temple teaching' (Matt. 26⁵⁵). It was the traditional custom of the Rabbis to sit while they taught (Matt. 23²), and Jesus normally adhered to it (Mark 4¹; 9³⁵; Luke 4²⁰; 5³). Further, it was usual for him, in the synoptic tradition, to go up into a mountain to teach (Matt. 5¹; 24³).

3

scribes and the Pharisees: Scribes are not mentioned elsewhere in John, though this particular phrase is frequent in the synoptics.

The woman is not brought to Jesus for a formal 'verdict', for he was not the proper authority (in the eyes of the Jews) to formulate it; but his opinion was sought in the expectation and hope that what he would say, one way or another, would give the Jews a lever against him. Other examples of this kind of 'trap' are given, e.g. in Mark 12¹³, ¹⁸.

5

'in the law Moses commanded us to stone such': In a case of ordinary adultery the penalty for both parties was death, though the manner of its execution was not specified. But in the particular case of a betrothed virgin, the penalty for adultery was death by stoning. It is therefore to be assumed that this is the sort of case brought to Jesus. The 'trap' which his opponents hoped to spring upon Jesus consisted in this: if he said 'Stone her' they could report him to the Roman authorities as one

inciting to murder or to riot; if he said 'Let her go' they could denounce him to their own people as a blasphemer who did not really care for the sacred law of Moses. In some ways, therefore, this story reproduces the dilemma presented by Mark in his report of the question about tribute money (Mark 12$^{14-17}$).

6

This they said to test him: cf. Mark 12^{13}ff., ^{18}ff.; 3^2; 10^2; Luke 6^7.

Jesus bent down and wrote with his finger on the ground: It is impossible to know why Jesus bent down, though from the fact that he stood up to face the woman's accusers and then bent down again, it would appear that Jesus wished to avoid any suggestion that he was taking up the position of a judge. That Jesus wrote on the ground is another statement that cannot be filled out with any certainty, though the word used for 'write', *kategraphen*, is found in the Septuagint and in some papyri with the meaning 'to register'. If this be the meaning here, Bernard's suggestion (I.C.C., II, p. 719) that the emphasis must then be placed on the words *on the ground*, which he renders 'in the dust', indicating that Jesus would have no permanent record. If that be so, the linking of the story with the statement shortly to be made, '*I judge no one*', becomes the more probable. Sin, even of this kind, can be forgiven, and blotted out.

7

as they continued to ask him: The scribes pressed Jesus for an answer, and would not let him escape.

he stood up: The Greek word here occurs again only in Luke 13^{11}; 21^{28}.

'*Let him who is without sin among you be the first to throw a stone at her*': This saying inevitably brings to mind the teaching of the Sermon on the Mount (Matt. 5^{27}ff.) where Jesus says: 'Every one who looks at a woman lustfully has already committed adultery with her in his heart.' But Jesus is doing more than suggest that all the present accusers are guilty of the offence of adultery interpreted in this way. The word used for *without sin* means 'innocent' *simpliciter*. The implication of the invitation for anyone who is completely innocent of sin to throw the first stone is not only that every man is guilty in this regard, but also that only someone completely innocent of all sin really has the right to take the action demanded by the law of the accusers in such cases, viz. to cast the first stone. The only one really able to condemn, really able to exact the penalty is a perfect being – God, and the Son of God present here in the flesh.

8

And once more he bent down and wrote with his finger on the ground: The accusers have been faced. Jesus has made it plain that there can be no 'capital punishment' inflicted on this occasion. He therefore resumes his writing on the ground.

9

But when they heard it, they went away, one by one, beginning with the eldest: If the synoptic locus for this story be, as the present writer believes, after the Triumphal Entry, the disappearance of those seeking to entrap Jesus is paralleled in the synoptics (Mark 12^{12}, etc.).

the eldest leave the scene first; they are, to use a more familiar translation, 'the elders', i.e. if the title be official, members of the Sanhedrin. It would be natural for such men to be members of the present deputation, and equally natural for them to be the first to depart; for it would have been their duty, presumably, to have 'cast the first stone', to have initiated the execution of the prescribed penalty had Jesus demanded it. They depart, and are followed by the other scribes, until Jesus and the woman are left alone.

10

Jesus looked up and said to her, 'Woman, where are they? Has no one condemned you?' The verb translated *looked up* is not the one usually accepted at this point of the narrative. Most editors of the text give the same word here as in v. 6. where it is stated that Jesus 'stood up'. At the earlier stage he was willing to act as a judge, though his judgement was very different from what the scribes expected; now he is prepared to act as judge again, and the 'innocent' one, who now stands alone, speaks the divine judgement on sin. But first he establishes the fact that no human religious authority has claimed the right to act as judge. But where they resign their rights, Jesus claims his, and exercises them.

11

The woman replied to Jesus quite simply: No one had ventured to pass or execute a sentence upon her.

'Neither do I condemn you; go, and do not sin again': *Condemn* is perhaps better rendered 'pass sentence', for the particular form of the verb (*katakrino*) means more than 'judge', and expresses those functions that a judge in a court has to undertake when offenders are found guilty. Unlike the story in Luke 7$^{36-50}$ the woman here is not represented as penitent; nor is Jesus depicted as saying anything about positive forgiveness. Yet the whole context, of a woman taken in the very act of adultery, being brought to Jesus for summary judgement to be passed upon her, cannot but raise the question of forgiveness. If forgiveness includes a restoration of right relationships between offended and

offender, then the woman cannot be said to have entered into that relationship at this point. But in so far as she is left with the injunction '*do not sin again*', it is made clear that no final condemnation has been passed by the one truly holy being who has the sole right to condemn. So the *pericope adulterae* is revealed as a story illustrating what Jesus meant when later in 8¹⁵ he said: 'You judge according to the flesh, I judge no one. Yet even if I do judge, my judgement is true, for it is not I alone that judge, but I and he who sent me.' The story of the woman underlines the significant differences between the 'judges' of Israel-after-the-flesh and the one divine Judge of the whole people of God who are to be gathered in by the coming of the Word in the flesh.

Index of References

OLD TESTAMENT

OTHER ANCIENT AUTHORS AND LITERATURE

Index of Names

Index of Subjects